The MICHELIN Guide

New York City

RESTAURANTS

2012

Manufacture française des pneumatiques Michelin

Société en commandite par actions au capital de 504 000 004 EUR
Place des Carmes-Déchaux — 63000 Clermont-Ferrand (France)
R.C.S. Clermont-Fd B 855 200 507
No part of this publication may be reproduced in any form without the prior
permission of the publisher.

© **Michelin, Propriétaires-éditeurs**
Dépot légal Octobre 2011
Made in Canada
Published in 2011

The MICHELIN Guide
One Parkway South
Greenville, SC 29615 USA
www.michelinguide.com
michelin.guides@us.michelin.com

Dear Reader

*W*e are thrilled to present the seventh edition of our
MICHELIN Guide to New York City.

*Our dynamic team has spent this year updating our selection to
wholly reflect the rich diversity of New York City's restaurants
and hotels. As part of our meticulous and highly confidential
evaluation process, our inspectors have anonymously and
methodically eaten through all five boroughs to compile
the finest in each category for your enjoyment. While these
inspectors are expertly trained food industry professionals, we
remain consumer driven: our goal is to provide comprehensive
choices to accommodate your comfort, tastes, and budget. Our
inspectors dine, drink, and lodge as 'regular' customers in order
to experience and evaluate the same level of service and cuisine
you would as a guest.*

*We have expanded our criteria to reflect some of the more
current and unique elements of New York City's dining scene.
Don't miss the scrumptious "Small Plates" category, highlighting
those establishments with a distinct style of service, setting, and
menu; and the further expanded "Under $25" listings which also
include a diverse and impressive choice at a very good value.*

*Additionally, you may follow our Michelin Inspectors on
Twitter @MichelinGuideNY as they chow their way around
town. Our anonymous inspectors tweet daily about their unique
and entertaining food experiences.*

*Our company's two founders, Édouard and André Michelin,
published the first MICHELIN Guide in 1900, to provide motorists
with practical information about where they could service and
repair their cars, find quality accommodations, and a good meal.
Later in 1926, the star-rating system for outstanding restaurants
was introduced, and over the decades we have developed many
new improvements to our guides. The local team here in New
York enthusiastically carries on these traditions.*

*We sincerely hope that the MICHELIN Guide will remain your
preferred reference to the city's restaurants and hotels.*

Contents

Peter L. Wrenn / MICHELIN

Contents

John Peden / NYBG

5

The Michelin Guide

"This volume was created at the turn of the century and will last at least as long".

This foreword to the very first edition of the MICHELIN Guide, written in 1900, has become famous over the years and the Guide has lived up to the prediction. It is read across the world and the key to its popularity is the consistency in its commitment to its readers, which is based on the following promises.

→ Anonymous Inspections

Our inspectors make anonymous visits to hotels and restaurants to gauge the quality offered to the ordinary customer. They pay their own bill and make no indication of their presence. These visits are supplemented by comprehensive monitoring of information—our readers' comments are one valuable source, and are always taken into consideration.

→ Independence

Our choice of establishments is a completely independent one, made for the benefit of our readers alone. Decisions are discussed by the inspectors and the editor, with the most important decided at the global level. Inclusion in the guide is always free of charge.

→ The Selection

The Guide offers a selection of the best hotels and restaurants in each category of comfort and price. Inclusion in the guides is a commendable award in itself, and defines the establishment among the "best of the best."

How the MICHELIN Guide Works

→ Annual Updates

All practical information, the classifications, and awards, are revised and updated every year to ensure the most reliable information possible.

→ Consistency & Classifications

The criteria for the classifications are the same in all countries covered by the Michelin Guides. Our system is used worldwide and is easy to apply when choosing a restaurant or hotel.

→ The Classifications

We classify our establishments using ⚔️⚔️⚔️⚔️-⚔️ and 🏨🏨🏨🏨-🏠 to indicate the level of comfort. The ✤✤✤-✤ specifically designates an award for cuisine, unique from the classification. For hotels and restaurants, a symbol in red suggests a particularly charming spot with unique décor or ambiance.

→ Our Aim

As part of Michelin's ongoing commitment to improving travel and mobility, we do everything possible to make vacations and eating out a pleasure.

The Michelin Guide

How to Use This Guide

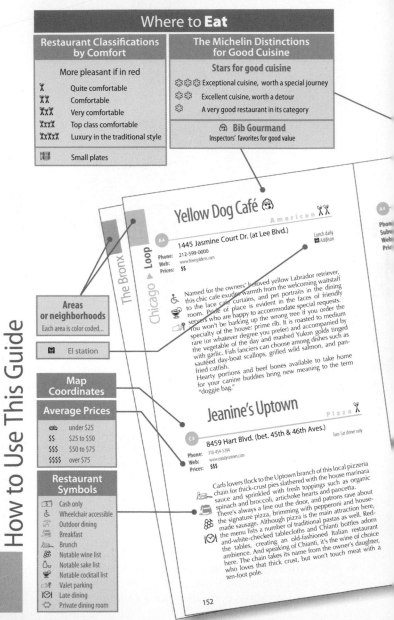

Where to **Eat**

Restaurant Classifications by Comfort

More pleasant if in red

X	Quite comfortable
XX	Comfortable
XxX	Very comfortable
XxxX	Top class comfortable
XxXxX	Luxury in the traditional style
🎐	Small plates

The Michelin Distinctions for Good Cuisine

Stars for good cuisine

😊😊😊 Exceptional cuisine, worth a special journey

😊😊 Excellent cuisine, worth a detour

😊 A very good restaurant in its category

😊 Bib Gourmand
Inspectors' favorites for good value

Yellow Dog Café 😊

American XX

A4

1445 Jasmine Court Dr. (at Lee Blvd.)

Phone: 212-599-0000
Web: www.llovegoldens.com
Prices: $$

Lunch daily
🚇 Addison

Named for the owners' beloved yellow Labrador retriever, this chic cafe exudes warmth from the welcoming waitstaff to the lace cafe curtains, and pet portraits in the dining room. Pride of place is evident in the faces of friendly servers who are happy to accommodate special requests. You won't be barking up the wrong tree if you order the specialty of the house: prime rib. It is roasted to medium rare (or whatever degree you prefer) and accompanied by the vegetable of the day and mashed Yukon golds tinged with garlic. Fish fanciers can choose among dishes such as sautéed day-boat scallops, grilled wild salmon, and pan-fried catfish.

Hearty portions and beef bones available to take home for your canine buddies bring new meaning to the term "doggie bag."

Jeanine's Uptown

Pizza X

C4

8459 Hart Blvd. (bet. 45th & 46th Aves.)

Phone: 310-454-5294
Web: www.eatatjeannies.com
Prices: $$$

Tues-Sat dinner only

Carb lovers flock to the Uptown branch of this local pizzeria chain for thick-crust pies slathered with the house marinara sauce and sprinkled with fresh toppings such as organic spinach and broccoli, artichoke hearts and pancetta. There's always a line out the door, and patrons rave about the signature pizza, brimming with pepperoni and house-made sausage. Although pizza is the main attraction here, the menu lists a number of traditional pastas as well. Red-and-white-checked tablecloths and Chianti bottles adorn the tables, creating an old-fashioned Italian restaurant ambience. And speaking of Chianti, it's the wine of choice here. The chain takes its name from the owner's daughter, who loves that thick crust, but won't touch meat with a ten-foot pole.

Areas or neighborhoods
Each area is color coded...

🚇 El station

Map Coordinates

Average Prices

⊗	under $25
$$	$25 to $50
$$$	$50 to $75
$$$$	over $75

Restaurant Symbols

💲	Cash only
♿	Wheelchair accessible
🌳	Outdoor dining
🍳	Breakfast
🥂	Brunch
🍷	Notable wine list
🍶	Notable sake list
🍸	Notable cocktail list
🚗	Valet parking
🕐	Late dining
🚪	Private dining room

152

8

Where to **Stay**

Average Prices	Hotel Symbols	Hotel Classifications by Comfort
Prices do not include applicable taxes	149 rooms Number of rooms & suites	More pleasant if in red
$ under $200	♿ Wheelchair accessible	🏠 Quite comfortable
$$ $200 to $300	Exercise room	Comfortable
$$$ $300 to $400	Spa	Very comfortable
$$$$ over $400	Swimming pool	Top class comfortable
	Conference room	Luxury in the traditional style
Map Coordinates	Pet friendly	
	Wireless	

The Fan Inn

135 Shanghai Street, Oakland

Phone: 650-345-1440 or 888-222-2424
Web: www.superfaninnoakland.com
Prices: $$

45 Rooms
5 Suites

...oused in an Art Deco-era building, the venerable Fan Inn ...ontly underwent a complete facelift. The hotel now fits ...with the new generation of cheekly understated hotels ...ring a Zen-inspired aesthetic, despite its 1930s origins.

...othing neutral palette runs throughout the property, ...uated with exotic woods, bamboo, and fine fabrics. ...e lobby, the sultry lounge makes a relaxing place for ...mixed cocktail or a glass of wine.

...eens and down pillows cater to your comfort, while ...n TVs, DVD players with iPod docking stations, ...less internet access satisfy the need for modern ...For business travelers, nightstands convert to ...les and credenzas morph into flip-out desks. ...ter, fax or scanner? It's just a phone call away. ...st, the hotel will even provide office supplies.

...ull of the accommodations here are suites, ...ury factor ratchets up with marble baths, ...ng areas, and fully equipped kitchens. ...Inn doesn't have a restaurant, the nearby ...rly everything you could want in terms of ...dumplings to haute cuisine

315

a's Palace ✿ ✿

italian XXXX

euther Pl. (at 30th Street)   Dinner daily

$309
8 Av
nyaslabulouspalace.com

Home cooked Italian never tasted so good than at this unpretentious little place. The simple décor claims no big-name designers, and while the Murano glass light fixtures are chic and the velveteen-covered chairs are comfortable, this isn't a restaurant where millions of dollars were spent on the interior.

Instead, food is the focus here. The restaurant's name may not be Italian, but it nonetheless serves some of the best pasta in the city, made fresh in-house. Dishes follow the seasons, thus ravioli may be stuffed with fresh ricotta and herbs in summer, and pumpkin in fall. Most everything is liberally dusted with Parmigiano Reggiano, a favorite ingredient of the chef.

For dessert, you'll have to deliberate between the likes of creamy tiramisu, ricotta cheesecake, and homemade gelato. One thing's for sure: you'll never miss your nonna's cooking when you eat at Sonya's.

153

Manhattan ▶ Chelsea

San Francisco ▶ Civic Center

How to Use This Guide

9

Peter L. Wrenn / MICHELIN

Manhattan

Chelsea

Restaurants in this artsy neighborhood–the hub of New York's gallery scene–feature flavors from around the globe, encompassing everything from French bistros to sushi bars and contemporary Spanish fare. Old World Puerto Rican luncheonettes on and around 9th Avenue (where patrons are accommodated in English or Spanish, and the *café con leche* packs a heady wallop) provide a striking contrast to the mega-hip places that punctuate Chelsea today. For heavenly pizza, try the much-hyped **Co.**, home to iconoclast Jim Lahey's blistered and crispy pies. The Chef/owner and founder of **Sullivan Street Bakery**, fires his pizza in a wood-burning oven imported from Modena, and the lines of folks eager to taste them stretch out the door. If that's not hip enough, there's always the scene at **Buddakan**, that tried and trendy temple of modern Asian fare, brought to New York by Philadelphia restaurateur wunderkind Stephen Starr.

In the burgeoning area known as the West Club District, patrons of nightspots like Mansion, Guest House, Home, and Marquee are grateful for all-night restaurants like the **Punjabi Food Junction**, offering a tasty self-serve Indian buffet. Also in the open-late category, quintessential New York spot **The Half King** dishes up good all-American grub. Named for an 18th century Seneca Indian chief, Half King also sponsors book readings on Monday nights, thanks to co-owner and writer Sebastian Junger, author of *War*, and co-director of the documentary, *Restrepo*.

Chelsea Market

No food-finding excursion to this area would be complete without a visit to the **Chelsea Market**. The 1898 Nabisco factory–where the Oreo cookie was first made in 1912–reopened in 1997 as an urban food market. Interspersed throughout its brick-lined arcades with stores selling flowers, meats, cheeses, artisan-made breads, and other gourmet essentials are cafés, bakeries, and eateries. Drop by to peruse their wares, stock your pantry, and have a bite to eat while you're at it.

Treat yourself to organic farm-fresh cuisine and biodynamic wines at **The Green Table** and **The Cleaver Co.** Seafood lovers can pick up a luscious lobster roll or some freshly steamed lobsters at **The Lobster Place**, New York's leading purveyor of these sea creatures. If you have kids in tow, a stop at **L'Arte del Gelato** is a must. Some new welcome additions to the market are **Dickson's Farmstand** for their serious meats and **Lucy's Whey** for fine cheeses. No matter your preference, a trip to the market will nourish you for hours of gallery-hopping on the district's western flank.

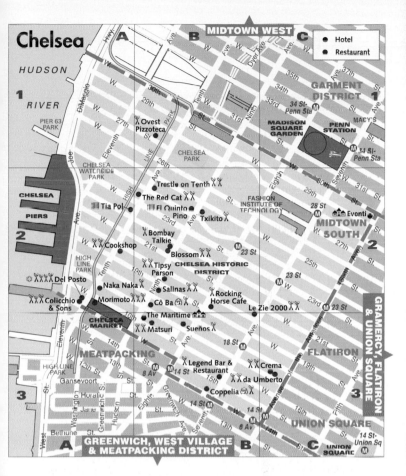

Chelsea

HUDSON RIVER

MIDTOWN WEST

- Hotel
- Restaurant

GARMENT DISTRICT

PIER 63 PARK

Ovest Pizzoteca

CHELSEA WATERSIDE PARK

MADISON SQUARE GARDEN

PENN STATION

MACY'S

34 St-Penn Sta

CHELSEA PARK

34 St-Penn Sta

CHELSEA PIERS

Trestle on Tenth

The Red Cat

Tia Pol

El Quinto

Pino   Txikito

FASHION INSTITUTE OF TECHNOLOGY

Eyonti

MIDTOWN SOUTH

Bombay Talkie

Cookshop

Blossom

23 St

HIGH LINE PARK

Tipsy Parson

Del Posto

Naka Naka

Salinas

CHELSEA HISTORIC DISTRICT

23 St

Colicchio & Sons

Morimoto

Cô Ba

Rocking Horse Cafe

Le Zie 2000

23 St

CHELSEA MARKET

The Maritime

Matsuri   Sueños

18 St

MEATPACKING

HIGH LINE PARK

Gansevoort

Horatio

Jane

Legend Bar & Restaurant

8 Av   14 St

FLATIRON

Crema

da Umberto

Coppelia

GRAMERCY, FLATIRON & UNION SQUARE

Bethune   St.

14 St

8 Av

UNION SQUARE

14 St-Union Sq

UNION SQUARE

GREENWICH, WEST VILLAGE & MEATPACKING DISTRICT

Upstairs, the Chelsea Market pavilion houses the studios and test kitchens for the Food Network. Continue your stroll through Chelsea and follow the meaty scents to **Salumeria Biellese** for some great cured products. After these salty snacks, **La Bergamote Patisserie** is the perfect landing spot for satisfying a sweet tooth. And while in the neighborhood, consider dining with a view of Lady Liberty on one of the dinner cruises that departs from Chelsea Piers, an ever-evolving recreational waterfront area located along the West Side Highway between 17th and 23rd streets. Comprising four historic piers along the Hudson River, the complex now houses state-of-the-art sports facilities, including a spa, ice skating rink, and bowling alley. **Chelsea Brewing Company**, overlooking the Hudson River, is a glorious spot to close your day. Satiate your palate with one of their unique beers like the Checker Cab Blonde Ale.

Blossom

B2

187 Ninth Ave. (bet. 21st & 22nd Sts.)

Subway: 23 St (Eighth Ave.)   Dinner nightly
Phone: 212-627-1144
Web: www.blossomnyc.com
Prices: $$

Who says vegan can't be sexy? This charming café hits all the right ambience notes: it's convivial without being loud, intimate without being claustrophobic, and the delicate mirrors and flickering votives offer the space a sultry dose of visual depth.

Though the city's demand for organic, nutritious meals continues to soar, not many restaurants are offering the kind of inventive, dynamic cuisine that Blossom is (along with its neighboring sister, Cocoa V Chocolate Boutique Wine & Dessert Bar). Witness a spirited black-eyed pea cake with chipotle aïoli; woodsy strips of grilled seitan over asparagus tips, shiitake mushrooms, and roasted cherry tomatoes; or the vegan Blossom cheesecake, a creamy concoction with an irresistible apricot purée.

Bombay Talkie

B2

189 Ninth Ave. (bet. 21st & 22nd Sts.)

Subway: 23 St (Eighth Ave.)   Dinner nightly
Phone: 212-242-1900
Web: www.bombaytalkie.com
Prices: $$

Located along a charming row of storefronts in Chelsea, the hip Indian restaurant, Bombay Talkie, knows the key to its popularity is in its consistency. Take a seat below the cool murals depicting Bollywood movie stars, and pick your meal off a menu boasting sections like "from the roadside" and "street bites."

Try a plate of *koliwada macchi*, an Indian rest stop staple of crispy fish served with shoe string potatoes; *malai kofta*, dumplings stuffed with cheese and coconut, and bathed in a cashew-yogurt sauce; or *Bombay bhel*, served with wheat flour chips and rice puffs, tossed with a bright lime, mint, onion, and green mango salsa. The double-decker standby offers two stories of seating and a long communal table, but reservations are still recommended.

Cô Ba 😊

B2

110 Ninth Ave. (bet. 19th & 20th Sts.)

Subway: 23 St (Eighth Ave.)   Lunch Mon – Fri
Phone: 212-414-2700   Dinner nightly
Web: www.cobarestaurant.com
Prices: $$

Chelsea may cradle a collage of cuisines, but it is also home to Cô Ba, a canteen that nurtures the true tenor of Vietnam. After an inspirational home cooking stint in his motherland, Chef/owner Steven Duong inaugurated this charming street stall. Shoe box-sized Cô Ba is anything but kitsch; in fact, it is the very picture of wistful elegance with charming artwork and well-set tables.

Here, Duong lures diners with Vietnam's more unique culinary repertoire that may include such delectable delights as *bahn mi thit*, a sinful version of the faithful smeared with honey-plum glazed pork and pâté; *bun cha ca Hanoi*, turmeric and dill-infused flaky white fish; and *thit ba roi kho*, caramelized pork belly bobbing in coconut milk with tofu and quail eggs.

Colicchio & Sons

A2

85 Tenth Ave. (bet. 15th & 16th Sts.)

Subway: 14 St - 8 Av   Lunch & dinner daily
Phone: 212-400-6699
Web: www.colicchioandsons.com
Prices: $$$

Chef Tom Colicchio continues to build his empire with this recent offering residing in the revamped Craftsteak. The multi-faceted ambience is comprised of the Tap Room with bar seating, and a wood-burning pizza oven accompanied by a daylight-flooded dining room bedecked in a dramatic and earthy aesthetic. It's all quite inviting, clamor notwithstanding. As one would hope and expect from a venue by this celebrity chef, the preparations monitor the season's bounty in a collection of plates that may bring pillowy bundles of potato gnocchi given a butter sauce sheen and dressed with malt-vinegar potato chips and American caviar; or slices of roasted Hudson Valley rabbit roulade paired with a savory crêpe folded over wilted stinging nettles.

Cookshop

A2

American ✗✗

156 Tenth Ave. (at 20th St.)

Subway: 23 St (Eighth Ave.) Lunch & dinner daily
Phone: 212-924-4440
Web: www.cookshopny.com
Prices: $$

The honest, super-focused menu at Chef Mark Meyer and his wife, Vicki Freeman's, Cookshop, defines a new generation of Manhattan restaurants: with a well-sourced (often local), seasonal menu that rotates faster than Mario Andretti's wheels, but is consistently soulful. Wonderfully al dente *garganelli* pasta arrives tossed with fresh tomatoes and Grana Padano; while soft, house-smoked Hampshire pork laced with smoky-vinegary sauce, is tucked into a fresh sesame potato roll with a thump of coleslaw.

The bright, airy space is dotted with green plants and fresh flowers, and by day the big picture windows offer a flood of natural light and visions of the Highline. By night, the space dims and the hip local crowd fills the space with an energetic buzz.

Coppelia

B3

Latin American ✗

207 W. 14th St. (bet. Seventh & Eighth Aves.)

Subway: 14 St (Seventh Ave.) Lunch & dinner daily
Phone: 212-858-5001
Web: www.coppelianyc.com
Prices: $$

Visionary Chef Julian Medina (of Toloache fame) and his unstoppable team are at it again. Enter sensational Coppelia to find a breezy Caribbean vibe, moan-worthy dishes, and jaw-dropping desserts courtesy of the talented Pichet Ong. The space is reminiscent of a 50s luncheonette and rocks bright yellow walls, red-topped tables, checkered floors, and vintage-style banquettes. Grab a spot on the gorgeous marble bar and let the fiesta begin.

Favorites include superb guacamole with tortilla, yucca, and plantain chips; four variations of exquisite empanadas; cheese *croquetas*; decadent mac and cheese with *chicharrón*; and luscious pernil (roasted pork) served over yucca purée. The carrot cake with manchego cheese frosting and lime is out of this world.

Crema

C3

Mexican ❌❌

111 W. 17th St. (bet. Sixth & Seventh Aves.)

Subway: 18 St
Phone: 212-691-4477
Web: www.cremarestaurante.com
Prices: $$

Lunch & dinner daily

Hidden below street level on a Chelsea block dominated by consignment shops, Crema doesn't boast its charms to the world. Rather, this little restaurant relies on Chef Julieta Ballesteros' solid grasp of modern, upscale Mexican cooking to lure them in.

Inside, you'll find a narrow room with smooth, colorful walls, a cactus garden and a bar area sporting lovely glass vats of *agua loca*—a Mexican sangria not to be missed. All the better to wash down a perfectly balanced bowl of cream of corn bobbing with plump crab meat and micro cilantro; a tortilla pie layered with fresh ingredients and tender shredded chicken; or a decadent slice of pecan pie with spiced Mexican eggnog and vanilla ice cream. Come lunchtime, $15.95 scores you an entrée, soup, and side dish.

da Umberto

C3

Italian ❌❌

107 W. 17th St. (bet. Sixth & Seventh Aves.)

Subway: 18 St
Phone: 212-989-0303
Web: www.daumbertonyc.com
Prices: $$$

Lunch Mon – Fri
Dinner Mon – Sat

After 23 years, da Umberto continues to raise the bar for this city's understanding and appreciation of Northern Italian cuisine, thanks to their exacting attention to detail and charming, sure footed service. The payoff for this kitchen's discipline is found in the creamy, perfectly cooked risotto; fork-tender rabbit, stewed in a fragrant caper-studded sauce; and seductively sweet ricotta cheesecake in a buttery crust. An interesting wine list, antipasto, and announced specials are worthy highlights.

The unassuming façade contrasts with the stylish businessmen and lunching ladies that fill its sophisticated dining room. A quiet restraint in both clientele and setting is testament to the fact that here, you are dining among those who are in the know.

Del Posto ✤

Italian 🍴🍴🍴🍴

A2

85 Tenth Ave. (bet. 15th & 16th Sts.)

Subway: 14 St - 8 Av
Phone: 212-497-8090
Web: www.delposto.com
Prices: $$$$

Lunch Mon – Fri
Dinner nightly

Joe Vaughn

In an island-city short on real estate, this Batali-Bastianich collaboration is indeed a temple—our Versailles—to grand (if at times grandiose) Italian cuisine. Del Posto is a massive version of upscale business dining that somehow landed in Chelsea rather than midtown, or even Vegas. Thin-skinned city food wonks may fear they've wandered west into the mainland, but once inside, the interior is opulent, with rich-toned burgundy and blue, theater-like balconies, oversized windows, and oversized window treatments covering them. Service runs with a robotic efficiency that feels more scripted than hospitable, as if striving to live up to a cliché.

Still, everyone has reserved in advance and lined up at the door to pay a premium for what has been hailed as some of the city's best Italian food. Menus are fixed as five or seven courses; pray that yours will begin with a perfectly cooked chilled lobster served with a complex chili sauce, broccoli rabe, fried onions, and a roasted chili pepper that combine with haunting excellence. Technical missteps in the kitchen may result in an overcooked chop or underdone pasta, but forgive this in favor of unearthing the menu's true gems.

El Quinto Pino

Spanish

B2

401 W. 24th St. (bet. Ninth & Tenth Aves.)

Subway: 23 St (Eighth Ave.)   Dinner nightly
Phone: 212-206-6900
Web: www.elquintopinonyc.com
Prices: 😊😊

Chelsea has enough tapas joints to give the Barcelona metropolis a run for its money, but El Quinto Pino is a worthy member of this crowded landscape. This Lilliputian spot aims to return tapas to its original concept— these are quick snacks rather than sit-down meals. This is an ideal stop for a distinctively authentic *ración* or two and *una copa* or three.
Despite its lack of traditional table seating and constant reshuffling in the kitchen, this warm, narrow, Spanish-tiled bar has been mobbed since its debut. Credit goes to the small, creative blackboard menu of tapas like uni panini, squeezed onto bread slathered with Korean mustard oil; and the Menu Turistico, featuring a revolving set of regional Spanish dishes.

Legend Bar & Restaurant

Chinese ✗

B3

88 Seventh Ave. (bet. 15th & 16th Sts.)

Subway: 14 St   Lunch & dinner daily
Phone: 212-929-1778
Web: www.legendrestaurant88.com
Prices: 😊😊

The chefs manning these stoves are phenomenally well-versed in Sichuan food (one might suspect their skill inspired the name). Legend is the newest incarnation of the short-lived Vietnamese spot, Safran, which may be why their superlative Sichuan menu is laden with missable Vietnamese dishes. Happy hour is big here, while the rest of the Asian-accented space caters to solid Sichuan feasts.
Vivid colors and a clean décor welcome you inside, while the lower level displays round tables outfitted with lazy Susans; and the orange upholstery pairs perfectly with such zesty offerings as spicy conch topped with slivered scallions; braised, diced rabbit with pickled peppers swimming in a red chili oil; and and rice balls of sesame paste floating in sweet milk.

Le Zie 2000

B3

172 Seventh Ave. (bet. 20th & 21st Sts.)

Subway: 23 St (Seventh Ave.)   Lunch & dinner daily
Phone: 212-206-8686
Web: www.lezie.com
Prices: $$

Inside this pastel dining room, Le Zie 2000 continues to embody wholesome Italian cuisine. Outside, a small patio remains a fine place to while away the sunny days.

Begin meals in the Venetian tradition by sharing the antipasti sampling–*cicchetti*–which includes several of the region's savory classics and is served with its signature starch, grilled polenta. Among several fine *paste* and heartier *secondi piatti* is the ever-popular Le Zie mac 'n cheese with truffles.

With an entrance on 20th Street, Le Zie features a cute, dimly lit, very comfy back lounge with light tasting and cocktail menus, served by a friendly bartender. All wines from Le Zie's extensive list of some 200 labels representing all of Italy's viticultural regions are available here.

Matsuri

B3

369 W. 16th St. (bet. Eighth & Ninth Aves.)

Subway: 14 St - 8 Av   Dinner nightly
Phone: 212-243-6400
Web: www.themaritimehotel.com
Prices: $$

Although set in a hotel known for hip young patrons, Matsuri remains well-run, delicious, and deserving of the coos and superlatives that its jaw-dropping interior provokes. Step inside the cavernous dining room, with its enormous curved ceiling, sake collection lining the wall, and beautiful misshapen paper lanterns to soak in the grandeur. Mystifying acoustics ensure a sleek, unspoiled ambience.

Finally, settle in for decadent Japanese fare, which may include a silky, red miso soup infused with scallion and ginger, elegantly floating a tender lobster claw at its center; or a fresh young sea bass, deep-fried with ponzu-*momiji* sauce. The menu's seasonality makes every day an ideal time to dine here—especially for fall and wintertime hot pots.

Morimoto

Fusion 🍴🍴🍴

88 Tenth Ave. (at 16th St.)

Subway: 14 St – 8 Av
Phone: 212-989-8883
Web: www.morimotonyc.com
Prices: $$$

Lunch Mon – Fri
Dinner nightly

Located in the super-trendy western nook of Chelsea, Morimoto has been packing them in on nights when even its most famous neighbors stand nearly empty. The draw is as much the starkly sexy interior as the cuisine, which is bold enough to match it. Sail beyond Morimoto's billowing curtains and into the sultry cement-and-metal filled space, where you'll be greeted by more beautiful people than you can shake a Jimmy Choo at.

On the plate, find upscale Japanese fusion (heavy on the fusion, light on the Japanese) courtesy of the great Masaharu Morimoto, whose acclaimed restaurant empire has quickly grown to span the globe. Here, try the signature dishes, such as Tuna pizza or yellowtail "pastrami" *togorashi* with gin crème fraîche and candied olives.

Naka Naka

Japanese 🍴

458 W. 17th St. (at Tenth Ave.)

Subway: 14 St – 8 Av
Phone: 212-929-8544
Web: www.nakanakany.com
Prices: $$$

Dinner Tue – Sun

Like a mouse bucking a sleek cat, little Naka Naka has stayed put while everything around it has caved to the ever-changing landscape where Chelsea borders the Meatpacking District. The winning concept of this homespun Japanese restaurant is simple– a small, pretty room tucked into a timeworn, pre-war building off 10th Avenue, where you'll discover a low-slung, horseshoe-shaped bar and a few well-spaced tables.

Save for the servers kneeling to take your order or ferrying food back and forth, the only commotion in this haven is on the plate, where you might discover a perfectly charred Spanish mackerel in sake paste, paired with a fried green horn pepper and roasted cherry tomato; or a fresh lobe of creamy uni, with Japanese pickles and grated radish.

Ovest Pizzoteca

Italian ✗

513 W. 27th St. (bet. 10th & 11th Aves.)

Subway: 23 St (Eighth Ave.) Lunch & dinner daily
Phone: 212-967-4392
Web: www.ovestnyc.com
Prices: $$

 Fine fare is rare in these parts, so Ovest Pizzoteca's (of the lauded Luzzo's) arrival into Chelsea's Club Row stirred up big buzz. Ravenous revelers follow the alluring aromas of pies and panini to this Italian idol–whose wood-and-gas burning oven crackles until first light–much to their delight. Open garage doors cede a glimpse of this mod, chic warehouse with industrial lighting and a wooden ceiling.

Veteran chefs prepare tasty treats like *alici marinate*–deliciously tart anchovies–in vinegar and olive oil; *polpettine* in a shiny tomato purée; *la pizza piccante* made pure with tomato sauce, cherry peppers, and sausage; and *pastiera Napoletana* with berries and vanilla. So let slide the loud crowd and yield to Luzzo's best on this side of the west.

The Red Cat

American ✗✗

227 Tenth Ave. (bet. 23rd & 24th Sts.)

Subway: 23 St (Eighth Ave.) Lunch Tue – Sat
Phone: 212-242-1122 Dinner nightly
Web: www.redcatrestaurants.com
Prices: $$

 This clever, cozy, and perpetually hip Jimmy Bradley joint is packed wall-to-wall seven nights a week. And no wonder: with an interior fitted out in rich red banquettes and Moorish light fixtures that radiate warmth in winter and read sultry come summer, a downright sexy cocktail list and scrumptious, always inventive American fare, The Red Cat is what you might call a restaurant triple threat.

Book ahead and you too can get in on dishes like the curried sweet potato soup, served with a dollop of crème fraîche; supremely fresh bluefish, expertly grilled and finished with potatoes, green olives, and pepper salsa; or a warm plum shortcake, bursting with soft quartered plums and topped with maple whipped cream and cinnamon crème anglaise.

Rocking Horse Cafe

Mexican 🍴

B2

182 Eighth Ave. (bet. 19th & 20th Sts.)

Subway: 14 St - 8 Av   Lunch & dinner daily
Phone: 212-463-9511
Web: www.rockinghorsecafe.com
Prices: $$

This easygoing Chelsea standby serves up solid Mexican fare in a vivid, sophisticated dining space fitted out with shimmering blue mosaic tiles, tangerine colored walls, beet red accents, and creamy jumbo lanterns. At the bar, big mesh containers hold mounds of the house-made tortillas and a cheerful crowd lines the stools, downing seriously good (and strong) margaritas while they wait to be seated.

In the dining room, couples and friends line the tables, tucking into creative spins on Mexican favorites like a marvelous *ensalada de calamares*, spiked with fresh cracked black pepper, cool cilantro, and a lick of *crema*; a fresh batch of Niman Ranch pork *carnitas*; or a traditional, but irresistible *tres leches con platanos* strewn with candied pecans.

Salinas

Spanish 🍴🍴

B2

136 Ninth Ave. (bet. 18th & 19th Sts.)

Subway: 18 St   Dinner nightly
Phone: 212 776-1990
Web: www.salinasnyc.com
Prices: $$$

You'll be salivating over the Spanish food (and the scantily clad hostesses) in no time at Salinas. Set behind wrought-iron gates on a busy stretch of Ninth Ave., this restaurant invites diners to an Iberian world of delicious treats and seductive spaces. Sure, it's tapas, but Chef Bollo's elegant take is a tad different than the tried and true classics found throughout the city.

There's a host of seasonal starters (summer months showcase clams with *pocha* beans and artichokes beside a spicy and oh-so-yummy ceviche). From Spanish flatbread peppered with thyme, dry aged Mahón cheese to *porcella*, slow-roasted suckling pig matched with grilled apricots and bathed in a wine reduction, there is nothing like sampling a cavalcade of culinary delights.

Sueños

B3

311 W. 17th St. (bet. Eighth & Ninth Aves.)

Subway: 14 St - 8 Av
Phone: 212-243-1333
Web: www.suenosnyc.com
Prices: $$

Dinner Tue – Sun

With its entrance tucked down an alley and requiring a walk along a virtual gangplank, Sueños is as downright good as it is audacious to succeed in its somewhat tired state, amid more fashionable neighbors. Nonetheless, this is a bright and charming Mexican spot that rises above the more familiar ethnic eateries that dot the boroughs.

In a city dominated by male chefs, Sue Torres brings success and life to her dishes through the little touches, like the fresh tortillas being churned out by hand in the dining room; or the guacamole, made to order with ripe chunks of avocado and bright tomato, paired with a basket of salty, house-made chips. An interesting chile-tasting menu and chile-rubbed goat with sweet plantain purée are not to be missed.

Tia Pol

A2

205 Tenth Ave. (bet. 22nd & 23rd Sts.)

Subway: 23 St (Eighth Ave.)
Phone: 212-675-8805
Web: www.tiapol.com
Prices: ⊖⊖

Lunch Tue – Sun
Dinner nightly

You can't shake a stick in Chelsea without hitting a tapas joint these days, but Tia Pol sets the standard. Although the bare bones space, a narrow dining room tucked behind a steel-patch door on Tenth Avenue, isn't much to marvel at—one whirl with Tia Pol's affordable Spanish wine list and delicious Basque small plates and you'll be rubbing elbows at the perpetually packed bar in no time.

Kick the night off with a cheese and charcuterie platter loaded with silky hams and garlicky chorizo; then dig into dishes like a chewy, toasted baguette laced with pickled onions and tender veal tongue, cooked *a la plancha*; smoky, paprika-dusted slices of chorizo finished in a sherry reduction; and tender lamb skewers rubbed with fragrant Moorish spices.

Tipsy Parson

A m e r i c a n XX

156 Ninth Ave. (bet. 19th & 20th Sts.)

Subway: 18 St

Lunch & dinner daily

Phone: 212-620-4545

Web: www.tipsyparson.com

Prices: $$

New Yorkers know the small plates drill by heart now: start slow and spend a mint. Tipsy Parson, a jewel in Chelsea compliments of Tasha Gibson and Julie Wallach, is as fine a place to do the dance as ever, with a homey, multi-room layout dressed in flower-fabrics, bric-à-brac, and French doors.

The menu features a nice selection of Southern fare, including cheeses from Georgia, Tennessee, Virginia, and South Carolina; an Ambrosia salad (with marshmallows); and buttermilk chive biscuits. Try the deviled eggs and fried pickles, *rumaki*, and oysters; and tender fried Mississippi-farmed catfish aside horseradish and mustard-laced potato salad. Don't miss the apple pie, featuring Northern Spy apples and cinnamon custard, served in a hot cast iron skillet.

Trestle on Tenth

C o n t e m p o r a r y XX

242 Tenth Ave. (at 24th St.)

Subway: 23 St (Eighth Ave.)

Lunch & dinner daily

Phone: 212-645-5659

Web: www.trestleontenth.com

Prices: $$

This inviting little gem is tiny in comparison to the behemoth restaurants thriving in and around Chelsea these days, but it packs a mighty big punch. Duck inside and you'll find an intimate, minimally-dressed interior featuring a wall of exposed brick; contemporary art; blonde wood ceilings; and a pretty outside garden that opens up seasonally.

Grab a seat and tuck into exceptional fare like a silky cauliflower soup, bobbing with fragrant herbs and tender, garlicky escargots; the homemade *metzgete* plate (served for a short window in January) utilizing every part of the pig, which might include exceptional blood sausage, liver sausage, and pork belly; or crispy roast chicken with summer vegetables in a fragrant, beautifully clear consommé.

Txikito

Manhattan ▶ Chelsea

B2

Spanish ✗

240 Ninth Ave. (bet. 24th & 25th Sts.)

Subway: 23 St (Eighth Ave.)
Phone: 212-242-4730
Web: www.txikitonyc.com
Prices: $$

Lunch Tue – Sat
Dinner nightly

The rise of the tapas movement is a fascinating one: what began as a Spanish snack of small plates paired with alcohol has grown so popular that people willingly spend as much as they would on a proper meal.

Good thing that tiny Txikito (pronounced *chick-KEE-toe*) offers so many wonderful reasons to indulge, with a knowledgeable waitstaff, proper silverware (though fingers, toothpicks, and perhaps forks are all one traditionally uses for tapas), and a simple, if slightly weathered décor. The menu is Chef Alex Raij's ode to Basque cuisine, featuring mouthwatering *pintxos* like *boquerónes* (marinated white anchovies); smoky eggplant purée; and a fan of boiled egg. Spanish wines and sangria spiked with gin, made refreshing with mint, complete the experience.

Good food without spending a fortune? Look for the Bib Gourmand 🏠.

Chinatown & Little Italy

As different as *chow mein* and chicken cacciatore, these two districts are nonetheless neighbors, though in recent years, their borders have become blurred with Chinatown voraciously gulping up most of Little Italy.

The end of California's Gold Rush brought the arrival of New York's first Chinese in the 1870s. The immigrant influx arrived energetically, setting up garment factories, markets, and restaurants in the quarter, which has inexorably spread into Little Italy and the Lower East Side. It is documented that New York cradles the maximum number of Chinese immigrants in the country and specifically, Queens, followed by Manhattan, holds one of the largest Chinese communities outside Asia. Immigrants from Hong Kong and mainland China (most recently Fujian province), populate Manhattan's Chinatown, each bringing their own distinct regional cuisines.

Chinatown Chow

Chowing in Chinatown can be both delectable and delightfully affordable. Elbow your way through the crowded streets and find a flurry of food markets, bubble tea cafés, bakeries, and eateries both large and small. Feast on freshly pulled noodles; duck into an ice cream parlor for a scoop of avocado or black sesame; or breeze past a market window and gander the crocodile meat and frogs on display (with claws!). Haggle over the freshest fish and produce at the storefronts and then sneak under the Manhattan Bridge for a *banh mi*. Klezmer meets Cantonese at the Egg Rolls and Egg Creams Festival, an annual summer street celebration honoring the neighboring Chinese and Jewish communities of Chinatown and the Lower East Side. Partygoers pack the streets for Chinese New Year (the first full moon after January 19th), with dragons dancing down the avenues accompanied by costumed revelers and fireworks.

LITTLE ITALY

The Little Italy of Scorsese's gritty, authentic *Mean Streets* is slowly vanishing into what may now be more aptly called Micro Italy. The onetime stronghold of a large Italian-American population (once spanning from Canal Street north to Houston, and from Lafayette to the Bowery) has dwindled to a mere corridor— Mulberry Street between Canal and Broome streets. Chinatown is quickly devouring Mulberry Street, the main drag and the tenacious heart of the area. But the spirit of the origins still pulses in century-old family-run markets, delis, gelato shops, and mom-and-pop trattorias. Established in 1892, **Alleva Dairy** (known for their homemade ricotta) is the oldest Italian cheese

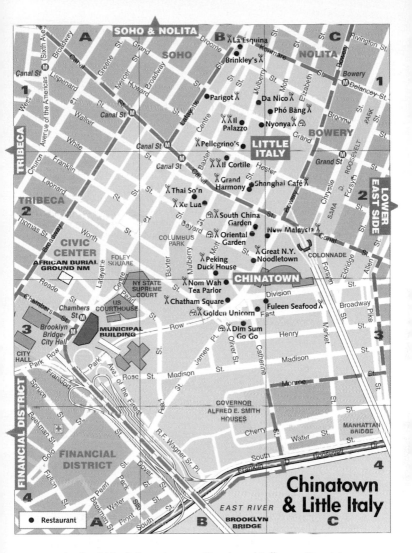

Chinatown & Little Italy

- Restaurant

store in the U.S. A few doors down at **DiPalo's Fine Foods** find imported *sopressata*, *salumi*, and stunning wine selections. Renowned for its Italian pastries and strong espresso, devotees frequent the beloved **Ferrara's Bakery and Café** on Grand Street. On weekends from May to mid-October, Mulberry Street is a pedestrian zone, creating one big alfresco party—the Feast of San Gennaro in September is particularly raucous. While these days you can get better Italian food elsewhere in the city, tourists still gather to treasure and bathe in the nostalgia of Mulberry Street.

Brinkley's

B1

406 Broome St. (bet. Centre & Lafayette Sts.)

Subway: Prince St   Lunch & dinner daily
Phone: 212-680-5600
Web: www.brinkleysnyc.com
Prices: $$

Brinkley's, a new gastropub tucked into the old Bar Martignetti space, is turning out to be quite the sleeper hit. Straddling a prime corner of real estate in Nolita, the restaurant (which is still owned by the Martignetti brothers) has good neighbors in nearby shop, Despaña, and the new Crosby Street Hotel; and the space is charmingly weathered, with a sexy, spirited design that reads retro in all the right ways.

A ridiculously skilled (and professional) team man the stoves, pushing out a menu that might include sardines mashed into a gorgeous tomato, fennel, and shallot strewn pulp; noodles of zucchini worked into a gorgeous carbonara, featuring smoky Virginia bacon and a tender poached egg; or a silky, exceptionally tasty pumpkin meringue pie.

Chatham Square

Chinese ✕

B3

6 Chatham Sq. (at East Broadway)

Subway: Canal St (Lafayette St.)   Lunch & dinner daily
Phone: 212-587-8800
Web: N/A
Prices: 🍳

Situated on a thriving stretch of the Bowery known as "Chatham Square," this lively, well-priced spot draws a mostly Chinese crowd for its fantastic daytime dim sum and evening classic Cantonese.

Large round tables line the colorful dining space where friendly servers wheel around carts of delicious dumplings, puffs, buns, and soups at lunch. The rolling dim sum show has become a rarity so sidle up next to some strangers at a shared table and indulge in delectable steamed dumplings–with at least ten varieties of fillings–or baked turnovers surrounding a savory mound of shredded roast pork. Sticky rice, congee, and dumpling soups provide some warmth. Feeling the funk? Brave the durian puffs—cigar-shaped pastries filled with a funky-fruity custard.

Da Nico

Italian 🍴

B1

164 Mulberry St. (bet. Broome & Grand Sts.)

Subway: Canal St (Lafayette St.) Lunch & dinner daily
Phone: 212-343-1212
Web: www.danicoristorante.com
Prices: $$

Dining here is an Italian-American celebration of garlic, tomatoes, and the traditional flavors typically associated with this culture—and neighborhood. From the coal fired oven comes a variety of pizzas, all made using a crust recipe that has been passed down through generations of the Luizza family (of the Mulberry Street empire). The ample selection of well-made favorites may include fried calamari, homemade minestrone, and huge portions of pastas. Entrées are likewise copious, from chicken Sorrentino to veal saltimbocca, and everything in between.

Weather permitting, opt to sit on the back patio. This enclosed outdoor terrace nearly doubles the restaurant's seating space and provides a bucolic ambience, removed from the neighborhood commotion.

Dim Sum Go Go 😊

Chinese 🍴

B3

5 East Broadway (at Chatham Sq.)

Subway: Canal St (Lafayette St.) Lunch & dinner daily
Phone: 212-732-0797
Web: N/A
Prices: 😊😊

Wake us up before you go-go to this Chinatown classic where the food is damn good; the dim sum is Hong Kong level; and the Cantonese is worth a shot. With over 24 varieties of mouthwatering dim sum served well into the evening (dim sum is traditionally a lunch thing) and a killer Cantonese menu, this bright, funky restaurant is a guaranteed good time; even if you do have to spend a little more than you would out in Sunset Park.

Head upstairs for a lively dinner scene or duck into the sleek downstairs room for a quick bite. Silky cellophane noodles arrive laced with crab and Chinese chives; while crab meat soup bobbing with tender bits of smoked ham, is served with fried Shanghai bread. Oh and you simply must not miss the otherworldly roast pork buns.

Fuleen Seafood

Chinese ✗

C3

11 Division St. (bet. Catherine & Market Sts.)

Subway: Canal St (Lafayette St.) Lunch & dinner daily
Phone: 212-941-6888
Web: www.fuleenrestaurant.com
Prices:

 From their variety of hard- and soft-shell crab dishes to the ever-popular snails in black bean sauce or geoduck clams "two different ways," this Cantonese cuisine does impressive things with gourmet ingredients. The large round tables of this upscale Chinatown mainstay are filled with gregarious groups from the local, discerning Chinese community—a testament to its success. Yet all are welcome here, as the polite staff graciously guides you through the menu, making helpful recommendations.

Garlicky, green vegetables are an essential accompaniment to meals here, perhaps complementing a whole fish, presented raw tableside before being expertly steamed and dressed with ginger and scallions. Landlubbers will unearth plenty of options on the sizeable menu.

Golden Unicorn

Chinese ✗

B3

18 East Broadway (at Catherine St.)

Subway: Canal St (Lafayette St.) Lunch & dinner daily
Phone: 212-941-0911
Web: www.goldenunicornrestaurant.com
Prices: $$

With its rolling carts of dim sum doing outrageous weekend lunch business and multiple stories of both Chinese and Manhattan foodie families gathering around large tables of Cantonese specialties, Golden Unicorn is a quintessential spot for Chinatown cuisine.

True, the décor feels a bit worn, waits are guaranteed at peak dim sum times (11:00 A.M.-2:00 P.M.), and all groups must be on their game to flag the speeding carts, but this perennial favorite is undeniably fun and delicious. Those in the know arrive early to avoid crowds and lessen competition for the best selection of roast duck, fried sticky pork dumplings, steamed bean curd skin rolls, and snow pea shoot buns.

Evening brings solid Cantonese specialties and nice banquet menus for large groups.

Grand Harmony

Chinese 🍴

B2

98 Mott St. (bet. Canal & Hester Sts.)

Subway: Canal St (Lafayette St.)   Lunch & dinner daily
Phone: 212 226-6603
Web: N/A
Prices: 😊😊

Is this, hands down, *the* best dim sum in Gotham? Probably not. Still, Grand Harmony pleases and teases its Chinese troops with an attractive banquet hall bedecked in red and gold, overflowing with chintzy decorations, gilded accents, and vibrant columns. Come midday, the huge space jams with crowds pouring in for that daytime indulgence—dim sum.

Dinner unveils a mélange of Cantonese food, but dim sum (at pretty prices) is the going game. Keep an eagle eye on those expert ladies rolling around carts of delicious *gai lan* (steamed Chinese broccoli, perfectly crisp, with oyster sauce); piping hot barbecue pork buns; fried tofu skin wrapped around pork, shrimp, and cabbage; or vermicelli tossed with pickled vegetables, dried squid, seafood, and scallions.

Great N.Y. Noodletown

Chinese 🍴

B2

28 Bowery (at Bayard St.)

Subway: Canal St (Lafayette St.)   Lunch & dinner daily
Phone: 212-349-0923
Web: N/A
Prices: 😊😊

You don't come for the ambience. With its closely jammed tables, roast ducks hanging in the window, and menus tucked under glass-topped tables, Great N.Y. Noodletown is down-market Chinatown at its drabbest. What you come for is the food–which, served daily from 9:00 - 4:00 A.M.–is not only delicious but remarkably cheap. Who could argue with a big bowl of perfectly roasted duck and tender noodles in a steaming broth for $4?

Best bets include any of the roasted meats served over fluffy rice; and, of course, duck, in all its crispy, fatty succulence. Don't miss the specials located on the table tents, where you'll find irresistible house delights like salt-baked soft shell crab (a must do when it's in season) and Chinese flowering chive stir-fries.

Il Cortile

B2

125 Mulberry St. (bet. Canal & Hester Sts.)

Subway: Canal St (Lafayette St)
Phone: 212-226-6060
Web: www.ilcortile.com
Prices: $$

Lunch & dinner daily

Beyond this quaint and charming façade lies one of Little Italy's famed mainstays, ever popular with dreamy eyed dates seeking the stuff of Billy Joel lyrics. The expansive space does indeed suggest a nostalgic romance, with its series of Mediterranean-themed rooms, though the most celebrated is the pleasant garden atrium (*il cortile* is Italian for "courtyard"), with a glass-paneled ceiling and abundant greenery.

A skilled line of chefs present a wide array of familiar starters and entrées, from eggplant rollatini to chicken Francese; as well as a range of pastas, such as *spaghettini puttanesca* or *risotto con funghi*. More than 30 years of sharing family recipes and bringing men to one bent knee continues to earn Il Cortile a longtime following.

Il Palazzo

B1

151 Mulberry St. (bet. Grand & Hester Sts.)

Subway: Canal St (Lafayette St.)
Phone: 212-343-7000
Web: N/A
Prices: $$

Lunch & dinner daily

This "palace" on Little Italy's celebrated Mulberry Street rises to every expectation of a good, traditional Italian-American meal. A tuxedo-clad host ushers guests into a long room with stucco walls and linen-draped tables. Beyond, the sunken dining room recalls a winter garden of lush greenery and natural light. Sidewalk seating is lovely and popular among tourists watching tourists.

Old-world dishes reign here, beginning with a basket of focaccia and bowl of Roman egg-drop soup. The classics continue with the likes of *vitello alla pizzaiola* (veal scallopini sautéed with tomato, onions, mustrooms, roasted pepper, and fresh basil); or *gamberoni alla scampi* (jumbo shrimp sautéed in a garlic-white wine sauce. Lunchtime frittata specials offer good value.

La Esquina

Mexican ✗

B1

106 Kenmare St. (bet. Cleveland Pl. & Lafayette St.)

Subway: Spring St (Lafayette St.)   Lunch & dinner daily
Phone: 646-613-7100
Web: www.esquinanyc.com
Prices: $$

When La Esquina opened in 2005 it was a breath of bright air, offering enjoyably fresh cuisine that stood tall among the paltry selection of Manhattan Mexican. Thankfully, the city's south-of-the-border dining scene has evolved since then. However, La Esquina remains a worthy option. More playground than restaurant, the multi-faceted setting takes up an iconic downtown corner and draws a hip crowd to the grab and go taqueria; 30-seat café, and lively subterranean dining room and bar amplified by a nightly DJ soundtrack.

Chef Akhtar Nawab has joined the operation and keeps the spirit not just alive but kicking with classic renditions of tortilla soup; *mole negro enchiladas*; as well the likes of *carne asada* of black Angus sirloin with *mojo de ajo*.

New Malaysia

Malaysian ✗

C2

46-48 Bowery (bet. Bayard & Canal Sts.)

Subway: Canal St (Lafayette St.)   Lunch & dinner daily
Phone: 212-964-0284
Web: N/A
Prices: ☜☜

Hidden in the Chinatown arcade accessed from either Bowery or Elizabeth, New Malaysia is the spot to go to in Manhattan for regional Malaysian. Some dishes are better than others, so reserve stomach space for the kitchen's strengths.

Asam laksa is a bowl of soupy, funky heaven, and the fried anchovies are a glorious and addictive could-be bar snack. *Roti canai* comes with a masterful coconut curry so delish you'll want to drink it up; and the fried *belacan* ladies fingers with shrimp is a complex, haunting stir fry. *Nasi lemak* and *beef rendang* are also killer but don't expect the skinny jeans to fit after all that coconut.

Insulin levels will spike with one of the Malaysian beverages, or colorful sweet shaved ices that bring sugary to a whole new level.

Nom Wah Tea Parlor

Chinese ✗

B3

13 Doyers St. (bet. Bowery & Pell St.)

Subway: Canal St (Lafayette St.)   Lunch & dinner daily
Phone: 212-962-6047
Web: www.nomwah.com
Prices: ⊜⊜

Possibly the most senior dim sum den along the still, back streets of Chinatown, Nom Wah Tea Parlor endured a face-lift when old man Wally handed over charge to young Wilson Tang. Renouncing a future in finance, Wilson took rule with an aim to refresh the model. While this may seem dubious, a parade of booths and tables topped with red-and-white vinyl spikes a nostalgic sense.

"The original egg roll" is a big hit and features delicious tempura-fried tofu skin wrapped around crunchy vegetables. Cheery servers follow this tasty, unique creation with other dim sum like a rice roll with fried dough splashed with sweet sauce; and roasted eggplant stuffed with crabmeat. While the house special pan fried dumplings may be salty, they are some of *the* best in town.

Nyonya 😊

Malaysian ✗

B1

199 Grand St. (bet. Mott & Mulberry Sts.)

Subway: Canal St (Lafayette St.)   Lunch & dinner daily
Phone: 212-334-3669
Web: www.penangusa.com
Prices: ⊜⊜

A Malaysian marvel in Manhattan, Nyonya is replete with regulars and City Hall suits. The space, now a bit brighter and larger, retains its Chinatown aesthetic and buzzes with gruff servers. But keep faith, as they hold the keys to some magnificent Malaysian.

Teasing your taste buds is a fluffy oyster omelette anointed with sweet chili sauce. A specialty from the massive menu and perfect for the prudent is beef satay with peanut sauce; while the house special crabs massaged with ground chili and dried shrimp is best for the bodacious.

A bevy of classic beverages gorgeously gratifies Malay faithfuls like *Assam laksa* rich with herbs, lemongrass, noodles, and sardine flakes; and *nasi lemak*, a mélange of coconut rice, chicken, anchovies, veg, and eggs.

Oriental Garden

Chinese 🍴

B2

14 Elizabeth St. (bet. Bayard & Canal Sts.)

Subway: Canal St (Lafayette St.)   Lunch & dinner daily
Phone: 212-619-0085
Web: www.orientalgardenny.com
Prices: $$

A single room makes up this garden of Chinese delights. Robed in warm shades of beige and red, and packed with tables that expand just as readily as your waistline, Oriental Garden is a precious jewel much sought both for daytime dim sum and top quality Cantonese.

Jammed by noon, dim sum is ordered from carts or the printed menu. The carts carry crowd-pleasers but tune them out and order the steamy chive dumplings, crisp baked roast pork triangles, and juicy roast duck. After the dumplings digest, Cantonese takes over. The fish tanks lining the entryway are a good indication of where to start. First-rate preparations of these global swimmers include the seasonal Australian crystal crabs, oysters with ginger and scallions, or lobster "country style."

Parigot

French 🍴

B1

155 Grand St. (at Lafayette St.)

Subway: Canal St (Lafayette St.)   Lunch & dinner daily
Phone: 212-274 8859
Web: www.parigotnyc.com
Prices: $$

In the neck of Nolita, Parigot is that hugely favored French bistro teeming with traditional fare. Francophiles come here to be comforted by classics such as mussels Parigot; escargot with garlic-parsley butter; Basque omelette; and coq au vin. Smaller groups from around the way might share an *assiette de charcuterie* or *assiette de fromages* (heaping platters of French meats or cheeses), all the while picturing themselves cruising along the prestigious Champs-Élysées.

With French music wafting through a wood-furnished dining room whose cheery walls are hung with photos of cafés, a meal at Parigot feels like a mini French vacation nicely capped with a salad Niçoise uniting hard boiled eggs, anchovy fillets, and tuna flakes with a tangy Dijon vinaigrette.

Peking Duck House

B2

28 Mott St. (bet. Chatham Sq. & Pell St.)

Subway: Canal St (Lafayette St)
Phone: 212-227-1810
Web: www.pekingduckhousenyc.com
Prices: $$

Lunch & dinner daily

Only rookies open the menu at Peter Luger steakhouse—and the same ought to apply to any restaurant named after a menu item. So, while you may stumble onto a few gems like the fragrant wonton soup, the bird is the word at this group-friendly Chinatown joint.

Despite its boorish name, the Peking Duck House is a touch classier than her Chinatown sisters, with a contemporary polish that won't frighten your Midwestern cousin. Service may slow down at the more elegant midtown location, but both locations wheel out the golden brown duck with proper flare, and carve it into mouthwatering slices. Your job is easy: fold the freshly carved meat into fresh pancakes, sprinkle with scallion, cucumbers, and a dash of hoisin sauce...then devour.

Pellegrino's

B1

138 Mulberry St. (bet. Grand & Hester Sts.)

Subway: Canal St (Lafayette St)
Phone: 212-226-3177
Web: N/A
Prices: $$

Lunch & dinner daily

On a warm summer day, Pellegrino's quaint sidewalk tables look upon the heart of Little Italy. You will likely find both regulars and tourists frequenting this local mainstay, since the long, narrow dining room is attractive, the umbrella-shaded outdoor tables are inviting, and the service is courteous. Children are welcome at family friendly Pellegrino's; in fact, half-portions are offered for smaller appetites.

The food stays true to its Italian-American roots with large portions of balanced pasta, meat, and fish selections. Linguini alla Sinatra, the signature dish named for the beloved crooner, teems with lobster, shrimp, mushrooms, and pine nuts in a light red clam sauce. Tasty, classic desserts are likewise a draw to this popular destination.

Pho Băng

C1

Vietnamese 🍴

157 Mott St. (bet. Broome & Grand Sts.)

Subway: bet. Broome & Grand Sts.
Phone: 212-966-3797
Web: N/A
Prices: 🪙🪙

Lunch & dinner daily

$

Hangover? Craving? In need of a quick, tasty meal? Pho Băng is where it's at for restorative bowls of bubbling *pho*, served up in a flash and on the cheap. Park it in the simple space and start with a plate of delicious fried Vietnamese spring rolls (*cha gio*) served with lettuce and mint leaves for wrapping; or try the tasty rice "crêpe," (*bahn cuon nhan thit cha lua*), stuffed with black mushrooms, pork, sprouts, and ham—a real treat and rare find here in New York, so don't skip it.

Finally, follow the lead of your fellow diners and slurp up one of seventeen varieties of hearty *pho*. Try the *pho tai gau*— fresh eye of round, brisket, and rice noodles in a flavorful beef broth, served with sprouts, basil, and lemon, all for less than eight bucks.

Shanghai Café

B2

Chinese 🍴

100 Mott St. (bet. Canal & Hester Sts.)

Subway: Canal St (Lafayette St.)
Phone: 212-966-3988
Web: N/A
Prices: 🪙🪙

Lunch & dinner daily

$

Head to this contemporary Chinatown spot when the craving hits for good Shanghai-style cuisine at a fair price. Dumpling assemblers beckon diners in from the front window, crafting the tiny, succulent juicy buns, and adding them to massive steamers. Filled with crabmeat and/or pork, these juicy little jewels explode with flavor in your mouth. A hands-down favorite, "steamed tiny buns," as the menu calls them, appears on nearly every occupied table, sometimes in multiple orders. In addition, the enormous menu cites a decision-defying array of Shanghainese classics including cold and hot starters, soups, and seafood and noodle dishes. Have a taste and you'll agree that Shanghai Café ranks a bun above the usual Chinese fare on this stretch of Mott Street.

South China Garden 😊

B2

22 Elizabeth St. (bet. Bayard & Canal Sts.)

Subway: Canal St (Lafayette St.)   Lunch & dinner daily
Phone: 212-964-2229
Web: N/A
Prices: 💰💰

Though the official name of this Chinatown restaurant is currently South China Garden, the city's "Chinese in the know foodies" call this place by its old moniker: Cantoon Garden. Call it anything you want for now—if they keep dishing up Cantonese fare this good, you're likely to be calling it your favorite new restaurant by bill time.

The atmosphere is simple, bright, and clean (hey, you don't come here for romance), and the waitstaff is young and eager to guide newcomers. Anything plucked off the massive menu is likely to deliver, but don't miss the wok-fried lobster massaged with soy, ginger, and scallions. Another hit is the salt-baked shrimp and the crisped baby bok choy perfumed with garlic is a perfect accompaniment to this meal.

Thai So'n

B2

89 Baxter St. (bet. Bayard & Canal Sts.)

Subway: Canal St (Lafayette St.)   Lunch & dinner daily
Phone: 212-732-2822
Web: N/A
Prices: 💰💰

Even along competitive Baxter Street, Thai So'n is a neighborhood standout for high-quality Vietnamese fare and tremendous value. The atmosphere may feel like a catering hall with minimal focus on comfort, but this does not dissuade the groups and families seeking the huge and authentic Vietnamese menu of fresh, fiery, and flavorful cuisine.

Ignore the Chinese selections (popular with the nearby City Hall crowds) and start with frogs legs in chili-lemongrass sauce, then go with the *pho*: comforting bowls of rice noodles and delicately sliced raw beef that instantly cook when scalding broth is poured overtop. Garnish this with ample condiments and wash it down with a *tra da chanh* (a Vietnamese Arnold Palmer) for a traditionally delicious experience.

Xe Lua

B2

86 Mulberry St. (bet. Bayard & Canal Sts.)

Subway: Canal St (Lafayette St)   Lunch & dinner daily
Phone: 212-577-8887
Web: www.xeluanewyork.com
Prices: 💰

A cheery orange sign splashed in yellow, blue, and green blazons this lovely spot's name in both English and Vietnamese, while tropical themes outfit the interior in royal blue, bamboo, and a floor-to-ceiling mural of boats, sea, and sky.

The expansive menu features a flavorful assortment of appetizers, stir fries, clay pots, noodles, and rice dishes, with headings like "Porky," "Froggy Style," and "Chicken Little" to express their quirky humor. Dive into one of fourteen varieties of *pho*—these steaming bowls of rice noodle soup are all under seven dollars. Heartier appetites are satisfied with the *pho xe lua*, a massive bowl of noodles, brisket, tendon, tripe, and meatballs swimming in a rich beef broth. The staff is pleasant, quick, and efficient.

Park your car without a problem when you see 🅿 for valet parking.

East Village

This storied bohemia is no longer rampant with riots, rockers, and radical zeitgeist, but remains crowned as Manhattan's uncompromising capital of counter-culture. East Villagers may seem tamer now that CBGB is closed, but they are no less creative, casual, and undeniably cool.

The neighborhood's bars and eateries exhibit the same edge, and denizens craving a nightly nosh have plenty to choose from. **Momofuku Milk Bar**, turns out a spectrum of delectable baked goods and soft serve ice cream in seasonal flavors like cereal milk and caramel apple until midnight. Crispy Belgian fries from **Pomme Frites** are heightened by sauces like curry-ketchup and smoked-eggplant mayo. For burgers, **Paul's** may have the best in town. **Crif Dogs**—open until 4:00 A.M. on weekends—deep fries their dogs for the perfect post-pub-crawl snack.

Many eateries, cafés, second-hand shops, and vendors line these blocks with specialties from pork (**Porchetta**) to macaroni & cheese (**S'mac**) in a distinctly East Village way. Speaking of cheese, **The Bourgeois Pig** draws celebrities on the "down-low" with its pots of fondue; equally stellar is **Luke's Lobster**, a seafood shack offering the freshest of product directly from Maine.

Perhaps most spirited, and in keeping with the kitschy downtown feel, is Japantown—a decidedly down-market and groovier "Harajuku" version of its Midtown East sibling. Along St. Marks Place look for the red paper lanterns of hip yakitori spots like **Taisho**, or smell the *takoyaki* frying and sizzling *okonomiyaki* at **Otafuku**; and explore divey *izakayas* like **Go** or **Village Yokocho**. Among the area's sultry sake dens, few can rival subterranean **Decibel**—serving an outrageous selection of sake and *shochu* in its hideaway setting. Devout bargain-hunters will relish **Xi'an Famous Foods**—their menu is made up of regional Chinese cuisine from the Shaanxi province, an area made famous after the discovery of the Terracotta Army.

While Japantown may tuck its lounges down a nondescript stairway, everything along the "Curry Row" stretch of East Sixth Street smacks of festivities, with spices as bold as the neon lights that dot the awnings. While these inexpensive spots may cater to NYU students, they also offer a great spread of South Asian food.

For a bit of old-world flavor, an afternoon at **Veniero's Pasticceria & Caffè** is in order. Established in 1894, this friendly staple draws long lines (especially around holiday time) for its traditional Italian baked goods. **Sigmund Pretzel Shop** is famed for its

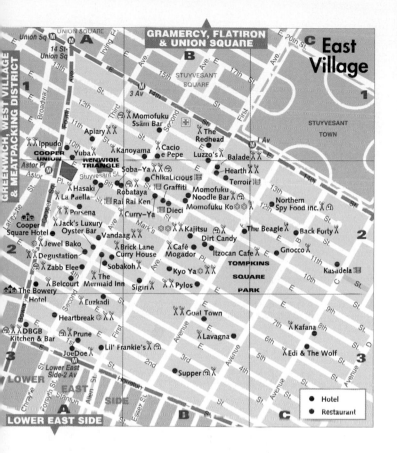

GREENWICH, WEST VILLAGE & MEATPACKING DISTRICT

LOWER EAST SIDE

STUYVESANT SQUARE

STUYVESANT TOWN

TOMPKINS SQUARE PARK

• Hotel
• Restaurant

---

handmade pretzels dressed with dips like beet-horseradish mayo. The beloved, family-run **Veselka** has been serving Ukrainian treats for over 50 years, representing the area's former Eastern European population.

For specialty items, **East Village Cheese** is a premier vendor—find an ample selection here, minus the mark-up of gourmet emporiums. It goes without saying that liquor flows freely in the East Village. There are an abundance of dive bars, but those with a more urbane palate will be happy that this neighborhood is at the nexus of cutting-edge mixology. **Angel's Share** (hidden in a Japanese restaurant on Stuyvesant Street); **PDT**, or Please Don't Tell (accessed through Crif Dogs); **Death & Co.** on East Sixth Street; and **Mayahuel** (with its south-of-the-border spin) all offer an epicurean approach to cocktail service garnering them accolades.

Apiary

A1

60 Third Ave. (bet. 10th & 11th Sts.)

Subway: 14 St - Union Sq   Dinner nightly
Phone: 212-254-0888
Web: www.apiarynyc.com
Prices: $$

   Bringing a unique elegance and maturity to its East Village locale, Apiary's intimate space is buzz-worthy. Envisioned by Ligne Roset, the contemporary furniture design company, the sleek room features burgundy and brown upholstered chairs beneath chandelier-shaped plastic sconces.

The modern menu follows suit, with the likes of golden brown sweetbreads with deep-crimson romesco sauce—its alluring flavors a wonderful departure from tradition. From the emerald-green olive oil and excellent breads to thick, caramelized pork chops with black beans and chunky guacamole, to desserts like a buttery blackberry financier, Executive Chef Scott Bryan (formerly of Veritas) keeps the menu concise and tasty.

Prix-fixe and tasting menus are also offered.

Back Forty

C2

190 Ave. B (at 12th St.)

Subway: 1 Av   Lunch Sat – Sun
Phone: 212-388-1990   Dinner nightly
Web: www.backfortynyc.com
Prices: $$

   Chef/owner Peter Hoffman satiates city slickers seeking the country life with this popular tavern's array of fresh-from-the-farm themed preparations. The casual setting evokes heartland charm with its tables topped by brown paper mats that display the menu, walls adorned with found objects and agricultural tools, as well as an inviting backyard dining area.

Snacks and starters, such as pork jowl nuggets with jalapeño jam, are represented alongside seasonal garden side dishes like a cauliflower gratin. A core menu of hearty entrées may include the excellent, succulent braised lamb shank, perfectly manageable in size, slicked with a rich meat jus reduction, then plated with creamy celery root purée and sweet-sour apple chutney.

Balade

Lebanese ✗✗

B2

208 First Ave. (bet. 12th & 13th Sts.)

Subway: 1 Av
Phone: 212-529-6868
Web: www.baladerestaurants.com
Prices: 🍲

Lunch & dinner daily

Honing in on the cuisine of Lebanon, Balade is a welcoming and tasty Middle Eastern experience fronted by a cheerful red awning. The spotless room is accented with tile, brick, and wood; and each table bears a bottle of private label herb-infused olive oil.

The menu begins with a glossary of traditional Lebanese ingredients and the explanation that *Balade* means "fresh, local." The meze; grilled meat-stuffed sandwiches; and Lebanese-style pizzas called *manakeesh* topped with the likes of lean ground beef, chopped onion, and spices are all fresh-tasting indeed. House specialties are also of note, like the *mujaddara crush*—a platter of lentils and rice topped by crispy fried onions and a salad of cool chopped cucumber and tomato.

The Beagle

Contemporary ✗

B2

162 Ave. A (bet. 10th & 11th Sts.)

Subway: 1 Av
Phone: 212-228-6900
Web: www.thebeaglenyc.com
Prices: $$

Dinner Tue – Sun

Headed by a pair hailing from Portland, OR, this East Village newbie rocks an old timey look that fashions a weathered concrete floor, French doors dressed up with curtains, and walls spruced up by duo-chromatic flora and fauna wallpaper into a winsome perch. The pleasingly petite café is an especially tempting suggestion for a cocktail. Complex concoctions such as the Astor Painless Anesthetic are poured from a white tiled bar; and the menu includes wooden board small plates accompanied by a shot—fried sweetbreads with caramelized fennel matched with a taste of Calvados is one fine example.

Olive oil poached halibut with fingerling potatoes and fish fumet-*onnaise*; and dark chocolate custard with caramelized corn flakes hint at the fun cuisine.

Belcourt

Mediterranean ✗

84 E. 4th St. (at Second Ave.)

Subway: Astor Pl
Phone: 212-979-2034
Web: www.belcourtnyc.com
Prices: **$$**

Lunch Sat – Sun
Dinner nightly

Brimming with mix-and-match wood furnishings, antique mirror panels, and reclaimed signage, one might be misled to assume that this young and charming neighborhood favorite is from a bygone era. The relaxed look is classic Paris brasserie; the cuisine is anything but.

Chef/partner Matt Hamilton, who sharpened his skills at Five Points and Prune, takes a fresh approach to a seasonally themed menu that sways toward the Mediterranean. Offerings may include a sauce-slurping stew of steamed clams, chewy coarse-ground sausage, and tender white beans all sparked by bold salsa verde; or moist pan-fried Long Island fluke beautifully complemented by a decadent scallion and crème fraîche sauce, garnished with sweet and tender roasted greenmarket carrots.

Brick Lane Curry House

Indian ✗

306-308 E. 6th St. (bet. First & Second Aves.)

Subway: Astor Pl
Phone: 212-979-2900
Web: www.bricklanecurryhouse.com
Prices: **$$**

Lunch & dinner daily

Located on Curry Row and named after London's own, Brick Lane is a 6th Street standout featuring numerous influences lifted from across the pond. Beers are available by the half or full pint, an Underground map adorns the wall, and meltingly soft cheddar cheese stuffs the tasty *paratha*.

Despite the Anglo-culinary whimsy, Brick Lane's heart belongs to curry with a selection of fifteen varieties that include Goan, spiked with green chilies and a tangy bite. Prepared with your protein of choice, the selection even includes the *phaal*, said to be so spicy it is accompanied by a disclaimer warning guests of "physical or emotional damage" that may result. However, this may also be a reminder of the thoughtful, friendly, and efficient service staff here.

Cacio e Pepe

Italian ✗

B1

182 Second Ave. (bet. 11th & 12th Sts.)

Subway: 3 Av   Dinner nightly
Phone: 212-505-5931
Web: www.cacioepepe.com
Prices: $$

With its subdued temperament and pleasant service, this casual and charming Italian can be trusted to satisfy, from the warm greeting everyone receives upon entering to the cannoli—a lovely finale to any meal here. The rustic menu of traditional Roman dishes features a house specialty from which the establishment takes its name: house-made *tonnarelli* tossed with pasta water, olive oil, cracked black pepper, and a showering of pecorino cheese. Yet there is much more to be discovered, such as cuttlefish over soft polenta or *bucatini all'Amatriciana*.

The wine list is short but carefully selected to highlight less-familiar producers in the most notable Italian regions. In warm weather, the pretty backyard garden makes an idyllic dining area.

Café Mogador

Moroccan ✗

B2

101 St. Mark's Pl. (bet. First Ave. & Ave. A)

Subway: 1 Av   Lunch & dinner daily
Phone: 212-677-2226
Web: www.cafemogador.com
Prices: ☺☺

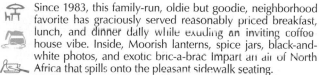

Since 1983, this family-run, oldie but goodie, neighborhood favorite has graciously served reasonably priced breakfast, lunch, and dinner daily while exuding an inviting coffee house vibe. Inside, Moorish lanterns, spice jars, black-and-white photos, and exotic bric-a-brac impart an air of North Africa that spills onto the pleasant sidewalk seating.

Mediterranean small plates like roasted eggplant with creamy tahini and fresh pita make a fine prelude to the Moroccan house specialties, such as fluffy couscous, *bastilla*, or perhaps the *merguez* sausage platter served with *harissa*. Traditional, spicy-sweet, slowly simmered, lamb and chicken tagines are moist, tender, and always popular in sauces of apricots and prunes or piquant green *charmoula*.

ChikaLicious

B2

203 E. 10th St. (bet. First & Second Aves.)

Subway: Astor Pl
Phone: 212-475-0929
Web: www.chikalicious.com
Prices: ⊜

Dinner Thu – Sun

Named for Pastry Chef/owner Chika Tillman, this sweet spot presents an all-encompassing dessert experience that somehow manages to impress without overkill. The chic white space offers counter seating overlooking a lab-clean kitchen where the team prepares elegant jewels that start as butter, sugar, and chocolate. À la carte is offered, but the best way to appreciate this dessert bar is to select the prix-fixe menu. Feasts here may begin with an amuse-bouche of Darjeeling tea gelée with milk sorbet, followed by a mascarpone semifreddo topped with espresso granita, then finish with the pillowy cubes of coconut-marshmallow petits fours.

Dessert Club across the street tempts with cookies, cupcakes, and shaved ice for a grab-and-go fix.

Curry-Ya

Japanese ✗

B2

214 E. 10th St. (bet. First & Second Aves.)

Subway: Astor Pl
Phone: 866-602-8779
Web: www.nycurry-ya.com
Prices: ⊜

Lunch & dinner daily

From the co-owner of Soba-Ya, comes this tasty newcomer, specializing in Japan's unique version of curry—*yoshoku*. This culinary icon belongs in the repertoire of Western style dishes that have become a part of the Japanese palate. Characterized by a mild sweetness and restrained heat, Curry-Ya's rich sauce is garnished with pickled vegetables, short grain rice, and is available with a selection of accompaniments like *panko*-crusted Berkshire pork cutlet, organic chicken, and grilled hamburger. The small menu also offers inspiring starters like a salad of *yuba* and snow peas with green olive dressing.

The bright space, warmed by pale pink walls and blonde wood stools, offers seating for 14 at a marble counter set in front of the white-tiled kitchen.

DBGB Kitchen & Bar 😋

A3

French ♟♟

299 Bowery (bet. First & Houston Sts.)

Subway: Lower East Side 2 Av
Phone: 212-933-5300
Web: www.danielnyc.com
Prices: $$

Lunch & dinner daily

Superstar Chef Daniel Boulud's popular take on casual downtown eats features an earthy shaded dining room that evokes the Bowery's past as a hub for restaurant supplies: shelves are stocked with dry goods and crockery, the wraparound exposed kitchen displays gleaming surfaces, and the restroom walls recall pages of vintage cookware catalogs. The kitchen's playful spirit is evident in the eclectic menu of impressive dishes, including mouthwatering burgers, a globally-inspired selection of sausages, and creative ice cream sundaes. More gilded fare has featured the likes of velvety potato soup seasonally embellished with green garlic, sweet peas, and ramps; and a richly satisfying bowlful of house-made saffron tagliolini with veal Bolognese.

Degustation

A2

Spanish ♟♟

239 E. 5th St. (bet. Second & Third Aves.)

Subway: Astor Pl
Phone: 212-979-1012
Web: N/A
Prices: $$

Dinner nightly

This discreet and understated East Village tapas bar from Jack and Grace Lamb, also of Jewel Bako next door, bears the chic vibe New Yorkers would expect from this stylish couple. Slate-tiled walls, red leather placemats, and sleek place settings make the dimly lit space feel elegant and intimate. Sushi bar-style seating is arranged on a counter facing the open kitchen, where small plates are artfully prepared by this fresh-faced and well-trained team. Creative offerings may include tiny golden *croquetas* with fine bits of ham and green apple, or wild mushroom salad with lamb bacon.

The knowledgeable, smartly attired staff thoughtfully tends to each guest, often guiding them through the menu and making suggestions from the all-Spanish wine list.

Dieci

B2

228 E. 10th St. (bet. First & Second Aves.)

Subway: Astor Pl
Phone: 212-387-9545
Web: www.dieciny.com
Prices: 🍝🍝

Dinner nightly

Dieci fuses Italian and Japanese cuisines for a successful marriage of taste and creativity. The tiny step-down setting is easy to miss but conquers its spatial challenge with comfortable seating centered on a dark-wood dining counter that juts out from the kitchen; a handful of small tables bolster the accommodations.

The menu is under the direction of Chef Takanori Akiyama and presents a unique array of small plates that include meaty bites such as yuzu-pepper organic chicken *kara-age*; unexpected sushi, as in shrimp and uni wrapped in prosciutto; and pastas such as an intermingling of slender, springy ramen and spicy lamb Bolognese. Desserts are also impressive, as in silky Earl Grey crème brûlée with house-made Tahitian vanilla bean gelato.

Dirt Candy 😊

B2

430 E. 9th St. (bet. First Ave. & Ave. A)

Subway: 1 Av
Phone: 212-228-7732
Web: www.dirtcandynyc.com
Prices: $$

Dinner Tue – Sat

Accommodating fewer than twenty in a boutique-sized space, Chef/owner Amanda Cohen keeps a watchful eye on each and every diner as she skillfully crafts vegetarian fare from the tiny rear kitchen. Certified by the Green Restaurant Association, the bright room has glass paneled walls and closely packed tables furnished with Arne Jacobsen chairs.

Both devotees and skeptics alike are impressed by this menu of unique items featuring such preparations as portobello mousse with truffle oil-slicked toast and pickled pear compote; or golden crisped blocks of semi-firm tofu draped with Kaffir lime beurre blanc. Yield to temptation with desserts like light and spongy zucchini-ginger cake served à la mode with deliciously smooth cream cheese ice cream.

Edi & The Wolf

C3

102 Ave. C (bet. 6th & 7th Sts.)

Subway: 1 Av
Phone: 212-598-1040
Web: www.ediandthewolf.com
Prices: $$

Lunch Sat – Sun
Dinner nightly

Chefs Eduard Frauneder and Wolfgang Ban, the dynamic duo behind Seäsonal, have brought their wares downtown with the arrival of this *heuriger*—a casual neighborhood wine tavern common in Austria. The dark and earthy den is chock-full of reclaimed materials including a 40-foot rope salvaged from a church, now coiled above the tiny bar.

The crux of the offerings is comprised of small and shared plates such as cured and dried *landjäger* sausage accompanied by house-made mustard and pickles. Entrées fall under the heading of "schnitzel & co." and offer a highly recommended wiener schnitzel, which starts with a pounded filet of heritage pork encased in an incredibly delicate and crunchy coating dressed with Austrian-style potato salad and lingonberry jam.

Euzkadi

A3

108 E. 4th St. (bet. First & Second Aves.)

Subway: Lower East Side - 2 Av
Phone: 212-982-9788
Web: www.euzkadirestaurant.com
Prices: $$

Dinner nightly

Haven't heard of Euzkadi? Maybe you've been living in a cave. While some restaurants dish out great food but disappoint in the décor department, this one-of-a-kind place delivers both. With textured, exposed walls painted with prehistoric-style cave drawings, thick, velvet curtains shutting out all sunlight, and soft, low lighting, diners can be cave dwellers—even if just for the evening. This cocoon-like restaurant is a great find, despite its cramped quarters.

Of course, no caveman ate this well. The menu covers all the bases of traditional Basque cooking, including tapas and the house specialty, *paella mariscos*. Loaded with fish and shellfish, and redolent of saffron, the paella comes sized for two in a traditional cast-iron pan.

Gnocco

Italian ✗

C2

337 E. 10th St. (bet. Aves. A & B)

Subway: 1 Av
Phone: 212-677-1913
Web: www.gnocco.com
Prices: $$

Lunch Sat – Sun
Dinner nightly

This quaint Alphabet City Italian is a top local hangout, perfectly suiting the casual, neighborhood vibe. The dining room's rustic charm is accented by rough hewn plank flooring, exposed brick, and large windows that overlook the colorful scenes of Tompkins Square Park. In summer, the shaded back terrace with vine-covered walls and pretty murals is a great place to enjoy the namesake specialty, *gnocco*: crispy, deep-fried pillows of dough served with thin slices of *prosciutto di Parma* and salami.

Enjoyable homemade pastas, a lengthy listing of thin-crusted pizzas, and heartier main dishes comprise the tasty offerings here, served by an attentive and gracious staff. The fluffy and creamy lemon and mint semifreddo is always a pleasant finish.

Goat Town

Contemporary ✗✗

B3

511 E. 5th St. (bet. Aves. A & B)

Subway: Lower East Side - 2 Av
Phone: 212-687-3641
Web: www.goattownnyc.com
Prices: $$

Lunch Sat – Sun
Dinner nightly

Overseen by a talented pair of restaurant professionals, this Alphabet City newcomer has the goods to back up its instantly lovable style. Installed with a collection of hand-built appointments, Goat Town rocks a rustic vibe underscored by a candlelit glow, fun crowd, and upbeat soundtrack.

The theme is bistro-influenced in offerings such as steak tartare, a nightly oyster list, and specials like French onion soup made with dark beer. Skilled cooking lets the high quality produce shine, like lacinato kale salad tossed with bits of butternut squash and country ham; or a textbook *meunière* made of Long Island fluke dressed with perfectly browned butter and a creamy puddle of cauliflower purée. For a finale, the New York cheesecake is a must.

Graffiti

R2

224 E. 10th St. (bet First & Second Aves.)

Subway: 1 Av

Phone: 212-464-7743

Web: www.graffitinyc.com

Prices: $$

Dinner Tue – Sun

Credibly doted on since it's inception in 2007, this cub of Chef/owner Jehangir Mehta (of Jean Georges luster) is still going strong and baby boy is quite the dreamboat. Dressed with tightly-packed square communal tables and beaded ceiling lights, petite Graffiti may be dimly lit, but an exposed brick wall glossed with a metallic finish and hugging framed mirrors is all brightness.

Feeding a pack of 20 on newspaper-wrapped tables are Indian-inspired sweet and savory small plates of watermelon and feta salad cooled by vibrant mint sorbet; eggplant buns spiked with toasty cumin; green mango *paneer*; and zucchini hummus pizza. If you forget to order the green chili shrimp, you can hit "Mehtaphor" in the Duane Street Hotel for a taste of this spiced delight.

Hasaki

A2

210 E. 9th St. (bet. Second & Third Aves.)

Subway: Astor Pl

Phone: 212-473-3327

Web: www.hasakinyc.com

Prices: $$$

Lunch Wed – Sun
Dinner nightly

Opened in 1984 and still going strong, this unassuming, no-reservations spot on a tree-lined stretch of the East Village is quietly housed just below street level. The dining room has a clean and spare look, with seating available at a number of wood tables or at the sizeable counter manned by a personable chef.

Hasaki's longevity is attributed to the high quality of its products, which infuses the dining experience with a sense of seriousness and purpose. Skillfully prepared and reasonably priced, delicate sushi and sashimi share the spotlight with shabu-shabu, green tea noodles, and crisp tempura. The menu is supplemented by fascinating daily specials that tend to sell out quickly. Before 6:30 P.M., the generous "Twilight" menu is cherished.

55

Heartbreak ✿

German ✕✕

29 E. 2nd St. (at Second Ave.)

Subway: Lower East Side - 2 Av
Phone: 212-777-2502
Web: www.heartbreakrestaurant.com
Prices: $$

Lunch Sat – Sun
Dinner nightly

Heartbreak

You mustn't be fooled by the corner upon which it sits, because your heart truly *will* melt upon entering this Swiss-German *urbanista*. Divulging an au courant décor are lush lumber floors, chaste walls, and tables armed with soothing grey chairs and leather banquettes. If that doesn't pop, the splash of red accents surely will.

Casual yet stylish, Heartbreak has won the hearts of many, including families, girly-gaggles, and jet-setters. They're all here for a bright, boozey spree (beers and wines are most notable) by dint of a dramatic bar. Attended by a warm, welcoming staff, most winning in this boundless, well-tread space is Chef Ingrid Roettele's preparations (and presence)— her performance both behind the stoves and on the floor is a true spectacle.

Drawing a dazzling cast of city types is an involved and prettily-priced menu. Boisterous clans swoon over the house fondue perfect with a Riesling; while the flawless kitchen flaunts *currywurst* (golden brown sausage dressed with a curry-spiked ketchup); *choucroute garni* (smoked pork chop and bacon with a deadly side of Riesling-sauerkraut); and Black Forest cake studded with dark chocolate and supple black cherries.

Hearth

Mediterranean ✗✗

B2

403 E. 12th St. (at First Ave.)

Subway: 1 Av
Phone: 646-602-1300
Web: www.restauranthearth.com
Prices: $$$

Dinner nightly

Simple wooden tables; walls lined with wine glasses and copper pots; a cozy little bar overlooking the kitchen—Hearth's welcoming, candlelit interior sets the stage for the comforting Mediterranean meal to come.

The menu effortlessly skates between old-world classics and seasonal dishes punched up with inspired touches of creativity that work beautifully. Try the spring onion soup, bobbing with rich knobs of sea urchin and tender brioche croutons; fresh Columbia River sturgeon wrapped in crispy prosciutto and paired with ruby-red beets, zingy horseradish, trout eggs, and chervil; or homemade lasagna, fat with fresh ricotta, saffron, and lemon rind. Paired with a gorgeous red plucked off the temptingly descriptive wine list? Mediterranean bliss.

Ippudo

Japanese ✗✗

A1

65 Fourth Ave. (bet. 9th & 10th Sts.)

Subway: 14 St - Union Sq
Phone: 212-388-0088
Web: www.ippudo.com/ny
Prices: ❤❤

Lunch & dinner daily

A wall covered in soup bowls is your clue of what to order at this first stateside outpost of the popular Japanese chain, opened by the renowned "King of Ramen" Shigemi Kawahara. Ramen-hungry diners are given a boisterous welcome from the youthful, energetic staff upon entering; expect the same at the farewell. With most seating arranged at communal oak-topped tables and prominently displayed open kitchen, Ippudo feels laid-back and fun yet sleek. The classic *shiromaru* ramen is a deeply satisfying bowl of rich pork broth and excellent, slender, fresh-made noodles garnished with sliced pork and cabbage.

If left with a bowlful of extra broth, simply tell your server "kae-dama" and for a small charge you'll receive an additional bowl of noodles.

Itzocan Cafe

Mexican 🍴

B2

438 E. 9th St. (bet. First Ave. & Ave. A)

Subway: 1 Av   Lunch & dinner Tue – Sun
Phone: 212-677-5856
Web: www.itzocanrestaurant.com
Prices: $$

With seating for less than 16, Itzocan is *muy pequeño*, but its menu of bold Mexican fare is certainly big on flavor. Quality ingredients abound in a lunchtime listing of quesadillas and burritos, but at dinner Chef/owner Fermin Bello offers more distinctive plates like braised flank steak with Burgundy-chile *pasilla* and semolina dumplings. Finishing the *queso fundido*, a molten cheese dip spiked with poblano peppers and chorizo, requires a group effort. The short list of entrées displays dashes of creativity yet remains hearty and flavorful. Desserts include a cheesecake-dense yogurt flan, dressed with chocolate sauce and candied almond slices.

The predominantly grey interior is brightened with colorfully painted tables and glazed flowerpots.

Jack's Luxury Oyster Bar

Seafood 🍴

A2

101 Second Ave. (bet. 5th & 6th Sts.)

Subway: Lower East Side - 2 Av   Dinner nightly
Phone: 212-253-7848
Web: N/A
Prices: $$$

Tucked into a busy Second Avenue block, this date-friendly oyster bar may be tiny in stature but is not short of personality thanks to owners (and namesake) Jack and Grace Lamb. Here, find a tempting raw bar that includes oysters as well as confident cooking in the substantial listing of small plates. These may include creamy duck liver pâté capped with port gelée or butter-poached lobster, in addition to a cheese selection and small dessert menu. The dining counter overlooking the open kitchen is a popular seating option, though the cozy wood-topped tables up front are also enjoyable.

The intimate space has a romantic glow of a rustic cabin yet maintains a distinctly downtown feel, with plaid walls, painted wainscoting, and glass votives all in red.

Jewel Bako ✿

A2

239 E. 5th St. (bet. Second & Third Aves.)

Subway: Astor Pl
Phone: 212-979-1012
Web: N/A
Prices: $$$

Dinner nightly

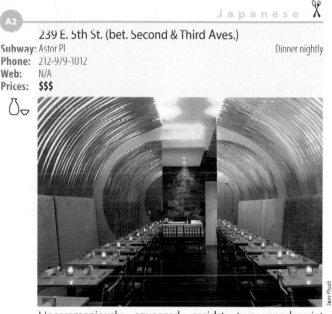

Swee Phuah

Unceremoniously squeezed amidst two nondescript façades, find a tiny lighted glass cube displaying a single flower, and a door discreetly marked "Jewel Bako." Maybe it's the fish shipped daily from Japan, or maybe the very committed owners, Jack and Grace Lamb, are behind the success, but somehow this famed *sushi-ya* gets better with each meal. Everything from the decor to the glassware, evidences the Lambs' impeccable style.

With one chopstick planted firmly into tradition and the other dipping playfully into whimsy, this is a must for sushi aficionados. Whether going for a platter of the day's freshest sushi or indulging in pristine omakase, Jewel Bako's greatest feat may be its spectacular consistency. The quality of fish is excellent, seasonal variety is appropriate, and depth of flavor can seem unending. Expect the likes of crisped salmon skin over micro-greens; ruby-red tuna topped with caviar, ginger, and scallions; or creamy uni topped with shiso.

Polite servers show an eye for detail and just the level of interest to ensure that you are enjoying your meal. Let them guide you to the perfect sake, with such spirit that the sashimi before you threatens to come back to life.

59

JoeDoe

A3

45 E. 1st St. (bet. First & Second Aves.)

Subway: Lower East Side - 2 Av
Phone: 212-780-0262
Web: www.chefjoedoe.com
Prices: $$

Lunch Sat – Sun
Dinner Tue – Sun

The snug setting of this downtown offering from Chef/partner Joe Dobias has an appealingly rustic and rugged aura. Wood and brick construct a stage that is sprinkled throughout with whimsical and nostalgic bric-a-brac. Seating is bolstered by the bar which doubles as a comfortable dining counter. Speaking of which, don't miss out on a spread of killer cocktails including the homemade celery soda and gin.

The chef's highly enjoyable menu emerges from a tiny but organized kitchen and displays a vibrant personality in dishes that have feature a gorgeous chilled carrot soup, thick and creamy with ground almonds, and flecked with cacao nibs for a bitter crunch; or slow roasted rabbit sauced with tomatillo salsa and matched with a round of fried dough.

Kafana

C3

116 Ave. C (bet. 7th & 8th Sts.)

Subway: 1 Av
Phone: 212-353-8000
Web: www.kafananyc.com
Prices: $$

Lunch Sat – Sun
Dinner nightly

Translating to "café" in Serbian, Kafana has a heartwarming ambience that beckons one to stay for a while. Exposed brick walls decorated with mirrors, vintage photographs, rough-hewn wood tables topped with votives and flowers, and boldly patterned banquettes outfit the intimate space, attended by a genuinely friendly staff. In one corner sits the small bar, with a charmingly low-tech antique cash register.

Kafana offers worldly diners an exotic cuisine not often found in Manhattan. The list of hearty Serbian specialties includes a phyllo pie filled with cow's milk feta and spinach, grilled meats, or slow-cooked stews prepared with large, tender white beans perfumed with garlic and paprika, topped with slices of smoky peasant sausage.

Kajitsu ✿ ✿

B2

414 E. 9th St. (bet. First Ave. & Ave. A)

Subway: 1 Av

Dinner Tue – Sun

Phone: 212-228-4873

Web: www.kajitsunyc.com

Prices: $$$

Kajitsu

Serving the Shojin cuisine of Zen Buddist monasteries, Kajitsu explores the vast culinary pleasures and complexities of food that does not "take life." Much more than a simple vegetarian restaurant, this is a very sophisticated dining experience founded entirely on a seasonal assortment of vegetables, beans, and grains.

A tranquil sense of finery pervades the demure and slender space. Delicately etched cups of sake are poured from polished steel carafes and their array of Japanese ceramics thrown by pottery masters make each dish seem more beautiful. This all may sound serious, but the vibe is reserved and comfortable. Friendly servers are thoroughly versed and happy to explain the intricacies of each dish. The food is subdued and elegant and may reveal an *okara* roll, a summer roll of turnip purée punched up with wasabi root; or vegetable consommé bobbing with fluffy and fragrant mountain yam dumplings. Thick cauldrons of richly flavored soy-sesame stew stocked with seasonal vegetables moisten crisp nests of soba noodles, for a variety of flavors that seem to whisper forth.

While the four-course *kaze* menu is lovely, the seven-course *hana* dinner is more elaborate and impressive.

Manhattan ▶ East Village

Kanoyama

B1 — Japanese

175 Second Ave. (at 11th St.)

Subway: 3 Av — Dinner nightly
Phone: 212-777-5266
Web: www.kanoyama.com
Prices: $$

Positive energy emanates from this tiny sushi spot where the amiable young staff caters to a clientele that is fanatical about their nigiri, sashimi, and maki—everything here is both reliable and impressive. Take a seat at the counter for a view of the chefs' amazing knife work and warm banter to fully appreciate petite Kanoyama's chill, downtown feel.

Daily fish specials display incredible variety and the menu supplements with even more choice, which may be best represented in the highlighted chef's recommendations. Kanoyama offers good value considering the quality, but that buttery toro or creamy uni can add up quickly.

Reservations are not accepted on Friday and Saturday nights, but there are plenty of lively bars nearby to ease the wait.

Kasadela

C2 — Japanese

647 E. 11th St. (bet. Aves. B & C)

Subway: 1 Av — Dinner nightly
Phone: 212-777-1582
Web: www.kasadela.com
Prices: ㉍

This simply furnished, low-key *izakaya* offers an array of traditional Japanese snacks best washed down with an iced cold beer or sake; just remember that here, your glass of sake can be embellished with gold leaf for a small fee, said to promote better health.

Located in Alphabet City, the space is often quieter early in the evening and stays open late enough to satisfy the cravings of the neighborhood's nocturnal scenesters. Patrons arrive here seeking honest, good-valued satisfaction, in the likes of creamy and smooth Japanese-style potato salad; addictively sweet and salty glazed chicken wings; or the classic fare of *tori kawa*: charred skewers of rich chicken skin. Finish with a crème caramel that would do any talented pastry chef proud.

Kyo Ya ✿

J a p a n e s e 🍴🍴

B2

94 E. 7th St. (bet First Ave. & Ave. A)

Subway: Astor Pl
Phone: 212-982-4140
Web: N/A
Prices: $$$

Dinner nightly

Kyo Ya

Everything about this unassuming East Village haunt is alluring: a hint of incense, the rice-paper lanterns, the zen-like slate and stone surfaces, modern staircase, and floor-to-ceiling glass wall that lend a light and airy feel to the subterranean space. Each of the three distinct dining nooks is comfortable and attractive, but the kitchen counter has the advantage of being presided over by the gracious and talented Chef Chikara Sono.

The outstanding service team is so informative that they preempt questions and assist diners in appreciating each dish as an enlightening experience. Food is treated deftly and sparely; tastes and textures are carefully brought to each plate with purpose, as if to fulfill an ancient culinary ritual. Purity of ingredients is highlighted in a cooling summertime *sakizuke* of vegetables simmered and steeped in delicate dashi. Following this, expect fragrant soup bathing a ball of sweet shrimp mousse; or marinated strips of squid with braised lotus root and stunningly carved eggplant topped by pickled plum sauce.

The vibe here is low-key and clientele is in the know; as un-Manhattan as this sounds, Kyo Ya seems contented to keep it that way.

La Paella

A2

214 E. 9th St. (bet. Second & Third Aves.)

Subway: Astor Pl
Phone: 212-598-4321
Web: www.lapaellanyc.com
Prices: $$

Lunch Wed – Sun
Dinner nightly

On a street known for Asian dining spots, La Paella recalls the charm of an old-world Iberian inn with rustic furnishings, wooden ceiling beams draped with bundles of dried flowers, and wrought-iron accents. A fresco of a picador on the parchment-colored wall completes the scene. Ideal for groups (though often crowded with them), the menu encourages sharing with its sizable tapas offering as well as the house specialty: paella, sized for two or more. Several variations of this namesake dish include the Basque, with chorizo, chicken, and clams over saffron-scented rice.

The cozy, dimly lit space makes it a delicious date spot for couples enjoying a bottle of Spanish wine, immune to the spirited sounds of sangria-fueled merrymaking.

Lavagna

B3

545 E. 5th St. (bet. Aves. A & B)

Subway: Lower East Side - 2 Av
Phone: 212-979-1005
Web: www.lavagnanyc.com
Prices: $$

Lunch Sat – Sun
Dinner nightly

The steady stream of regulars frequenting this very popular and charmingly low-key trattoria is immediately evident at Lavagna. The gracious staff often greets guests by name, though this same courteous attention is given to first-time visitors. The warm service is enhanced by the cozy dining room, featuring a visible kitchen, wood-topped bar, framed mirrors, pressed-tin ceiling, and white linen-covered tables glowing in the candlelight.

The Italian menu includes a concise listing of *pizzette*, perhaps topped with roasted wild mushrooms, fontina, and white truffle oil fired in the wood-burning oven. Fresh pastas, *secondi*, and excellent desserts complete the offerings. Sunday nights feature a reasonably priced three-course set menu from 5:00-7:00 P.M.

Lil' Frankie's 😊

Italian 🍴

A3

19 First Ave. (bet. 1st & 2nd Sts.)

Subway: Lower East Side - 2 Av
Phone: 212-420-4900
Web: www.lilfrankies.com
Prices: 💰💰

Lunch & dinner daily

Dinnertime always seems like a party at this offshoot of the ever-popular Frank, featuring a greenery-adorned dining room and a bar area lovingly nicknamed after owner Frank Prisinzano's father, "Big Cheech." The classic East Village space is furnished with a combination of wood and marble-topped tables, colorful benches, and brick walls with black-and-white portraits, fashioning a shabby-chic backdrop.

Cooked to crispy perfection in a wood-burning oven, Naples-style pizza, with toppings like homemade sausage and wild fennel, star on the menu. Equally impressive is the lineup of antipasto and pastas, handmade with the freshest ingredients. Come with a crowd or expect to wait, reservations are accepted only for parties of six or more.

Luzzo's

Pizza 🍴

B1

211-13 First Ave. (bet. 12th & 13th Sts.)

Subway: 1 Av
Phone: 212-473-7447
Web: www.luzzosnyc.com
Prices: 💰💰

Lunch Tue – Sun
Dinner nightly

Luzzo's is easily spotted by its long line of hungry faces patiently waiting to score a table, especially on a Friday night when the rustic setting of rough-hewn plank flooring and exposed brick adorned with copper cookware can suddenly feel like an NYU dining hall.

Despite the masses, this consistently top-rated pizzeria is a fun night out. Its Naples-born owner and noted *pizzaiolo* does things his own way to produce a stellar pie while defying some of the strict mandates set by the Neapolitan-pizza politburo, most notably baking his pizzas in a mix of wood *and* coal. The results are delectable, as in the pizza *diavolo*—crusty, puffy, and tender with a hint of smoke and topped with tomato, creamy mozzarella, and salty-spicy slices of hearty salami.

The Mermaid Inn

Seafood 🍴

A2

96 Second Ave. (bet. 5th & 6th Sts.)

Subway: Astor Pl   Dinner nightly
Phone: 212-674-5870
Web: www.themermaidnyc.com
Prices: $$

When schedules and seasons don't inspire a trip to the Cape, The Mermaid Inn offers a polished yet comfortably rustic take on those familiar sea-sprayed fish shacks. Dark wood furnishings, walls decorated with nautical maps, and a quaint backyard dining area give the setting an undeniable charm. The concise menu begins with a first-rate raw bar and continues with deftly prepared offerings like P.E.I. mussels steamed in an aromatic broth, or the lobster sandwich served on a grilled bun. Their addictive crunchy, golden, Old Bay fries are an essential side dish. A complimentary demitasse of creamy pudding ends things sweetly.

Two additional Manhattan locations (in Greenwich Village and the Upper West Side) continue to spread the wealth.

Momofuku Noodle Bar 🐷

Asian 🍴

B2

171 First Ave. (bet. 10th & 11th Sts.)

Subway: 1 Av   Lunch & dinner daily
Phone: 212-777-7773
Web: www.momofuku.com
Prices: 🍜

This spot launched Chef David Chang's ascent into celebrity chef-dom. The ever-popular destination and its hoards of hungry fans may reside in bigger digs now, but this restaurant is still a "lucky peach" (the name's Japanese translation). Momofuku's gutsy menu is fashioned with Asian street food in mind: steamed buns of chicken, shiitake, or pork are offered alongside generous bowls of house-made ramen in dark, subtly flavored broth. The trendsetting chef put fried chicken on the foodie map with his order-in-advance feast featuring two treatments of bird with sauces and greenmarket sides.

Whether sitting at the counter or communal tables, join the devotees slurping noodles elbow-to-elbow and watching the chefs' sleight of hand in the open kitchen.

Momofuku Ko ✿ ✿

163 First Ave. (bet. 10th & 11th Sts.)

Subway: 1 Av
Phone: 212-777-7773
Web: www.momofuku.com
Prices: $$$$

Lunch Fri – Sun
Dinner nightly

Noah Kalina

This sliver of a restaurant has East Villagers crying Momo-mia for Chef David Chang's truly inspired and extraordinarily unique cooking. Just follow the throngs of foodies making a beeline to the cut-out metalwork façade and reverently entering the modern, minimalist space comprised of twelve chunky stools at a dining counter. As with its four sibling restaurants, Momofuku Ko feels as if every design note, every serving piece, every spotlight's angle is intended to highlight the very impressive food.

Each night, Chef Chang's team serves a multi-course contemporary menu that derives its inspiration from...who knows? But whatever his muse may be, there is almost no deviation and it is always delicious.

From the hip and attentive staff, expect to be served a sleek, sloped bowl layered with salty-sweet pine-nut brittle, Riesling gelée, and litchis with a hunk of frozen foie gras torchon shaved over the top, producing an incredibly rich cloud of flavors and textures that literally melt in the mouth. Still for many, desserts are a destination here and arrive in outrageously creative combinations like freshly fried parsnip donut holes served with parsnip ice cream and hazelnut brittle.

Momofuku Ssäm Bar 😊

B1

207 Second Ave. (at 13th St.)

Subway: 3 Av   Lunch & dinner daily
Phone: 212-777-7773
Web: www.momofuku.com
Prices: $$

Restless Chef David Chang somehow always manages to wow the taste buds of even the most jaded foodies. At this freewheeling culinary playground, he offers an exuberant contemporary menu so far-reaching that it somehow all makes sense. Rest assured, this kitchen only serves dishes that they themselves find delicious—and the cocktail list demonstrates the same voracity as the menu.

The signature steamed pork buns remain a draw, but raw bar items like cracked Jonah crab claws and country hams are likewise praiseworthy. Seasonal dishes cater to the familiar, while variety meats entertain more daring diners, as do the famed mad scientist desserts.

Loud and crowded, the chic and minimalist space is perpetually mobbed by its sophisticated clientele.

Northern Spy Food Co. 😊

C2

511 E. 12th St. (bet. Aves. A & B)

Subway: 1 Av   Lunch & dinner daily
Phone: 212-228-5100
Web: www.northernspyfoodco.com
Prices: 😊😊

Espousing a country kitchen aesthetic, this inviting café is framed by reclaimed hickory flooring, a wood-slat banquette painted robin's egg blue, and tables fashioned from salvaged bowling alley lanes.

Chef Nathan Foot and his team serve up a Bay Area sensibility in a value-driven menu of seasonal, locally-sourced fare that is always enjoyable. Lunchtime offerings include impressive sandwiches such as the crispy chicken thigh and poached egg or wild mushroom and cheddar, washed down by an old-timey coffee seltzer. Dinner serves up house-made head cheese; heritage pork meatballs with marinara; and Long Island market fish with anchovy butter. A list of local beers accompanies the wine list; and Sunday nights bring a reasonable prix-fixe menu.

Porsena

Italian ✗✗

A2

21 E. 7th St. (bet. Second & Third Aves.)

Subway: Astor Pl
Phone: 212-228-4923
Web: www.porsena.com
Prices: $$

Dinner nightly

New Yorkers love Sara Jenkins. Her cooking is adroit, uncomplicated, and just so good—a combination that has diners flocking to her newest establishment, Porsena. Bigger than closet-sized Porchetta, this spot, furnished with a mix-and-match assortment of chairs and touches of red and grey as well as a comfortable bar counter, is a hugely accommodating space.

Inspired by the chef's childhood time in Rome, the menu starts off with the likes of wilted escarole salad, bitter and smoky, dressed with garlic vinaigrette. The heart of the menu is its focus on *pasta asciutta* (dried pasta) that may be deliciously prepared as *pennette col cavolfiore*—a lusty balance of mini penne, roasted cauliflower, capers, and black olives showered by toasted breadcrumbs.

Prune 😊

Contemporary ✗

A3

54 E. 1st St. (bet. First & Second Aves.)

Subway: Lower East Side - 2 Av
Phone: 212-677-6221
Web: www.prunerestaurant.com
Prices: $$

Lunch & dinner daily

Packed with simple furnishings and attended to by a friendly staff, the popularity of this endearing breadbox of a restaurant never seems to fade. On a warm day when the front doors open, few Manhattan restaurants can match its ambience. From her kitchen in back, Chef/owner (and best-selling author) Gabrielle Hamilton has impressed serious diners since 1999.

The deceptively modest menu changes often but the chef's signature style shines through in items that are fuss-free yet display an undeniable level of skill and talent. A meal here may feature a crisp-skinned fillet of Tasmanian sea trout set atop a bundle of frisée and crowned by a dollop of perfect homemade mayonnaise; or a creamy, sweet/tart lime custard graced with crumbly oatmeal shortbread.

Pylos

Greek ✗✗

128 E. 7th St. (bet. First Ave. & Ave. A)

Subway: Astor Pl
Phone: 212-473-0220
Web: www.pylosrestaurant.com
Prices: $$

Lunch Wed – Sun
Dinner nightly

Taking its name from the Greek translation of "made from clay," this contemporary taverna features a ceiling canopy of suspended terra-cotta pots and whitewashed walls with lapis-blue insets. The restrained décor produces a chic Mediterranean vibe that perfectly suits its lusty, home-style, deliciously refined cuisine—courtesy of noted Greek food authority Diane Kochilas.

Moussaka, a classic Greek comfort favorite, is beautifully presented here as a dome filled with layers of browned meat and silky eggplant, encrusted in slender potato slices, finished with layer of golden-browned béchamel. Sides may include *spanakorizo*, wilted spinach rice flecked with feta crumbles; while custard-filled phyllo drenched in mountain honey ends things sweetly.

Rai Rai Ken

Japanese ▤

214 E. 10th St. (bet. First & Second Aves.)

Subway: Astor Pl
Phone: 212-477-7030
Web: N/A
Prices: ⊜⊜

Lunch & dinner daily

This sliver of a spot specializes in slurp-inducing, soul-satisfying ramen that stands out among the city's recent proliferation. The setting is utilitarian: 14 low stools are situated at the busy counter overlooking a narrow kitchen lined with bubbling pots. Besides the caddies of chopsticks and paper napkins, there's just enough room for a deep, rich, brimming bowl at each setting.

The menu shines through in its brief listing of four near-addictive, remarkably complex broth variations such as *shio*, *shoyu*, miso, and curry. Each is chock-full of garnishes, like fishcakes or roasted pork, and nests of fresh, springy noodles. Before leaving, be sure to grab a business card; loyal diners are rewarded with a complimentary bowl after ten visits.

The Redhead

G a s t r o p u b ✗

B1

349 E. 13th St. (bet. First & Second Aves.)

Subway: 1 Av   Dinner nightly
Phone: 212-533-6212
Web: www.theredheadnyc.com
Prices: $$

This lil' ole East Village charmer lures an ardent following nightly with its stocked bar, substantial list of well-poured libations, and distinctly Southern appeal. Stop here for a creative cocktail, best enjoyed with the near-addictive bacon-peanut brittle, because this menu reminds us that "everything is better with bacon." Then, continue on to the rear dining area with exposed brick walls and a red velvet banquette. Everything here is done simply, radiating a warm, laid-back charm.

The menu's Southern accent is appetizingly evident in the kitchen's preparations that feature low country shrimp, pan-seared trout, and buttermilk fried chicken served with cornbread. The tasty dessert menu of puddings, tarts, and cakes cleverly unites "gastro" and "pub."

Robataya 😊

J a p a n e s e ✗

A2

231 E. 9th St. (bet. Second & Third Aves.)

Subway: Astor Pl   Lunch Wed – Sun
Phone: 212-979-9674   Dinner nightly
Web: www.robataya-ny.com
Prices: $$

This latest (and such fun) venture from restaurateur Bon Yagi features a front room with a 26-seat counter lined with salivating diners and platters of ultra fresh vegetables, fish, and meats to be grilled and served by a paddle wielding team of chefs perched behind the counter.

The *robatayaki* menu offers up flavorfully grilled dishes, from silky eggplant to sheets of dried sardines, seasoned with imported salt, brushed with soy or teriyaki, or dressed with miso. The menu shows a plethora of options but is usually supported by cold, warm, and seasonal appetizers; fried dishes like *yuba gyoza*; and iron pots of steamed rice (*kamameshi*) topped with snow crab.

Table seating is available in the rear dining room for those who prefer a more tranquil experience.

Sigiri

B2

91 First Ave. (bet. 5th & 6th Sts.)

Subway: 1 Av	Lunch & dinner daily
Phone: 212-614-9333	
Web: www.sigirinyc.com	
Prices: 💰💰	

For a delicious taste of something different, round the corner of 6th Street to First Avenue, and climb to Sigiri's small second floor dining room. This humble Sri Lankan establishment stands above its neighbors for wonderfully prepared, intriguingly fragrant cuisine that needs neither a colorful light display nor boisterous greeter. Instead, the warm and sedate room features sienna walls and simple tables with bright cloths.

Specialties are numerous and may include *string hopper kotthu*, a stir-fry of impossibly thin and fluffy rice noodles tossed with eggs, chicken, and vegetables, accompanied by a cup of coconut gravy; or spoon-tender chunks of eggplant *moju*, spiced with dried red chili. In lieu of alcohol, fruit cordials or apple-iced tea is offered.

Sobakoh

A2

309 E. 5th St. (bet. First & Second Aves.)

Subway: Lower East Side - 2 Av	Lunch Fri – Sun
Phone: 212-254-2244	Dinner nightly
Web: N/A	
Prices: 💰💰	

Before entering Sobakoh, stop for a minute to appreciate Chef/owner Hiromitsu Takahashi, sequestered to his temperature- and humidity-controlled glass booth, forming layers of organically grown buckwheat flour dough into first-rate noodles. This ritual is performed several times daily by the smiling chef and is the foundation of the seasonally arranged offerings at this Japan-meets-East Village soba spot. Service can be sluggish, so start with a classic Japanese snack, like the refreshing daikon salad dressed with yuzu, wasabi, and bonito flakes, while waiting for your bowlful of *uni ikura soba*—chilled buckwheat noodles heaped with creamy sea urchin and plump salmon roe.

The inexpensive prix-fixe menu offered nightly is even cheaper before 7:00 P.M.

Soba Ya 🎭

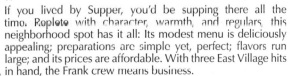

A2

Japanese ✕✕

229 E. 9th St. (bet. Second & Third Aves.)

Subway: Astor Pl
Phone: 212-533-6966
Web: www.sobaya-nyc.com
Prices: 💰💰

Lunch & dinner daily

In a neighborhood replete with tempting Japanese dining options, Soba-Ya has been sating noodle cravings with awesome buckwheat soba and hearty udon–all homemade daily–for more than a decade. Enterprising co-owner Bon Yagi, also of Curry-Ya, favors authenticity over flash in his establishments, and this popular soba spot fashioning a traditional Japanese aesthetic is no exception.

Sit among the largely Japanese lunchtime clientele to savor and slurp cold, refreshing soba attractively served in a red-black bento box neatly stocked with the likes of dashi-poached vegetables, fresh and deliciously glazed salmon, or crisp shrimp tempura. Complete this meal with a pot of hot broth added to your remaining soy-based dipping sauce for a warming finish.

Supper 🎭

B3

Italian ✕

156 E. 2nd St. (bet. Aves. A & B)

Subway: 1 Av
Phone: 212-477-7600
Web: www.supperrestaurant.com
Prices: $$

Lunch Sat – Sun
Dinner nightly

If you lived by Supper, you'd be supping there all the time. Replete with character, warmth, and regulars, this neighborhood spot has it all: Its modest menu is deliciously appealing; preparations are simple yet, perfect; flavors run large; and its prices are affordable. With three East Village hits in hand, the Frank crew means business.

A substantial menu keeps company with nightly specials and a killer wine list; diners pack the low-lit, sultry front room for a slice of action from the open kitchen. Find more intimacy in the back, or pick the private room for a dinner party starring veal *polpettini* bobbing in *sugo*; roasted chicken massaged with rosemary and garlic; and *spaghetti al limone*, sauced with white wine, cream, lemon zest, and Parmesan.

Terroir

Italian 🍽

B2

413 E. 12th St. (bet. First Ave. & Ave. A)

Subway: Astor Pl
Phone: 646-602-1300
Web: www.wineisterroir.com
Prices: $$

Dinner nightly

Step inside Terroir, from Hearth partners Chef Marco Canora and sommelier Paul Grieco, and you will be seduced by the spirit of this place; the passion is palpable. What else would you expect from a sommelier who describes this wine bar as his sandbox? Park yourself on one of the 24 seats and enjoy flipping though the whimsical menu—a vinyl binder adorned with stickers and markings galore that looks like the work of a trouble-making grade-schooler.

The clever line up of fermented beverages includes Kosher wines, cider, and mead; and is accompanied by enjoyably prepared morsels like crunchy red wine risotto balls strewn with braised oxtail; or a slice of strawberry tart that was featured as part of a seasonal Riesling-inspired prix-fixe.

Vandaag

European 🍴🍴

A2

103 Second Ave. (at 6th St.)

Subway: Astor Pl
Phone: 212-253-0470
Web: www.vandaagnyc.com
Prices: $$

Lunch & dinner daily

Kind of Dutch, sort of Danish, wholly intriguing, Vaandag is a unique Northern European gift to downtown diners. The chic room of hard surfaces and cool colors is populated by an equally cool crowd starting dinner with a highly recommended cocktail, as in the West of 2nd, combining Holland-style gin with mezcal and pomegranate molasses.

The fanciful menu is vividly rendered, and each offering boasts layer upon layer of flavor. Specialties include delicately sweet sea urchin bisque (sea urchin shells and Armagnac are used to flavor the stock) stunningly capped by a brioche crostini spread with basil seeds and uni; or perfectly grilled quail, infused with a Thai-inspired curry, and paired with Brussels sprouts tossed with puffed wild rice and mint.

Yuba

Manhattan ▶ East Village

A1

Japanese ✕

105 E. 9th St. (bet. Third & Fourth Aves.)

Subway: Astor Pl
Phone: 212-777-8188
Web: www.yubanyc.com
Prices: **$$**

Lunch Mon – Sat
Dinner nightly

This new sushi den is helmed by a chef who worked previously for the beloved Bar Masa. Here, their menu not only presents sushi—impressively knifed and deliciously fresh—but also an affection for yuba. This delicate and silky tofu skin is offered in a number of guises that include yuba maki, grilled miso yuba, and risotto-style uni rice.

A nightly prix-fixe menu features pairings like uni and yuba in *tosazu* sauce; Kumamoto oyster topped with caviar; sweet corn tempura; and a procession of nigiri that perhaps include soy-brushed blue fin tuna, live sea scallop with Himalayan sea salt and yuzu zest, and *mirugai* (geoduck clam).

Yuba is spare and contemporary as one would expect, but it's also a tad sexy with a dark grey interior and dim lighting.

Zabb Elee

A2

Thai ✕

75 Second Ave. (bet. 4th and 5th Sts.)

Subway: Astor Pl
Phone: 212-505-9533
Web: www.zabbelee.com
Prices: 🥜🥜

Lunch & dinner daily

Proclaim you've found a great new Thai spot, and people listen; announce it's in Manhattan, and crowds race you to the door. This spicy sparkler eschews the high design look common to others in its category, opting instead for a reticent look of pale tones jazzed up by patterned tile and light green shutters.

The food speaks, or should we say shouts, for itself, honing in on Northern Thailand for a vibrant profusion of Isaan specialties. Chef Ratchanee Sumpatboon delivers knockouts such as *som tum poo plara* (green papaya salad with preserved crab and fried pork rind); *pukk boong moo korb* (sautéed morning glory with crispy pork); and *pad ped moo korb* (fried pork mingling with Thai eggplant in a ginger curry sauce fragrant with green peppercorns).

Financial District

Widely considered the financial center of the world, the southern tip of Manhattan is flooded by hard-driving Wall Street types. When it's time to eat, they love a hefty steak, especially when expense accounts are paying the bill. And though expense accounts may be shrinking these days, bigger is still better at stalwarts like **Delmonico's**, which opened in 1837 as America's first fine-dining restaurant. The restaurant that introduced diners to now-classic dishes such as eggs Benedict, lobster Newburg, and baked Alaska, continues to pack 'em in for the signature Angus boneless rib eye, aka the Delmonico steak.

Reinventing the Public Market

New is replacing old as the publicly owned Tin Building and New Market Building–home to the former Fulton Fish Market–house tenants in the form of **The New Amsterdam Market**, a seasonal marketplace where butchers, grocers, fishmongers, artisan cheese producers, and other vendors hope to create a regional food system. With a stated mission "to reinvent the public market as a civic institution in the City of New York," this non-profit organization dedicates itself to promoting sustainable agriculture and regionally-sourced food, while offering space for independent purveyors to sell on behalf of farmers and producers. Check their website (www.newamsterdampublic.org) for event dates. One of the district's largest tourist draws, South Street Seaport is surrounded by eateries from family-friendly Irish pubs to the historic **Fraunces Tavern**. Innkeeper Samuel Fraunces purchased this three-story, 18th century brick mansion at the corner of Pearl and Broad streets in 1762.

The Financial District has traditionally catered to power-lunchers by day and business travelers by night. However, that's all changing rapidly as the area becomes increasingly residential. What you will discover is a smorgasbord of bars, restaurants, and food services catering to the local residents. These blossoming culinary gems incite buttoned-up Wall Street suits to loosen their collars and chill out over a plate of steak frites at **Les Halles Downtown**—the brasserie affiliated with bad boy chef and Travel Channel celebrity, Anthony Bourdain. Front Street has attracted a surprising spate of Italian eateries counting **Il Brigante**, with its dough-spinning *pizzaiolo* who belongs to the United States Pizza Team, among their number.

Another newbie, **Barbarini Alimentari** raises the bar with gourmet groceries and an upscale menu of Italian fare. The ultimate in express lunch, NY's food-carts are hugely popular in the FiDi. For a

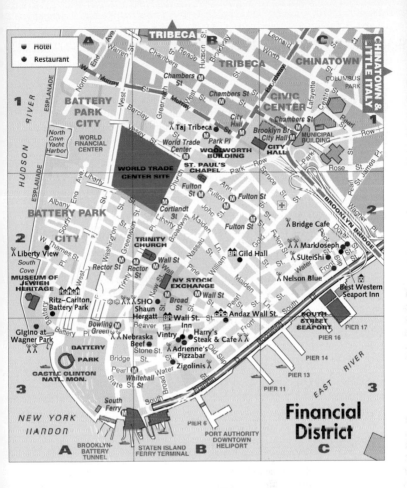

Hotel
Restaurant

TRIBECA

TRIBECA

CHINATOWN

COLUMBUS PARK

CIVIC CENTER

BATTERY PARK CITY

HUDSON RIVER

ESPLANADE

North Cove Yacht Harbor

WORLD FINANCIAL CENTER

Chambers St

Chambers St

City Hall

Taj Tribeca

World Trade Center

Park Pl

WOOLWORTH BUILDING

Chambers St

Brooklyn Br City Hall

MUNICIPAL BUILDING

CITY HALL

ST. PAUL'S CHAPEL

WORLD TRADE CENTER SITE

BROOKLYN BRIDGE

Fulton

Cortlandt St

Fulton St

Fulton St

Fulton St

BATTERY PARK CITY

Liberty View

South Cove

MUSEUM OF JEWISH HERITAGE

TRINITY CHURCH

Wall St

Rector St

Rector St

NY STOCK EXCHANGE

Wall St

Gild Hall

Bridge Cafe

MarkJoseph

SUteiShi

Nelson Blue

Best Western Seaport Inn

Ritz-Carlton, Battery Park

Gigino at Wagner Park

SHO

Shaun Hergatt

Wall St. Inn

Andaz Wall St.

Bowling Green

Nebraska Beef

Vintry

Harry's Steak & Cafe

Adrienne's Pizzabar

Zigolinis

SOUTH STREET SEAPORT

PIER 17

PIER 16

PIER 14

DATTERY PARK

Bridge St

Stone St.

Old Slip

EAST RIVER

CASTLE CLINTON NATL. MON.

Whitehall St

Pearl

Water

Franklin

PIER 13

PIER 11

NEW YORK HARBOR

South Ferry

PIER 6

Financial District

BROOKLYN-BATTERY TUNNEL

STATEN ISLAND FERRY TERMINAL

PORT AUTHORITY DOWNTOWN HELIPORT

A

B

C

quick nosh at a bargain price, follow your nose to **Alan's Falafel Cart** on Cedar Street; then for something sweet, head to **Financier Patisserie** on charming, cobblestoned Stone Street, one of the narrow, sinuous streets laid out in the 17th century by New York's Dutch settlers. Wash it all down with an espresso at **Zibetto's** on Fulton Street. Despite the economic downturn, restaurants downtown are as busy as ever, with former Wall Street wonders drowning their worries in martinis and Manhattans; and reviewing their portfolios over burgers and beer. Events like the Stone Street Oyster Festival, sponsored by the same folks who operate Financier Patisserie and Ulysses pub, play to the area's strengths. What better way to lift your spirits and celebrate the local Blue Point harvest in September than by slurping oysters and swilling libations outdoors on Stone Street?

Adrienne's Pizzabar

Pizza ✗

B3

54 Stone St. (bet. Coenties Alley & S. William St.)

Subway: Bowling Green
Phone: 212-248-3838
Web: www.adriennespizzabar.com
Prices: 💰

Lunch & dinner daily

When the clock strikes noon, Adrienne's is always abuzz with Financial District business types hungering for these delectable pizzas. With their thin crusts, slightly chunky sauce, and fresh toppings, these pies are a classic on all fronts—the square shape is true to the venerable Sicilian-American version.

Yet with so many new neighborhood residents, Adrienne's is now just as packed at night, when diners linger to appreciate the oak paneling and other upscale touches, while indulging in heartier baked dishes like lasagna. Outdoor tables along Stone Street are lovely perches for watching the neighborhood reinvent itself at dinner. Desserts are divine, which is no surprise as the owners are also behind the wildly popular Financier Patisserie chain.

Bridge Cafe

American ✗

C2

279 Water St. (at Dover St.)

Subway: Brooklyn Bridge - City Hall
Phone: 212-227-3344
Web: www.bridgecafenyc.com
Prices: $$

Lunch Sun – Fri
Dinner nightly

Set along the touristy cobblestoned street that is today's Water Street, the Bridge Cafe–which claims to be New York's oldest drinking establishment–was standing here when the area was better known for brothels and saloons than J. Crew and Banana Republic.

And so if the food is simply good, but not heroic, at this Manhattan mainstay, one can let a few details slide—especially for brown liquor enthusiasts looking to cruise the restaurant's extensive list of bourbons, malts, and Scotches. The menu lists some refreshingly light fare like a soft shell crab BLT; grilled wild Pacific salmon; and avocado and watercress salad. But a spot-on buffalo burger, topped with chili, bacon, and pepper jack on a chipotle aïoli-slathered bun really hits the spot.

Gigino at Wagner Park

A3   Italian ✗✗

20 Battery Pl. (in Wagner Park)

Subway: Bowling Green   Lunch & dinner daily
Phone: 212-528-2228
Web: www.gigino-wagnerpark.com
Prices: $$

Impress your buddies after an afternoon romp to Ellis Island with this Southern Italian gem, and you'll be hailed a genius. Harbor views abound at this relaxing Italian restaurant, tucked into the ground floor of a wedge-shaped building in the Financial District's far-flung Wagner Park, but you'll want to call ahead to reserve a seat on the outdoor terrace. If you don't score it, you'll find a fairly soothing oasis inside as well, with a creamy white dining room dancing in blinking lights from the harbor.

Kick dinner off with a rich lentil soup flooded with tender braised escarole, diced tomato, and sweet onion; and then move on to a silky braised lamb shank served with a white bean and mint risotto; and bread pudding with rum and vanilla sauce.

Harry's Steak & Cafe

B3   American ✗✗

1 Hanover Sq. (bet. Pearl & Stone Sts.)

Subway: Wall St (William St.)   Lunch & dinner Mon – Sat
Phone: 212-785-9200
Web: www.harrysnyc.com
Prices: $$

Mornings may begin with a bell, but Wall Street's powerbrokers ring in its end at Harry's Steak & Cafe. A beloved watering hole for decades, this Wall Street institution was reincarnated into two distinct spaces: a café and a steakhouse. Handsome and clubby with a gleaming black walnut bar and copper ceilings, the cafe defines relaxed elegance, while the more serious steakhouse feels secreted away with a sophisticated intimacy.

Beef is what's on tap at Harry's, so expect old-fashioned boys' club dining and precise service. The more casual cafe menu features a few deep-pocketed riffs on American favorites like the Kobe hot dog (only on Wall Street), while the steakhouse focuses on classic preparations of its excellent quality, rich, and juicy beef.

Liberty View

A2

21 South End Ave. (below W. Thames St.)

Subway: Rector St (Greenwich St.)   Lunch & dinner daily
Phone: 212-786-1888
Web: www.libertyviewrestaurant.com
Prices: $$

You may find better food in Chinatown, but few places can rival these gorgeous vistas of the Hudson River, Ellis Island, and the Statue of Liberty. This well-set Chinese restaurant holds true to its name, offering eye-popping views of Lady Liberty from its prime ground-floor location (with outdoor seating) at the tip of Battery Park City.

When you do finally peer down to the menu, keep in mind that the chef is from Shanghai, so focusing on those regional offerings are a good bet. Crisp, pan-fried dumplings or the thin, steamed pockets of crab and pork soup dumplings are tasty options, and the Shanghai fried rice is perfectly delicate and light. Those with nautical aspirations can grab a picnic of Chinese goodies before sailing from North Cove Marina.

MarkJoseph

C2

261 Water St. (bet. Peck Slip & Dover St.)

Subway: Brooklyn Bridge - City Hall   Lunch Mon – Fri
Phone: 212-277-0020   Dinner Mon – Sat
Web: www.markjosephsteakhouse.com
Prices: $$$

Rising from the shadows of the Brooklyn Bridge in the South Street Seaport Historic District, MarkJoseph's caters to both Wall Street wunderkinds and tourists with deep pockets. The cozy dining room is a notch above the standard steakhouse design, with art-glass vases and pastoral photographs of the wine country adding sleek notes.

At lunch, regulars devour hearty half-pound burgers (though a turkey variety is also offered). At dinnertime, prime dry-aged Porterhouse, sized for two to four, takes center stage. Classic accompaniments may include crisp salads, seafood cocktails, and sides like creamed spinach. The wine list offers a nice choice of hefty varietals, as well as some interesting old-world selections to accompany that bone-in ribsteak.

Nebraska Beef

B3

Steakhouse ✗✗

15 Stone St. (bet. Broad & Whitehall Sts.)

Subway: Bowling Green
Phone: 212-952-0620
Web: www.nebraskasteakhousenyc.com
Prices: $$$

Lunch & dinner Mon – Fri

It's easy to miss the door that marks the entrance to this beloved Financial District watering hole-cum-steakhouse (look for the red and gold sign out front), but not the raucous happy hour crowd that floods the narrow bar leading to the restaurant. Smile and squeeze through, to discover a much calmer scene inside: a dark, wood-paneled dining room with a clubby, in the know vibe.

This is one Wall Street oasis where the past and present comfortably co-exist—the martinis flow freely, the garlic bread melts in your mouth, and the hand-picked, 28-day, dry-aged ribeye still arrives sizzling, perfectly charred, and juicy as sin. If you're short on time or looking for lunch options, you can also grab a steak sandwich, salad, or burger on the fly.

Nelson Blue

C2

New Zealand ✗

233-235 Front St. (at Peck Slip)

Subway: Fulton St
Phone: 212-346-9090
Web: www.nelsonblue.com
Prices: $$

Lunch & dinner daily

Tucked into a bustling old corner of Front Street near the South Street Seaport, dominated by old pubs and workhorse happy hour restaurants, Nelson Blue offers a quirky, delicious detour from the usual haunts. The solid fare and never-ending beer taps are the main draw here, but the fun-loving ambience–notice hand-crafted artifacts like a Maori war canoe, a handsome oval bar, and a long communal wood table–only adds to the fun.

The New Zealand-based menu offers a range of straightforward fare like a Thai chicken soup humming with coconut, curry, lotus root, lemongrass, and sizzling rice; tender grilled lamb lollipops laced with a delicious rosemary-mustard sauce; and Nelson Blue's classic curried lamb pot pie paired with creamy mashed potatoes.

SHO Shaun Hergatt ✿ ✿

B2

Contemporary 🍴🍴🍴

40 Broad St. (bet. Beaver St. & Exchange Pl.)

Subway: Broad St
Phone: 212-809-3993
Web: www.shoshaunhergatt.com
Prices: $$$

Lunch Mon – Fri
Dinner Mon – Sat

Lucy Schaeffer

SHO Shaun Hergatt truly shows off in its stylish lair; glimpse a dramatic stage ruled by Asian inspiration—Chinese calligraphy brushes and Tibetan metal necklaces hang throughout exuding an air of lost treasures. Find your way (through a tunnel of wine) to present day, perhaps at the bar packed with ritzy revelers.

Diners, steer clear of the less-than-ravishing lounge, and insist on sitting in the glorious dining room where the immaculate kitchen is on full display behind a wall of glass. Dressed with metallic silks and warm tones, find chic tables endowed with silver, crystal, and a gilded conch shell cradling an amuse-bouche of foie gras spheres rolled in squid ink-flavored panko crumbs. Otoro carpaccio may star in another course, finished with young red shiso and green onion; while posing atop porcelain plates is glossy pork belly with purple radishes.

The black-suited staff is efficient, and forgive the odd young'un if he seems a tad rattled—a cake tranche layered with huckleberry compote and sweet pear sorbet can have that effect. So, whether you compose your own 3-course prix-fixe or sing the à la carte tune here, all pieces work in harmony to render a stunning meal.

SUteiShi

C2

Japanese ✗

24 Peck Slip (at Front St.)

Subway: Fulton St
Phone: 212-766-2344
Web: www.suteishi.com
Prices: $$

Lunch Mon – Sat
Dinner nightly

In a neighborhood starved for good eats, this colorful and spacious haven makes the grade. Make no mistake: it's not mind-blowing sushi you'll find here, but guests who stick to the inventive rolls or lunchtime bento boxes will be rewarded with a very good meal in a welcoming atmosphere.

Make your way into SUteiShi's sleek, red lacquer-accented dining room and you'll find a sushi bar with a wood-weaved backdrop, a few bonsai plants and the requisite "Hello Kitty" porcelain doll. Don't miss the *ikura* wrapped with King salmon and topped with bright salmon roe; the super-fresh uni; or the strangely appealing black sesame brulée that reads more like a pudding, and arrives accompanied by two sesame wafers, bright slices of strawberries, and ripe blueberries.

Taj Tribeca

B1

Indian ✗

18 Murray St. (bet. Broadway & Church St.)

Subway: Park Place
Phone: 212-608-5555
Web: www.tajtribeca.com
Prices: $$

Lunch & dinner daily

Set along one of the more culinary challenged strips of lower Manhattan, just east of City Hall, Taj Tribeca is a nearly new Indian restaurant with a superb (albeit tiny) bar, exposed brick walls, and mile-high ceilings.

With such lovely design at play, one begins to wonder if the food could be elevated too—and the good news is that it is. Sure, they have the requisite lunch buffet (New Yorkers might picket without it), but the regular à la carte offerings remain ambitious and fresh. Try the compelling Goan shrimp curry headlining pitch-perfect heat and spice, shot with cool coconut milk, and served with fluffy basmati rice topped with perfectly caramelized fried onions. Save room for the warm carrot pudding, fragrant with green cardamom and clove.

Vintry

B3

57 Stone St. (bet Coenties Alley & Hanover Sq.)

Subway: Bowling Green
Phone: 212-480-9800
Web: www.vintrynyc.com
Prices: $$

Lunch & dinner daily

Vintry is a gem in a sea of standard bars on the very charming, pedestrian-only, cobbled Stone Street, with a sparkle that is light years away from the typical frat party-style taverns that dominate this stretch. From its rare African redwood and rainforest marble bar to its bone-like maple vines, the interior combines rare elements to fashion a swanky yet unique setting.

First and foremost, this is a temple to brown booze (no clear spirits served here) and boasts tremendous whiskey and wine lists. Bigwigs and budget-conscious alike can find something to fit their tastes (note the wire-covered wall cabinet housing the big guns). The concise menu has everything from lamb meatballs, truffle mushroom *cavatelli*, and swordfish *au poivre* to complement.

Zigolinis

B3

66 Pearl St. (at Coenties Slip)

Subway: Wall St (William St.)
Phone: 212-425-3127
Web: www.zigolinis.com
Prices: $$

Lunch & dinner daily

With its lovely chandeliers, silk fabric, and stylish filament bulbs, this sexy downtown restaurant is a breath of fresh air among the staid options that typify the Financial District dining scene.

The Italian–leaning–American menu is broad and appealing, with an ample offering of salads and appetizers. Vegetable wraps are a quick, healthy lunch option, while sharable small plates feature more interesting fare, such as Philly cheesesteak dumplings, enveloped in wonton wrappers and served with A1 aïoli, or the perfectly crisp fried calamari with sundried tomato coulis.

These owners know they've found a good thing: note their quick-serve "deli" outpost located next door, as well as a casual Zigolinis serving Neapolitan-style pizza in Hell's Kitchen.

Gramercy, Flatiron & Union Square

Gramercy Park, anchoring its namesake neighborhood, is steeped in history, old-world beauty, and tranquility. But, its extreme exclusivity is the stuff of legends among life-long New Yorkers, few of whom have set foot on its pretty yet private paths. This may be where tourists have an advantage, because outside of the residents whose home address faces the square, Gramercy Park Hotel guests are among the few permitted entrance. The staff accompanies guests to the daunting cast-iron gate, allows them in, and reminds them of the number to call when they wish to be let out again, perhaps to explore this lovely enclave filled with charming cafés and beautiful brownstones. Still this is New York, so walk a few blocks in any direction to discover the neighborhood's diverse offerings.

Curry Hill

North of the park find Gramercy's very own "Curry Hill" with an authentic range of satisfying, budget-friendly restaurants. Food enthusiasts should visit **Kalustyan's**—a spice-scented emporium specializing in a mind-boggling wealth of exotic products ranging from orange blossom water, to thirty varieties of dried whole chillies. A few blocks to the west, find the very open, tranquil, and welcoming Madison Square Park, which boasts its own

unique history and vibe. This was the home of the city's first community Christmas tree in 1912, the original location of Madison Square Garden arena, and site of New York's very first baseball club, the Knickerbockers of 1845. It is therefore only fitting that greeting park visitors is the original and scrumptious **Shake Shack**, serving its signature upscale fast food to a legion of followers from an ivy-covered kiosk. Burgers and Chicago-style dogs are always popular, but the house-made creamy custard has its cultish followers checking the online "custard calendar" weekly for their favorite flavors, like red-velvet or salted caramel. Barbecue fans should time their visits here with the Big Apple Barbecue Block Party held in June. This weekend-long event features celebrity pit masters displaying and serving their talents to throngs of hungry aficionados.

One of this neighborhood's most famous and frequented features is **Eataly NY**, founded by Oscar Farinetti and brought stateside by business partners Mario Batali and Joe Bastianich. This massive mecca offers a glamorous market place and dining hall replete with Italian products and food stalls showing off fresh pasta, organic breads, domestically-raised meats, fresh fish from the Fulton Fish Market, Neapolitan-style pizza, gelato, and a coffee bar. Nearby Union Square may be

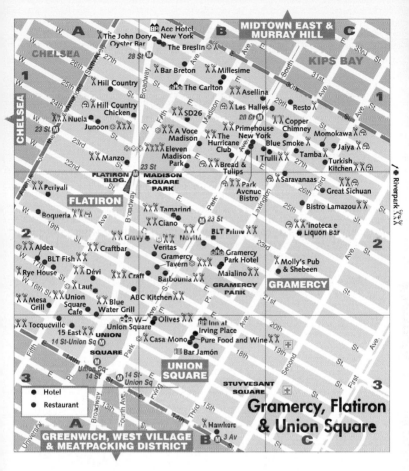

Gramercy, Flatiron & Union Square

known as an historic downtown park with playgrounds and tiered plazas that occasionally hosts political protests and rallies, but today the square is best known for its year-round **Greenmarket**.

Housed in the newly renovated Union Square Park is a beautiful array of seasonal produce, baked goods, fresh meat, seafood, dairy, plants, and flowers are still available every Monday, Wednesday, Friday, and Saturday. Early in the day, it is not uncommon to spot chefs

dressed in their whites selecting the day's supplies. Beyond the market's borders, find a nice bottle of wine to complement that farm-to-table meal from the comprehensive **Union Square Wines and Spirits**, or the regionally-specific **Italian Wine Merchants**. Further testament to Union Square's reputation as the center of Manhattan food shopping is the presence of **Whole Foods** and the city's very first **Trader Joe's**, all within blocks of one another.

ABC Kitchen

💥💥

A2

35 E. 18th St. (bet. Broadway & Park Ave. South)

Subway: 14 St - Union Sq   Lunch & dinner daily
Phone: 212-475-5829
Web: www.abckitchennyc.net
Prices: $$

The super-busy Super-Chef Jean-Georges Vongerichten weaves a bit of green into his rich tapestry of dining venues with this invigorating eatery at ABC Carpet & Home. Rooted in a farm-to-table ethos, diners sup on an assortment of seasonal and consciously procured preparations that feature market-inspired small plates; wood-fired whole wheat crusted pizzas; clever entrées like crackling skinned suckling pig topped with bacon marmalade, and fun desserts that include a slice of banana chip ice cream cake.

The chic setting showcases a white-washed interior warmed by reclaimed ceiling beams, soy candles, and that trademark ABC touch: mix and match chandeliers. The room's furnishings and handmade service pieces are available for purchase online.

Asellina

💥💥

B1

420 Park Ave. South (at 29th St.)

Subway: 28 St (Park Ave. South)   Lunch & dinner daily
Phone: 212-317-2908
Web: www.togrp.com/asellina
Prices: $$

From hospitality company The One Group, and housed in the glassy new Gansevoort Park Avenue hotel, Asellina offers a gratifying and updated vision of Italian dining. Bedecked with terra brick walls, concrete flooring, exposed filament bulbs, and sienna-toned leather furnishings, the lofty room glimmers with chic rusticity.

A long list of *antipasti* kicks off the menu with the likes of swordfish carpaccio with pink peppercorns, oven-dried tomato, and orange zest. Pizza topped with nuggets of suckling pig, *robiola*, and tart shallots caramelized in red wine vinegar, is one of several flatbread offerings; and more substantial fare features excellent pastas like the hearty but not heavy rigatoni with crumbled sausage, wild fennel, and Pecorino Sardo.

Aldea ✿

A2

31 W. 17th St. (bet. Fifth & Sixth Aves.)

Subway: 14 St – 6 Av
Phone: 212-675-7223
Web: www.aldearestaurant.com
Prices: $$

Lunch Mon – Fri
Dinner Mon – Sat

Jerry Errico

Chef George Mendes is the star at this forever pleasing Flatiron restaurant, the name of which means village in Portuguese. Birch, leather, glass, and cool colors deliver a tastefully modern vision of a sun-bleached coastal locale and one is greeted by a sense of calm upon settling in at Aldea. Seating is supplemented by an elegant mezzanine and counter overlooking the pristine kitchen where Chef Mendes stands sentry over his talented team.

Mendes has honed his craft under many influential talents including David Bouley, Alain Ducasse, and Kurt Gutenbrunner. His concise menu bears a unique concept forged by the chef's Portuguese-American background and experiences, and unfolds a carte that serves such delicious *petiscos* like sea urchin toast, a divine marrying of earth and sea featuring creamy cauliflower purée topped by sweet briny lobes of uni. The chef's signature *arroz de pato* reveals a succulent *soccarat* studded with tender duck breast, impressively cooked to medium-rare, and woven with crunchy skin, chorizo, and sweet tangerine.

Desserts at Aldea are as studied as they are sinful, as in a passion fruit parfait with a swish of velvety chocolate and almond meringue kisses.

A Voce Madison ❀

Italian ✗✗

B1

41 Madison Ave. (entrance on 26th St.)

Subway: 28 St (Park Ave. South)
Phone: 212-545-8555
Web: www.avocerestaurant.com
Prices: $$$

Lunch Mon – Fri
Dinner Mon – Sat

Evan Sung

Steps from the glorious Madison Park, and flanked by a barrage of skyscrapers, lies this Italian sparkler. Find your way through a sidewalk dining terrace before entering A Voce Madison's sleek dining room which unfolds a stunning study of nature's tones. Floor-to-ceiling windows bestow a gorgeous glow upon brown leather chairs with chrome cages. While maintaining a minimalist aura, wooden branch accents and a massive bar (wooden, naturally!) feed an earthy interest.

Yet what is wrought best in this classically modern space is Missy Robbins' warm and rustic menu. If you're looking for privacy, reserve a large table and conduct your affairs away from the eavesdroppers. Patronized by surrounding suits, notice a well-orchestrated staff also pander to a coterie of fashionable fat-cats.

Austere tables are juxtaposed with lively conversations about gnocchi knobs sprinkled with tangy *caprino* and goat milk butter. Crowds may also clamor for rosemary- and garlic-roasted chicken with a deliciously salted skin; or poached *ipologlosso* (halibut) with *Castelluccio* lentils. Finally, rest assured that you will have only sweet dreams after a lick of the *zuppa inglese* crested with lemon granite.

Barbounia

B2

250 Park Ave. South (at 20th St.)

Subway: 23 St (Park Ave. South)
Phone: 212-995-0242
Web: www.barbounia.com
Prices: $$

Lunch & dinner daily

Favored by the nearby business crowd and residents alike, this big and bustling space boasts exotic touches throughout. Fat columns and arched openings abate the room's scale, while pillow-lined banquettes, a knobby-wood communal table, and open kitchen equipped with a wood-burning oven allude to the menu's bazaar of Mediterranean flavors, highlighting Greece and Morocco as well as Southern France and Italy.

The sunny flavors of the region shine in the selection of creamy spreads accompanied by a slab of freshly baked flatbread. Branch out to explore a tempting array of mezes, oven-roasted whole fish, or house specialties like lamb terra-cotta—a stew perfumed with sweet spices, covered with a crusty bread lid, and baked in an earthenware dish.

Bar Breton

B1

254 Fifth Ave. (bet. 28th & 29th Sts.)

Subway: 28 St (Broadway)
Phone: 212-213-4999
Web: www.barbreton.com
Prices: $$

Lunch & dinner daily

Chef Cyril Renaud does his native Brittany proud at the comfortable and ever-tempting Bar Breton. This inspired brasserie respects French tradition while boasting enough creativity to endear it in the hearts of savvy diners and those lucky local business lunch crowds.

The cozy front barroom yields to a back dining area done in a pale palette enlivened by artwork. The setting provides a simple enough backdrop in which to focus on the myriad ways to indulge in the *galette*, or buckwheat crêpe. Expect these savory treats to arrive in any number of guises, such as "lasagna" with creamy crabmeat filling, nutty Parmesan, and sweet shellfish foam. Non-*galette* dishes include a classic bœuf Bourguignon and the BB burger deluxe with a Nutella shake.

91

Bar Jamón

B3

125 E. 17th St. (at Irving Pl.)

Subway:	14 St - Union Sq	Lunch Sat – Sun
Phone:	212-253-2773	Dinner nightly
Web:	www.barjamonnyc.com	
Prices:	**$$**	

A nibble at tiny Bar Jamón, with its brilliant by-the-glass list of Spanish wines (shared with big sister Casa Mono next door), may convince you that Chef Andy Nusser is the unsung hero of the Batali empire. Though the restaurant is the size of a closet, everything is done deliciously and with panache.

This mouthwatering menu so creatively breaks the tired tapas mold that arrival more than 15 minutes past opening almost guarantees a wait (stick to weekend off-hours). Luscious slices of jamón serrano or the famed Iberico from Spain's *pata negra* (black hoofed) pigs and a long list of cheeses and accompaniments star on a menu of small plates washed down by more than 600 choices of Spanish wine. A *cuarto* from the impressive list is de rigueur.

Bistro Lamazou

C2

344 Third Ave. (bet. 25th & 26th Sts.)

Subway:	23 St (Park Ave. South)	Lunch & dinner daily
Phone:	212-481-8550	
Web:	www.bistrolamazou.com	
Prices:	**$$**	

This new Gramercy bistro from Aziz and Nancy Lamazou, proprietors of the namesake cheese shop a few doors away, is housed in a glossy dining room that bears an airy mien warmed up by sunny hues. The comfortable bar is a nice spot for a snack.

Understandably, the menu is prefaced by an offering of cheeses and charcuterie before delving into a lineup of preparations that cruise the Mediterranean. Starters may include a delightful salad of endive spears topped with candied walnuts and julienned apple that is dressed with creamy Roquefort-lime vinaigrette and basil oil. Entrées bring the likes of rack of lamb with black-olive crust and Moroccan chicken tagine. The *calisson de Provence* with mixed berry sorbet is a fitting finale for true sugar fiends.

BLT Fish

A2

21 W. 17th St. (bet. Fifth & Sixth Aves.)

Subway: 14 St - 6 Av
Phone: 212-691-8888
Web: www.bltfish.com
Prices: $$$

Lunch Mon — Fri
Dinner nightly

BLT Fish presents two options to hungry seafood fans. On the ground floor, the Fish Shack offers an extensive raw bar, beachfront-worthy lobster rolls, and fish and chips. The upstairs dining room bears all the hallmarks of BLT's casual elegance: dark wood furnishings, contemporary touches, a white tiled open kitchen, and a wine list to be pondered. A glass ceiling adds drama and views of the night sky.

Exceptionally fresh shellfish or line-caught, hand-cut fish may be simply brushed with olive oil and grilled; but the menu also boasts more ingenious offerings, like the semi-smoked King salmon with avocado hollandaise. Thoughtful and sophisticated extras throughout the meal enhance the experience.

Lunch is only served weekdays at the Fish Shack.

BLT Prime

B2

111 E. 22nd St. (bet. Lexington Ave. & Park Ave. South)

Subway: 23 St (Park Ave. South)
Phone: 212-995-8500
Web: www.bltprime.com
Prices: $$$

Dinner nightly

Though this city offers a world of dining options, it still savors its meat and potatoes. Here at elegant BLT Prime, cuts of USDA prime and certified Black Angus and American Wagyu are fancifully presented sizzling hot in a cast-iron pan and glistening with herbed butter. The menu allows diners to lavishly adorn their steaks with an array of homemade sauces, as well as a "beef temp" guide to ensure that the medium rare steak you order is exactly what suits you. The humble potato achieves greatness in nine different sides, and the Gruyère popovers start meals with a warm and tasty welcome.

The handsome room and bar area, popular with local, after-work crowds, feature rich tones of butterscotch and mocha, and sleek zebrawood tables.

Manhattan ▶ Gramercy, Flatiron & Union Square

Blue Smoke

B1

116 E. 27th St. (bet. Lexington Ave. & Park Ave. South)

Subway: 28 St (Park Ave. South)   Lunch & dinner daily
Phone: 212-447-7733
Web: www.bluesmoke.com
Prices: $$

Blue Smoke, where hickory and applewood infuse the "low and slow" smoked meats in a real barbecue pit, proves that jazz and barbecue are nothing if not a winning combination. The proof lies in the ravishing pulled pork platter—think of a mountain of tender, shredded meat studded with bits of crisped skin heaped precariously atop a slice of house-baked white bread and accompanied by a caddy of sauces. Starters like deviled eggs and shrimp corn dogs as well as stellar desserts, by pastry chef Jennifer Giblin, bookend this fabulous feast.

Families and groups may choose the upstairs dining, but the same food can be enjoyed downstairs at Jazz Standard, complete with live music. Owner Danny Meyer stamps the restaurant with his signature of gracious service.

Blue Water Grill

A2

31 Union Sq. West (at 16th St.)

Subway: 14 St - Union Sq   Lunch & dinner daily
Phone: 212-675-9500
Web: www.bluewatergrillnyc.com
Prices: $$

Facing the Union Square Greenmarket, perennially popular Blue Water Grill is housed in a former, century-old bank, whose grand rooms now bustle with eager guests and a well-trained service team. Still, it retains a stately air with its soaring molded ceiling, gleaming marble, and windows overlooking the terraced dining area, ideal for warmer weather.

The crowd-pleasing menu focuses on seafood, but offers something for everyone. Highlights include a raw bar and sushi or maki selections, as well as fish entrées, simply grilled or accented with international flavors, as in big eye tuna with miso-black garlic vinaigrette. Find live jazz nightly in the downstairs lounge; or private group dining in the Vault Room, a former repository for gold bullion.

Boqueria

Spanish 🍴🍴

A2

53 W. 19th St. (bet. Fifth & Sixth Aves.)

Subway: 18 St (Seventh Ave.) Lunch & dinner daily
Phone: 212-255-4160
Web: www.boquerianyc.com
Prices: $$

 Channeling the little bars that surround the legendary *Mercat de la Boqueria* in Barcelona, this upscale tapas spot is among the city's better destinations for an Iberian bite. Despite the crush of occupants each evening, the attractive setting provides a comfortable perch either in the rear room furnished with high tables or at the front counter flaunting plates of *tortilla Española*.

Seamus Mullen has departed but the kitchen, now headed by a Barcelona native with an impressive resume, soldiers on. Treats here have featured crunchy *croquetas* filled with a creamy combination of octopus and tomato; house-made pork sausage paired with crisped garbanzo beans and syrupy red wine reduction; and *torrija*, a stunning Spanish rendition of French toast.

Bread & Tulips

Italian 🍴🍴

B1

365 Park Ave. South (at 26th St.)

Subway: 28 St (Park Ave. South) Dinner nightly
Phone: 212-532-9100
Web: www.breadandtulipsnyc.com
Prices: $$

This stretch of Park Avenue South tends to have the dime-a-dozen variety of restaurant, but chew on this...Bread & Tulips is something worth ducking into. It's very New York in that exposed brick walls, dark polished wood floors, and filament bulb light fixtures kind of way. The young staff is smartly dressed in striped aprons and silk scarves. It's loud, so save the serious talk for later.

The wood-burning oven is from Modena and the artisan pies (topped with foraged mushrooms, ramps, watercress, and taleggio cheese) taste as if they dropped from heaven. It could end there, but with starters like King salmon belly crudo, and entrées like handmade *trofie* pasta topped with a zesty lamb ragù, why would you give up before the going gets greater?

The Breslin ✿

Gastropub 🍴

B1

16 W. 29th St. (at Broadway)

Subway: 28 St (Broadway)　　　　　　　　Lunch & dinner daily
Phone: 212-679-1939
Web: www.thebreslin.com
Prices: $$

Melissa Hom

When Chef April Bloomfield opened the Spotted Pig years ago, her instant success earned accolades and acclaim for introducing NY to her signature nose-to-tail philosophy. Since then, her skills and passion have proven that she is no flash in the pan, but a true force to be reckoned with—this is immediately evident at her Ace Hotel gastropub, The Breslin.

Word of this white-hot spot is out, and the masses are a-coming. All of them. So be prepared to wait amid Chef Bloomfield's enthusiasts in fever pitch. Still, creative cocktails and a nice selection of beer help push those dreamy thoughts of scrumpets with mint vinegar and terrine boards to the back of everyone's mind. Once seated in the high-ceilinged room, with its vintage vibe and animal figurines, expect the casual yet very well-informed staff to guide you through the massive menu. Offerings may reveal chicken liver parfait with Madeira jelly, crispy sweetbreads, or pig's foot for two; as well as adeptly prepared vegetable sides, like crunchy-crackly duck-fat fries.

Those keen on avoiding lines can grab a group and reserve the lamb or suckling pig dinner, for a memorable feast that is dramatic and delicious in its simplicity.

Casa Mono

B3

52 Irving Pl. (at 17th St.)

Subway: 14 St - Union Sq
Phone: 212-253-2773
Web: www.casamononyc.com
Prices: $$

Lunch & dinner daily

Casa Mono

A stroll around leafy Irving Place can leave you wondering whether downtown could be any more charming. The answer is "yes" when stepping over the threshold to Casa Mono, where you'll find yourself immersed in a somewhat tiny world of tapas with a bone-shaking soul.

From its rustic setting to an action-packed open kitchen and stunning antique mosaic-tiled floor, this place first pleases the eyes. Round up a small group of only your best pals, since you'll be knocking knees and getting cozy at the diminutive tables. If the forever-alluring aromas lure you inside without reservations, find a seat at the kitchen-view counters.

Although Chef Andy Nusser headed this hot spot for years, he has passed the baton to Anthony Sasso who keeps the menu inventive with dishes that spark, please, tantalize, and always distinguish themselves from the pack of cookie-cutter gourmet copycats. Dishes may be traditional, as in the *bacalao croquettas*, but come alive with a citrusy, slightly sweet aïoli. From the big, smoky flavors of house-made chorizo; *gambas* with gazpacho vinaigrette; to octopus with fennel and scarlet grapefruit, the offerings here display as much passion as promise of expertise.

Ciano

Italian ✗✗

B2

45 E. 22nd St. (bet. Broadway & Park Ave. South)

Subway: 23 St (Park Ave. South)   Lunch & dinner daily
Phone: 212-982-8422
Web: www.cianonyc.com
Prices: $$$

Park Avenue South is packed with spots (some good, some gut-wrenching), but Ciano is the latest to hit the scene. Located in the former home of Beppe, Ciano retains the rustic Tuscan farmhouse look and feel. Headed by Cru alum Shea Gallante, there's plenty of hype to go around.

The market-inspired Italian menu is cluttered with too many choices and has its fair share of hits and misses. Homemade pastas can be inconsistent (sometimes overcooked with flavorful condiments, and at other times melt-in-your-mouth but with a lackluster finish); however, crisped duck breast with garlic *sformato* is knock-out. Portions are large, so don't be pressured to over order. Service is at times spotty and disorganized, but don't let that distract from the lovely tiramisu.

Copper Chimney

Indian ✗✗

C1

126 E. 28th St. (bet. Lexington Ave. & Park Ave. South)

Subway: 28 St (Park Ave. South)   Lunch & dinner daily
Phone: 212-213-5742
Web: www.copperchimneynyc.com
Prices: 💶

This attractive and sleek dining room with a hip décor and fun vibe impresses with Northern and Southern Indian fare that stands well above the array of local options. The appetizer selection may include lovely *malai kofta*, perfectly browned and simmered in a delicious, creamy saffron sauce. Main courses incorporate a wide range of traditional ingredients, while emphasizing refined preparation and elegant presentation. Non-meat eaters will be happy with the ample selection of flavorful vegetarian items. Delicately puffed *kulcha*, served hot and dusted with cilantro and mint, is a great foil to any rich, leftover sauces (and the best way to sop them up).

The contemporary setting is further enhanced by a second floor lounge area.

Craft

American 🍴🍴🍴

B2

43 E. 19th St. (bet. Broadway & Park Ave. South)

Subway: 14 St - Union Sq
Phone: 212-780-0880
Web: www.craftrestaurant.com
Prices: $$$$

Dinner nightly

This hot spot from celebrity chef/owner Tom Colicchio is honest-to-goodness city chic. It's dim and moody—reading the menu in the dark can make you feel older than that harried exec in the corner. It's American as only a city chef can do, with more twists and turns than a drive on the autobahn. Colicchio's a good guy though—note the shout-outs to farmers and producers of these quality ingredients.

Confused by the seemingly simple choices? Broken down, it's really just sophisticated snacks with a "pick and choose" mentality. It was Miss Scarlet in the Library with a candlestick holder, er, it's halibut, braised in beurre blanc, in a copper dish. Keep grazing...you'll go from pork trotter and crisp-a-licious shishito peppers to s'mores stat.

Craftbar

Contemporary 🍴🍴

A2

900 Broadway (bet. 19th & 20th Sts.)

Subway: 14 St - Union Sq
Phone: 212-461-4300
Web: www.craftrestaurant.com
Prices: $$

Lunch & dinner daily

Flaunting Craft's trademark style, Craftbar offers fine cooking garnished by the space's industrial good looks and pretty occupants—all a perfect match for its Gramercy environs.

With an extensive menu of something for just about everyone, it's no wonder that Craftbar always draws a crowd. Raw, cured, and fried snacks, local cheeses, and small plates offer a tasty prelude to the range of product-focused fare that has featured stuffed rabbit saddle dressed with golden raisin chutney, and pan-seared branzino draped over a peak of ratatouille. Brown sugar cake with a caramelized pineapple ring and crème fraîche ice cream makes saving room for dessert a requisite indulgence.

Revel in the boundless wine list, with many selections by the glass.

Dévi

A2

8 E. 18th St. (bet. Broadway & Fifth Ave.)

Subway: 14 St - Union Sq
Phone: 212-691-1300
Web: www.devinyc.com
Prices: $$

Lunch Mon – Fri
Dinner nightly

One of Manhattan's most bewitching Indian restaurants, Dévi is awash in warm colors, rich jewel-toned fabrics, and intricate wood carvings.

The proficient kitchen, led by founder and cookbook author Suvir Saran, sends forth a divine menu of regional specialties that highlight creative range. A host of good looking diners are invited to compose their own tasting menu of three or four courses from a spread that includes grilled Georges Bank scallops propped by dabs of red pepper chutney, candied strips of bitter orange peel, and sweet and sour florets of Manchurian-style cauliflower; decadent jackfruit biryani studded with carmelized onions potatoes; or shrimp *haree* curry, a spicy green mélange of coconut milk, curry leaves, cilantro, and smoky cumin.

15 East

A3

15 E. 15th St. (bet. Fifth Ave. & Union Sq. West)

Subway: 14 St - Union Sq
Phone: 212-647-0015
Web: www.15eastrestaurant.com
Prices: $$$

Lunch Mon – Fri
Dinner Mon – Sat

Chef Masato Shimizu apprenticed in Japan for seven years before making his way to the Big Apple—a training you'll be thanking the sweet heavens for the minute you eyeball a gorgeous ceramic tile of his supremely fresh sashimi. Tucked into a charming four-story building overlooking 15th Street, just steps from Union Square, this modest little sushi den boasts a beautifully detailed interior decked out in gauzy white curtains, lush gray walls, and dangling geometric lanterns.

But what really matters is on your plate: tender braised octopus dusted with salt; Santa Barbara sea urchin served in its spiny shell and topped with shiso leaf; melt-in-your-mouth toro; delicate squid ribbons with lemon zest; and perfectly fried whole shrimp tempura.

Eleven Madison Park ✾ ✾ ✾

B1

11 Madison Ave. (at 24th St.)

Subway: 23 St (Park Ave. South)
Phone: 212-889-0905
Web: www.elevenmadisonpark.com
Prices: $$$$

Lunch Mon – Fri
Dinner Mon – Sat

Francesco Tonelli

New York nights are filled with endless amazement and Eleven Madison Park is one grand surprise party. This space remains stunning with grand ballroom ceilings, natural light, terrazzo floors, and art deco lithographs. But if you haven't been in a while, you are in for a treat; from spirited service to exciting cuisine, this is a restaurant reborn.

Chef Daniel Humm starts guests with single ingredients simply listed on the bill of fare as "chicken" or "eggplant," but uses his formidable skill in ways that are more wondrous and playful than formal, with spectacular results. Do not be frustrated with the menu's lack of description or if the waiter seems tight-lipped about what is to come. That "chicken" may arrive as a roulade stuffed with morels and foie gras, with puréed potato, and pristine shavings of black truffle. An "apple" dessert may involve tart balls of fruit infused with cilantro, served with curry curd on a plate shellacked with caramel. From the tableside cocktail service fit for a king, to the house-made granola gifted upon departure, nothing here misses its mark.

While such culinary talent is a gift, the chef's dedication to the evolution of his craft is a true rarity.

Gramercy Tavern ✿

Contemporary ✗✗✗

42 E. 20th St. (bet. Broadway & Park Ave. South)

Subway: 23 St (Park Ave. South)   Lunch & dinner daily
Phone: 212-477-0777
Web: www.gramercytavern.com
Prices: $$$

Ellen Silverman

Set mid-block along venerable Gramercy Park, the commotion fades away the moment you step inside—or at least once you pass through the lively Tavern and into any of the comfortable interior rooms, adorned with arches, paintings, murals, drapes, and copper sconces. Count on polished servers to arrive at the tables with an almost-bookish knowledge of Chef Michael Anthony's daily menu, and be ready to share it with the assembled bigwigs, celebrities, and casual diners alike.

What has made this restaurant so great for 18 years? That starts with spot-on appetizers, like sunchoke salad, served both puréed and roasted with a lemon vinaigrette and perfect black lentils that burst in the mouth. Sparkling mains include a plump, golden-brown pork croquette on a bed of red cabbage and *aji dulce* finished with spiced-port sauce. Neither of these dishes should let you forget about the desserts, including the creamy peanut-butter *semifreddo* sandwiched between chocolate macarons. The well-sourced wine list offers an impressive range of selections by the glass.

At times, Gramercy Tavern seems so inviting that you can almost imagine yourself dining at a great aunt's house, were she prone to excellence.

Gravy

American ✗✗

32 East 21st St. (bet. Broadway & Park Ave. South)

Subway: 23 St (Park Ave. South)   Dinner nightly
Phone: 212-600-2105
Web: www.gravyny.com
Prices: $$

Gravy adds to the city's growing number of Southern-inspired venues, offering a contemporary spin on down-home favorites in a setting that sports classic Flatiron bones. The large grey and brick-accented dining room features a bar flanked by columns, red vinyl booths, and opaque ceiling pendants suspended from the high ceiling above. Starters include the likes of crawfish gumbo fritters, while heartier offerings have featured Sullivan Island bog—a low-country treat comprised of impeccable shellfish and grilled tasso ham atop a moist mound of Carolina red rice sweetened with tomatoes, diced bell peppers, and sliced okra, all given a faint hit of spice. Tempting sides include crackling creamed corn and a trio of grits: honey, cheesy, and porky.

Great Sichuan 😊

Chinese ✗✗

363 Third Ave. (bet. 26th & 27th Sts.)

Subway: 28 St (Park Ave. South)   Lunch & dinner daily
Phone: 212-686-8866
Web: www.greatsichuan.com
Prices: $$

This under-the-radar Sichuan restaurant, tucked into a bustling stretch of Third Ave., is a find you'll want to tell your friends about stat. A simple dining room, fitted out in wood details, white linens, and stone tile floors, belies the bold and flavorful fare ahead. Dishes are fresh and authentic—not to mention spicy enough to put some hair on your chest.

Skip the American-style offerings and set your sights on one of the chef's Sichuan specialties; or the authentic Mao section, which features mouthwatering goodies like cured pork with green garlic shoots, or braised pumpkin with ginger and scallions. Another highlight is the whole steamed fish, smothered in pickled chili peppers, sweet red bell peppers, caramelized white onion and green scallion.

Hawkers

B3

225 E. 14th St. (bet. Second & Third Aves.)

Subway: 14 St - Union Sq   Lunch & dinner daily
Phone: 212-982-1688
Web: www.hawkersnyc.com
Prices: ⊗⊗

Hawkers takes its cue from the open-air food stalls strutting local specialties commonplace throughout Southeast Asia. The slender room, embellished by a collection of silhouettes and street-theme graffiti art set against a bright red background, showcases a two-sided dining counter and a laid-back crew.

The menu is gently priced and serves up a variety of fresh and tasty snacks such as Thai sausage, chicken *satay* burger, and five-spice pork roll encased in a delicately crisp bean curd skin. Several fried rice and noodle preparations form the heart of Hawkers' offerings: the Maggi, named after a popular brand of instant noodles, features ramen served up as a fluffy stir-fry stocked with sliced tomato, egg, bean sprouts, and green onion.

Hill Country

A1

30 W. 26th St. (bet. Broadway & Sixth Ave.)

Subway: 28 St (Broadway)   Lunch & dinner daily
Phone: 212-255-4544
Web: www.hillcountryny.com
Prices: $$

This Texas-size roadhouse has won over the hearts and stomachs of smoked brisket deprived New Yorkers. Always a rollicking good time, Hill Country's food stations, dispensing some of NY's best barbecue and country fare, set it above the booming competition.

The crew behind the stoves here have clearly honed their skills— successfully fueling Hill Country's massive smokers with cords of oak to recreate a truly Texan Hill Country experience. Grab Flintstone-size ribs by the pound, sausages by the link, stamp your meal ticket, and head to the trimmings counter for home-style sides. Then, settle in for some live country music, making this a festive spot for groups and families.

Those seeking a more subdued setting can order takeout or delivery.

Hill Country Chicken 🐷

A1

1123 Broadway (at 25th St.)

Subway: 23 St (Broadway) Lunch & dinner daily
Phone: 212-257-6446
Web: www.hillcountrychicken.com
Prices: 💰💰

The city's fried chicken rivalry has gotten more delicious with the arrival of Hill Country Chicken. Like its barbecue-themed sibling, Texas serves as the inspiration for this self-described chicken joint, which can accommodate 100 in a country kitchen-style space in sunny yellow and sky blue. Service involves lining up to order, but the crew is swift and friendly. The first order of business is deciding on a variety of naturally raised chicken (classic or Mama El's rocking a skinless, cracker-crumb crust), but there's no wrong choice. Each piece is crunchy, juicy, and incredibly flavorful.

Pimento cheese-topped mashed potatoes; biscuits baked on premises; and a slew of awesome pies proves that Hill Country is much more than a one hit wonder.

The Hurricane Club

B1

360 Park Ave. South (at 26th St.)

Subway: 28 St (Park Ave. South) Lunch Mon – Fri
Phone: 212-951-7111 Dinner nightly
Web: www.thehurricaneclub.com
Prices: $$

A tiki bar as envisioned by the design impresarios at AvroKO and Chef Craig Koketsu (of Park Avenue), The Hurricane Club offers the sips and eats of faraway lands in a pretty setting worthy of a movie backdrop. The multi-room space, vast by NYC standards, is embellished with glossy black and dark croc-embossed banquettes brightened by mirror panels, potted greenery, and large windows dressed with cascading ivory shades; the center bar is crowned by strands of crystal beads.

The assortment of libations provide a quenching prelude to an upscale Polynesian-ish menu of pu pu platters stocked with *croque monsieur* spring rolls; and family-style preparations of sticky and succulent ribs, noodles, and rice. Order-in-advance luau dinners are also offered.

'inoteca e Liquori Bar 😊

Italian ✗✗

C2

323 Third Ave. (at 24th St.)

Subway: 23 St (Park Ave. South)   Lunch & dinner daily
Phone: 212-683-3035
Web: www.inotecanyc.com
Prices: $$

Most sophisticated of its clan, 'inoteca e Liquori Bar brings its beloved small plates to Gramercy. Awash in candlelight, the chic dining space is an earthy rainbow of marble paneling; the separate, bustling bar is a bright corner with large windows and marble tables. With a cocktail menu of more than thirty-five masterful classic and vintage libations, heightened with fresh juices, infusions, and chilled with crystal clear blocks of ice, this is where 'inoteca's theme is at its best.

To complement the skillfully crafted wines, the excellent Italian wine bar cuisine features *antipasti*, panini, and decadent pastas, like baked rigatoni with cauliflower and herbed breadcrumbs. Sidewalk dining is a lovely spot for the inexpensive, prix-fixe brunch.

I Trulli

Italian ✗✗

C1

122 E. 27th St. (bet. Lexington Ave. & Park Ave. South)

Subway: 28 St (Park Ave. South)   Lunch & dinner daily
Phone: 212-481-7372
Web: www.itrulli.com
Prices: $$$

Equal parts dining room and *enoteca*, the charming I Trulli has been going strong for more than 15 years. From the roaring fireplace to the breezy outdoor garden, this place oozes warmth and the ambience is chic country comfort. Every detail including the domed white walls and oven is designed to recall the distinctive architecture of the region's *trullo*, or stacked-stone homes.

I Trulli celebrates the wine and food of Southern Italy's Puglia region. The wine bar has a terrific selection of all-Italian wines and a tempting taste of small dishes, while the dining room focuses on heartier selections, handmade pastas, and regional specialties such as *fave e cicoria*.

Desserts show off the chef's proud roots as a pastry artist and provide a strong, and sweet, finish.

Manhattan ▶ Gramercy, Flatiron & Union Square

Jaiya ⊛

C1

396 Third Ave. (bet. 28th & 29th Sts.)

Subway: 28 St (Park Ave. South)
Phone: 212-889-1330
Web: www.jaiya.com
Prices: ⊛⊛

Lunch & dinner daily

After twenty years in the same location, this beloved spicy stalwart now has been revitalized with a slicker look. The furnishings may now feature deep-hued woods, dark tables, padded beige walls, and a contemporary bar. Still, rest assured that the vast, budget-friendly menu remains as delicious as ever.

Start with a hot and crisp spring roll filled with glass noodles and bean sprouts while considering the proteins for customizing Jaiya's heaping stir-fried dishes fragrant with basil, garlic, and Kaffir lime. Curry listings encourage the same liberty, highlighting a host of creamy coconut curries, spiced with chilies and sweet with fresh basil, filled with the likes of succulent shrimp and fresh tilapia, accompanied by a cone of hot sticky rice.

The John Dory Oyster Bar

B1

1196 Broadway (at 29th St.)

Subway: 28 St (Broadway)
Phone: 212-792-9000
Web: www.thejohndory.com
Prices: $$

Lunch & dinner daily

Rejoice: Chef April Bloomfield's John Dory Oyster Bar has returned! Housed in the Ace Hotel New York, the vibe is now low-key and fun for all. Set in a high-ceilinged corner space, the frequented setting boasts original details like a mosaic tile floor and chic touches such as ebony subway tile, comfortable seating in crayon-bright blue and green, and a gorgeous raw bar.

The menu adheres to its oyster bar ethos and offers an array of seafood small plates that everyone piles high on petite copper-topped tables. Dishes include *hiramasa* crudo topped with ginger and shards of crisped skin; delicate *carta de musica* sandwiching a lusty combination of *bottarga* and chili; and the signature oyster pan roast capped by a garlic-rubbed crostini topped with uni.

Junoon ✿

Indian XXX

A1

27 West 24th St. (bet. Fifth & Sixth Aves.)

Subway: 23 St (Sixth Ave.)
Phone: 212-490-2100
Web: www.junoonnyc.com
Prices: $$$

Lunch Mon – Fri
Dinner nightly

Ruggero Vanni

Junoon's dramatic façade is a fitting omen of what lies within. Entrée this stunning Indo arena and you will be swept away by its palatial ambience. A bar/lounge lives up front and is embellished with two antique *jhoolas* (swings) carved from Burmese teak. Junoon is the very picture of an Indian palace. Carved stone panels (set in a reflecting pool) line the trail separating two dining rooms—sultry lighting, ornate mirrors, earthy tones, and wood moldings set the scene for a regal repast.

A polite and *pukka* staff feed a flood of Indian diners old-world classics mingled with modern elegance; while sleekly-suited sommeliers show you the way around a fine wine list. From the main dining room, watch the kitchen's tour de force. With a mission to sate the tastes of date-night duos, corporate barons, and other devotees, they bring you *patthar*—lamb shoulder golden-crusted with papaya juice and *garam masala*.

Find your mouth watering for shrimp *ghassi* bathed in tamarind and coconut; or a lovely rendition of *sarson ka saag*, mustard greens puréed with ginger and cumin. The *kulfi* trio (mango, cardamom, and cherry) cools you down, while the passion fruit bombe promises to explode in your mouth.

Laut

A2

15 E. 17th St. (bet. Broadway & Fifth Ave.)

Subway: 14 St - Union Sq

Phone: 212-206-8989

Web: www.lautnyc.com

Prices: $$

Lunch & dinner daily

Laut

Alive with the haunting flavors of Southeast Asia, the cuisine at Laut extracts the specialties of Malaysia, Singapore, and Thailand for a meal that is a standout among its peers.

The room, located off of a busy stretch of Union Square, is simple yet the ambience is everything but; and parades an attractive space where red brick walls are embellished with images of flora sketched with colorful chalk, and the smiling staff attends to eager and hungry diners seated at dark wood tables.

The kitchen is now under the stewardship of Malaysian-born Executive Chef Ngan Ping "Tommy" Lai. He hails from the town of Rasa which translates to "taste." Take that as an auspicious sign, as Laut's offerings present well-prepared renditions of regional favorites such as *Asam laksa*—a bowlful of rice noodles bobbing in a spicy-sour broth fragrant with lemongrass and mint; *nasi lemak*—a lusty stir-fried combination of rice strewn with bits of egg, coconut chicken curry, pickled vegetables, and dried anchovies; and *masak Asam pedas*—a clay pot of pristine, plump pieces of shrimp (or red snapper) afloat with vegetables in a textured but stimulating sauce of tamarind, turmeric, mint, chilies, and garlic.

Les Halles 🙂

French 🍴

C1

411 Park Ave. South (bet. 28th & 29th Sts.)

Subway: 28 St (Park Ave. South) Lunch & dinner daily
Phone: 212-679-4111
Web: www.leshalles.net
Prices: $$

Hugely loved bad boy chef-at-large, Anthony Bourdain, may have put this beloved brasserie (his home base) on the map, but the simple, unfussy French cooking is the true draw. This is that rare spot renowned for leaving French classics untouched and absolutely delicious. The timeless brasserie menu may start the day with breakfast "Parisien" of brioche French toast, and end with a terrine *maison*; onion soup gratinée; *boudin aux pommes*; and *chocroute garnie* to accompany the budget-friendly wine list.

After 8:00 P.M. and until midnight daily, the lights go down, music goes up, and hip yet unpretentious crowds pour into their perennial favorite, housed in a century-old building. Tiny, tight tables put the outdoor seats in high demand during warm weather.

Maialino

Italian 🍴🍴

B2

2 Lexington Ave. (at 21st St.)

Subway: 23 St (Park Ave South) Lunch & dinner daily
Phone: 212-777-2410
Web: www.maialinonyc.com
Prices: $$

Danny Meyer's reworking of the Gramercy Park Hotel's dining venue has rendered a chicly casual Italian spot with a rustic theme conceived by the Rockwell Group. Accessed by a separate street entrance, the expanse up front is bright and lively with plenty of counter seating at the bar; while the back area, with its glossy dark wood accents, is furnished with tables dressed in blue-and-white checked tablecloths.

An alumnus of Babbo and Gramercy Tavern rules the kitchen; and the Roman trattoria menu offers a selection of salami and *antipasti*. This is followed by pastas symbolic of the region such as an excellent *tonnarelli cacio e pepe*, and a short list of hearty *secondi* that includes crispy fried suckling pig's foot with braised lentils.

Manzo

A1

Italian ✗✗

200 Fifth Ave. (at 23rd St.)

Subway: 23 St (Broadway)   Lunch & dinner daily
Phone: 212-229-2180
Web: www.eataly.com
Prices: $$$

Mario Batali and friends have a hit on their hands with Eataly NY. Originally founded by Oscar Farinetti in Turin, Italy, this dining emporium not only exhibits a collection of stations proffering freshly prepared Italian specialties, but also is home to fine dining at Manzo ("beef" in Italian).

Away from the fray, this formal option boasts an inviting bar pouring impressive wines and is overseen by a polished team. A nose-to-tail influence is seen in starters that include blood sausage and crispy sweetbreads. Pastas are excellent, as in the *girasoli di mortadella* with pistachios and scallions. Game and seafood are sprinkled throughout, but meat shines on the list of *secondi*, as in Porterhouse of domestically raised *Razza Piemontese* beef for two.

Mesa Grill

A2

Southwestern ✗✗

102 Fifth Ave. (bet. 15th & 16th Sts.)

Subway: 14 St - Union Sq   Lunch & dinner daily
Phone: 212-807-7400
Web: www.mesagrill.com
Prices: $$$

Responsible for launching Chef Bobby Flay to cookbook and Food Network stardom, Mesa Grill still buzzes nightly even after two decades of service—a particularly impressive achievement in this fickle city. The lofty room, colored with Southwest accents, sees its share of tourists hoping to catch a glimpse of the famous celebrity chef and native Manhattanite; but even if the chef is absent, a glass-walled kitchen entertains with views of his team putting a creative spin on Southwest cuisine.

Flay's trademark style results in a solid menu of vibrant preparations that can include a roasted garlic shrimp tamale; grilled mahi mahi with refreshing pineapple and onion salsa alongside creamy roasted poblano rice; or a moist, toasted-coconut layer cake.

Millesime

B1

Seafood XX

92 Madison Ave. (at 29th St.)

Subway: 28 St (Park Ave. South)
Phone: 212-889-7100
Web: www.millesimerestaurant.com
Prices: $$$

Lunch daily
Dinner Mon – Sat

Moving on from San Francisco's Aqua, Chef Laurent Manrique brings his seafood prowess to Gotham at the revamped Carlton hotel dining room. The brasserie setting retains its elegant bones but has been given a more casual makeover: lipstick-red banquettes, tables set with crisp linens and shiny, Eiffel Tower-shaped salt and pepper shakers, as well as a tempting raw bar beneath a Tiffany stained-glass dome.

Millesime means "vintage" in French, and the menu follows suit with a mix of classics, like pike quenelles in luscious lobster sauce, with contemporary dishes, like grilled Caesar salad. Diners compose their own entrées by selecting from excellent fish fillets that are grilled on the *plancha*, dressed with a choice of sauces, and paired with tasty sides.

Molly's Pub & Shebeen

C2

Gastropub X

287 Third Ave. (bet. 22nd & 23rd Sts.)

Subway: 23 St (Park Ave. South)
Phone: 212-889-3361
Web: www.mollysshebeen.com
Prices:

Lunch & dinner daily

A stop at Molly's Pub & Shebeen isn't just for celebrating St. Patrick's Day-style revelry the remaining 364 days of the year. The utterly charming setting, friendly service, and heartwarming fare make it much more than the standard Irish watering hole. The setting, first established in 1895, has had various incarnations but has been sating a loyal following since 1964. Wood smoke perfumes the air, rustic furnishings are arranged on a sawdust-covered floor, and a seat at the original mahogany bar couldn't be more welcoming. The ambience of this pub (or *shebeen*, which is an illicit drinking establishment) has few peers.

Stick with the list of house specialties (lamb stew, corned beef and cabbage, and Shepherd's pie) for an authentic experience.

Momokawa 😊

Japanese ✕

C1

157 E. 28th St. (bet. Lexington & Third Aves.)

Subway: 28 St (Park Ave. South) Dinner nightly
Phone: 212-684-7830
Web: www.momokawanyc.com
Prices: $$

Fans of Japanese cuisine will cheer at the authenticity of the expansive menu served at this impressive charmer. The location may come as a surprise, tucked away on a busy Curry Hill block, but the sparsely decorated small room is reminiscent of the type of place Tokyo salarymen might frequent for drinks and a delicious bite before the long commute home.

You can opt for one of their set menus (either the $60 prix-fixe or $55 seasonal course menu) or go for the à la carte affair kicking things off with seasonal appetizers such as miso eggplant, or soy-marinated rice cake; from there sashimi follows; and then cooked items like simmered beef with daikon, fried sardines with shishito peppers, and beef sukiyaki make for a lovely finish.

Novitá

Italian ✕✕

B2

102 E. 22nd St. (bet. Lexington Ave. & Park Ave. South)

Subway: 23 St (Park Ave South) Lunch Mon — Fri
Phone: 212-677-2222 Dinner nightly
Web: www.novitanyc.com
Prices: $$

For a solid Italian meal in Gramercy, this sweet little trattoria is worth wandering into. Tucked just below street level, along quiet 22nd Street, Novitá is delightfully unpretentious given its tony zip code, with a pretty, straightforward décor featuring sunny yellow walls, wide windows, and beautiful fresh flowers strewn about the room.

Ditto on the food. The daily specials can be pricey (be sure to ask in advance) but are lovely additions to a regular menu that might reveal crimson red tuna, fried in paper-thin pastry and served with a silky mayo and balsamic reduction; perfectly roasted Australian rack of lamb with sautéed baby spinach and garlic; or a soft square of *millefoglie* sporting rich vanilla cream and fresh sprigs of mint.

Nuela

A1

43 W. 24th St. (bet. Broadway & Sixth Ave.)

Subway: 23 St (Sixth Ave.)
Phone: 212-929-1200
Web: www.nuelany.com
Prices: $$$

Dinner nightly

This natty newcomer to the Flatiron district gorgeously illustrates regional traditions and creative touches on each pan-Latin plate. The space is vast and the crowd comfortably spread, but the décor is hot and spicy with orange-covered banquettes set against red walls—a nice compliment to Nuela's bold menu.

The eye-popping scene is completed by sterling servers carrying skewers of jiggly pork belly confit and exceptionally poached octopus glossed with shisito mayo; or braised oxtail empanadas atop parsley root purée. In addition to a menu dedicated to ceviche, the pinnacle of achievement may be in an entrée of beautifully cooked lamb chops given a flashy Latin edge when paired with *tacu tacu*—a cake of rice and beans seasoned with *aji amarillo*.

Olives

B3

201 Park Ave. South (at 17th St.)

Subway: 14 St - Union Sq
Phone: 212-353-8345
Web: www.toddenglish.com
Prices: $$$

Lunch & dinner daily

Despite his usual disdain for larger, commercial dining affairs, cooking personality and branded Chef Todd English offers a serious culinary experience from his NYC foothold on the first floor of the W Hotel-Union Square. The spacious, modern hotel-ish setting is divided into a popular lounge area and high-ceilinged dining room with comfortable furnishings and an open kitchen fronted by a curved dining counter.

English's rendering of Mediterranean flavors enlivened with a contemporary touch is on display in items like escargot flatbread with Montrachet goat cheese; king crab pappardelle with preserved lemon; and lamb Porterhouse with pistachio vinaigrette.

The prix-fixe lunch menu showcases ingredients sourced from the nearby greenmarket.

Park Avenue Bistro 😊

B1

377 Park Ave South (bet. 26th & 27th Sts.)

Subway: 28 St (Park Ave. South)
Phone: 212-689-1360
Web: www.parkavenuebistronyc.com
Prices: $$

Lunch Mon – Fri
Dinner Mon – Sat

Classic bistro favorites are the strength of this cheerful and immaculately shiny spot. Affable service and walls brightened by the artwork of emerging artists lighten the hearty and soulful mood of the menu, as does the petite section of outdoor dining set on this bustling thoroughfare.

The impressively prepared, classic menu may include a salad of crisp and bitter frisée tumbled with shredded bits of duck confit and crisp bacon; or fork-tender coq au vin bathed with a mouth-coating wine reduction with traditional garnishes set atop a mound of creamy mashed potatoes. Follow these fine examples of Park Avenue Bistro's time-honored cuisine with a tart of thinly sliced apples atop butter-drenched puff pastry with a scoop of vanilla bean ice cream.

Periyali

A2

35 W. 20th St. (bet. Fifth & Sixth Aves.)

Subway: 23 St (Sixth Ave)
Phone: 212-463-7890
Web: www.periyali.com
Prices: $$$

Lunch Mon – Fri
Dinner nightly

In a city that prides itself on offering what's new and what's next, the owners of Periyali deserve credit for their sincere dedication to what works—serving their own brand of sophisticated Greek fare in an inviting and elegant setting since 1987. The fresh-looking, gauzy interior, and shimmering fish-shaped accents transport diners to a light and breezy Mediterranean locale, complete with friendly, unobtrusive service.

The gracious staff attends to a mixed crowd of devoted regulars who know that the strength of Periyali's kitchen is in such attractive and tempting preparations of Greek classics as rich bowls of lemony *avgolemono* soup; skillfully charred yet tender marinated octopus; and *garides saganaki*—sautéed shrimp with feta and tomatoes.

Primehouse New York

Steakhouse 🍴

B1

381 Park Ave. South (at 27th St.)

Subway: 28 St (Park Ave. South)　　Lunch & dinner daily
Phone: 212-824-2600
Web: www.primehousenyc.com
Prices: $$$

A glossy and grand ambience sets this steakhouse apart from the recognizable herd of traditionalists. Here, chic multi-room spaces sport walls covered in pale marble and ebony tiles, sleek furnishings, and an impressively stocked smoke glass-walled wine cellar. However, style does not trump substance. The focus remains on well-prepared cuts of prime Black Angus beef from Creekstone Farms, KY, aged in-house. Many non-steak options include "ocean meats" or raw bar combinations like the "East Meets West" coastal oyster selection. Attentive servers wheel trolleys throughout the room, ladling soups and preparing Caesar salads tableside. Remember to save room for the very tempting dessert offerings.

The sexy bar lounge is a top stop for after-work cocktails.

Pure Food and Wine

Vegan 🍴

B3

54 Irving Pl. (bet. 17th & 18th Sts.)

Subway: 14 St - Union Sq　　Lunch & dinner daily
Phone: 212-477-1010
Web: www.purefoodandwine.com
Prices: $$

Carnivores beware: this restaurant's name means what it says. A disciple of the raw-food movement, Pure Food and Wine serves only raw vegan dishes. This means that to preserve vitamins, enzymes, minerals, and flavors in the food, nothing is heated above 118°F.

Dishes like a compressed heirloom tomato, fennel, and avocado salad, or a Lapsang-smoked portobello mushroom with caper potato salad don't just taste good, they're good for you—especially if you buy into the purported health benefits. Regardless, the kitchen uses only the freshest organic produce and there is no sense of deprivation with desserts like a deceptively decadent non-dairy ice cream sundae.

During the summer, seating spills out to the backyard dining space ringed with greenery.

Resto

C1

Contemporary ✗

111 E. 29th St. (bet. Lexington Ave. & Park Ave. South)

Subway: 28 St (Park Ave. South) Lunch & dinner daily
Phone: 212-685-5585
Web: www.restonyc.com
Prices: $$

Sporting a less distinctly Belgian accent than when it first opened, Resto's comfortable dining room beckons to a steady stream of Gramercy residents who find this chicly spare and friendly spot the perfect setting to unwind at day's end or while away an afternoon.

Moules frites is still a specialty, dessert highlights include a Belgian chocolate tasting, and the marble bar's Belgian-focused beer list remains extensive. Yet Resto's highly enjoyable menu now represents a globally inspired array ranging from shrimp and grits to savory house-made lamb and feta sausage on a bed of wilted Swiss chard. The frites remain killer—golden brown, crispy tender, perfectly salted, made even more outrageously delicious when paired with a flavor-spiked mayonnaise.

Riverpark

C1

Contemporary ✗✗✗

450 E. 29th St. (bet. First Ave. & the East River)

Subway: 28 St (Park Ave. South) Lunch & dinner daily
Phone: 212-729-9790
Web: www.riverparknyc.com
Prices: $$

Backed by Chef Tom Colicchio and housed in the newly constructed Alexandria Center, Riverpark sits on the extreme edge of Manhattan's East Side. The modernist box feels light and airy, even at night, and is outfitted with ample river views, limestone flooring, sleek furnishings, and beautiful tabletops. The preparations showcase a skilled kitchen in a menu that hooks the best of each season. Meals include the likes of tortelloni stuffed with rich goose meat, bathed in a clear, deep-violet huckleberry consommé; diver scallops plated with a host of garnishes such as butternut squash purée, hen of the woods mushrooms, roasted pear, and kale chutney that steals the show; and for dessert, a meringue-topped lemon tart paired with citrus *mostarda* ice cream.

Rye House

American ✗

A2

11 W. 17 St. (bet. Fifth & Sixth Aves.)

Subway: 14 St (Sixth Ave.)   Lunch & dinner daily
Phone: 212-255-7260
Web: www.ryehousenyc.com
Prices: $$

As its name would suggest, Rye House offers a tavern-inspired look and easygoing vibe fueled by an impressive selection of amber liquor. The front bar provides a comfortable perch from which to sip a mint julep or single-malt Scotch, but those who wish to dine sacrifice the bar's ambience for the back area's greater comfort and enjoy the kitchen's concise and enjoyably prepared selection of playful pub grub.

The small plate offerings include the likes of crunchy and well-seasoned fried dill pickle slices, Sloppy Joe sliders, and drunken mussels bathed in Belgian-style ale. The list of entrées may be short but items such as roasted chicken dressed with spoonbread, braised greens, and buttermilk-enriched jus prove this is food to be savored.

Saravanaas 😊

Indian ✗

C2

81 Lexington Ave. (at 26th St.)

Subway: 28 St (Park Ave. South)   Lunch & dinner daily
Phone: 212-679-0204
Web: www.saravanabhavan.com
Prices: ☜☜

With its corner location and attractive two-room setting, Saravanaas stands out from the Curry Hill crowd. The brightly lit room is set with lacquered tables and high-backed ivory upholstered chairs that seem a far cry from the taxi driver cafeterias dotting this strip of Lexington.

The reason this beloved Gramercy location is forever bustling with locals and tourists alike is for vegetarian food that is as good as it is serious, with a wide array of specialties, curries, breads, and weekend-only biryani on offer. However, table-long *dosas*, paired with a plethora of chuntneys (think coconut and chili) and fiery *sambar* are *the* main attraction. Don't miss the *aloo paratha*: this butter-drenched, puffy flatbread filled with spiced potatoes is excellent.

SD26

B1

Italian 🍴🍴

19 E. 26th St. (bet. Fifth & Madison Aves.)

Subway: 28 St (Park Ave. South)
Phone: 212-265-5959
Web: www.sd26ny.com
Prices: $$

Lunch Mon – Fri
Dinner nightly

This regional Italian restaurant formerly known as San Domenico now inhabits a 14,000 square foot dining hall replete with a crowd-pleasing array of features—a wine bar, generously sized lounge area, multiple dining rooms, open kitchen, and jumbo *salumeria* station.

The offerings are as wide-ranging as the space, with good value found at both the lunch prix-fixe and small plates served at the wine bar. Given the size and scope of SD26, the service can sometimes flounder but here are three reasons that prove the kitchen gets it right: silky strands of whole wheat fettucine dressed with luscious wild boar ragout; braised beef cheeks, melt-in-your-mouth tender, paired with a dollop of white polenta; and a spot on *baba* with sweet, juicy orange sauce.

Tamarind

B2

Indian 🍴🍴🍴

41-43 E. 22nd St. (bet. Broadway & Park Ave. South)

Subway: 23 St (Park Ave. South)
Phone: 212-674-7400
Web: www.tamarinde22.com
Prices: $$

Lunch & dinner daily

At Tamarind, regional Indian cuisine is tempered by an elegant ambience featuring courteous, polished service, and an upscale, urban space.

The hefty menu offers a virtual tour through the flavors of Goa, Punjab, Madras, and Calcutta. Airy breads, aromatic tandoori dishes, piquant curries, and delectable vegetarian specialties are prepared by an ardent brigade of cooks who combine both familiar and unconventional flavors as in the rosemary naan. A peek inside the dining room's glassed-in kitchen is sure to stimulate your taste buds. Lunchtime offers a reasonable fixed-price menu.

For a casual bite, try the petite Tea Room located next door for its lighter fare of sandwiches, pastries, and Indian specialties, with a recommended tea pairing.

119

Tamba

C1

Indian ✗

103 Lexington Ave. (bet. 27th & 28th Sts.)

Subway: 28 St (Park Ave. South)   Lunch & dinner daily
Phone: 212-481-9100
Web: www.tambagrillandbar.com
Prices: $$

Slow down in Curry Hill—Tamba is that cozy, colorful spot one might easily pass, and miss their chance for excellent, wallet-friendly Indian cuisine, as well as great service that soars above other nearby *desi* diners.

Hindi for copper, Tamba showcases Indian delicacies as glorious and gleaming as the copper vessels that carry them. Leaving aside the insanely popular, inexpensive lunch buffet, true gourmands know to branch out and explore the unique menu. They may begin with a faithful rendition of the famed street snack Chicken 65 (made pungent with garlic, ginger, and other spices), before moving on to flavorful entrées like spicy prawn *vindaloo*; delicious pepper mutton fry; and *paneer makhni*—buttery paneer cubes dancing in a rich tomato-cream sauce.

Tocqueville

A3

Contemporary ✗✗

1 E. 15th St. (bet. Fifth Ave. & Union Sq. West)

Subway: 14 St - Union Sq   Lunch & dinner Mon – Sat
Phone: 212-647-1515
Web: www.tocquevillerestaurant.com
Prices: $$

Lovingly run by proprietors Chef Marco A. Moreira and his wife Jo-Ann Makovitsky, Tocqueville offers a creative approach to seasonal cuisine in a stately dining room located just one block from the Union Square Greenmarket. During the summer months, the restaurant's three course greenmarket menu showcases its bounty at both lunch and dinner. Celebrate each season with the likes of green garlic velouté or house-made gnocchi with a tousle of wilted Swiss chard and grated *ricotta salata*. The 300-label wine list features selections from little-known regions around the world as well as a number of sakes.

Lush fabrics, vintage mirrors, and bold art fashion an elegant décor—a soothing respite in which to enjoy this roster of inspired creations.

Turkish Kitchen ☺

Turkish   ✗✗

386 Third Ave. (bet. 27th & 28th Sts.)

Subway: 28 St (Park Ave. South)
Phone: 212-679-6633
Web: www.turkishkitchen.com
Prices: ☺☺

Lunch Sun – Fri
Dinner nightly

There are so many good Turkish restaurants floating around Manhattan's East Side these days, it's getting harder to choose among the competition. Here's a tip: you'll almost never go wrong placing your chips on this quirky, jewel-toned mainstay which boasts a lively dinner scene; an attentive service staff ready to walk newcomers through the extensive offerings, and a lunch menu stacked with great value (including a four-course prix-fixe).

The restaurant's grilled meats; stuffed cabbage; and *manti*, spiced ground beef dumplings in a rich dill chicken broth capped by a dollop of yogurt, are all standouts. Or try the *iskender* kebab—seasoned lamb, sliced paper-thin off a rotisserie and served over crispy pita bathed in garlic-yogurt and rich tomato sauce.

Union Square Cafe

American   ✗✗

21 E. 16th St. (bet. Fifth Ave. & Union Sq. West)

Subway: 14 St - Union Sq
Phone: 212-243-4020
Web: www.unionsquarecafe.com
Prices: $$$

Lunch & dinner daily

Since 1985, New Yorkers have held a special place in their hearts for this inviting yet refined institution that first launched the career of über-restaurateur Danny Meyer.

Today, tables may be more likely populated by tourists than local foodies, but NY bar-dining was pioneered here, where seats are welcoming and the winning staff is gracious. Arrive here before the crowds for a great burger or perhaps a three-course meal of excellent, Italian-rooted American cuisine and sampling of wines by the glass. The nearby greenmarket figures largely into the planning of the menu, as in the fall vegetable *farratto* served with New Zealand venison loin and Concord grape pan sauce.

The tremendous wine list is diverse, special, and reasonably priced.

Veritas ✿

Contemporary 🗙🗙

B2

43 E. 20th St. (bet. Broadway & Park Ave. South)

Subway: 23 St (Park Ave. South)   Dinner nightly
Phone: 212-353-3700
Web: www.veritas-nyc.com
Prices: $$$

Veritas

Veritas may have undergone a chef change, but one fact remains gospel—it is still a hallowed oasis in Gotham's industrial-chic Flatiron District. Other restaurants have moved in, but Veritas soars due to its welcoming demeanor, masterful menu, and imposing wine list. Let the genial hostess lead you into a svelte dining room where the bar is front and center. You can dine here, but to forgo the beauty in the back with brick walls hugging slender mirrors, warming Cognac-blushed leather seating, soft lighting, and wall-sized wine racks, would be quite tragic.

As if to remind you of their forte, pieces of (cork) art and tidy ebony tables set the tone for Chef Sam Hazen's neat, contemporary fare. He shepherds the turf as well-timed servers endow you with accurately assembled and memorable dishes like maple-brined Wooly pork pan-seared to rosy perfection, matched with a log of fried shredded shoulder meat, and bathed in reduced *saba*; or the farmer's market tasting of fluffy risotto mingling mushrooms, ramps, and Parmesan.

To the hum of jazz tunes, wine savants sip as sweet fiends savor the "dark and stormy" sticky toffee pudding kissed with a quenelle of ginger and lime ice cream.

Greenwich, West Village & Meatpacking District

Greenwich, West Village & Meatpacking District

Manhattan ▶

Artistic, poetic, and edgy: these ideals are the Village's identity. Thank the Beat Generation for this, because fifty years later, many still seek out this neighborhood for its beloved street cafés brimming with struggling artists, philosophical meanderings, and revolutionary convictions. Perhaps due to the prominence of NYU, local residents still embrace the liberal, intellectual, bohemian spirit that, in many ways, is the heart of this city.

Nevertheless, the belly of this area is equally worthy of attention and praise; even the humble **Peanut Butter and Co. Sandwich Shop** flaunts its creative side with peanut-buttery concoctions like the Elvis, which is grilled with bananas and honey (bacon is optional). Or, pick up a jar to-go, flavored with the likes of maple syrup, white chocolate, or chili powder. Nearby, **Mamoun's** has been feeding NYU students some of the best falafel in town for generations; topping one with their killer hot sauce is a must. In Washington Square Park, savvy students and foodies stand shoulder-to-shoulder in line for **N.Y. Dosas**, wrapped in delicate rice and lentil flour crêpes, served with character and flair. Peer into the assortment of old-time Italian bakeries and shops along Bleecker Street, where **Faicco's Pork Store** has been offering its specialties for

over 100 years—take home a sampling of their fresh and perfectly seasoned sausages or a tray of *arancini* (fried rice balls), though etiquette dictates that one must be eaten warm, before leaving the store. Yet the neighborhood's most noteworthy storefront may be **Murray's Cheese Shop**. This is Manhattan's definitive cheesemonger, run by a deeply informed staff, happy to initiate hungry neophytes into the art and understanding of their countless varieties (enthusiasts note that classes are also available, exploring the meaning of terroir or cheese-pairing fundamentals). If seeking a more lowbrow spot, try **Dirty Bird** for fried or rotisserie chicken. Rest assured that these birds are locally sourced from an Amish farm, and are free-range, vegetarian fed, and antibiotic free—all necessary qualifications for any self-respecting takeout joint in downtown bohemia. Of course, no Village jaunt is complete without pizza—with some of the finest to be found coal-fired and crisp, only by the pie, at the original **John's**. For a quick slice, stop by **Joe's** for traditional thin-crust, or **Famous Ray's**, but be prepared to use a fork here. A visit to **Cones** is equally enticing, where uniquely textured Argentine ice cream is available in both expected and unforeseen flavor combinations.

West Village

For a nearly royal treat, stop by **Tea and Sympathy**, offering tea-time snacks or full Sunday dinners of roast beef and Yorkshire pudding. The storefront also sells prized English wares, ranging from teas to pots to jars of clotted cream. No matter where you grab your picnic, one of the best places to enjoy it is Hudson River Park, watching the urban vista of roller skaters and marathoners. Pier 45 is a particularly lovely spot, at the end of Christopher Street, across the Westside Highway. Steps away is **Il Cantuccio**, a boutique Tuscan bakery that boasts a regional variant of biscotti from Prato. The influential James Beard Foundation sits in the historic 12th Street townhouse that was once home to the illustrious food writer.

While strolling back through chic boutiques and camera-ready brownstones, peek down quaint Perry Street for yet another *very* NY moment: a glimpse at where Carrie Bradshaw (of *Sex and the City*) "lived." For a quick but excellent bite, be sure to stop in at **Taïm** for killer falafels and refreshing smoothies. Then, let the overpowering aromas of butter and sugar lead you to the original **Magnolia Bakery**. Filled with pretty little pastel-flowered cupcakes and prettier couples donning Jimmy Choo shoes, this is the Village's official date night finale.

Another sweet spot is **Li-Lac**, dispensing chocolate-covered treats and nostalgic confections since 1923. One of the West Village's most celebrated landmarks may be the **Corner Bistro**, whose pub fare has been at the heart of the "Best Burger in Town" debate for decades. Another "bar's bar" incarnate that strives to embody everything a cheap beer and retro juke hope to effuse is the **Rusty Knot**. Kick back and grab some Po' boys or pickled eggs to go with that pint. For a more refined late-night scene, expert mixologists can be found creatively pouring "long drinks and fancy cocktails" at **Employees Only**. Likewise, bartenders approach celebrity status at **Little Branch**, where an encyclopedic understanding of the craft brings dizzying and delectable results.

Meatpacking District

Further north is an area known as the Meatpacking District. Just two decades ago, its cobblestoned streets were so desolate that only the savviest young Manhattanites knew that its empty warehouses held the city's edgiest clubs. Young hipsters take note: the Meatpacking has already arrived, repopulated, and regrouped with seas of sleekly designed lounges serving pricey cocktails to the fashionable minions, as if in defiance of these cautious times. Luxury hotels have risen, and storied bistros so infamously festive that they once defined the neighborhood have fallen. Completing this picture is the High Line, an abandoned 1934 elevated railway that is now transformed into a 19-block long park.

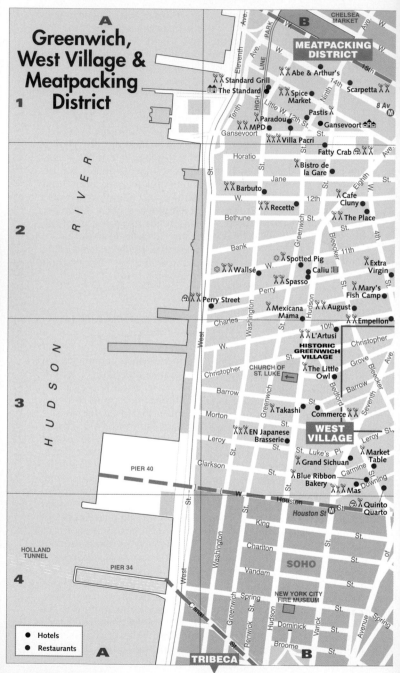

Greenwich, West Village & Meatpacking District

A

B

CHELSEA MARKET

MEATPACKING DISTRICT

Standard Grill
The Standard
Abe & Arthur's
Spice Market
Scarpetta
Pastis
Paradou
MPD
Gansevoort
Villa Pacri
Fatty Crab
Horatio St.
Bistro de la Gare
Jane St.
Barbuto
Cafe Cluny
Recette
The Place
Bethune
Bank St.
Spotted Pig
Wallsé
Caliu
Extra Virgin
Spasso
Mary's Fish Camp
Perry Street
Mexicana Mama
August
Empellon
Charles St.
L'Artusi
HISTORIC GREENWICH VILLAGE
CHURCH OF ST. LUKE
The Little Owl
Barrow
Takashi
Commerce
WEST VILLAGE
EN Japanese Brasserie
Leroy
Market Table
Grand Sichuan
Blue Ribbon Bakery
Mas
Houston St.
Quinto Quarto
King
Charlton
SOHO
Vandam
NEW YORK CITY FIRE MUSEUM
Spring
HOLLAND TUNNEL
PIER 34
Dominick
Broome

PIER 40

RIVER

HUDSON

● Hotels
● Restaurants

TRIBECA

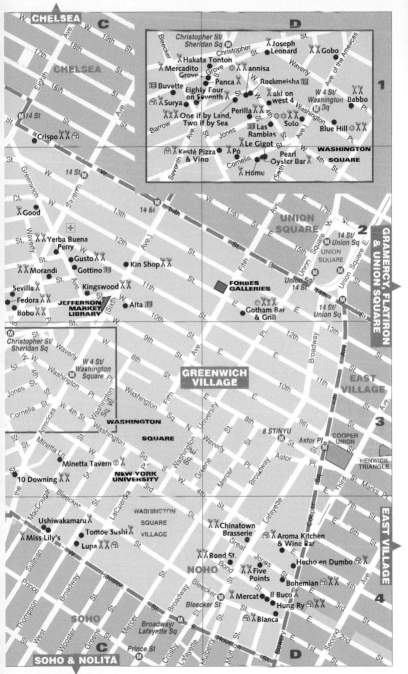

Abe & Arthur's

American 🍴🍴

B1

409 W. 14th St. (bet. Ninth & Tenth Aves.)

Subway: 14 St - 8 Av   Dinner nightly
Phone: 646-289-3930
Web: www.abeandarthurs.com
Prices: $$$

Housed in a former nightclub, this serious Meatpacking newcomer offers an enjoyably prepared menu that is both creative and hearty. The front bar sports a sexy dark wood and glossy tiled look, while the high-ceilinged rear dining room is tastefully appointed with creamy tan leather seating, parchment ceiling pendants, and backlit scrims adorned with graffiti-like imagery.

Steaks are a popular option here, procured from Creekstone Farms, embellished with myriad sauces and sides. Starters include the likes of tuna tartare tacos, served as a mound of diced tuna scattered with crunchy mini-tortilla shells for a do-it-yourself aesthetic; non-steak entrée options may include seared sea scallops with crisped foie gras and cauliflower-almond purée.

aki on west 4

Japanese 🍴

D1

181 W. 4th St. (bet. Sixth & Seventh Aves.)

Subway: W 4 St - Wash Sq   Dinner nightly
Phone: 212-989-5440
Web: N/A
Prices: $$

Set in a red-brick row house, Aki's tiny dining room feels like an intimate parlor. Add to this a warm, polite staff and a menu that displays a distinct personality, and it is easy to see why this spot continues to attract a loyal following.

Chef/owner Siggy Nakanishi once served as private chef to the Japanese Ambassador to Jamaica and his menu reflects a sweet and sunny personality. Daily specials are presented as a tabletop photo display; the chef's menu offers a selection of creative preparations that may include the eel napoleon appetizer composed of panko-crusted tofu, delicate eel tempura, and pumpkin purée. Other dishes include finely prepared sushi and rolls, as in the Jamaica roll, stuffed with jerk chicken and hearts of palm, of course.

Alta

Contemporary

C2

64 W. 10th St (bet. Fifth & Sixth Aves.)

Subway: Christopher St - Sheridan Sq   Dinner nightly
Phone: 212-505-7777
Web: www.altarestaurant.com
Prices: $$

Rusticity is reinvented at this popular West Village tapas bar. While the wood-burning fireplace, exposed brick, and antique Moorish flooring evoke haciendas past, the little bites coming out of its kitchen are undeniably, deliciously modern.

Traditions are given contemporary twists as tapas are pulled into the 21st century with dishes like carpaccio of beef topped with a spicy horseradish-infused crème fraîche foam. The four pieces of seared tuna *tataki* come bathed in a sweet basil cloud perfumed with preserved lemons; and the lamb meatballs, blended with rice, sesame seeds, and dates, have a depth uncommon in such a simple dish. For parties of seven or more, Alta offers "The Whole Shebang," every dish on the menu at a reasonable discount.

Aroma Kitchen & Wine Bar

Italian

D4

36 E. 4th St. (bet. Bowery & Lafayette St.)

Subway: Bleecker St   Dinner nightly
Phone: 212-375-0100
Web: www.aromanyc.com
Prices: $$

This welcoming spot radiates an amiable vibe from its edge of the Village, thanks to co-owners Alexandra Degiorgio and Vito Polosa. Simple, warm, and rustic, the cozy room's focal point is its dark-wood dining counter. In fair weather, the space opens to provide additional sidewalk seating and alleviate the throng of enthusiastic regulars.

This wine bar menu begins with hearty appetizers like meatballs with Neapolitan ragù and smoked mozzarella along with expertly prepared pastas such as *paccheri gratin*. The unique and fairly priced wine list contains many varietals rarely found outside Italy.

annisa ❀

Contemporary 🍴🍴

D1

13 Barrow St. (bet. Seventh Ave. South & W. 4th St.)

Subway: Christopher St - Sheridan Sq   Dinner nightly
Phone: 212-741-6699
Web: www.annisarestaurant.com
Prices: $$$

Annisa

After a devastating fire that kept it closed for 10 months, beloved Annisa ("women" in Arabic) has reopened its doors to prove its resilience as well as its unchanged status as one of the best Village options for sophisticated dining.

From its charming setting within a historic district, Annisa seems inviting both outside and in, with stunning windows, upholstered walls, and a cozy yet exquisite elevated dining room. A polite, professional service team does not miss a beat in orchestrating meals here.

The contemporary menu focuses on flavors and combinations that are thought provoking and very tasty. Dinners reveal such understated and complex starters as succulent wild boar with tempura-covered *unagi* and crunchy apple slices with a minty lime vinaigrette—a perfect combination of sweet, tart, and earthy tastes. Pan-roasted monkfish may be paired with savory cabbage, silky langoustine, pressed *ankimo* medallions, and finished with a sultry chicken liver sauce. Desserts, like poppyseed bread and butter pudding with fragrant Meyer lemon curd, can be moist and buttery, or even add a note of whimsy, as in the coconut-vanilla popsicle with candied ginger, chocolate truffle, and fresh mint.

August

B2

European 🍴🍴

359 Bleecker St. (bet. Charles & 10th Sts.)

Subway: Christopher St - Sheridan Sq
Phone: 212-929-8727
Web: www.augustny.com
Prices: $$

Lunch Sat – Sun
Dinner nightly

Always popular August has no problem drawing crowds, so it's commendable that instead of resting on its laurels, this establishment embraces change.

The dining room has been reworked to offer tall tables; and the kitchen is now under the dominion of Executive Chef Jordan Frosolone, recently of Hearth. Thankfully, some things remain the same. The wood-burning oven is still ablaze and the backyard is as charming a spot as ever. That oven, where the personable chef keeps a watchful eye, plays a starring role in the preparation of August's European-roaming specialties that may include roasted sweetbreads with macadamia nuts and pickled ramps; tomato-basil pizza; and crisped skin Lola duck breast with thigh confit and grilled apricot.

Babbo

D1

Italian 🍴🍴

110 Waverly Pl. (bet. MacDougal St. & Sixth Ave.)

Subway: W 4 St - Wash Sq
Phone: 212-777 0303
Web: www.babbonyc.com
Prices: $$$

Dinner nightly

You can babble all you want about the latest this or that, but judging from the crowds that are three deep, you know Babbo's still got it. This Mario Batali mainstay doesn't cut any corners or lines—reservations are a must for table seating, though you can pop in and sit at the bustling bar. From the on-the-move staff (the real deal and not actors biding their time) to the rock-and-roll music, the place is busier than Grand Central Terminal.

Staff shuttle plates of pasta and other Italian specialties to eager customers who come as much for the convivial ambience as they do for the *crostino* with chickpeas. Say what you want about the grilled and briny beef tongue, but for a true taste of *la dolce vita*, order the superbly light and delicate panna cotta.

131

Barbuto

B2

775 Washington St. (at 12th St.)

Subway: 14 St - 8 Av
Phone: 212-924-9700
Web: www.barbutonyc.com
Prices: $$

Lunch & dinner daily

Those who wax poetic on the virtues of the perfect roast chicken need look no farther. Located on a quiet stretch of the West Village just steps from MePa, Chef Jonathan Waxman's Barbuto plays up its locale and industrial bones with concrete flooring, painted-over brick walls, and garage doors that open up to create an atmospheric indoor/outdoor vibe.

Still, that chicken is what best expresses Barbuto's refined simplicity—the roasted bird has a coarse pepper-freckled auburn skin and tender ivory flesh moist with flavorful juices, further enhanced by a splash of bright and briny salsa verde. This dish is admirably supported by the likes of grilled octopus salad with fennel and pink grapefruit or a cookie-like chocolate hazelnut *crostata*.

Bianca 😮

D4

5 Bleecker St. (bet. Bowery & Elizabeth St.)

Subway: Bleecker St
Phone: 212-260-4666
Web: www.biancanyc.com
Prices: $$

Dinner nightly

Curtained windows lead the way to this unassuming spot, perfect for a date or catching up with friends. With plank flooring, candlelit tables set with blue-striped kitchen towels used as napkins, shelf-lined walls displaying delicate floral-trimmed china, and an open kitchen tucked in the cozy back, Bianca's casual personality extends through to every detail, including the cuisine.

The Northern Italian-themed menu strives to remind guests that simplicity is always satisfying, especially with starters like *gnocco fritto*. Other specialties may include a traditional Emilia-Romagna style lasagna or fennel-studded sausage simmered with cannellini beans.

Generous portions and a moderately priced Italian-focused wine list contribute to Bianca's large following.

Bistro de la Gare

Mediterranean ✗

B2 626 Hudson St. (bet. Horatio & Jane Sts.)

Subway: 14 St – 8 Av   Lunch & dinner Tue – Sun
Phone: 212-242-4420
Web: www.bistrodelagarenyc.com
Prices: $$

Equally talented and no less charming are Chef/owners Maryann Terillo and Elisa Sarno who have created a wonderfully low-key neighborhood bistro that exudes the aura of an old favorite even though it is new to the scene. The quaint room is simply done with tan walls hung with sepia photography, and is furnished with wooden chairs and white paper-topped tables. Like the décor, the menu follows suit lending a simplistic approach to a listing that boasts Mediterranean influences.

Starters include the likes of blistered-skin grilled sardines with warm cannellini bean salad; entrées may offer a roasted baby chicken cloaked with walnut crumbs; and desserts feature a slice of olive oil cake decked in a compote of plumped raisins and dried figs.

Blue Ribbon Bakery

Contemporary ✗

B3 35 Downing St. (at Bedford St.)

Subway: Houston St   Lunch & dinner daily
Phone: 212-337-0404
Web: www.blueribbonrestaurants.com
Prices: $$

The origin of this very New York bistro begins with the discovery of an abandoned brick oven that brothers Eric and Bruce Bromberg found in the basement of a bodega. This sparked the idea for a bakery, and in 1998 Blue Ribbon Bakery joined the duo's family of popular and impressive dining venues. The sunny corner spot charms with mustard-yellow walls and creaky wood-plank flooring; downstairs the heady aroma of freshly baked bread wafts throughout exposed brick alcoves.

Excellent sandwiches star on the roster of lunchtime fare, like shrimp salad with roasted tomato mayonnaise tucked into slices of lightly toasted challah. Dinner brings eclectic possibilities like leeks vinaigrette, grilled sardines, fried chicken, and ice cream parlor desserts.

Blue Hill ✿

American 🍴🍴

75 Washington Pl. (bet. Sixth Ave. & Washington Sq. Park)

Subway: W 4 St - Wash Sq
Phone: 212-539-1776
Web: www.bluehillnyc.com
Prices: $$$

Dinner nightly

Thomas Schauer

There is no longer any question: Blue Hill has emerged as a world-class dining destination. As a longtime proponent of local, seasonal ingredients, Chef Dan Barber and his team prepare a bill of fare that relies almost solely on the small-farm network located within a few hundred miles of the city. Of course, the daytrip-worthy farm at Stone Barns (home to Blue Hill's Westchester outpost) purveys the bulk of his kale (and beets, green garlic, etc). However, extraordinary produce alone does not make this the sleek restaurant that it is; rather, the kitchen's talent and creativity have earned its attention and accolades.

A simple bowl of corn soup tells a story in itself. What began as an heirloom kernel planted at Stone Barns was harvested, dried, ground, and prepared as a golden custard-like soup with such sweet intensity and confounding purity of flavor that it can only be described as "corny." Slate cheese boards are a veritable education in America's top producers, accompanied by the likes of tart green apple marmalade, dense raisin bread, and candied walnuts.

Chef Dan Barber's presence is not only felt in each dish but regularly observed in the understated, elegant dining room.

Bobo

181 W. 10th St. (at Seventh Ave.)

Subway: Christopher St - Sheridan Sq   Lunch Sat – Sun
Phone: 212 488-2626   Dinner nightly
Web: www.bobonyc.com
Prices: $$

Tucked into a gorgeous West Village brownstone meant to invoke a dreamy Parisian apartment, the sexy, relaxed Bobo is built to inspire coos. Make your way through the first floor bar area and you'll find a second floor dining room awash in dark wood, pale blue walls, and whitewashed brick, stuffed with eclectic charms like gilded mirrors and beaded lighting. Chef Patrick Connolly lends a light, seasonally focused touch to Bobo's menu, with dishes like a novel BLT that arrives as a butter lettuce cup filled with tenderly roasted Berkshire pork, mayonnaise, slow cooked tomato, and toasted bread crumbs; or roasted salmon with mushroom broth, served with plump white cannellini beans and baby carrots, then topped with slivers of fried shiitake.

Bohemian 😊

57 Great Jones St. (bet. Bowery & Lafayette St.)

Subway: Bleecker St   Dinner nightly
Phone: 212-388-1070
Web: www.playearth.jp
Prices: $$

This intriguing dining den is secreted away down an unmarked hallway and fronted by a thick glass door. Despite the stealth locale, the staff couldn't be more welcoming or courteous as they attend to diners amid polished concrete floors, white walls, and mid-century furnishings in emerald green, turquoise, and cognac—in a space that once served as a studio for artist Jean-Michel Basquiat.

Bohemian's bill of fare features snacks and small plates such as a decadent mushroom croquette topped with uni. However, the true highlight is the exceptional *washugyu* from Japanese Premium Beef offered in several guises—as a sashimi of short rib; steak of the day; or as luscious mini burgers dressed with lettuce, slow roasted tomato, and pecorino on tender brioche.

Bond Street

D4

Japanese ✗✗

6 Bond St. (bet. Broadway & Lafayette St.)

Subway: Bleecker St   Dinner nightly
Phone: 212-777-2500
Web: www.bondstrestaurant.com
Prices: $$$$

There is no name to mark the three-story brownstone that houses dark and swanky Bond Street—only a brown dot on a banner. And so the scene is set: always stylish, always hopping, Bond Street is where moneyed trendsters find high-end sushi that looks as beautiful as it tastes. Here, pudding-sweet uni is attractively served in a purple shell, then laced with a necklace of diced cucumber and crowned with a golden leaf. Painstakingly beautiful presentations here are as likely to drop some jaws as they are to flash some bling. However, as many "oohs" and "aahs" are bound to follow the first bite of this delicious and inventive cuisine.

As expected, deep pockets are de rigueur, with appetizers that start at $16 and prices rising steeply from there.

Buvette

C1

French

42 Grove St. (bet. Bedford & Bleecker Sts.)

Subway: Christopher St - Sheridan Sq   Lunch Mon – Fri
Phone: 212-255-3590   Dinner nightly
Web: www.ilovebuvette.com
Prices: ⊗⊗

Rolling stone Chef Jody Williams moves from Italy to France at her newest venture set in the former home of the Pink Teacup. Despite the Lilliputian space, Buvette oozes charm and all are well taken care of—the affable staff weaves lithely through the full house, greeting guests with a warm smile and displaying a chalkboard of daily specials to diners at the counter and low tables.

French tapas are the theme, including cheeses, charcuterie, tartines, and Escoffier-esque vegetable dishes such as artichokes à la Grecque. Heartier options may include coq au vin, in a mini cast iron pot, stocked with all the classic elements. End on a sweet note with the chocolate mousse, dense enough to cut with a knife, and capped by a cloud of whipped cream.

Cafe Cluny

A m e r i c a n ✗

284 W. 12th St. (at W. 4th St.)

Subway: 14 St - 8 Av
Phone: 212-255-6900
Web: www.cafecluny.com
Prices: $$

Lunch & dinner daily

With its winsome glow, this quintessential neighborhood restaurant (from the owner of TriBeCa's Odeon) is one of the Village's most chic meeting spots, no matter the time of day. The popular corner-set bar and multi-room interior, are lined with caricatures of celebrity regulars and a wall installation of shadowy bird cutouts that come alive in the candlelit space. Open daily from 8:00 A.M. until midnight, the kitchen continuously puts a classic touch on everything from homemade granola with sheep's milk yogurt at breakfast, to evening meals of crisp pumpkin and goat cheese fritters with warm lentil salad and smoked paprika, or olive oil poached cod with Pommeray mustard vinaigrette. Service is affable, able, and attracts a devoted following.

Caliu

S p a n i s h 🍽

557 Hudson St. (bet. Perry & W. 11th Sts.)

Subway: Christopher St - Sheridan Sq
Phone: 212-206-6444
Web: www.calilutapas.com
Prices: 🐢🐢

Lunch & dinner daily

The mission at this low-key tapas spot, helmed by a Peruvian chef and alum of Boqueria and Casa Mono, is to present a distinctive menu that is focussed and authentic in its offering of Spanish tapas. Served *frías* and *calientes*, the creative carte piques interest with the likes of *sobrassada*—a dense and chewy chorizo with an uncommonly rich spreadable center; and baguette toasts cradling dollops of roasted red pepper and almond romesco topped with fresh mint. Warm preparations include the likes of quick-sautéed calamari dressed with a jet-black vinaigrette enriched with squid ink. The room is spare but comfortable; tumblers of wine and a skilled kitchen ensure that diners leave this bona fide tapas den happy and sporting a warm, satisfied glow.

Manhattan ▶ Greenwich, West Village & Meatpacking District

Chinatown Brasserie

Chinese XX

D4

380 Lafayette St. (at Great Jones St.)

Subway: Bleecker St
Phone: 212-533-7000
Web: www.chinatownbrasserie.com
Prices: $$

Lunch & dinner daily

You'll think you've died and gone to dim sum heaven at Chinatown Brasserie, a dreamy little spot that says to heck with the usual tea time rules. Here, the Chinese small plates–along with a wealth of Cantonese specialties and fusion fare–are served all day long in a chic downtown space featuring floor-to-ceiling silk curtains, oversize lanterns, and a sexy mod lounge downstairs replete with koi pond. With kids? Check out the family-friendly brunch.

The playful, but polished, modern dim sum menu might reveal tender, translucent steamed shrimp and snow pea dumplings; ethereally light and silky roast pork buns; crispy curry-laced black bass and avocado tarts; or warm, fluffy pillows of custard *bao* topped with a crunchy swirl of sugar.

Commerce

Contemporary XX

B3

50 Commerce St. (near Barrow St.)

Subway: Christopher St - Sheridan Sq
Phone: 212-524-2301
Web: www.commercerestaurant.com
Prices: $$

Lunch Sat – Sun
Dinner nightly

Commerce sits on a picture perfect West Village block, and although it's only been open since 2007 the lovingly restored space dates back to being a depression-era speakeasy. Belly up to the bar with its backdrop of polished wood veneer; or grab a seat in the convivial dining room that shows off earthy-toned terrazzo flooring and walls accented with glazed ivory tile.

Chef Harold Moore's menu melds seasonal and global inspiration and brings forth items such as a BLT soup, a cool, creamy green purée livened by buttermilk and stocked with slivered heirloom tomatoes, crushed bacon, and brioche croutons. Entrées have featured a Korean-style pork chop; and desserts are fun—envision a tall wedge of birthday cake, adorned with a candle for deserving diners.

Crispo 🐛

C1

240 W. 14th St. (bet. Seventh & Eighth Aves.)

Subway: 14 St (Seventh Ave.)   Dinner nightly
Phone: 212-229-1818
Web: www.crisporestaurant.com
Prices: $$

Its convenient 14th Street address may help draw crowds, but Chef/owner Frank Crispo's impressive Northern Italian fare is what keeps fans returning again and again. The large room fills up easily and is effortlessly comfortable with attentive service In a rustic ambience punctuated by filament light bulbs, mahogany panels, and vintage tile work.

The menu begins with a lengthy listing of small plates starring prosciutto, carved in the dining room on the chef's antique Berkel slicers, as well as daily specials like grilled artichokes glossed with a lemony butter sauce. Pastas are expertly prepared and may include a silky twirl of fettucine topped with sweet and plump head-on prawn scampi. For dessert, panna cotta is a voluptuous experience.

Do not confuse ✕ with
❀ ! ✕ defines comfort,
while ❀ are awarded for
the best cuisine. Stars
are awarded across all
categories of comfort.

Eighty Four on Seventh

C1

Contemporary 🍴

84 Seventh Ave. South (bet. Bleecker & Grove Sts.)

Subway: Christopher St - Sheridan Sq
Phone: 212-255-7150
Web: www.84nyc.com
Prices: $$

Lunch Sat – Sun
Dinner Tue – Sun

Despite the hullabaloo that ensues along this trafficked stretch of Seventh Ave., you would be remiss for not noticing Eighty Four on Seventh's demure arrival to the West Village dining landscape.

The skilled kitchen team crafts impressive platters that may include fried zucchini blossoms stuffed with sweet lumps of blue crab and dabbed with lemon-tarragon aïoli; luscious beer-brined brick chicken (roasted chicken nirvana) bolstered by smashed fingerling potatoes and vermouth jus; and a comforting composition of banana cake, brown butter ice cream, and salted caramel sauce. Espresso-stained furnishings and a reclaimed church pew are laid out in a spare room with white painted brick walls hung with blackboards announcing drink specials and clever quotes.

Empellón

B2

Mexican 🍴🍴

230 W. 4th St. (at 10th St.)

Subway: Christopher St - Sheridan Sq
Phone: 212-367-0999
Web: www.empellon.com
Prices: $$

Lunch Sat – Sun
Dinner nightly

Alex Stupak, wd~50's former pastry chef extraordinaire, switches gears from sweet to savory at this new venture and brings along a temptingly creative and heartfelt rendition of Mexican cuisine with creamy textures, sweet spices, and tangy roasted chiles aplenty. The tasteful setting features dark-stained furnishings in a whitewashed room with pizzazz from a colorful mural and a bar that gets plenty of action.

The kitchen prepares a roster of heavily stuffed tacos, such as a tasty mélange of shredded chicken with chili- and cilantro-spiked green chorizo. Other treats include a *queso fundido* of braised beef short ribs baked with a blanket of Sheep's milk ricotta, or warm and crunchy chips with a duo of smoked cashew and roasted *arbol* chili salsas.

EN Japanese Brasserie

B3

435 Hudson St. (at Leroy St.)

Subway: Houston St
Phone: 212-647-9196
Web: www.enjb.com
Prices: $$$

Lunch Mon – Sat
Dinner nightly

Industrial chic meets Tokyo mod in this hot spot *izakaya* with soaring heights, warm tones, brick walls, and regal fittings. EN's open kitchen pays homage to authentic Japanese palates, but also reveals ingenuity in its own inventions.

This West Village favorite draws a swank set with its sophisticated fare. Diners sip from the thorough sake selection and await specialties like house-made tofu skin (*yuba*) or perhaps the chef's kaiseki menu starring a Kyoto-style seaweed or lobster tempura with plum salt. Fresh, succulent sashimi and hot treats like delicate crab *chawan mushi* or beautifully marbled Kobe short ribs grilled over a hot stone are menu highlights. End meals with an earthy-sweet soup bobbing with rice dough, red beans, and green tea ice cream.

Extra Virgin

B2

259 W 4th St (at Perry St.)

Subway: Christopher St - Sheridan Sq
Phone: 212-691-9359
Web: www.extravirginrestaurant.com
Prices: $$

Lunch Tue – Sun
Dinner nightly

Co-owned by two Queens natives, this invitingly laid-back spot sits on an idyllic tree-lined corner. There are touches of rusticity throughout the space, with rough-hewn wood tables, exposed brick walls, and framed mirrors; the vibe here is as chill and enjoyable during days as evenings.

Extra Virgin's Mediterranean menu offers crowd-pleasing fare like a starter salad of warm pistachio and breadcrumb-crusted goat cheese with roasted beets, generously showered with crisp, julienned Granny Smith apple. The kitchen's seriousness is evident in touches like the addition of bright and flavorful sweet peas, roasted yellow peppers, and black olives to the rigatoni with sausage; or the apple tart paired with sour cream ice cream and warmed dark caramel sauce.

Manhattan ▶ Greenwich, West Village & Meatpacking District

Fatty Crab 😊

Malaysian ✗✗

643 Hudson St. (bet. Gansevoort & Horatio Sts.)

Subway:	14 St - 8 Av
Phone:	212-352-3592
Web:	www.fattycrab.com
Prices:	$$

Lunch & dinner daily

Zak Pelaccio's signature dish could be made with mung beans, and it would still knock the socks off the uninitiated. As it is, the namesake dish at Fatty Crab, a creative Malaysian joint tucked into a cozy storefront in the Meatpacking District, is made with mouthwatering chunks of Dungeness crab, bobbing in a rich, messy chili sauce that is part sweet, part savory—and wholly freaking amazing. Don't forget to grab the bread on your table to sop up every drop of this delicious specialty.

The front patio and small dining room filled with a few-too-many dark wood tables fill up fast, so arrive early for dinner (a second location on the Upper West Side takes reservations); or swing by for a late afternoon lunch and you'll have the place mostly to yourself.

Fedora

Contemporary ✗✗

239 W. 4th St. #A (bet. Charles & 10th St.)

Subway:	Christopher St - Sheridan Sq
Phone:	646-449-9336
Web:	www.fedoranyc.com
Prices:	$$

Dinner nightly

Originally opened in 1952, Fedora was recently taken over by Gabriel Stulman. The restaurateur has an affinity for all things vintage, and this freshened-up space has been kept lovingly intact, down to the blazing neon signage out front. The retro setting–polished brass, black-and-white photos, and jelly jars used as votive holders–pours creative libations at a mahogany bar and seats diners along a black leather banquette.

Rich and meaty plates abound as in Wagyu tongue with celeriac remoulade; crispy pig's head with sauce *gribiche*; and a "surf and turf" of fried sweetbreads and seared octopus with port wine enriched butter sauce. If possible, save room for a creative dessert like the silky cheesecake panna cotta drizzled with passion fruit nectar.

Five Points

D4 American 🍴🍴

31 Great Jones St. (bet. Bowery & Lafayette St.)

Subway: Bleecker St
Phone: 212-253-5700
Web: www.fivepointsrestaurant.com
Prices: $$

Lunch & dinner daily

The pulse of Chef Marc Meyer's first success continues to beat as strongly as when it opened a decade ago. This neighborhood favorite blends relaxed ambience, polished service, and seasonally-focused fare with a near-Californian sensibility that is utterly irresistible to its nightly stream of food-savvy sophisticates.

Beyond the energetic bar is a quieter back dining room anchored by a tree trunk bedecked with greenery and surrounded by tables wrapped in brown paper. After ordering from a menu that boasts local, seasonal ingredients, a welcoming bread basket paired with homemade pickles winks at Chef Meyer's take on urbane rusticity. Offerings may go on to include fresh ham redolent of cloves, served with local peach relish and creamed collards.

Gobo

D1 Vegetarian 🍴🍴

401 Sixth Ave. (bet. 8th St. & Waverly Pl.)

Subway: W 4 St - Wash Sq
Phone: 212-255-3902
Web: www.goborestaurant.com
Prices: 💰💰

Lunch & dinner daily

With its nourishing global vegetarian cuisine and peaceful Zen-inspired décor, Gobo offers a tasty and tranquil timeout from Manhattan's bustle. Muted tones and warm wood accents dominate the airy dining room that is attended by a suitably laid-back staff.

Gobo's inexpensive menu of "food for the five senses" begins with healthy beverages like freshly squeezed juices and soy milk-based smoothies as well as organic wines. Ambitious starters easily tempt without pushing the vegetarian envelope in the likes of *roti canai* and homemade hummus. Larger plates offer an appetizing Asian influence in satisfying and flavorful vegetable protein dishes such as the healthful stir-fry of ginger-marinated seitan with lightly sautéed kale and steamed rice.

Good

American ✗

C2

89 Greenwich Ave. (bet. Bank & 12th Sts.)

Subway: 14 St - 8 Av
Phone: 212-691-8080
Web: www.goodrestaurantnyc.com
Prices: $$

Lunch Tue — Sun
Dinner nightly

Yes, it's true: this charming neighborhood favorite lives up to its preordained reputation, and has done so since opening in 2000. The pale, earthy, and appealing dining room has a soothing, intimate, and laid-back air, as if to whisper, "Stop by anytime." This echoes through the cozy bar and stretch of sidewalk seating.

The menu proffers a greatest-hits list of comfort food favorites that are given a globally-inspired turn. Fish tacos are stuffed with the selection of the day; macaroni and cheese is studded with green chilies beneath a tortilla crumb-crust; and grilled lamb sirloin arrives with chickpea polenta and creamed Swiss chard.

Good offers a hearty lunch menu and nicely priced combo specials; weekend brunch is washed down by clever cocktails.

Gottino

Italian 🍽

C2

52 Greenwich Ave. (bet. Charles & Perry Sts.)

Subway: Christopher St - Sheridan Sq
Phone: 212-633-2590
Web: N/A
Prices: 🍸🍸

Lunch & dinner daily

Despite the departure of its founding chef, this charming *enoteca* continues to serve as a lovely respite in which to savor a variety of highly enjoyable small plates. Knobby wood, a marble dining counter, and blackboard with wine list highlights set against exposed brick craft the rustically endearing setting.

An assortment of snacks is prepared on view by the skilled and attentive staff, and nibbling sophisticates will find much to choose from. Small bites include crostini, freshly toasted in a press and slathered with mint-flecked artichoke confit; and roasted Lilliputian apples stuffed with pork sausage. Heartier plates feature *pizzoccheri*—a baked and bubbling intermingling of buckwheat pasta, melted green cabbage, speck, and fontina.

Gotham Bar and Grill ✥

Contemporary ✕✕✕

D2

12 E. 12th St. (bet. Fifth Ave. & University Pl.)

Subway: 14 St - Union Sq
Phone: 212-620-4020
Web: www.gothambarandgrill.com
Prices: $$$

Lunch Mon – Fri
Dinner nightly

David Cavallo

For decades Gotham has baffled the fickle NY restaurant scene by consistently remaining one of its hottest spots. It may favor mass appeal over innovation, but this food is serious, solid, and brings complete pleasure to every bite.

The lovely, unassuming exterior seems to belie the fact that inside this enormous open space–dotted with chandeliers and flower arrangements worthy of contemplation–the tables are humming with money and power. But by the grace of servers who never stop smiling and a kitchen that doesn't disappoint, the business crowds are clearly focused on dining.

Artistic presentations may begin with a cold-smoked Tasmanian sea trout, cut into thin, decorative ribbons and glistening within the culminating layers of braised baby fennel, tart celery hearts, and Meyer lemon confit. Marinated in a soy-miso reduction, served with bok choy, shiitake mushrooms, and lemongrass-ginger sauce, black cod becomes a thing of east-meets-western beauty. Rather than simply trying to sate a sweet tooth, desserts like the ethereal soufflé Belle Helen highlight a range of flavors and textures with pear-infused crème anglaise, dark chocolate tinged with orange, and warming spices.

Grand Sichuan

Chinese ✗

B3

15 Seventh Ave. South (bet. Carmine & Leroy Sts.)

Subway: Houston St
Phone: 212-645-0222
Web: www.thegrandsichuan.com
Prices: 🥟

Lunch & dinner daily

♿
☂

This latest outpost of the well-run chain strives to offer a more healthy Chinese option in this Sichuan-focused menu. The enjoyable, delicious fare includes excellent shredded chicken with sour cabbage; chewy *dan dan* noodles layered with spicy minced pork; and a mouthwatering braised whole fish with hot bean sauce. In addition to the expansive "American Chinese," "Classic Sichuan," and "Latest" sections of menu offerings, dining here features a thoughtful touch—both small- and large-sized portions are offered, allowing guests to feast without fear of over doing it.

The pleasant room may be restrained in its décor, but boasts large windows overlooking a stretch of Seventh Avenue and is graciously attended to by the polite, uniformed staff.

Gusto

Italian ✗✗

C2

60 Greenwich Ave. (at Perry St.)

Subway: 14 St (Seventh Ave.)
Phone: 212-924-8000
Web: www.gustonyc.com
Prices: $$

Lunch & dinner daily

☂
🍷
🍽

Although Gusto's kitchen has been a revolving door of notable talent, this sleek and sexy Village trattoria continues to impress. The menu balances warm antipasti, such as the surprisingly light seafood *fritto misto*, with enticing house-made pastas, like organic spinach and ricotta dumplings in sage butter. Equally pleasing is the simply yet beautifully prepared risotto, perhaps made with the straightforward flavors of lemon and fresh basil. If offered, the luscious, mauve-colored fig gelato, powerful with the flavor of ripe fruit, is not to be missed—especially when enjoying the ample sidewalk seating on a warm evening.

The neatly plated food suits the tailored interior's whitewashed walls, velvet banquettes, crystal chandelier, and Missoni bar stools.

Hakata Tonton

J a p a n e s e ✖

61 Grove St. (bet. Bleecker St. & Seventh Ave.)

Subway: Christopher St - Sheridan Sq   Dinner nightly
Phone: 212-242-3699
Web: www.tontonnyc.com
Prices: $$

A new cuisine has taken root in New York. Enter this tiny red and yellow dining room to be educated in this other facet of the Japanese culinary repertoire: *tonsoku* (pigs' feet, ears, and the like).

Varied *tonsoku* dishes may include a luxurious slow roasted pork or *oreilles du cochon* (French in name only) which are an explosion of crunchy, cool, creamy, sweet, sticky, and vinegary flavors. Truer to its Italian roots, *tonsoku* carbonara is made with smoky bacon and is a good choice for wary newbies. A "rare cheesecake" of piped cheese and sour cream is a very smart and completely delicious take on the traditional dessert.

The plain-Jane décor sits in stark contrast to the rich and porky fare that diners will come rushing back for.

Hecho en Dumbo 🐶

M e x i c a n ✖

354 Bowery (bet. 4th & Great Jones Sts.)

Subway: Bleecker St   Lunch & dinner daily
Phone: 212-937-4245
Web: www.hechoendumbo.com
Prices: $$

Adios DUMBO, this Mexico City-style spot has now taken up residence in Manhattan. The room sports an edgy downtown vibe with reclaimed wood and mismatched chairs; a back dining counter offers diners a view of the kitchen led by Mexico City native Daniel Mena.

Antojitos (small bites) and contemporary fare shape the made-from-scratch menu built around house-made tortillas, *bolillo* bread, and *queso Oaxaca*. Tasty treats may include *pescadillas*: fried turnovers of crispy tortilla filled with shredded tilapia, diced onion, and chiles. The *molletes* is (for lack of a better reference) the ultimate Mexican version of grilled cheese, served toasted and open-faced, topped with black bean purée, *queso* Chihuahua, and crumbles of homemade pork belly chorizo.

Home

Contemporary 🍴

D2

20 Cornelia St. (bet. Bleecker & W. 4th Sts.)

Subway: W 4 St - Wash Sq
Lunch & dinner daily
Phone: 212-243-9579
Web: www.homerestaurantnyc.com
Prices: $$

This intimate Cornelia St. dining room has persevered through the years and continues to offer great tastes of Americana in a setting that is welcoming and warm—all apt characteristics for an eatery called Home. Everyone seated in their black spindled chairs or back garden seats, is happy to see this unassuming, unpretentious whitewashed little space thriving. The kitchen honors sourcing and seasonality in its range of comforting specialties that have included a freshly prepared vegan purée of tomato and sweet basil representing the soup of the day; and a hearty oyster Po'boy featuring hefty and briny, cornmeal-crusted Willapa Bay oysters, spice-tinged rémoulade sauce, on a fresh ciabatta roll alongside a tangle of Old Bay sprinkled shoestring fries.

Hung Ry 🐸

Asian 🍴🍴

D4

55 Bond St. (bet. Bowery & Lafayette St.)

Subway: Bleecker St
Lunch & dinner Tue – Sun
Phone: 212-677-4864
Web: www.hung-ry.com
Prices: 🐸🐸

This new spot with the catchy name (say it fast…cute, right?) takes the standard noodle shop and gives it an updated twirl, offering bowlfuls of excellent produce and hand-pulled strands (thin or wide) freshly made to order. The selection is seasonal and the degree of skill impressive, as showcased by the mutton-focused version—its meaty broth is warmed by sweet spices, stocked with lamb sausage, belly, liver, salted cabbage, and persimmon. Bolstering the menu are starters like the utterly fresh vegetable plate, a timely composition of pickled daikon, carrot, Asian pear salad, and baby beets with toasted pumpkin seeds.

The chic space is outfitted with an open kitchen and is decorated with organic paint, birch veneer, and sacks of local flour.

Il Buco

Italian

47 Bond St. (bet. Bowery & Lafayette St.)

Subway: Bleecker St
Phone: 212-533-1932
Web: www.ilbuco.com
Prices: $$

Lunch Mon – Sat
Dinner nightly

Il Buco offers guests the idyllic Tuscan farmhouse fantasy without leaving Manhattan. This artist's studio-cum-restaurant shines with sunny charm and quirky warmth through chicly rustic tables, wood floors, copper plates, and antiques.

However, with delightful service, an extraordinary sommelier, and superlative market-driven Italian cuisine, Il Buco does not rely on looks alone. The chef is a stickler for quality, and the product-focused menu celebrates the seasons, as in an amazingly simple salad of crisp and earthy Tuscan black kale with anchovy vinaigrette. Plentiful appetizers are followed by homemade pastas and daily-changing entrées, such as pan-fried prawns with Sicilian sea salt, a hint of rosemary, and delicious kick of hot pepper.

Joseph Leonard

Contemporary

170 Waverly Pl. (at Grove St.)

Subway: Christopher St - Sheridan Sq
Phone: 646 429-8383
Web: www.josephleonard.com
Prices: $$

Lunch Tue Sun
Dinner nightly

Joseph Leonard serves an enjoyable carte of well-prepared contemporary fare devoted to the season and bearing a faint French accent in country pâté with pickled onions and baguette; pan-seared Long Island fluke with creamy lemon rice and soy reduction; and a tall wedge of classic carrot cake. Breakfast is served as well and includes the likes of *saucisson à l'ail* with eggs and hashbrowns.

This chicly curated corner setting, owned by Gabriel Stulman, sports rough-hewn wood-plank flooring, raw walls, and book-filled shelves. The space is installed with a winsome assemblage of vintage pieces including a zinc bar and fridge that looks like it was lifted from the set of *I Love Lucy*, that lend a unique air to this always welcoming establishment.

Manhattan ▶ Greenwich, West Village & Meatpacking District

Kesté Pizza & Vino 🐶

D2

271 Bleecker St. (bet. Cornelia & Jones Sts.)

Subway: W 4 St - Wash Sq
Phone: 212-243-1500
Web: www.kestepizzeria.com
Prices: 💰

Lunch & dinner daily

Co-owner Roberto Caporuscio was born and raised near Naples, is a former mozzarella producer, and is the current American-chapter president of the *Associazione Pizzaiuoli Napoletani*. When it comes to creating authentic Neopolitan-style pizza, he knows what he's doing.

A list of salads are offered as a starting point for the main event—distinctively charred, crusty, tender pies scented with wood smoke and baked on a layer of volcanic stone. Fashioned from mostly imported ingredients (flour, tomatoes, cheese, and olive oil) there are eighteen varieties of pizza with a specific combination of toppings (the menu states no changes allowed). The *salsiccia* is crowned with local basil and sweet, meaty crumbles procured from across the street at Faicco's.

Kingswood

C2

121 W. 10th St. (bet. Greenwich & Sixth Aves.)

Subway: 14 St (Seventh Ave.)
Phone: 212-645-0044
Web: www.kingswoodnyc.com
Prices: $$

Lunch Sat – Sun
Dinner nightly

Kingswood's mirthful spirit is evident from the moment you step inside. The inviting bar is habitually packed by a good-humored crowd, while beyond, the dining room is abuzz with its own sleek rusticity and warmth. Bathed in a flattering glow, diners sit in long communal tables and caramel-leather banquettes set against a softly lit glass-walled installation and votive candles.

The contemporary menu displays boldly flavored accents while paying homage to its owner's native Australia, as in the house burger with cheddar and sweet chili sauce; Goan fish curry; and beer battered fish and chips. Here, surf and turf may mean crisp-skinned salt cod and fork-tender pork cheeks dressed in a dark reduction of meaty jus with creamy, smoked mashed potatoes.

Kin Shop

C2

Thai ✗✗

469 Sixth Ave. (bet. 11th & 12th Sts.)

Subway: 14 St (Seventh Ave.)
Phone: 212-675-4295
Web: www.kinshopnyc.com
Prices: $$

Lunch & dinner daily

Chef/owner Harold Dieterle has flirted with Thai food in the past at his lovely Perilla, but now fully affirms his serious commitment to this cuisine at Kin Shop. His buzzing new venture gets its name from the Thai word "to eat," and one does this very well in this pretty dining room boasting whitewashed brick, batik canvases, and a beachy color scheme.

The approach is contemporary and offers a mouthwatering sojourn. Curries include banana leaf steamed rabbit bathed in sour yellow curry with eggplant chutney; while noodles feature pan-fried rice vermicelli tangled with roasted chilies and crab. Even the condiments deserve undivided attention—the addictive chili jam is made even more delicious when paired with freshly griddled, buttery *roti*.

L'Artusi

B3

Italian ✗✗

228 W. 10th St. (bet. Bleecker & Hudson Sts.)

Subway: Christopher St - Sheridan Sq
Phone: 212-255-5757
Web: www.lartusi.com
Prices: $$

Dinner nightly

L'Artusi's façade may be demure, but this attractive dining room offers a fun, buzz-worthy vibe to elevate its upscale rendition of Italian-rooted fare, anchored by small plates. The large space, with gray and ivory stripes aplenty, offers three dining counters, table service, and a quieter mezzanine. An open kitchen adds to the lively air.

The impressive Italian wine list, complete with maps, is laid out with a gravitas that demands attention. The well-versed staff is pleased to suggest the best pairings to complement pastas such as buckwheat *pizzoccheri* with Brussels sprouts, fontina, and sage. Salads of chicory dressed in Parmesan, lemon, and anchovies, or crudo plates of beef carpaccio with horseradish *crema* are wonderful ways to start a meal here.

Las Ramblas

D1

Spanish

170 W. 4th St. (bet. Cornelia & Jones Sts.)

Subway: Christopher St - Sheridan Sq
Phone: 646-415-7924
Web: www.lasramblasnyc.com
Prices: ⬤⬤

Lunch Sat – Sun
Dinner nightly

Sandwiched among a throng of attention-seeking storefronts, mighty little Las Ramblas is easy to spot, just look for the crowd of happy, munching faces; the scene spills out onto the sidewalk when the weather allows. Named for Barcelona's historic commercial thoroughfare, Las Ramblas is a tapas treat.

A copper-plated bar and collection of tiny tables provide a perch for snacking on an array of earnestly prepared items. Check out the wall mounted blackboard for *especiales*. Bring friends, it's that kind of place, to fully explore the menu, which serves up delights such as succulent head-on prawns roasted in a terra-cotta dish and sauced with cava vinegar, ginger, and basil; or béchamel creamed spinach topped by a molten cap of Mahón cheese.

Le Gigot

D2

French

18 Cornelia St. (bet. Bleecker & W. 4th Sts.)

Subway: W 4 St - Wash Sq
Phone: 212-627-3737
Web: www.legigotrestaurant.com
Prices: $$

Lunch & dinner Tue – Sun

Looking perfectly at home on its quaint tree-lined street, Le Gigot is quietly and confidently alluring. The petite bistro boasts personable yet polished service, inlaid wood flooring, olive-colored velvet banquettes, and butter-yellow walls hung with blackboards displaying the day's specials, such as lobster salad or bœuf Bourguignon. This intimate setting is a perfect match for the classic French fare.

The salad of endive, apple, and Roquefort, studded with toasted walnuts and dressed with sweet vinaigrette hinting of mustard seed, is simplicity at its most delicious. The duck confit, with its velvety rich meat cloaked with fabulously crisped skin and a bubbling, golden block of potato and celery root gratin, is one of the best in the city.

The Little Owl

B3

90 Bedford St. (at Grove St.)

Subway: Christopher St - Sheridan Sq   Lunch & dinner daily
Phone: 212-741-4695
Web: www.thelittleowlnyc.com
Prices: $$

Perched on a winsome corner of the West Village, Chef Joey Campanaro's Little Owl continues to hold a dear place in the hearts of diners near and far who appreciate that simple food and great food can be one and the same. The broccoli soup (a pure, silky purée enriched with a trace of cream and crowned by a crouton of bubbling, aged cheddar) is among the best examples of this.

The small corner room is quaint and despite this establishment's popularity, the service team is completely attitude-free. The wee kitchen is on display, and the focused crew turns out a rousing roster of preparations that bear an affinity for Mediterranean cuisine such as seared cod with *bagna cauda* vinaigrette, and gravy meatball sliders, a hands-down house specialty.

Lupa 😊

C4

170 Thompson St. (bet. Bleecker & Houston Sts.)

Subway: W 4 St - Wash Sq   Lunch & dinner daily
Phone: 212-982-5089
Web: www.luparestaurant.com
Prices: $$

This ever-popular Roman trattoria has been skillfully sating wolfish appetites for years and continues to fall under the hegemony of culinary heavyweights schooled in the immense bounty offered by the Italian table. Lupa's setting is rustic and charming with that timeless combination of sienna-toned walls, terra-cotta tile flooring, and wood furnishings. The service team is notable for their knowledge and courteousness.

Stop at the bar for a carafe of *vino* from the all-Italian wine list and nibble on house-cured specialties. Then move on to a focused selection of fare such as capon and pork terrine with celery *conserva*; and impressive *primi* like *tonnarelli* dressed with chunks of heritage pork ragù. A short list of *secondi* anchors the offerings.

Market Table

B3

54 Carmine St. (at Bedford St.)

Subway: W 4 St - Wash Sq   Lunch & dinner daily
Phone: 212-255-2100
Web: www.markettablenyc.com
Prices: $$

Sophisticated cooking is on display at this quaint and urbane café brought to you by Joey Campanaro and Chef Mike Price. Open all day, the bright, two-room space features brick walls lined with shelves of pantry staples, warm wood furnishings, large plate-glass windows, and a boisterous energy that rarely quiets down.

The kitchen, open for hungry eyes to enjoy, excels at turning out a seasonally respectful assortment of presentations that are just as skilled as they are simple. Case in point: The beet salad is composed as a rainbow of roasted roots paired with crunchy-creamy goat cheese fritters; and the strip steak is enhanced by irresistible and decadent fontina-potato purée. Even a humble slice of apple pie will not only please but also impress.

Mary's Fish Camp

B2

64 Charles St. (at W. 4th St.)

Subway: Christopher St - Sheridan Sq   Lunch & dinner Mon – Sat
Phone: 646-486-2185
Web: www.marysfishcamp.com
Prices: $$

Mary Redding opened this tiny Florida-style fish shack in a West Village brownstone in 2000 and has been enjoying wild success ever since. Her ever-debated lobster rolls are among the city's finest examples, overflowing with succulent chunks of meat, slathered in mayonnaise and piled on a buttery hot dog bun—messy but are definitely worth it! Yet this small spot features an extensive menu that goes well beyond, with particular focus on Key West cuisine such as conch fritters, and the bounty of New England waters. Accompaniments like Old Bay fries and regional desserts reflect American flair with homespun simplicity.

Bear in mind that only seafood is served here, reservations are not accepted, and the counter couldn't be better for solo dining.

Mas

B3

39 Downing St. (bet. Bedford & Varick Sts.)

Subway: Houston St
Phone: 212-255-1790
Web: www.masfarmhouse.com
Prices: $$$

Dinner nightly

The rustic exterior of this lovely, and beloved, establishment bears a chic rusticity that stands out from its already picturesque West Village location. The intimate space is evocative of a Provençal farmhouse, and its elegance promotes hush tones. Weathered wood planks, a communal dining table, and a sandstone bar effectively convey the charming vision.

CIA trained chef, Galen Zamarra, who honed his skills working in David Bouley's kitchen, pays homage to his finely sourced ingredients by producing delicious, seasonal fare. Dinner may reveal roasted sea scallops splashed with sweet corn soup; Long Island duck breast with olive-glazed turnips and Port-stewed cherries; and end with local strawberries paired with buttermilk pound cake and sorbet.

Mercadito Grove

D1

100 Seventh Ave. South (at Grove St.)

Subway: Christopher St - Sheridan Sq
Phone: 212-647-0830
Web: www.mercaditorestaurants.com
Prices: $$

Lunch Sat – Sun
Dinner nightly

Largest in the Mercadito chainlet, Grove has a devoted following that fills its pastel-painted chairs and corner sidewalk seating nightly. Starters range from a small list of fresh ceviches to flautas filled with chicken and black beans. Recommendations include any of the *platos fuertes* that make up the menu's concise selection like the adobo-marinated *pollo a las brasas*, available as a half or whole bird.

Tacos are likewise popular and are prepared with homemade tortillas, perhaps stuffed with beer-battered mahi mahi as in the *estilo Baja*. Hungry night owls should note that their NYC locations offer an all-you-can eat taco special late in the evening.

Each dish attests to why Mercadito now includes outposts in Miami and Chicago.

Mercat

D4

45 Bond St. (bet. Bowery & Lafayette St.)

Subway: Bleecker St
Phone: 212-529-8600
Web: www.mercatnyc.com
Prices: $$

Dinner nightly

Brick walls, subway tiles, and plank flooring line this hip yet inviting tapas den, whose name translates to "market" in Catalan. Owner Jaime Reixach hails from Barcelona, and the two American chefs he hired have both spent extensive time in the area, giving the cooking an authentic leg up and over New York's endless string of Spanish tapas bars.

The rich and authentic tastes of Catalonia are clear in decadent little plates like such as coca bread toped with duck, pears, spinach, and hazelnuts; or house-made *botifarra* sausages, served with butter beans and mushrooms. At its center, the marble bar-lined room features a station piled high with sweet-scented jamon and cheeses.

The Spanish wine list highlights cavas, sherries, and seasonal sangrías.

Mexicana Mama

B2

525 Hudson St. (bet. Charles & 10th Sts.)

Subway: Christopher St - Sheridan Sq
Phone: 212-924-4119
Web: N/A
Prices: ⊜⊜

Lunch & dinner Tue – Sun

Cute and charming, Mexicana Mama showcases the homespun flavors of the Mexican kitchen. The space, painted deep blue, barely seats 20 and is so small that a trip to the bathroom necessitates a walk through the open kitchen for an up close and personal view of the crew at work, where everything looks tidy and tempting.

A blackboard announces the day's mouthwatering specials, such as apricot and chipotle-glazed chicken or coconut-marinated fish. The printed menu offers the likes of grilled corn slathered with chipotle mayonnaise and a showering of *cojito* cheese; or *queso flameado*—molten cheese topped with spicy Mexican chorizo and thin strips of roasted poblano pepper, attractively presented with fresh tortillas for a delicious and fun make-your-own feast.

Minetta Tavern ❀

Gastropub ✗

C3

113 MacDougal St. (at Minetta Ln.)

Subway: W 4 St - Wash Sq
Phone: 212-475-3850
Web: www.minettatavernny.com
Prices: $$$

Lunch Sat – Sun
Dinner nightly

Ngoc Minh Ngo

One of the more eclectic haunts in town, Minetta Tavern oozes history and charm. Crowding in every strata of society (from the sedulous to the uninformed, the young to the old, and the blue-blooded to the bourgeois), dining at this Rat Pack chic lair is both interesting and undeniably New York. Scene aside, glimpse Minetta Tavern's stunning staff gleefully deal with the droves.

The patina-coated walls are comforting and reek of the golden years; listen very carefully as nearby romantics tell the tales of times past. Like every proud tavern, Minetta makes you feel right at home. Find solace in the snug front room hosting a princely bar and plush banquettes; or squeeze in the back room with its larger tables and order up a fabulous cocktail to go with those buzz-worthy dishes.

This novel gastropub may be famously favored and appropriately exclusive, yet its menu is a coherent lineup of classics like beef tartare dressed with anchovies and capers, crowned by a quivering quail egg and *pommes gaufrettes*. The signature Black Label burger is juicy, but the expertly-aged and charred bone-in NY Strip, decadent *pommes aligot*, and frothy Grand Marnier soufflé reign supreme.

Miss Lily's

C4

Jamaican 🍴

132 W. Houston St. (at Sullivan St.)

Subway: Houston St
Phone: 646-588-5375
Web: www.misslilysnyc.com
Prices: 💶

Lunch & dinner daily

Jerk chicken gets the scenester treatment at Miss Lily's, brought to you by La Esquina's Serge Becker. Up front, the look conjures a retro takeout joint, with orange Formica booths, linoleum flooring, and a backlit menu board above the open kitchen. The back dining room is larger and has reggae record jackets lining the walls. Loud music, a gorgeous staff, and a blithe crowd create a festive vibe.

Glossy packaging aside, the Jamaican specialties served here are well done. Curry goat brings bone-in pieces of pasture-raised meat in a tasty sauce bright with turmeric, sweet spices, and the slow burn of Scotch bonnet pepper. As for that chicken, it's charred and smoky, accompanied by mango-ginger chutney and a bottle of the tangy, spicy marinade.

Morandi

C2

Italian 🍴🍴

211 Waverly Pl. (bet. Charles St. & Seventh Ave. South)

Subway: 14 St (Seventh Ave.)
Phone: 212-627-7575
Web: www.morandiny.com
Prices: $$$

Lunch & dinner daily

Morandi has all the requisite charm one would expect from a Keith McNally trattoria that recalls Tuscany with all its glorious clichés, antique-tiled floors, brick archways, and walls lined with straw-wrapped Chianti bottles. Dotted with a mishmash of tables, well-dressed patrons shielded by designer shades are bathed in a warm glow even at high noon, thanks to parchment shaded ceiling fixtures.

They come to pay homage to a rustic menu that may begin with seasonal *antipasti* before moving on to a classic panzanella marrying beefsteak and heirloom tomatoes, fresh basil, and slivers of red onions; *spaghetti neri*, squid ink pasta rolling with tender calamari, octopus, shrimp, and mussels; and light, spongy *budino limone* licked with buttermilk ice cream.

MPD

B1

French ✗✗

73 Gansevoort St. (bet. Greenwich & Washington Sts.)

Subway: 14 St - 8 Av   Lunch & dinner daily
Phone: 212-541-6991
Web: www.mpdnyc.com
Prices: $$

Short for *mon petit déjeuner* (my breakfast), the acronym used as the moniker of this spacious boîte references both its Gallic roots as well as its Meatpacking District location. As expected, the look here is chic, clad in whitewashed brick and warmed by chocolate brown furnishings; deep booths offer a comfy perch for those who want to feel like a VIP. Despite the DJ booth behind the maitre d' stand, there is as much substance as style here, thanks to the kitchen.

Carpaccio-style *cru de salmon* is served as paper-thin tartare with crème fraîche and a drizzle of preserved lemon purée; and the beautifully cooked saffron-crusted rack of lamb is even tastier when paired with the Périgord truffle and potato croquettes featured among the sides.

One if by Land, Two if by Sea

Contemporary ✗✗✗

D1

17 Barrow St. (bet. Seventh Ave. South & W. 4th St.)

Subway: Christopher St - Sheridan Sq   Lunch Sun
Phone: 212-255-8649   Dinner nightly
Web: www.oneifbyland.com
Prices: $$$

Step into this oh-so-agreeable 18th century carriage house and it's easy to forget you're in Manhattan. Long known as one of the city's most romantic dining rooms, this establishment enjoys the reputation of being the place to pop the question, or least the spot for a romantic rendezvous. The brick-lined space exudes old-world sophistication—tables are topped with a rose and taper candle, the room looks out onto an ivy-cloaked courtyard, and there's live piano music.

The food is delectable, whether you're in the mood for love or not, and proffers a contemporary slant in its collection of courses that can include Maine scallop sashimi with stone fruit; fettucine with Sicilian pistachio pesto; and poached day boat cod with green garlic-citrus *nage*.

Manhattan ▶ Greenwich, West Village & Meatpacking District

159

Panca

Peruvian ✗

D1

92 Seventh Ave. South (bet. Bleecker & Grove Sts.)

Subway: Christopher St - Sheridan Sq   Lunch Thu – Sun
Phone: 212-488-3900   Dinner nightly
Web: N/A
Prices: $$

The exciting flavors of *Novo Andean* cuisine headline this contemporary spot, where Peruvian ingredients are prepared with Asian and American techniques. Outside, a sidewalk dining area sits along the hubbub of Seventh Avenue; the interior is simple and cool with citron walls and a stacked-stone bar displaying the bottles of *pisco* to be mixed into cocktails.

Discreetly tucked into the dining room's corner is the ceviche station, where ocean-fresh seafood inspires vibrant preparations of *tiraditos* like the five *elementos* made with the fish of the day, red onions, key lime juice, chiles, and pink Hawaiian sea salt. *Lomo saltado* highlights the cuisine's fusion in an entrée of beef tenderloin stir fried with vegetables, *aji Amarillo*, and soy sauce.

Paradou

French ✗

B1

8 Little W. 12th St. (bet. Greenwich & Washington Sts.)

Subway: 14 St - 8 Av   Lunch Fri – Sun
Phone: 212-463-8345   Dinner nightly
Web: www.paradounyc.com
Prices: $$

Paradou offers a bit of Provence and a welcome respite from the spate of gargantuan, over-the-top-posh restaurants populating the Meatpacking District. Here, a casual yet energetic crowd shares a carefree French spirit while relaxing over crisp glasses of Champagne and bowls of plump mussels *du jour* or traditional bouillabaisse.

The whimsical covered "magical garden" tent offers winter enchantment with heat lamps warming the space during colder evenings, but comes down in spring and summer. Enjoy unlimited Champagne cocktails, truly al fresco, during their weekend brunch. Live music and "Paradou Happenings" are scheduled regularly.

The all-French wine list offers some reasonably priced selections to complement the classic and rustic bistro menu.

Pastis

French 🍴

9 Ninth Ave. (at Little W. 12th St.)

Subway: 14 St – 8 Av
Phone: 212-929-4844
Web: www.pastisny.com
Prices: $$

Lunch & dinner daily

This lovingly recreated bistro is the first success story of the Meatpacking District, then a nascent neighborhood. Even now, it remains a trendy and popular place that is just as much fun during the day as evening, squeezing in a fashionable (and often famous) flock from breakfast through dinner. Inside, the timeless bistro décor (decorative mirrors, long zinc bar, walls lined with vintage Pastis ads) has that hip, informal charm so difficult to replicate; outside, the sidewalk seating was designed with Bellini-sipping and sunshine in mind.

The menu is good and satisfying, focusing on neighborhood favorites like steak *frites*. The cocktail list, as expected, leans heavily on the anise-flavored aperitif from which the restaurant takes its name.

Pearl Oyster Bar

Seafood 🍴

18 Cornelia St. (bet. Bleecker & W. 4th Sts.)

Subway: W 4 St - Wash Sq
Phone: 212-691-8211
Web: www.pearloysterbar.com
Prices: $$

Lunch Mon – Fri
Dinner Mon – Sat

In 1997, Chef/owner Rebecca Charles opened Pearl Oyster Bar in memory of her grandmother and the childhood summers they spent in Maine. Today, she serves a slice of New England to the heart of Manhattan; though many imitations and variations can be found, Pearl is a NY classic. This beloved eatery has a small dining room, a counter handling a brisk business for shellfish aficionados, an accompanying cookbook, and long lines out the door.

The classic New England menu offers small and large plates of pristine seafood as well as their hallowed lobster roll. Try this with one of their carefully selected wines or beers on tap. Pearl is a true, tried American restaurant, so don't even try to end meals with an espresso (the chef refuses to serve it).

Manhattan ▶ Greenwich, West Village & Meatpacking District

Perilla

Contemporary XX

D1

9 Jones St. (bet. Bleecker & W. 4th Sts.)

Subway: W 4 St - Wash Sq
Phone: 212-929-6868
Web: www.perillanyc.com
Prices: $$

Lunch Sat – Sun
Dinner nightly

This casually elegant Village fave, with its unaffected vibe, showcases the talents of partners Chef Harold Dieterle and General Manager Alicia Nosenzo. He is a CIA graduate and premier winner of the reality television hit "Top Chef"; and she is a San Francisco native who has honed her front of the house skills at impressive establishments on both coasts.

Up front is an inviting bar and the rear dining room, with its zebrawood tables and warm lighting, is attended to by an eager staff, forthcoming with suggestions on the seasonally respectful menu. Reflecting global influences, the chef spices a beautifully prepared snapper crudo with pickled radish and *tom yum* broth, and transforms game hen into bacon-wrapped roulades sauced with pomegranate molasses.

Perry Street 😊

Contemporary XX

B2

176 Perry St. (at West St.)

Subway: Christopher St - Sheridan Sq
Phone: 212-352-1900
Web: www.jean-georges.com
Prices: $$

Lunch & dinner daily

Contrasting the theatrics of Spice Market is Jean-Georges Vongerichten's cool and current Perry Street. Sheer fabrics cling to large windows, letting sunlight drench this gorgeous, ground-level dream. Stroll past a lounge lit with dazzling fixtures to a wispy dining room featuring white and light wood, leather upholstery, and close-knit tables.

Emulating this minimalist aspect is the service and food. Cozy up at the bar or a corner table to savor an Alsatian white alongside such tidy, angular presentations of Arctic char sashimi crowned with fried fish skin; and organic fried chicken with Meyer lemon marmalade, mushroom "stuffing", and mashed potatoes. If that doesn't entice you, the $28 lunch and $38 dinner menu offer ace value and must not be missed.

The Place

B2

310 W. 4th St. (bet. Bank & 12th Sts.)

Subway: 14 St - 8 Av
Phone: 212-924-2711
Web: www.theplaceny.com
Prices: $$

Lunch Sat – Sun
Dinner nightly

Set deep within the West Village, The Place is the kind of cozy, grotto-style den that makes you feel all grown-up. Rendezvous-like, guests climb below street level to find a bar aglow with flickering votive candles. Wander back a bit, and you'll find rustic beams and white tablecloth seating; two outdoor terraces beckon when the sun shines.

The guileless name of the "place" and timeless look of the century-old setting is nicely juxtaposed by a wholly contemporary menu that roams the globe: Duck confit-filled parcels served with grain mustard and braised red cabbage is a lovely autumnal treat, while entrées please year round with dishes like a cheddar-capped shepherd's pie; Long Island duck breast with tamarind sauce; and Cuban-style pork chops.

Pó

D2

31 Cornelia St. (bet. Bleecker & W. 4th Sts.)

Subway: W 4 St - Wash Sq
Phone: 212-645-2189
Web: www.porestaurant.com
Prices: $$

Lunch Wed – Sun
Dinner nightly

This longtime neighborhood favorite, opened in 1993, continues to attract a devoted following for its understated yet sophisticated ambience and creative Italian fare.

During the day, the slender dining room is light and breezy, especially in warmer weather when the front door is propped open and ceiling fans swirl overhead. At night, this quaint spot tucked away on tree-lined Cornelia St. feels timeless and perfectly romantic.

Egg dishes and panini are available at lunch. The dinner menu features a contemporary slant that may include starters like house-cured tuna dressed with white beans, artichokes, and chili-mint vinaigrette; freshly made gnocchi draped with lamb ragù; and entrées that include grilled skirt steak with Gorgonzola butter.

Manhattan ▶ Greenwich, West Village & Meatpacking District

Quinto Quarto 😋

Italian 🍴

B3

14 Bedford St. (bet. Downing & Houston Sts.)

Subway: Houston St
Phone: 212-675-9080
Web: www.quintoquarto.com
Prices: 🍝🍝

Lunch & dinner daily

This newly opened *"osteria Romana"* is named after a neighborhood that once served as Rome's Meatpacking District. Its enticingly rustic menu is served in an intimate setting that beams warmth; the dark-wood furnishings, exposed brick walls, and friendly service offer a charmingly heavy Italian accent.

The adept kitchen paves the way to the Eternal City with a listing of regional specialties that include a luscious *bucatini all'Amatriciana*, a tangle of perfectly cooked strands dressed with carrot and onion sweetened tomato sauce, bacon, and pecorino cheese. Entrées may include roasted bone-in pieces of tender rabbit wildly fragrant with rosemary, sage, and accompanied by crisped potatoes. Dessert offers a short listing of jam-filled *crostatas*.

Recette

Contemporary 🍴🍴

B2

328 W. 12th St. (at Greenwich St.)

Subway: 14 St - 8 Av
Phone: 212-414-3000
Web: www.recettenyc.com
Prices: $$$

Lunch Sat – Sun
Dinner Mon – Sat

Straddling a charming, tree-lined corner in the heart of the West Village, Recette has a few things going for it straight off the bat: it's cute, intimate, and decidedly low-lit. Date night, anyone?

But with Jesse Schenker, a much-buzzed-about young chef, on board–not to mention a pastry chef rumored to hail from Per Se–there's a lot more to Recette than good looks and location. The menu's focus is on globally-inspired small plates, perfectly suited to share with friends or indulge in solo. Witness tender, marinated hamachi paired with fresh uni and a soft pile of mache, blood orange gelée, jalapeño, and harissa foam; or perfectly-seared squab meat served with Anson Mills grits, date purée, a poached egg, and shaved Parmesan.

Rockmeisha

D1

Japanese

11 Barrow St. (bet. Seventh Ave. South & W. 4th St.)

Subway: Christopher St - Sheridan Sq   Dinner Tue – Sun
Phone: 212-675-7775
Web: N/A
Prices: 🍴🍴

Regional specialties hailing from the chef's homeland of Kyushu, the large island in Southern Japan, are the way to go at this laid-back, fun, and tasty *izakaya*.

Like its name, the menu takes on a musical theme in listing its dishes as "goldies" such as the likes of *takosu*, thick slices of dense octopus bobbing in a refreshing yuzu-zested soy vinegar sauce; while their "greatest hits" may feature the *tonsoku*, a crispy pork foot that is rich to the point of being voluptuous, accompanied by raw cabbage and a dab of citrusy-spicy *yuzu kosho* to cut the richness.

The intimate space is decorated with a touch of kitsch (think poison warning signs), curious little cartoon drawings lining the walls, and rock music pulsing in the background, of course.

Scarpetta

B1

Italian 🍴🍴

355 W. 14th St. (bet. Eighth & Ninth Aves.)

Subway: 14 St - 8 Av   Dinner nightly
Phone: 212-691-0555
Web: www.scarpettanyc.com
Prices: $$$

In a town where location is everything, it takes critically acclaimed Chef Scott Conant to pull this one off. Stuffed between a diner and a comedy club on bustling West 14th Street, Scarpetta is in a strange place to merit attention from serious eaters—yet they come in droves for the wickedly good food, the impeccable service, and clever wine list.

If you're in the mood to people-watch, grab a seat in the stylish bar area; or retreat back to the slick, pretty dining room where dinner might unveil a beautiful pile of fresh cavatelli chockablock with juicy braised rabbit, tender peas, ripe tomatoes, and creamy pecorino; or oven-roasted halibut wrapped in crispy lardo and surrounded by a seasonal succotash of fiddlehead ferns, fava beans, and ramps.

Sevilla

Spanish Spanish ✗

C2

62 Charles St. (at W. 4th St.)

Subway: Christopher St - Sheridan Sq
Phone: 212-929-3189
Web: www.sevillarestaurantandbar.com
Prices: $$

Lunch & dinner daily

With a long and colorful history since first opening its doors in 1941, charmingly nostalgic Sevilla remains a rarity among Manhattan's dining scene. The roaming menu harks back to traditional Spanish fare, heaping and hearty; the kind enjoyed long before our commonplace exposure to the cuisine became focused on small plates.

The majority of Sevilla's reasonably priced dishes are built around simply prepared seafood and chicken dressed with a number of primary sauces featuring almond, garlic, wine, and the prominent green sauce—parsley-packed and punched with garlic. Starters include the *ajo* soup, a clear chicken broth infused with the nutty essence of roasted garlic and enriched with egg; the smooth, classic flan is a fitting finale.

Spasso

Italian ✗✗

B2

551 Hudson St. (bet. Perry & 11th Sts.)

Subway: Christopher St - Sheridan Sq
Phone: 212-858-3838
Web: www.spassonyc.com
Prices: $$

Lunch Sat – Sun
Dinner nightly

This newcomer adds to the wealth of Italian small plates available in the West Village. Housed in the former home of Alfama, the convivial room boasts a gracious mien with a touch of rusticity; seating options include a comfortable bar and dining counter near the kitchen where one can watch prosciutto shaved, salads prepped, and gooey chocolate caramel *crostata* sliced and plated.

The kitchen, headed by an alum of Lupa and Convivio, serves up an array of contemporary Italian. Bites include eggplant "*arancini*" and whipped house-made ricotta flavored with the sweet taste of roasted tomato. There are plenty of heartier options as well, such as silky ravioli pockets filled with spring peas and chopped prawns; and *secondi* like trout saltimbocca.

Soto ✿✿

Japanese ✗✗

D1

357 Sixth Ave. (bet. Washington Pl. & W. 4th St.)

Subway: W 4 St - Wash Sq

Dinner Mon — Sat

Phone: 212-414-3088

Web: N/A

Prices: $$$

Tokia Kuniyoshi

There are no signs to mark your arrival at Soto. The minimalist room can feel stark, bright, a touch clinical, and a bit slow to come alive each evening. But when Chef Kosugi arrives at his station behind the bar and presents your first course of the night, close your eyes to the fireworks that are about to explode. *Itadakimasu!*

This may be a luxe spot for sushi, but the extraordinary caliber of fish and finesse with which it is prepared leaves no doubt that Soto is a worthy place to splurge on the chef's full omakase. Meals may begin with a block of beguiling tofu, half black and sesame flavored, half white with pure soy, dense yet impossibly soft beneath soy foam and freshly grated wasabi.

The menu goes on to explore the seas with minute-steamed sea bream so tender that it verges on resembling custard; lobster-uni mousse encased in rounds of lotus root; and squid with quail egg nested in strands of nori. Presented in a leaf-lined wooden tray, the nigiri is a vision to behold with its array of brightly hued, opaque and delicate, torched and brilliantly raw creations. Mind that this may arrive as your fifteenth (or was it fourteenth?) course, so do remember to pace yourself.

Spice Market

B1

403 W. 13th St. (at Ninth Ave.)

Subway: 14 St - 8 Av   Lunch & dinner daily
Phone: 212-675-2322
Web: www.spicemarketnewyork.com
Prices: $$

   Now a Meatpacking mainstay, Spice Market continues to attract the area's well-dressed, fun-loving scenesters, who come here regularly to graze on Chef Jean-Georges Vongerichten's culinary romp through Asian street food.

This 12,000 square-foot former warehouse realized by Jacques Garcia sexes up marketplace stalls with deep shades of red, violet, and gold; a large teak pagoda takes center stage, while wooden arches divide the seating areas. Enjoy the visual feast of this lively, colorful, and very successful spot that now claims outposts from Istanbul to Qatar.

The Chef's skill and trademark style is evident in vibrant dishes of deeply flavorful spiced chicken samosas with cilantro yogurt or elegantly modernized bowls of coconut-rich *laksa*.

Standard Grill

B1

848 Washington St. (bet. Little W. 12th & 13th Sts.)

Subway: 14 St - 8 Av   Lunch & dinner daily
Phone: 212-645-4100
Web: www.thestandardgrill.com
Prices: $$

   Classy comfort food is the name of the game at this jaunty grill that draws the "in" crowd. Despite the scene, the cooking is worth every penny. The raw bar or cheese fondue for a crowd make a fine start before moving on to the likes of grilled cobia fillet with a caramelized coating of chermloula marinade. Is that lobster Thermidor on the menu? Yes. And high- and lowbrow desserts include baked Alaska and cookies with local milk.

Perched beneath the Highline, the Standard Grill serves up a choice of seating: a bright and airy front lounge, breezy sidewalk, and knockout dining room—clubby and sophisticated—replete with wood paneled walls, subway tile-clad vaulted ceiling, comfy red leather booths, and tables sporting menswear-inspired linens.

Surya ⊛

C1

302 Bleecker St. (bet. Grove St. & Seventh Ave. South)

Subway: Christopher St - Sheridan Sq   Lunch & dinner daily
Phone: 212-807-7770
Web: www.suryany.com
Prices: $$

This sleek Indian restaurant serves a slice of the East with a definitive New York look (read: no bright colors and no sequin-studded artwork at Surya). Polished dark wood floors, a cushioned banquette, ivory walls, and a back garden fashion a clean aesthetic and very pleasant ambience. Toto, we're definitely not in Delhi anymore.

It might look New York, but the taste is pure India. Take one bite of the lamb Chettinad or the halibut *moli* and you'll be transported in no time. Choose from a variety of regional specialties and tandoor preparations. You'll find everything from the familiar (*vindaloo*) to the rare (*surra putto*, cubes of shark with green pepper and curry leaf).

It's more limited than at night, but the lunch menu delivers a good value.

Takashi

B3

456 Hudson St. (bet. Barrow & Morton Sts.)

Subway: Christopher St - Sheridan Sq   Dinner Tue – Sun
Phone: 212 414-2929
Web: www.takashinyc.com
Prices: $$

This Korean-style Japanese newcomer is all about beef, raw and cooked, with cuts of *horumon* (the Japanese term for offal) calling out to all carnivores—especially the adventurous ones. Takashi serves the likes of cow's liver, heart, sweetbreads, and tongue presented as slices of the tip, middle, and back for a full experience. These tabletop grill offerings arrive either seasoned with salt, garlic, and sesame oil; or marinated in a special sauce which evokes the Japanese-born chef's Korean heritage. Ribeye and *kalbi* pleases diners seeking the familiar. The contemporary room features a counter facing the personable crew as well as table seating arranged against a wall bearing whimsical instructions and illustrations on blackboard painted walls.

Spotted Pig ✿

Gastropub ✗

B2

314 W. 11th St. (at Greenwich St.)

Subway: Christopher St - Sheridan Sq

Phone: 212-620-0393

Web: www.thespottedpig.com

Prices: $$

Lunch & dinner daily

The Spotted Pig

Tucked into a West Village corner that's quiet, tree-lined, and bewitching is NY's dream neighborhood pub, The Spotted Pig. Born and bred by English chef extraordinaire, April Bloomfield, this classic speakeasy's carefully worn interior is now well-trodden after these past years. Straight out of the UK, The Spotted Pig feels and looks as it should—not so much comfortable as it is accurate.

Hang your coat, grab a stool, and gloat over food that's far beyond chicken wings. The Pig is young, informal, and hip. It may wear a pinch of attitude, but is mighty efficient and learned. The bar is the best place for a lazy lunch starring simple yet heavenly dishes kissed with Italian flair, namely a giant fried duck egg over ramps and tickled with sherry vinaigrette; or the appropriately favored Cubano mingling fatty, delicious pork with Gruyère and jalapeños.

The scene upstairs is no less encompassing—nothing flashy, just tight tabletops with delightfully unembellished presentations. Dinner is more boisterous than lunch and requires copious amounts of booze to go with garlic-infused beets and greens, or a richly-rustic walnut torte glossed with dark chocolate and crème fraîche.

10 Downing

C3

10 Downing St. (bet. Bleecker & Hudson Sts.)

Subway: Houston St

Lunch & dinner daily

Phone: 212-255-0300

Web: www.10downingnyc.com

Prices: $$

This popular downtown hot spot has seen a few changes in recent years, including the departure of Chef Jason Neroni and consulting chef, Katy Sparks—a kitchen overhaul that left San Francisco alum, Chef Jonathan Leiva, manning the ship. Meanwhile, all the regulars want to know is if the food still rocks, the décor's still cheeky and the vibe's just right?

The answer is decidedly yes. Fitted out with upside-down antlers, a white marble-topped bar, and French doors that swing open come summer, 10 Downing's menu is built around a collection of small plates, appetizers, and sides; along with a selection of seasonal entrées like tender lemon- and herb-roasted chicken, accompanied by a bundle of fresh arugula, golden raisins, and grilled radicchio.

Tomoe Sushi

C4

172 Thompson St. (bet. Bleecker & Houston Sts.)

Subway: Spring St (Sixth Ave.)

Lunch Tue – Sat

Phone: 212-777-9346

Dinner nightly

Web: N/A

Prices: ⊖⊘

Tomoe focuses on value and quality rather than soigné appearances. Its tile floor has been dulled by a steady stream of sushi aficionados, the simple furnishings aren't conducive to leisurely meals, and the décor is limited to hand-drawn signs displaying specials. Still, regulars enthuse over these supple morsels prepared by the efficient team behind the counter and presented by swift, casual servers.

Characterized by pieces that err on the side of heft, this sushi has a foundation of rich, thickly cut slices of fish, minimal embellishment, and fine technique. The kitchen also prepares a long list of cooked dishes that display a creative hand, as in steamed buns filled with teriyaki-brushed silken tofu, pickled garlic, and a dollop of mayonnaise.

Ushiwakamaru

C4

Japanese ✗

136 W. Houston St. (bet. MacDougal & Sullivan Sts.)

Subway: B'way - Lafayette St Dinner nightly
Phone: 212-228-4181
Web: N/A
Prices: $$$$

Manhattan's sushiphiles crave a taste of Chef Hideo Kuribara's outrageously fresh creations. Most nights, this casual and simple den (you wouldn't know it from the name!) is packed with regulars, ordering drinks from kimono-clad waitresses and watching the kitchen staff hold court at the sushi bar. Some of the area's finest fish is the true draw here, and the local set can rest assured of this even as they sit down to a table full of buttery *negi* toro roll and *anago*. True foodies relish the outstanding uni and *ikura*, piece by piece. Also, their selection of sake is the perfect complement to a meal here.

Inside its small basement location, this lively downtown gem is dressed in white linen and soothing blonde wood tones. Just remember to book ahead.

Villa Pacri

B1

Mediterranean ✗✗✗

55 Gansevoort St. (bet. Greenwich & Washington Sts.)

Subway: 14 St - 8 Av Dinner Tue – Sat
Phone: 212-924-5559
Web: www.villapacri.com
Prices: $$$

Villa Pacri is proof that you can have it all. This multi-level restaurant-cum-lounge has a little bit of everything spread over five floors, from a basement/underground lounge to a rooftop deck, with a first-floor café and Villa Pacri–the grown-up's choice–in between. This inviting room looks like the offspring of an Italian villa and a California shabby-chic cottage (think wood floors, exposed brick walls, and white wood chairs).

It's a scene, and many are there for the people-watching, but the well-executed Italian cooking is delicious and the staff is well-trained. Irresistible pasta dishes will have you licking your plate clean, while desserts are worth the splurge—just beware that bills can be bigger than the next table's TriBeCa loft.

Wallsé ✿

B2

344 W. 11th St. (at Washington St.)

Subway: Christopher St - Sheridan Sq
Phone: 212-352-2300
Web: www.wallse.com
Prices: $$$

Lunch Sat – Sun
Dinner nightly

Wallsé

This Austrian favorite is a real New Yorker. Situated on a corner that embodies what everyone dreams downtown neighborhoods should resemble, Wallsé resides among tree-lined, cobblestoned streets and historic townhouses all bathed in rose-colored light as the sun sets over the Hudson just blocks away. Inside, the two dining rooms pay tribute to the arts and fashion a sophisticated atmosphere with colorful modern paintings. Tables are filled with a well-to-do clientele who appreciate that dining here is an event to be savored.

As if the effortlessly modern Village-meets-Vienna space were influencing the cuisine, Wallsé is blooming into a more contemporary version of itself. The cuisine is decidedly Austrian, but embraces creative twists with starters like marinated raw tuna, topped with a scoop of chopped tuna tartare, accompanied by braised onions and artichokes; or entrées of lightly smoked breast and crisp leg of squab with roasted salsify and black truffles. Yet these dishes may simply be preparing you for an extraordinary finish.

Desserts must never be skipped here, especially with incomparable preparations like *Mozartkugel* with pistachio-nougat sabayon and Sicilian pistachios.

173

Yerba Buena Perry

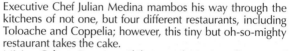

Latin American XX

C2

1 Perry St. (at Greenwich Ave.)

Subway: 14 St (Seventh Ave.)   Dinner nightly
Phone: 212-620-0808
Web: www.ybnyc.com
Prices: $$

Executive Chef Julian Medina mambos his way through the kitchens of not one, but four different restaurants, including Toloache and Coppelia; however, this tiny but oh-so-mighty restaurant takes the cake.

Mixing Cuban, Peruvian, Chilean, and Mexican flavors and traditions, upscale Medina delivers a signature flavor. Even familiar dishes have unexpected flair as in the ribeye ceviche dressed with spicy red pepper sauce, completed with corn kernels and sea urchin lobes. In the hands of this kitchen, even simple shrimp assume a lobster-like meatiness, complemented with their own Rio de Janeiro-style tomato salsa.

The tightly packed room is comfortable but can feel cramped, so hope to make new friends to share the meaty *Parrillada* and a trio of fab fries.

The sun is out – let's eat alfresco! Look for 🏠.

Harlem, Morningside & Washington Heights

Flanked by Riverside and Morningside parks and home to stately Columbia University, Morningside Heights is a lovely quarter of the city, and known for some of the best breakfast spots in town. Sandwich shops and eateries line these avenues, where quick, inexpensive meals are a collegiate necessity. Resident academics and Ivy leaguers are found darting to and from class or lounging at the **Hungarian Pastry Shop** with a sweet treat and cup of tea. Considered a landmark, this old-world bakery has been open for more than three decades and is a focal point for students and gatherings. Across the street, Saint John the Divine, a gorgeous Gothic revival and a formidable presence on Amsterdam Avenue offers beauty, history, and wonderful community outreach programs. Special occasions call for an evening at Butler Hall's **Terrace In The Sky**. Rather than be misled by the plain building in which it's housed, prepare yourself for the expansive views of the city and fine continental fare. In the summer, enjoy a drink in the breeze on the alluring outdoor terrace. To the north is Harlem—a true feast for the stomach and soul. Fifth Avenue divides the neighborhood into two very unique areas: West Harlem, an epicenter of African-American culture; and East Harlem, a diverse Latino quarter affectionately known as "El Barrio."

WEST HARLEM

West Harlem still retains a kind of sassy edge as it gives way to slow, welcomed gentrification—one of its most visible borders is at

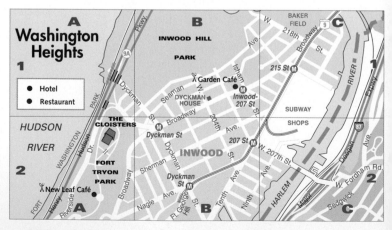

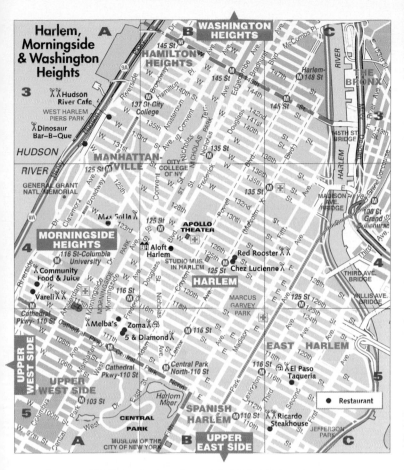

Harlem, Morningside & Washington Heights

WASHINGTON HEIGHTS

HAMILTON HEIGHTS

145 St
145 St
137 St-City College
135th
135 St
Harlem 148 St
145 St

THE BRONX

145TH ST BRIDGE

HUDSON RIVER

MANHATTAN-VILLE

CITY COLLEGE OF NY

135 St

MADISON AVE. BRIDGE

125 St

GENERAL GRANT NATL. MEMORIAL

WEST HARLEM PIERS PARK

Hudson River Cafe
Dinosaur Bar-B-Que

MORNINGSIDE HEIGHTS

116 St-Columbia University

Community Food & Juice

Vareli

Cathedral Pkwy-110 St

Melba's
5 & Diamond

Max So Ia

125 St
123rd

APOLLO THEATER

Aloft Harlem
STUDIO MUS. IN HARLEM
125 St

Red Rooster
Chez Lucienne

HARLEM

Zoma

116 St

MARCUS GARVEY PARK

THIRD AVE. BRIDGE

125 St 126th
125th
124th

WILLIS AVE. BRIDGE

EAST HARLEM

116 St
El Paso Taqueria

UPPER WEST SIDE

Cathedral Pkwy-110 St

Central Park North-110 St

116 St

103 St

Harlem Meer

CENTRAL PARK

SPANISH HARLEM

110 St

Ricardo Steakhouse

JEFFERSON PARK

MUSEUM OF THE CITY OF NEW YORK

UPPER EAST SIDE

| | Restaurant |

Fairway, a Tri-State area staple that lures shoppers off the West Side Highway for their mind boggling offerings and sensational produce. For a taste of the area's history, sift through the impressive literary collection at The Schomburg Center for Research in Black Culture on Lenox Avenue, or spend a sunny afternoon among the quaint row houses in the historic districts of Sugar Hill and Hamilton Heights. In the evening, slip into famed 70-year old **Lenox Lounge** for jazz and drinks and grab a seat at one of the banquettes. Harlem Week is an annual festival that features art, music, and food each August. While there, cool off with a cone of red velvet cake ice cream if the natural ice cream stand is around.

Food factors heavily into Harlem culture—both east and west of Fifth Avenue—and the choices are as diverse as the neighborhood itself. From Mexican to Caribbean to West African, the culinary delights abound. Locals line up around the block at **Famous Fish Market** for deep-fried faves such as fish and chips or baskets of crispy shrimp. To further indulge your fried food fantasy, entrée **Charles** for Chef Charles Gabriel's acclaimed buffet and sinfully delicious fried chicken. For dangerously spiced Senegalese food, head to **Afrika Kine**; or shop around **Darou Salam Market** for West African groceries. **Carrot Top Pastries** entices locals with sweet potato pies, while **Raw Soul**, a health-focused Harlem spot, offers a menu of vegan "living foods" and ongoing cooking classes designed to educate seekers of well-being.

EAST HARLEM

In East Harlem, visit **Itzocan Bistro** for a unique brunch menu and a great selection of pastries. **Amor Cubano**'s *lechon* is savored amidst a vibrant atmosphere of live Cuban music. For Caribbean delights stop into **Sisters**; or peruse the taco trucks and taquerias along the Little Mexico strip of East 116th Street in the heart of one of New York's many Mexican communities. A remnant of the former Italian population of East Harlem, **Rao's** is a New York institution. Run out of a small basement and frequented by the likes of Donald Trump and Nicole Kidman, Rao's is one of the most difficult tables to get in all of Manhattan.

The original patrons have exclusive rights to a seat here and hand off their reservations like rent-controlled apartments. Better try to get in good with the owner if you can. **Patsy's** is still holding strong in Harlem, burning it's coal oven and sometimes its pizza.

WASHINGTON HEIGHTS

The diverse Washington Heights offers a plethora of food choices from trucks to charming restaurants, perfect for the late-night crowd. The Tony award-winning musical *In The Heights* pays loving tribute to the ebullient Washington Heights neighborhood where Dominican and Puerto Rican communities have taken root. Latin beats blast through the air; and bright, refreshing Puerto Rican piragua carts can be found on almost every corner selling shaved ice soaked in a rainbow of tropical flavors. Try *jugos naturales*—juices made from cane sugar and fresh fruits like pineapple and orange—for a healthy treat.

Great fish markets and butcher shops dot the streets, and less than ten bucks will get you a delicious plate of *pernil* with rice and beans at any number of eateries. Duck into **La Rosa Fine Foods**, a wonderful Latin gourmet market, for fresh fish, meat, and produce; or **Nelly's Bakery** for a creamy cup of *café con leche* and a *guayaba con queso* (guava and cheese pastry). **Piper's Kilt**, a standing relic in Inwood, represents the former Irish and German population of the area. Settle into a booth at the lively "**Kilt**" with some Irish nachos and a perfect pint.

Chez Lucienne

B4

French

308 Lenox Ave. (bet. 125th & 126th Sts.)

Subway: 125 St (Lenox Ave.)
Phone: 212-289-5555
Web: www.chezlucienne.com
Prices: $$

Lunch & dinner daily

French drifts between patrons and staff at this classic bistro in Central Harlem, overlooking historic Lenox Ave. Turquoise banquettes and brick walls line the narrow space, where servers don the Parisian bistro uniform (black bowties, white aprons) and present tasty French fare from the semi-open kitchen.

The affordable menu focuses on the homey simplicity inherent to great food, made even more reasonable with daily pricing specials—a rustic *pâté de maison* splashed with "chutney" is one among the faves. The talented founders, Jerome Bougherdani and Chef Matthew Tivy (both of Daniel), chose this unlikely area (now teeming with hot spots) and are successfully drawing foodies from across the borough.

Live jazz on weekends celebrates the historic environs.

Community Food & Juice

A4

American

2893 Broadway (bet. 112th & 113th Sts.)

Subway: Cathedral Pkwy/110 St (Broadway)
Phone: 212-665-2800
Web: www.communityrestaurant.com
Prices: $$

Lunch & dinner daily

Community Food & Juice might be the most exciting place to arrive in this pocket of Morningside Heights yet. Not just because the highly sustainable, locally-sourced food is spectacular, or because the owners arrive via the lauded Clinton Street Baking Company—but because the homey vibe makes you want to come back every night of the week. Unfortunately, so does the rest of the neighborhood—and most nights, you'll find a healthy wait for a table (they don't take reservations). Your reward for all that patience? A piping hot, homespun matzo ball chicken soup dancing with tender carrots, celery, and fragrant herbs; a pan-seared Vietnamese chicken sandwich done *bahn mi*-style; or rich butterscotch pudding sporting a smooth dollop of whipped cream.

Dinosaur Bar-B-Que

A3

Barbecue ✗

700 W. 125th St. (at Twelfth Ave.)

Subway: 125 St (Broadway)
Phone: 212-694-1777
Web: www.dinosaurbarbque.com
Prices: $$

Lunch & dinner daily

They've finally moved! This Harlem institution, steps below the imposing Riverside Drive, may now be larger but it is no less loud. Still, their barbecue is as good as its rocking reputation and the welcoming staff is perfectly equipped to manage the scores of rib lovers waiting for tables. The décor feels timeless—complete with a line of Harleys parked outside.

Dinosaur's undiminished popularity is thanks to the menu of rich, lip-smacking specialties piled high with a range of Southern flavors, from sweet and smoky to tangy and sultry. Whether going for a full rack of dry-rubbed ribs glazed with their propriety sauce; Creole-spiced deviled eggs flecked with sour cornichons; or a Big Ass pork shoulder, all is quenched with a bevy of frosty beers.

El Paso Taqueria

C5

Mexican ✗

237 E. 116th St. (bet. Second & Third Aves.)

Subway: 116 St (Lexington Ave.)
Phone: 212-860-4875
Web: www.elpasotaqueria.com
Prices: 🐷🐷

Lunch & dinner daily

Sweet tacos! After a long-standing Mexican food drought, New York City is finally (happily) awash in the stuff. And does it come as any surprise that one of the more notable places in town is located deep in the heart of Spanish Harlem?

Housed along demographically diverse 116th Street, El Paso Taqueria has a nice lineup of Poblano standards (the dedicated owner, who is often on-site, is from Puebla), with a menu that might feature *tamales oaxaqueños*, a plate of warm fluffy corn tamales filled with sweet chicken, wrapped around tender corn masa, and topped with *salsa de chile pasilla* and soft cheese; or melt-in-your-mouth New Zealand lamb cooked in a maguey leaf and served simmering in a brick-red chile sauce. Save room for the killer sangrias.

5 & Diamond

Contemporary ✗

A5

2072 Frederick Douglass Blvd. (bet. 112th & 113th Sts.)

Subway: Cathedral Pkwy/110 St (Central Park West)   Lunch & dinner daily
Phone: 646-684-4662
Web: www.5anddiamondrestaurant.com
Prices: $$

This is no dime a dozen place. Located in a former hardware shop, David Martinez has taken the helm and nails it with his Mediterrean-meets-Manhattan cuisine. It's tiny in here so expect to hear neighbors' happy squeals, but who wants to talk anyway when you can fill your mouth with seared scallops with Fuji apple and date purée; or house-made linguini topped with Swiss chard, coco beans, and cockle clams with citrus-butter sauce. Chatham cod wrapped in thin, buttery phyllo is delicate, glistening, and crisp; while the sweet and maple-y pecan tart is a nod to the area's Southern roots.

The place buzzes, due in large part to its servers who bustle to and fro, but snag a seat at the bar to catch the game or spark up a conversation and you're money.

Garden Café

Contemporary ✗

B1

4961 Broadway (bet. 207 & Isham Sts.)

Subway: Inwood - 207 St   Lunch & dinner daily
Phone: 212-544-9480
Web: www.gardencafenyc.com
Prices: $$

A chocolate brown awning dips over this sweet Inwood favorite, where a charming vibe and broad, contemporary menu that leans heavily on Latin American staples keep locals cheery. Inside, bare bistro tables and leather banquettes sit against golden-hued walls, while sultry jazz soothes the air.

Sit in the quaint outdoor garden and savor the special sangria and dark-grain breadbasket with tasty olive tapenade, but beware that dishes here are deliciously oversized. Peruse the daily specials or simply start with the likes of flavorful corn tortilla soup before delving into the perfectly charred stuffed poblano—bursting with tender shrimp simmered in peppers and chorizo, served with Spanish rice, black beans, *pico de gallo*, and fresh corn tortillas.

181

Hudson River Cafe

American ✕✕

A3

697 W. 133rd St. (at Twelfth Ave.)

Subway: 125 St (Broadway)
Phone: 212-491-9111
Web: www.hudsonrivercafe.com
Prices: $$

Lunch Sun
Dinner nightly

Though it brought high-end dining to an otherwise casual food 'hood, fun is still the main point at Hudson River Cafe—a Harlem eatery tucked beneath the unique arched steel underpass of Riverside Drive, with wickedly strong cocktails, live music pouring out of the doors on weekends, and bold Latin-American flavors.

Try the delicate empanadas to start, then move on to the delicious Harlem paella, bursting with juicy chorizo, Serrano ham, chicken, smoky duck, wild mushrooms, and truffle oil; and finish with a warm tropical carrot dessert loaded with spicy cinnamon and raisins, then topped with an excellent coconut ice cream. One note going in: lest you get too caught up in the fun and food to see your check clearly, an automatic tip is added to all bills.

Max SoHa

Italian ✕

A4

1274 Amsterdam Ave. (at 123rd St.)

Subway: 125 St (Broadway)
Phone: 212-531-2221
Web: www.maxsoha.com
Prices: $$

Lunch & dinner daily

Locals seeking an unpretentious touch of neighborhood familiarity–especially amid Columbia University's rapid expansion through Morningside Heights–need look no further than Max SoHa. The warm, rustic interior, clad in weathered woods, exposed brick, and colorful ceramics, purrs with coziness and fashions an idyllic atmosphere for comforting Italian fare.

Menu highlights include the well-made, simple, and satisfying pastas and *risotti*; while equally delicious daily specials can be found posted on two chalkboards hanging near the kitchen and bar. On a sunny day, grab a sidewalk table, order a glass from the lovely, affordable Italian wine selection, and enjoy the cacophony of intermingling languages and discourse in this area swarming with change.

Melba's

Southern ✗

A5

300 W. 114th St. (at Frederick Douglass Blvd.)

Subway: 116 St (Frederick Douglass Blvd.)
Phone: 212-864-7777
Web: www.melbasrestaurant.com
Prices: $$

Lunch Sat – Sun
Dinner nightly

This popular Morningside Heights joint stays elbow-to-elbow most nights despite small digs, loud music, and a slow-as-molasses staff. In fact, that's all part of the charm for the regulars that crowd into Melba's to listen to music, drink, and, of course, eat.

Solidly ensconced in what is recognized as Harlem's Gold Coast, Melba's custom chandeliers, plush banquettes, and exposed brick are cozy-chic incarnate. From the Southern bill of fare, go for down-home comfort, like Southern-fried chicken or eggnog waffles, while those looking to stay on the soulful lighter side stick to Melba's grilled vegetable Napoleon. No matter what, the heartbreakingly moist coconut layer cake infused with butter cream and dusted with coconut flakes is a must.

New Leaf Café

American ✗

A2

1 Margaret Corbin Dr. (in Fort Tryon Park)

Subway: 190 St
Phone: 212-568-5323
Web: www.newleafrestaurant.com
Prices: $$

Lunch & dinner Tue – Sun

Plumb in the heart of bucolic Fort Tryon Park stands the gorgeous stone edifice that houses New Leaf Café. Built in the 1930s and revitalized in 2001 by the New York Restoration Project, the cottage-like structure flaunts a vintage charm with its arched brick doorways and windows, shaded by a bevy of lush trees. The interior is as enchanting with dark woods, stone walls, and seasonal artwork outfitting the amber-lit rooms; picturesque views of the verdant surroundings add to the allure.

Fresh, carefully sourced ingredients make for a wonderful menu of seasonal dishes. Savor the fantastically flavorful free-range chicken: moist on the inside, crisp on the outside— perfect. To end, the brioche bread pudding with homemade rum raisin ice cream is a must.

Red Rooster

American ✗✗

B2

310 Lenox Ave. (bet. 125 & 126th Sts.)

Subway: 125 St (Lenox Ave.)   Lunch & dinner daily
Phone: 212-792-9001
Web: www.redroosterharlem.com
Prices: $$$

Kudos to Marcus Samuelsson, chef and Harlem resident, for opening a restaurant that's so fun and enticing it attracts a coterie of hip and savvy diners north of 96th St., adding to the already lively throng of proud Harlemites who've embraced this spot from the get-go. The room boasts a bustling bar, an open kitchen, and a plethora of original works from neighborhood artists.

The melting pot menu tickles many fancies with a satisfying show of skill, offering the likes of Helga's meatballs revved up by pickled cucumbers, lingonberries, dill, and sour cream; crispy and succulent fried yard bird smeared with white gravy and sparked by hot sauce; and slabs of crumbly corn bread teamed with salted honey butter and spicy tomato jam.

Ricardo Steakhouse

Steakhouse ✗✗

C5

2145 Second Ave. (bet. 110th & 111th Sts.)

Subway: 110 St (Lexington Ave.)   Dinner nightly
Phone: 212-289-5895
Web: www.ricardosteakhouse.com
Prices: $$

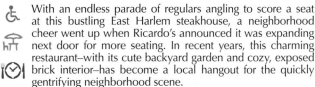

With an endless parade of regulars angling to score a seat at this bustling East Harlem steakhouse, a neighborhood cheer went up when Ricardo's announced it was expanding next door for more seating. In recent years, this charming restaurant–with its cute backyard garden and cozy, exposed brick interior–has become a local hangout for the quickly gentrifying neighborhood scene.

Kick things off with flaky empanadas or tender calamari salad, grilled *a la plancha*; and then get down to business with one of the house's spectacular cuts of beef. A T-bone special arrives perfectly charred, impressively thick and well-marbled, laced in a green peppercorn sauce and paired with mashed potatoes, French string beans, and a buttery handful of sautéed shrimp.

Vareli

A4

Mediterranean 🍴🍴

2869 Broadway (bet. 111th & 112th Sts.)

Subway: Cathedral Pkwy/110 St (Broadway)   Lunch & dinner daily
Phone: 212-678-8585
Web: www.varelinyc.com
Prices: $$

Stuffed into the foodie wasteland that surrounds Columbia University, one step into this gorgeous little restaurant and you know you're onto something good. With its barrel-shaped ceilings, polished copper bar, and lovely upstairs dining room replete with Japanese rock water wall, this Morningside looker is young—but exceptionally clever.

Owner George Zoitas ushers in superb ingredients from his nearby market—then lets Israeli chef, Amitzur Mor (who worked at Bouley), spin them into lip-smacking Mediterranean fare like tender grilled octopus, laced with *labneh* yogurt and tossed with chickpeas, Moroccan olives, and serrano peppers; or a juicy, sumac-rubbed pork chop paired with grilled Swiss chard, roasted artichokes, and preserved lemon.

Zoma 🐾

A5

Ethiopian 🍴

2084 Frederick Douglass Blvd. (at 113th St.)

Subway: 116th (Frederick Douglass Blvd.)   Dinner nightly
Phone: 212-662-0620
Web: www.zomanyc.com
Prices: 🐚🐚

Ethiopian date night? If you're headed uptown to Harlem, look no further. Nestled among the new landscape of beer gardens and coffeehouses that flank this quickly-morphing area of Morningside Heights, sophisticated Zoma feels smart, cool, and modern—with a spare white interior lined in beautiful exotic relics and intricately woven fabrics.

The menu hits a similarly understated but classy note, with ample yet reasonably priced portions of authentic dishes like *timatim fitfit*, a refreshing starter of *injera* and tomato salad tossed with sweet onions, cilantro, and jalapeño peppers, dressed in a lemony olive oil; or *awaze tibs*, a slowly simmered lamb dish laced with onions, spicy green peppers, and the fragrant hint of cardamom and coriander.

Lower East Side

Clockwise from the north, this neighborhood is bounded by Houston Street, the East River, Pike Street, and the Bowery. While it has proudly retained the personality of its first wave of hard-working settlers, the area has embraced a steady change to its landscape brought on by artsy entrepreneurs lured to these formerly overlooked parts. A mostly low-lying neighborhood, with the exception of a few high-rise apartments and towering reminders of a recent real estate boom, the Lower East Side feels village-like in its stature with a palpable creative spirit.

Eastern European Eats

Before checking out the scene as it looks today, visit the Lower East Side Tenement Museum for a glimpse of the past. This restored structure dates back to 1863 and depicts what life was like for the swells of immigrant families, primarily Eastern European Jews that settled here in the early part of the last century fleeing famine and war, making this neighborhood the most densely populated area in the country. For a taste of yore, head to **Russ & Daughters** on Houston Street. Opened in 1914, this beloved institution is a nosher's dream, and is famed for its holiday specialties, selection of smoked fish, and all things delicious, otherwise known as "appetizing."

ORCHARD STREET

Orchard Street, long the retail heart of this nabe was once dominated by the garment trade with stores selling fabrics and notions. Tailors remain in the area, offering inexpensive while-you-wait service, but boutiques selling handmade jewelry, designer skateboards, and handcrafted denim have also moved in. Shoppers looking to cool their heels should drop by **Il Laboratorio del Gelato** for an indulgent scoop—their gleaming new location tempts Houston Street passersby with a seasonally-changing roster of gelati.

For purchases with a more daily purpose, the **Essex Street Market** houses numerous purveyors of fresh produce, meat, and fish under one roof. The market is truly a gourmet's delight—it features two cheesemongers, a coffee roaster, a chocolatier, and **Shopsin's General Store**, a crazy joint notorious for its encyclopedic menu and cranky owner. By the 1950s, the melting pot that defined the LES became even more diverse with a new tide of immigrants, this time from Puerto Rico and other parts of Latin America.

This population continues to be the dominant force today. For a sampling of home-style Latino fare (like mofongo and pernil), try **El Castillo de Jagua** on the corner of Essex and Rivington streets.

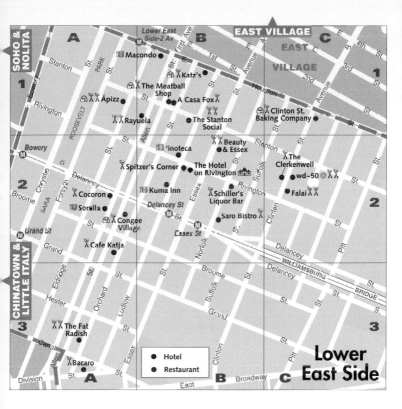

RIVINGTON STREET

Rivington Street embodies this area's hybrid of old and new. Located here is **Streit's Matzo Factory**, in operation since 1925, and **Economy Candy**, an emporium for old-fashioned sweets since 1937. During the day, the mood is pretty chill, perfect for idling in any one of the nearby coffee shops.

For a nutritious pick-me-up, **Teany** specializes in vegan vittles served in a café setting. Read: a plethora of teas and a super special brunch on weekends. Come evening, the street fills with meandering groups strolling to and from a number of popular dining

spots. South of Delancey Street, Grand Street is home to well-maintained residential complexes and shops that cater to a cadre of longtime residents.

Carb-addicts should be afraid, very afraid, as this street is home to **Kossar's Bialys**, several kosher bakeries, and **Doughnut Plant**, where the owner offers an updated take on his grandfather's doughnut recipe in flavors like Valrhona chocolate. For that quintessential deli accent at home, head to **Pickle Guys** on the corner of Essex Street, stocked with barrel upon barrel of...you guessed it... pickles.

A Casa Fox

B1

173 Orchard St. (bet. Houston & Stanton Sts.)

Subway:	Lower East Side - 2 Av	Lunch Wed – Sat
Phone:	212-253-1900	Dinner Tue – Sat
Web:	www.acasafox.com	
Prices:	**$$**	

Chef/owner Melissa Fox dishes out savory home-style Latin American cuisine in an attractively rustic setting replete with an open kitchen, gracious service team, variously sized wooden tables topped with bottles of homemade *picante* sauce, exposed brick, and plaster-coated walls. Family keepsakes offer a heartwarming glow by the working fireplace.

The menu reflects inspiration from the chef's Nicaraguan mother and offers an array of small plates such as tender-crusted empanadas, perhaps filled with smoked Gouda and finely diced portobello mushroom. A portion of the menu is devoted to slowly simmered stews presented in a terra-cotta bowl like the *arroz con pollo*—fluffy tomato-stained rice studded with white meat, green olives, and sweet peas.

Ápizz 😋

A1

217 Eldridge St. (bet. Rivington & Stanton Sts.)

Subway:	Lower East Side - 2 Av	Dinner Tue – Sun
Phone:	212-253-9199	
Web:	www.apizz.com	
Prices:	**$$**	

It's hard not to fall in love with Ápizz. The room–dressed with honey-toned wood furnishings, amber glass votive holders, and slender mirror panels–has a bewitching rosy glow fueled by the star of the restaurant's open kitchen, a wood-fired brick oven. The motto here is "one room, one oven," and this area prettied by polished copper pots, dried flowers, and platters of produce is the command post for the preparations that follow on the menu.

The flame-kissed specialties bear a sophisticated rusticity as in a vibrant pile-up of warm octopus, diced potato, and cherry tomatoes; the L.E.S. pizza topped with chorizo; and *fazzoletti e granchio*—fresh handkerchief pasta with spicy tomato sauce and sweet nuggets of excellent quality lump crabmeat.

Bacaro

Italian ✗

A3

136 Division St. (bet. Ludlow & Orchard Sts.)

Subway: East Broadway   Dinner Tue – Sun
Phone: 212-941-5060
Web: www.bacaronyc.com
Prices: $$

From the owners of Peasant comes Bacaro, which takes its name and inspiration from the pub-like wine bars of Venice, and has a warm, inviting glow that sets it apart from its edgier surroundings. The sexy subterranean dining room (a former gambling parlor) evokes an ancient cellar with brick archways, weathered plaster, salvaged ceiling beams, and candlelit alcoves, which are perfect for groups. The marble-topped bar, illuminated by a blown glass chandelier, is a lovely spot to enjoy a *crostini di giorno*, or explore the all-Italian wine list.

The menu highlights Venetian traditions in offerings like tender octopus and cubed potato dressed with olive oil and parsley, or hearty dishes of creamy lasagna Treviso with smoked mozzarella and radicchio.

Beauty & Essex

Contemporary ✗✗

B2

146 Essex St. (bet. Rivington & Stanton Sts.)

Subway: Delancey St   Dinner nightly
Phone: 212-614-0146
Web: www.beautyandessex.com
Prices: $$

Chef/partner Chris Santos (also of The Stanton Social) shows off his prowess at creating utterly intriguing small plates at this chic new multi-room bôite. The tempting roster offers ginger-glazed General Tso's monkfish garnished with broccoli and rice croquettes; sashimi of tuna, tonnato-style; and braised short rib tamales. The extensive menu is also hearty as in dishes like *garganelli* with spicy veal ragù baked in an earthenware crock.

A vestibule fashioned as a pawn shop fronts the dazzling setting which is outfitted in an earthy palette contrasted with metallic touches; upstairs there's a bar arranged against a backdrop of crystal decanters, and a small dining room featuring a collection of vintage lockets hung on the walls.

Cafe Katja

Austrian ✕

A2

79 Orchard St. (bet. Broome & Grand Sts.)

Subway: Delancey St
Phone: 212-219-9545
Web: www.cafe-katja.com
Prices: $$

Dinner nightly

Cozy in scale yet big in spirit, Cafe Katja turns out an impressive rendition of genuine old-world specialties focusing on the owner's native Austria. The candlelit brick and tan room casts a welcoming glow and is intimately furnished with a mere row of tables supplemented by a bar set adjacent to the tiny back kitchen.

The crock of homemade liverwurst, dense and silky, is accompanied by an array of house-pickled vegetables and thick slices of whole grain bread, making a fine bar meal, especially when washed down by a well-chosen selection of beers and Austrian wines. Heartier plates feature the likes of homemade Emmentaler sausage—coarse ground, filled with hollows of melted cheese, and accompanied by ethereal quark cheese dumplings.

The Clerkenwell

Gastropub ✕

C2

49 Clinton St. (bet. Rivington & Stanton Sts.)

Subway: Delancey St
Phone: 212-614-3234
Web: www.clerkenwellnyc.com
Prices: $$

Lunch Sat – Sun
Dinner Tue – Sun

The Clerkenwell brings the pub-inspired world of beef pie and mushy peas to Clinton Street's already diverse diningscape. Emanating a warm and comfortable vibe to complement its cuisine, the pint-sized space features button-tufted banquettes, a visible kitchen in back that provides diners with a bit of a show, and a comfortable, graciously-tended bar. A wine list is offered but a crisp, cold lager on tap is a much more appropriate way to wash down the contemporary pub grub. Offerings include the likes of a pea and leek tart with poached egg; slow-roasted pork belly with parsnip purée; or plump sausages cradled in Yorkshire pudding and topped with red onion marmalade.

The scattering of tables set out front make a great spot to people watch.

Clinton St. Baking Company 😊

C1

4 Clinton St. (bet. Houston & Stanton St.)

Subway: Lower East Side - 2 Av
Phone: 646-602-6263
Web: www.clintonstreetbaking.com
Prices: 💰💰

Lunch daily
Dinner Mon — Sat

Stop by this L.E.S. institution on just about any afternoon and chances are pretty good that you'll be greeted by a crowd waiting patiently for a table and their turn to partake in a menu of brunch-y delights, offered until 4:00 P.M. daily (6:00 P.M. on Sundays). Revered for his skill with carbohydrates, Chef Neil Kleinberg crafts buttermilk biscuits, brioche French toast, *huevos rancheros*, and an assortment of pancakes (think wild Maine blueberry or chocolate chunk) that are, in a word, awesome.

Simple wood furnishings and two small dining counters outfit the room, and the service is as gracious as one would hope. Dinnertime brings a quieter scene and comfort food favorites like fish tacos; spicy shrimp and grits; or buttermilk fried chicken.

Cocoron

A2

61 Delancey St. (bet. Allen & Eldridge Sts.)

Subway: Delancey St
Phone: 212-925-5220
Web: N/A
Prices: 💰💰

Lunch & dinner Tue — Sun

Heartwarming soba is the specialty at this new stall-sized spot. The room offers a handful of tables and is dominated by a hefty counter facing the busy little kitchen. Service is all smiles, and those needing assistance in making their selections are in good hands.

Eight varieties of soba are offered. Besides being delicious, each one claims to have special restorative powers like the stamina soba—a pot of meaty rich broth boasting a sweet and salty essence and stocked with exceptional pork (ground and sliced), *tsukune*, burdock root, and shiitake, accompanied by buckwheat noodles for ample slurping. Side dishes are very fresh and include snacks such as kimchi, miso coleslaw, potato salad, and *okara*—the pulp leftover from soy milk production.

Congee Village ☺

A2

100 Allen St. (at Delancey St.)

Subway: Delancey St   Lunch & dinner daily
Phone: 212-941-1818
Web: www.congeevillagerestaurants.com
Prices: ⊛⊛

Porridge for dinner may not tempt at first, but with 30 varieties of *congee* (also known as *jook*), this attractive spot specializing in Cantonese cuisine stays busy winning over even the most wary. Their soothing specialty, popular throughout China, is served bubbling hot in an earthenware pot, ready to be seasoned with an assortment of tableside condiments. Besides the namesake signature, sample the likes of dim sum; braised abalone with oyster sauce; or Manila clams in black bean sauce. House special plates are reserved for the adventurous.

Located on the fringe of Chinatown, the well-maintained, multilevel space covered in bamboo and stone has a warm ambience. Large tables, a buzzing bar, and private rooms fill it with the revelry of a town square.

Falai

C2

68 Clinton St. (bet. Rivington & Stanton Sts.)

Subway: Lower East Side - 2 Av   Dinner Tue – Sat
Phone: 212-253-1960
Web: www.falainyc.com
Prices: $$

Falai triumphs in standing above Clinton Street's myriad eating and drinking options. The white-on-white dining room is a sexy, polished sliver of flattering lighting, gleaming marble, and close-knit tables hugging an open kitchen. Chef/owner Iacopo Falai began his career as a pastry chef and now attends to his growing empire of Italian eateries.

Dinner at Falai is sure to enchant, but here's a bit of advice—order a pasta. The list changes often and creations include *pappardelle alle mandorle*, pocked with ricotta, dressed with brown butter and summer truffle, and slathered with carrot sauce. Moving on, there's crisp-skinned branzino paired with fregola and sweet/sour eggplant; and desserts reveal a boozy *baba au rhum* with lemon chantilly to finish.

The Fat Radish

Contemporary XX

A3

17 Orchard St. (bet. Canal & Hester Sts.)

Subway: East Broadway
Phone: 212-300-4053
Web: www.thefatradishnyc.com
Prices: $$

Lunch Sat – Sun
Dinner nightly

When this former sausage factory was transformed into a handsome boîte brimming with a chic coterie, The Fat Radish became a classic Lower East Side success story. Bedecked with a poured concrete bar, exposed brick walls, and touches of salvaged wood, the space is embellished with fresh flowers, warm candlelight, and colorful art softening the room's industrial carriage.

The free-spirited kitchen tickles the palate with a gift of radishes dressed with olive tapenade. The eclectic carte presents an intriguing array that may include handmade tagliatelle tossed with chunky puréed broccoli rabe, sundried tomato, and anchovy breadcrumbs; or tart and fragrant monkfish *vindaloo* over a toothsome mound of wild rice accompanied by *raita* and long bean chutney.

'inoteca

Italian ▤

B2

98 Rivington St. (at Ludlow St.)

Subway: Delancey St
Phone: 212-614-0473
Web: www.inotecanyc.com
Prices: ☺☺

Lunch & dinner daily

This charmingly rustic wine bar, with its knobby wood furnishings and wraparound sidewalk seating, has been a foodie favorite since 2003, and is perhaps the definitive dining destination of the Lower East Side, thanks to owners Jason and Joe Denton. Open all day long, 'inoteca continuously tempts with Chef Eric Kleinman's menu of lovingly simple yet sophisticated Italian fare in an ambience that beckons guests to stop by anytime.

The offerings may include a quick lunchtime salad of grilled mushrooms with *Piave vecchio*; an after-work respite in a glass of chilled lambrusco and a few slices of *coppa*; or a dinnertime sampling of small plates. Yet the heart of the menu is a listing of panini, like heritage beef *bollito* with watercress and horseradish.

Katz's 🍝

Deli ✗

B1

205 E. Houston St. (at Ludlow St.)

Subway: Lower East Side - 2 Av
Phone: 212-254-2246
Web: www.katzdeli.com
Prices: 🍝🍝

Lunch & dinner daily

One of the last-standing, old-time Eastern European spots on the Lower East Side, Katz's is a true NY institution. It's crowded, crazy, and packed with a panoply of characters weirder than a jury duty pool. Tourists, hipsters, blue hairs, and everybody in between flock here, so come on off-hours. Because it's really *that* good.

Walk inside, get a ticket, and don't lose it (those guys at the front aren't hosts—upset their system and you'll get a verbal beating). Then get your food at the counter and bring it to a first-come first-get table; or opt for a slightly less dizzying experience at a waitress-served table.

Nothing's changed in the looks or the taste. Matzoh ball soup, pastrami sandwich, potato latkes—everything is what you'd expect, only better.

Kuma Inn

Asian

B2

113 Ludlow St. (bet. Delancey & Rivington Sts.)

Subway: Delancey St
Phone: 212-353-8866
Web: www.kumainn.com
Prices: 🍝🍝

Dinner nightly

Pan-Asian tapas are the theme at this second floor dining room not much bigger than some of the chic boutiques found in this exciting neighborhood. A veteran of Daniel and Jean Georges, New York City-born Chef/owner King Phojanakong offers well prepared, flavor-packed fare that reflects the multicultural influences of his Thai-Filipino background. The menu is best suited for grazing so bring reinforcements to ensure you hit all the chef's specialties that include sautéed Chinese sausage with Thai chili-lime sauce; sake-braised beef with Asian root vegetables; and *arroz Valenciana* with chicken, seafood, and sausage.

Genteel service and a background soundtrack of the chef's favorite tracks add to the ambience of the minimally decorated room.

Macondo

B1

Latin American

157 E. Houston St. (bet. Allen & Eldridge Sts.)

Subway: Lower East Side - 2 Av
Phone: 212-473-9900
Web: www.macondonyc.com
Prices: $$

Lunch Sat – Sun
Dinner nightly

The vibe at this fun spot from the owners of Rayuela matches that of its high-traffic location. Weather permitting, the front bar opens onto the street and is abuzz with thirty-somethings sipping refreshing, fruit-forward cocktails. Inside, the long, narrow space is accented by shelves of Latin provisions, an open kitchen, rows of communal tables, and low, lounge-like booths towards the back.

Crowds come here to linger (until 3:00 A.M. on weekends) over the pan-Latin array of small plates exploring Venezuela, Brazil, Mexico, and beyond. Perfect for a group, the menu is divided into a large selection of shareable snacks, such as *cocas* (flatbreads) topped with tuna escabeche and goat cheese. Their toasty, warm *bocadillos* are especially popular.

The Meatball Shop 😊

B1

Italian

84 Stanton St. (bet. Allen & Orchard Sts.)

Subway: Lower East Side - 2 Av
Phone: 212-982-8895
Web: www.themeatballshop.com
Prices: 😊😊

Lunch & dinner daily

Be prepared to enjoy more than just meatballs here. Of course they *are* the focal point of the tempting menu—whether served as a hero, sliders, or "naked" in a bowl—and are available in a number of variations such as classic beef, spicy pork, and a daily offering. The thrilling and tasty sides include fresh (creamy) polenta and collards with garlic confit to complete your meal. The compact room is a perfect fit for its cool and comfortable locale and is equipped with a communal dining table, dining counter outfitted with swivel stools, and brick-red painted walls hung with old photos. Diners get to watch the steady stream of action in the open kitchen.

The success has spilled over to Brooklyn with the opening of an outpost in Williamsburg.

Rayuela

Latin American ✕✕

165 Allen St. (bet. Rivington & Stanton Sts.)

Subway: Lower East Side - 2 Av
Phone: 212-253-8840
Web: www.rayuelanyc.com
Prices: $$

Lunch Sat – Sun
Dinner nightly

This sleek Lower East Side gem helped kick off the neighborhood's wave of Pan-Latin fusion spots—and locals quickly embraced its hip vibe and deeply flavorful food. Years later, the loyalty remains: despite more and more competition, Rayuela continues to pack them in.

What's the secret? For starters, dark wood, sexy lighting, and great music make this a comfortable setting for an important date or night out with friends. Moreover, the food continues to be solid: Try the red snapper, marinated in a ginger-soy-citrus sauce with a flurry of bright julienned peppers, cucumbers, and red chili peppers; the gorgeous seafood paella humming with lemongrass, coconut milk, and ginger; or mouthwatering corn arepas with *cabra* cheese and sweet agave nectar.

Saro Bistro

Eastern European ✕

102 Norfolk St. (bet. Delancey & Rivington Sts.)

Subway: Delancey St
Phone: 212-505-7276
Web: www.sarobistro.com
Prices: $$

Lunch Sat – Sun
Dinner Tue – Sun

Inspired by the cooking of his Yugoslavian grandmother, Israeli-born Chef/owner Eran Elhalal serves cuisine that tours the Balkans from his quaint bistro. The petite 22-seat room is comfortable and pleasantly arranged with papered walls, wood furnishings, and dried flower arrangements. Tables are set with vintage flatware, mismatched floral-rimmed china, and a glass filled with slender green chilies to spice up your meal.

The menu offers a rich trip through this unique and eclectic region with specialties that include a daily offering of savory pie accompanied by kefir; grilled *cevapcici* kebabs served with zucchini fritters and a quenelle of fresh cheese; homemade linguini with clams; and slow-roasted lamb shoulder with braised cabbage.

Schiller's Liquor Bar

B2

European ✗

131 Rivington St. (at Norfolk St.)

Subway: Delancey St   Lunch & dinner daily
Phone: 212-260-4555
Web: www.schillersny.com
Prices: $$

Schiller's, like Keith McNally's wildly successful Balthazar and Pastis, touts a magical mix—like the most popular girl in high school, it has just the right combination to pop in a crowd. However, its components are breezy retro-bistro good looks, solid (if not inventive) brasserie fare, and a prime location straddling a sunny corner of the Lower East Side. The straightforward menu may not require much contemplation, but be sure to remember a side of their perfect frites.

As to how best to describe the atmosphere that draws locals, day trippers, and low-key celebrities alike, we direct you to the cheeky house wine list, categorized into *cheap*, *decent*, or *good*. A terrific cocktail selection rounds out the drink list, including a spot-on Pimm's Cup.

Sorella

A2

Italian 🍴

95 Allen St. (bet. Broome & Delancey Sts.)

Subway: Delancey St   Dinner Tue – Sun
Phone: 212-274-9595
Web: www.sorellanyc.com
Prices: $$

For a leisurely yet serious offering of small plates, step inside Sorella's narrow, whitewashed brick dining area and glass-enclosed atrium. The Northern Italian menu is broken down to offer a selection of cheeses, meats, and *qualcosina*, which translates as "a little something." This selection of finely tuned dishes may include the likes of gnocchi with Castelrosso cream sauce and brown butter-slicked pears; and crispy veal sweetbreads with quince bacon marmalade—both delicious and impressive.

Complement a meal here with a tempting selection from their expansive list of wines by the glass; Sorella's features twenty-five choices, each priced under $15.

Next door, Stellina is a sweet spot for gelato, snacks, and pink boxes of handmade *grissini*.

Spitzer's Corner

B2

101 Rivington St. (at Ludlow St.)

Subway: Delancey St
Phone: 212-228-0027
Web: www.spitzerscorner.com
Prices: ⊛

Lunch & dinner daily

This modern New York gastropub strives to highlight its honest, local sensibilities; but most importantly, this spot perfectly complements the casual cool of a weekend night on the Lower East. With old pickle-barrel slats for walls and a zinc bar, the multi-room space is effortlessly stylish and comfortable, much to the pleasure of the trendy crowds who pile in, despite the no-reservations policy. Happily, they chill at the bar or settle into a long, sleek bench while nursing a selection from the 40 smartly chosen beers on tap, or the small but studied by-the-glass wine list.

The menu offers a host of salads and sandwiches, but those looking for a proper meal can go with plates of hand-cut French fries, truffled mac' and cheese, and Kobe sliders.

The Stanton Social

B1

99 Stanton St. (bet. Ludlow & Orchard Sts.)

Subway: Lower East Side - 2 Av
Phone: 212-995-0099
Web: www.thestantonsocial.com
Prices: $$

Lunch Sat – Sun
Dinner nightly

A beloved haunt in the LES, The Stanton Social has a richly tailored design that pays homage to the haberdashers and seamstress shops that once dotted this trendy nabe. Vintage hand mirrors, woven leather straps, and wine shelves laid out in a herringbone pattern outfit the low-lit, dark-wood furnished cave.

Opened in 2005, this grand boîte is still going strong; a testament to the enjoyable cuisine on offer. The generous order of globally-inspired preparations, executed under the watch of Chef/partner Chris Santos, brings on cooking with gusto and includes sliders, a house signature; hand-pulled chicken arepas kicked with tomatillo sauce and pickled jalapeños; and rounds of crispy eggplant Parmesan finished with mozzarella, micro basil, and basil oil.

wd~50 ✿

Robert Polidori

Contemporary 🍴🍴

C2

50 Clinton St. (bet. Rivington & Stanton Sts.)

Subway: Delancey St
Phone: 212-477-2900
Web: www.wd-50.com
Prices: $$$

Dinner Wed – Sun

♿

Wd~50's wooden façade is as imposing as it should be, set among the bodegas and boutiques of Clinton Street. Geometric angles and primary colors compose the casually elegant interior space, as if pointing everyone's attention to the open kitchen located along the back wall. The clientele is sophisticated and intent on contemplating Chef Wylie Dufresne's extraordinarily creative menu that reinterprets classics with fine-dining modernity. The informative staff will be happy to elaborate.

Visually, dishes are unexpected. A cold fried-chicken appetizer may be a single block of pressed white and dark meat that has been fried, sliced, chilled, and topped with dollops of house-made ricotta and glistening caviar. Yet taste is never forgotten, as the plate is completed with chicken skin cracklins and Tabasco gelée. A sense of surprise continues with an impossibly thick lamb skirt steak, subtle in flavor and cooked sous-vide to a perfect medium-rare, with crunchy pistachio polenta and savory apricot purée.

Consistency carries through to dessert, with options such as spice cake that has the coconut-crunchy exterior of a donut, spiced with *ras el hanout*, and filled with sweetened coconut cream.

Midtown East & Murray Hill

Started by the Vanderbilts in the 19th century, then saved from the wrecking ball with the help of Jacqueline Kennedy Onassis in the 20th century, Grand Central Terminal has somehow become a 21st century foodie haven.

Grand Central Terminal

A perfect day at the world's largest train station begins with a coffee amid the work-bound masses from **Joe's**. Lunch options range from the multi-ethnic food court offerings (**Café Spice** for Indian, **Mendy's** for kosher, **Zocalo** for Mexican), to the prized concourse restaurants situated beneath the celestial ceiling murals. Nonetheless, one of Manhattan's most beloved icons, the **Oyster Bar**, has been tucked into the cavernous lower level since 1913. Be sure to first visit the "whispering gallery" located near its entrance, where low, ceramic arches allow whispers to sound like shouts.

Come happy hour, Grand Central continues to inspire with **Campbell Apartment**—for those who meet the dress code. This 1920s office of railroad mogul John W. Campbell was restored and re-opened as one of the area's swankier stops for a famously dry martini. Those seeking a quiet night of home cooking can simply walk across the concourse to visit the market, for a stunning array of gourmet items. Fishmongers, produce stands, butchers, bakeries, and possibly the best spices in the city are all found here.

Grand Central is a perfect microcosm of its eastern midtown home, because stretching through this neighborhood is the same diversity of shopping and dining. Residents of Beekman and Sutton boast their very own top fishmonger (**Piscayne**), cheese shop (**Ideal Cheese**), butcher (**L. Simchik**), bagel and lox shop (**Tal**), and to complete any dinner party, florist (**Zeze**). One of the area's better-kept secrets is **Dessert Delivery**, specializing in delivering expertly baked treats. Luckily, it is free from the ongoing cupcake war between **Buttercup** and **Bruce's**, with **Magnolia** and **Crumbs**' arrival and following. Also find some of the best chocolate in town, from **Richart** to **Teuscher** and **Pierre Marcolini**. While **Dag Hammarskjold Greenmarket** may by dwarfed by Union Square, it has just the right amount of everything to satisfy its neighbors.

Japantown

Within these distinctly commuter, residential, and internationally-focused midtown nooks, is a very sophisticated Japantown, with casual *izakayas* and secreted-away hostess clubs lining the area east of Lexington. For a light lunch or snack, sample *onigiri* at **Oms/b**, or try the modern takeout yakitori, **Kushi-Q**. True Japanophiles *should* stop by **Cafe Zaiya**

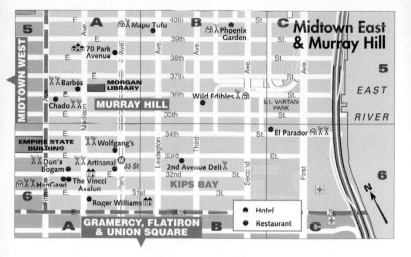

for their mouthwatering array of udon dishes (maybe the *kitsune?*); or the reputed **Japanese Culinary Center** filled with gorgeous Japanese tabletop items like glassware, shiny knives, ceramics, as well as kitchenware, unique ingredients, and imported delicacies. Another udon hot spot is **Onya**, showcasing a variety from *kamaage* and curry udon, to vegetable soup udon.

MURRAY HILL

Along the neighborhood's eastern border is the famous United Nations building. In the spirit of this landmark, the **Delegates Dining Room** at the UN sponsors food festivals that spotlight a different cuisine each month. Just remember to make a reservation for this buffet lunch and arrive early, allowing extra time to clear security.

Younger and quieter than its northern neighbor, Murray Hill has its own distinct restaurant vibe. Here, faster and casual

finds thrive, populated by hungry twenty-somethings seeking a slice of pizza or hearty cheesesteak. Afterwards, they move on to their favored Third Avenue watering holes to hoot and holler with college buddies over Bud Lights while catching the snowboarding championships. This is the Murray Hill of recent college grads spilling out onto sidewalks of **Bar 515** or perhaps **Third and Long**. However, this is only one Murray Hill. The other Murray Hill rises with the sun over pristine brownstones and apartment towers, awakening young families who gather amid blooming flowers at St Vartan Park or chat with neighbors over chopped liver, smoked fish, knishes, and other Jewish delicacies at **Sarge's Deli**. These are the (slightly) senior locals of Murray Hill—they love it here and will remain faithful residents until well-after the frat party has ended.

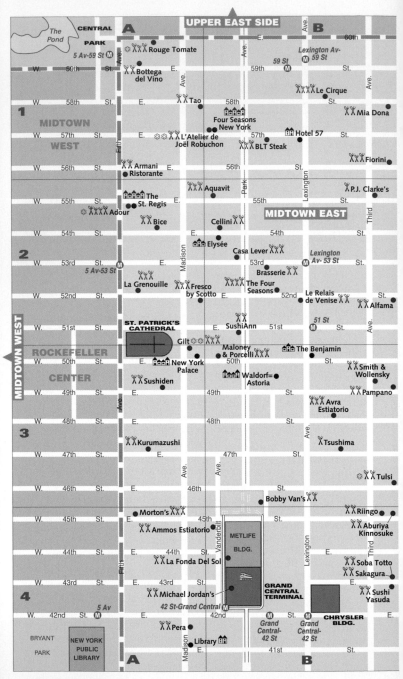

The Pond

CENTRAL PARK

5 Av-59 St Ⓜ

Rouge Tomate

Bottega del Vino

Lexington Av-59 St

59 St Ⓜ

Tao

Le Cirque

Four Seasons New York

Mia Dona

MIDTOWN WEST

L'Atelier de Joël Robuchon

Hotel 57

BLT Steak

Fiorini

Armani Ristorante

The St. Regis

Aquavit

P.J. Clarke's

MIDTOWN EAST

Adour

Bice

Cellini

Elysée

Casa Lever

La Grenouille

Fresco by Scotto

The Four Seasons

Brasserie

Lexington Av-53 St Ⓜ

Le Relais de Venise

Alfama

ST. PATRICK'S CATHEDRAL

SushiAnn

51 St Ⓜ

Gilt

Maloney & Porcelli

The Benjamin

ROCKEFELLER CENTER

New York Palace

Waldorf= Astoria

Smith & Wollensky

Sushiden

Pampano

Avra Estiatorio

Kurumazushi

Tsushima

Tulsi

Bobby Van's

Riingo

Morton's

Aburiya Kinnosuke

Ammos Estiatorio

METLIFE BLDG.

La Fonda Del Sol

Soba Totto

Sakagura

Michael Jordan's

GRAND CENTRAL TERMINAL

Sushi Yasuda

42 St-Grand Central Ⓜ

5 Av Ⓜ

CHRYSLER BLDG.

Pera

Grand Central-42 St Ⓜ

Grand Central-42 St Ⓜ

BRYANT PARK

NEW YORK PUBLIC LIBRARY

Library

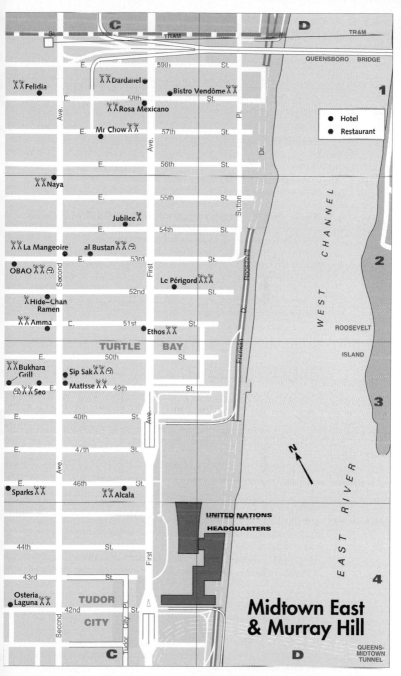

C

TRAM

D

TRAM

St.

QUEENSBORO   BRIDGE

E.

59th

St.

1

X X Felidia

X X Dardanel

58th

St.

Bistro Vendôme X X

Ave.

E.

X X Rosa Mexicana

St.

Pl.

E.

Mr Chow X X

57th

St.

Ave.

E.

56th

St.

Dr.

X X Naya

E.

55th

St.

Sutton

CHANNEL

Jubilee X

54th

St.

X X La Mangeoire

al Bustan X X ☺

53rd

St.

Roosevelt

E.

First

WEST

OBAO X X ☺

Second

Le Périgord X X X

52nd

St.

X Hide-Chan
Ramen

ROOSEVELT

X X Amma

E.

51st

St.

Ethos X X

Franklin

ISLAND

TURTLE   BAY

50th

St.

X X Bukhara
Grill

Sip Sak X X ☺

☺ X X Seo

Matisse X X

49th

St.

3

E.

48th

St.

Ave.

E.

47th

St.

N

E.

Ave.

46th

St.

Sparks X X

X X Alcala

EAST   RIVER

UNITED NATIONS

HEADQUARTERS

44th

St.

First

43rd

St.

4

Osteria
Laguna X X

TUDOR

42nd

Second

Tudor City Pl.

St.

CITY

C

D

Midtown East
& Murray Hill

QUEENS-
MIDTOWN
TUNNEL

● Hotel
● Restaurant

Aburiya Kinnosuke

B4

213 E. 45th St. (bet. Second & Third Aves.)

Subway: Grand Central - 42 St
Phone: 212-867-5454
Web: www.aburiyakinnosuke.com
Prices: $$

Lunch Mon – Fri
Dinner nightly

The route may be dark and narrow, but this particular one leads to a real and honest *izakaya* replete with crowning cocktails for you to sample the night away. Aburiya Kinnosuke has a bit of a split personality: by day, it's an upscale bento box haven filled with chirpy midtowners; come nighttime, it turns into an authentic, intimate lair. Action freaks should hit the counter, while the rest can peel off into a private nook.

Robata is the real deal here so go for the *tsukune*—deliciously grilled chicken meatloaves dunked in cold poached egg. Also excellent and incredibly popular are their daily specials, menu additions, and value set menus ("course") which require advance booking. It's all very Japanese at night, so don't flake on those reservations!

al Bustan

C2

319 E. 53rd St. (bet. First & Second Aves.)

Subway: Lexington Av - 53 St
Phone: 212-759-5933
Web: www.albustanny.com
Prices: $$

Lunch & dinner daily

With a fresh location comes a whole new outlook on food, service and ambience, and suddenly this tired Lebanese favorite–a longtime staple among the United Nations power crowds–is turning heads again.

They didn't physically move far: al Bustan now resides along a sleepy patch of 53rd Street, just a few blocks from the old digs—but the space is quite stunning, with a lofty, brick-walled space featuring enormous crystal chandeliers, white leather chairs, and handsome dark wood accents. And the food, which used to go through the motions, now seems to leap off the plate: gorgeous Lebanese meze like *fattoush*, *hommos bi lahmeh*, and *foul medamas* are not to be missed; and prix-fixe options at $45 or $50 a head offer a nice way to sample from the menu.

Adour ⅋

A2

Contemporary 𝕏𝕏𝕏𝕏

2 E. 55th St. (at Fifth Ave.)

Subway: 5 Av - 53 St

Phone: 212-710-2277

Web: www.adour-stregis.com

Prices: $$$$

Dinner Tue – Sat

Brice Buck

The St. Regis may be posh, but it instantly fades into the background once you've moved beyond its lounge and crossed the threshold into its culinary pride and joy, Adour. The main dining room stuns with its detailed moldings, delicate archways, and illuminated wine cases. Relish the view as you pass through this splendor, because unless you are a captain of industry, you will likely be relegated to a satellite room. Have no fear, as every tourist and celebrant can attest that these banquettes are just as plush and the champagne flutes just as sparkling.

Whether admiring the gorgeous space or considering Chef Didier Elena's menu, the elegance is effortless, modern, and very French. Meals here may begin with a contemporary "salade Niçoise" of sweet crab over crisp, micro-chopped vegetables, hard-boiled quail egg, and vinaigrette gelée. Perfect rectangles of rhubarb sable with rhubarb-Sauternes ice cream hint that sometimes the best is saved for last. Let the standout sommelier guide you to the right wine.

The servings here are forever "adoured," so let slide the kitchen's inconsistency for a delicious bite of their lamb loin, cooked perfectly, and paired with Parmesan-rich polenta.

Alcala

C3

Spanish ✕✕

342 E. 46th St. (bet. First & Second Aves.)

Subway: Grand Central - 42 St   Lunch Mon – Fri
Phone: 212-370-1866   Dinner nightly
Web: www.alcalarestaurant.com
Prices: $$$

You won't find a lot of the garlic-heavy Spanish staples that Americans have come to know so well at this charming little neighborhood restaurant, located across the street from the United Nations headquarters. Instead, you'll find the rustic, often simple, cuisine found throughout Northern Spain and the Basque region, with a kitchen that is not afraid to bring the pork.

Businessmen, UN tourists, and Spanish ex-pats alike pile into Alcala for its cozy-as-home vibe; pretty (enclosed) garden; and welcoming staff. Try the *espinacas*, a delicious baked casserole with spinach, pine nuts, raisins, and sheep's milk cheese; or a decadent *arroz con leche*. Finally, sample one of their tasty tapas (both hot and cold) dishes, perfectly chased by a mean house sangria.

Alfama

B2

Portuguese ✕✕

214 E. 52nd St. (bet. Second & Third Aves.)

Subway: Lexington Av - 53 St   Lunch & dinner daily
Phone: 212-759-5552
Web: www.alfamanyc.com
Prices: $$

It's been a few years since Alfama shuttered its West Village location, but thankfully Tarcisio Costa and Miguel Jerónimo found a midtown space to call their own. There's no mistaking that inimitable Portuguese flair—blue-and-white ceramic tiles and pottery add rustic touches, while the illuminated glass tile map of the world on the wall is an attractive focal point.

Choose from *petiscos*–the Portuguese version of tapas–like brandy flambéed sausage, shrimp turnovers, and rabbit meatballs. Seafood stews, and cod and shrimp gratin are heartier choices. *Galito gerlhado*, grilled chicken with *piri piri* and fried yucca, is one of many faves, but seafood is the star. Three courses for under $30 at lunch, makes Alfama popular with midtowners.

Amma

C2

Indian ✕✕

246 E. 51st St. (bet. Second & Third Aves.)

Subway: 51 St
Phone: 212-644-8330
Web: www.ammanyc.com
Prices: $$

Lunch & dinner daily

Make your way up a few stairs to enter Amma's home, an elegant parlor arranged with close-knit, white-robed tables set atop carpeted floors. This is indeed Indian food—brought to you in a colonial-style townhouse in frenzied midtown. Amma's "living room" feels bright with big windows, saffron-tinted walls, chaste artwork, and a chandelier twinkling upon an affluent set.

Brimming at lunch with delicacies like *prawn masala* steeped with coconut, Amma becomes romantic at night. In keeping with its mien, warm yet vigilant servers present you with Indian hospitality at its finest—in the form of *tandoori* sea bass with plantain dumplings; *bagharey baingan* (eggplant stuffed with a spicy peanut sauce); and *bhindi ka raita*, all soaked up by a basket of breads.

Ammos Estiatorio

B4

Greek ✕✕

52 Vanderbilt Ave. (at 45th St.)

Subway: Grand Central - 42 St
Phone: 212-922-9999
Web: www.ammosnewyork.com
Prices: $$$

Lunch & dinner Mon – Sat

Duck into sunny and sophisticated Ammos, right across from Grand Central station, and leave gray skies behind. Favoring a certain modern Mediterranean-meets-Manhattan elegance, this upscale Greek brightens the midtown lunch crowds with white market umbrellas hanging from the ceiling, warm yet efficient service, and a well-run kitchen serving time-honored favorites with contemporary flair.

The fresh and modern boosts are clear in *spanikopita*, prepared with well-flavored feta and spinach between two crisp, golden layers of phyllo, jazzed up with light tomato sauce and mint olive oil. Salads, the Ammos fries, and a three-course prix-fixe are most popular at lunch, while quieter dinners feature a large selection of entrées and fresh fish by-the-pound.

Aquavit

B2

Scandinavian ✗✗✗

65 E. 55th St. (bet. Madison & Park Aves.)

Subway: 5 Av – 53 St   Lunch & dinner daily
Phone: 212-307-7311
Web: www.aquavit.org
Prices: $$$$

If you equate Scandinavian style with IKEA, think again. There's nothing bare bones or budget about Aquavit's sensational Scandia style. Divided into three spaces with a café, lounge, and dining room (separate moods and menus), it's a jewel box of high-end design. Design divas ooh and aah over the Arne Jacobsen chairs and Quistgaard salt and pepper shakers.

An affluent crowd of Euros comes here for the grown-up sophistication and classic dining. The dining room, where three courses or a tasting menu are a must, is the most serious but certainly where the kitchen shows off. Aquavit's myriad dishes are artfully presented and highly contemporary—think "toast" painted with beef, roe, and quail egg; or hay-crusted sweetbreads set elegantly with fava beans.

Armani Ristorante

A1

Italian ✗✗

717 Fifth Ave. (at 56th St.)

Subway: 5 Av – 59 St   Lunch daily
Phone: 212-207-1902   Dinner Mon – Sat
Web: www.armani5thavenue.com
Prices: $$$

Ascend the three-story spiral staircase, past elegant floors of the eponymous clothing line, to arrive in a stunning space cloaked in dramatic, high-design spectacle. Perched above posh 5th Avenue over the Armani store, this dining room is styled with floor-to-ceiling windows bedecked in twinkling strands of fiber-optic lights, round futuristic furniture, and black ceilings and floors.

While its impressive design may align well with haute couture, the well-groomed (yet ill-informed) service staff falls short, and the food itself can be pedestrian; still, dishes do satisfy. Expect the likes of excellent quality veal filet, Parmesan-encrusted sea bass, or crispy meringue stacked with nutty praline semifreddo, topped with sticky-sweet *amarena* cherries.

Artisanal

French ✗✗

A6

2 Park Ave. (entrance on 32nd St.)

Subway: 33 St   Lunch & dinner daily
Phone: 212-725-8585
Web: www.artisanalbistro.com
Prices: $$

Terrance Brennan's much-loved restaurant serves a whole roster of bistro delights (think chicken paillard, tuna niçoise, and steamed mussels) but the real fans of Artisanal treat the place like their own private cheese club. Brennan has a passion for the stuff, and the restaurant has oodles of varieties as well as an on-site cheese cave—that you can enjoy it in a lively, upscale brasserie only makes it even more fun.

Choose a glass of wine from the extensive list, and get to work on a perfectly prepared basket of *gougères*, followed by one of the house fondues; or an irresistible *croque monsieur*, sporting tender prosciutto, soft Gruyere, and a delicious lick of browned béchamel, paired with a crunchy stack of house-made chips.

Avra Estiatorio

Greek ✗✗✗

B3

141 E. 48th St. (bet. Lexington & Third Aves.)

Subway: 51 St   Lunch & dinner daily
Phone: 212-759-8550
Web: www.avrany.com
Prices: $$$

Let's face it, Midtown, awash in gray and black, can sometimes have you singing the blues. But wait! Next time you're feeling a little low, get your dose of sunshine inside Avra. This appealing and bright space, with plenty of outdoor seating, brings the warmth of the Greek islands to the concrete jungle. This dressed-up taverna is always jammed with midtowners, business types, and tourists who come for the comfortable sophistication and the pleasing menu. Whether here for brunch, lunch, or dinner, the mostly Greek menu is large and offers everything from *saganaki* and souvlaki to fresh grilled fish (on display at the back).

The prices and the less-than-sunny staff could be seen as drawbacks, but the delicious food and pleasant setting shine through.

Barbès

Mediterranean ✕✕

21 E. 36th St. (bet. Fifth & Madison Aves.)

Subway: 33 St

Lunch & dinner daily

Phone: 212-684-0215

Web: www.barbesrestaurantnyc.com

Prices: $$

Look for the *hamsa* door knocker (a symbol of protection) and push open that heavy wooden door to an exotic world that will have you mistaking midtown for Morocco. Named for the Parisian neighborhood marked by its North African denizens, Barbès doles out a dusky sensuality with its burnt orange walls, hammered copper-topped bar, and seductive tunes.

Holy hummus, this menu has it all from spreads like *zaalouk* with roasted eggplant and tomato, to Moroccan mussels with heady garlic, tomato, and crushed pepper. Grilled meat skewers, wraps, salads, and sandwiches are on tap, while hungry honeys should go with entrées like grilled shrimp with pesto couscous and coriander-harissa sauce, or tagine of chicken with preserved lemon and green olives.

Bice

Italian ✕✕

7 E. 54th St. (bet. Fifth & Madison Aves.)

Subway: 5 Av - 53 St

Lunch & dinner daily

Phone: 212-688-1999

Web: www.bicenewyork.com

Prices: $$$

In a neighborhood teeming with subdued, upscale façades, Bice cuts a cheerful figure with its bright canopies and stream of people walking to and fro. Perhaps it can't help but give off some of that upbeat Milan bustle—the restaurant, which now boasts 40 locations world-wide, began in Italy's most fashionable city.

Judging from the longevity of this location, the formula (solid upscale Northern Italian cuisine in unique city-specific settings) works. Open for lunch and dinner, Bice stays thumping day and night with fashionable diners tucking into tender tagliolini with lobster, shiitake mushrooms, blistered tomatoes, chunky tomato sauce, and a float of basil chiffonade; or crispy *cantuccini*, laced with roasted almonds or chocolate biscotti.

Bistro Vendôme

C1

405 E. 58th St. (bet. First Ave. & Sutton Pl.)

Subway: 59 St
Phone: 212-935-9100
Web: www.bistrovendomenyc.com
Prices: $$

Lunch & dinner daily

Bistro Vendôme brings a breath of fresh air to somewhat stuffy Sutton Place, with this revived townhouse that was occupied for years by the formal and fussy March. Now bright and airy with three levels and an outdoor terrace at the top, this classic restaurant nails the European bistro in its look and feel. While neighborhood denizens (of a certain age) may crowd the place, it remains surprisingly family friendly with a children's menu.

The kitchen delivers the classics exactly as they were conceived. From the escargot bathed in a rich parsley and garlic-butter sauce, to mussels Provençale with frites, and floating islands of meringue in crème anglaise with toasted almonds and spun sugar—each dish is solid, traditional, and just as it should be.

BLT Steak

B1

106 E. 57th St. (bet. Lexington & Park Aves.)

Subway: 59 St
Phone: 212-752-7470
Web: www.bltrestaurants.com
Prices: $$$$

Lunch Mon – Fri
Dinner nightly

For an unexampled and global version of an American steakhouse, BLT Steak is your place. Leave your troubles behind when you enter this lively, perennially packed, and elegant steakhouse, which not only dishes up beautifully-executed classic cuts alongside Kobe and Wagyu, but a heady dose of daily specials, fresh fish, and exquisite side dishes as well.

Adding to the big spirit are a bunch of delicious, unfussy sides like towering (and tempting) stacks of crunchy onion rings. Clever little portions of hen of the woods mushrooms and a chopped vegetable salad will make you wonder why you need the meat at all. The grand finale, be it a flavor-packed hanger steak or the Porterhouse for two licked with a blue cheese sauce, always screams money.

Bobby Van's

B3

230 Park Ave. (at 46th St.)

Subway: Grand Central - 42 St
Phone: 212-867-5490
Web: www.bobbyvans.com
Prices: $$$$

Lunch Mon – Fri
Dinner Mon – Sat

This scene is so powerful that it intoxicates. A regular flock of bankers and brokers (entering through the passageway beneath the Helmsley Building at 46th and Park) seek this clubby and boisterous favorite for its scene, pricey wines, and those towering shellfish platters, served with flourish and perhaps a gruff edge.

After starters like the popular steakhouse wedge salad with fried onions and bacon, arrives the meaty main attraction. These steaks are cooked exactly as ordered and carved tableside, with sides like fried zucchini served family-style.

After work, the bar is adorned with addictive house-made potato chips and offers a lighter menu as it comes alive with well-shaken martinis.

Note that Bobby Van's has four other locations in Manhattan.

Bottega del Vino

A1

7 E. 59th St. (bet. Fifth & Madison Aves.)

Subway: 5 Av - 59 St
Phone: 212-223-2724
Web: www.bottegadelvinonyc.com
Prices: $$$$

Lunch & dinner daily

Owner Severino Barzan picked a prize location (just off Fifth Avenue) for this alluringly rustic wine tavern. The front half of this delicious sun-drenched space is Bar Quadronno—sister of sensational Via Quadronno and home to one of the best cappuccinos in town.

Ideal for an Italian-stlye meal, this pricey pearl is adorned with painted columns, dark-wood walls, cozy banquettes, and a stylish Euro-crowd sipping on phenomenal Italian wines (served in hand-blown, lead-free, caricature-sized glasses) and supping on traditional Northern Italian fare. Pasta dishes and house specialties best display the kitchen's talent. Elegant and delicate, homemade ravioli filled with Gorgonzola *dolce* and paired with a nutty pistachio sauce is nothing short of amazing.

Brasserie

B2

Contemporary ✗✗

100 E. 53rd St. (bet. Lexington & Park Aves.)

Subway: Lexington Av - 53 St
Phone: 212-751-4840
Web: www.rapatina.com/brasserie
Prices: $$$

Lunch & dinner daily

Whether it's Brasserie's location in the Seagrams building or the simple fact that this been a midtown fixture since 1959, everyone here seems to expect Don Draper to walk in at any moment. And what an entrance he would make, since all guests have to descend a set of stairs before snagging a seat. Mod in that "meet George Jetson" kind of way, Brasserie is a see-and-be-seen spot for suits.

Strike a deal or schmooze with clients over this country club-style cuisine. With offerings like onion soup gratinée chock-full of caramelized onions beneath a classic Gruyère crown; white asparagus crêpes topped with chervil-lemon-butter sauce and lobster; and striped bass over a bed of new potatoes, this food may seem familiar but it is equally wonderful.

Bukhara Grill

C3

Indian ✗✗

217 E. 49th St. (bet. Second & Third Aves.)

Subway: 51 St
Phone: 212-888-2839
Web: www.bukharany.com
Prices: $$

Lunch & dinner daily

Blazing Bukhara Grill's dusky space exudes sophistication, drama, and a dash of kitsch. The upper level leans contemporary; while the rustic and timbered dining room is dressed in tables carved from tree-trunks, Indian artwork, and stoneware. Sink into a lush booth and gaze at imposing masters manning fiery tandoors.

Waiters in traditional garb present upscale diners with foods from India's Northwest Frontier region. Bite into juicy chicken *malai kebab* marinated in ginger, garlic, and spices; *aloo bukhara korma* starring saucy lamb chunks dancing with apricots and potatoes; and the forever beloved *kurkuri bindi*—crispy okra tossed with onions, spices, and coriander. Piles of puffy bread, straight out of the oven, reveal a committed chef and kitchen.

Casa Lever

Italian ✕✕✕

B2

390 Park Ave. (entrance on 53rd St.)

Subway: Lexington Av - 53 St   Lunch & dinner Mon – Sat
Phone: 212-888-2700
Web: www.casalever.com
Prices: $$$

In the basement of the landmark Lever House is now the new restaurant, Casa Lever, and though the general scene hasn't changed too much–a unique, retro-modern dining room shaped like a hexagon, where well-heeled Upper East Siders clink glasses in slick, elevated booths–the elegant Italian dishes seem to have taken a step in a very delicious direction. Kick things off with a plate of nicely seared calamari, served with fresh spring peas, sautéed baby carrots, and rendered pieces of *guanciale*; and then move on to perfectly al dente pockets of homemade ravioli filled with braised duck and laced with brown butter and mushrooms. Finish with a fresh square of moist tiramisu that arrives plated with lovely *langue du chat* and *palmier* cookies. *Perfetto.*

Cellini

Italian ✕✕

B2

65 E. 54th St. (bet. Madison & Park Aves.)

Subway: Lexington Av - 53 St   Lunch Mon – Fri
Phone: 212-751-1555   Dinner nightly
Web: www.cellinirestaurant.com
Prices: $$$

With its pleasant informality, lively atmosphere, efficient service, and high quality selection of deliciously simple Italian classics, Cellini appeals to all. Even old-school Italian-American standards, like grilled Atlantic calamari, are served with the care and culinary attention often reserved for fancier food. Good flavors and skill are demonstrated in pasta offerings, like their signature spaghetti and meatballs or seafood risotto, brimming with shellfish, roasted artichokes, and shallots in a white wine-lobster broth.

A concise, well-chosen wine list featuring Italian labels plus crowd-pleasers from around the world, a polite waitstaff well-versed in the menu, and undeniable warmth justify Cellini's popularity among locals and tourists alike.

214

Chado

A5

Japanese ✗✗

4 E. 36th St. (bet. Fifth & Madison Aves.)

Subway: 34 St - Herald Sq
Phone: 212-532-2210
Web: www.chadonyc.com
Prices: $$

Lunch Mon – Fri
Dinner nightly

♿

🍴

This chic, upscale sushi restaurant arrives courtesy of a partnership between Omar Balouma, of Barbès, and Étienne Deyans of Tapis Rouge. The black-and-white decor may be a bit of a departure from the classic Japanese aesthetic, yet the space feels sleek and pretty with exposed brick walls and hardwood floors. Throw in a rotating roster of special maki and a wide spectrum of pristine fish, and you've got yourself a heck of a place to throw down a few nigiri.

The menu rounds the usual sushi bases (and it is lovely sushi indeed), but also offers appetizers like sautéed oysters with garlic-chive sauce and organic egg; and dinner options like pistachio shrimp with crab roe, or sea bass with sake-infused roasted seaweed sauce.

Dardanel

C1

Turkish ✗✗

1071 First Ave. (bet. 58th & 59th Sts.)

Subway: 59 St
Phone: 212-888-0809
Web: www.dardanelnyc.com
Prices: $$

Lunch & dinner daily

Dardanel's ocean-themed exterior stands out against the rather bleak block on which it sits. Inside, it feels bright and contemporary with sleek white banquettes and dark wood tables, creating a lovely atmosphere where a warm vibe complements the Mediterranean and Turkish fare.

The house *manti* are reason alone for a visit; these divine micro-versions of the Turkish dumplings are tenderly soaked in a yogurt-garlic sauce. Otherwise, starters, house specialties, and grilled meats are the way to go—try the flavorful zucchini pancakes, or shrimp casserole (brick-oven baked with tomatoes, peppers, and mushrooms in a creamy tomato sauce, topped with *kasserie* cheese).

The place hums with a mix of neighborhood locals—a cozy spot for a casual dinner or date.

Don's Bogam

Korean ✗✗

17 E. 32nd St. (bet. Fifth & Madison Aves.)

Subway: 33 St
Phone: 212-683-2200
Web: www.donsbogam.com
Prices: $$

Lunch & dinner daily

K-town gets a kick in the pants from this exciting, group-friendly mod spot. The contemporary room features a few different seating options, but big parties will want to head for the sleek, modern floor-level tables fitted out with tabletop grills and specially designed cavities for dangling your feet. The menu is typically massive—with a bevy of lunch and dinner specials (served both à la carte and as sampler barbecue combos) and a *banchan* parade accompanying everything. The atypical thing is the quality and freshness arriving in plates like *mandu*, traditional Korean pork and vegetable dumplings; grilled and marinated barbecue shrimp; or barbecue *bulgogi*, a heavenly pile of tissue-thin beef flash-cooked with cabbage, sprouts, and noodles.

El Parador 😊

Mexican ✗✗

325 E. 34th St. (bet. First & Second Aves.)

Subway: 33 St
Phone: 212-679-6812
Web: www.elparadorcafe.com
Prices: $$

Lunch & dinner daily

For over 50 years, El Parador has been pleasing generations of New Yorkers with killer margaritas, tasty Mexican food, accommodating staff, and its "you want it, you got it" ethos (don't hesitate to order something not found on the menu). Do not be deterred by its Midtown Tunnel location or façade that suggests it is a spot where real drinkers drink. Its warm interior offers some of the best tasting Mexican-influenced food around, as in the taco tray—spilling with savories from beef *picadillo* to chorizo, it is as fun and satisfying to prepare as to eat. Equally tasty are the nachos: crisp tortillas spread evenly with toppings and cleanly sliced for easy eating. Wash it down with a sip (or several) of their excellent tequila and perfect margaritas.

Ethos

Greek ✗✗

C2

905 First Ave. (at 51st St.)

Subway: 51 St
Phone: 212-888-4060
Web: www.ethosrestaurants.com
Prices: $$

Lunch & dinner daily

Ethos has been reborn! A renovation brought sparkle to this standby (just across from Beekman and its ritzy residents) and transformed the lifeless room to a vibrant picture of Mykonos with whitewashed walls, cozy cushions, and light wood trim. Gleaming china, glassware, and an upbeat soundtrack finish off the polish, and transport you to the Greek islands...for a night.

While the mezze makes for a delicious meal on its own, the menu remains appealing (minus a few favorite kitchen items) with abundant salads and grilled whole fish. *Pikilia* (assortment of spreads) is as tasty as before, and those Ethos chips of zucchini and eggplant with *tzatziki* are a must. The new servers can be pushy, but hopefully a face-lift is planned for them as well!

Felidia

Italian ✗✗

C1

243 E. 58th St. (bet. Second & Third Aves.)

Subway: Lexington Av - 59 St
Phone: 212-758-1479
Web: www.lidiasitaly.com
Prices: $$$

Lunch Mon – Fri
Dinner nightly

For the past 25 years, Felidia has attracted a huge, loyal, and diverse following of well-heeled regulars. TV personality and cookbook author Lidia Bastianich's flagship is housed in a cozy brownstone with a copper-topped bar, warm colors, polished wood, and seating on two levels. Wine racks prominently showcase the restaurant's vast, mostly Italian, and very impressive list.

While Lidia is no stranger here, Sicilian-born Chef Fortunato Nicotra skillfully mans the stoves, where for more than a decade he has turned out tempting pastas like spinach tagliatelle with braised Hudson Valley duck and mushrooms; or pear and fresh pecorino-filled ravioli; as well as regional fare and tasting menus. Many dishes are elegantly finished in the dining room.

Fiorini

B1

209 E. 56th St. (bet. Second & Third Aves.)

Subway: Lexington Av - 53 St
Phone: 212-308-0830
Web: www.fiorinirestaurant.com
Prices: $$$

Lunch Mon – Fri
Dinner Mon – Sat

Lello Arpaia and his son, Dino, are masters at the hospitality trade, and they run their Italian eatery, Fiorini, (which translates to little flower) so tightly that you can't help but leave with a special fondness for the place. Make your way past the elegant front bar, and you'll find an intimate, honey-toned dining room aglow in warm pastels and buzzing with a quietly professional service staff.

Modern, straightforward Italian best describes the menu, where you'll find any number of comfort classics along with a lineup of fresh, silky pastas like a perfectly luscious al dente spaghettini *alla carbonara*, tossed with organic egg, fresh Pecorino Romano, cracked pepper, and sweet crumbles of bacon. Polished off with the house espresso? Perfect!

The Four Seasons

B2

99 E. 52nd St. (bet. Lexington & Park Aves.)

Subway: 51 St
Phone: 212-754-9494
Web: www.fourseasonsrestaurant.com
Prices: $$$$

Lunch Mon – Fri
Dinner Mon – Sat

In a day when restaurants try to draw in crowds by populist appeal, The Four Seasons is unabashed in its embrace of power and privilege. Opened in 1959, this time capsule of mid-century swagger is a design delight. Those who go already know that the walnut-paneled Grill Room is *the* place to be for lunch, while the iconic tree-anchored Pool Room is a great scene for evening dining.

Diners who don't circle the same orbit as the cast of celebrity regulars may bristle at the astronomic prices of the menu. But it's still worth a visit, for seasonal preparations such as plump sweet corn ravioli with rock shrimp and chanterelles; delicately crisped fried soft shell crabs; refreshingly tart raspberry summer pudding; or just for a leisurely cocktail at the bar.

Fresco by Scotto

A2

Italian ✗✗✗

34 E. 52nd St. (bet. Madison & Park Aves.)

Subway: 5 Av – 53 St
Phone: 212-935-3434
Web: www.frescobyscotto.com
Prices: $$$

Lunch Mon – Fri
Dinner Mon – Sat

Despite a location near Rockefeller Center that draws on expense accounts and nearby NBC executives (perhaps the same ones who just produced the Scotto family recipe demonstrations on The Today Show), Fresco by Scotto exudes a comfortable yet cosmopolitan aura. Unobtrusive service and sound Italian-American cuisine enhance the dining room's simple elegance.

Lunch and dinner menus list rustic and robust dishes, including "Fresco Originals" like penne gratin, a hearty pasta with julienned *prosciutto di Parma*, peas, fontina, provolone, Parmigiano, finished with cream and cracked pepper. Equally enticing are their grilled sweet sausages, seasoned with cheese and parsley, in roasted pepper and onion ragù.

Try Fresco on the go for a quick lunch fix.

HanGawi 🏵️

A6

Korean ✗✗

12 E. 32nd St. (bet. Fifth & Madison Aves.)

Subway: 33 St
Phone: 212-213-0077
Web: www.hangawirestaurant.com
Prices: $$

Lunch & dinner daily

Don't worry about wearing your best shoes to HanGawi; you'll have to take them off at the door before settling in at one of the restaurant's low tables. In the serene space, decorated with Korean artifacts and soothed by meditative music, it's easy to forget you're in Manhattan.

The menu is all vegetarian, in keeping with the philosophy of healthy cooking to balance the *um* and *yang*. You can quite literally eat like a king here starting with vermicelli delight (sweet potato noodles), perfectly crisp kimchi and mushroom pancakes, devastatingly delicious tofu clay pot in ginger sauce, and the regal kimchi stone bowl rice made fragrant with fresh veggies. Of course, you'll have to rejoin the crowds outside. Still, it's nice to get away... now and Zen.

Gilt ❀ ❀

A3

455 Madison Ave. (bet. 50th & 51st Sts.)

Subway: 51 St
Phone: 212-891-8100
Web: www.giltnewyork.com
Prices: $$$$

Dinner Tue – Sat

The New York Palace

From its home at the New York Palace Hotel, Gilt's façade is so steeped in the drama and history of its stately Italian Renaissance style that it seems a shame to go inside. But of course, the interior is replete with more leaded glass, carved woods, plaster friezes, marble hearths, and glittering Gilded Age glamour than you can shake an over-sized fire iron at. Yet this is all just a starting point for a restaurant that seems so effortlessly exquisite.

The dining room is blissfully opulent and the service team is excellent, but all are focused on the gustatory adventure that is sure to encompass a meal here.

An amuse-bouche may begin as an homage to a classic cauliflower custard but then take a brilliant creative leap with squid ink *lavash.* Entrées such as Mangalitsa pork prove not only the kitchen's skill but also its great effort to source top ingredients. Here, a seemingly simple dish of pork becomes otherworldly when glazed to a deep and regal brown, served with chestnuts, stewed apples, and supremely briny oysters. Desserts are truly unique, as in beautiful rounds of perfectly poached pears, stunningly stacked and scented with pistachio streusel and milky-sweet pecorino.

Hide-Chan Ramen

Japanese ✗

C2

248 E. 52nd St. (bet. Second & Third Aves.)

Subway: Lexington Av - 53 St
Phone: 212-813-1800
Web: N/A
Prices: 🍜

Lunch Mon – Fri
Dinner nightly

Food is everyone's focus at this buzzing ramen shop. While their menu offers a few Japanese delicacies (maybe the best *gyoza* in town), regulars come here for one item alone: the deliciously slurpy ramen. You can customize yours (fatty broth please!), but to skip the classic *Hakata tonkotsu*, with its delectable piggy flavor, would be such a shame. Likewise, the *Hakata kuro ramen* is really something special—splashed with a nutty black garlic purée, it approaches divinity.

Climb a flight of stairs to arrive at this cozy ramen canteen. Perch at the counter or a private table (surrounded by textured cement walls and paper signs advertising sake and specials), as you wait for steamed buns, wrapped around an excellent slice of pork, drizzled with kewpie mayo.

Jubilee

French ✗

C2

347 E. 54th St. (bet. First & Second Aves.)

Subway: Lexington Av 53 St
Phone: 212-888-3569
Web: www.jubileeny.net
Prices: $$

Lunch Sat – Sun
Dinner nightly

Don't tell Turtle Bay, but the secret is out on their beloved neighborhood bistro. With its charming, Old Europe ambience and cozy, close-knit tables, Jubilee was securing two-tops for locals long before the rest of Manhattan decided to horn in on the action. No wonder—the French-Belgian menu is a heady lineup of bistro comfort classics like duck leg confit, escargots, profiteroles, and Prince Edward Island mussels (the house specialty) prepared five different ways.

A warm goat cheese salad arrives brimming with roasted tomatoes and drizzled in a honey and sherry vinaigrette; while a plate of tender mussels is broiled up Provençale-style in garlic and parsley butter, and paired with an addictive stack of crispy frites and a vibrant green salad.

Kurumazushi

Japanese ✗✗

7 E. 47th St. (bet. Fifth & Madison Aves.)

Subway: 47-50 Sts - Rockefeller Ctr   Lunch & dinner Mon – Sat
Phone: 212-317-2802
Web: www.kurumazushi.com
Prices: $$$$

Hidden in the second story of a bland office building, Kurumazushi is marked by little more than a few plain letters on a nondescript door. Push past this red herring and head upstairs to find impeccable service and a small room dressed in red, white, and black.

This is the house of Toshihiro Uezu, an omakase master of the first order—trust in this chef's choice succession of outstanding sushi (best toro in town), which seems to have swam here from the Tokyo market before its expert preparation. Some loyalists might argue that behind the counter the deft touch of the chef has become inconsistent, yet a dinner here will nonetheless blow your socks off for quality of fish. Of course, so might the hefty bill—a price likely overshadowed by that creamy toro.

La Fonda Del Sol

B4

Spanish ✗✗

200 Park Ave. (entrance on Vanderbilt Ave.)

Subway: Grand Central - 42 St   Lunch & dinner Mon – Sat
Phone: 212-867-6767
Web: www.patinagroup.com
Prices: $$

La Fonda del Sol might just have it all. Good location? Only the best, since this "café in the sun" is located in the MetLife tower. Lively scene? You bet. It's the kind of place that rocks a mix of corporate types and those who've unknotted their ties to tie one on. Good food? La Fonda del Sol doesn't mess around with its Spanish tapas and main dishes. It is a sensational twist on snack time here, where a bustling crowd keeps the energy level through the roof.

Like its Adam Tihany-designed setting, no drama is spared when it comes to presentation. Hay-roasted Colorado lamb is plated like a present after its dome is opened tableside. Spanish influences are ever-present, from the chicken empanada with piquillo pepper sauce to garlic shrimp "*cazuelita*."

La Grenouille

French

A2

3 E. 52nd St. (bet. Fifth & Madison Aves.)

Subway: 5 Av - 53 St	Lunch Tue – Fri
Phone: 212-752-1495	Dinner Mon – Sat
Web: www.la-grenouille.com	
Prices: $$$$	

Like the Judi Dench of French dining, La Grenouille is a respected holdout from another era in Manhattan's fine dining scene—one where white-coated servers fussed over you in a setting fit for royalty. But as over-the-top as the dining room might appear nowadays (think high coffered ceilings, plush red banquettes, and opulent flower arrangements), there is something comforting for the well-heeled regulars who have been calling this Masson family mainstay its second home (one where you're required to wear jackets) since 1962.

Quickly disappearing old-world dishes like *quenelles* and *rognons* share menu space with dishes like duck confit, served over warm green lentils; and tender chicken paillard, paired with crispy sage and tender squash gnocchi.

La Mangeoire

French

C2

1008 Second Ave. (bet. 53rd & 54th Aves.)

Subway: Lexington Av - 53 St	Lunch Sun – Fri
Phone: 212-759-7086	Dinner nightly
Web: www.lamangeoire.com	
Prices: $$	

Gorgeous, top-notch ingredients; simple, lovely, and authentic Provençal preparations by a critically-acclaimed chef, a sunny ambience that transports you up and out of midtown and into the South of France—what's not to love here? La Mangeoire may have been around for a while, but Chef Christian Delouvrier, who manned the stoves at an impressive number of starred restaurants, gave this neighborhood favorite the booster shot it richly deserves. The quality here has never been better.

Try the delicious *pizzette antiboise*, topped with caramelized onions, anchovies, and black olives; the wickedly fresh *moules*; or the irresistible blueberry clafoutis tart paired with crème anglaise, red fruit coulis, and sweet whipped cream.

L'Atelier de Joël Robuchon ✿ ✿

Contemporary ✕✕

B1

57 E. 57th St. (bet. Madison & Park Aves.)

Subway: 5 Av - 59 St
Phone: 212-829-3844
Web: www.joel-robuchon.net
Prices: $$$$

Dinner nightly

Durston Saylor

The I.M. Pei-designed Four Seasons Hotel is certainly a fitting home for world-renowned Chef Joël Robuchon. But beyond the heavily marbled hotel landing, lies an intimate space, sultry with burgundy tones and black lacquer that lend a Japanese-inspired look. The mood is relaxed; the service is personalized, interactive, and engaging.

At its center is a u-shaped dining counter–a reminder that this *atelier* is indeed something of a studio–where comfortably perched guests stop chatting and lean forward in anticipation of this open-air kitchen's great theater. The spectacle alone has many regulars returning time and again. Vivid and distinct in so many ways, the cooking of Chef Xavier Boyer is a complex and eloquent display of technical mastery and very fine taste, best experienced through the "decouverte" menu. Some dishes, like caramelized eel, may have you waxing poetic about the flavors of pure ocean waters; others, like quail stuffed with foie gras, are reminders that this carries the name of culinary genius. Bloomberg should probably ban Robuchon's outrageously buttery signature potatoes.

Though playing with their iPad wine list is fun, allow the outstanding sommelier to help.

Le Cirque

Contemporary 🍴🍴🍴🍴

B1

151 E. 58th St. (bet. Lexington & Third Aves.)

Subway: 59 St
Phone: 212-644-0202
Web: www.lecirque.com
Prices: $$$$

Lunch Mon – Fri
Dinner Mon – Sat

Nestled into One Beacon Court, this legendary restaurant remains dramatic with huge curving windows, billowing tents draped above the main dining room, and circus motifs gracing the walls. As popular as the décor is the ever-charming host, Sirio, who famously tends to this loyal, old-money clientele, who come here as much for the memories as for the lovely contemporary cuisine.

Offerings may include sautéed Gulf shrimp with Kaffir lime, hearts of palm, and carrot confit; or pavé of veal with pear, pecorino, and coffee-cardamom jus. Impressive desserts may include sweet, green pistachio macaroons topped with pistachio paste and fresh raspberries, plated tableside.

The café is another popular dining option, offering a focused menu and excellent value.

Le Périgord

French 🍴🍴🍴

C2

405 E. 52nd St. (off First Ave.)

Subway: 51 St
Phone: 212-755-6244
Web: www.leperigord.com
Prices: $$$

Lunch Mon – Fri
Dinner nightly

With a nostalgic feel that dates back to the 1960s, Le Périgord is a beloved period piece that cossets diners at lavish tables with hand-painted Limoges and fresh roses. Adding further elegance are the tuxedo-clad waiters who proffer formal service to diplomats from the nearby United Nations. This is one of the few places in New York where one still dresses for dinner and bears witness to the beauty in tradition.

The time-honored menu is likewise a classic, celebrating French culinary traditions in an outstanding preparation of foie gras, as well as nearly forgotten favorites, like *île flottante*. Offerings go on to include dishes so perfectly suited to this suddenly unique ambience that they are difficult to find in other NYC restaurants.

Le Relais de Venise

Steakhouse ✗✗

B2

590 Lexington Ave. (at 52nd St.)

Subway: 51 St
Phone: 212-758-3989
Web: www.relaisdevenise.com
Prices: $$

Lunch & dinner daily

There is no menu at Le Relais de Venise L'Entrecôte, a Parisian restaurant with a prime location set along thumping Lexington Avenue. There is only one $24.95 option, but it is a delightful option indeed—green salad with tangy mustard vinaigrette and walnuts, followed by juicy steak served in two parts (because you wouldn't want the rest of it to get cold, would you?) laced with the house's mouthwatering secret sauce, with all the crunchy frites you can eat.

With a Parisian décor and waitresses darting around in saucy French maid get-ups, this is a lively joint—all the more reason to pluck a glass of *vino* off the extremely affordable list, sit back and relax. By the time the dessert menu rolls around, you'll have forgotten how stressful decisions can be.

Maloney & Porcelli

American ✗✗✗

B3

37 E. 50th St. (bet. Madison & Park Aves.)

Subway: 51 St
Phone: 212-750-2233
Web: www.maloneyandporcelli.com
Prices: $$$

Lunch Mon – Fri
Dinner nightly

Much more than a steakhouse, this upbeat and versatile spot is sure to exceed expectations. Note that the first sign of this excess is clear in portion control, with entrée-sized starters, and a Flintstone-sized Porterhouse that has you bringing the bone home for Dino. Pleasant surprises are equally evident in crowd-pleasing offerings like tuna and avocado tartare or the outrageous house signature, crackling pork shank with firecracker applesauce.

Wine glasses and peppermills are also enormous, supplementing the philosophy that more is more. Unfortunately, this also extends to the check—a reminder that these big meals carry big prices. Nonetheless, it is appropriately jammed with an expense-account crowd, and the bar remains very popular post-work.

Mapo Tofu ⑧

B5

338 Lexington Ave. (bet. 39th & 40th Sts.)

Subway: Grand Central - 42 St   Lunch & dinner daily
Phone: 212-867-8118
Web: N/A
Prices: ⊛⊛

Just when you think you're sated, this Sichuan Shangri-la bestows you with another boon. At Mapo Tofu it's not just about tofu, but their sumptuous Sichuan; it's not about spicy, but the expert marriage of spices; and it's not about ambience—a slim room with tables and slapdash servers—but the genius locale and superior spread that hoists it into a league of its own.

Start this Sichuan safari with sliced conch steeping in roasted chili vinaigrette; string beans with bamboo shoots and pork are an incredible item; and braised fish, tofu, and cellophane noodles carry a fiercely flavorful chili broth. Camphor tea-smoked duck; *dan dan* noodles with pork; and wok tossed prawns with spiced salt and Sichuan peppercorns are stunning, flavor-ridden plates.

Matisse

C3

924 Second Ave. (at 49th St.)

Subway: 51 St   Lunch & dinner daily
Phone: 212-546-9300
Web: www.matissenyc.com
Prices: $$

Matisse might be smack dab in midtown, but this tightly packed, sun-filled bistro looks and feels more downtown. Informal without being casual, this single room restaurant with a front row seat to the action of Second Avenue has that typical New York lack of elbow room, but forever lively and whizzing spirit.

Young and old area denizens are lured by the simple and classic French cooking with a reasonable price tag. The menu presents an appealing range of comfort foods, such as caramelized onion tarte and *croque monsieur*. Sunday brunch delivers the goods with omelets and French toast alongside other usual suspects.

Some of the dishes are presented on delightfully rustic wooden boards and exude charm thereby displaying Matisse's stylish flair.

227

Mia Dona

Italian 🍴🍴

B1

206 E. 58th St. (bet. Second & Third Aves.)

Subway: 59 St
Phone: 212-750-8170
Web: www.miadona.com
Prices: $$

Lunch Mon – Fri
Dinner Mon – Sat

Mamma mia, Donatella has done it again! Donatella Arpaia seems to have the Midas touch when it comes to restaurants and midtown's Mia Dona is her latest success story. With its glammed-up trattoria style (travertine limestone floors and old farm tools hung on whitewashed brick walls), it should come as no surprise that the menu focuses on country cooking.

It's all about Maria Mama's *polpette*, so don't even think of skipping these parcels of juicy perfection. You can even pick up a cup or a sammy overflowing with these delicious meat treats from the hip street cart outside. Her spicy sauce can make you sweat but is worth every drop. Gorgeous Mia Dona also struts paninis, soups, salads, and grilled fish, but really, can you still be hungry?

Michael Jordan's

Steakhouse 🍴🍴

B4

Grand Central Terminal

Subway: Grand Central - 42 St
Phone: 212-655-2300
Web: www.michaeljordansnyc.com
Prices: $$$

Lunch & dinner daily

Beneath Grand Central Terminal's painstakingly restored celestial mural, Michael Jordan's always offers dining under the stars. Wood paneling and photos of sleek locomotives bring art deco glamour to the lofty mezzanine.

At dinner, expect generous filets, ribeye, and Porterhouse (for two) cuts of well-prepared prime Angus beef and traditional steakhouse sides—be sure to try the Jordan family's macaroni and cheese. Golden beet carpaccio with grilled asparagus and goat cheese is a nice alternative to the ever-decadent warm garlic bread with Gorgonzola fondue. Lunch adds lighter fare and a reasonable prix-fixe menu.

The elliptical mahogany bar is an agreeable setting for a happy hour beverage; while the wine salon is great for a cocktail party.

Morton's

Steakhouse ✕✕✕

551 Fifth Ave. (entrance on 45th St.)

Subway: 5 Av
Phone: 212-972-3315
Web: www.mortons.com
Prices: $$$

Lunch Mon – Fri
Dinner nightly

Part of a Chicago born chain with outposts across the country, Morton's understands exactly how to empower the weekday corporate crowds and charm weekend tourists with its fun, formulaic experience.

It all starts with a cart: as the servers recite and explain the menu, a cart is rolled to your table, bearing plastic-wrapped samples of the exact cuts of Prime, aged beef, which will be prepared exactly to your liking. Alongside these meats are virtually every raw ingredient used to round out the menu, from massive potatoes to live lobsters. Gimmicks aside, the food here is high quality and delicious.

As one of the older siblings, this midtown Morton's embraces a clubby décor of mahogany paneling and jewel tones that sets the steakhouse standard.

Mr Chow

Chinese ✕✕

324 E. 57th St. (bet. First & Second Aves.)

Subway: 59 St
Phone: 212-751-9030
Web: www.mrchow.com
Prices: $$$$

Dinner nightly

This Mr Chow dates back to 1979 but still lures nightly the Who's Who of Manhattan. Actor, artist, restaurateur, and Renaissance man Michael Chow added interior design to his talents in creating this chic black-and-white dining room draped with a red fabric mobile. The team of white-jacketed servers may lack warmth, but makes packed-in diners feel posh and pampered.

Regulars and cognoscenti do not request the menu; have your waiter order for you (though do ask for the fried seaweed), and don't be shy about dislikes. Find yourself distracted from your meal when the oft-performed noodle-making demonstration begins. It's impressive, as will be the rapidly mounting check. Note the other high-profile, international outposts, as well as a TriBeCa sibling.

Naya

Manhattan ▶ Midtown East & Murray Hill

Lebanese ✗✗

C2

1057 Second Ave. (bet. 55th & 56th Sts.)

Subway: Lexington Av - 53 St   Lunch & dinner daily
Phone: 212-319-7777
Web: www.nayarestaurants.com
Prices: $$

In a city starved for good Lebanese food, Naya is a sight for sore eyes. Owner Hady Kfoury, worked the front-of-house at both Daniel and Payard before bringing in Lebanese chef, Rafic Nehme, to open this tiny, but impeccably sleek space, with its mod, all-white décor and narrow lineup of glossy, angular booths.

The modern Lebanese menu rounds the usual meze bases before introducing a handful of entrées and tempting Lebanese wines. Try the juicy *kafta kebab*, a savory, mint-seasoned kebab of ground lamb, paired with fluffy rice pilaf and grilled vegetables; or a glistening, golden tower of flaky baklava cigars drizzled with honey.

If pressed for time, visit Naya Express—the popular fast food version that gives Chipotle a run for their lunchtime money.

OBAO ☺

Asian ✗✗

C2

222 E. 53rd St. (bet. Second & Third Aves.)

Subway: Lexington Av - 53 St   Lunch & dinner daily
Phone: 212-308-5588
Web: www.obaonyc.com
Prices: ☜☜

Who knows what possessed Michael Huynh to drop this fantastic new Vietnamese restaurant in Midtown East, but anyone tired of slogging to Chinatown is in for one heck of a treat.

The restaurant has a contemporary urban feel, with a smattering of booths and a communal table toward the center of the back room; and while the Vietnamese dishes are the strongest (especially the *pho*), the menu also dabbles in cuisine from Laos and Singapore, adding creative touches that truly work. Don't miss the fragrant curried catfish satay; the Laos beef salad tossed with pineapple, shallots, and mint; or the beef *luclak* with tomatoes and crisp watercress, washed down with Vietnamese coffee or coconut juice straight from the shell.

230

Osteria Laguna

C4

Italian ✕✕

209 E. 42nd St. (bet. Second & Third Aves.)

Subway: Grand Central - 42 St
Phone: 212-557-0001
Web: www.osteria-laguna.com
Prices: $$

Lunch Mon – Fri
Dinner nightly

A little bit corporate (it is midtown, after all) and a little bit casual (daytrippers from nearby Grand Central), Osteria Laguna has nailed its audience and delivers a perfect blend to suit both worlds. Inside, It's delightfully rustic, complete with the requisite Italian ceramic plates and wooden chairs with rush seating.

Crowd-pleasers like pastas, pizzas from the wood-burning oven, *antipasti*, salads, and grilled meats and fish dishes comprise the menu at this better-than-average Italian. The friendly service can be spotty, but the perfectly crisped wood-fired pizzas are always spot on. The portions are abundant, perhaps even too much given the tiny tables, but the prices aren't, so you can treat your out-of-town friend and keep the change.

Pampano

B3

Mexican ✕✕

209 E. 49th St. (bet. Second & Third Aves.)

Subway: 51 St
Phone: 212-751-4545
Web: www.modernmexican.com/pampano
Prices: $$$

Lunch Mon – Fri
Dinner nightly

This vivid Mexican restaurant is a duet between Mexicateur, Richard Sandoval (who owns sister restaurant, Maya), and legendary tenor, Placido Domingo. The combination hits all the right notes—think coastal Mexican cuisine meets an elegant East Side setting, and you're getting warm. The chic interior, drawn in ivory tones and green palm trees, renders the two-level space open and airy; and there's a great terrace upstairs when the weather plays nice.

The menu's favorites include bowls of ceviche or the *empanadas de camaron* dressed with vibrant salsas, followed by deep entrées like the *pez espada mérida*, a thick fillet of swordfish atop a potato-caper fondue with a fresh pea shoot and Asian pear salad all swimming in a smooth achiote-habañero sauce.

Pera

Turkish ✗✗

A4

303 Madison Ave. (bet. 41st & 42nd Sts.)

Subway: Grand Central - 42 St   Lunch & dinner daily
Phone: 212-878-6301
Web: www.peranyc.com
Prices: $$

This perennially-packed Mediterranean brasserie attracts a loud lunchtime crowd of office workers, while at nighttime the scene is populated by intimate duos. The establishment, named after an upscale neighborhood in Istanbul, warms the heart with its chocolate-brown color scheme and grand display kitchen boasting an open flame grill station.

The expert kitchen churns out a throng of mouthwatering fare, like fig *pidette*—a dense flatbread spread with strips of Turkish-style dried beef, *rucola*, dried figs, and cumin-infused yogurt drizzles; the cubed watermelon and feta salad massaged with fragrant basil oil is a warm weather must; and roasted whole fish is offered to be de-boned and comes delightfully dressed with blistered tomatoes and candied lemon.

Phoenix Garden 🍃

Chinese ✗

B5

242 E. 40th St. (bet. Second & Third Aves.)

Subway: Grand Central - 42 St   Lunch & dinner daily
Phone: 212-983-6666
Web: www.thephoenixgarden.com
Prices: 🍪🍪

You can take the restaurant out of Chinatown, but you can't take the Cantonese out of this midtown favorite—which serves up authentic dishes at a great value. By day, the office suits set pours in for quick lunches; by dinner, Phoenix Garden lights up with a fun, diverse crowd looking to check out the mouthwatering daily specials.

While the house's tasty Peking duck is not always on the menu, you can certainly try to request it—a deliciously crispy affair that gets rolled into neat little pancakes with hoisin, scallion, and cucumber. Meanwhile, don't miss the steamed chive dumplings, plump with tender shrimp; the succulent pepper and salty shrimp; or the sautéed snow pea shoots in a lovely crabmeat sauce, with tender mushrooms and snow peas.

P.J. Clarke's

Gastropub ✗

B2

915 Third Ave. (at 55th St.)

Subway: Lexington Av - 53 St   Lunch & dinner daily
Phone: 212-317-1616
Web: www.pjclarkes.com
Prices: $$

The original is always the best: that's why it's been duplicated. It might sound trite, but this midtown institution started serving drinks and meals to men in suits before your father's father was born. It feels old and traditional because it is, yet somehow this spot manages to keep improving. No fluff, no fuss, no reservations at P.J. Clarke's, where the staff is likely to throw a "hon" or two into the conversation.

The crowd-pleasing menu offers old-time classics like chilli and tasty burgers (note the fries are extra), but seafood and steakhouse dishes are popular. Salads and appetizers are not only numerous, but those thick-cut potato chips with salty Maytag blue cheese dip and massive chopped salads seem to get better with each visit.

Riingo

Fusion ✗✗

B4

205 E. 45th St. (bet. Second & Third Aves.)

Subway: Grand Central - 42 St   Lunch & dinner daily
Phone: 212-867-4200
Web: www.riingo.com
Prices: $$

From the Japanese word for "apple" (as in the Big Apple), this is a stylish, contemporary space just off the Alex Hotel lobby, incorporating ebony, bamboo, and accents like custom-made ceramic sake sets. The day-long menu thoughtfully reinterprets Japanese and American cuisines, going well beyond typical hotel dining. At the front of the restaurant, a small bar and lounge with a few sidewalk tables offer a pleasant, quiet terrace for an innovative cocktail or choice of light snacks, like cassava chips with yuzu sour cream.

The very creative kitchen menu features the likes of duck dumplings in five-spice consommé, near-perfect tuna sandwiches, and an extensive raw-bar selection. Riingo also offers a full range of sushi and maki of impressive quality.

233

Rosa Mexicano

Mexican ✗✗

C1

1063 First Ave. (at 58th St.)

Subway: 59 St
Phone: 212-753-7407
Web: www.rosamexicano.com
Prices: $$

Lunch Sat – Sun
Dinner nightly

This oldie but goody is why the brand name is now found throughout the country, but this original location is by far the best. The dining room's Mexican hacienda style is cozy; its tightly packed tables only add to the lively ambience. Rosa Mexicano strikes a rare balance with its broad appeal: find young professionals downing pomegranate margaritas alongside couples with children perusing the "Young Amigos" menu.

Specialties like *queso fundido* (cheese casserole with chorizo) and *alambre de camarones* (jumbo shrimp grilled with veggies and served aside *pico de gallo*) pack a flavorful punch. There is nothing gimmicky about the tableside guacamole—it may be the city's best and is a worthy accompaniment to the homemade tortillas and excellent salsa.

Sakagura

Japanese ✗✗

B4

211 E. 43rd St. (bet. Second & Third Aves.)

Subway: Grand Central - 42 St
Phone: 212-953-7253
Web: www.sakagura.com
Prices: $$$

Lunch Mon – Fri
Dinner nightly

With its killer sake list and delicious small plates, this unassuming sake den has gotten deservedly popular in the last few years. For those who can find it (hint: it's in the basement by way of the back stairs), plan for a swinging night out in Tokyo by way of midtown. Grab a seat at the long counter to amp up the fun and watch the libations flow.

Though the menu is built to complement the sake, the food more than merits its own applause. A soft boiled egg bobs alongside fresh uni and salmon roe in a lovely dashi (*onsen tamago*); while grilled eel is layered with Japanese cucumber and seaweed in a light rice wine vinegar vinaigrette (*uzaku*); and chicken is marinated in sake and ginger-infused soy sauce, then fried to sweet perfection (*tori karaage*).

Rouge Tomate ❃

Contemporary 🗶🗶🗶

A1

10 E. 60th St. (bet. Fifth & Madison Aves.)

Subway: 5 Av   Lunch & dinner Mon – Sat
Phone: 646-237-8977
Web: www.rougetomatenyc.com
Prices: $$$

Katie Sokoler

Exquisitely located just a stone's throw of NY's flagship boutique, Reem Acra, and across from beloved Barney's, Rouge Tomate is the upscale capital of genteel ladies and powerhouse players. A gorgeous restaurant with a gracious poise, Rouge Tomate aims to initiate its devotees into seasonally-inspired, modern American cuisine that is at once nutritious and delicious.

This street-level arena is quite a stunner. The chaste décor is mighty mod and straddles the line between vibrant (red splashes) and soothing (warm hues of ivory and amber); while the easily stylish lair downstairs is hallowed for private parties.

With a bevy of fuss-free accoutrements, this delightfully Spartan sanctum doesn't detract from Chef Jeremy Bearman's fare. While the service may not be as finely tuned as his balanced approach to food, sophisticates come to imbibe refreshing cocktails alongside thinly sliced *walu* crudo, freshly prepared with avocado, yuzu, and jalapeño; Moroccan-style duck breast atop *fregola sarda*, lovingly blended with Medjool dates, turnips, and Marcona almonds; and an elegantly assembled cheese course chaperoned by green apple and celery salad with a *gewürztraminer* and peppercorn syrup.

2nd Avenue Deli

Deli ✗

B6

162 E. 33rd St. (bet. Lexington & Third Aves.)

Subway: 33 St
Phone: 212-689-9000
Web: www.2ndavedeli.com
Prices: 🍴🍴

Lunch & dinner daily

While the décor may be more deli-meets-deco and there's a tad less attitude, this food is every bit as good as it was on Second Avenue. Ignore the kvetching and know that this is a true Jewish deli filled with personality, and one of the best around by far.

The menu remains as it should: Kosher, meat-loving, and non-dairy, with phenomenal pastrami, pillowy rye, tangy mustard, perfect potato pancakes, and fluffy matzoh balls in comforting broth. Have the best of both worlds with the soup and half-sandwich combination.

Carve a nook during midday rush, when in pour the crowds. The deli also does takeout (popular with the midtown lunch bunch), and delivery (grandma's pancakes at your door). Giant platters go equally well to a bris or brunch.

Seo 🐶

Japanese ✗✗

C3

249 E. 49th St. (bet. Second & Third Aves.)

Subway: 51 St
Phone: 212-355-7722
Web: N/A
Prices: $$

Lunch Mon – Sat
Dinner nightly

This is not your average neighborhood standby, and yet Seo–tucked into a residential street in midtown's booming Japanese culinary scene–draws as many locals as it does lunchtime regulars and weekend adventurers looking for the real deal. Thus, it's best to make reservations early.

The secret lies in Seo's one-two punch of pairing a tranquil dining room and long dining counter with a kitchen staff dedicated to the acumen of faithful Japanese food. Skip the sushi and dive into the wildly flavorful and perfectly prepared *Inaniwa* udon; or juicy broiled cod, glazed in a spot-on miso sauce, and flanked by Japanese plum and ginger root. Keep an eye out for the *chawan mushi*—a silky egg custard that should not be missed if it appears on the daily specials.

Sip Sak 🐾

Turkish ✗✗

C3

928 Second Ave. (bet. 49th & 50th Sts.)

Subway: 51 St   Lunch & dinner daily
Phone: 212-583-1900
Web: www.sip-sak.com
Prices: $$

An NY personality and maestro of Turkish cuisine, Orhan Yegen has been at it again. After a drastic face-lift including a pressed tin ceiling and marble-topped tables, Sip Sak is now the very picture of a Parisian bistro. This mad Turk may dance around his tables (and staff), but his is top-notch, classic Turkish food and is perhaps the best in the city.

The U.N. posse and locals convene to devour Yegen's tempting fare. Taste his terrific Turkish in flaky *pacangas* rolled with spiced beef and fried cheese; delicious *manti* in a yogurt puddle; lamb *adana* atop fried pita with a dollop of *cacik*; and pumpkin soaked in rosewater and honey.

Bi Lokma, a few blocks away, offers a lovely takeout lunch and sit-down dinner in an informal setting.

Smith & Wollensky

Steakhouse ✗✗

B3

797 Third Ave. (at 49th St.)

Subway: 51 St   Lunch Mon — Fri
Phone: 212-753-1530   Dinner nightly
Web: www.smithandwollensky.com
Prices: $$$$

Long before Manhattan's steakhouse craze reached epic proportions, there was Smith & Wollensky. The NY flagship opened in 1977, and over 30 years later, it is still jumping—it's historic green and white façade is a welcome beacon to neighborhood power players during the week; while families and tourists keep businesss booming over the weekends. Now you too can have your "Devil Wears Prada" moment as they deliver to your desk, no assistant required!

The owners may have plucked the names Smith and Wollensky out of a phone directory, but they were considerably more careful choosing their USDA prime beef, which they dry-age and hand-butcher on premises. The result, paired with mouthwatering mashed potatoes or hashbrowns, is steakhouse nirvana.

Soba Totto

Japanese ✗✗

B4

211 E. 43rd St. (bet. Second & Third Aves.)

Subway: Grand Central - 42 St
Phone: 212-557-8200
Web: www.sobatotto.com
Prices: $$

Lunch Mon – Fri
Dinner nightly

This fairly young Japanese restaurant arrives courtesy of the family behind the popular Aburiya Kinnosuke, Yakitori Totto, and Totto Ramen. Like their other ventures, Soba Totto offers incredibly fresh, authentically prepared Japanese specialties in a stylishly-appointed, low-lit dining room. There's a counter where you can watch the chefs go to town, and lots of nooks and crannies for private conversations.

At lunch, midtowners flood in for rejuvenating soba noodles and traditional Japanese lunch sets; come dinner, the menu expands to include small plates, starters, and a wide selection of yakitori—the remarkable little chicken skewers, featuring unique parts like liver, soft knee bone, and tail, which put Totto on the map at some of their other venues.

Sparks

Steakhouse ✗✗

C3

210 E. 46th St. (bet. Second & Third Aves.)

Subway: Grand Central - 42 St
Phone: 212-687-4855
Web: www.sparksnyc.com
Prices: $$$$

Lunch Mon – Fri
Dinner Mon – Sat

Phenomenal steaks, exceptional Scotch, frosty martinis, big expense accounts, seating for nearly 700, and carnivorous crowds exuding a raucous, masculine vibe are the fundamentals of Sparks. Service is speedy and efficient, if rough around the edges, throughout the gigantic, bi-level dining space. This is enhanced by large tables and 19th century landscapes of the Hudson River Valley that line the wainscoted walls. There will be time to appreciate the ambience while inevitably waiting for your table among the masses at the bar.

On the menu, go straight to the flavorful, buttery, and perfectly cooked prime sirloin, accompanied by unbeatable creamed spinach. Complete this consistently excellent, powerhouse experience with a bottle of big red wine.

SushiAnn

B2

Japanese ✕✕

38 E. 51st St. (bet. Madison & Park Aves.)

Subway: 51 St
Phone: 212-755-1780
Web: www.sushiann.com
Prices: $$

Lunch Mon – Fri
Dinner Mon – Sat

Lucky are those who wander into this midtown den steered by one of the best teams of sushi chefs in town. Nestled into a corporate no man's land along 51st Street, it's hard from the outset to see what separates SushiAnn from the pack of smooth-blonde-wood-and-black-lacquered-tray sushi joints that line this pocket of Manhattan.

As in every honest *sushi-ya*, take a seat at the bar (where there is a $30 minimum), get to know one of the chefs, and benefit from the relationship. Skip the menu and tables and go for the omakase—incredibly fresh mackerel served with ponzu and minced ginger sauce; fatty blue fin fanned over shiso leaf and kelp; smoky slices of grilled giant clam; rich torched sardine—all of it is carefully explained by the knowledgeable staff.

Sushiden

A3

Japanese ✕✕

19 E. 49th St. (bet. Fifth & Madison Aves.)

Subway: 5 Av - 53 St
Phone: 212-758-2700
Web: www.sushiden.com
Prices: $$$

Lunch Mon – Fri
Dinner Sun – Fri

Close your eyes to the California rolls, forget everything you've heard from the gaijin crowds, and open yourself to experience this classic, skillfully prepared, very authentic *sushi-ya*. These chefs are no mere amateurs—best to order omakase, allowing the talented professionals to create a delicious parade of seasonal, simply adorned, outrageously fresh fish.

Regardless of recent competition in the form of more modern and stylish spots, Sushiden is more subtly elegant, and remains popular for its traditional food and excellent service. It is an especially big hit with the business lunch crowd that jams the place at midday, so be sure to make reservations.

Another Sushiden location feeds the West Side business crowd in a larger but less warm setting.

239

Sushi Yasuda

Japanese ✗✗

B4

204 E. 43rd St. (bet. Second & Third Aves.)

Subway: Grand Central - 42 St
Phone: 212-972-1001
Web: www.sushiyasuda.com
Prices: $$$$

Lunch Mon – Fri
Dinner Mon – Sat

Attention rule breakers: this glorious sushi spot ain't for you. Late for your reservation? It will be forfeited. Lingering too long after eating? You will be informed that time is up. Sushi-loving diehards can handle the tough love though, and come back time and time again for the spectacularly fresh fish. Left in the capable hands of Mitsuru Tamura after Naomichi Yasuda's departure, this beloved spot still maintains its loyal following.

Grab a spot on the sleek bamboo sushi counter and give over to the chef's superb recommendations, which will be circled on the menu. Tasty slices of kanpanchi (amberjack) and *aji* (mackerel) are brushed with soy and served over rice; while the exquisite *hotate* (scallop) is sprinkled with a touch of sea salt.

Tao

Asian ✗✗

A1

42 E. 58th St. (bet. Madison & Park Aves.)

Subway: 59 St
Phone: 212-888-2288
Web: www.taorestaurant.com
Prices: $$$

Lunch Mon – Fri
Dinner nightly

This former cinema is now (literally) a lively, massive, and über-popular temple of all foods pan-Asian, dramatically outfitted with a Chinese scroll draped across the ceiling and 16-foot statue of Buddha towering over a reflecting pool. The theater's former balconies remain packed, accommodating 300 diners on three levels. The fusion cuisine has a crowd-pleasing combination of Hong Kong, Chinese, Thai, and Japanese dishes, including sushi and sashimi. Perfect for sharing, the well-prepared menu offers everything from small plates of shrimp tempura with garlic-chili sauce and squab lettuce wraps, to wasabi-crusted filet mignon.

The loyal after-work business crowd turns younger and trendier on weekends, ordering hip libations like the lychee martini.

Tsushima

Japanese ✗

B3

141 E. 47th St. (bet. Lexington & Third Aves.)

Subway: Grand Central - 42 St
Phone: 212-207-1938
Web: N/A
Prices: $$

Lunch Mon – Fri
Dinner nightly

Once frequented by a handful of in-the-know diners, Tsushima is a sleeper no more. This midtown Japanese lair is jam-packed with business diners and neighborhood dwellers seeking fantastic value (especially at lunch) and terrific quality. It's not big, but it is bright and upbeat with a long, narrow space that is stylish in a spare Tokyo-meets-Manhattan way. Service is speedy, which is perfect for those who need to get back to a meeting after slurping some soup and nibbling some sushi—options are authentic but nod to spicy tuna-craving Americans. Lunch specials are generous, plentiful (choose from maki, sushi, bento boxes, and more) and inexpensive. The omakase for dinner is well worth the extra expense, when the sushi chefs are less rushed.

Wild Edibles 🍴

Seafood ✗

B5

535 Third Ave. (bet. 35th & 36th Sts.)

Subway: 33 St
Phone: 212-213-8552
Web: www.wildedibles.com
Prices: $$

Lunch & dinner daily

Wild Edibles is plain neat. This utterly charming fish shop, smack dab in harrowing midtown, is flooded with warmth and great seafood. With stations in Grand Central, this fabulous retailer remains unequalled—notice a smattering of dark-wood tables, subway tiles, and a bar joined to the seafood counter unveiling the freshest (and finest) seafood. Relish the quiet at lunch, and do as the regulars do in seeking out straight-from-the-source seafood. Take off with an outstanding warm seafood salad mingling fennel, arugula, and creamy white beans; and then fly high with the Canadian club oyster flight with three pours of wine or beer. The New England (or Orleans) mussels are sumptuously sopped up by Old Bay fries. Rushed? Take your 'catch' and sauce to-go.

Tulsi ❀

Indian 🍴🍴

B3

211 E. 46th St. (bet. 2nd & 3rd Aves.)

Subway: Grand Central - 42 St
Phone: 212-888-0820
Web: www.tulsinyc.com
Prices: $$

Lunch Mon – Sat
Dinner nightly

Tulsi Restaurant/Melissa Hom

An important symbol in Hinduism, Tulsi or holy basil translates to the "incomparable one," a suitable tag for this midtown Indian marvel. Stylish both inside and out, the clean and breezy décor is masked in glass and a pearl palette, and simulates an Indian fantasy. The odd splash of color (green-draped booths) and regal tints of gold, lend to Tulsi an air of exotic fancy.

Saunter into a veiled nook where attractive linen-dressed tables and plush, high-backed chairs set the stage for an opulent dining experience. The service may verge on erratic, but one thing is static: Executive Chef/owner Hemant Mathur's regional creations are original, dashing, and studied. Haunting your mind (and taste buds) for days is a pumpkin ginger soup fragrant with fenugreek seeds; and pungent pea and lamb croquettes splashed with tamarind-date chutney.

Gander a pack of businessmen and locals swoon over his Bombay chicken curry perfumed with *garam masala*, tamarind, and coconut milk, and *Hyderabadi fish murtabak*, a "casserole" of *chapattis* and fish hobnobbing in a rich curry of *kokum* and chilies. Cork this enticing gala with a sweetly spiced duck *moilee*, chased by *jalebis* joined with spiced almond milk.

Wolfgang's

A6

Steakhouse ✗✗

4 Park Ave. (at 33rd St.)

Subway: 33 St
Phone: 212-889-3369
Web: www.wolfgangssteakhouse.com
Prices: $$$$

Lunch & dinner daily

  What started for the fomer waiter of the esteemed Peter Luger has evolved into now five locations going strong—a decision that has yielded mouthwatering results. Located in the former Vanderbilt Hotel dining room, this 1912 landmark space is dressed with elegant tables and showcases a gorgeous terra-cotta ceiling courtesy of famed architect, Rafael Guastavino.

The setting is handsome, but the steak's arrival refocuses all attention on the strapping Porterhouse (for two, three, or four) served sizzling and paired with fried onion rings; sautéed mushrooms; and German potatoes...extra crispy please! If you really want something to knaw on before the meat makes its way, order a perfect martini and slice by slice of Canadian bacon—you're not here for a diet.

Your opinions are
important to us. Please
write to us at:
michelin.guides@
us.michelin.com

Midtown West

New York is a city of incomparable diversity, evident in every quiet, tree-lined neighborhood, ethnic enclave, and luxury high-rise. The truth remains, however, that there is only one street in all five boroughs to be boldly hailed Restaurant Row. Consider that its famed location–where celebrity chefs prepare all-you-can-eat pasta alongside promising sushi bars–is in a neighborhood named Hell's Kitchen is further testament to its dedication to great food.

Restaurant Row

Still, this is an area that insists on reinvention. Hence, Restaurant Row (perhaps due to its uneven reputation) is becoming known as Little Brazil near Sixth Avenue, where samba and street food are celebrated late summer each year on Brazilian Day. A few steps farther west and the city's eclectic identity comes to life again, where a walk down Ninth Avenue offers a world of goods. A wonderful start (or finale) can be found at **Amy's Bread**, whose crusty baguettes supply countless restaurant kitchens, while colorful cakes or cookies tempt passersby. Meanwhile across the avenue, **Poseidon Bakery** is rumored to be the very last place in America to still make its own phyllo dough by hand—a taste of the *spanakopita* will prove it. Regardless of its name, **Sullivan Street Bakery**'s one and only retail outlet is actually on 47th,

between 10th and 11th avenue (a location so perilously far west in the Manhattan mindset that its success proves its worth in gold). Absolutely anything artisanal and delicious can be found nearby at the **Amish Market**, filled with fine produce, meats, and an array of specialty items. A sweet side-trip is the **Little Pie Company**, whose beloved wares are rolled, filled, and baked in its glass-paneled display kitchen.

While this stretch of Hell's Kitchen is rich with markets and restaurants, those highlights familiar to any theater-going tourist or Lincoln Tunnel-bound commuter who has been stuck in its traffic, include a juicy and moist burger from the **Film Center Café**. To unearth its hidden treasures, travel south of Port Authority Bus Terminal and visit a string of unassuming storefronts, starting with **Ninth Avenue International Foods**. These olives, spices, and spreads are a serious business, but it is the renowned *taramosalata* (as if prepared by the gods atop Mount Olympus themselves) that finds its way into restaurants throughout the city. Stop by **Giovanni Esposito and Son's** meat market for a sampling of their Italian sausages. For sandwiches, **Manganaro's** is the true inventor of the original six-foot Italian-American "hero." These are among the family-owned landmark businesses that have quietly been shaping New York's food scene for a better part of the century. Truffle fiends will find a spectacular selection at stylish **Urbani Truffles**, happily located on West End Avenue and 60th Street.

Street Eats

While this is an area often choked by traffic and overpopulated with hungry office workers, New Yorkers demand outstanding food, no matter the venue. Under the guidance of the Vendy Awards and the blog (midtownlunch. com), discover a moveable line of fast, satisfying street-food vendors. Highlights include sausage and schnitzel from **Hallo German Food Stand** and the **Treats Truck** (check the web or follow on Twitter for upcoming locales). Those seeking a more stable location to grab a fantastic burger, fries, or milkshake will not be disappointed at Le Parker Meridien's **burger joint**. Foodies in need of a rarer treat know to head south to K-town—the type of New York neighborhood that sneaks up and floors you. Its instant, unmistakable Asian vibe owes largely to the prominence of karaoke bars, authentic grocers, and countless spots for fresh tofu or handmade dumplings. Throughout Midtown West, it is clear that equal attention is paid to cuisine as to arranging storybook holiday mannequins behind the velvet ropes of Saks Fifth Avenue. As if to illustrate the point, the Japanese bakery, **Minamoto Kitchoan**, channels elegance and subtlety in its

impossibly beautiful rice cakes, bejeweled with plum wine gelée or golden sprinkles. The exquisite packaging makes these the penultimate hostess gift for any uptown dinner party. On the other end of the spectrum, **AQ Café** puts every effort into serving three outstanding meals a day to its throngs of midtown devotees (four, if counting the fabulous pastries). In the same vein, French-influenced **Petrossian Boutique** offers fine caviar and delectable croissants to their parade of patrons. **Marketa** is great for Greek food fanatics, after which a shot of espresso at **FIKA** (where the Swedes display their passion and skill for the Italian elixir) tastes divine. Wind up the affair with a stirring cocktail at the chic **Empire Room** housed in the Empire State Building.

TIME WARNER CENTER

No visit here is complete without a tribute to the gargantuan feat that is the Time Warner Center, presiding over regal Columbus Circle. Here, world-renowned chefs indulge both themselves and their patrons with earth-shattering success. The good news is that the economic downturn has eased demands for reservations (the bad news is the price tag). Still, a range of pleasures can be found here, from **Bouchon Bakery**'s classic French *macarons*, to the eye-popping style and sass of **Clo** Wine Bar.

Midtown West

A   B

DEWITT CLINTON PARK

HUDSON RIVER

INTREPID SEA, AIR & SPACE MUSEUM

CIRCLE LINE FERRY TERMINAL

LINCOLN TUNNEL

395

1

2

W. 52nd
W. 51st
W. 49th
W. 47th
W. 45th
W. 42nd
W. 41st
W. 39th

DiMaggio Hwy.
Joe DiMaggio Hwy.
Eleventh Ave.
Tenth Ave.

Print

Daisy May's BBQ

Landmark Tavern

44 & X
Hell's Kitchen

Esca
West Bank Café

JACOB K. JAVITS CONVENTION CENTER

● Hotels
● Restaurants

PORT AUTHORITY BUS TERMINAL

Mercato

3

4

Broadway
Central Park South
CENTRAL PARK
The Pond

South Gate
Petrossian
Jumeirah Essex House
BLT Market
The Ritz–Carlton, Central Park

Trattoria Dell'Arte
Seäsonal
Radiance Tea House
57 St-7 Av
Le Parker Meridian
57 St
The Plaza

Molyvos
Gordon Ramsay at The London
The Blakely
Estiatorio Milos
Nobu Fifty Seven
Brasserie 8 1/2

Maze at The London
Abboccato
BG

The London NYC
Osteria del Circo
chom chom
Chambers

Mr. Robata
Remi
Má Pêche

Le Bernardin
Ben Benson's
Benoit

Piano Due
The Peninsula New York

The Michelangelo
China Grill
MOMA
The Modern

21 Club

5 Av-53 St

Oceana
Brasserie Ruhlmann
Del Frisco's
ROCKEFELLER CENTER

7 Av
Seventh Ave.
Avenue of the Americas (Sixth Ave.)
Fifth Ave.
Madison Ave.

49th St.
50th St.
51st St.
52nd St.
53rd St.
54th St.
55th St.
56th St.
58th St.

Staghorn
34 St-Penn Sta
Nick & Stef's

MADISON SQUARE GARDEN
PENN STATION

Ninth Ave.
Eighth Ave.

CHELSEA
28 St
27th St.

A   B   CHELSEA

246

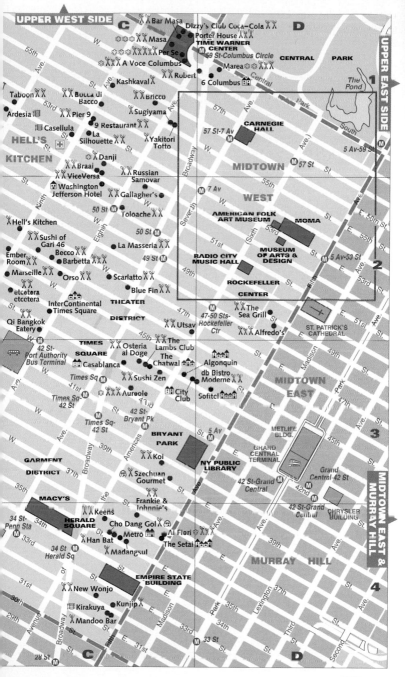

Abboccato

Italian ✗✗

A3

136 W. 55th St. (bet. Sixth & Seventh Aves.)

Subway: 57 St
Phone: 212-265-4000
Web: www.abboccato.com
Prices: $$$

Lunch Mon – Sat
Dinner nightly

Housed within Blakely Hotel, Abboccato is smart, attractive, and expertly run under the watchful eye of seasoned restaurateurs—the Livanos family is also behind nearby Oceana. A sophisticated yet rustic dining room, bar area ripe for people watching, attentive service, and pretty *terrazza* that almost swings onto the sidewalk boast their characteristic style and provide a sophisticated antidote to this bustling midtown location.

The Italian menu meanders through the Peninsula, and each offering is a regional specialty like spaghetti carbonara, made here with house-cured duck prosciutto. An additional menu is dedicated exclusively to *cicchetti*. The dessert offerings are not extensive but remember the classics, such as pignoli macaroons or cannoli.

Alfredo's

Italian ✗✗✗

D2

4 W. 49th St. (bet. Fifth & Sixth Aves.)

Subway: 47-50 Sts - Rockefeller Ctr
Phone: 212-397-0100
Web: www.alfredos.com
Prices: $$$

Lunch & dinner daily

Make your way past the hungry 30 Rock tourists that mob Alfredo's and be rewarded with pizza and pasta delicious enough to make your *nonna* blush. When that unshakable desire to have a classic dish of fettucini Alfredo rears its hungry head, is there any other spot in New York? No. Still, the wise gourmand goes further to explore a solid menu of enjoyable fare, including the enormous Valtellina pizza—it's perfectly crispy, paper-thin crust bursting with fresh toppings like creamy Gorgonzola, soft mozzarella, ripe pears, and truffle oil.

Their consistent success is thanks to the love and attention of a polished, professional kitchen and warm servers passionate about the cuisine; these are assets Alfredo's has in spades, no matter how busy it gets.

Ai Fiori ❀

C4

Italian ✕✕✕

400 Fifth Ave. (bet. 36th & 37th Sts.)

Subway: 34 St - Herald Sq

Lunch & dinner daily

Phone: 212-613-8660
Web: www.aifiorinyc.com
Prices: $$$$

Evan Sung

Ai Fiori seems very much "among the flowers," as if blossoming from its home above the impressive Setai hotel entrance. Within the dining room, certain elements may remind you that this is a hotel restaurant, but designers have worked their magic in contriving a space that is attractive, contemporary, and extremely high-end. This is all warmed by a gracious and well-trained staff.

Through a modern Italian menu, Chef Michael White expresses his knack for putting together an expert kitchen team capable of great things. Dishes find inspiration from the Italian and French Rivieras, balancing rustic favorites with elegant presentations. Starters might include Mediterranean sardines beautifully cooked over a rich tomato confit, or bowls of chilled potato and leek soup poured over plump oysters, drizzled with leek and chorizo oil. However, pasta courses steal the show, with outstanding options such as house-made *trofie al nero* with a Ligurian crustacean ragout of sepia, scallops, and spiced *mollica*.

Desserts show creative genius through tropical fruit, passion fruit coulis, and *crema di coco* all soaking in rum alongside their baba. Lunchtime offers unique bargains with $38 prix-fixe menus.

Ardesia

C1

510 W. 52nd St. (bet. Tenth & Eleventh Aves.)

Subway: 50 St (Eighth Ave.)   Dinner nightly
Phone: 212-247-9191
Web: www.ardesia-ny.com
Prices: $$

Thanks to the talented ladies of Ardesia , this far western stretch of Hell's Kitchen is suddenly stylish and chic. Parked at the base of a swanky new high rise, this sleek spot is the result of owner Mandy Oser and Chef Amorette Casaus's collective hard work, and a favorite for locals seeking scrumptious small plates.

Sit and savor a glass at the white marble bar and admire the floor-to-ceiling blackboards displaying their terrific wine selection. Or, lounge on a sexy brown velvet banquette while nibbling the likes of crispy crostini slathered in an epic, house-made goat milk ricotta; chunks of sweet-slathered, tender pork belly atop cubes of tart apple; or the smoky duck *bánh mì*, loaded with house-cured duck, pickled veggies, and *sriracha* aïoli.

Barbetta

C2

321 W. 46th St. (bet. Eighth & Ninth Aves.)

Subway: 50 St (Eighth Ave.)   Lunch & dinner Tue – Sat
Phone: 212-246-9171
Web: www.barbettarestaurant.com
Prices: $$$

Standing proud since its 1906 opening, Barbetta proves that the "new" in New York need not be taken literally. From its gilded furnishings to its candelabra and crystal chandeliers, this dining room celebrates an old-world aesthetic. At the ornate tables, find true-blue New Yorkers who, as regulars, have been treated like family here for more than century (though outsiders may detect a hint of indifference from the service staff).

Consistency is the theme here, and some of the menu items, such as *minestrone giardiniera*, have been served since the very beginning. Good, traditional Italian food with a few throwbacks–capped off by a selection from the dessert trolley–prove that this just might be your grandfather's favorite Italian restaurant.

Aureole ✿

Contemporary ✗✗✗

C3

135 W. 42nd St. (bet. Broadway & Sixth Ave.)

Subway: 42 St - Bryant Pk
Phone: 212-319-1660
Web: www.charliepalmer.com
Prices: $$$$

Lunch Mon – Fri
Dinner nightly

Eric Laignel

The Bank of America tower is a welcome addition to the city skyline. Above, the sleek skyscraper strikes a pose, illuminating the night sky with its colorful spire; below, ever-popular Aureole stands sentry as a beacon of fine dining in the area.

The capacious Adam Tihany-designed space brims with possibility. With its elevated ceiling, expanse of glass, and handsome details, the front bar room beckons those who fancy a cocktail or à la carte bite. The back dining room swaddles its occupants in soft lighting, plush furnishings, and fine materials for a prix-fixe meal. Wine aficionados, take a moment to glimpse the eye-catching bottle lined catwalk and engage with the crackerjack team for counsel navigating the astute list.

Charlie Palmer's Aureole has seen its share of talent come and go in the short existence of its new incarnation, but thankfully the cuisine remains consistent regardless. The cooking is impressive and makes room for elegant preparations—tender, charred octopus tentacle dressed with *vadouvan*, hummus, and shaved spring vegetables; or slow-braised veal cheeks sparked by cornichon mustard sauce, silky cabernet reduction, and an earthy morel ragout.

A Voce Columbus ⚚

Italian 𝓧𝓧𝓧

C1

10 Columbus Circle (in the Time Warner Center)

Subway: 59 St - Columbus Circle

Lunch & dinner daily

Phone: 212-823-2523

Web: www.avocerestaurant.com

Prices: $$$

Bruce Buck

Two words that best describe this Italian diva? Expert and exceptional. Housed in the gourmet Time Warner Center, delight in this shining showroom's façade (a gorgeous mall rife with a hotel, shopping, and residences), before shimmying into its grand interior.

Like big sis A Voce Madison, mellow tones rule the dining room with khaki-clothed designer chairs and glossy wood tables sitting atop polished planks. Statuesque windows let sunlight drench this decadent den, where many revelations are to be had. Besides its spirited bar and blanket views, A Voce Columbus' glass-walled kitchen looms large and lures many with Missy Robbins' warming and sincere Italian eats.

Favored by a brew of media moguls (CNN is in the south tower) and devout locals, her menu is a veritable registry of superb products handled with care, and reveals freshly-baked focaccia sprinkled with ricotta and basil, and tagliatelle twirled in chicken liver sauce studded with caramelized onions, truffles, and Parmesan. Tingling your taste buds is crumb-crusted *baccalà* spiced with *nduja*; while a crispy Mela-apple Charlotte kissed with brown butter gelato and raisins, offers you a peek into honeyed nirvana.

Bar Masa

C1

Japanese ✗✗

10 Columbus Circle (in the Time Warner Center)

Subway: 59 St - Columbus Circle

Phone: 212-823-9800

Web: www.masanyc.com

Prices: $$$

Lunch & dinner Mon – Sat

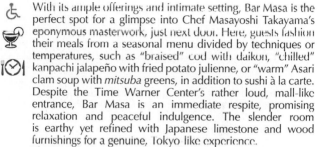

With its ample offerings and intimate setting, Bar Masa is the perfect spot for a glimpse into Chef Masayoshi Takayama's eponymous masterwork, just next door. Here, guests fashion their meals from a seasonal menu divided by techniques or temperatures, such as "braised" cod with daikon, "chilled" kanpachi jalapeño with fried potato julienne, or "warm" Asari clam soup with *mitsuba* greens, in addition to sushi à la carte. Despite the Time Warner Center's rather loud, mall-like entrance, Bar Masa is an immediate respite, promising relaxation and peaceful indulgence. The slender room is earthy yet refined with Japanese limestone and wood furnishings for a genuine, Tokyo-like experience.

The popular bar area offers well-chosen wines and creative cocktails.

Becco

C2

Italian ✗✗

355 W. 46th St. (bet. Eighth & Ninth Aves.)

Subway: 42 St - Port Authority Bus Terminal

Phone: 212-397-7597

Web: www.becco-nyc.com

Prices: $$

Lunch & dinner daily

Tucked into the Theater District's ambitious, highly competitive restaurant row, Becco's been rocking out killer Italian fare since it debuted in 1993. You can thank owners Lidia Bastianich and son, Joseph, for that—the former has been instrumental in informing the American public (through television and her cookbooks) about the distinction between Italian and Italian-American dishes, and demystifying Italian regional cooking in general.

How this translates to your plate is a culinary delight—dishes like creamy polenta wrapped in a crispy jacket of *Montasio* cheese arrive with scrumptious slices of speck; while grilled swordfish is laced with pumpkin seed oil and paired with spaghetti squash, stewed cherry tomatoes, and roasted pumpkin seeds.

Ben Benson's

A4

Steakhouse ✕✕

123 W. 52nd St. (bet. Sixth & Seventh Aves.)

Subway: 7 Av
Phone: 212-581-8888
Web: www.benbensons.com
Prices: $$$

Lunch Mon – Fri
Dinner nightly

From this office building ground floor, Ben Benson's has spent over 25 years serving prime cuts of USDA meats and other classic American fare to contented power brokers and politicians (regulars' names are engraved on brass plaques). The huge, rotating menu features perfectly cooked steaks and chops, but remembers to include something for everyone, as in the selection of salads or even chicken Parmigiana. Seafood fans will be happy to find shrimp scampi; and the cold poached salmon is a rare find. Oenophiles rejoice in the impressive wine list.

The high-ceilinged dining room, expertly staffed by smartly attired servers, is airier than many of the steakhouses in town. For pleasant alfresco dining, head to the spacious sidewalk terrace in warmer weather.

Benoit

A4

French ✕✕

60 W. 55th St. (bet. Fifth & Sixth Aves.)

Subway: 57 St
Phone: 646-943-7373
Web: www.benoitny.com
Prices: $$

Lunch & dinner Mon – Sat

What started as the Manhattan outpost of a century-old Parisian classic has grown, matured, and indeed come into its own as an elegant French bistro with genuine New York style. One step inside reveals layer upon lovely layer of red accents, polished brass, frosted glass, and modern chairs that combine to make this a very special place.

Be sure to begin with a range of hors d'oeuvres that showcase the kitchen's potential, from lentil salad topped with quail eggs to the excellent rillettes and *baccalau*. While some dishes are touched with innovations, others highlight good quality and tradition, as in the hand-cut steak tartare. Desserts are not to be missed—the rum baba, topped tableside with rum and dollops of whipped cream, is simply outstanding.

BG

American ✗✗

754 Fifth Ave. (at 58th St.)

Subway: 5 Av   59 St   Lunch & dinner daily
Phone: 212-872-8977
Web: www.bergdorfgoodman.com
Prices: $$$

How many Burnettes does it take to feed a bevy of Bergdorf Blondes? Just one if it's the talented Darryl Burnette—the chef hired by the luxury department store to create an inviting seventh-floor menu for its discerning clientele. Luckily, Burnette comes armed with a heavy-hitting resume (Spice Market and Métrazur), and a knack for spinning out delicate luncheon goodies like tender coins of ahi tuna tartare, layered with ripe avocado and crunchy tobiko.

The afternoon tea, served daily, is a perfect fit for the Parisian-styled salon, with its hand-painted wallpaper, 18th century chairs, and celebrated views of Central Park. Those looking for a soup or sandwich, *sans* pomp, can wander over to Bar III, located in the men's store across the street.

BLT Market

American ✗✗

1430 Sixth Ave. (at 59th St.)

Subway: 5 Av - 59 St   Dinner Tue — Sat
Phone: 212-521-6125
Web: www.bltrestaurants.com
Prices: $$$

Tucked into the ground floor of the historic Ritz-Carlton Central Park, BLT Market's dining hall is the very picture of a stylish, market-themed affair replete with floor-to-ceiling windows flooding light into a big, open room dressed in wood-sculpted credenzas.

With Tourondel's credentials at the helm, this market fare doesn't come cheap, but you'll find only the finest ingredients in the rotating menus that might feature tender pigs in a blanket, slathered in an herby garlic oil and excellent Dijon mustard; spice-crusted yellowfin tuna set atop a tangy, creamy aïoli and paired with roasted beets in vinaigrette and frisée salad; or glazed Long Island duck and Hudson Valley foie gras with Bosc pear-ginger compote and wild mushrooms.

Blue Fin

C2

1567 Broadway (at 47th St.)

Subway: 49 St
Phone: 212-918-1400
Web: www.bluefinnyc.com
Prices: $$$

Lunch & dinner daily

It's inside the W Hotel so you know it's going to look good and Blue Fin doesn't disappoint with its two-tiered dining room, sweeping staircase, and baby grand piano. The scene is buzzy on the first floor and at the sushi bar, so if you're looking for quieter digs, head upstairs.

Blue Fin is a seafood spot—would you have guessed? Maybe it's the light blue walls with the motion of the ocean hanging installation. There's sushi and a raw bar, as well as an assortment of everything from grilled octopus salad to Atlantic striped bass. Desserts, like the key lime mojito tart, are where it's at. Honestly, who can resist the adorable "going to the theater" treat with selections like gooey and warm chocolate chip cookies or caramel popcorn to-go?

Bocca di Bacco

C1

828 Ninth Ave. (bet. 54th & 55th Sts.)

Subway: 50 St (Eighth Ave.)
Phone: 212-265-8828
Web: www.boccadibacconyc.com
Prices: $$

Dinner nightly

Nestled into the theater district, rustic yet sultry Bocca di Bacco is a consummate favorite for its great selection of wines, appealing nibbles, and décor that harks back to the *cantine* of Italy with NYC art gallery accents. Solo diners seek the front bar—a sexy perch to snack, sip, and savor.

Through its wine bar identity, the menu spotlights pristine ingredients and products. The array of easygoing dishes may include grilled octopus with a well-dressed potato salad; juicy and tender *fegatini di pollo* (sautéed chicken livers) floating in a sweet onion and port wine reduction; or penne with Gorgonzola, green peas, and walnuts that are all sweetness and crunch.

Although nights can get busy and boisterous, the kitchen remains skilled and competent.

Braai

C1

329 W. 51st St. (bet. Eighth & Ninth Aves.)

Subway: 50 St (Eighth Ave.)
Phone: 212-315-3315
Web: www.braainyc.com
Prices: $$

Lunch Fri – Sun
Dinner nightly

With a meaty menu that includes ostrich and African road runner grilled over the *ysterhout* wood of African olive trees, this South African restaurant has quickly created a buzz. Opened in 2008, Braai (Afrikaans for barbecue) may not have the smooth service of its popular sister bar, the nearby South African wine bar Xai Xai; but this is just the kind of restaurant the Theater District needs. The sultry, arched ceilings, gnarled wooden beams, and creative fare more than satisfy, as if every day here is Braai Day (which is actually 9/24).

Save room to linger over your wine with a classic South African dessert like the *malva* pudding—a moist, delicate bread pudding dish of Dutch origin, served on a thin bed of fragrant granadilla-amarula custard.

Brasserie 8 1/2

B3

9 W. 57th St. (bet. Fifth & Sixth Aves.)

Subway: 57 St
Phone: 212-829-0812
Web: www.brasserie8andahalf.com
Prices: $$$

Lunch Sun – Fri
Dinner nightly

Nestled into the unique Skidmore building, the sweeping, tangerine-colored staircase that delivers you into Brasserie 8 1/2 is a bit more theatrical than the menu's predictable performance, but this Patina Group restaurant impresses nonetheless. Settle into the main dining room with its eye-popping hues and original artwork of Henri Matisse and Fernand Léger—to find solid, contemporary, prettily plated French offerings. From the seasonal game menu, expect the likes of stuffed pheasant with apples, foie gras, cabbage, and an apple cider reduction.

Though its thoughtful design and well-spaced tables will impress company, it also caters well to solo guests, whether at the handsome, elevated mezzanine or one of the two sleek bars anchoring the room.

Brasserie Ruhlmann

French ✗✗

A4

45 Rockefeller Plaza (bet. Fifth & Sixth Aves.)

Subway: 47-50 Sts - Rockefeller Ctr
Phone: 212-974-2020
Web: www.brasserieruhlmann.com
Prices: $$$

Lunch daily
Dinner Mon – Sat

Named for the French designer, Emile-Jacques Ruhlmann, this midtown brasserie sweeps you from the cacophony of touristy Rockefeller Center and into a heady vision of old-school Paris, surrounded by dark panels, red velvet, and perhaps a few personalities from nearby NBC Studios.

A commendable team heads the kitchen, spinning a solid roster of brasserie classics into delicious artistry. A poached artichoke arrives tender, meaty, and succulent, with a white rémoulade topped with black olive tapenade spooned into its center; while a pristine Dover Sole Meunière is served whole, beautifully browned, alongside *pommes fondant* and a bright bundle of sautéed spinach. A decadent and elegant cookie plate almost prepares you for the outside world again.

Bricco

Italian ✗✗

C1

304 W. 56th St. (bet. Eighth & Ninth Aves.)

Subway: 57 St - 7 Av
Phone: 212-245-7160
Web: www.bricconyc.com
Prices: $$

Lunch Mon – Fri
Dinner nightly

It's a bit of a challenge to spot this cozy nook in the swirling hubbub of nearby Columbus Circle, but its well worth the effort. Romantic little spots like Bricco are a rarity in this neck of the woods, and owner, Nino Catuogno, knows it—those autographed lipstick kisses lining the ceiling and popular, female-friendly bar prove it.

Couples can head back to the intimate main room for the comforting menu of delicious pizzas (visibly made to order in the brick oven); fat ribbons of whole wheat pasta in meaty ragù; or tender filet mignon dancing in brandy and cream, and sprinkled with crunchy peppercorns. Save room for a fragrant dessert of deep purple pears, poached in wine and liqueur.

The love is now extended to its new sibling, Bricco Blu.

Casellula

C1

American

401 W. 52nd St. (bet. Ninth & Tenth Aves.)

Subway: 50 St (Eighth Ave.)
Phone: 212-247-8137
Web: www.casellula.com
Prices: 💲💲

Dinner nightly

After running the cheese program at The Modern, Brian Keyser partnered with Joe Farrell to open this simple but charming cheese and wine café off of Ninth Avenue. Inside, a wonderfully attentive staff tends the small bar and handful of wood tables, set against simply adorned brick walls and rustic rows of wine bottles.

With over 30 varieties of excellent cheese, each is clearly organized from fresh to bloomy and beyond. The kitchen's offerings may include delights like a crisp "pig's ass" *panino* made from a crusty baguette, moist, sweet slices of roast pork, and drizzled with a thick chipotle aïoli; goose-breast Reuben with *Fontina Val d'Aosta*, house slaw, and creamy horseradish; or a decadent chocolate cake, with each layer soaked in fresh cream.

China Grill

A4

Asian

60 W. 53rd St. (bet. Fifth & Sixth Aves.)

Subway: 7 Av
Phone: 212-333-7788
Web: www.chinagrillmgt.com
Prices: 💲💲💲

Lunch Mon – Sat
Dinner nightly

Opened more than 20 years ago, this first China Grill continues to be a perennial favorite and serves as the flagship of Jeffrey Chodorow's international restaurant organization. The sprawling interior, designed by Jeffrey Beers, is housed on the ground floor of the CBS building and features a multi-level dining room of soaring 30-foot ceilings accented with white canopy light fixtures. The long bar area is a popular spot to unwind after a long day at the office.

Large tables provide the perfect spot to dine with a group; the food is good, fun, and is best enjoyed when shared. Served family style, the Asian-influenced menu may include perfectly fried rice topped with creamy, diced avocado, or delicate pancakes generously filled with tender lobster.

Cho Dang Gol 😊

Korean ✗

C4

55 W. 35th St. (bet. Fifth & Sixth Aves.)

Subway: 34 St - Herald Sq
Phone: 212-695-8222
Web: www.chodanggolny.com
Prices: 💰💰

Lunch & dinner daily

K-town may boast its barbecue joints, but Cho Dang Gol has its own calling in tofu, that creamy little bean curd that sets hearts a-jumping. The restaurant is named for a South Korean village famous for this specialty; one imagines those locals would approve of this fresh, silky house-made version. Here, tofu finds its way into more than two dozen dishes, including hot and crispy pancakes, filled with ground pork and vegetables; or a cast iron pot, loaded with sweet and spicy octopus. A spicy prime-rib casserole is perfect for sharing.

At first glance, Cho Dang Gol is warm and sentimental with cute Korean artifacts and rustic wooden tables, but don't expect like-minded service. When the house gets packed, servers respond with brusque efficiency.

chom chom

Korean ✗✗

A3

40 W. 56th St. (bet. Fifth & Sixth Aves.)

Subway: 57 St
Phone: 212-213-2299
Web: www.chomchomnyc.com
Prices: $$

Lunch & dinner daily

Somehow, chom chom landed well north of its K-town compatriots to happily bring its soul-shaking Korean cuisine to a neighborhood away from the clamor. The vibe at this Korean corridor is mod and folksy (vertically cut trees drape the walls), but the food is flavorfully faithful. Sip a soju at the bar before diving into a menu that favors fun to tradition.

Chom chom wears many hats, but everything is crested with serious ingredients. Begin with a few "kapas" (Korean tapas) like spicy pork buns; succulent sweet potato *japchae* with paper-thin beef and vegetables; and *bo ssäm* with braised and seared pork belly, spicy batons of root vegetables, and fresh Boston lettuce. Simpler dishes highlight amazing quality, as in broiled wild salmon.

Daisy May's BBQ

B2 Barbecue 🍴

623 Eleventh Ave. (at 46th St.)

Subway: 50 St (Eighth Ave.)   Lunch & dinner daily
Phone: 212-977-1500
Web: www.daisymaysbbq.com
Prices: 😊😊

Trek to the ends of the earth (known to some as Eleventh Avenue), and the barbecue gods will reward you. Welcome to Daisy May's BBQ USA—where Chef/owner (and cookbook author) Adam Perry Lang's smoky, succulent 'cue served up in a big old dining hall (think school lunchroom meets barn) counts everyone from Oprah to bike messengers to midtown suits as fans.

Three chalkboards list the pig specials: a whole pig for up to 12 people (should you be blessed with so many friends); half a pig; and a few daily specials. The house pulled pork, a mound of tender, glistening sweet and smoky pork, is a fan favorite for good reason. A limited selection of beer and wine is available to wash it all down, but our money's on the irresistibly sweet and minty iced tea.

db Bistro Moderne

D3 Contemporary 🍴🍴

55 W. 44th St. (bet. Fifth & Sixth Aves.)

Subway: 5 Av   Lunch & dinner daily
Phone: 212-391-2400
Web: www.danielnyc.com
Prices: $$$

This stylish Daniel Boulud bistro is an ideal upscale spot for drinking and dining pre- or post-theater. Its moneyed clientele looks perfectly at home in the sophisticated space, which is divided into a lively, red-accented front room and a much quieter, comfortable, more refined elevated back room.

Boulud's French-inflected menu showcases the chef's consistency and formidable skills in dishes like country duck pâté that somehow become richer and more decadent with each bite. The lovely chocolate clafouti is garnished with outstanding vanilla ice cream and chocolate sorbet. Yet most famously, the humble burger is recreated with foie gras, black truffles, and short ribs—a monument that helped ignite New York's gourmet burger renaissance.

Danji ⌘

Korean 🍴

346 W. 52nd St. (bet. Eighth & Ninth Aves.)

Subway: 50 St (Eighth Ave.)
Phone: 212-586-2880
Web: www.danjinyc.com
Prices: $$

Lunch Mon – Fri
Dinner Mon – Sat

James Park/2be Photography & Design

Masa and Daniel veteran Hooni Kim is making headlines with his own venture, a contemporary and crowning Korean boîte in Hell's Kitchen. Tucked into a handsome, narrow space, Danji is outfitted with shimmering silk panels; an arrangement of earthenware pots; a bar streaming a line of primo libations; and those ever-popular Edison bulbs gently lighting the space.

An eminently engaging staff invites a posse of cosmopolites to perch at the bar or at one of the pretty blonde (wood) counters accoutered with glossy white-framed stools. Kim draws on his heritage and culinary training to craft both traditional and modern Korean dishes which proudly flaunt an array of first-rate products.

Kick things off with tender, shredded brisket in a delicate miso stew wafting with silky tofu, chunky root vegetables, and fingerling potatoes; and then move on to *bulgogi* beef sliders mingled with roasted bone marrow, spicy pickled cucumber, and scallions all snuggled into a toasted brioche bun. A sublime yellowtail sashimi, folded over a crunchy kelp and sesame salsa might very well be Danji's "signature," and is a fitting epitome of this ravishing rookie's seamless progression from classic to current.

Del Frisco's

A4

Steakhouse   🍴🍴🍴

1221 Sixth Ave. (at 49th St.)

Subway: 47-50 Sts - Rockefeller Ctr   Lunch Mon – Fri
Phone: 212-575-5129   Dinner nightly
Web: www.delfriscos.com
Prices: $$$

Prime, aged, corn-fed beef is the main attraction at this sprawling outpost of the Dallas-based steakhouse chain. Portions range from a six ounce filet to the 24-ounce Porterhouse to make any Texan proud.

The menu may begin with a suitably rich feast of turtle soup or caviar, but then does an about face with offerings of angel hair pasta or creamed corn. This may be as much a testament to its dedication to please every palate as it is to the fact of its outrageous financial success. Complementing its midtown locale in the McGraw-Hill Building, Del Frisco's showcases a large L-shaped bar, linen-covered tables, and window panels stretching to the second floor. The mezzanine dining area, accessible by a sweeping staircase, enjoys a quieter ambience.

Dizzy's Club Coca-Cola

C1

Southern   🍴🍴

10 Columbus Circle (in the Time Warner Center)

Subway: 59 St - Columbus Circle   Dinner nightly
Phone: 212-258-9595
Web: www.jalc.org
Prices: $$

It took legendary jazz great, Wynton Marsalis, plenty of smooth-talking to convince the city and developers that the Time Warner Building should permanently house Jazz at Lincoln Center; but the terrific Dizzy's Club Coca-Cola, a jazz hall-cum-restaurant, is all the proof needed to greenlight a visit here.

Housed on the 5th floor of the North tower at the Frederick P. Rose Hall, this swanky little gem has glossy windows overlooking Central Park, and the cooking is as tasty as the rotating performers are talented. Expect a loose and comfy lineup of Southern staples like low country shrimp and grits with local cheddar sauce, caramelized onions, and smoked Tasso ham; Cajun jambalaya with diver scallops and andouille; or babyback ribs with moppin' sauce.

Ember Room

Asian ✕✕

C2

647 Ninth Ave. (bet. 45th & 46th Sts.)

Subway: 42 St - Port Authority Bus Terminal   Lunch & dinner daily
Phone: 212-245-8880
Web: www.emberroom.com
Prices: $$$

The Ember Room is certainly a hot thing to hit Hell's Kitchen recently. It packs a serious pedigree–Todd English and Ian Chalermkittichai are two bold-faced names on the lineup– but this place is drop-dead gorgeous too. Push back the velvet curtains and see that you've died and gone to heaven. A ceiling covered with golden temple bells, a Carrara marble bar, and a 25-foot distressed wood wall covered with gold-leaf calligraphy—it's all stunning.

With looks this good, who cares about the food? Well, they do. The kitchen turns out sensational Thai-spiced dishes like roasted scallops with smoked bacon and kohlrabi, and Thai pastrami meatballs. Chocolate baby back ribs, and barbecue beef tongue with a sea salt and jalapeño kick are to do die for.

Esca

Seafood ✕✕✕

B2

402 W. 43rd St. (bet. Ninth & Tenth Aves.)

Subway: 42 St - Port Authority Bus Terminal   Lunch Mon – Sat
Phone: 212-564-7272   Dinner nightly
Web: www.esca-nyc.com
Prices: $$$

Helmed by avid fisherman and Chef David Pasternack and team Batali-Bastianich, it is no wonder that Esca introduced New Yorkers to something new. Though it may lay a bit off the well-worn midtown path, this spot is credited with putting *crudi*, a sort of Italian sashimi, on the culinary map. On occasion, this estimable seafood favorite loses its way, but when it's good, it's fantastic—from the table of Italian-style vegetables to the bluefish trio. The talented staff has a gift for patiently steering newcomers to the perfect Italian wine. Bathed in creamy yellow walls, dark timbers, and soft light, Esca's rustic charms are undeniable.

Enthusiasts sail onward to Eataly, where Chef Pasternack runs the fish department, and pick up a copy of his book.

Estiatorio Milos

Greek

A3

125 W. 55th St. (bet. Sixth & Seventh Aves.)

Subway: 57 St
Phone: 212-245-7400
Web: www.milos.ca
Prices: $$$

Lunch Mon – Fri
Dinner nightly

It's mod meets the Med in midtown at Estiatorio Milos. This sleek space has cornered the market on industrial chic with its light-filled, atrium-style dining room, raw cement columns and walls, and exposed ducts. Antiqued flooring and decorative objects add a Greek aspect to this otherwise New York-centric space.

Hugely patronized by local businesses and corporate casts, the food here is as polished as the crowd. The kitchen's signature is its simple, yet elegant, preparations of incredibly fresh fish, filleted or left whole. Silky tender and perfectly grilled octopus transports diners straight to the Cyclades, while the meze platter brings together the flavors of Greece with roasted stuffed peppers, olives, *tzatziki*, *taramasalata*, and fava bean purée.

etcetera etcetera

Italian

C2

352 W. 44th St. (bet. Eighth & Ninth Aves.)

Subway: 42 St - Port Authority Bus Terminal
Phone: 212-399-4141
Web: www.etcrestaurant.com
Prices: $$

Lunch Wed & Sun
Dinner nightly

Hip and modern, etcetera etcetera is a breath of fresh air in the often staid Theater District. The modern and contemporary design punctuated by pops of bright orange has a Milan-meets-Miami sensibility, but the crowd is never too cool for school.

The kitchen turns out seriously solid and well-prepared dishes. Pasta and risotto dishes, such as the homemade basil spaghetti with jumbo lump crab and sweet roasted peppers, can be halved and served as appetizers. The entrées (crispy Cornish hen, braised lamb shank) are hearty and offer beautifully balanced flavors and textures. Etcetera etcetera proves that looking good does not always mean spending a fortune—the $35 prix-fixe three-course dinner is an exceptional value.

44 & X Hell's Kitchen

American ✕✕

622 Tenth Ave. (at 44th St.)

Subway: 42 St - Port Authority Bus Terminal
Phone: 212-977-1170
Web: www.44andx.com
Prices: $$

Lunch & dinner daily

With its jumbo windows overlooking a prime people-watching corner of 44th Street and 10th Avenue, this Hell's Kitchen mainstay is a classic choice day or night, no matter the season, and no matter how huge this high-rise heavy neighborhood gets. On warm summer afternoons, guests await outdoor tables under the big striped awning in front; come wintertime, the carved wooden bar beckons.

The staff can be flaky on occasion, though it's probably par for the course with waiters sporting cheeky "Heaven" and "Hell" t-shirts. Best to belly up and join the fun over inventive American fare like stacked roasted beets with piped ribbons of tangy goat cheese; or moist turkey meat loaf wrapped in smoky bacon. Next door, sibling 44&X boasts an intimate back garden.

Frankie & Johnnie's

Steakhouse ✕✕

32 W. 37th St. (bet. Fifth & Sixth Aves.)

Subway: 34 St - Herald Sq
Phone: 212-947-8940
Web: www.frankieandjohnnies.com
Prices: $$$

Lunch Mon — Fri
Dinner Mon — Sat

You get a slice of history with your perfectly-seared ribeye at this storied Garment District steakhouse. The renovated townhouse–with its masculine sensibility and cozy wood-paneled library-turned upstairs dining room–used to belong to the actor John Drew Barrymore, and it is the second of three sibling restaurants that began in 1926 (the first restaurant is a stone's throw away and the third location resides in Rye, New York).

Served by a professional, all-male brigade, the food is pure steakhouse bliss: think silky Clams Casino, topped with crispy bacon and scallions; tender, bone-on ribeye, seared to perfection; irresistibly crunchy hashbrowns; and buttery, flaky apple strudel, delivered with a side of fresh whipped cream and mint sprig.

Gallagher's

C2

Steakhouse ✗✗

228 W. 52nd St. (bet. Broadway & Eighth Ave.)

Subway: 50 St (Broadway)
Phone: 212-245-5336
Web: www.gallaghersnysteakhouse.com
Prices: $$$

Lunch & dinner daily

Established in 1927 next to what is now the Neil Simon Theater, this culinary character and true New Yorker (with outposts in New Jersey and Florida) satisfies carnivores with beef grilled over hickory coals. This focus is clear upon entering to face rows of assorted cuts hanging, patiently aging, in the glass-enclosed meat locker. Inside the wood-paneled dining room, charmingly gruff waiters in gold-trimmed blazers efficiently tend red-checked tables, alongside walls lined with nostalgic photographs of Broadway stars, politicians, and athletes.

While meals are not cheap, the quality shines. Classic salads and creamy desserts are delicious bookends to any meal here. The $30 prix-fixe lunch is an excellent option for the budget conscious.

Han Bat

C4

Korean ✗

53 W. 35th St. (bet. Fifth & Sixth Aves.)

Subway: 34 St - Herald Sq
Phone: 212-629-5588
Web: N/A
Prices: 🍴🍴

Lunch & dinner daily

Pop into this 24-hour K-town spot for traditional, tasty Korean comfort food. Unlike the surrounding mega-barbecue joints, Han Bat favors a cozy, familial vibe and belly-warming specialties. In place of in-table grills, find *dol sot bi bim bap* (sizzling clay pots of crisp-seared rice topped with beef, pickles, eggs, and many condiments); plates of addictive *mandoo* (Korean dumplings stuffed with pork and vegetables); savory bowls of *sul run tang* (sliced beef in a milky beef broth); and a spicy stew of kimchi and tofu. Whether stopping in for a lunch special or late-night, post-karaoke snack, there is something for everyone on the ample, well-organized menu.

Authentic and intrepid foodies should sample the *u jok sara moo chim*—"jello" from ox legs.

Gordon Ramsay at The London ✿ ✿

Contemporary XXXX

151 W. 54th St. (bet. Sixth & Seventh Aves.)

Subway: 7 Av

Dinner Tue – Sat

Phone: 212-468-8888
Web: www.gordonramsay.com
Prices: $$$$

Gordon Ramsay at The London

Is this dining room effete? Absolutely not. But entering this space feels like a privilege reserved for upper echelons, with subtleties and splendor lost on the plebs. Picture Gatsby toying with his sterling cigarette case at the next table, while others remark that the room evokes the inside of an oyster shell. Whether or not this sparks your interest, know that the staff is superbly orchestrated, the wines are impressive, and that dining here is a luxurious experience.

While Gordon Ramsay no longer dons his whites here, Chef Markus Glocker continues to put forth a highly skilled and contemporary cuisine (at times inconsistently) available as three- or five-course menus. To begin, expect the likes of sweet, golden-brown scallops served with curry-spiced cauliflower, crunchy chickpeas, and compressed mango. Entrées shine with the likes of veal tenderloin, served as a riff on beef Wellington, tucked into a layer of thin bread, pan-fried to crispiness, and dressed with an outstanding sauce of reduced veal jus and summer truffles.

For dessert, the Meyer lemon pudding cake paired with strawberry meringue and scoops of Champagne sorbet makes a refreshingly pink finish.

Hell's Kitchen

C2

Mexican ✕

679 Ninth Ave. (bet. 46th & 47th Sts.)

Subway: 50 St (Eighth Ave.)
Phone: 212-977-1588
Web: www.hellskitchen-nyc.com
Prices: $$

Dinner nightly

Upscale Mexican food is clearly enjoying its heyday on the city's culinary scene, but Hell's Kitchen was way ahead of the curve. Named for its western midtown locale, this hip, progressive Mexican eatery has been packing them in from day one with their complex, spiced-to-order food and great service to boot. Be forewarned that the vibe here can go from lively to raucous at prime times, so best to arrive early.

Everything is lovingly prepared, from the tuna tartare with mini-tostadas and spicy guacamole to wickedly good empanadas stuffed with warm, gooey-sweet, caramelized banana, and topped with a bittersweet chocolate sauce. Entrées may feature heaping plates of tender, shredded pork, braised to perfection and folded into soft, warm tortillas.

Kashkaval

C1

Mediterranean ✕

856 Ninth Ave. (bet. 55th & 56th Sts.)

Subway: 50 St (Eighth Ave.)
Phone: 212-581-8282
Web: www.kashkavalfoods.com
Prices: $$

Lunch & dinner daily

Kashkaval is a little Mediterranean grocery-cum-wine bar-cum-perfect neighborhood eatery.

Inside this scruffy little storefront, the dedicated staff and gracious owners are scurrying to accommodate locals picking up garlicky spreads, cheeses, and exotic oils from the front grocery, while the ever-growing lines of regulars happily wait for a precious table or stool to be vacated in the back dining room.

At its heart, this Mediterranean menu embodies what every diner wants: quality ingredients, careful cooking, good prices, and smiles to boot. Offerings may include the tender and moist turkey meatballs or Middle Eastern tapas, featuring baba ganoush, lentil salad, and *muhammara*—highly spiced chopped nuts with red pepper flakes, bound together with oil.

Keens

C4

72 W. 36th St. (bet. Fifth & Sixth Aves.)

Subway: 34 St - Herald Sq
Phone: 212-947-3636
Web: www.keens.com
Prices: $$$

Lunch Mon – Fri
Dinner nightly

Dating back to 1885, Keens steakhouse is imbued with a palpable sense of history that sets it apart from the average midtown chophouse. A collection of dining rooms build the setting, each arranged with dark wood furnishings, linen-draped tables, and chock-full of Gilded Age charisma—a vestige of Keens' men-only, smoker's club days is displayed in their collection of long-stemmed, clay churchwarden pipes lining the ceiling.

Mouthwatering slabs of broiled meat star here; and the hand-selected prime cuts of beef are dry-aged in house. Icy platters of oysters and bananas Foster are classic bookends to any feast.

The Pub Room offers lighter fare, and the bar pours one of the most extensive selections of single malt Scotch around.

Kirakuya

C4

2 W. 32nd St. (bet. Fifth & Sixth Aves.)

Subway: 34 St - Herald Sq
Phone: 212-695-7272
Web: www.kirakuya-nyc.com
Prices: $$

Lunch Mon – Fri
Dinner Mon – Sat

Though it resides in K-town, this sake bar and restaurant is Japanese to the hilt. On the second floor of a nondescript building overlooking jumbled 32nd Street, the sultry Kirakuya starts to soothe your nerves long before your first gulp of sake: the spacious room, divided by deep mahogany wood accents, features an elegant bar and high-backed wood banquettes.

Chef Michihiro Kumagai meanders from traditional *izakaya* offerings, fusing Italian ingredients (think anchovy sauce and prosciutto) with classic Japanese technique. At lunch soba and udon are stellar, but don't miss dinner delights like the *unagi don*, a dish of sweetly-glazed, grilled eel, paired with rice, shredded egg, and miso soup; or juicy pork tempura wrapped around okra pods.

Koi

Fusion 🍴🍴

C3

40 W. 40th St. (bet. Fifth & Sixth Aves.)

Subway: 42 St - Bryant Pk
Phone: 212-921-3330
Web: www.koirestaurant.com
Prices: $$$

Lunch Mon – Fri
Dinner nightly

This stunning, über-trendy New York offshoot of the West Hollywood flagship, with siblings in Las Vegas and Bangkok, is aptly located among the young and affluent in the Bryant Park Hotel. An enormous canopy dominates the dining room; underneath it, elements of feng shui dictate the eye-popping design, in spite of the pulsating music.

The easygoing pan-Asian menu leans toward Japan, with an array of sushi, sashimi, and maki. More original fare may include *sansho*-rubbed hanger steak with *aji-amarillo* sauce, or bowls of creamy, coconut-rice pudding crème brûlée.

From the black-clad waitstaff and attractive plating, to the A-list crowd, cool is the operative word at Koi—perhaps replacing warmth from the staff. The Cellar Bar is equally chic.

Kunjip

Korean 🍴

C4

9 W 32nd St. (bet. Broadway & Fifth Ave.)

Subway: 34 St - Herald Sq
Phone: 212-216-9487
Web: www.kunjip.net
Prices: ⊜⊜

Lunch & dinner daily

Craving a cup of burdock tea and some kimchi at 2:00 A.M? Kunjip is open and ready to serve you. This place doles out traditional Korean food 24 hours a day seven days a week and the line is out the door. It's in the heart of bona fide K-town steps from Herald Square, so you know it's the real deal.

Service is speedy and the place is bustling so it helps to know what you're ordering. You can't go wrong with the restorative *dogani-tong*, a soup of simmered ox knees, which could be your stand-in for chicken noodle any day. Move on to the *goong joong dduk boki*, a thin fried rice cake of scallions and beef; or the *kam ja-tang*, an amazingly tender fall-off-the-bones meat soup. *Jok bal*, sliced pig's feet topped with a fishy sauce is refreshingly different.

La Masseria

Italian ✕✕

C2

235 W. 48th St. (bet. Broadway & Eighth Ave.)

Subway: 50 St (Eighth Ave.)
Phone: 212-582-2111
Web: www.lamasserianyc.com
Prices: $$

Lunch & dinner daily

This Theater District favorite takes your average red-sauce Italian joint, and–like the better Broadway shows outside its door–heightens the everyday into true art. Dressed to look like a *Pugliese* farmhouse, guests are greeted by stone and stucco walls, exposed wood beams, and great old photos; not to mention a few benevolent rounds of cheek-kissing and hand shaking from the chic regulars flocking in.

And yet when it comes to the food, La Masseria leaves the theatrics at the door. You'll find no silly distractions on a plate of tender, grilled artichoke hearts topped with buttery taleggio; a spot-on penne in a light tomato sauce with bacon, radicchio, and smoked mozzarella; or silky grilled salmon fillet in creamy Dijon mustard sauce.

The Lambs Club

American ✕✕

C3

132 W. 44th St. (bet. Broadway & Sixth Ave.)

Subway: Times Sq - 42 St
Phone: 212-997-5262
Web: www.thelambsclub.com
Prices: $$$

Lunch & dinner daily

Ask any Gotham foodie to rattle off New York's top restaurateurs and the name Geoffrey Zakarian is sure to come up. One amongst his recent ventures, The Lambs Club, is hidden just off the luxurious Chatwal Hotel's lobby, and sexily outfitted in rich red leather seating, a fireplace, and a wall adorned with black-and-white photos. It's dark and sultry, all right—but the moodiness ends there. Expect wait service to be perfectly friendly and professional.

From there, things only get better: dinner might include ruby red beef tartare with pickled chanterelles, cornichons, and chewy country toast; soft white gazpacho chockablock with fresh peekytoe crab, grapes, and tangy crème fraîche; and slow-roasted pork belly and seafood with tender, braised leeks.

Landmark Tavern

American ✗✗

B2

626 Eleventh Ave. (at 46th St.)

Subway: 50 St (Eighth Ave.)
Phone: 212-247-2562
Web: www.thelandmarktavern.org
Prices: $$

Lunch & dinner daily

If you find yourself in the foodie nether regions of Midtown West, here's some relief. Originally opened in 1868 as an Irish saloon that catered to local dock workers, Landmark Tavern later served time as a mediocre restaurant in desperate need of repairs. And repairs it got with its 2005 transformation into these handsome new digs, replete with carved mahogany paneling, shiny beveled mirrors, and a clever new menu to match.

Though it's not quite the ambitious operation it was on the heels of the revamp, Landmark's commitment to high minded pub fare is still very much intact. Try the hazelnut-crusted Scotch eggs, rolled with sausage and served over organic baby greens; or a fluffy shepherd's pie filled with buttery root vegetables and fragrant meat.

La Silhouette

French ✗✗

C1

362 W. 53rd St. (bet. Eighth & Ninth Aves.)

Subway: 50 St (Eighth Ave.)
Phone: 212-581-2400
Web: www.la-silhouettenyc.com
Prices: $$$

Lunch & dinner daily

Hell's Kitchen may boast a glut of restaurants, but serious diners tend to shun the area for mediocre food. But wait! La Silhouette has come to the rescue. This darling is easy to miss, but step inside and you'll be glad you didn't blink.

Three distinctive rooms define the interior, but the clear winner is the "suspended" space floating above a sunken dining room. Warm, hospitable service is a treat, but really it's the New York-y French food (think bagel chips with fluffy goat cheese) that leaves a lasting memory. *Pâtes imprimées* with sheets of pasta moistened by a rich and silky broth and filled with braised rabbit and wild mushrooms; or a perfectly cooked mustard-crusted lamb with stuffed artichokes walk the line between sophistication and comfort.

Le Bernardin ✿ ✿ ✿

A4

Seafood 🍴🍴🍴🍴

155 W. 51st St. (bet. Sixth & Seventh Aves.)

Subway: 50 St (Broadway)
Phone: 212-554-1515
Web: www.le-bernardin.com
Prices: $$$$

Lunch Mon – Fri
Dinner Mon – Sat

Lyn Hughes Photography

Le Bernardin will unveil a new look after extensive renovations, and her many suitors will be eager to eye her up and down. Yet as one of NY's reigning restaurants, much is sure to remain unchanged: it will be upscale yet never stuffy; service will remain professional but personable; and Chef Eric Ripert will continue to breathe new life and inspiration into this superlative cuisine.

The prix-fixe menu may offer such "barely touched" options as perfectly cooked langoustines, but their sweetness is terrifically heightened by the tremendous depth and richness of a wild mushroom salad with white balsamic vinaigrette. Chef Ripert's formidable talents shine with the Southeast Asian flavors of charred sepia and shrimp layered over a green papaya and apple "summer roll" bathed in chilled carrot-lime broth. The sense of balance and elegance returns again and again with each dish, as in seared rare kingfish with golden pea tendrils and morels in sweet-pea wasabi sauce. While lunchtime caters to a more corporate clientele, dinner at Le Bernardin is an elevated social affair.

The wine list is—in a word—blockbuster. Consider enlisting the help of their very able and unpretentious sommeliers.

Madangsui

Korean ✗

C4

35 W. 35th St. (bet. Fifth & Sixth Aves.)

Subway: 34 St – Herald Sq
Phone: 212 564 9333
Web: www.madangsui.com
Prices: $$

Lunch & dinner daily

If the Korean-speaking waitstaff doesn't tip you off to this K-town joint's authenticity, then perhaps the mind-blowing barbecue, cooked directly at your table, will. Located about a block north of midtown's Korean restaurant hub, Madangsui's clean, glass-fronted façade offers a reprieve from the flurry outside. Inside, soothing leather banquettes and cream colored walls promise more sanity, but the excited hum toward the kitchen reveals a restaurant that is getting its (much deserved) fifteen minutes.

Don't miss the short beef ribs bobbing in a hot beef broth laced with cellophane noodles; spot-on oyster pancakes, studded with green scallions; or the Metropolitan beef and pork combo, which gives delicious new meaning to dinner theater.

Mandoo Bar

Korean ✗

C4

2 W. 32nd St. (at Fifth Ave.)

Subway: 34 St – Herald Sq
Phone: 212-279-3075
Web: N/A
Prices: ⊜⊜

Lunch & dinner daily

Whether steamed, fried, spicy or not, Mandoo is always Korean for "dumpling," and every kind you can dream up is served here as unique, tidy little bundles. This postage stamp-sized K-town favorite keeps its massive number of customers happy with its array of freshly made, unassuming Korean fare, dished out fast enough to keep weekend shoppers on the move.

Meals may begin with the likes of pan-fried dumplings filled with pork and vegetables (*goon mandoo*); bite-sized and boiled baby *mandoo*; or the combo *mandoo*, with fillings of seafood, vegetables, and pork. Korean-style spicy beef soup (*yuk kae jang*) and acorn or buckwheat flour noodle dishes tossed with citrus vinaigrette, sesame seeds, scallions, and cilantro are fine and worthy accompaniments.

Má Pêche

Fusion ✗✗

15 West 56th St. (bet. Fifth & Sixth Aves.)

Subway: 57 St
Phone: 212-777-7773
Web: www.momofuku.com
Prices: $$

Lunch Mon – Sat
Dinner nightly

For years, New Yorkers have been momofuku-mad for Chef David Chang, and with good reason: his edgier downtown originals are lauded for displaying a rare, gutsy brilliance. Meanwhile, this muted and rather austere midtown space is a good option for uptown folk who prefer reservations and a more restrained kitchen.

Skills, talent, and excellent ingredients do prevail in the likes of a perfectly cooked, massive pork chop, and unique presentation of pan-braised Brussels sprouts that sing with flavor. And this is where the meal will end.

The restaurant's entrance, beyond of glass counter stocked with famous Milk Bar soft-serve, crack pies, and sweets, teases your meal's finale—a dessert which is neither offered nor permitted to be enjoyed at tables. Ever.

Marseille

French ✗✗

630 Ninth Ave. (at 44th St.)

Subway: 42 St - Port Authority Bus Terminal
Phone: 212-333-2323
Web: www.marseillenyc.com
Prices: $$

Lunch & dinner daily

Marseille marries the charm of a classic French bistro with the inimitable style of New York City. The sexy, soft golden glow, convivial spirit, and superlative Theater District location make it a popular choice for everyone from tourists craving a taste of Broadway to colleagues cooling off after a day's work. The skilled and truly professional kitchen prepares an impressive cuisine bursting with pronounced, balanced flavors. From salads and seasonal specials to more French-formed entrées like steak frites, there is something for everyone. Hungry diners appreciate that the portions lean toward American sensibilities; and the budget-conscious value the prix-fixe lunch and dinner menus. Don't skip out without the frites—they may be the best in the city.

Marea

Seafood XXX

240 Central Park South (bet. Broadway & Seventh Ave.)

Subway: 59 St Columbus Circle

Phone: 212-582-5100

Web: www.marea-nyc.com

Prices: $$$$

Lunch Sun – Fri
Dinner nightly

Daniel Krieger

Among the boldly moneyed, their beautiful companions, and area publishing professionals with expense accounts, this is *the* place to go. Buzzing at street-level along Central Park South, the packed room has a high-spirited design with red lamps, swanky leather seating, undulating panels of glossy woods and honey onyx, and decorative seashells to convey the Italian menu's theme.

That each dish is prepared with culinary expertise is not lost on even the most novice diner. Here, Chef Michael White's foray into seafood is yet another expression of his talent. An ample raw selection, including fresh mackerel crowned with butternut-squash caponata, lead to outstanding pastas or decadent dishes like silky *burrata* topped with perfectly poached lobster, batons of pickled eggplant, bloomed basil seeds, peeled red grapes, and mâche drizzled with olive oil. A few landlubbing offerings are available, but knowing of their superb branzino golden brown and gently set upon roasted eggplant purée with grilled ramps and apricot *mostarda*–should be enough to convince you otherwise.

Desserts provide the perfect finish with scoops of pink grapefruit sorbet over white chocolate mousse sweetened with honey.

277

Maze at The London

A3

151 W. 54th St. (bet. Sixth & Seventh Aves.)

Subway: 57 St   Lunch & dinner daily
Phone: 212-468-8888
Web: www.gordonramsay.com
Prices: $$

The Maze at The London is the younger and more spirited sister of Gordon Ramsay at the London. And, since we're speaking of royalty, it's a bit like those Middleton Girls, and Maze is definitely the Pippa to Gordon Ramsay's Kate. Sexy and elegant, this restaurant is less serious than its counterpart, but still attracts a well-coiffed and deep-pocketed crowd of jacket-wearing tourists and tycoons. It's chic-Paris in its smoky mirrored, teal banquetted, shimmering glass art deco glory.

Like its setting, the food is Frenchified. Roast chicken breast is glistening and topped with "potato chips"; black risotto is decadently buttery with St. Georges mushrooms; and chocolate fondant is textbook perfect coated with a green cardamom caramel for a perfect finish.

Mercato

B3

352 W. 39th St. (bet. Eighth & Ninth Aves.)

Subway: 42 St - Port Authority Bus Terminal   Lunch & dinner daily
Phone: 212-643-2000
Web: www.mercatonyc.com
Prices: $$

This best selling Italian trattoria in Hell's Kitchen arrives courtesy of Puglian-born Fabio Camardi, a onetime partner at Cacio e Vino. With a charming décor featuring weathered farm tools; vintage signs; a small back-lit wooden bar; and a walk-in wine room, the vibe is decidedly rustic, almost cave-like, at Mercato.

All the better to settle in for a luscious glass of red wine and get things started with a plate of plump, wickedly fresh sardines, grilled to perfection and coated with a lip-smacking *salmoriglio*; and then move on to a heaping *tiella* chockablock with mussels, cherry tomatoes, fluffy rice, and potatoes, served tableside from the cast iron skillet, and finish with *fave e cicoria*, fava purée with sautéed chicory and EVOO.

Masa ✿ ✿ ✿

Japanese 🍴🍴

C1

10 Columbus Circle (in the Time Warner Center)

Subway: 59 St - Columbus Circle
Phone: 212-823-9800
Web: www.masanyc.com
Prices: $$$$

Lunch Tue – Fri
Dinner Mon – Sat

Manhattan ▶ Midtown West

Despite its touristy Time Warner location, this is one of the city's most impressive restaurants. Pull back that heavy wooden door with reverence and bow thy head, supplicant, upon entering the temple of Masa. The beautiful, Zen-like space stuns from every angle with massive plantings, water elements, and a wooden sushi counter that is sanded nightly and shines with pristine cleanliness. There are a few tables for groups, but that would mean neglecting this extraordinary opportunity to experience the magic and education in watching these spectacular chefs. They are convivial and amazingly dedicated to the great Chef Masa Takayama and his eponymous cuisine.

Of course, this is a Japanese restaurant, but the menu is more unique and intricate than expected, as if bearing the signature of an expatriate chef and his decades in America. Now Japan is missing out.

Dishes begin with the finest ingredients and fish that may have swam directly to the restaurant and jumped onto the counter in worthy self-sacrifice. The signature toro tartare is incomprehensibly simple yet lush; *hamo* shabu shabu is a thing of rare beauty; and an inexplicable alchemy transforms broth into elixers between courses.

The Modern ❀

Contemporary 🍴🍴🍴

A4

9 W. 53rd St. (bet. Fifth & Sixth Aves.)
Subway: 5 Av - 53 St   Lunch & dinner daily
Phone: 212-333-1220
Web: www.themodernnyc.com
Prices: $$$

Ellen Silverman

No courses in art history will prepare you for the first time that long, narrow runway spills you into this dazzling restaurant, a most beautiful starlet in the USHG empire. The wall-sized photograph of a serene forest in the bar may be eye-catching, but the soaring glass overlooking the MoMA's renowned sculpture garden is an unparalleled showstopper. A design feat in itself, the dining room's vaulted ceilings, polished metals, and deep-blue carpeting combine to effect warmth in this light-flooded space, best appreciated at night. Chef Gabriel Kreuther's classical training shines through this menu that deliciously indulges his sense of creativity. Meals may begin with the likes of pumpkin mousse and silky-syrupy pomegranate soup, or a perfectly cooked *sepia* risotto with tangy Granny Smith apples and earthy beluga lentils. The fallow venison loin's incredible flavor and exceptional tenderness are reminders that this food is not something one tastes everyday.

Updated flavors and excellent combinations carry through to dessert, with offerings such as a warm tart of figs in balsamic reduction, topped with pignoli compote and served alongside a lovely scoop of olive-oil ice cream.

Molyvos

Greek ✗✗

871 Seventh Ave. (bet. 55th & 56th Sts.)

Subway: 57 St - 7 Av
Phone: 212-582-7500
Web: www.molyvos.com
Prices: $$

Lunch Mon – Sat
Dinner nightly

Part of the Livanos family restaurant empire, which boasts Oceana as its crown jewel, Molyvos (named for the owner's birthplace on the island of Lesvos) brings the home-style dishes of Greece to midtown.

Chef/partner (and cookbook author) James Botsacos can claim his fair share of the restaurant's success. Dishes highlight the freshest fish, whether grilled whole or skewered with marinated Gulf shrimp and summer vegetables. Equally enticing is the Greek-style hamburger, perhaps best enjoyed with a glass of Greek wine.

A block south of Carnegie Hall, Molyvos is well-situated for those attending a performance. Order the modestly priced pre- and post-theater menu and the attentive staff will be sure to pace your meal in time with the performance.

Mr. Robata

Japanese ✗✗

1674 Broadway (bet. 52nd & 53rd Sts.)

Subway: 50 St (Broadway)
Phone: 212-757-1030
Web: www.mrrobata.com
Prices: $$$

Dinner Mon – Sat

Squeezed between an ample supply of chain restaurants and a discreet gentlemen's club, this unexpected find is putting its culinary neighbors to shame. The serene and elegant setting is marked by the centerpiece blonde-wood sushi bar, lined with high, cushioned chairs, so grab a seat where the action is and dig in.

Specialty maki rolls with names like "Stay With Me" (asparagus, mango, and jalapeño, wrapped in seared salmon, and topped with yuzu-miso sauce) or "Call Me Later" are as cheeky as they are tasty, but offerings fired up on the *robata* grill are where it's at. Try the free-range chicken breast (*jidori muneniku*) or pork toro (belly) served up with passion fruit ponzu and wasabi cream cheese.

Swing by until 3:00 A.M. for a post-party bite.

New Wonjo

C4

23 W. 32nd St. (bet. Broadway & Sixth Ave.)

Subway: 34 St - Herald Sq
Phone: 212-695-5815
Web: N/A
Prices: $$$

Lunch & dinner daily

Truth be told, New Wonjo–a no-frills, turn-and-burn Korean joint nestled into bustling 32nd Street–is not going to give the reigning outer borough darlings a run for their money anytime soon. But if you're looking for some decent Korean food in midtown, you could do a lot worse than this modest, two-level eatery, fitted out with tabletop barbecue grills.

Moreover, after a management overhaul in spring of 2010, the kitchen now falls under the sights of Chef Hwang Han Joo, who reputedly boasts over 40 years of Korean culinary experience. Taste the experience in dishes like *kam ja jun gol*, a fragrant, flavorful casserole of spicy pork bone, potato, and vegetables; or tenderly marinated cuts of brisket and short ribs, grilled to succulent perfection.

Nick & Stef's

B4

9 Penn Plaza (bet. Seventh & Eighth Aves.)

Subway: 34 St - Penn Station
Phone: 212-563-4444
Web: www.nickandstefs.com
Prices: $$$

Lunch Mon – Fri
Dinner Mon – Sat

Adjacent to Madison Square Garden and Penn Station is one of the neighborhood's better dining options: Nick & Stef's (named for partner Chef Joachim Splichal's twin sons). As part of the Patina Group, this steakhouse is known for serving consistently good food.

The menu balances its list of broiled steaks with a variety of hearty entrées including Nova Scotia lobster stuffed with crabmeat and organic roasted chicken. Meats are served unadorned, so make sure you order some glorious sides like herbed shoestring fries or garlicky sautéed spinach. Lunchtime also highlights salads, sandwiches, and embellished steakhouse burgers.

A suited clientele regularly fills this contemporary space, featuring warm tones and angled pine ceilings.

9 Restaurant

Contemporary ✗✗

C1

800 Ninth Ave. (at 53rd St.)

Subway: 50 St (Eighth Ave.)
Phone: 212-956-3333
Web: www.9restaurantnyc.com
Prices: $$

Lunch & dinner daily

9 Restaurant is a bright, contemporary spot in an area better known for bars and casual eats than a thrilling dining scene. Chef/owner Eric Hara, who has polished his resume at heavy-hitters like River Café, Davidburke & Donatella, and The Oak Room, mans the stove at this elegant and vibrant spot. Occupying a prominent corner of Ninth Avenue, 9 is dramatic and captivating with whimsical artwork and a garage door-style façade (open to sidewalk seating).

The menu may look familiar, but each dish has a distinctive edge. Spoon up some of the best matzo ball soup in the city—this beef-based soup with mushroom-studded matzo balls is definitely not your grandmother's. From skate schnitzel to bread pudding—it's all finished with an unexpected flair.

Nobu Fifty Seven

Japanese ✗✗✗

A3

40 W. 57th St. (bet. Fifth & Sixth Aves.)

Subway: 57 St
Phone: 212 757 3000
Web: www.noburestaurants.com
Prices: $$$$

Lunch & dinner daily

Despite remaining under fire for disregarding fish conservation, Chef Nobu Matsuhisa continues to succeed with his upscale chain. The entrance feels removed from the bustle of 57th Street, as David Rockwell's cavernous interior uses chandeliers of silvery abalone shells, sake barrels, towering ceilings, a long bar fashioned from a single piece of gnarled wood, and countless other details to dramatic effect. The restaurant attracts a cosmopolitan crowd that knows the promise of Nobu quality and has expense accounts to handle the hefty prices. Signatures dishes include perfectly fresh, paper thin pieces of yellowtail sashimi topped with jalapeño and fanned around a mound of cilantro, in a terrific combination of sweet, salty, hot, and cool flavors.

Orso

C2

322 W. 46th St. (bet. Eighth & Ninth Aves.)

Subway: 42 St - Port Authority Bus Terminal   Lunch & dinner daily
Phone: 212-489-7212
Web: www.orsorestaurant.com
Prices: $$

This intimate little restaurant–with its friendly staff and antique photos–is the late-night haunt of Broadway players in search of a post-show meal. It shows off their good taste too, for the food at this Restaurant Row darling rises well above the competition.

Occupying the ground floor of a charming brownstone, Orso offers simple, delicious Italian classics including a very nice selection of pizzas. The $24 *contorni* selection of five vegetable dishes like farro, roasted spinach, and broccoli in hot pepper flakes can turn into a meal in itself. From the moment they set the fresh and flavorful white bean dip and bread upon the table, the charming and knowledgeable staff is happy to help.

Be sure to call ahead, as pre-theater reservations book quickly.

Osteria al Doge

C3

142 W. 44th St. (bet. Broadway & Sixth Ave.)

Subway: Times Sq - 42 St   Lunch Mon – Fri
Phone: 212-944-3643   Dinner nightly
Web: www.osteria-doge.com
Prices: $$

Tucked into one of those theater-dominated cross streets that define this jumbled area of Times Square, the first thing Osteria al Doge has on the competition is its good looks: think sunny yellow walls, wrought-iron chandeliers, and bright Italian ceramic plates. Not to mention a long marble and wood bar where solo diners can settle into a comfortable padded stool and enjoy a little people-watching before the real show.

Back on the plates it's delicious Italian food tended to with love, like a plump tangle of fettuccine *verde* in a silky lamb ragù dotted with lemon rind and pitted black picholine olives, thin slices of tuna carpaccio drizzled with citrus olive oil, a dash of crunchy sea salt, and herbs; or a fresh lemon tart topped with strawberries.

Oceana ✿

Seafood ※※※

1221 Sixth Ave. (at 49th St.)

Subway: 47–50 Sts - Rockefeller Ctr
Phone: 212-759-5941
Web: www.oceanarestaurant.com
Prices: $$$

Lunch Mon – Fri
Dinner nightly

Paul Johnson

Oceana, seafood purveyor extraordinaire, has settled beautifully into its new home in Rockefeller Center. Enter to see a display of pristine fish at the front and be reminded of Oceana's seriousness of purpose. The sleek and contemporary dining room, with deep blue banquettes and stunning floral arrangements, is a flawless setting in which to savor Chef Ben Pollinger's superlative fare. Glass-enclosed private rooms and a chef's table in the kitchen are attractive options for power crowds hosting lunch meetings.

The superbly fresh seafood never falters in finding just the right global accent, as in creamy New England clam chowder, enhanced by smoky linguiça and a delicate piece of cod. The tapioca-crusted halibut is unbelievably moist, served with a flavorful *bagna cauda* sauce of olives, tomatoes, garlic, and chilies.

The mahi mahi is as appealing on the plate as to the palate, arriving golden-brown with a red dollop of mole poblano made with chilies, cinnamon, and cloves, set atop a banana leaf that hints of the dish's inspiration. Desserts are noteworthy, especially the boozy eggnog panna cotta and sour-cherry rice pudding, layered with custard and kirsch cherry truffles.

Osteria del Circo

A3

Italian ✕✕

120 W. 55th St. (bet. Sixth & Seventh Aves.)

Subway: 57 St	Lunch Mon – Fri
Phone: 212-265-3636	Dinner nightly
Web: www.osteriadelcirco.com	
Prices: $$$	

Ever fantasized about running away to join the circus? Fulfill that dream without all of the acrobatics at Osteria del Circo. This restaurant, run by the Maccioni clan of Le Cirque fame, offers a tasteful take on the Big Top. Its tent-like ceiling is complete with streaming fabric in a riot of colors and is punctuated by spinning circus performers and animal sculptures. There is a palpable buzz here—just one of the reasons there are so many regulars.

However, this menu isn't about peanuts and popcorn. Instead, look forward to deftly prepared Italian dishes like grilled branzino and milk-fed veal chops from the professional kitchen. The staff is warm and engaging—not surprising given the Maccionis' reputation for throwing open their arms to guests.

Petrossian

A3

French ✕✕✕

182 W. 58th St. (at Seventh Ave.)

Subway: 57 St - 7 Av	Lunch & dinner daily
Phone: 212-245-2214	
Web: www.petrossian.com	
Prices: $$$	

Settled along a tourist-filled stretch near Carnegie Hall in the ornate, Renaissance-style Alwyn Court building dating back to 1907, Petrossian makes no apologies for its old-world, bourgeois indulgence. And why should it? Its pedigree speaks for itself: this is the baby sister to Petrossian Paris, a French mainstay that's been going strong since the 1920's.

The original location, opened by two Armenian brothers, put caviar on the map, and the company remains the premier importer of Russian caviar. Not surprisingly, the New York branch specializes in the inky stuff—all the more reason to linger among the Lalique crystal sconces and etched Erté mirrors, and indulge in the house tasting, filled with ace caviar, foie gras, and delicious smoked fish.

Per Se ❀ ❀ ❀

C1

Contemporary XXXXX

10 Columbus Circle (in the Time Warner Center)

Subway: 59 St – Columbus Circle   Lunch Fri – Sun
Phone: 212-823-9335   Dinner nightly
Web: www.perseny.com
Prices: $$$$

Deborah Jones

Can something be too perfect? Can its focus be so singular, pleasure so complete, and technique so flawless that creativity suffers? Per Se proves that this fear is unfounded.

Far above the maddening cityscape below, Per Se resides on the Time Warner Center's highfalutin fourth floor. Arrive early and stop in the salon to sip Champagne alongside foodies relishing the fact that one doesn't need reservations to eat à la carte in the lounge. Inside the bi-level dining room, find well-spaced tables covered in understated finery, all with Central Park views beyond the modern fireplace.

Chef Thomas Keller's daily menu offers nine courses of wondrously conceived dishes, including a glorious vegetable tasting. Beginnings such as artichoke *barigoule en gelée* with fine herbs highlight delicate flavors, and may lead to a springtime terrine of whipped Meyer-lemon ricotta, shaved heirloom radishes, and English peas. Creative cheese courses may include sour apple mille-feuille with grated Gorgonzola. Extraordinary consistency carries through to the end, with an Asian-influenced dessert of black sesame ice cream in a pool of Champagne mango, or a composition of dark chocolate, malt, and caramel.

Piano Due

A4

151 W. 51st St. (bet. Sixth & Seventh Aves.)

Subway: 49 St
Phone: 212-399-9400
Web: www.pianoduenyc.net
Prices: $$$

Lunch Mon – Fri
Dinner Mon – Sat

With neighbors like critically-acclaimed Le Bernardin in your hood, there's not a lot of wiggle room for area restaurants to mail it in when it comes to food and ambience. Piano Due has both in spades—but you'll have to find it first.

Duck into always-hopping Palio Bar and make your way up (via an elevator) to this second-floor den, romantically dressed in antique mirrors, silk fabrics, and plush red chairs. Dinner might include a fresh tangle of tagliatelle tossed with Maryland lump crabmeat and *peperoncino*; or tender braised chicken with Italian sausage in white wine. From the service to the cutlery, Piano Due is all grace and elegance—but not so much so that the restaurant doesn't know a good deal. The $30 lunch prix-fixe is a steal.

Pier 9

C1

802 Ninth Ave. (bet. 53rd & 54th Aves.)

Subway: 50 St (Eighth Ave.)
Phone: 212-262-1299
Web: www.pier9nyc.com
Prices: $$$

Lunch & dinner daily

When hankering for seafaring favorites in Manhattan, steer your ship straight to Pier 9. This fresh and upbeat space, with whitewashed walls, aquamarine tiles, and bright colors, will instantly elevate your mood and have you feeling the wind in your hair. Sidewalk dining and an open-air back patio are hits during warmer months, but the bar is always rollicking.

Expect barefoot, casual-style seafood, where an outstanding rendition of New England clam chowder, blackened snapper tacos, and "Chicago-style" lobster hot dogs reign. The succulent lobster roll, piled high and dressed with little more than a hint of celery seeds, will have you canceling that trip to Maine. Order a Bloody Mary and raw bar items, but pay attention to the daily specials.

Porter House

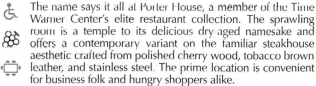

C1   Steakhouse XXX

10 Columbus Circle (in the Time Warner Center)

Subway: 59 St - Columbus Circle   Lunch & dinner daily
Phone: 212-823-9500
Web: www.porterhousenewyork.com
Prices: $$$$

The name says it all at Porter House, a member of the Time Warner Center's elite restaurant collection. The sprawling room is a temple to its delicious dry-aged namesake and offers a contemporary variant on the familiar steakhouse aesthetic crafted from polished cherry wood, tobacco brown leather, and stainless steel. The prime location is convenient for business folk and hungry shoppers alike.

Under the longtime charge of Executive Chef Michael Lomonaco, the expansive menu is steeped in tasty starters and sides like tomato and onion salad dotted with Maytag blue cheese, and rich truffle-mashed Yukon Golds to round out a carnivorous feast. A range of non-steak options is also offered, and the nostalgic take on dessert is worth saving room for.

Print

B1   American XXX

653 Eleventh Ave. (at 48th St.)

Subway: 50 St (Eighth Ave.)   Lunch & dinner daily
Phone: 212-757-2224
Web: www.printrestaurant.com
Prices: $$

Set among the car dealerships and new residential units that flank this lonesome section of Midtown West, Print may prove to be a pioneer in this burgeoning hood. As it is, anyone driving up the West Side Highway suddenly has a darn good reason to pull off the 42nd Street exit.

Set just off the lobby of the Kimpton Hotel Group's Ink48, Print is downright lovely, with stunning, mesh-covered windows, copper-topped tables, and rustic ceramics. The food, prepared by the talented husband-wife duo, Charles Rodriguez and Heather Carlucci-Rodriguez, is fresh, seasonal, and unapologetically simple—think juicy, slow-roasted pork sandwiches stuffed with sautéed broccoli rabe and fontina; or lip-smacking chocolate bread with raw honey and ricotta.

Qi Bangkok Eatery

Thai ✗✗

C2

675 Eighth Ave. (bet. 42nd & 43rd Sts.)

Subway: Times Sq – 42 St   Lunch & dinner daily
Phone: 212-247-8991
Web: www.qirestaurant.com
Prices: $$

This stretch of Eighth Avenue is dominated by gray and grimy storefronts, but wait, what is this cool white palace that stands before you...is it a mirage? Nope, it's the lovely and serene Qi Bangkok Eatery from standout star Pichet Ong. He sharpened his teeth with Jean-Georges and later developed his own spots downtown, but Qi Bangkok is the latest showcase for his talents. Large and loungey with a sleek white-on-white palette, the space is swanky and hip with a futuristic feel, while the food hails straight from Southeast Asia.

Fiery red pork with red turmeric curry is a trifecta of sweet, sour, and spicy flavors. Delicate dumplings with house-made chili sauce, rich coconut milk soup...even a curried seafood mousse...Thai any on for size.

Radiance Tea House

Asian ✗

A3

158 W. 55th St. (bet. Sixth & Seventh Aves.)

Subway: 57 St – 7 Av   Lunch & dinner daily
Phone: 212-217-0442
Web: www.radiancetea.com
Prices: ⊜⊜

In frenetic, fast-paced midtown, this serene oasis is a welcome relief. Beautifully carved mahogany tables sit atop natural wooden floors, while exotic teas line the shelves and infuse the air with their delicate fragrances. The space also accommodates a lovely gift and book store where tea is the principal subject.

The pan-Asian menu focuses on delicious soups, cold noodles, rice-flour rolls, and rice bowls. The handmade soupy-pork dumplings are a must—its tender wrappers are stuffed with ground pork and ginger-garlic swimming in savory pork both. Tea lovers rejoice: an international selection of over 150 varieties is available for your sipping pleasure, including the signature blend of green and black teas with rose, jasmine, and sunflowers.

Remi

A4

Italian ✗✗✗

145 W. 53rd St. (bet. Sixth & Seventh Aves.)

Subway: 7 Av
Phone: 212-581-4242
Web: www.remi-ny.com
Prices: $$

Lunch Mon – Fri
Dinner nightly

A convivial buzz winds through the various rooms of this Italian restaurant, from the thumping party room in the back to its atrium-enclosed shop, offering gourmet breakfast and lunch to-go. At the center of the party is a dining room with whimsical flying buttress archways, murals, mirrors, and glass chandeliers that recall the Veneto region.

Nevertheless, the true draw to this well-orchestrated production is its delicious menu that highlights easygoing, rustic Italian specialties as in sardines roasted with Vidalia onions, raisins, and pine nuts in sweet and sour sauce. Fresh pastas may include the *tonnarelli sciue' alla moda Napoletana*, with homemade *spaghetti alla chitarra*, clams, calamari, and shrimp mingling in a flavorful, spicy tomato sauce.

Robert

D1

Contemporary ✗✗

2 Columbus Circle (bet. Broadway & Eighth Ave.)

Subway: 59 St - Columbus Circle
Phone: 212-299-7730
Web: www.arkrestaurants.com
Prices: $$

Lunch & dinner daily

The booming restaurant scene growing around Columbus Circle (nearby Time Warner Center is a hotbed of high-end restaurants) gets another notch on its belt with the Museum of Arts & Design's new restaurant, Robert.

Named for famous party planner Robert Isabell, the L-shaped restaurant resides on the ninth floor (request a north-facing table for good views), and its super-modern design–which boasts blush and orange light boxes and video-art installations–leaves you wondering if the food will get any attention. A rich, smoky tomato soup licked with a whirl of cream; wickedly fresh wild mushroom cavatelli brimming with spicy pork sausage, earthy Tuscan kale, and cubes of pumpkin; and sweet, fatty pan-roasted Scottish salmon supplies the answer.

Russian Samovar

C2

256 W. 52nd St. (bet. Broadway & Eighth Ave.)

Subway: 50 St (Broadway)   Dinner nightly
Phone: 212-757-0168
Web: www.russiansamovar.com
Prices: $$

Which came first: the vodka or the celebs? It's hard to say when it comes to this hot spot, which caters to hockey players, Russian intellectuals, and vodka aficionados alike. Our bets are on that beautiful vodka selection, available in all kinds of flavors, qualities, and sizes (shot, carafe, or bottle). Nestled into the bustling Theater District, Russian Samovar is both quirky and elegant—with low lighting, glass panels, and frequent musicians playing the piano and violin. The staff, both attentive and sweet, can walk you through delicious fare like a fresh salmon caviar blini, prepared tableside; *pelmeni*, tender veal dumplings served with sour cream and honey mustard; or milk-cured Baltic herring, paired with pickled onions, potatoes, and carrots.

Scarlatto

C2

250 W. 47th St. (bet. Broadway & Eighth Ave.)

Subway: 50 St (Eighth Ave.)   Lunch & dinner daily
Phone: 212-730-4535
Web: www.scarlattonyc.com
Prices: $$

Done and done: this adorable trattoria is guaranteed to woo your date and finally put an end to those frustrating post-Saturday night wanderings. Dip down below street level and you'll find a lovely, exposed brick interior lined with wine bottles, mirrors, and still shots of Audrey Hepburn in *Roman Holiday*.

The menu doesn't offer too many surprises, but it does deliver solid, well-prepared Italian fare. Rosy-pink *carpaccio di manzo* arrives ultra-thin and topped with a creamy Parmesan-lemon dressing, a soft pile of arugula, and chewy slices of sourdough bread; while a bowl of *garganelli* gets a kick from an osso buco stew enlivened with rosemary; and fresh Atlantic salmon is baked with caramelized Vidalia onions and garlicky sautéed spinach.

The Sea Grill

D2

Seafood ✗✗

19 W. 49th St. (bet. Fifth & Sixth Aves.)

Subway: 47-50 Sts - Rockefeller Ctr
Phone: 212-332-7610
Web: www.patinagroup.com
Prices: $$$

Lunch Mon – Fri
Dinner Mon – Sat

This seafood grill overlooking Rockefeller Center's ice skating rink boasts one of the city's most famed locations. As expected, winter bookings start early at The Sea Grill, especially near the holidays, when skaters whizz by your windows filled with the best (and warmest) view of the Christmas tree. However, summertime is likewise charming, when the doors swing open and diners can enjoy an alfresco feel overlooking the Rink Bar.

Perhaps due to its tourist-driven locale, the fare is solid, rather than terrifically surprising. Offerings may include platters of chilled shellfish, teeming with lobster, crab meat, shrimp, and ceviche; Sea Grill chowder; or grilled specialties, like East Coast halibut. Save room for the memorable desserts.

South Gate

A3

Contemporary ✗✗✗

154 Central Park South (bet. Sixth & Seventh Aves.)

Subway: 57 St
Phone: 212-484-5120
Web: www.jumeirah.com
Prices: $$$

Lunch & dinner daily

Tucked into the first floor of the Jumeirah Essex House, South Gate is downright splendid in its sophistication. Designed by Tony Chi, the room owns a singular light and airy sexiness, with padded leather tables, creamy swivel chairs, and mirrored glass walls.

Executive Chef Kerry Heffernan's modern American menu elevates contemporary classics to current heights. Don't miss the creamy fried macaroni and cheese, crunchy with breadcrumbs and sporting a perfectly smoked tomato coulis; or the delicately poached lobster salad with ripe avocado and shaved fennel ribbons, beautifully tied together with a lemon emulsion. Spotty service can sometimes put a dent in an otherwise lovely evening, but a seat at the welcoming bar will certainly remedy the situation.

Seäsonal ✿

Austrian ✗✗

132 W. 58th St. (bet. Sixth & Seventh Aves.)

Subway: 57 St - 7 Av
Phone: 212-957-5550
Web: www.seasonalnyc.com
Prices: $$$

Lunch Mon – Sat
Dinner nightly

Seäsonal

Subtly set behind the luxurious Jumeirah Essex House, Seäsonal is one of those sleeper NY beacons that lived quite well through the economic turmoil of '08. Its reason for redemption may include a modest mien, despite being hedged by affluent residential buildings and store fronts.

It's not flashy, but in its understated elegance you'll find a service staff that is spot-on and oozes über charm. To assuage any further doubt, glimpse the dining room's handsome leather chairs, warming wood floors, and festive orchids and frills. Ivory walls and threaded lights rouse Seäsonal's chaste yet eager spirit. Speaking of spirit, the elliptical bar is ace for sipping; but if you can, grab your group and head for a table adorned with porcelain.

Gloat over the kitchen's "fresh" take on *steckrüben suppe*, a flawless mushroom consommé arranged with rock shrimp, rutabaga, *urfa*, and bone marrow; and *schweinebauch*, a piece of shiny pork belly made sweet and succulent with chestnut purée, chanterelles, and honey vinegar. Other devotees devour a classic *weiner schnitzel* paired with warm potato salad, or semolina pumpkin seed terrine dripping with poached fig compote and pumpkin seed ice cream.

Staghorn

Steakhouse ✗✗

B3

315 W. 36th St. (bet. Eighth & Ninth Aves.)

Subway: 34 St - Penn Station
Phone: 212-239-4390
Web: www.staghornsteakhouse.com
Prices: $$$

Lunch Mon – Fri
Dinner Mon – Sat

Does the word "steakhouse" conjure up images of old-school, slightly brusque waiters in white aprons and no frills good-old-boy décor? Well, think again. Staghorn steakhouse takes the bull by its, ahem, horns, and turns it completely on its head. The less-than-thrilling neighborhood may leave something to be desired, but inside this former warehouse is a wondrous space with an Asian-Zen ambience.

The look is modern but the food is classic, with typical sides like mashed potatoes and creamed spinach. Start with tasty baked clams or the Staghorn salad bursting with Roquefort and tomatoes. From well-aged Porterhouse steaks that ooze with juice to thick and meaty Kansas City bone-in sirloin, it's all about the beef to the chic carnivore at this temple.

Sugiyama

Japanese ✗

C1

251 W. 55th St. (bet. Broadway & Eighth Ave.)

Subway: 57 St - 7 Av
Phone: 212-956-0670
Web: www.sugiyama-nyc.com
Prices: $$$

Dinner Tue – Sat

Remember when hosts and servers actually seemed (gulp) happy to see you? When chefs were honored to have you choose their restaurant, and took the time to tell you so? Seems like a very long time ago to most jaded Manhattan eaters, but the lovely Sugiyama—a little Japanese superstar that looks, at first blush, like so many other kids in its class—offers hope that true hospitality exists.

That—and the kaiseki is off the hizzay. It might start with silky monkfish liver blended with fresh, custardy tofu, and paired with grated radish and ponzu sauce; and then move on to a spread of sashimi so bright it could rival a crayon box; tender braised octopus; crab wrapped in whisper-thin white radish; and glazed sea bass, grilled to smoky-sweet perfection.

Sushi of Gari 46

Japanese ✗✗

C2

347 W. 46th St. (bet. Eighth & Ninth Aves.)

Subway: Times Sq - 42 St
Phone: 212-957-0046
Web: www.sushiofgari.com
Prices: $$$$

Lunch Mon — Fri
Dinner nightly

This outpost of Chef Masatoshi "Gari" Sugio's much-loved sushi trifecta doesn't quite stack up to the near-surreal omakase experience that shot the original Upper East Side prodigy to fame, but coming this close to sushi perfection in the increasingly commercial Theater District is good enough. The pay-per-piece omakase show will put a sizable, albeit worthy, dent in your wallet, but those on a budget can always hit the reasonably-priced regular menu. The place to sit is at the action-packed bar, where you can watch the staff slice and dice their way through Japanese fare like a nori-wrapped bundle of warm rice topped with sweet King crab meat; or gorgeous ruby red tuna, brushed with soy and topped with creamy tofu sauce and freshly grated wasabi.

Sushi Zen

Japanese ✗✗

C3

108 W. 44th St. (bet. Broadway & Sixth Ave.)

Subway: 42 St - Bryant Pk
Phone: 212-302-0707
Web: www.sushizen-ny.com
Prices: $$$

Lunch Mon — Fri
Dinner Mon — Sat

Nestled among midtown's high-rises, this jewel of a sushi restaurant is a nice respite from the Bryant Park hustle and bustle—with soothing swaths of natural light flooding a small dining room with high ceilings, and a sidewalk seating section protected by fabric panels and potted green plants.

Chef Toshio Suzuki's team doles out a host of rolls, many of them going beyond the conventional preparations to employ seasonal fish and vegetables. Kick things off with a smoky white miso soup bobbing with Asari clams; and then move on to the Bara Chirashi Sushi, or sushi Zen style. "Bara" means little things, and here that translates to a neverending style of fish, sashimi, and vegetables served over rice. Save room for the *yokan*, a sweet, jellied dessert.

Szechuan Gourmet 😊

Chinese 🍴

C3

21 W. 39th St. (bet. Fifth & Sixth Aves.)

Subway: 42 St - Bryant Pk   Lunch & dinner daily
Phone: 212-921-0233
Web: www.szechuangourmetnyc.com
Prices: $$

Despite the exquisite pain inflicted by their wok tossed green chilies, legions line up for more of Szechuan Gourmet's spicy, tasty, and authentic delicacies. Away from the usual lunch bustle, hordes hustle at this midtown haven for their devilishly delicious repertoire of Sichuan specialties.

The attempt at ambience is a touch clichéd, but the kitchen's masterful marriage of ingredients amply atones with tofu crêpes stuffed with shiitakes; crispy lamb dusted with cumin and chilies; and bass fillets swimming in a smoky soup of cabbage and cellophane noodles. Rabbit pieces glazed with a sweet, spicy oil; and conch slivers in roasted chili vinaigrette will leave you smitten.

For a quieter (more delicious?) meal, stop by its baby sis on West 56th Street.

Taboon

Middle Eastern 🍴🍴

C1

773 Tenth Ave. (at 52nd St.)

Subway: 50 St (Eighth Ave.)   Lunch Sun
Phone: 212-713-0271   Dinner nightly
Web: N/A
Prices: $$

This far western neighborhood gem offers an always pleasant vibe and enticing air courtesy of the brick-walled, wood-burning oven (taboon) that greets entering guests and sets the whitewashed interior aglow. The crackling logs, fronted by neatly arranged platters of produce, exude a rustic mien and fuse deftly with the food and philosophy.

Fresh from taboon to table, rip into the house-made focaccia and await the lot of enticing specialties. Linger abroad with the likes of charred octopus confit with hearth-roasted apples and pickled cucumber; or succulent osso buco of lamb glossed with a meaty reduction, atop a pile of bulgur wheat.

A solid dining feat, Taboon is a pioneer of sorts in fusing Middle Eastern and Mediterranean flavors.

Toloache

C2

251 W. 50th St. (bet. Broadway & Eighth Ave.)

Subway: 50 St (Broadway)   Lunch & dinner daily
Phone: 212-581-1818
Web: www.toloachenyc.com
Prices: $$

Mexican dining is at its hottest in New York, with many thanks due to the unstoppable team behind Toloache, Yerba Buena, and their other rapidly expanding, successful outposts. Here in midtown, the phenomenon is elevated in a sophisticated yet festive two-story restaurant decked in brightly painted tiles, wood-beam ceilings, and punched-metal chandeliers.

A pleasure from start to finish, try the wonderfully smoky house chicken served over boldly flavored corn *pico de gallo* with a fried cheese-and-pinto bean dumpling, perhaps followed by a neat stack of cinnamon-dusted churros with chocolate and goat's milk caramel sauce.

A serious list of tequilas is on offer and a worthy follow-up to one of the many refreshing margaritas poured nightly.

Trattoria Dell'Arte

A3

900 Seventh Ave. (bet. 56th & 57th Sts.)

Subway: 57 St - 7 Av   Lunch & dinner daily
Phone: 212-245-9800
Web: www.trattoriadellarte.com
Prices: $$$

There's a downright contagious exuberance to Shelly Firemen's always-packed Carnegie Hall classic, Trattoria Dell'Arte. It might be the smart, confident service staff, or the overflowing, recession-be-damned antipasto bar. Maybe it's the cheeky welcome motto ("What's Italian for Carnegie Hall? Trattoria Dell'Arte."), or the Tuscan-styled rooms lined with mahogany wine racks and dripping candles, that keep people coming back again and again.

Expect to pay–perhaps a bit too steeply–for this kind of *io non lo so*, but the flaky, thin-crust pizzas and heady dishes of finely-sauced pastas do not disappoint. Save room for the irresistible Italian desserts, like an airy cheesecake wrapped in chocolate sponge cake, topped with piping-hot chocolate ganache.

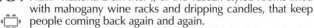

298

21 Club

A4

American ✗✗

21 W. 52nd St. (bet. Fifth & Sixth Aves.)

Subway: 5 Av – 53 St
Phone: 212-582-7200
Web: www.21club.com
Prices: $$$

Lunch Tue – Fri
Dinner Mon – Sat

Now in its 70th year, 21 Club (of the Orient-Express group) remains in the pantheon of restaurants and an inherent part of the NYC experience. Its unique history and speakeasy ambience are loved by glitterati and former presidents alike. Gentleman, embrace the classics and don your finest, though ties are no longer required.

Lantern-holding jockeys and bronze double doors lead back in time, into the old Manhattan world of wealth and tradition still celebrated over dry martinis and oysters, beneath the dining room's low canopy of vintage model toys.

The experienced staff serves a solid American menu that may include creamy cauliflower soup with mushrooms, lobster, and apples; perfectly fresh, grilled Dover sole; or gargantuan wedges of apple-crumb pie.

Utsav

C2

Indian ✗✗

1185 Sixth Ave. (enter on 46th St.)

Subway: 47-50 Sts - Rockefeller Ctr
Phone: 212-575-2525
Web: www.utsavny.com
Prices: 🍴🍴

Lunch & dinner daily

Push past the humdrum ground-floor bar seating, and make your way up the carpeted steps for a lovely surprise. This is Utsav – an upscale little hideaway perched high above the hustle and bustle of 46th Street, on an elevated bridge between two midtown office buildings. From here, the restaurant fashions a light, simple air with billowing fabrics, leafy green plants, and unique views.

The gorgeous, overflowing lunch buffet and bar-area takeout options bring office workers in by the droves. However, the à la carte and evening menus are equally worthy, with soft piles of blistered, piping hot naan; plump, juicy garlic chicken slathered in a tangy chili sauce; spicy, tender lamb stir-fried with coconut and curry leaves; and rich, smooth mango *lassi*.

ViceVersa

Italian 🍴🍴

C1

325 W. 51st St. (bet. Eighth & Ninth Aves.)

Subway: 50 St (Eighth Ave.)
Phone: 212-399-9291
Web: www.viceversarestaurant.com
Prices: $$

Lunch Sun – Fri
Dinner Mon – Sat

This urbane, sophisticated spot (pronounced VEE-chay versa) embodies everything that a European would love in Italian-American cuisine. Inside, the elegant dining room is a haze of muted earth tones with a long, wide bar for lingering or solo dining, and pretty enclosed garden area that opens in fair weather for alfresco meals. The beautifully choreographed service and attentive staff is a worthy attraction in itself.

Although the menu lists some Italian classics, the dishes themselves cater to the American palate, with creamy and boldly sauced pastas aplenty. Appetizers include the likes of *gnocchi di patate* with fresh favas, *guanciale*, and *Pecorino di Fossa* cheese; or perhaps the sautéed calamari and artichoke tart over fresh radicchio salad.

West Bank Café

American 🍴🍴

B2

407 W. 42nd St. (bet. Ninth & Tenth Aves.)

Subway: 42 St - Port Authority Bus Terminal
Phone: 212-695-6909
Web: www.westbankcafe.com
Prices: $$

Lunch & dinner daily

This beloved Theater District mainstay has kept its head above the all-too-choppy waters of Manhattan's dining scene since 1978 by offering delicious, progressive American food at honest prices. The flocks of regulars that squeeze into this simply adorned bistro most nights of the week are proof, though some of these guests may be heading to the Laurie Beechman Theater, located inside the café.

The vibe is lively, warm, and energetic, so settle into one of the leather banquettes and let the pleasant hum of jazz enhance your meal. Try the tender and beautifully charred steak, perhaps flanked by a salty tower of beer-battered onion rings. Bargains are available after 8:00 P.M., when two courses for $25 are served to non-theatergoers each evening.

Yakitori Totto

C1

J a p a n e s e 🍴

251 W. 55th St. (bet. Broadway & Eighth Ave.)

Subway: 57 St - 7 Av
Phone: 212 245 4555
Web: www.tottonyc.com
Prices: $$

Lunch Mon – Fri
Dinner nightly

Annoying foodie friend won't stop talking about their trip to Tokyo? Get a pen out. Some argue that Yakitori Totto's is amongst the best Japanese in the city; but we agree they are in the top two for yakitori—those tasty skewers of chicken, meats, vegetables, and other goodies, perfectly seasoned and cooked on a smoky charcoal grill. It's one of Japan's most popular street foods and this lively little den, tucked up a flight of stairs, elevates it to new heights.

House specialties like the chicken hearts, knees and necks are not to be missed, but even finicky eaters will find plenty to devour with dreamy little *tskune* (get them with the sauce); *teba*, so lovingly grilled you'll swear off buffalo sauce; and *nasu*, best enjoyed with miso paste.

Remember, stars
(✿✿✿…✿) are awarded
for cuisine only! Elements
such as service and décor
are not a factor.

SoHo & Nolita

SoHo (South of Houston) and Nolita (North of Little Italy) prove not only that New York has a penchant for portmanteaus, but that the downtown "scene" lives on now more than ever. What remains new and ever-changing are the subtle transformations that redefine these neighborhoods block by block. Despite the retail invasion that has taken over some of SoHo's eastern corners, it remains true to its promise of sun-drenched restaurants and open-air cafés filled with European sophisticates of a certain age, and supermodels lingering over salads. There are also plenty of tourists to admire them.

Shopping in SoHo

Those fortunate enough to live in what were once artists' lofts (now multimillion dollar condos) know that there are still a few foodie gems in this area heavily focused on restaurant dining. For your at-home tapas needs, **Despana** offers Spanish foods (and rare wines next door) as well as ingredients from oil-packed tuna to mouthwatering *bocadillos*. They will even prepare a traditional tortilla Española with advance notice. A visit to **Pino's Prime Meat Market**, a small butcher shop that carries some of the best meat in town should be followed by a respite at the original **Dean and Deluca**, filled with some of the cities

favorite cakes and coffees. While this is a true gourmet treat, be forewarned that its steep prices match the sleek location.

Nolita

Farther east is Nolita—a neighborhood as cool as its name. This is where a slightly hipper and hungrier downtown set flock (judging by its many offerings). These locals aren't living the typical midtown nine-to-five life and shun the *je ne sais quoi* of SoHo in favor of smallish spots that begin with the word "café." At the top of this list is **Café Habana**, offering its casual crowds a gritty diner vibe and amazing Mexico City-style corn on the cob (also available for takeout next door at **Café Habana To Go**). Equally hip hangouts can be found at **Café Gitane**, serving French-Moroccan; or **Café Colonial** for Brazilian food.

The ethos in Nolita is focused: do a single thing very well. This may have been inspired by **Lombardi's**, which claims to be America's very first pizzeria (founded in 1905) and still has lines outside the door. **Hoomos Asli** may not be attractive and its service is brisk, but they clearly put effort into the outstanding hummus, fluffy pitas, and falafels to accompany those tart, fresh lemonades whose memory will keep you cool for many summers to come.

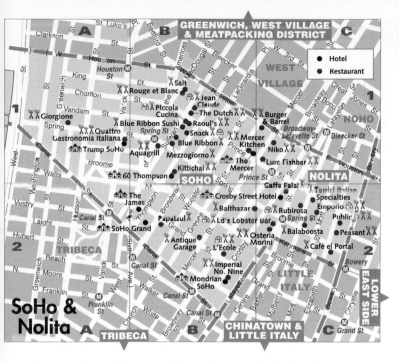

- Hotel
- Restaurant

A B C

WEST VILLAGE

St. Luke's Pl.
Clarkson St.
W. Houston St.
Houston St.
King St.
Charlton St.
Rouge et Blanc
Salt
Vandam St.
Giorgione
Spring St.
Quattro
Gastronomia Italiana
Piccola Cucina
Jean Claude
The Dutch
Blue Ribbon Sushi
Raoul's
Burger & Barrel
Broadway-Lafayette St
Trump SoHo
Aquagrill
Mezzogiorno
Blue Ribbon
Mercer Kitchen
Niko
Lure Fishbar
Kittichai
The Mercer
Broome St.
60 Thompson
SOHO
Prince St.
Caffe Falai
Torrisi Italian Specialties
The James
Crosby Street Hotel
Emporio
Public
SoHo Grand
Balthazar
Rubirosa
Spring St
Papatzul
Ld's Lobster Bar
Balaboosta
Peasant
Antique Garage
L'Ecole
Osteria Morini
Café el Portal
TRIBECA
Imperial No. Nine
LITTLE ITALY
Mondrian SoHo
NOHO
NOLITA
LOWER EAST SIDE

SoHo & Nolita

TRIBECA CHINATOWN & LITTLE ITALY Grand St

For the best fish tacos this side of California, head to **Pinche Taqueria**. However, if whiling away the afternoon in one of Manhattan's most idyllic outdoor gardens suits your mood, then visit **Le Jardin Bistro**. Even satisfying a sweet tooth is done with elevated style at **Pappabubble**, whose candies are crafted with an eye-popping sense of design. With equal ingenuity and old-school flair, **Rice to Riches** serves its celebrated bowls of rice pudding with creatively named toppings, like "Mischief" (buttery graham crackers) or "Nudge" (chilled espresso and cocoa). Cheesecake connoisseurs take note that **Eileen's Cheesecake** and its mind-boggling array of flavors has been chasing those Junior's fanatics back to Brooklyn. Even between feedings, this area promises to nurture your inner epicurean with a visit to the Bowery. The unrefined kitchen supply stores that line the neighborhood's eastern border are technically wholesale only, but some still sell for cash. Come here to stock up on sheet pans, rubber spatulas, and pu pu platters.

One of the greater challenges Nolita poses is the decision of where to end the day. Tucked into these streets are cozy bars, each with its own stylish NY feel, *sans* the masses besetting other neighborhoods. Date-like places such as **Pravda** with its assortment of vodkas or **Sweet and Vicious** for expert cocktails, are a fitting finale.

Antique Garage

B2

41 Mercer St. (bet. Broome & Grand Sts.)

Subway: Canal St (Broadway)
Phone: 212-219-1019
Web: www.antiquegaragesoho.com
Prices: $$

Lunch & dinner daily

As impossible as it sounds, try to imagine an adorable, inviting restaurant tucked into a renovated auto repair garage in SoHo. Its homey, unpretentious vibe is complete with beautiful rugs, dripping chandeliers, and cool antiques available for purchase. Live music is featured on weeknights. By day, the Antique Garage offers a quiet reprieve for SoHo shoppers; at night, couples revel in the intimacy of these close-knit tables and flickering candlelight.

As for the very good food, dishes are decidedly Turkish but hint at all regions of the Mediterranean. Expect salads of char-grilled eggplant rich with the flavors of smoke, mixed with olive oil and lemon, and served with pidé, a Turkish bread; or marinated chunks of perfectly grilled chicken shish kebab.

Aquagrill

B1

210 Spring St. (at Sixth Ave.)

Subway: Spring St (Sixth Ave.)
Phone: 212-274-0505
Web: www.aquagrill.com
Prices: $$

Lunch & dinner daily

If only Cheers had such good food! Much-loved Aquagrill is the kind of restaurant where everyone knows your name—well, at least the staff knows the names of the regulars who flank the front bar. The difference, of course, is the quality of seafood at Jeremy and Jennifer Marshall's seafood house, where the husband-and-wife duo divvy up responsibilities: she works the front of house, while he mans the kitchen.

Like any good chef with a fresh piece of fish, Marshall employs a light touch in dishes like his velvety soup loaded with plump, briny mussels; or the Maine lobster salad, laced with creamy avocado, zebra beets, and ruby-red grapefruit. Don't miss a few fresh oysters off the gorgeous raw bar, or the decadent handmade chocolate sampler.

Balaboosta

C2

214 Mulberry St. (bet. Prince & Spring Sts.)

Subway: Spring St (Lafayette St.)
Phone: 212-966-7366
Web: www.balaboostanyc.com
Prices: $$

Lunch Sat – Sun
Dinner nightly

Downtown foodies are already well aware of Israeli-born Chef Einat Admony thanks to her popular Taïm, located in the West Village and clearly marked by its lines out the door. Here at the chef's latest in Nolita, Balaboosta (a Yiddish expression meaning the perfect housewife) features a full-service dining experience in an attractively spare room with a petite bar area and a menu of expectedly enjoyable Middle Eastern cuisine.

A listing of small plates includes the crowd-pleasing hummus presented in a mortar and pestle, as well as falafel-wrapped meatballs served with herbed tahini sauce. Entrées display a contemporary sensibility as in the lamb three ways: a seared chop, a cut of loin wrapped in Swiss chard; and kibbeh on a pool of cool *tzatziki*.

Balthazar

B2

80 Spring St. (bet. Broadway & Crosby St.)

Subway: Spring St (Lafayette St.)
Phone: 212 965-1414
Web: www.balthazarny.com
Prices: $$$

Lunch & dinner daily

With its legendary red awning and brassy good looks, Keith McNally's ageless downtown darling has been a joyous zoo ever since it opened its doors in 1997.

All of this means that reservations are highly recommended, though there are a few ways to dodge the prime-time problems. Bar tables are open to walk-ins; breakfast hours are lovely; and the bakery next door serves scrumptious salads, sandwiches, and pastries to-go (not to mention devastating hot chocolate). At the restaurant, classic bistro fare abounds in a rotating list of daily specials, from trout on Monday to Sunday's *choucroute*. Of course, anyone seeking that timelessly Balthazar experience should attempt the towering feast of chilled oysters and *fruits de mer*—a true must-have.

Blue Ribbon

Contemporary 🍴

B1

97 Sullivan St. (bet. Prince & Spring Sts.)

Subway: Spring St (Sixth Ave.)   Dinner nightly
Phone: 212-274-0404
Web: www.blueribbonrestaurants.com
Prices: $$$

It's for good reason that the Blue Ribbon family is now liberally fanned out across the city. Meet the catalyst for it all—Blue Ribbon brasserie, a New York classic tucked into Sullivan Street. The restaurant's welcoming and engaging staff is a luxury in a neighborhood more inclined to make you feel plain than cherished—which is quite interesting, considering Blue Ribbon has its own celebrity following. Namely, the city's chef circuit, that regularly swings through post-shift (the kitchen serves until 4:00 A.M.) come to indulge in a range of rawbar delights, and flavorful comfort classics like the playful *pu pu* platter or gourmet fried chicken. So follow suit, bring a group, and dive into decadent delicacies like bone marrow with oxtail marmalade.

Blue Ribbon Sushi

Japanese 🍴

B1

119 Sullivan St. (bet. Prince & Spring Sts.)

Subway: Spring St (Sixth Ave.)   Lunch & dinner daily
Phone: 212-343-0404
Web: www.blueribbonrestaurants.com
Prices: $$$

Cooler than the traditional sushi den yet just as delicious, Blue Ribbon Sushi is yet another example of how these über-restauranteurs, the Bromberg brothers, have mastered their cultish art of the casually hip New York eatery. Here, they turn their attentions to the sea, where the team of talented chefs has but one all-important question for customers: Pacific or Atlantic? This is how the fresh-off-the-boat (or plane) sashimi and daily specials are delineated, although the spicy-tuna set can tread safer waters with dishes like the crispy rock shrimp tempura.

No reservations are taken at this discreet sushi den, so aim for off-hours or lunchtime, when you can command a booth for an afternoon feast. Late hours, until 2:00 A.M., are popular among chefs.

Burger & Barrel

American ✕✕

C1

25 W. Houston St. (at Greene St.)

Subway: Broadway - Lafayette St   Lunch & dinner daily
Phone: 212-334-7320
Web: www.burgerandbarrel.com
Prices: $$

It should come as no surprise that Burger & Barrel is busier than a barrel of monkeys. After all, it comes from the same owners that have worked their magic with Locanda Verde, Chinatown Brasserie, and Lure. Inside, it's as tight as it is cool with a classic pub feel. You won't be able to have a private conversation, but the eavesdropping is fantastic!

Renowned burgers (like the Puebla) deserve the headline, with tasty toppings like red-onion relish, roasted chili peppers, and creamy *queso fresco*, though there is more to this menu than meat. Comforting favorites go on to include fried chicken and sides like corn pudding or polenta fries. Desserts are to drool over, like the salty peanut-butter-brownie sundae, to round out a heart-stopping meal here.

Café el Portal

Mexican ✕

C2

174 Elizabeth St. (bet. Kenmare & Spring Sts.)

Subway: Spring St (Lafayette St.)   Lunch & dinner Mon — Sat
Phone: 212-226-4642
Web: N/A
Prices: 🅒🅒

In an area that has recently been attracting newcomers in large, hip spaces, Café el Portal defies this trend with its low-key design, casual ambience, and family-run feel. Despite its less than impressive digs, this restaurant serves some of the most authentic Mexican dishes in the city, such as the classic *pastel con tres leches*, made with fantastic vanilla sponge cake soaked in condensed milk. Everything is made in-house, from the fresh tortillas to the Mexican hot chocolate.

The tiny bar boasts a tequila collection with more bottles than the restaurant has seats, and the cocktail menu goes well beyond margaritas to include many non-alcoholic options. Reasonable prices and flavorful, fun food keep el Portal buzzing with locals and regulars.

Caffe Falai

C2

Italian ✗

265 Lafayette St. (bet. Prince & Spring Sts.)

Subway: Spring St (Lafayette St.) Lunch & dinner daily
Phone: 212-274-8615
Web: www.falainyc.com
Prices: $$

The elements come together to make for a delicious meal in Caffe Falai's delicate little jewel box interior, where white-framed mirrors hang from pure white walls, and the pretty round mosaic floor tiles light up under ornate glass chandeliers. All the more reason to linger over one–or two– of Chef Iacopo Falai's to-die-for pastries, lovingly displayed in the glass showcase by his kitchen.

The lunch and dinner menu entices just as much, with a comforting lineup of regional favorites from all over Italy, like an authentic bowl of minestrone, its scent delivering all the freshness of spring; or the ever-popular panini. Very well-made pastas are a highlight, but the focus of many meals here are the desserts—sensible gourmands save room for more than one.

The Dutch

B1

American ✗✗

131 Sullivan St. (at Prince St.)

Subway: Spring St (Lafayette St.) Lunch & dinner daily
Phone: 212-677-6200
Web: www.thedutchnyc.com
Prices: $$$

The pre-opening frenzy of Andrew Carmellini and The Dutch riled up everyone from foodies to fashionistas but here's one feeding frenzy that is well deserved. Go ahead and believe the hype—it's a hit.

They may have been waiting with baited breath, but the place is read-my-lips loud and packed with a crowd of downtown debs and their dons who are definitely not going dutch. Carmellini spins a wondrous web of Americana. "Oyster sliders" with mustard-pickled okra remoulade; chile- and scallion-studded corn bread; ruby red shrimp; fried green tomatoes—it's mod Midwest and slick South in the heart of so cool SoHo. The flavorful, tender rabbit pot pie is enough to make you think Glenn Close's character was really on to something in *Fatal Attraction*.

Ed's Lobster Bar

Seafood ✗

C2

222 Lafayette St. (bet. Kenmare & Spring Sts.)

Subway: Spring St (Lafayette St.)
Phone: 212-343-3236
Web: www.lobsterbarnyc.com
Prices: $$

Lunch & dinner daily

The delicacy and purity of seafood is epitomized in cute and convivial Ed's Lobster Bar. A sunny yet cool space with a good mix of food-savvy NYers, Ed's is that ideal sanctum for anyone who wishes to escape to New England for an hour. As if to ease the no-reservations policy, this saltwater gem offers a fine choice of seafood-friendly wines and beers that go down as smoothly as the oysters. The narrow space is dotted with tables, but true cheer is found at the marble bar. While side dishes are all enticing, faves like perfectly fried calamari; creamy and luscious chowder with succulent clams; and the stellar buttery lobster roll (piled with juicy meat tossed in mayo, celery, and dill) aside crispy fries and Ed's homemade pickles are sheer decadence.

Emporio

Italian ✗✗

C2

231 Mott St. (bet. Prince & Spring Sts.)

Subway: Spring St (Lafayette St.)
Phone: 212-966-1234
Web: www.auroraristorante.com
Prices: $$

Lunch & dinner daily

Having charmed Manhattan and Brooklyn with his Aurora restaurants, famed Riccardo Buitoni decided to try an even warmer, more cheery concept on the narrow streets of Nolita with Roman-inspired trattoria, Emporio.

Like his other ventures, this idyllic Italian eatery has loads of rustic appeal. The interior space feels close-knit and is meant to invoke a twenties-era grocery. Usually swarming with crowds on weekends, the menu epitomizes fresh ingredients in tasty preparations. Start with a mouthwatering plate of cured meats presented with grilled, olive oil-brushed bread before digging into dishes like squash blossoms, stuffed with cheese and anchovies; pizza laced with buffalo mozzarella, zucchini, and ricotta; and juicy, oven-roasted rabbit.

A1
Italian ✗✗

307 Spring St. (bet. Greenwich & Hudson Sts.)

Subway: Spring St (Sixth Ave.) Lunch & dinner daily
Phone: 212-352-2269
Web: www.giorgionenyc.com
Prices: $$

Tucked down a nondescript street on the burgeoning Hudson Square, Giorgione walks softly but carries a big stick. Owned and founded by Giorgio Deluca (of Dean & Deluca), the restaurant first gathered a following for its octopus salad—these days, it stays packed for its honest Italian fare.

Inside the narrow dining room you'll find sleek chrome tables, cool white leather seats, and icy blue walls—all the better to let one of the ace pizzas from the wood-burning oven warm you up. Specials rotate daily, but you might find a *rigatoni alla Norma* tossed with a judicious amount of silky eggplant, ripe tomatoes, and milky ricotta; or a flaky *crostata*, glazed with red currants and topped with mission figs, lemon rind, and a smear of mascarpone cheese.

Imperial No. Nine

B2
Seafood ✗✗

9 Crosby St. (bet. Grand & Howard Sts.)

Subway: Canal St (Lafayette St.) Lunch & dinner daily
Phone: 212-389-0000
Web: www.mondriansoho.com
Prices: $$$

Behold this stunning space: crystal chandeliers hanging from a pitched glass ceiling; elegant tea tables with wrought-iron garden chairs; glass walls shrouded in curtains, and an abundance of gorgeous greenery. Welcome to the long-awaited Imperial No. Nine, where Chef Sam Talbot is currently making his mark. Just off of the lobby of the equally breathtaking Mondrian Hotel, this atrium-like dream of a spot is firing up some seriously outstanding seafood.

Try the incredibly fresh jumbo fluke, topped with Chinese black vinegar, frozen coconut granite, and crispy garlic; or the mind-blowingly lavish lard and sea urchin—grilled rustic bread slathered with mustard caper sauce and topped with salty slices of lard and a whole "tongue" of sea urchin. Divine!

Jean Claude 😊

French ✗

B1

137 Sullivan St. (bet. Houston & Prince Sts.)

Subway: Spring St (Sixth Ave.)   Dinner nightly
Phone: 212-475-9232
Web: www.jeanclauderestaurant.com
Prices: $$

With its tight-knit tables, lived-in good looks, and soft French music quietly thrumming in the background, this romantic little bistro could be straight off of Paris' Left Bank. Luckily for Manhattan, though, the infinitely charming Jean Claude is smack in the middle of SoHo.

In winter, the room is decidedly cozy; while summer finds the front windows thrown open and couples lingering over the reasonably priced wine list, which boasts a nice carafe and half-carafe list. The French cooking is straightforward and delicious, with a solid lineup of bistro staples like tender *moules marinieres* and frites; seared hanger steak in a thyme, red wine and shallot reduction, paired with a sinful *gratin dauphinois*; and a spot-on rendition of crème brûlée.

Kittichai

Thai ✗✗

B1

60 Thompson St. (bet. Broome & Spring Sts.)

Subway: Spring St (Sixth Ave.)   Lunch & dinner daily
Phone: 212-219-2000
Web: www.kittichairestaurant.com
Prices: $$$

Good Thai food rarely doubles as a place to woo your sweetie, but dark and sultry Kittichai breaks the mold. Tucked into the trendy 60 Thompson hotel, the restaurant owns a jaw-dropping interior, replete with silk swaths, suspended orchids, and floating candles.

Thai hounds know there are more authentic places in the city to get their fix, but Kittichai makes up for the lack of heat with well-polished European touches. Try the spicy and sour oxtail soup, bobbing with Kaffir lime leaves and charred tomatoes; tender organic chicken, served in a delicious green, coconut-scented curry dancing with Thai eggplant and sweet basil; or a delicious Thai ice cream sundae with coconut jelly, passion fruit seeds, and palm seeds.

L'Ecole

French ✗✗

462 Broadway (at Grand St.)

Subway: Canal St (Broadway)
Phone: 212-219-3300
Web: www.frenchculinary.com
Prices: $$

Lunch daily
Dinner Mon – Sat

This fun, virtual classroom (courtesy of the French Culinary Institute) provides students their first opportunity to show their expertise, love, and respect for the art of traditional French cooking. However, this is a "learning experience" so there may be a few mistakes alongside a treasured moment of brilliance. Regardless, it is clear these students have mastered the use of top ingredients, where they shine in simple preparations like country pâté or roasted duck.

The classic French menu changes every six weeks, offering four- or five-course dinners as well as an inexpensive prix-fixe lunch.

Conscientious student servers cater to guests in an ambient "SoHo" space with images of a bustling restaurant kitchen and lofty windows overlooking Broadway.

Lure Fishbar

Seafood ✗✗

142 Mercer St. (at Prince St.)

Subway: Prince St
Phone: 212-431-7676
Web: www.lurefishbar.com
Prices: $$$

Lunch & dinner daily

Housed in the basement of the popular Prada showroom, Lure Fishbar easily has some of the best digs in town. Outside, SoHo's streets might be covered in beautiful old-school cobblestones and teeming with young gorgeous gazelles, but down here a tiki-trendy-meets-maritime motif (think tropical prints, angular porthole windows, and cozy booths) and fat seafood plates reign supreme.

A mean-looking sushi-counter and raw bar lets you know how seriously they take the food, though. A plate of yellowtail carpaccio arrives fresh as can be, topped with garlic-chili sauce, sesame oil, thin slices of avocado, and crispy, deep-fried shallots; while a wickedly fresh branzino is served whole, perfectly de-boned and laced with pesto, scallions, and crunchy shallots.

Mercer Kitchen

Contemporary ✕✕

B1

99 Prince St. (at Mercer St.)

Subway: Prince St   Lunch & dinner daily
Phone: 212-966-5454
Web: www.jean-georges.com
Prices: $$

A-listers and Hollywood types may flock to the latest "it" restaurant, but these trendy spots often shutter long before their cool quotient becomes cliché. Mercer Kitchen is that rare NY restaurant that has retained its hot spot reputation and celebrity guestbook for what seems like eons.

Showcasing a street-level bar (with stellar cocktails), a divvied up downstairs dining room, and subterranean lounge, Mercer Kitchen continues to offer well-executed and contemporary food like pizza flambée topped with smoky, fatty bacon and crème fraîche; delicately flavored tuna spring rolls with a soy purée; and baked salmon with potato salad and horseradish. Bold-faced names aren't only at the tables—Jean-Georges Vongerichten is still behind the scenes here.

Mezzogiorno

Italian ✕

B1

195 Spring St. (at Sullivan St.)

Subway: Spring St (Sixth Ave.)   Lunch & dinner daily
Phone: 212-334-2112
Web: www.mezzogiorno.com
Prices: $$

The big, bright blue awnings of this Italian veteran are a fixture on the SoHo scene. Its 100 interior collages—each one a local artist's unique interpretation of the restaurant's logo—are a lovely reminder of when the neighborhood was more artists than agents.

The real star of the show, of course, is the beautiful wood-burning oven, which juts out into the main dining room where all can marvel at its delicious, thin-crust pies. In addition to the extensive pasta offerings, try the myriad seasonal Italian specialties like *carciofi saltati*, a plate of tender artichoke hearts paired with crunchy pistachio, and laced with lemon and parsley—this is a perfect delight when spring hits and the raised terrace opens up for prime people watching.

Manhattan ▶ SoHo & Nolita

Niko

Japanese ❌❌

170 Mercer St. (bet. Houston & Prince Sts.)

Subway: Lafayette St
Phone: 212-991-5650
Web: www.helloniko.com
Prices: $$$

Lunch Mon – Fri
Dinner nightly

You can have it your way at Niko, since this SoHo Japanese joint is a half sushi bar and a half restaurant rife with Japanese creations. It's sleek and serene in that inimitable Asian way, but then throws in some SoHo funk for good measure and pride of place. It is overlooking Mercer Street in all its glory, after all, but don't worry, since you'll feel comfortable here whether you are in your Louboutins or loungewear.

Omakase is definitely the way to go to sample the succulent sushi and sashimi. The rice is perfect, the fish, with everything from giant clam, tilefish, octopus, and fluke, is delicious—it's a win-win. Leaning toward cooked? Go with the flavorful rock shrimp donburi or the moist and tender slow-roasted chicken with gingered cabbage.

Osteria Morini

Italian ❌❌

218 Lafayette St. (bet. Kenmare & Spring Sts.)

Subway: Spring St (Lafayette St.)
Phone: 212-965-8777
Web: www.osteriamorini.com
Prices: $$

Lunch & dinner daily

Chef Michael White's rustic tribute to Italy's Emilia-Romagna rarely misses a beat. Once through the heavy wooden door, the cozy, oft-crowded space decorated with curios, photos, and shelves of ingredients pulses with the satisfied expectations of contented diners. An expert staff moves efficiently between the bar, the chef's counter, and the dining room.

The food is uncompromising, luscious, and hearty. The simple *polpettine*, prosciutto and mortadella meatballs, burst with porky goodness in a chunky tomato sauce; the *gramigna* topped with sausage ragù is elegant and full-flavored. The *affogato* is an unexpected and transporting star of the show—this cloud of zabaglione gelato resting on an ocean of espresso is reason enough to return again and again.

Papatzul

B2   Mexican 🍴

55 Grand St. (bet. West Broadway & Wooster St.)

Subway: Canal St (Sixth Ave.)   Lunch & dinner daily
Phone: 212-274-8225
Web: www.papatzul.com
Prices: $$

This tiny, mouthwatering Mexican restaurant is a refreshing find in the model-festooned neighborhood. Its ambience is festive yet comfortable enough for lingering over conversations and effortlessly cool yet welcoming. Beyond the lively bar find closely-spaced tables with couples enjoying pitchers of margaritas. Laid-back service and genial prices add to the warmth, while the relaxed (*un*-Manhattan) pacing may add to its authenticity.

An outstanding start to any meal here is the house ceviche, bright with the flavors of lime, cilantro, and the freshest fish. The ample listing of *platos fuertes* may include the *budin al pasilla*, layered with chili sauce, shredded chicken, cheese, beans, and cream — totally decadent and rich with melted flavors.

Peasant

C2   Italian 🍴🍴

194 Elizabeth St. (bet. Prince & Spring Sts.)

Subway: Spring St (Lafayette St.)   Dinner Tue – Sun
Phone: 212-965-9511
Web: www.peasantnyc.com
Prices: $$

Things just keep getting better here at Peasant. A seasoned SoHo staple, this sublime spot continues to fire up terrific Italian with expert skill and consistency. Whitewashed brick walls and gorgeous wood-burning ovens stir up visions of an osteria, while the crackling hearth, complimentary bread, and sublime ricotta cheese seal the deal.

Sarde al forno—baked sardines with crispy breadcrumbs and grated lemon zest, served in a terra-cotta cassoulet—start things off beautifully. Fresh, hand cut pastas are cooked al dente perfectly, as in the *malfatti con coniglio* in a hearty and gamey braised rabbit ragù, served with root vegetables and milky *Parmigiano*. End with apple and quince tart, flaky, sweet, and moist, topped with a scoop of gelato.

Piccola Cucina 🐛

Italian ✕

B1

184 Prince St. (bet. Sullivan & Thompson Sts.)

Subway: Spring St (Sixth Ave.)　　　　　Lunch & dinner daily
Phone: 212-625-3200
Web: N/A
Prices: $$

If you think the best thing that Sicily exports is its sunshine, you obviously *have* been to Piccola Cucina. It lives up to its name (this place is teeny tiny), but don't underestimate the kick of this Italian spot.

Filippo Guardione owns the prize and his proud papà back home ships the best of Sicily to this NY kitchen. Starting with the excellent cannoli cream from Ragusa to the swordfish from Messina...even to the salt, it's like a culinary chamber of commerce dog and pony show. Take a few bites of the crispy *arancino*, perfect pasta, glistening sardines, or delicious eggplant and you'll think FedEx should be sainted for shipping such delights. Back to those cannolis: in one felt swoop you'll be transported to a Sicilian *pasticceria*. Need we say more?

Quattro Gastronomia Italiana

Italian ✕✕✕

A1

246 Spring St. (at Varick St.)

Subway: Spring St (Sixth Ave.)　　　　　Lunch & dinner daily
Phone: 212-842-4500
Web: www.trumpsohohotel.com
Prices: $$$

Quattro Gastronomia Italiana is a love letter to Italy. Its seductive design is culled straight from Milan while its cooking is driven by the talented Piemontese chef. Pair that with a terrific location at the base of the Trump SoHo hotel and you've got a winner—and a new cafeteria for the nabe's glamorous types. *Nota bene*: definitely go bling or you won't fit in with this bold and beautiful crowd.

Doubting foodies who think just because Trump's behind it the food won't be up to snuff are wrong. *Tajarin delle Langhe con battuto di carne*, a nest of handcut pasta tossed with *battuto*, and *vitello tonnato* are *bellissimi*; while branzino tartare is fresh and fabulous. Hey, you don't have a shoot tomorrow, so dig right in to that silky *torta di Piemonte*.

Public ❀

C2   F u s i o n ✕✕

210 Elizabeth St. (bet. Prince & Spring Sts.)

Subway: Spring St (Lafayette St.)   Lunch Sat – Sun
Phone: 212-343-7011   Dinner nightly
Web: www.public-nyc.com
Prices: $$$

Michael Weber

Shiny brass beacons and a few metal stairs indicate the entrance to Public, while wide open windows and carriage house-like beams enhance the industrial effect of this very posh and "public" SoHo arena. From its suave Monday Room (an adjoining wine suite) to a series of dining spaces, Public offers a rustic, rare, and sexy ambience in which to appreciate Chef Brad Farmerie's spirited and refined cuisine.

Find novel delights like grilled Kobe beef tongue with an eggplant-cumin relish, and satchels of snail and oxtail ravioli in smoked paprika oil—all served in a lavish dining room marked by billowing fabric and bare tables set with linen napkins. Adding to the originality, menus are presented on clipboards and resemble old-fangled order tickets; while literature from the 1940s and the innovative use of recycled materials recall the heart of public academia.

When the lights turn low and cast a sultry glow, witness an engaging staff steer chic and agreeable diners through a superior wine list as they imbibe the philosophy behind pork belly confit with apple purée, sage shortbread, and watercress; or a chocolate espresso cake licked with butterscotch ice cream and whiskey sabayon.

Manhattan ▶ SoHo & Nolita

Raoul's

French ✗✗

B1

180 Prince St. (bet. Sullivan & Thompson Sts.)

Subway: Spring St (Sixth Ave.)   Dinner nightly
Phone: 212-966-3518
Web: www.raouls.com
Prices: $$$

Whether by charms or talent, this beloved bistro has survived 30-plus years in one of the fussiest parts of town, somehow remaining popular, sophisticated, and stylishly unpretentious. The authentic French fare is prepared simply, but remains impressive with top ingredients and delicious flavors—as in the steak tartare with quail egg, or seared foie gras with Concord grape purée. The menu, exquisitely handwritten on chalkboards and presented by the amiable waitstaff, still appeals to savvy diners and connoisseurs hungry for meaty steaks and fries made crisp with duck fat.

The energetic atmosphere in the dimly lit main room is intoxicating, but those seeking a calmer spot for quiet conversation should try the bright upstairs space or tiny covered garden.

Rouge et Blanc

Contemporary ✗✗

B1

48 MacDougal St. (bet. Houston & Prince Sts.)

Subway: Houston St   Lunch Wed – Sun
Phone: 212-260-5757   Dinner Tue – Sun
Web: www.rougeetblancnyc.com
Prices: $$$

With a burlap-covered ceiling, reclaimed wood, handcrafted pottery, lanterns, and plants, Rouge et Blanc's Indochine-influenced décor leaves no one guessing its theme. This restaurant successfully renews the romance of French-influenced Vietnam in its interior; while behind the scenes, the kitchen delivers a contemporary Asian menu that highlights pristine ingredients.

Well-charred razor clams are sweet and smoky atop leek confit; and creamy yellowtail is served with Oregon black truffles, soy jus, and ugli fruit for a sweet and citrusy finish. Rich endings, like caramelized foie gras with apples, cocoa nibs, and vanilla-bean ice cream, are unusually appealing. Let the over-eager bussers know you are not in a hurry, then all can relax and enjoy.

Rubirosa 🐶

Italian ✗

C2

235 Mulberry St. (bet. Prince & Spring Sts.)

Subway: Spring St (Lafayette St.) Lunch & dinner daily
Phone: 212-965-0500
Web: www.rubirosanyc.com
Prices: $$

Boy oh boy...no pun intended. From its adorable all-male waitstaff (take a seat at the counter for *the* best flirting) to its mind-blowingly good Italian-American food, Rubirosa has it going on. You won't know if you're swooning over the hot waiter or the intoxicating smells wafting from the oven here. Rubirosa is SoHo by way of Staten Island—one of the owners has ties to Joe & Pat's in the old neighborhood.

Know that adage about never being too rich or too thin? This Italian sweet lives up to it with its perfect thin-crust pizzas and in-your-face delicious and rich meatball-studded lasagna. From the classic pizza sourced from a 50-year-old family recipe, to the rock-your-world *sfogliatelle*, it's proud Italian blue collar bliss served up with a smile.

Salt

American ✗

B1

58 MacDougal St. (bet. Houston & Prince Sts.)

Subway: Spring St (Sixth Ave.) Lunch & dinner daily
Phone: 212-674-4968
Web: www.saltnyc.com
Prices: $$

The expression "neighborhood restaurant" is bandied about on too casual a basis nowadays, but Salt genuinely deserves the moniker (though prices, too, are in step with this high-end neighborhood). This is a favorite spot where locals congregate, rub elbows, and catch up on gossip at communal tables in the middle of the tight, simply furnished, shabby-chic dining room. Others may choose a small table near the large front windows.

Long Island duck breast or Alaskan King salmon are some of the highlights from the brief menu that is a showcase in fresh and flavorful combinations, incorporating seasonal and local meats and produce. Under the section "Protein + 2," select any two sides to accompany the main dish—a classic American mealtime formula.

Snack ☻

B1

105 Thompson St. (bet. Prince & Spring Sts.)

Subway: Spring St (Sixth Ave.)   Lunch & dinner daily
Phone: 212-925-1040
Web: N/A
Prices: ☜☜

Snack may not be that quaint, laid-back Santorini *taverna*, but there is much to love in this bustling slip of a restaurant tucked into SoHo's quiet, leafy Thompson Street. The old black-and-white photos and shelves of Greek groceries fail to conjure far-off lands, but ignore the slightly erratic interior and strive to snag one of the four dining room tables. The Hellenic fare is authentic enough to transport at first bite. Just don't stop at the meze—entrées are equally satisfying.

Despite the moniker, most of the portions here are hearty, including a generously-sized shredded lamb sandwich, topped with ripe tomatoes, roasted red onions, a smear of aïoli, and fresh arugula; or a Greek salad bursting with creamy feta, kalamata olives, and oregano.

Torrisi Italian Specialties

C2

250 Mulberry St. (at Prince St.)

Subway: Spring St (Lafayette St.)   Lunch & dinner Tue – Sun
Phone: 212-965-0955
Web: www.piginahat.com
Prices: $$

Everyone's still buzzing about this unique Italian-American restaurant from seasoned Chefs Mario Carbone and Rich Torrisi. Reservations aren't accepted so dinner here requires some foresight. Eager hopefuls must line up prior to the start of service to snag a table. Once past the door, everyone eagerly awaits the feast in a charming space replete with red brick walls shelved with an array of ready-to-use products and wooden banquettes.

The nightly dinner is fixed, no substitutions allowed: 5 small *antipasti*, followed by pasta, choice of entrée, Italian ice, and dessert divinity via the cookie plate. Starters like creamy liverwurst with pickled red onion and grilled soft pretzel might be followed by *gemelli* with "dirty" duck ragout, and skate *Francese*.

TEN PELL
RESTAURANT

Lee Lee Beauty & Hair Salon
TEL:528-1381

FOR RENT
212-677-3806
212-349-6800

ve Design

12 Lee Lee Beauty & Hair

BEAUTY & STYLING HOUSE

TriBeCa

Catering to its local clientele of creative types, trendy TriBeCa is, quite simply, a cool place to eat. Here, splurge on meals in pricey restaurants (whose reputations and namesake celebrity chefs precede them), or go for more modest gastropub fare. On sunny days, snag an umbrella-shaded table outside—TriBeCa's famously wide sidewalks are hugely accommodating and among the city's top spots for star-gazing. This wedge of cobblestoned streets, galleries, design stores, and historic warehouses converted to multi-million-dollar lofts was named in the 1970s by a real-estate agent hoping to create a hip identity for the area. The acronym—which stands for Triangle Below Canal–describes an area that is not a triangle at all, but a trapezoid bounded by Canal Street, Broadway, Murray Street, and the Hudson River. Greenwich and Hudson streets are its main thoroughfares for dining and nightlife.

Drinking and Dining

In keeping with its independence and artistic spirit, TriBeCa offers a gourmet experience for any palate (or price tag). On Hudson Square, **City Winery** gives urban wine enthusiasts a place to make their own private-label wine by providing the grapes (a selection of varietals from international vineyards), the barrels, the storage, and the expertise. Also hugely beloved by wine connoisseurs is **Chamber Street Wines**. Those looking for something to enjoy with their wine will rejoice in the monthly events sponsored by **New York Vintners**, which may include free cheese tastings or lessons on making mozzarella. The neighborhood is loaded with wonderful bakeries, the most popular of which includes the **Duane Park Patisserie** for pastries and seasonal specialties; and **Tribeca Treats** for decadent and delicious chocolates. Since 1886, venerable **Bazzini** has occupied the building where company founder, Anthony Bazzini, first opened the business in 1886. Drop by to pick up some gourmet groceries or prepared foods for dinner, and don't leave without a bag of nuts or a jar of their old-fashioned cashew butter. **Puffy's Tavern** is a friendly neighborhood bar displaying five plasma-screen TVs for sports fans, happy-hour drinks, and hearty lunchtime signature Italian sandwiches. Speaking of local faves, **Bubby's** will cater to your homestyle food cravings; while **Zucker's Bagels & Smoked Fish** will remind you of *bubbe's* grub. Like every New York neighborhood, TriBeCa claims its own great pizza joints, as in the Roman-style *pizza al taglio* at hot spot **Farinella**. Owner Alberto Polo Cretara is a Neapolitan hip-hop artist who honed his pizza-making skills at the legendary Il Forno in Rome. Round up some friends to sample his tasty

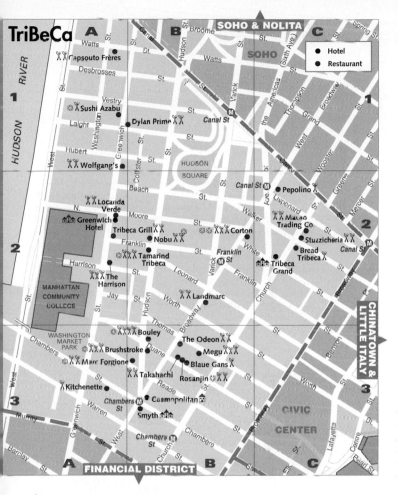

TriBeCa

A   B   C

Watts St.   Broome   St.   Spring St.

SOHO

Hotel
Restaurant

Capsouto Frères

Desbrosses   Watts   St.

HUDSON RIVER

Vestry   St.

Sushi Azabu

Laight   Dylan Prime   Canal St

Hubert

Wolfgang's

Collster   HUDSON SQUARE

Beach   St.

Canal St   Pepolino

Locanda Verde   N.

Moore   Walker   Macao Trading Co

Greenwich Hotel

Tribeca Grill   Corton

Nobu   White   Stuzzicheria

Franklin   St.   Bread Tribeca

Tamarind Tribeca   Franklin St   Tribeca Grand

Harrison   Leonard

The Harrison

MANHATTAN COMMUNITY COLLEGE   Jay   St.   Franklin   Church

Hudson   Worth   Landmarc

WASHINGTON MARKET PARK   Thomas

Bouley   Broadway   The Odeon

Brushstroke   Duane   Megu

Marc Forgione   Blaue Gans

Takahachi   Rosanjin

Kitchenette   Reade

Chambers St   Cosmopolitan

Warren   Smyth

Murray   Chambers   Chambers St

Barclay St

CHINATOWN & LITTLE ITALY

CIVIC CENTER

four-foot-long pies. Under the "dinner and a movie" category, the 2001 film *Dinner Rush* used TriBeCa as a stage. In fact, director Bob Giraldi shot this Mafia- and food-themed movie at one of his famed eateries—**Gigino Trattoria**. The plot tells the story of a night in the life of a chic TriBeCa restaurant, delving into sidelines such as food critics and ambitious chefs. Today this area is still associated with films of many stripes, thanks to the annual Tribeca Film Festival, created in 2002 by Robert DeNiro and others to revitalize the area after 9/11. This world-famous springtime event hosts twelve days of great films, special events, and community camaraderie. Throngs of locals, tourists, and film fiends flock here during this time to see the movies and experience TriBeCa's many wonderful restaurants.

Blaue Gans

B3

Austrian ✗

139 Duane St. (bet. Church St. & West Broadway)

Subway: Chambers St (West Broadway) Lunch & dinner daily
Phone: 212-571-8880
Web: www.wallse.com
Prices: $$

It's hard not to fall in love with Kurt Gutenbrunner's (of Wallsé fame) Blaue Gans, a restaurant that does a lot of things extremely well, while making the whole thing look completely effortless: modern, unpretentious Austrian cooking; cozy, urban ambience; excellent German beer and Austrian wine selection; and a crackerjack service staff. Need we go on?

The menu offers regular and seasonal dishes, and none of them miss—pillowy quark ravioli, sautéed with mint and brown butter; and tender free range chicken, perfectly fried in schnitzel batter and paired with a light, creamy potato and arugula salad. Start with a platter of schnitzels and wursts, and end on dessert (the apple strudel does nicely)—two moves that seem unnecessary but deliver big.

Bread Tribeca

C2

Italian ✗

301 Church St. (at Walker St.)

Subway: Canal St (Sixth Ave.) Lunch & dinner daily
Phone: 212-334-8282
Web: www.breadtribeca.com
Prices: $$

Still trendy among locals, celebrities, and corporate casts, this TriBeCa treasure is graced by large windows, soaring ceilings, creaky floors, and iron columns. The bar upfront is beloved by businessmen seeking happy hour drinks and nibbles, while an assembly line in the open kitchen routinely dispatches panini, pasta, pizza, and myriad entrées.

The menu goes on to include simple preparations that rise to the sublime through skill and quality of ingredients, as in the excellent *caprese* salad. Italian cravings are further indulged in rich saffron linguini twirled with shrimp, roasted tomatoes, and parsley; or pizza *carciofi* topped with artichokes, prosciutto, and Parmigiano Reggiano. A wonderfully fresh and creamy ricotta cheesecake is a fine finale.

Bouley ✿

Contemporary 𝗫𝗫𝗫𝗫

B3

163 Duane St. (at Hudson St.)

Subway: Chambers St (West Broadway)   Lunch & dinner Mon – Sat
Phone: 212-964-2525
Web: www.davidbouley.com
Prices: $$$$

Nicole Bartelme

Luxury embraces you upon entering this extraordinary château-inspired space, richly appointed with worldly imports, chandeliers that appear to drip jewels, carved wooden doors, murals, parquet floors, and arched ceilings that glint with gold. The entry vestibule is lined with impossibly fragrant apples, as if the king had ordered a bit of fruit. But of course, royal treatment is reserved for guests here, as the poised and attentive service staff would remind you throughout your meal.

An experience not readily replicated, dining here is transporting and festive as evidenced by the celebrants that fill its sparkling tables. While remaining true to his classic French culinary foundation, talented Chef David Bouley prepares a rather contemporary menu garnished with global influences. Starters are interesting and exciting as in earthy porcini flan with sweet Dungeness crab and black truffle dashi brightened with green yuzu. The subtle sweetness of pineapple-saffron sauce brings wonderful complexity to fresh black sea bass with chanterelles, sautéed spinach, and almonds.

A word to the wise: the restaurant's unmarked entrance is easily confused with the residential building next door.

Brushstroke ✿

Japanese ⚔⚔⚔

B3

30 Hudson St. (at Duane St.)

Subway: N/A
Phone: 212-791-3771
Web: www.davidbouley.com
Prices: $$$$

Dinner Mon – Sat

Brushstroke/Nicole Bartelme

In this third installation (what was Danube became Secession but is now Brushstroke) Chef David Bouley turns to Japan with Chef Isao Yamada to consider a more modern interpretation of traditional kaiseki menus.

Despite its many lives, the setting is ethereal and ideal for contemplating the series of courses that Japan has spent centuries trying to perfect. The style here is elemental and minimalist (rice paper diffuses natural light through oversized windows, wood planks line counters, charcoal metals cover columns) and finished with painstaking detail—the bar's wall is actually made of books.

This precise aesthetic carries through to the cuisine: before any item is plated, its serving vessel is misted for a slightly glimmering effect. Some dishes succeed in exploring more experimental than traditional tastes as in the green and white asparagus "terrine" in sea urchin sauce. Other courses may seem more classic such as the grilled duck "salad" with fantastic, custard-like Japanese eggplant and miso-mustard dressing. Yet as the dishes progress, there are moment's when the menu's ambition trumps taste.

This academic undertaking is a partnership with the esteemed Tsuji Cooking Academy.

Capsouto Frères

A1

French ✗✗

451 Washington St. (at Watts St.)

Subway: Canal St (Sixth Ave.)
Phone: 212-966-4900
Web: www.capsoutofreres.com
Prices: $$

Lunch Tue – Sun
Dinner nightly

This family owned French institution has been going strong since 1980—step inside this gorgeous landmark building, which dates all the way back to 1891, and you'll find howling steam pipes echoing against carved wainscoting, dark wooden floors, and large jacquard curtain-lined windows.

The menu is honest and focused, though quality slips in and out with different dishes: a foie gras terrine is not particularly good, but a *saucisson de Lyon en croute* with Madeira sauce delights. Don't miss the wine list—a unique, hand-chosen list by Jacques Capsouto (who leads the New York chapter of Compagnons du Beaujolais with wine tastings and monthly meals) carefully selected from all over the world, including unique lifts from countries like Israel.

Dylan Prime

B1

Contemporary ✗✗

62 Laight St. (at Greenwich St.)

Subway: Franklin St
Phone: 212-334-4783
Web: www.dylanprime.com
Prices: $$$

Lunch Sun – Fri
Dinner nightly

With a menu that boasts a parade of cuts like Porterhouse, filet mignon, or aged prime rib, Dylan Prime is undoniably a steakhouse. However, unlike many In this category, this menu boldly and deftly expands to offer very enjoyable American fare. Still, anyone considering a steak should try adding a chapeau—savory crust made with the likes of Maytag blue cheese and chives or mushroom and truffles. Featured on the separate lounge menu or at lunchtime, great value is served in the $14 Dylan Prime Burger, thick and juicy on a warm brioche.

The service is swift, but relaxed in this spacious setting located along a quieter strip of TriBeCa.

Inside, the mood is dark, sultry, and romantic, thanks to low lighting, cozy banquettes, and flickering votives.

Corton ✿ ✿

Contemporary 🗙🗙🗙

B2

239 West Broadway (bet. Walker & White Sts.)

Subway: Franklin St   Dinner Mon – Sat
Phone: 212-219-2777
Web: www.cortonnyc.com
Prices: $$$$

Richard Pare

There is no missing Chef Paul Liebrandt—if not for the film that documents his skyrocket to fame, look through the sliver of a window into Corton's kitchen, and you are sure to spot his imposing height towering over the staff.

Glimpse this scene and suddenly the restaurant itself seems taller, stark perhaps, but with very cool, modern character and an unerring sense of space that is a perfect reflection of its TriBeCa locale.

Yet just as tangible is Chef Liebrandt's enormous culinary skill and unbridled creativity. Corton's two prix-fixe menus are up-to-the minute compilations of seasonality, global inspiration, ambitious techniques, and whimsy. There are moments when the sheer volume of elements presented detracts from the brilliance, as in "the sea" with five unique preparations, a few otherworldly in their excellence (the sultry crab bisque), and a few uncharacteristically restrained (the deconstructed razor clam chowder). Yet it is as if we are briefly gazing at the artist's palette rather than the canvas before him—that sense of genius and contemplation returns with the impeccable roulade and terrine of poularde with black truffle purée, chestnut polenta, and flowering thyme.

The Harrison

Contemporary ✕✕✕

A2

355 Greenwich St. (at Harrison St.)

Subway: Franklin St
Phone: 212-274-9310
Web: www.theharrison.com
Prices: $$

Lunch Mon – Fri
Dinner nightly

With killer hand-crafted cocktails, cozy stay-a-while ambience, and the kind of *je ne sais quoi* most restaurateurs can only dream about, The Harrison hasn't missed a beat even with the brief health scare of Chef/owner Jimmy Bradley—a man who apparently can do hip-and-homey neighborhood restaurant in his sleep.

Grab a seat in the sexy, amber-soaked dining room and treat yourself to a spread of seasonal fare, like a Sunday special of slow braised ragù floating over rigatoni and topped with fresh ricotta, Parmesan, and bright ribbons of basil; perfectly-seared skate surrounded by a seasonal mélange of vegetables including shaved Brussel sprouts and tender potatoes cooked in a duck broth; or fluffy chocolate-filled beignets with quince sauce.

Kitchenette

American ✕

A3

156 Chambers St. (bet. Greenwich St. & West Broadway)

Subway: Chambers St (West Broadway)
Phone: 212-267-6740
Web: www.kitchenetterestaurant.com
Prices:

Lunch & dinner daily

Styled after an old-school luncheonette with black-and-white floor tiles, swiveling barstools and a long Formica-topped counter, Kitchenette stops just sort of kitsch when it comes to the food. This ain't your Momma's Betty Crocker, but delicious, real-deal home cooking—think freshly baked cornbread, decadent four-cheese macaroni, and silky turkey meatloaf. Washed down with a Boylan's bottled soda, a meal at Kitchenette could put a smile on the grumpiest man's face. The desserts are all made in-house and should not be missed: try the lemon and poppy seed layered cake, a fresh, mile-high slice of crumbly, buttery divinity laced with cream cheese frosting. For the Columbia University crowd, Kitchenette has a sister location in Morningside Heights.

Landmarc

B2

179 West Broadway (bet. Leonard & Worth Sts.)

Subway: Franklin St
Phone: 212-343-3883
Web: www.landmarc-restaurant.com
Prices: $$

Lunch & dinner daily

Rustic yet modern French bistro fare is made with flair here, largely thanks to the open grill, boldly placed just a few feet from the bar, bustling with patrons and cheery servers. This not only acts as a festive focal point for the room, but also transforms straightforward dishes like roast chicken into expertly charred, juicy centerpieces. Plated alongside mustardy French beans, the result is abundantly rich in flavor. The easy space (another location is in the Time Warner Center) is relaxed but trendy, featuring exposed brick walls and a narrow second-floor balcony that opens to the street in warm weather. The frugal oenophile will be happy to know that Landmarc's famed half-bottle list is still well-chosen, and gloriously within budget.

Locanda Verde

A2

379 Greenwich St. (at N. Moore St.)

Subway: Franklin St
Phone: 212-925-3797
Web: www.locandaverdenyc.com
Prices: $$$

Lunch & dinner daily

It may be located inside the Greenwich Hotel, but Locanda Verde feels more like a hip neighborhood hang out than a hotel restaurant. While this rustic Italian remains casual with more jeans than suits, the star power of owner Robert DeNiro and Chef Andrew Carmellini brings an upscale bent and downtown vibe to the crowd who looks as good as the space.

The comfort food-style menu headlines simple dishes like fire-roasted garlic chicken and *porchetta* sandwiches. Exemplary focaccia and blockbuster pastas can display an incredible brilliance and unique talent, as in the house-made penne with lamb Bolognese, topped with ricotta and just the right touch of mint. Perfectly executed in every way, this dish is some of the kitchen's best work.

Macao Trading Co.

Portuguese ✗✗

C2

311 Church St. (bet. Lispenard & Walker Sts.)

Subway: Canal St (Sixth Ave.)   Dinner nightly
Phone: 212-431-8642
Web: www.macaonyc.com
Prices: $$

Hidden just behind a red light on a quiet TriBeCa block, Macao Trading Co. is one of those opium-den-like joints that stays humming until 4:00 A.M. In other words, exactly the kind of place your suburban friends *think* you hang out in all the time.

So prove them right: because unlike so many other stylish restaurants that don't deliver, Macao gives as much attention to the food as to the drinks and sexy décor. Macao belonged to the Portuguese before they handed the island over to the Chinese in 1999, and the two cultures are given equal play time on the menu: Try the *bacalhau* tartare, a house cured salt cod topped with beets, fresh horseradish, and micro greens; or tender pork and lamb meatballs with smoked paprika tomato sauce and chorizo.

Megu

Japanese ✗✗✗

B3

62 Thomas St. (bet. Church St. & West Broadway)

Subway: Chambers St (West Broadway)   Dinner Mon – Sat
Phone: 212-964-7777
Web: www.megurestaurants.com
Prices: $$$

Sleek, gorgeous, and sexy Megu takes good advantage of this lofty, subterranean setting that has the heart of the Euro-scene thumping, while a midtown location provides Zen elegance for the diplomat crowd.

After a short descent down a row of stairs, visitors discover this jaw-dropping décor, replete with a carved ice Buddha hovering over a pool strewn with rose petals, all beneath a dramatic replica of a Japanese temple bell. Nevertheless, Megu's kitchen lives up to this grand-scale design, sourcing only the highest-quality ingredients, and turning out plates of bright, inventive Japanese delicacies, touched with influences farther afield. Extensive offerings may include inventive salads, fresh sushi, and desserts that verge on the ethereal.

Marc Forgione ✿

American 🗶🗶

134 Reade St. (bet. Greenwich & Hudson Sts.)

Subway: Chambers St (West Broadway)	Lunch Sun
Phone: 212-941-9401	Dinner nightly
Web: www.marcforgione.com	
Prices: $$$	

Daniel Krieger

Set on a tree-lined street, the rustic vibe emanating from this TriBeCa spot, courtesy of Chef Marc Forgione, is further enhanced by exposed brick, a dark painted ceiling, and furnishings like bookshelves, antique mirrors, and pillar candles—just imagine dining in the chicest of country barns. That look extends to the tables, which also exude an old-school Americana style with blue-band kitchen towels for napkins, small vases of wildflowers, and vintage flatware.

The menu is ever-changing but every dish promises hefty flavors in utterly enjoyable presentations. From the soft, warm potato rolls that arrive with caramelized onion butter, to desserts like the rum-soaked sponge cake with Meyer lemon syrup and a scoop of peppercorn-infused ice cream, the kitchen's high level of skill underscores each creation.

While many offerings remain rooted in Americana, they also display refinement, as in the plump and fluffy potato gnocchi afloat in a brick-red Bolognese sauce enriched with dry-aged beef and veal; or the crisp and delicate cod fillet in a pool of lobster emulsion with pasta and diced winter vegetables.

Remember to begin with a cocktail—their list is of special note.

Nobu

Japanese ✗✗

B2

105 Hudson St. (at Franklin St.)

Subway: Franklin St
Phone: 212-219-0500
Web: www.myriadrestaurantgroup.com
Prices: $$$$

Lunch Mon – Fri
Dinner nightly

The exemplary care, skill, and excellence of celebrity chef, Nobu Matsuhisa and partner, Drew Nieporent, have made Nobu (and its global outposts) a wildly popular formula for success, despite attacks from sustainable fishing advocates. Nevertheless, there have been lines out the door and demand for reservations for nearly two decades. Inside this former bank (the vault is used for wine storage) architect David Rockwell virtually started a movement in recreating the Japanese countryside with stylized birch trees and black river stones.

The talented kitchen serves contemporary Japanese fusion cuisine in creative and delicious specialties like fresh squid "pasta" with garlic sauce. Sharing multiple dishes may provide the most authentic "Nobu" experience.

The Odeon

American ✗✗

B3

145 West Broadway (at Thomas St.)

Subway: Chambers St (West Broadway)
Phone: 212-233-0507
Web: www.theodeonrestaurant.com
Prices: $$

Lunch & dinner daily

Occupying a prime piece of real estate smack in the middle of TriBeCa, The Odeon has been going strong since the 1980's—go at the right hour these days, and you're still likely to find the lawyers and City Hall types who put the place on the map perched on their bar stools.

Between the art deco architecture, wood framed-windows, and the lazy fans slowly rotating overhead, you'll feel like you've walked into a lovely brasserie in Lyon. The food matches the atmosphere—charming and noisy, laid-back but never absent-minded. Try the heirloom beet salad with silky shaved fennel, aged goat cheese, and blood orange vinaigrette; or a sushi-grade yellowfin tuna burger licked with wasabi mayonnaise and tucked between a toasted sesame seed bun.

Pepolino

Italian 🍴

C2

281 West Broadway (bet. Canal & Lispenard Sts.)

Subway: Canal St (Sixth Ave.)   Lunch & dinner daily
Phone: 212-966-9983
Web: www.pepolino.com
Prices: $$

Simple Tuscan fare, neither reimagined nor stripped down, is the recipe for success at this institution, where the two-floor dining space fills up nightly with neighborhood regulars. Named for a variety of wild thyme found in the Northern Italian region, Pepolino has been going strong since 1999— no easy feat in a town where restaurants measure their anniversaries like cat years.

You can thank original (and current) chef, Enzo Pezone, for steadily guiding diners through dishes like crispy pork feet terrine, donning a sinfully creamy inside and topped with sharp mustard and a flutter of Italian greens; or a light polenta soufflé paired with savory venison ragù. Don't miss the tomato-basil pâté, an opener guaranteed to please the whole table.

Stuzzicheria

Italian 🍴🍴

C2

305 Church St. (at Walker St.)

Subway: Canal St (Sixth Ave.)   Lunch & dinner daily
Phone: 212-219-4037
Web: www.stuzzicheriatribeca.com
Prices: $$

Talk about the best of both worlds. Straddling a bustling corner of Church Street in see-and-be-seen TriBeCa, this sleek new Italian restaurant is dedicated to the old school of home cooking. Owner Gerard Renny, author of the cookbook, *The Men of the Pacific Street Social Club Cook: Home-Style Recipes and Unforgettable Stories*, has set up a rotating menu of daily specials pulled from his East New York childhood. Think spaghetti and meatballs, baked pasta and ragù, and a rotating lineup of fresh Italian cheeses.

The kitchen realizes the vision perfectly, giving each dish a hearty but delicate spin. Witness a silky tangle of tagliolini laced with creamy pistachio and lemon peel pesto; or the falling-apart-in-all-the-right-ways short rib *braciole*.

Rosanjin 🏵

Japanese ✕✕

B3

141 Duane St. (bet. Church St. & West Broadway)

Subway: Chambers St (West Broadway)   Dinner Mon – Sat
Phone: 212-346-0664
Web: www.rosanjintribeca.com
Prices: $$$$

&

Peter Dressel

Rosanjin is a sanctuary for diners who appreciate the art of kaiseki: a traditional Japanese progression of courses flaunting careful skill and technique.

Walk slowly down Duane Street, as the restaurant's sign is small and easy to miss. Inside, the space is serene and comfortable (at times too quiet?) with slate floors, fabric-covered walls, mosaic-tiled accents, and cushioned armchairs. Upon being seated, settle in and simply wait for the first course to arrive; no bill of fare is presented as guests were asked to choose their menu at the time of booking.

Let there be no doubt that Rosanjin is dedicated to serious dining, as if the chef considers each course to be an opportunity to showcase his restrained attention to detail and respect for tradition. At the same time, meals are refined and studious. Expect such highlights like *temari* sushi of salmon and fluke; a pristine sashimi assortment presented with freshly grated wasabi; and clay pots of Kamadaki rice and Spanish mackerel. However, tempura courses are such a strong standout that those who opt for the kaiseki tempura menu will *not* be disappointed. A small but well-chosen selection of sake and *shochu* complete the experience.

Sushi Azabu ❀

A1

428 Greenwich St. (at Laight St.)

Subway: Franklin St
Phone: 212-274-0428
Web: www.greenwichgrill.com
Prices: $$$

Lunch Mon – Fri
Dinner nightly

Nishijima

Sushi Azabu's location alone seems a hallmark of authenticity, as it flaunts a Tokyo-like penchant for spaces not located at street-level. Here, guests approach the Greenwich Grill, stop at the bar, and eagerly await their green-light to enter the subterranean sushi den, decked with bamboo ceilings and river-stone floors.

The good news is that Sushi Azabu is an excellent spot for traditional sushi, all beautifully crafted from impeccable fish. The bad news is that you may be the only one here for the food, as this crowd seems more interested in spicy tuna than the explosively delicious omakase. The chefs here are talented, genuine, and bring a sense of fun to each meal that is lost on those who opt to sit in the rounded leather booths. Expect offerings such as jumbo Pacific oysters, sweet shrimp, Spanish mackerel, and Japanese uni that are all buttery and insanely redolent of fresh ocean waters. Cooked offerings are just as enticing, like terrifically hot and faintly smoky *chawan mushi* with lobster claw, ginger, *ginko* nuts, and shiitakes.

A playful love of tradition extends to the very authentic Japanese-style restrooms—consider it a necessary side trip during your visit here.

Takahachi

B3

Japanese ✕✕

145 Duane St. (bet. Church St. & West Broadway)

Subway: Chambers St (West Broadway)
Phone: 212-571-1830
Web: www.takahachi.net
Prices: $$

Lunch Mon – Fri
Dinner nightly

In a neighborhood dominated by the Japanese behemoths Nobu and Megu, unassuming Takahachi is a welcome reprieve for nouveau Japanese fare in TriBeCa—minus the fuss, high-flying theatrics, and exorbitant price tags. Those willing to forgo the sexier settings even find a little romance in the skylights of Takahachi's small, spare dining room come sunset.

Mainly, this is a true local favorite for families to gather over an array of Japanese fare. The menu may include bright, velvety sashimi; fresh tangles of sesame-dressed buckwheat soba noodles studded with shiitake mushrooms and avocado; or grilled appetizers like the supremely fresh black cod marinated in nutty and irresistible miso.

A second location welcomes a throng of laid-back East Villagers.

Tribeca Grill

A2

Contemporary ✕✕

375 Greenwich St. (at Franklin St.)

Subway: Franklin St
Phone: 212-941-3900
Web: www.myriadrestaurantgroup.com
Prices: $$$

Lunch Sun – Fri
Dinner nightly

Two decades ago, Drew Neiporent and Robert DeNiro turned a 1905 warehouse into a New York classic. Exposed pipes and brick walls preserved the past and set an architectural standard for many modern TriBeCa eateries. Celebrity investors, moneyed locals, and many more of the city's beautiful and powerful people meet here on a regular basis, perhaps before ducking into the Tribeca Film Festival headquarters, accessible from the restaurant.

The contemporary menu highlights dishes using thoughtfully sourced ingredients. The staff is efficient, well paced, and happy to bring the sommelier if guests have questions on the very impressive wine list. For a savory after-dinner treat, sample the extensive selection of artisanal cheeses with creative accompaniments.

Tamarind Tribeca ❀

Indian XXX

B2

99 Hudson St. (at Franklin St.)

Subway: Franklin St
Phone: 212-775-9000
Web: www.tamarinde22.com
Prices: $$$$

Lunch & dinner daily

Tamarind Tribeca

The wildly popular, lavish Indian restaurant of Gramercy Park gets a downtown sibling and baby sister is quite the looker. Rumor has it that this gorgeous and gargantuan space cost a cool five million to build and every cent of it shows. From its marble-topped bar pouring classy cocktails, wood-patterned floors, and spirited orange orchids, to glass windows and sky-high ceilings, there's glamour in every direction.

Settle into an elegant table or private booth for an intimate meal with friends. Executive Chef Eric McCarthy's contemporary menu is patiently explained to affluent patrons by a polite and proficient staff. They offer a culinary journey through India's vast regions: *bataki kosha*, tender shredded duck crêpes served with black salt and tangerine chutney; and *daab chingri*, prawns in a delicious coconut curry cooked with green chilies, curry leaves, and mustard seeds.

Seducing the South Asian set is a tandoor oven churning out a tandem of treats including *murgh angarey*, Cornish hen doused in *garam masala*, yogurt, and saffron; while others leave with a lilt after a whiff of *tres leches*, an Indian play on the Latin classic, crested with whipped cream and honeydew melon.

Wolfgang's

A1

Steakhouse ✗✗

409 Greenwich St. (bet. Beach & Hubert Sts.)

Subway: Franklin St
Phone: 212-925-0350
Web: www.wolfgangssteakhouse.com
Prices: $$$$

Lunch & dinner daily

If it ain't broke, don't fix it—Wolfgang's takes this adage to heart. The third outpost of this steakhouse mini-empire (the other two are in midtown), doesn't mess with tradition. Expect extraordinarily efficient yet gruff Eastern-European waiters, a clubby yet warm setting with well spaced tables and private dining rooms, a large bar populated by locals and FiDi types alike, and a classic Luger-like steakhouse menu served family style.

Giant, superbly cooked steaks are huge and meant for sharing, ideal for those who came with colleagues to soak up the market's losses with a perfect dry martini or dip into their expense accounts. The creamed spinach here is the stuff of legends, and addictive onion rings are thin, crisp, and impossibly juicy.

Look out for **red** symbols, indicating a particularly pleasant ambiance.

Upper East Side

The Upper East Side is a vast, mainly residential neighborhood with many faces ranging from prominent New York families to fresh from college prepsters. Closest to the park are posh spots catering to the Euro crowd and ladies who lunch. Walk further east to find young families filling the latest, casual sushi-ya or artisanal pizzeria. Along First and Second avenues, pubs are packed with raucous post-grads keeping the party alive.

The most upper and eastern reaches were originally developed by renowned families of German descent who built country estates in what has now become Yorkville. **Schaller & Weber** is one of the few remaining butchers carrying traditional Austro-German products including fantastic wursts for winter steaming or summer grilling, and the pungent mustards to accompany them. The Upper East Side has a greater concentration of gourmet markets than any other neighborhood in the city, most with a European feel. Each shop may be more packed than the next, yet has made processing long lines an art of inspired efficiency. **Agata & Valentina** specializes in everything Italian with a considerable regional cheese selection. **Citarella** pumps its mouthwatering aroma of rotisserie chickens out the storefront to entice passersby; but the seafood selection is where they find nirvana. **Grace's Marketplace** is a longtime favorite, loved for its cramped corners and cascading displays. Insiders frequent their trattoria, showcasing quality ingredients carried in the store. However, the true champion of everything uptown and gourmet, is Eli Zabar and his ever-expanding empire. **E.A.T.** has been a Madison Avenue darling since 1973, selling baked goods and takeout foods alongside its casual café. Later branches include his **Vinegar Factory** and newer mega-mart **Eli's**.

However, there are plenty of smaller purveyors to patronize. **Lobel's** and **Ottomanelli** are among the cities best remaining classic butcher shops, both offering the best meats and pragmatic cooking advice. **William Greenberg Jr.** bakes New York's favorite cookie, the black-and-white, along with to-die-for *babka*. **Glaser's** looks and tastes of everything Old World. And on the high end, **Lady M's** boutique and couture cakes blend right in with its chic Madison Avenue neighbors. For any foodie, Kitchen Arts & Letters has the largest stock of food and wine publications in the country; and owner Nach Waxman is as good a source of industry insight as any book or blog.

Upper East Side

A   B   C

Daniel
Nello
Le Bilboquet
Le Caprice
Lowell
Park Avenue
JoJo
Geisha
Fig & Olive
Lexington Av-63 St
Philippe
Regency
Fishtail by David Burke
David Burke Townhouse
58th
Lexington Av-59 St
59 St
Madison
Park
Lexington
Third

CENTRAL PARK
SPANISH HARLEM

E. 99th St
E. 97th St
E. 95th St
96 St

NATIONAL ACADEMY MUSEUM
GUGGENHEIM MUSEUM
81 St–Museum of Natural History
93rd
91st
Nick's
Parlor Steakhouse
Café Sabarsky
Centolire
San Matteo
Taco Taco
89th
87th
86 St
86th
85th
83rd
THE METROPOLITAN MUSEUM OF ART

CENTRAL PARK
Andre's Café
Maz Mezcal
Kings' Carriage House
The Lake
Boathouse Central Park
The Mark Restaurant by Jean–Georges
The Mark
Flex Mussels
Beyoglu
Donguri
Wa Jeal
Shalezeh
Il Riccio
Taste
Spigolo
The Surrey
The Carlyle
Café Boulud
Shanghai Pavilion
Cascabel Taqueria
Caravaggio
Untitled
MXco Cantina
Quatorze Bis
WHITNEY MUSEUM
77 St
Lusardi's
Orsay
Atlantic Grill
Uva
THE FRICK COLLECTION
J.G. Melon
Mezzaluna
Guild of Cari
Garden Court Café
Persepolis
75th
Innes Wood Foundry
JOHN JAY PARK
ASIA SOCIETY AND MUSEUM
73rd
Szechuan Chalet
72nd
Sushi Sasabune
68 St–Hunter College

UPPER WEST SIDE

Central Park West
Transverse
West Dr.
East Dr.
Fifth Ave.
Madison Ave.
Park Ave.
Lexington Ave.
Third Ave.
Second Ave.
First Ave.
York Ave.

Roosevelt Channel

L'Absinthe
Lexington Av-63 St
65th St
Lexington Av-59 St
ROOSEVELT ISLAND
Maya
Tori Shin
Sushi Seki
El Porrón
Marché du Sud
Tiella
Bentley
59 St
MIDTOWN EAST
57th
E. 60TH ST. METROPORT HELIPORT
Roosevelt Island
Lexington Av-53 St
QUEENSBORO BRIDGE
TRAM
West Main
Ridge Dr.

● Hotel
● Restaurant

341

Andre's Café

Eastern European ✗

C2

1631 Second Ave. (bet. 84th & 85th Sts.)

Subway: 86 St (Lexington Ave.)
Phone: 212-327-1105
Web: www.andrescafeny.com
Prices: 🍴🍴

Lunch & dinner daily

This charming café details deliciously old-fashioned baked goods from a bakery of the same name established in Queen's in 1976. Tiny, tidy, and welcoming, the exterior proudly boasts this establishment's Hungarian heritage with a red, white, and green awning. A temptingly-arranged display of sweet and savory strudels, tortes, and cakes greet guests upon entering. Table service is available in the rear, and before delving into dessert, there is a full menu of hearty old-world fare offered daily.

Weekday meal specials come complete with a salad or soup and a selected yet sinful pastry, and can include home spun traditional favorites like chicken *paprikash*, swathed in a luscious paprika cream sauce and accompanied by freshly made *nokedli*.

Atlantic Grill

Seafood ✗✗

B3

1341 Third Ave. (bet. 76th & 77th Sts.)

Subway: 77 St
Phone: 212-988-9200
Web: www.atlanticgrill.com
Prices: $$

Lunch & dinner daily

Swimmingly similar to its downtown sibling Blue Water Grill and Upper West Side newbie at Lincoln Center, Atlantic Grill hooks a very NY clientele with a vast, Asian-accented menu focused on the sea. Sushi and raw bar offerings are still beloved, as are entrées like nori-wrapped bigeye tuna with sticky rice, and other options that satisfy fish-free appetites.

The large, alluring space is frequented by a well-dressed, fun-loving crowd occupying two rooms—one features a nautical blue and white theme; and the other is sunny with a terrazzo floor, wicker chairs, and potted palms. Fair weather sidewalk seating is in high demand, as is weekend brunch; and the intent service team perfectly completes the offerings at this long-time crowd-pleaser.

Beyoglu 😊

Turkish ✕

1431 Third Ave. (at 81st St.)

Subway: 77 St
Phone: 212-650-0850
Web: N/A
Prices: $$

Lunch & dinner daily

Sharing may not come naturally to everyone, but when dining at Beyoglu, arrive with a crowd and prepare to pass your plates to fully experience the delicious range of Mediterranean meze that earns its praise. Most of the recipes–and some wine and beer offerings–come from Turkey, though Greek and Lebanese accents can be found throughout. Warm and tender pita bread makes a delightful accompaniment to anything on the menu. Thick homemade yogurt with spinach and garlic; grilled shrimp; and marinated octopus are a short sampling of the wide selection.

If grazing doesn't satisfy, choose from a list of larger daily specials, perhaps including *tavuk izgara*, char-grilled breast of free-range chicken, and *kilic sis*, swordfish kebabs served with rice pilaf.

Boathouse Central Park

American ✕✕

The Lake at Central Park (E. 72nd St. & Park Dr. North)

Subway: 68 St - Hunter College
Phone: 212-517-2233
Web: www.thecentralparkboathouse.com
Prices: $$

Lunch & dinner daily

This unique locale offers Manhattan's only lakeside dining experience. Built in 1954, Loeb Boathouse is a pleasant multi-venue operation that includes a charming outdoor bar perched along the water and a lovely glass-walled dining room offering views of the lake, greenery, and skyline beyond—there isn't a bad seat in the house.

Highlighting American ingredients and sensibilities, the menu features an updated approach with items such as beef carpaccio dressed with syrupy balsamic and a Parmesan *frico*; braised chicken thighs with plumped prunes and glazed endive; and a brownie-dense chocolate tart capped with ginger ice cream. While lunch and brunch are served year-round, note that dinner is only offered during warmer months (April through November).

Café Boulud ✿

B3

20 E. 76th St. (bet. Fifth & Madison Aves.)

Subway: 77 St
Phone: 212-772-2600
Web: www.danielnyc.com
Prices: $$$$

Lunch & dinner daily

Bill Milne

This superbly sophisticated café presents itself with beguiling simplicity. The interior palette is a refined white with red accents and modern art hanging on the walls; outside offers lovely sidewalk seating during spring and summer. Everything is just as tasteful as its well-to-do crowd of ladies lunching on salads, but to stop there would be a mistake. While the menu is divided into Chef Daniel Boulud's categories of inspiration (classics, seasons, world cuisine, and vegetables), the food is fantastically complex, as if in spite of the monikers.

In the kitchen, Chef Gavin Kaysen ensures that each tempting dish and contemporary presentation is just as delicious as it sounds. Balanced and bright flavors are highlighted in a starter of adobo-marinated sea scallop with dried pineapple chips, thinly sliced radish, and a fine brunoise of pineapple and red onion. The pleasures of technical grace are clear in entrées such as crisp-skinned duck breast on a mound of confit and silky black Venere rice.

To end with a butterscotch gâteau with mascarpone cream, bourbon glaze, and brown-sugar ice cream may be divine, but those linen-lined baskets of warm and homey madeleines are Proustian.

Café Sabarsky

Austrian ✗

B2

1048 Fifth Ave. (at 86th St.)

Subway: 86 St (Lexington Ave.)
Phone: 212-288-0665
Web: www.kg-ny.com
Prices: $$

Lunch Wed – Mon
Dinner Thu – Sun

In addition to the renowned art displayed at the intimately scaled Neue Galerie, find Chef Kurt Gutenbrunner's charming café modeled after a late 19th century Viennese *kaffehause*, complete with dark wood-paneled walls and formally attired servers. The museum, housed in a 1914 Beaux-Arts mansion, was conceived by cosmetic mogul Ronald Lauder and art dealer Serge Sabarsky to display their collections of early 20th century Austrian and German art.

The traditional menu features savory fare like sautéed bratwurst over riesling sauerkraut, along with an indulgent listing of classic sweets like apple strudel. Beverages include a very nice selection of German and Austrian wines by the glass, tremendous coffee offerings, and divine hot chocolate.

Caravaggio

Italian ✗✗✗

A3

23 E. 74th St. (bet. Fifth & Madison Aves.)

Subway: 77 St
Phone: 212-288-1004
Web: N/A
Prices: $$$

Lunch & dinner Mon – Sat

This ambitious newcomer adds a dose of elegance to the city's Italian dining scene. Caravaggio's slender dining room, decorated with silk-covered walls, sleek leather seating, and evocative, original artwork exudes a cool palette that, at times, mirrors the disposition of the formally attired waitstaff. The menu is enhanced by a lengthy list of daily specials that is verbally recited in minute detail. Be sure to pay attention, because you wouldn't want to miss out on the likes of *Amarone* risotto—a magenta-hued mound of starchy perfection piled with taleggio cheese, and drizzled with syrupy balsamic vinegar. But fret not, because the printed menu offers other gems as well, like monkfish osso buco dressed with braised fennel, *garganelli*, and paprika jus.

Manhattan ▶ Upper East Side

Cascabel Taqueria

Mexican ✗

C3

1538 Second Ave. (at 80th St.)

Subway: 77 St
Phone: 212-717-8226
Web: www.nyctacos.com
Prices: 🍴🍴

Lunch & dinner daily

From its new, bigger home, this tasty little spot still serves up quite a nice taco. The menu is concise and in keeping with the focused taqueria theme, with selections that include double layered corn tortillas filled with house-made chorizo and smoked paprika onions; roasted wild shrimp with fresh oregano, garlic, and chili oil; or chipotle-braised Amish chicken topped with chicken *chicaharrón*. Interesting (and deliciously healthful) sides include a bowl of fluffy organic quinoa topped with Cotija cheese and cilantro. The space is a daylight-filled room complete with a TV-equipped bar and dining room in zesty shades of lime green and lemon yellow, and tables topped with caddies of salsas.

A few doors up, is baby sibling Cantina by Cascabel.

Centolire

Italian ✗✗

B2

1167 Madison Ave. (bet. 85th & 86th Sts.)

Subway: 86 St (Lexington Ave.)
Phone: 212-734-7711
Web: www.pinoluongo.com
Prices: $$$

Lunch & dinner daily

Restaurateur, Pino Luongo, opened Centolire as a homage to his native Tuscany. Downstairs, the all-day café features a menu of salads and panini, with house-made focaccia stuffed with the likes of braised radicchio, Gorgonzola, and honey. For a more elegant experience, take the glass-enclosed elevator upstairs to the spacious second-floor setting, sunlit by large windows overlooking Madison Avenue, and attractively appointed with colorful fabrics and antique kitchen tools.

The smartly attired service team graciously attends to diners, occasionally stopping to prepare Caesar salad tableside. The classically infused menu includes homemade pastas and entrées such as *stracotto di manzo*, Tuscan-style braised brisket with sautéed spinach.

Daniel ✿✿✿

A1

French XXXXX

60 E. 65th St. (bet. Madison & Park Aves.)

Subway: 68 St - Hunter College
Phone: 212-288-0033
Web: www.danielnyc.com
Prices: $$$$

Dinner Mon – Sat

Eric Laignel

Year after year and night after night, Daniel remains the place to go for an ultra-luxurious meal among NY's movers and shakers. Find yourself in a luxurious room, stunning the moneyed crowd with modern art, overflowing floral displays and a glass-enclosed wine wall. Rest assured that the layout of this gorgeous place gives everyone a head-turning grand entrance. Amid soaring ceilings and cozy nooks, the world outside melts away with maximum posh and precision; here, your every comfort is considered (perhaps Madam's purse would like its own ottoman?).

Daniel is a tribute to the finest traditions of French cooking, yet is never dated. This is cerebral, sensuous, and stimulating food prepared with dazzling acuity. Florida frog legs and Jerusalem artichoke soup is a symphony of tastes (black garlic, rock chives, earthy mushrooms) that express an understanding of harmonious flavors and fragile ingredients. The duo of Vermont quail is supremely moist, its tender breast wrapped with maple-sweet and smoky bacon, served with glazed celery, leg confit, and pillow-soft gnocchi.

Somehow, Chef Daniel Boulud enhances each flavor with the next, as if layering the pleasures without distraction.

David Burke Townhouse

A1

133 E. 61st St. (bet. Lexington & Park Aves.)

Subway: Lexington Av - 59 St
Phone: 212-813-2121
Web: www.davidburketownhouse.com
Prices: $$$

Lunch & dinner daily

David Burke's refreshed Upper East Side restaurant, housed in a quaint, red-bricked building with a white-furnished lounge features an elegantly appointed space dressed with handsome red banquettes amidst tall white walls adorned with Roman shaded mirrors and bright artwork.

An immaculately attired service staff might kick things off with a warm Gruyère and poppy seed popover, and then move on to Burke's signature brand of bold, contemporary cuisine (now executed by Picholine alum, Executive Chef Carmine DiGiovanni) that may reveal crisp and angry lobster; and Hudson Valley rabbit degustation with date-mustard spread and spring onions. The reasonably priced lunch prix-fixe offers all this elegance at a pretty price.

Donguri

C2

309 E. 83rd St. (bet. First & Second Aves.)

Subway: 86 St (Lexington Ave.)
Phone: 212-737-5656
Web: www.dongurinyc.com
Prices: $$$

Dinner Tue – Sun

The ongoing construction of the Second Avenue subway may have obscured Donguri's already unassuming location, but this demure Japanese still draws a devout following. Its steady clientele of high-powered international bankers, neighborhood couples, and Japanese ex-pats longing for a taste of home speaks to its sophistication and authenticity.

With just 24 seats, Donguri has a minimalist décor and is lovingly attended by a polite team. Deliciously straightforward preparations may include wonderfully fresh sashimi (though no sushi); flash-fried and sublimely crunchy sweet-corn tempura; rice bowls of grated mountain yam, luscious sea urchin from Maine, and yuzu zest; or a refreshing finale of delicate grapefruit gelée, honey-sweet and blushing pink.

El Porrón

Spanish 〽️

B4

1123 First Ave. (bet. 61st & 62nd Sts.)

Subway: Lexington Av - 59 St
Phone: 212-207-8349
Web: www.elporronnyc.com
Prices: $$

Lunch & dinner daily

The tapas movement shows no signs of ceasing anytime soon, but this welcome neighborhood addition, more than does the small plate craze justice with its energetic ambience featuring upbeat Spanish tunes; a lively crowd chugging down delicious sangria come nighttime; and finger-licking authentic Spanish cuisine.

Chef Gonzalo Bermeo's menu is as playful as the room, gracefully dancing between traditional entrées and scrumptious paellas made to order; classic tapas like tender chicken with ratatouille or a sizzling *cazuela* filled with garlic shrimp, white wine, and olive oil; and original creations like tender veal meatballs, slow-cooked in a fragrant leek and tomato stew then finished with toasted sliced almonds.

Fig & Olive

Mediterranean ✖️

B1

808 Lexington Ave. (bet. 62nd & 63rd Sts.)

Subway: Lexington Av - 63 St
Phone: 212-207-4555
Web: www.figandolive.com
Prices: $$$

Lunch & dinner daily

The bounty of the Mediterranean's olive groves is not only featured on the menu of this casually elegant Upper East spot (with midtown and Meatpacking locations), but is also available for purchase in gift-worthy packaging. Each dish—from salad Niçoise to grilled branzino—is accented with a specific extra virgin oil, carefully selected to highlight their extensive stock. Dinners begin with an olive oil trio to sample (though your server will choose which ones you try).

Inside the bright, sunny space, shoppers find a soothing respite in light Mediterranean plates of ceviche, a sampling of crostini, or pastas and grilled fare. The wine list echoes the same regions of origin as the fragrant oils, with many selections available by the glass.

Fishtail by David Burke

Seafood ✕✕✕

B1

135 E. 62nd St. (bet. Lexington & Park Aves.)

Subway: Lexington Av - 63 St
Phone: 212-754-1300
Web: www.fishtaildb.com
Prices: $$$

Lunch Sun – Fri
Dinner nightly

This fitting addition to Chef David Burke's oeuvre features a sophisticated setting throughout two levels of a cozy townhouse. The first floor is an oyster bar and lounge popular with the after-work crowds, while the upstairs dining room is wrapped in deep red and bedecked with accents that colorfully convey the ocean theme.

The menu focuses on seafood, of which 80% is caught through sustainable fishing methods—perhaps from the chef's own boat. The preparations are stamped with the chef's unique touch, whether simply prepared as a whole, roasted striped bass, or more creatively interpreted in the pan-roasted Atlantic salmon with braised bok choy and two curries. Regardless of your selection, these dishes show the hand of a skilled kitchen.

Flex Mussels

Seafood ✕

B2

174 E. 82nd St. (bet. Lexington & Third Aves.)

Subway: 86 St (Lexington Ave.)
Phone: 212-717-7772
Web: www.flexmusselsny.com
Prices: $$

Dinner nightly

Despite its strong name, Flex Mussels is actually a fun, casual, and intimate seafood shack with uptown polish. Usually packed to the gills, the slim bar area features pretty touches like flowers, slender mirrors, and a dining counter. The back dining room is spare, contemporary, more subdued, and fills up quickly.

The menu features the namesake bi-valve, hailing from Prince Edward Island, priced by the pound, steamed in more than twenty globally-inspired guises, like the "PEI" featuring lobster stock and drawn butter; or "San Daniele" with prosciutto, caramelized onions, white wine, and garlic. No matter the choice, your best accompaniment is a side of piping-hot, hand-cut skinny fries.

Flex now has a downtown sibling in the West Village.

Garden Court Café 😊

B3

Asian ✗

725 Park Ave. (at 70th St.)

Subway: 68 St - Hunter College
Phone: 212 570-5202
Web: www.asiasociety.org
Prices: $$

Lunch Tue – Sun

Tucked into the glass-enclosed, plant-filled lobby of the Asia Society, this café is a far cry from your garden-variety museum restaurant. Though it doesn't generate much fanfare, it is worth seeking out, not only for its quiet ambience, but for the light Asian dishes that expertly fuse East and West.

Serving lunch only, from Tuesday through Sunday, the menu draws Asian inspiration in its offerings that may include herb-crusted salmon with lemongrass, Thai basil, and mint. The bento box features two chef selections along with rice and salad.

Everything here is done with quality, right down to the careful presentation and very good service—and the museum's entry fee is not required. Don't miss the museum gift shop for its wonderful wares.

Geisha

A1

Japanese ✗✗

33 E. 61st St. (bet. Madison & Park Aves.)

Subway: Lexington Av - 59 St
Phone: 212-813-1112
Web: www.geisharestaurant.com
Prices: $$$

Lunch Mon – Fri
Dinner Mon – Sat

Set in the ritzy Upper East Side, and starring a series of intimate dining nooks, Geisha is an adored hot spot whose scene is as warm as it is modern—a smattering of Asian effects like earthy hues, wood panels inlaid with floral accents, and a mighty print of a geisha portrait should help you catch the drift.

Lounge beats thump in the background as grand dames discuss posh private schools with their suited men. If that doesn't fit your mood, take a seat at an orange resin counter and be greeted by a bowl of edamame. A bright skylight or blazing fireplace casts a delicious glow on Geisha's prix-fixe delights like mayo-free spicy tuna roll; vegetable udon floating with carrots and bok choy; and fluffy coconut blancmange trickled with chocolate curls.

Il Riccio

Italian 🍴

B3

152 E. 79th St. (bet. Lexington & Third Aves.)
Subway: 77 St   Lunch & dinner daily
Phone: 212-639-9111
Web: www.ilriccioblu.com
Prices: $$

This low-key Italian, and its smiling cadre of charming staff, is just the right spot to recharge after an afternoon perusing the fabulous neighborhood boutiques or meandering through the nearby Metropolitan Museum of Art. Inside, the space offers a cozy feel with warm ochre walls, simple furnishings, and an assemblage of photographs, though regulars know to head back to the enclosed garden to enjoy their meals.

The cooking here is fuss-free, pasta-focused, and lovingly dedicated to the Amalfi Coast. Dishes may include arugula and roasted red pepper salad with marinated fresh anchovies; spaghetti with crab meat and fresh tomatoes; grilled fish dressed simply with olive oil and fresh lemon; and a straightforward selection of dessert pastries.

J.G. Melon 😊

American 🍴

B3

1291 Third Ave. (at 74th St.)
Subway: 77 St   Lunch & dinner daily
Phone: 212-744-0585
Web: N/A
Prices: 😊😊

J.G. Melon is the kind of place that parents tell their children they used to frequent when they were young in the city; nothing changes here, and that is part of the allure. It's a multi-generational watering hole for the masses, feeding Upper East Siders burgers and beers in a convivial setting that never seems to forget itself. The key here is the burger: griddled and served on a toasted bun, it's one of the best in the city. Couple this with a bowl of the crispy round fries and a cool draft and you've got the answer to why this spot has been packed for years. BLTs, salads, steaks, and omelets round out the menu.

Tables may be tight and the waits can be long, but the service is jovial and it's come-as-you-are and…did we mention the burger?

JoJo

B1

Contemporary ✗✗

160 E. 64th St. (bet. Lexington & Third Aves.)

Subway: Lexington Av - 63 St
Phone: 212-223-5656
Web: www.jean-georges.com
Prices: $$$

Lunch & dinner daily

With its snug velvet banquettes; romantic, tapestry-framed archways; and seductive, bordello-low lighting, Jean-Georges Vongerichten's first-born New York restaurant (at last count, the maestro had no less than seven Manhattan establishments) is a welcome reprieve from its stuffy Upper East Side cousins, earning the little red townhouse a special place on the neighborhood scene. The sophisticated locals still come in droves.

Given the tony 10021 zip code, the compact à la carte menu is surprisingly reasonable, and might include a crispy, pan-fried terrine filled with a soft pocket of warm Coach Farms goat cheese; tart lemon spätzle chockablock with fresh, roasted lobster; or apple *pain perdu* paired with a smooth scoop of green apple sorbet.

Jones Wood Foundry

C3

Gastropub ✗

401 E. 76th St. (bet. First & York Aves.)

Subway: 77 St
Phone: 212-249-2771
Web: www.joneswoodfoundry.com
Prices: $$

Lunch Sat – Sun
Dinner nightly

The moniker of this pleasing Yorkville pub refers to when the neighborhood was merely a stretch of heavily forested land. Although that bucolic ideal has been replaced by tower-lined corridors, the eatery offers a taste of the Old World tucked away from the fray. A narrow wood bar area welcomes guests, while a pretty courtyard dining room and larger rear space offer plenty of breathing room.

Chef/partner Jason Hicks garners inspiration from his childhood in England to beget a spot-on lineup of enjoyable pub-grub. A "toast" list includes a soft boiled farm egg and soldiers; steak and kidney pie is presented as golden-brown pastry stuffed with a stew of chopped beef and vegetables; and a delightfully boozy sherry trifle caps off any meal here.

Kings' Carriage House

C2

251 E. 82nd St. (bet. Second & Third Aves.)

Subway: 86 St (Lexington Ave.)
Phone: 212-734-5490
Web: www.kingscarriagehouse.com
Prices: $$

Lunch & dinner daily

Picture the mist rolling in when dining at this bona fide facsimile of an Irish manor, warmly run by Elizabeth King and husband Paul Farrell (of Dublin). Since 1994, this elegantly countrified setting has been an old-world rarity, complete with creaky floors, murals, linen-draped tables with lacy overlays, antique china, and vintage silverware accenting the multiple dining rooms. A collection of china teapots is even available for purchase.

The nightly prix-fixe menu offers an updated take on classically prepared cuisine that complements the romantic ambience beautifully, as in the roasted filet mignon with a medallion of tarragon Cognac sausage and port wine demi-glace. Afternoon tea is quite popular, so be sure to reserve in advance.

L'Absinthe

B4

227 E. 67th St. (bet. Second & Third Aves.)

Subway: 68 St - Hunter College
Phone: 212-794-4950
Web: www.labsinthe.com
Prices: $$$

Lunch & dinner daily

A true charmer, L'Absinthe is a uniquely enjoyable classic neighborhood bistro that can claim few peers. The warm and amiable setting boasts an authentically continental elegance that is enhanced by an understated, sophisticated clientele.

The flawless menu offers a culling of preparations that are seasonal and contemporary in theme, but the real draw here are Chef Jean-Michel Bergougnoux's "brasserie classics" like the *choucroute royale Alsacienne*, presented as a heaping platter of expertly prepared pork: Garlicky sausage, *boudin blanc*, belly, and ham; also await caraway-spiced braised cabbage and boiled potatoes. Another classic, the *baba au rhum* is deliciously done—a boozy moist cake slathered with *crème pâtissière* and *brunoise* of tropical fruits.

Le Bilboquet

A1

French ✕

25 E. 63rd St. (bet. Madison & Park Aves.)

Subway: Lexington Av - 63 St
Phone: 212-751-3036
Web: N/A
Prices: **$$**

Lunch & dinner daily

This Upper East Side institution still draws a chic and pampered crowd to its attractive but minuscule setting that is part bistro and part Euro-social club. Named for a 16th century game, scoring a table in this butter-yellow room can be quite challenging. But once past the door and settled into a plush banquette, consider yourself among the in-crowd; enjoy the scene, brightened by bold artwork and vivid flowers. The support staff is as well dressed as the clientele and politely speed things along.

The pleasant cooking here is solid throughout the classic menu that may offer the likes of country pâté made of duck and served with perfectly toasted baguette, cornichons, and ground Dijon mustard; or a pan-seared, crispy skin fillet of sea bass.

Le Caprice

A1

Contemporary ✕✕✕

795 Fifth Ave. (bet. 60th & 61st Sts.)

Subway: 5 Av - 59 St
Phone: 212-940-8195
Web: www.capriceny.com
Prices: **$$$**

Lunch & dinner daily

Taking up residence in the extensively renovated Pierre, this London export has elicited a faithful following among the city's elite. The cutting-edge brasserie setting renders a bar area that is generous in length and comfort; and an art deco dining room, that is at once resplendent and dramatic with sparkling chrome fixtures, and encased in gleaming black and white marble.

The menu offers straightforward cuisine marked by excellent product, and even a few of the English classics manage to shine through. Fish and chips, a tough find in this town, is made exquisite and upscale with pristine cod fillets cloaked in a featherlight golden batter and accompanied by mint-flecked mushy peas, decadent tartar sauce, and a side of excellent fries (chips).

Lusardi's

Italian ✗✗

C3

1494 Second Ave. (bet. 77th & 78th Sts.)

Subway: 77 St
Phone: 212-249-2020
Web: www.lusardis.com
Prices: $$$

Lunch Mon – Fri
Dinner nightly

A neighborhood mainstay since 1982, brothers Luigi and Mauro Lusardi continue to run an impressive operation. Tastefully appointed with pumpkin-colored walls and deep-toned woodwork, the dining room is warmly attended by a beaming staff that suits Lusardi's comfortable elegance and old-world vibe.

Fresh ingredients and careful preparation go into the Northern Italian fare such as *crespelle Fiorentina*, a cylinder of pan-fried eggplant filled with a fluffy blend of spinach and ricotta then bathed in bright and creamy tomato sauce. Many of the preparations feature an appetizingly rustic presentation as in the *fegato alla Veneziana*—chunks of chicken liver sautéed with sweet onions and white wine, then piled onto a nest of coarse ground polenta.

Marché du Sud

French ✗

B4

1136 First Ave. (bet. 62nd & 63rd Sts.)

Subway: Lexington Av - 59 St
Phone: 212-207-4900
Web: www.marchedusud.com
Prices: ⬭⬭

Lunch & dinner daily

Who says you can't be all things to all people? Open all day, this bakery/gourmet grocery/wine bar/restaurant seems to be wearing many hats without a glitch. Walk by the interesting imported products—you can pick up a jar of mustard on your way out. Snag a menu, printed on the back of Paris Match and other French language magazines, and you'll soon see that *Alsatian tarte flambée* is de rigueur here. Go for tradition and you'll enjoy this thin, flaky crust topped with Gruyère, bacon, and onions; or go house-style with crème fraîche, duck confit, and black truffle-foie gras.

Chef/owner Adil Fawzi hails from Morocco, so the Marocaine, topped with hummus, harissa, merguez, cheese, and lemon confit is a sure bet. Don't worry *cherie*, there's dessert too.

The Mark Restaurant by Jean-Georges

Contemporary 𝐗𝐗𝐗

B2

25 E. 77th St. (at Madison Ave.)

Subway: 77 St
Phone: 212-606-3030
Web: www.themarkrestaurantnyc.com
Prices: $$$

Lunch & dinner daily

Snuggled inside the posh kingdom of the recently revamped Mark Hotel, The Mark Restaurant is the latest hot spot for the ladies-who-lunch crowd. This bastion of Upper East Side exclusivity hits all the right marks with its eye-catching, light-filled, contemporary décor. It's not just the ladies who are dressed to the nines; even the staff is sharply attired in black and cream uniforms.

Jean-George Vongerichten and his Chef de Cuisine Pierre Schutz, formerly of Vong, are at it again with a crowd-pleasing menu. The choices are surprisingly straightforward, with selections like sweet pea soup; and fresh linguini with clams, chili, and parsley. Go ahead and put away that green tea opera cake. The city's best plastic surgeons are just a block or two away.

Maya

Mexican 𝐗𝐗

B4

1191 First Ave. (bet. 64th & 65th Sts.)

Subway: 68 St - Hunter College
Phone: 212-585-1818
Web: www.richardsandoval.com
Prices: $$

Dinner nightly

Maya continues to impress as one of the city's finest examples of upscale Mexican cuisine. To add to the spark, it now offers increased accommodations with their recently redone bar and lounge, that serves divine mango margaritas—still perfect after all these years. Service may lag a bit but the kitchen excels, serving up a contemporary version of Mexican classics in a colorful and chic dining room.

Here, Mexican flavors are captured with modern style, combining seamlessly and deliciously in *entradas* such as *quesadillas surtidas*, fried masa dough filled with Oaxaca cheese, chile poblano *rajas*, and doubly dressed with salsas. Creative and classic *platos fuertes* may include tequila-flambéed shrimp paired with decadent black bean and Gouda *huarache*.

Maz Mezcal

C2

316 E. 86th St. (bet. First & Second Aves.)

Subway: 86 St (Lexington Ave.)
Phone: 212-472-1599
Web: www.mazmezcal.com
Prices: $$

Lunch Sat – Sun
Dinner nightly

Simple, bountiful Mexican food leaves locals and families eager to return to Maz Mezcal, located on a busy stretch of 86th Street. Eduardo Silva (who has long been a part of Mexican dining on the Upper East) hosts his family's eastside stalwart, where a low-key party begins almost every night, spilling into the street in warm weather.

The flavorful fare includes an assortment of enchiladas, flautas, tostadas, and burritos to create your own Tex-Mex-style platter, or choose from the house combinations named for Mexican beach towns. Specialties may include traditional mole poblano made with seven distinct chile varieties and bittersweet chocolate.

Dishes are tailored to mild palates, but the kitchen is happy to accommodate those who prefer food *picante*.

Mezzaluna

B3

1295 Third Ave. (bet. 74th & 75th Sts.)

Subway: 77 St
Phone: 212-535-9600
Web: www.mezzalunany.com
Prices: $$

Lunch & dinner daily

After a whopping 25 years in the business, this old Upper East Side cat could show the new crop of wood-burning ovens popping up across the city a thing or two. Mezzaluna (named for the crescent-shaped knife, which you'll find rendered 77 different ways on the restaurant's art-strewn walls) manages to feel both fresh and comforting to the throngs of loyal regulars who keep it packed day and night.

What's their secret? Simple, unfussy Italian food that's made with pristine ingredients and careful attention to detail—not to mention a wood-burning oven that pushes out perfectly bubbling pies; a thoughtful Italian wine list; and a warm, convivial staff bolstered by a friendly, hands-on owner who can often be found milling about his dining room.

MXco Cantina

Mexican ✗

B3

1491 Second Ave. (at 78th St.)

Subway: 77 St
Phone: 212-249-6080
Web: www.mxcony.com
Prices: ⬭⬭

Lunch & dinner daily

Sure, those from the other coast lament the authenticity of New York's Mexican spots, but the situation is improving, thanks to the welcomed addition of MXco Cantina. The family-friendly, casual, anytime vibe and budget-friendly pricing are all appreciated, but its biggest draw is a menu devised by consulting Chef Julieta Ballestros, from Crema in Chelsea.

The list of goodies offers a range of generously stuffed tacos, like Coca-Cola braised *carnitas*, built upon excellent corn tortillas spread with black bean purée and accompanied by a shot of roasted tomato salsa. *Penca de nopal*, grilled prickly pear salad; and chorizo *sope*, griddled masa patties topped with fresh chorizo also populate a menu bolstered by quesadillas, burritos, and flautas.

Nello

Italian ✗✗

A1

696 Madison Ave. (bet. 62nd & 63rd Sts.)

Subway: 5 Av - 59 St
Phone: 212 980-9099
Web: N/A
Prices: $$$$

Lunch & dinner daily

Nello offers a chic and polished yet satisfying Italian dining experience, fashionably perched among pricy boutiques and astronomical real estate. The bright and airy room (resplendent with marble, ivory walls hung with black-and-white safari scenes, and thick linen-covered tables dressed with white flowers) is overseen by a well-orchestrated, suit-clad service team. Everything here radiates privilege and optimism. Even the menu's typeface appears elegant...and expensive.

While high prices and celebrity sightings do not ensure an enjoyable meal, the flavorful offerings like San Daniele prosciutto and melon; neat mounds of perfectly prepared pasta; and hearty entrées of osso buco should bring enough pleasure to help ease the potential sticker shock.

Nick's

C2

Pizza ✗

1814 Second Ave. (at 94th St.)

Subway: 96 St (Lexington Ave.)   Lunch & dinner daily
Phone: 212-987-5700
Web: www.nicksnyc.com
Prices: ⊜⊜

    Due to a blockade of equipment needed for the ongoing construction of the Second Avenue subway line, Nick's may be a bit harder to spot but still ranks highly on Upper East Siders' short list of pizza favorites. This Manhattan location of the Forest Hills original, named for owner Nick Angelis, has cozy surroundings with tables overlooking the dough-tossing *pizzaiolos* and jovial service.

In addition to the excellent, bronzed, crackling thin-crust pizzas, a variety of Italian-American pastas (referred to as "macaroni") and entrées are available as full or half portions for family-friendly dining. Offerings may include veal scaloppini with lemon and butter or an enjoyable tangle of linguini with white clam sauce infused with roasted garlic cloves.

Orsay

B3

French ✗✗

1057 Lexington Ave. (at 75th St.)

Subway: 77 St   Lunch & dinner daily
Phone: 212-517-6400
Web: www.orsayrestaurant.com
Prices: $$

    Orsay gets high marks for its authenticity. Dripping with detail, the art nouveau setting exudes brasserie-style class from every corner, with hand-laid mosaic tiles, mahogany paneling, custom lighting, and a pewter-topped bar. The deep awning out front protects Orsay's clientele as they sip, sup, and socialize on this fashionable stretch of Lexington Avenue.

The menu features a more classic tone than before since the kitchen now claims Chef Antoine Camin, formerly of La Goulue, as its own. His celebrated cheese soufflé is still fortifying denizens of well-heeled Upper Eastsiders (if only at lunch).

Orsay's polished staff manages to graciously jockey a room full of power brokers while making all feel decorously comfortable and suitably pampered.

Park Avenue

Contemporary ✕✕

A1

100 E. 63rd St. (at Park Ave.)

Subway: 59 St
Phone: 212-644-1900
Web: www.parkavenyc.com
Prices: $$$

Lunch & dinner daily

While many restaurants pay the utmost attention to seasonality on the plate, Park Avenue extends it to the décor. Every three months, it shutters for 48 hours to re-emerge as a celebration of spring, summer, fall, or winter. In a sort of architectural trompe l'oeil, a series of panels were devised to frame the dining room and create a fresh backdrop that changes throughout the year.

The beautifully prepared menu displays the same determined playfulness with boosts from ingredients such as fig carpaccio with goat cheese in autumn, or wintertime plates of stout-braised lamb shank with aged-cheddar polenta and green apples. The cocktail menu is likewise enticing.

One constant: the decadent and shareable "chocolate cube" is a dessert menu fixture.

Parlor Steakhouse

Steakhouse ✕✕

C2

1600 Third Ave. (at 90th St.)

Subway: 86 St (Lexington Ave.)
Phone: 212-423-5888
Web: www.parlorsteakhouse.com
Prices: $$$

Lunch & dinner daily

This sexy, contemporary Upper East Side steakhouse, straddling a busy corner of 3rd Ave. and 90th St., has managed to stay under the radar for almost two years. But what a shame, for this neighborhood find boasts clubby, welcoming good looks (think plush fabric and masculine dark stripes); first-class steaks cooked to juicy perfection; and a mean Belgian beer selection.

Kick your night off with one of the rotating daily specials, such as soft shell crabs, delicately fried and served with a kicky gherkin-spiked rémoulade; and then move on to the succulent bone-in ribeye, topped with roasted garlic cloves and served with a bevy of traditional sauces (béarnaise, horseradish, herb fresh lime, and red wine reduction) to choose from.

Persepolis

B3

1407 Second Ave. (bet. 73rd & 74th Sts.)

Subway: 77 St
Phone: 212-535-1100
Web: www.persepolisnyc.com
Prices: $$

Lunch & dinner daily

Alluring cuisine served in a classic Upper East Side setting keeps this longtime neighborhood treasure on the short list of the city's finer Persian restaurants. An attractive room with red-toned wood furnishings, landscapes paintings, and gracious service fashion a convivial scene in which to enjoy the range of fragrant specialties.

One bite of the house tabbouleh reveals the seriousness of the kitchen; it is neatly plated, sparked by a bright and tasty balance of lemon and garlic, and vibrant green from a profusion of fresh parsley. The array of grilled marinated meats is impressive as well, but the stews deserve particular attention, as in the *khorest gaimeh*—cubes of beef filet braised with split peas, pickled lime, tomato sauce, and hints of cinnamon.

Philippe

A1

33 E. 60th St. (bet. Madison & Park Aves.)

Subway: Lexington Av - 59 St
Phone: 212-644-8885
Web: www.philippechow.com
Prices: $$$

Lunch Mon – Sat
Dinner nightly

From former Mr Chow chef, Philippe Chow (no relation), this luxe Chinese is elegant but not too fancy to be delicious. Inside, the stage is set with linen-draped tables, chopsticks in wooden boxes, and celebrity sightings. The support staff pairs white jackets and mandarin collar uniforms with red canvas sneakers—this whimsical departure from formality is juxtaposed by the stately monochromatic color scheme that flows throughout the multi-room space.

The satisfying menu features starters like scallion pancakes and shrimp toasts as well as a list of dumplings and noodles prepared by a dedicated noodlemaster. Specialties include Peking duck and Beijing chicken with walnuts and sweet brown sauce.

Enthusiasts can visit Philippe in both Miami and L.A.

Quatorze Bis

C3

French 🍴🍴

323 E. 79th St. (bet. First & Second Aves.)

Subway: 77 St
Phone: 212-535-1414
Web: N/A
Prices: $$

Lunch Tue – Sat
Dinner nightly

With its lipstick-red façade and sunny yellow awning, Quatorze Bis easily stands out along this high-rise stretch of the Upper East. The pleasant interior, frequented by a mature, well-dressed crowd, displays a continental flair with framed vintage posters, mirrored panels painted with the wine list, and comfortable red-velvet banquettes. The friendly waitstaff greets patrons with a small blackboard to present the day's specials.

The menu's roster of satisfying French classics is executed with savoir faire, as in the terrine *maison* and a savory tart of bacon, leek, and Gruyère. Grilled sirloin with light and crispy frites and decadent sauce béarnaise followed by the excellent hot apple tart is testament to the timelessness of true bistro cooking.

San Matteo

C2

Pizza 🍴

1739 Second Ave. (at 90th St.)

Subway: 86 St (Lexington Ave.)
Phone: 212-426-6943
Web: www.sanmatteopanuozzo.com
Prices: 💷💷

Lunch Fri – Sun
Dinner nightly

Upper East Siders have been counting their blessings since this convivial pizza newcomer moved into the neighborhood. The space is tiny and rustic, but also inviting and gracious.

More than 20 varieties of Neapolitan-style pizza temptingly emerge from the hand-built, wood-fired oven. Add to this a unique regional specialty hailing from Campania called *panuozzo*. Simply stated, it's a cross between a calzone and a panino, comprised of a puffy plank of freshly baked pizza dough stuffed with an array of fine quality ingredients such as roasted pork, mozzarella, and baby arugula for the *panuozzo di Bartolomei*. Co-owner Fabio Casella is an authority on Italian cheeses and, as one would hope, the excellent toppings here include house-made mozzarella.

Shalezeh 😊

B2

1420 Third Ave. (bet. 80th & 81st Sts.)

Subway: 77 St

Phone: 212-288-0012

Web: www.shalezeh.com

Prices: $$

Lunch & dinner daily

♿

Warm, ambient, and comfortably upscale, this Persian favorite is the perfect compliment to its busy Upper East Side environs. Inside, the service is attentive and tables are filled with a decidedly sophisticated, international crowd.

The kitchen is as talented as it is clearly dedicated to presenting this traditional bill of fare. Meals here should begin with a rich (and thick) yogurt, spinach, and garlic spread. Entrées like chicken kebabs are truly tasty, whether marinated in saffron and onions, or ground with herbs; but the accompanying sour cherry rice threatens to steal the show (ditto the lentil, raisin, saffron version). Rustic desserts highlight the region's powerful tastes, as in the trio of cherry, pomegranate, and rosewater ice cream.

Shanghai Pavilion

B3

1378 Third Ave. (bet. 78th & 79th Sts.)

Subway: 77 St

Phone: 212-585-3388

Web: N/A

Prices: 😖

Lunch & dinner daily

Shanghai Pavilion may be considered upscale neighborhood Chinese, yet it rises above its many peers with attractive surroundings and service with a smile—these are your first hints that there is an underlying seriousness to the cooking here. The polished, unobtrusive staff does much to draw these well-heeled local residents, but the list of celebration-worthy, order-in-advance specialties earns their devotion.

Shanghai and Cantonese regional favorites abound, as with the slurp-inducing steamed juicy dumplings. While enjoying these toothsome treats, the efficient servers stealthily restock your soup spoon with the next bun from the tabletop bamboo steamer. Other house specialties may include red-cooked chicken and braised beef with dried chilies.

Spigolo

Italian ✕✕

C3

1561 Second Ave. (at 81st St.)

Subway: 86 St (Lexington Ave.)
Phone: 212-744-1100
Web: www.spigolonyc.com
Prices: $$

Lunch Sat – Sun
Dinner nightly

With fewer than 25 seats, a copper-topped bar, menu marked by bold flavors, and serious service, beloved Spigolo (meaning "corner" in Italian) is a place wistfully wished to be a trusted secret. However, crowds hungry for a sophisticated meal know all too well of this impressive Italian, owned and warmly operated by husband-and-wife team Scott and Heather Fratangelo (who also happens to be the very talented pastry chef).

Clams and oysters on the half shell are popular to start, followed by excellent pastas or rustic entrées like braised chicken with porcini mushrooms and pearl onions over soft polenta. The wonderful dessert selection may prove irresistible, especially when faced with their assortment of house made cobblers, cookies, and *gelati*.

Sushi Sasabune

Japanese ✕

C3

401 E. 73rd St. (at First Ave.)

Subway: 77 St
Phone: 212-249-8583
Web: N/A
Prices: $$$

Lunch Tue – Fri
Dinner Tue – Sat

Nestled in the Upper East Side, this third outpost of the Sasabune family is paradise for devoted followers who appreciate premium quality fish and palatable price tag. The style of rice preparation is likewise a draw here, with more assertive vinegar and a warmer temperature.

Since Sasabune only serves sushi and sashimi omakase, this is no place for newbies or picky eaters. In fact, the restaurant's motto clearly states: "No Spicy Tuna. No California Roll. TRUST ME." So, those hankering for tempura should steer clear.

Aficionados or anyone sincerely seeking outstanding fish will find a home here, amid the parade of butterfish, stuffed squid, and local oysters. This wholly gratifying experience justifies the cult status of this modest spot.

Sushi of Gari ✿

C3

402 E. 78th St. (bet. First & York Aves.)

Subwa: 77 St   Dinner nightly
Phone: 212-517-5340
Web: www.sushiofgari.com
Prices: $$$

Sushi of Gari

This residential area, filled with flower shops and bodegas, somehow launched one of Manhattan's most dynamic sushi empires, by the grace and talents of Chef Masatoshi "Gari" Sugio. Since 1997, this has been something of a local beacon, spilling light onto the sidewalks and comforting its crowds with warm welcomes, hot cleansing towels, and very creative sushi. The contemporary room is simple and spare, as if to ensure that everyone's focus is on the cadre of chefs, their work and wares displayed in glass cases.

When the great "Gari" stands among his chefs, the restaurant comes alive as he lavishes his talents on those lucky enough to be seated at the counter. On such nights, toro with puréed daikon and ponzu sauce might begin your meal; while the fish is superb, it exceeds fantasy with flavors that pair to reveal the quirky genius behind this small empire. Signature touches appear as supremely fresh salmon is tucked over bubbling-hot roasted tomatoes and subtle garlic sauce, eliciting "oohs" and "aahs" from the surrounding tables.

The fish is exceptional and sauces are deliciously innovative no matter the night; however, this star shines its brightest when the master is in.

Sushi Seki

Japanese ✗

B4

1143 First Ave. (bet. 62nd & 63rd Sts.)

Subway: Lexington Av - 59 St

Phone: 212-371-0238

Web: N/A

Prices: $$$

Dinner Mon - Sat

Beloved Sushi Seki fills up nightly with a devoted following that represents a cross section of city life: neighborhood families, business colleagues, novices looking to broaden their horizons, and even celebrity chefs enjoying a late night snack. Although the décor of this well-worn sushi den doesn't make much of an impression with its dark carpeting, simple furnishings, and unadorned walls, what goes on behind the counter is truly special.

The menu offers enjoyable appetizers and cooked fare, but sushi is where Seki shines. The original special recipe platter serves up a stellar nigiri array–rich salmon topped with warmed tomato; butter-sautéed scallop; tuna with tofu cream; and silky *amaebi*–as well as a crunchy, creamy, spicy shrimp tempura roll.

Szechuan Chalet

Chinese ✗✗

B3

1395 Second Ave. (bet. 72nd & 73rd Sts.)

Subway: 68 St - Hunter College

Phone: 212-737-1838

Web: N/A

Prices: ☜☜

Lunch & dinner daily

Uptown dwellers rejoice at the opening of this new Chinese standout. Spicier fare prevails, but the kitchen shows a talent for balancing flavors and offering quality. The menu is large, so focus on the chef's specials and regionally specific dishes that include Sichuan pork dumplings red with chili-spiked oil or shredded chicken in a fiery vinaigrette, served chilled and doused with a creamy sesame sauce. The "chili fish pond" (mind the pun) is a red chili-oil based broth brimming with fish and vegetables, capped by a flotilla of Sichuan peppercorns and dried red chilies.

Graciously attended by professional staff, the fresh and contemporary space is adorned with red upholstery, pale walls, inked landscapes, and a sparkly blue-accented ceiling.

Taco Taco 🐷

C2

Mexican ✗

1726 Second Ave. (bet. 89th & 90th Sts.)

Subway: 86 St (Lexington Ave.)　　　　　　　Lunch & dinner daily
Phone: 212-289-8226
Web: N/A
Prices: 🪙

With prices as palatable as the food, the reputation of this budget-friendly neighborhood darling extends far beyond its Upper East enclave. The tacos alone are worth a visit— soft corn tortillas are abundantly filled with the likes of pork marinated with smoked jalapeños, simply adorned with onion and cilantro. Still, this colorful spot offers much more than its namesake with both authentically Mexican and Tex-Mex offerings like burritos, *tortas,* and house specials.

The bar stocks a variety of tequilas, but a *michelada* (beer seasoned with lime and Tabasco, served on the rocks with a salted rim) makes for a refreshing thirst quencher, as do the *agua frescas* in flavors like *horchata,* hibiscus, and tamarind. Downtown sister Mole shares a similar menu.

Taste

B3

American ✗✗

1413 Third Ave. (at 80th St.)

Subway: 77 St　　　　　　　　　　　　Lunch & dinner daily
Phone: 212-717-9798
Web: www.elizabar.com
Prices: $$

Located on what may as well be known as "Eli's block," Taste is part of Eli Zabar's vast operation that includes a sprawling market, wine store, flower shop, and even an ice cream stand. This attractive dining room is appointed with a striking inlaid tile floor, tobacco-brown walls, and mocha-hued furnishings. At night, the rich colors are lightened by tables dressed in orange Frette linens.

The impressive menu focuses on seasonality and simplicity in offerings like peekytoe crab salad with honeydew purée; olive-oil poached salmon with greenmarket string beans; and for dessert, peach and fig tart baked in the wood-burning oven, served with vanilla ice cream.

Breakfast and lunch is self-service, with a wide variety of items priced by the pound.

Tiella

Italian XX

B4

1109 First Ave. (bet. 60th & 61st Sts.)

Subway: Lexington Av - 59 St
Phone: 212-588-0100
Web: www.tiellanyc.com
Prices: $$

Lunch Mon – Sat
Dinner nightly

Although this forgotten stretch of First Ave, steps from the Roosevelt Island Tramway and Queensboro Bridge, is busy and unattractive, Tiella's Southern Italian specialties and classic hospitality are reason enough to seek it out. This neighborhood fave is housed in a room as slender as a train car, outfitted with espresso-dark wood furnishings set against ivory walls and exposed brick.

Tiella draws its name from the petite pans used to produce wood-oven pizzas that are characterized by a uniquely delicate crust. Toppings are fresh and balanced, as in the *Caprese* with creamy mozzarella, sweet cherry tomatoes, and fragrant basil. An inventive pasta listing, several *secondi*, and starters such as a *bellisima* block of eggplant Parmigiana complete the menu.

Untitled

American X

B3

945 Madison Ave. (at 75th St.)

Subway: 77 St
Phone: 212-570-3600
Web: www.whitney.org
Prices: ⊗⊗

Lunch Tue – Sun
Dinner Fri – Sun

Operated by the Union Square Hospitality Group, this new daytime dining venue is ensconced on the lower level of the Whitney Museum of American Art. The bright setting, designed by the Rockwell Group, is furnished with blonde wood booths and a comfortable dining counter facing a blackboard wall that spotlights the menu's comprehensive listing of local product.

An array of breakfast fare is served all day, accompanied by brunch-y sips, such as a grapefruit Campari mimosa. Keep powered up for a tour of the art with the likes of crispy kale with beets, almonds, and yogurt vinaigrette washed down by a fresh apple-ginger sparkler; or indulge with a pimento cheese and caramelized onion-topped burger followed by a wedge of Brooklyn-baked pie.

Tori Shin ✿

B4

1193 First Ave. (bet. 64th & 65th Sts.)

Subway: 68 St - Hunter College   Lunch & dinner daily
Phone: 212-988-8408
Web: www.torishinny.com
Prices: $$

Atsushi Kono

Irasshaimase! Beyond sliding wood doors, hear the staff's unified call welcoming you to this lively yet rather upscale *yakitori*-ya and know that you are in for an uncommon treat—certainly for this side of the globe.

The smoky essence of Tori Shin permeates everything, as the *noki* charcoal imported from Japan slowly burns, luring diners inside with its aroma, and searing each delicacy with menacing heat. There are three tables, but most diners are perched around the horseshoe-shaped counter at the restaurant's core. Here's some salutary advice: first-timers should join the herds and go for the chef's omakase. Sprinkling *shichimi* on chicken and chatting with the masters over the nuances of each sublimely grilled morsel occupies everyone's full attention. Meals may begin with excellent quality house-pickled cucumber and daikon, before moving on to skewers of perfectly grilled chicken breast with *yuzukosho*, *tsukune* (chicken meatballs), livers, or decadent bacon-wrapped tomatoes.

Everything is organic here, the chickens arrive specially from their own farm, and ingredients are handled with meticulous care and great skill. Simply put, Tori Shin is the best *yakitori-ya* in the country.

Uva

Italian 🍴

1486 Second Ave. (bet. 77th & 78th Sts.)

Subway: 77 St
Phone: 212-472-4552
Web: www.uvawinebar.com
Prices: $$

Lunch Sat – Sun
Dinner nightly

Bathed in an amber glow, this rustic wine bar conjures the comforts of Italian country dining, amid exposed brick walls, wooden tables, mounted sconces, a copper-clad bar, and very gracious service. This lived-in décor is complemented by an upbeat vibe, especially when dining in the charming back garden, weather permitting.

The well-selected wines include more than 30 choices by the glass; while the substantial, wine-bar themed menu begins with *bruschette*, flatbreads, cured meats, and all-Italian cheeses. The kitchen is equally adept in preparing heartier *secondi*, such as homemade gnocchi with creamy black truffle and chive sauce.

Desserts are wonderfully simple and a late menu starting at 11:00 P.M. keeps everyone happy well into the night.

Wa Jeal

Chinese 🍴🍴

1588 Second Ave. (bet. 82nd & 83rd Sts.)

Subway: 86 St (Lexington Ave.)
Phone: 212-396-3339
Web: www.wajealrestaurant.com
Prices: 🥜

Lunch & dinner daily

Specializing in the heated fare of the Sichuan province, Wa Jeal is spicing up the Upper East. The upscale room is comfortable with an uncharacteristically cozy atmosphere and gracious service.

The menu offers popular lunch specials and an array of regional favorites, but for a much more distinctive experience dive into the chef's menu, with its assortment of cold or hot appetizers and specialties that demonstrate the kitchen's complexity and strength. Dishes are both fresh and tantalizing, as in poached chicken dressed with soy, crushed dried red chili, and sesame oil boasting the unique, sensational tingle of Sichuan pepper; a mung bean jello salad that is at once cool and spicy; and lean strips of camphor tea-smoked duck boasting a salty-sweet allure.

Upper West Side

Proudly situated between two of Manhattan's most celebrated parks, home to venerable Lincoln Center, and the beloved Natural History Museum, the family-friendly Upper West Side is one of the city's most distinct neighborhoods. It has a near-cultish belief in its own way of doing things–whether it's because they boast some of *the* best cafés namely **Épicerie Boulud** that has it all from breakfast, sandwiches, soups, and salads, to coffee, pastries and *gelati*, or that life here means constantly tripping through the set of *Law and Order*–these residents cannot imagine being elsewhere.

Hollywood's New York

First and foremost, the Upper West is a neighborhood for strolling. Its sidewalks are lined with quaint brownstones, as well as more daunting architectural feats, like the Dakota (where *Rosemary's Baby* was filmed). Imagine rambling apartments filled with bookish locals arguing with equal gusto over the future of opera, or whether the best sturgeon is at **Murray's** or **Barney Greengrass**. If a scene from *Hannah and Her Sisters* comes to mind, you are beginning to understand this neighborhood.

Medley of Markets

This enthusiasm extends to all aspects of life—particularly food. For shopping, the **Tucker Square Greenmarket** is popular and anchored on West 66th Street (aka "Peter Jennings Way"). Equally celebrated is the original **Fairway**, filled with reasonably-priced gourmet treats. Intrepid shoppers should brave its famously cramped elevator to visit the exclusively organic second floor.

No visit to the Upper West Side is complete without **Zabar's**– home of all things gourmet and kosher–to ogle the barrels of olives and grab a few knishes. Another cyber haunt is www.thekoshermarketplace.com— they have everything! If planning an Italian themed evening, visit Cesare Casella's **Salumeria Rosi**. This neighborhood jewel offers an excellent and enormous selection of cured meats, while their small plates will leave you hungering for more. Finally, get your fish fix at **Luke's Lobster**, a spin-off of the original in the East Vilage. This fine seafood haven presents a wealth of seafood rolls including the all-time favorite (and most delicious) lobster roll.

If in need of refreshment, stop by **Soutine Bakery**, a quiet little storefront with jaw-dropping cakes; or opt for the legendary chocolate chip cookies from **Levain**. Of course, one of **Magnolia's** (many) outposts is sure to gain a quick cupcake following. For a more savory snack, grab a "Recession Special" at **Gray's Papaya**—the politically outspoken (check the window slogans) and quintessentially Upper West hot dog chain.

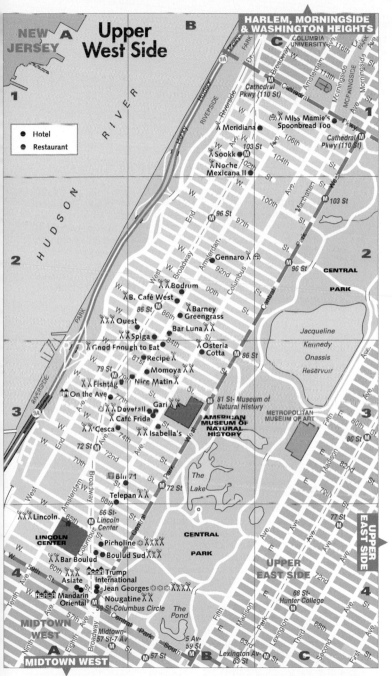

Upper West Side

NEW JERSEY

A   B   C

1

COLUMBIA UNIVERSITY

NEW YORK

HUDSON RIVER

RIVERSIDE DR

● Hotel
● Restaurant

Cathedral Pkwy (110 St)

Miss Mamie's
Spoonbread Too

Cathedral Pkwy (110 St)

Meridiana

103 St

Sookk
Noche
Mexicana II

103 St

96 St
97th

100th

2

Gennaro

96 St

CENTRAL

PARK

Bodrum

B. Café West

86 St

Barney
Greengrass

Ouest

Bar Luna

Jacqueline
Kennedy
Onassis
Reservoir

Spiga

Good Enough to Eat

Osteria
Cotta

Recipe

86 St

Momoya

Nice Matin

3

Fishtag

On the Ave

Gari

81 St-Museum of
Natural History

Dovetail

Café Frida

AMERICAN
MUSEUM OF
NATURAL
HISTORY

METROPOLITAN
MUSEUM OF ART

86 St

'Cesca

Isabella's

72 St

82nd

The Lake

Blu 71

Telepan

72 St

77 St

Lincoln

66 St-
Lincoln
Center

Picholine

LINCOLN
CENTER

Bar Boulud   Boulud Sud

CENTRAL

PARK

UPPER
EAST SIDE

72nd

68 St-
Hunter College

4

Asiate

Trump
International

Jean Georges

Mandarin
Oriental

Nougatine

59 St-Columbus Circle

The Pond

5 Av-
59 St

68th

63 St

MIDTOWN
WEST

Midtown-
57 St-7 Av

57 St

Lexington Av-
63 St

Asiate

A4

Fusion 🍴🍴🍴

80 Columbus Circle (at 60th St.)

Subway: 59 St - Columbus Circle
Phone: 212-805-8881
Web: www.mandarinoriental.com
Prices: $$$$

Lunch & dinner daily

There may be no finer view of Central Park than the jaw-dropping vista through floor-to-ceiling windows at Asiate, an elegant fusion restaurant perched on the 35th floor of the Mandarin Oriental hotel. Yet this natural beauty, unfurled like a lush carpet against the steep geometry of New York's skyline, is in fact rivaled by Asiate's own splendor fashioned with wine walls, stylized branches suspended from the ceiling, shimmering fabrics, and semi-private leather booths. Nonetheless, Asiate proves its own worth as a restaurant with a masterful waitstaff and impeccably trained kitchen. Mediterranean sensibilities are expressed, yet dishes highlight Asian flavors, as in honey-miso glazed wild salmon, with spiced mandarin orange and ginger gastrique.

Bar Boulud

A4

French 🍴🍴

1900 Broadway (bet. 63rd & 64th Sts.)

Subway: 66 St - Lincoln Center
Phone: 212-595-0303
Web: www.danielnyc.com
Prices: $$$

Lunch & dinner daily

Bright and airy by day, sexy and booming by night—Daniel Boulud's fresh, young, and unfussy Bar Boulud wears two different, albeit charming, hats for lunch and dinner. The restaurant's casual elegance starts with the wine barrel marking the entrance, and continues through to the service which reads polished, but relaxed, and the ample grape list, divided into four whimsical categories: Discoveries, Classics, Legends, and Heartthrobs.

The food doesn't stray far from the classics in Boulud's wheelhouse but airs on the simple side, with wine-friendly plates of pâté, terrine, and charcuterie (a must-do—specific team members trained under the legendary Parisian charcutier, Gilles Vérot) doing some heavy lifting on a terrific French comfort menu.

Bar Luna

B2

Italian 🍴🍴

511 Amsterdam Ave. (bet. 84th & 85th Sts.)

Subway: 86 St (Broadway)
Phone: 212-362-1098
Web: www.barlunanyc.com
Prices: $$

Lunch Sat – Sun
Dinner nightly

Long-time restaurateur Turgut Balikci illuminates the Amsterdam Avenue dining scene with this sexy eatery, while ex-West Branch talent runs the kitchen. The stylish interior sports bare wood tables and striped banquettes against weathered brick walls donning fuchsia-framed mirrors and stunning glossy photos. Bursts of yellow bring warmth to the space, softly lit by hanging lamps and fairy lights.

Nurse a pre-dinner cocktail at the spacious, friendly bar before tackling the sublime menu offerings, such as the spoon-tender rabbit richly braised with white wine, anise, and green olives. Pair the meal with a carafe of rosé, and perhaps finish it with a juicy cube of brioche bread pudding, studded with poached black cherries, doused in caramel.

Barney Greengrass

B2

Deli 🍴

541 Amsterdam Ave. (bet. 86th & 87th Sts.)

Subway: 86 St (Broadway)
Phone: 212-724-4707
Web: www.barneygreengrass.com
Prices:

Lunch Tue – Sun

New York's venerable "Sturgeon King" has earned its title and position as an Upper West Side institution.

In addition to serving breakfast and lunch until 5:00 P.M., they do double duty as a vibrant carry-out business and now take Internet orders. The place is darling, whether eating in or taking out; the deli sandwiches–piled high with pastrami or homemade egg salad, and served with a big, bright, crunchy pickle–are among the best in the city.

Order a heaping plate of sturgeon, house-cured gravlax, or clear, flavorful bowl of matzoh ball soup at this Formica-clad jewel and take a trip back in time; this food is the real thing. Service without ceremony but unique NY attitude makes a trip to Barney Greengrass an authentic and essential experience.

B. Café West

B2

Belgian ✗

566 Amsterdam Ave. (bet. 87th & 88th Sts.)

Subway: 86 St (Broadway)
Phone: 212-873-0003
Web: www.bcafe.com
Prices: $$

Lunch Sat – Sun
Dinner nightly

It used to be that finding a good spot along this Upper West stretch was like looking for a needle in a haystack. Well, needle found! B. Café West (the original "East" is on the Upper East Side) is now a go-to spot. This postage stamp of a restaurant stands out for its charming style, seemingly endless selection of Belgian-only beers, and delicious comfort food that is authentic and satisfying. The rustic, faux traditional style may feel a bit cliché, but no one seems to mind.

First, choose from their impressive beer list (you can't go wrong), then slurp some *moules* swimming in savory broth, and crunch those addictively crispy frites. From beef croquettes to smoked ham-wrapped endive with béchamel and Gruyère, this is Belgian comfort food to the hilt.

Bin 71

A3

Italian

237 Columbus Ave. (bet. 70th & 71st Sts.)

Subway: 72 St
Phone: 212-362-5446
Web: www.bin71.com
Prices: $$

Lunch Wed – Sun
Dinner nightly

With its low-slung ceiling and pretty marble bar packed with an endless stream of happy, buzzing patrons, this charming Italian wine and tapas bar is still going strong. With over thirty wine varieties available by the glass, and bottles from as far-reaching places as Slovenia, there's a *vinoversity* to be had here.

Choose from a delicious roster of small plates, all quick and easy enough to get you in and out in time to make a show at nearby Lincoln Center: Plump, juicy meatballs puddled in a lip-smacking lemon-and-white wine broth; fresh, oven-roasted oysters laced with thin ribbons of fennel, sweet butter, and salty capers; or moist olive oil cake paired with tender braised apples and a smooth dollop of whipped cream.

Bodrum

B2

Turkish ✕✕

584 Amsterdam Ave. (bet. 88th & 89th Sts.)

Subway: 86 St (Broadway)
Phone: 212-799 2806
Web: www.bodrumnyc.com
Prices: $$

Lunch & dinner daily

This Upper West Side Turkish restaurant is the very definition of a cozy and comfortable neighborhood spot. Regulars pack the place throughout the day for its inviting, Mediterranean feel; warm-weather sidewalk seating; and the delicious, well-priced fare.

Though not a traditional feature of Turkish spots, there's a wood-burning oven for thin, European-style pizzas, which are a popular choice among chatting locals. The bulk of the very appealing menu features traditional Turkish specialties like crunchy and fresh shepherd salad with a smattering of sumac, and grilled chicken *Baharat*. Flavorful and healthy dishes keep the neighborhood coming back for more, as do the lunch and dinner specials that are as light on the wallet as they are on the waistline.

Boulud Sud

A4

Mediterranean ✕✕✕

20 W. 64th St. (bet. Broadway & Central Park West)

Subway: 66 St - Lincoln Center
Phone: 212-595-1313
Web: www.danielnyc.com
Prices: $$$

Dinner nightly

Tucked around the corner from all things Boulud is the prim and proper Boulud Sud. The bar draped at the entrance is lined with people gawking at the 120-seat dining room glitzed with arched white ceilings, plush banquettes, wood panels, and sheer curtains that buffer the bustle of Lincoln Center.

This chic, windowed arena mingles foodies with newbies; find them lounging in metal framed chairs while noshing under paintings evocative of Van Gogh. Tasteful is the theme and tasty is the fare presented by sharp servers who meet your every need whether it may be crispy artichokes *alla Romana*; harissa-coated lamb laid across roasted eggplant and honey-laced eggplant purée; and Provençal *moelleux*, an olive oil cake crowned with strawberries and lemon icing.

Café Frida

Mexican ✗

B3

368 Columbus Ave. (bet. 77th & 78th Sts.)

Subway: 81 St - Museum of Natural History   Lunch Sat – Sun
Phone: 212-712-2929   Dinner nightly
Web: www.cafefrida.com
Prices: $$

Sporting bright fuchsia walls, pretty wrought-iron chandeliers, and cozy wooden tables, this pretty little hacienda manages to be festive, classy, and rustic all at the same time. Add in the fluffy handmade tortillas; fresh organic produce; and intricate Mexican specialties, and you'll think you've died and gone to Puebla.

The gorgeous homemade margaritas (compliments of Mixologist Junior Merino) and serious tequila list only lulls you deeper into the dream. Café Frida's menu, served up by a friendly and knowledgeable staff, might reveal a fragrant chicken soup bobbing with tender white hominy, potatoes, and tomatillo; or *enchiladas suiza*, stuffed with juicy shredded chicken and laced with a tart tomatillo purée and cool lick of *crema*.

'Cesca

Italian ✗✗

A3

164 W. 75th St. (at Amsterdam Ave.)

Subway: 72 St   Dinner nightly
Phone: 212-787-6300
Web: www.cescanyc.com
Prices: $$

Tucked into 75th Street, just off Amsterdam Ave., the sexy 'Cesca keeps perfect company with a spate of new condos that were built into this Upper West Side nook over the last few years. The space is stylish and sprawling, with dark, low-ceilings, deep brown velvet banquettes, and iron chandeliers; while the waitstaff is attentive, professional, and eager to please. Everyone is in good spirits at 'Cesca, it would seem.

But how's the food, you wonder? Not wildly innovative, but very fresh and very well-made. Witness a luscious *minestra* studded with cubes of sweet, aromatic *cotecchino*, chard, chickpeas, tomato, and herbs; chewy orecchiette humming with homemade lamb sausage, pecorino, and rainbow Swiss chard; and tender, slow-roasted Long Island duck.

Dovetail ✿

American   ✗✗

B3

103 W. 77th St. (at Columbus Ave.)

Subway: 81 St - Museum of Natural History

Phone: 212-362-3800

Web: www.dovetailnyc.com

Prices: $$$

Lunch Fri – Sun

Dinner nightly

Emilie Baltz

With such easy access to the sacred Museum of Natural History and just off lively Columbus Ave., Dovetail is that lovely little find admired by pundits and tourists alike for its seasonally-driven food and jovial mood. This American idol may be rimmed by bustle, but an elegant entryway with glass-encased wine racks and a gracious hostess with a quiet manner, promises to soothe your every nerve.

Find a deluge of charm in a single dining room crisply attired in wood furnishings that are as simple as they are warming. Keeping with the cool caprice, are polished servers who coach a sober Upper West Side set on Chef John Fraser's delightfully chaste offerings. Unleash the "adult" in you and dive into sophisticated dishes like chilled corn soup sweetened with blueberries and piquant with paprika; an "everything" salmon fillet crusted with bread crumbs and poppy seeds poised atop potato purée deliciously tickled with cucumbers, dill, and salmon roe; and a milk chocolate gianduja washed with apricot-lavender sherbert.

Dovetail is praised and preferred by many for its two Friday $24 lunch menus; Monday vegetarian menu; and "Sunday Suppa"—all flashing tempting treats at fantastic value.

Fishtag

Manhattan ▶ Upper West Side

Seafood ✗✗

A3

222 W. 79th St. (bet. Amsterdam Ave. & Broadway)

Subway: 79 St	Lunch Sat – Sun
Phone: 212-362-7470	Dinner nightly
Web: www.fishtagrestaurant.com	
Prices: $$$	

Nestled in the lower floor of a townhouse, this iconic space has been completely transformed into the polished new home of the celebrated chef, Michael Psilakis. A warm marble front bar opens to a refined, white-walled room with exposed brick and classic wood panes. Here, the well-informed, engaged staff happily and patiently guides patrons through the two menus that strive to describe the nuances of each dish via color codes and wine suggestions.

Meals may begin with a spectacular selection of buttery cold-smoked sablefish, "pastrami" salmon, and smoked tuna with a range of accompaniments, from citrus to chickpea confit, that attest to the kitchen's brilliance. The sea urchin crudo in ocean water is exactly as it sounds: perfect, sensible, and delicious.

Gari

Japanese ✗✗

B3

370 Columbus Ave. (bet. 77th & 78th Sts.)

Subway: 81 St - Museum of Natural History	Lunch & dinner daily
Phone: 212-362-4816	
Web: N/A	
Prices: $$$	

The Columbus Avenue outpost of Sushi of Gari (there are three in Manhattan) fashions a hip aesthetic with contemporary Asian décor and large glass windows facing the sidewalk.

While ingredients are top quality and everything is made to order, there is strong focus on mass appeal here, as more guests order à la carte rather than put themselves in the skillful hands of the sushi chefs and try the highly recommended omakase, where the true beauty of Gari lies. A fine mix of sushi, including signatures by Chef Masatoshi "Gari" Sugio, and cooked dishes are all prepared with a modern touch. European influences are evident in items like duck and lamb chops.

Offering a well-chosen list of sake and wine, plus professional service, Gari is packed nightly.

Gennaro 😊

B2

Italian 🍴

665 Amsterdam Ave. (bet. 92nd & 93rd Sts.)

Subway: 96 St (Broadway)
Phone: 212-665-5348
Web: www.gennaronyc.com
Prices: $$

Dinner nightly

Expect a wait at this bright, boisterous trattoria; the throngs of regulars flooding in know that Gennaro can't be beat for a delicious neighborhood Italian meal, and that no reservations are taken. Soak in the friendly vibe and enjoy the unpretentious space, filled with colorful ceramics, until you can settle into one of the snug tables (roomy ones seem to go to the regulars). Still, the food is worth it.

Join the crowds in starting with the antipasto, before moving on to the inspired offering of pasta, like perfectly tender *bucatini*, dusted with freshly cracked pepper and cheese. The daily specials' list is nearly as long as the regular menu, but be sure to ask about prices—these can be considerably steeper than their everyday offerings.

Good Enough to Eat

B3

American 🍴

483 Amsterdam Ave. (bet. 83rd & 84th Sts.)

Subway: 79 St
Phone: 212-496-0163
Web: www.goodenoughtoeat.com
Prices: $$

Lunch & dinner daily

The title of the place pretty much says it all—it's good enough to eat here, all right, and you could do so from morning 'till night if you wished. This family-friendly comfort food haven offers breakfast, lunch, and dinner (not to mention takeout), and the Upper West Side locals, for one, can't get enough of Chef/owner Carrie Levin's simple, but mouthwatering renditions of tender, home-cooked meatloaf; flaky fish and chips; and crunchy stacks of buttermilk-fried onion rings.

The homey atmosphere matches the food, with a whimsical mix of folk art, cow accents–lots of 'em–and large "candies" hanging from the ceiling. A cozy area in front offers a great solo meal—add a little frost on the window, and you'll dream you've gone home for the holidays.

Isabella's

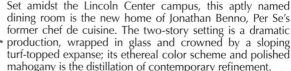

Mediterranean ✗✗

B3

359 Columbus Ave. (at 77th St.)

Subway: 81 St - Museum of Natural History
Phone: 212-724-2100
Web: www.isabellas.com
Prices: $$

Lunch & dinner daily

For over two decades, this popular NY dining institution has boasted and rightfully earned some of the area's best sidewalk real estate. Lovely interiors and Mediterranean flavors make Isabella's a worthwhile legacy. However, bi-level dining, outdoor seating (weather permitting), and competition from its neighbor, Shake Shack, does nothing to ease long waits for tables, especially during weekend brunch which features a variety of Benedicts, from crab to BLT-inspired.

Music keeps tempo with the bustling activity, while the charming and professional staff tends to diners relishing the likes of herb-roasted chicken. Regulars know two things: For a small corkage fee, they may BYO; and always save room for the generous warm brownie sundae.

Lincoln

Italian ✗✗✗

A4

142 W. 65th St. (bet. Amsterdam Ave. & Broadway)

Subway: 66 St - Lincoln Center
Phone: 212-359-6500
Web: www.lincolnristorante.com
Prices: $$$$

Lunch Wed – Sun
Dinner nightly

Set amidst the Lincoln Center campus, this aptly named dining room is the new home of Jonathan Benno, Per Se's former chef de cuisine. The two-story setting is a dramatic production, wrapped in glass and crowned by a sloping turf-topped expanse; its ethereal color scheme and polished mahogany is the distillation of contemporary refinement.

The kitchen melds excellent product and Italian inspiration to produce an assemblage of crowd-pleasing creations that oscillate between rustic and elegant. A sip from the Negroni bar is highly recommended before delving into *primi* such as *gigli* with hunks of Peekytoe crab, Santa Barbara sea urchin, and Meyer lemon; roasted chicken breast tucked with fresh herbs and wilted watercress; and standout desserts.

Jean Georges ❀ ❀ ❀

A4

Contemporary 🍴🍴🍴🍴

1 Central Park West (bet. 60th & 61st Sts.)

Subway: 59 St - Columbus Circle Lunch & dinner Mon — Sat
Phone: 212-299-3900
Web: www.jean-georges.com
Prices: $$$$

Thomas oef

This is the playground of the very chic, very New York, and very, *very* moneyed. It is a place where one goes to be treated like royalty amid the natural beauty of Central Park, urban theater at Columbus Circle, and a dining room that enhances its windowed walls with soothing tones of silver.

As local splendor sets this scene, the expert service staff recalls Europe from a bygone era, when dishes were finished tableside by waiters donning waistcoats and matching slacks.

While quality of ingredients and mastery of skills are paramount here, Chef Jean-Georges Vongerichten's creative talent and subtle Asian bent is the stuff of his famed genius. His empire may be expanding around the globe, but here in Manhattan, Chef Mark Lapico remains true to the eponymous chef's sensibilities with the likes of beautiful baby beets with tart yogurt, golden-crisp shallots, and a surprising hit of pure chili-pepper fire—a spicy and memorable kiss at the end. Fun desserts may pay tribute to a seasonal darling, such as rhubarb, served as golée with lemongrass glace, vanilla and coconut pearls, and rhubarb pickles. Finish with a few inches of *guimauve* (marshmallow) in seasonal flavors. *Parfait!*

Meridiana

Italian   %

C1

2756 Broadway (bet. 105th & 106th Sts.)

Subway: 103 St (Broadway)   Dinner nightly
Phone: 212-222-4453
Web: N/A
Prices: $$

Where good eats are concerned, there's often wisdom in the masses. A loyal Upper West Side following has kept this Italian mainstay going strong for almost two decades in an otherwise fickle food hood. Much of the restaurant's ongoing success can be attributed to Chef/owner Gianni "Johnny" Nicolosi and his wife, Pilar, who know how to keep the atmosphere easy—think rhythmic ceiling fans, towering palm trees, and pretty frescos—and the food straight-up delicious.

Try the silky spaghetti with tender diced calamari, basil, tomato, and squid ink; and then move on to the juicy chicken and sausage, mixed with peppers, potatoes, and a flutter of fragrant rosemary and olives; or an un-traditional Sicilian zabaglione semifreddo with chocolate ice cream.

Miss Mamie's Spoonbread Too

Southern   %

C1

366 W. 110th St./Cathedral Pkwy. (bet. Columbus & Manhattan Aves.)

Subway: Cathedral Pkwy/110 St (Central Park West)   Lunch & dinner daily
Phone: 212-865-6744
Web: www.spoonbreadinc.com
Prices: ☜☜

This venerable Morningside Heights institution doesn't coast on its reputation as a homey Southern haven just north of Central Park. The food is as good as ever, the atmosphere is easygoing and welcoming, and the music is soulful yet unobtrusive.

Fresh and expertly made classics rule the menu, but the daily specials board offers gems that should not be ignored. Here, find the likes of crazy chicken, perfectly fried and juicy with a generous helping of three sides and gravy. The smothered pork chops are tender and wonderfully tangy; the yams are soft and spicy; and the banana pudding is the stuff of dreams. Sit back and soak in a super-sweet iced tea or the Spoonbread punch and relax—food made with such care can take its time getting to your table.

Momoya

B3

Japanese ✗✗

427 Amsterdam Ave. (bet. 80th & 81st Sts.)

Subway: 79 St
Phone: 212-580-0007
Web: www.themomoya.com
Prices: $$$

Lunch & dinner daily

It's a bit more sophisticated than its Chelsea sister (think curvy wood and painted brick walls, slate floors, and cream leather booths), but there's nothing pretentious or fussy about Momoya. Instead, this sushi restaurant with its swift service, consistently good sushi, and fair prices, has won the hearts of Upper West Siders.

The sleek setting doesn't hurt either. Given the location, Momoya's menu isn't altogether a surprise, so await familiar favorites like spicy tuna rolls and sashimi platters with eel, toro, Spanish mackerel, and sea urchin. Dessert is often an after-thought at Japanese restaurants, but the delicious *mille crêpes* with green tea and crème anglaise is perfectly delicate and provides a cool and light finish to a satisfying meal.

Nice Matin

B3

Mediterranean ✗

201 W. 79th St. (at Amsterdam Ave.)

Subway: 79 St
Phone: 212-873-6423
Web: www.nicematinnyc.com
Prices: $$

Lunch & dinner daily

Named after the daily newspaper published in a major city on France's Côte d'Azur, Nice Matin transports diners to the sun-drenched Mediterranean coast.

Niçoise dishes here exhibit as many vibrant flavors and colors as appear in the room's luminous décor. Fashioned as a coastal brasserie, Nice Matin asserts its unique personality by avoiding all the decorative clichés found in many Gallic-style restaurants; lights dangle from the tops of high pillars that spread umbrella-like against the ceiling, and tables are covered with Formica.

Starting with their wonderful breakfasts of poached eggs Provençal or fresh scones, the menu finds inspiration in wandering the wider Mediterranean region, from a perfectly cooked risotto to a traditional bouillabaisse.

Noche Mexicana II

B1

842 Amsterdam Ave. (at 101st St.)

Subway: 103 St (Broadway)
Phone: 212-662-6900
Web: www.noche-mexicana.com
Prices: $$

Lunch & dinner daily

Sequels are usually better known for missing the mark rather than hitting it, but Noche Mexicana II bucks the trend. This Upper West Side pearl known for its fluffy tamales moved to bigger and brighter digs this year, closing its original some blocks north. These higher reaches of Amsterdam Ave. aren't the prettiest, but once inside this bright, upbeat spot, you'll never look back.

Moist corn meal tamales with succulent pork and green mole sauce; spicy *camarones Mexicana*; tempting *guajilio* chili with tender chicken—you can't go wrong. Other surefire hits include *tingas*, *taco cesina* (preserved beef), and the *pipian de pollo*, shredded chicken served with toasted pumpkin and sesame seeds and cooked with jalapeño and *guero* chile peppers...*muy bueno*!

Nougatine

A4

1 Central Park West (at 60th St.)

Subway: 59 St - Columbus Circle
Phone: 212-299-3900
Web: www.jean-georges.com
Prices: $$

Lunch & dinner daily

If you're in the nabe and in need of a charming spot to rest your weary feet after shopping and trotting, dash to Nougatine. On the Upper West Side, this beautiful catch dons a stunning outfit (with glorious Central Park views, modern artwork, ornate marble floors, and flower splashes) that is only matched by its delicious food (they shares stoves with revered sibling, Jean Georges).

Keep an eagle eye out for the boisterous waitstaff, as they swerve around tables like NY cabbies rife with 'tude. Listen to their chatter while diving into an elegant sweet pea purée heaped with Beaufort and crunchy croutons; Peekytoe crab cake salad tossed with sugar snap pea remoulade; and a buttery seasonal (pear) tart rich with crème fraîche and black currant sorbet.

Osteria Cotta

B3

Italian 🍴

513 Columbus Ave. (bet. 84th & 85th Sts.)

Subway: 86 St (Broadway)
Phone: 212 873-8500
Web: N/A
Prices: $$

Lunch Sat – Sun
Dinner nightly

This neighborhood newcomer is already the go-to spot for those NYers who are tired of trendy and seek a taste of home without the hassle. Osteria Cotta is decidedly more comfortable than chic, featuring wood beams, wrought-iron banisters, exposed brick walls, and wood-framed glass doors that open out to Columbus Avenue to define its rustic look.
There's a roaring oven for pizza that also turns out a truly perfect roasted chicken. For some old-fashioned comfort, try the lasagna Bolognese: rich, creamy, with thick sheets of chewy pasta, satiny pillows of cheese and kissed with the flavors of fennel and pork—it might be more than poor *nonna's* heart can bear. Don't miss the Nutella- and ricotta-filled dessert calzone for a little sachet of heaven.

Ouest

B2

Contemporary 🍴🍴🍴

2315 Broadway (bet. 83rd & 84th Sts.)

Subway: 86 St (Broadway)
Phone: 212-580-8700
Web: www.ouestny.com
Prices: $$$

Lunch Sun
Dinner nightly

The last decade saw a slew of serious eateries marching into the Upper West—notably this popular outpost from the trailblazing Chef/owner Tom Valenti.
As with his other ventures, Chef Valenti's top priorities are both hospitality and his kitchen, where nothing is overlooked and everything is delicious. Expect edgy riffs on American comfort foods like plump, house-made potato gnocchi with short rib ragout and herbed ricotta or pan-roasted rack of lamb with chickpea purée.
The sleek dining room is masculine yet undeniably comfortable, attended by gracious servers leading groups to beautiful, circular red leather banquettes, guaranteed to keep the conversations intimate. Solo diners enjoy seats at the gorgeous and well-tended mahogany bar.

Picholine ✿

Contemporary ✕✕✕✕

A4

35 W. 64th St. (bet. Broadway & Central Park West)

Subway: 66 St - Lincoln Center
Phone: 212-724-8585
Web: www.picholinenyc.com
Prices: $$$$

Dinner nightly

Picholine

Quietly sitting in the shadows of a jewel that is Lincoln Center, Picholine is quite the theater-lover's dream come true. The entryway is subtle, and the dining rooms have just the right hint of regality for grandes-dames dressed to the nines on their way to the ballet. Yes, the large crystal chandeliers, decorative moldings, white columns, and padded gray upholstery do smack of old money, but starry-eyed young celebrants ensure it is equally appropriate for special occasions.

The first, longer dining room is fronted by a lively bar perfect for solo dining and tables that may have the best eavesdropping in the city (enthusiasts take note); the second room is cozier and intimate. The service team is a rather gentlemanly set: regimented, polite, and proper.

The menu encompasses a range of dishes from both land and sea that strive to evoke the Mediterranean. An elegant amuse-bouche of poached quail egg in a toasted brioche purse topped with American sturgeon caviar is a worthy prelude to the likes of beautifully presented creamy fava-stuffed agnolotti in pesto, topped with baby asparagus and Parmesan foam. The wine and cheese selection offer an impressive expanse of culture and time.

Recipe

B3

American ✗

452 Amsterdam Ave. (bet. 81st & 82nd Sts.)

Subway: 79 St
Phone: 212-501-7755
Web: www.recipenyc.com
Prices: $$

Lunch Sat – Sun
Dinner nightly

This sweet little sliver of a restaurant arrives courtesy of the team behind Land, a beloved Thai spot located a few steps away. With Recipe, they turn their well-focused attention to contemporary American fare —and the result is yet another reason to deem the Upper West Side the city's fastest rising food corridor.

In a simple space dressed in whitewashed walls, reclaimed knickknacks, and industrial light fixtures, you'll find a straightforward menu touting a rustic lineup that highlights exceptionally fresh fish and downright sultry desserts. Dishes may include seared duck breast, cooked exactly as requested, then glazed with a beautiful mustard baste and set over wild rice, alongside a generous helping of steamed and roasted vegetables.

Sookk

B1

Thai ✗

2686 Broadway (bet. 102nd & 103rd Sts.)

Subway: 103 St (Broadway)
Phone: 212-870-0253
Web: www.sookkrestaurant.com
Prices: $$

Lunch & dinner daily

From the hip folks behind the downtown lounge, Room Service, this tiny Thai joint draws Upper West Siders in droves —and it's not hard to see why. Unique dishes are cooked up in the style of Yaowarat (a district in Northwest Bangkok) which marries Thai, Sichuan, and Cantonese cuisines. Warm up with savory white lemongrass soup of poached chicken, chili oil, and mushrooms; or the delectable chicken pumpkin curry in spicy coconut milk. The mussel turnip cake may sound like an acquired taste, but plump green mussels stir fried with ginger and tamarind, with pan-fried turnips, eggs, and bean sprouts are a funky crowdpleaser.

Bedecked in bright colors, mesh lanterns, and red banquettes, the space is attractive top to bottom (check out the restrooms).

Spiga

B2

Italian ✗✗

200 W. 84th St. (bet. Amsterdam Ave. & Broadway)

Subway: 86 St (Broadway)   Dinner nightly
Phone: 212-362-5506
Web: www.spiganyc.com
Prices: $$$

When neighborhood residents want to treat themselves to a memorable Italian meal, they head to Spiga. Replete with shelves lined in wine bottles, a beamed ceiling, and affable service, the handsome setting also claims a creative kitchen turning out a heap of specialties influenced by Puglia and the northern reaches of the country.

Kick things off with a salad of mixed beans studded with the crunch of celery and slivered red onion—stunning in its simplicity. Then move on to herb-crusted lamb chops, coated with a flurry of fresh rosemary made fragrant by the hot oven, accompanied by sautéed broccoli rabe and a block of creamy potato gratin. Finish with the apple and pear strudel enrobed in a tender crust and paired with a scoop of ginger ice cream.

Telepan

A3

American ✗✗

72 W. 69th St. (bet. Central Park West & Columbus Ave.)

Subway: 66 St - Lincoln Center   Lunch Wed — Sun
Phone: 212-580-4300   Dinner nightly
Web: www.telepan-ny.com
Prices: $$$

Tucked behind a green awning near Lincoln Center, Chef/owner Bill Telepan's namesake restaurant is firmly dedicated to sustainability and organic products both inside this kitchen and out (he also cooks healthy meals for school children in Washington Heights). All the while, his Hungarian roots mingle with his locavore philosophy with delicious results as in the house-smoked fish with black radish and sour cream set atop a fluffy blini.

The wonderfully conceptualized menu flaunts multiple options for tasting courses as well as à la carte dining. Dishes may range from a humble vegetable and bread soup and lobster Bolognese, to delish desserts like the pumpkin-cheesecake sundae.

Inside, the pecan-wood tones and crackling fireplaces are a pleasant backdrop.

John Peden/The New York Botanical Garden

The Bronx

The only borough attached to the mainland, the Bronx is marked by contrasts. Although abandoned apartment buildings and massive housing projects once overran the borough's south section, private foundations and grassroots movements are successfully revitalizing these areas. As always, grand mansions and lush gardens still characterize the northern areas of Riverdale and Fieldston.

BELMONT

Hispanics, African-Americans, Irish-Americans, West Indians, and Albanians comprise much of the current population. Though a host of Italians once settled in the Belmont area, today they only reside as shop proprietors.

Thanks to the 19th century journalist John Mullaly, who led a movement in the late 1800s to buy and preserve inexpensive parcels of land, 25 percent of the Bronx today consists of parkland. This includes Pelham Bay Park, with its sandy Orchard Beach. Here, step into pizza paradise–**Louie and Ernie's**–for a slice of heaven.

Beyond, City Island is a gem of a coastal community, much like New England with its quaint inns and seafood spots. During the summer, stroll down City Island Ave., and into **Lickety Split** for a scoop of divine ice cream. Belmont's most renowned street and Italian food mecca, Arthur Avenue,

lures from far and wide. Tear into warm, freshly baked breads from **Terranova**, **Madonia**, or **Addeo**—the choices are plenty. Dive into a ball of warm and creamy mozzarella at **Joe's Deli** (open on Sundays!). The pistachio-studded mortadella from **Teitel Brothers** or *salumi* from **Calabria Pork Store** are also perfect salt licks for tigers on the prowl.

Gourmet Getaway

Check out **The Arthur Avenue Retail Market**, a covered oasis built by Mayor LaGuardia to prevent pushcart vendors from crowding busy streets. The dwindling vendors inside sell quality Italian pasta, homemade sausage, olive oil, notorious heroes, heirloom seeds, and hand-rolled cigars.

Although the Belmont section is now mainly known as Little Mexico and Ecuador, it has a world of Eastern European treats. Visit **Tony & Tina's Pizza**, but skip the Italian stuff. Instead, devour Albanian or Kosovar *burek*—these flaky rolls are packed with pumpkin purée and are *sine qua non*.

Gustiamo's warehouse, now open to retail, will delight your palate with simple Italian specialties that include a variety of regional oils and vinegars; pastas and rice; classic recipe favorites like San Marzano tomatoes; seafood; sweets and coffee; and attractive gift baskets. In the same vein, **Honeywell Meat Market** (their butchers in particular) can teach newbies a thing or two about breaking down a side of beef. Bronxite's will revel in the heart satisfying *chicharron de cerdo* at pork-central **El Bohio Lechonera** in nearby Crotona Park. Take yourself out to a ball game at the Yankee Stadium and snack from **Lobel's** cart (the ultimate butcher shop); or if you're lucky enough to have premium seats, enjoy one of their expertly dry-aged steaks.

Comfort Foods

The Eastchester, Wakefield, and Williamsbridge sections of the Bronx cradle a number of communities and their tasty eats and treats. The spicy, smoky tidbits of the Caribbean have become a local staple. Visit Vernon's **New Jerk House** for mouthwatering jerk chicken, and end with something sweet from **Kingston Tropical Bakery**. Or for Italian, drop by **G & R Deli** on Williamsbridge Road for big flavors in their homemade sausages or rich meaty sauce sold by the quart. End at **Sal & Dom's** for flaky *sfogliatelle*.

Asia comes alive at **Pho Saigon No.1**—peek in and discover that authentic Vietnamese food has officially arrived in the Bronx. For a flurry of Cambodian delights, step into the **Phnom Penh-Nha Trang Market** across the street. The hamburger craze continues uptown at the **Bronx Ale House** and the established **Bruckner Bar & Grill**.

A Latin Affair

A unique blend of Latin American spots populates the South Bronx, with the largest concentration hailing from Puerto Rico. On Willis Avenue, Mott Haven's main drag, bright awnings designate Honduran diners, Mexican bodegas, and Puerto Rican takeout. Fenced off empty lots allow for older folks to chat, play cards, and linger over authentic dishes from their homeland.

Vital to New York's food business is the **Hunts Point Food Distribution Center**, a 329-acre complex containing a mass of food wholesalers, distributors, and food processing businesses. The mega complex includes **The Hunts Point Meat Market**, **Hunts Point Terminal Produce Market**, and **The Fulton Fish Market**, a wholesale triumvirate where the city's restaurateurs and market owners come to pick their goods.

RIVERDALE

Riverdale may not be widely known for its dining culture and culinary treasures, but **Liebman's** is still considered one of the finest kosher delis in the Bronx. They comfort local masses with dishes like steamy soups, hot dogs, and brisket.

At the primped **Mother's Bake Shop**, stop to savor the traditional *babkas* and challahs; and **Skyview Wines** carries a rare selection of kosher wines, thereby completing your culinary journey with some meat, sweet, and spirit.

Hop, skip, and a jump from the last stop on the 1 line, follow your nose (cause it always knows!) to **Lloyd's Carrot Cake** for one or several slices of their famously divine carrot cake or layer cakes including homemade red velvet, German chocolate, and pineapple-coconut.

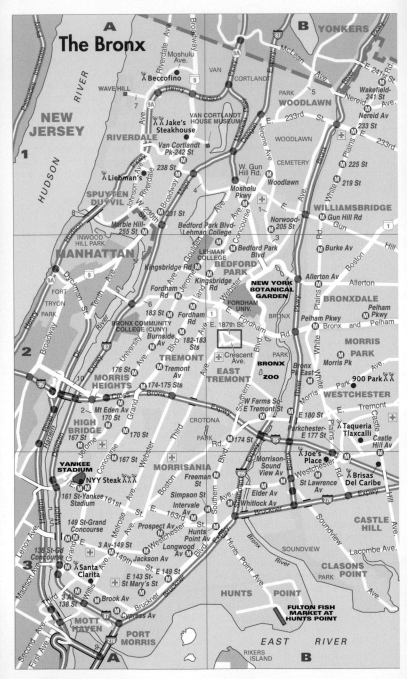

The Bronx

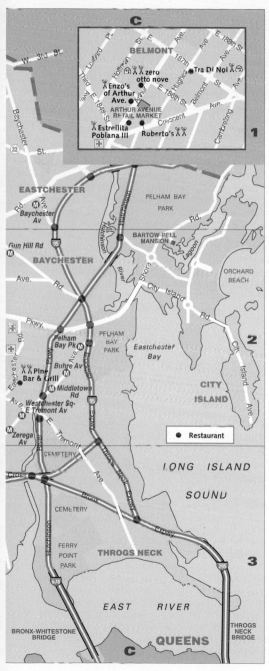

Beccofino

A1

5704 Mosholu Ave. (at Fieldston Rd.)

Subway: Van Cortlandt Park-242 St (& bus BX9)   Dinner nightly
Phone: 718-432-2604
Web: N/A
Prices: $$

Tucked into the quaint, family-oriented Bronx neighborhood of Riverdale, Beccofino sets a pretty, idyllic stage straight away—with large inviting windows overlooking a leafy, residential street and a rustic osteria interior fitted out with exposed brick walls, terra-cotta floors, and a handful of tables wrapped in deli paper.

Beccofino's menu is pure Italian-American comfort, with hand-crafted dishes that prioritize fresh ingredients over inventiveness. Most nights, you'll find a healthy list of hand-written daily specials, along with dishes like warm mozzarella in *carrozza*, served with a side of chunky marinara; tender, sausage-stuffed cremini mushrooms; and savory veal chop *à la forestière*, paired with roasted potatoes and fresh winter vegetables.

Brisas Del Caribe

B3

1207 Castle Hill Ave. (bet. Ellis & Gleason Aves.)

Subway: Castle Hill Av   Lunch & dinner daily
Phone: 718-794-9710
Web: N/A
Prices: 🍴🍴

This popular eatery stays packed to the rim day and night with those looking for solid Puerto Rican fare at bargain basement prices. Tucked into a multi-ethnic enclave of the Bronx dotted with 99 Cent stores, 1950s coffee houses, and Korean grocers, Brisas Del Caribe's waiters bounce around the bright, airy room at a good clip and seem to like it when you can woo them with a bit of Spanish. But don't be dissuaded if you don't talk the talk—anyone and everyone is welcome here. It just might take a little longer to order is all.

Don't miss the spot-on *mofongo*, a crispy, delicious mountain of plantain studded with tender shredded chicken; or the killer Cubano sandwich, stuffed with sweet and salty shredded pork, cheese, sliced pickles, and mayo.

Enzo's of Arthur Ave

Italian ✗

C1

2339 Arthur Ave. (bet. Crescent Ave. & 186th St.)

Subway: Fordham Rd (Grand Concourse)   Lunch & dinner daily
Phone: 718-733-4455
Web: N/A
Prices: $$

With its old-fashioned tiled floors, bistro tables, and pressed-tin ceiling, this offshoot of the original Enzo's (located at 1998 Williamsbridge Rd.) might look like your average red-sauce joint, but Enzo's takes *nonna's* spaghetti-and-meatballs to a new level.

Yes, it's super informal and the menu is best shared with a gaggle of friends, but owner Enzo DiRende (whose father co-founded Arthur Ave.'s legendary Dominick's) kicks the standbys up a notch with his devotion to sourcing local vendors—a smart thing when your hood is teeming with killer Italian markets. The fresh, crusty baguettes are baked across the street; the delicious cured meats are sourced from a local pork store; and the vanilla-scented cheesecake is baked around the corner.

Estrellita Poblana III

Mexican ✗

C1

2328 Arthur Ave. (bet. Crescent Ave. & 186th St.)

Subway: Fordham Rd (Grand Concourse)   Lunch & dinner daily
Phone: 718-220-7641
Web: N/A
Prices: 🍝🍝

🕐 The smallest of its brethren, this adorable Arthur Avenue spot serves up the same mouthwatering Mexican as the other two, but in sweeter surroundings. The sparkling room is like a tiny, immaculate jewel box with powder blue walls, wood wainscoting, and purple hand-cut flowers atop each table.

At the heart of this local favorite is the food—homemade, fresh, honest, and satisfying. Though the friendly staff speaks little English, the menu is clear and the specials delicious. Start with the likes of *budin Azteca*, corn tortillas with layers of shredded chicken, cheese, and chile with a spicy-nutty mole sauce. Specials punctuating the menu may include their fantastic *pozole* of tender hominy and pork.

Take note: tamales are available on weekends only.

Jake's Steakhouse

Steakhouse 🍴🍴

A1

6031 Broadway (bet. Manhattan College Pkwy. & 251st St.)

Subway: Van Cortlandt Park-242 St   Lunch & dinner daily
Phone: 718-581-0182
Web: www.jakessteakhouse.com
Prices: $$$

Got baseball on the docket but beef on the brain? This multi-level, 126-seat Bronx steakhouse might be one of the best-kept secrets for Yankees fans headed north after the game. Located across from Van Cortland Park, just off the last stop of the 1 train, Jake's Steakhouse offers superior steaks for reasonable prices, in a warm, masculine interior.

Kick things off with the tender house crab cake, chockablock with fresh lump meat; and then move on to the star of the show—a hand-selected, wet-aged slab of premium T-bone, sliced off the bone and laced in natural beef jus. Any cut can be gussied up with melted gorgonzola, crunchy frizzled onions, and port wine sauce, but with steak this good, you might not need the bells and whistles.

Joe's Place

Puerto Rican 🍴

B3

1841 Westchester Ave. (at Thieriot Ave.)

Subway: Parkchester   Lunch & dinner daily
Phone: 718-918-2927
Web: www.joesplacebronx.com
Prices: $$

The Bronx loves its hometown heroes: J. Lo, Dave Valentin, Sonia Sotomayor, and Joe Torres. Who? If you have to ask, you're not from the Bronx. That's because Torres owns one of the top spots in the Bronx for delicious Puerto Rican/ Dominican food.

From children to Congressmen, they're all here, and Joe chats up them all. This place draws regulars who all come to catch up with the jovial proprietor and for the classic dishes. Begin with *sopa de pollo*, that lovely hot mess of chicken and noodles that tastes just like *papi* ordered. Move on to the *mofongo* with shredded pork and a mash of deep fried-green plaintains. *Pastelillo* is a flaky, crusty triumph and the *bacalao guisado*, a flavorful cod stew with pimiento-stuffed olives and capers, is a surefire hit.

Liebman's

A1

Deli 🍴

552 W. 235th St. (bet. Johnson & Oxford Aves.)

Subway: 231 St (& bus BX 7)   Lunch & dinner daily
Phone: 718-548-4534
Web: www.liebmansdeli.com
Prices: 💷

Some things never change (phew!) and Liebman's is definitely one of those things. This iconic kosher deli has been stuffing sandwiches and ladling bowls of matzoh ball soup for over 50 years. Residents wax poetic about the place, but it's nothing special, just a true-blue deli. Walk in and it's like a Smithsonian set for a Jewish deli —a neon sign in the front window, the grill roasting hot dogs, and meat slicing machines.

The food is classic and soulful as in stuffed veal breast, potato latkes, pastrami and tongue sandwiches on nutty rye bread paired with tangy pickles...and even that old standby—noodle pudding. Order to-go, or take a load off and grab a seat at one of the booths. Just don't forget about that bowl of "cure-all" matzoh ball soup.

900 Park

B2

Italian 🍴🍴

900 Morris Park Ave. (at Bronxdale Ave.)

Subway: Bronx Park East   Lunch & dinner daily
Phone: 718-892-3830
Web: www.900park.com
Prices: $$

Easy, breezy, beautiful...900 Park. It might be located in the "other" Little Italy (Morris Park), but this stylish spot goes well beyond just fresh *cavatelli*. More St. Barts than Calabria, 900 Park hums with a great vibe and packed crowd spanning everyone from children to their grandparents.

Save the skinny jeans—these family-style meals will stuff you to the gills. Still, overindulging never felt so good with delicious starters like seafood-topped pizza and mussels fra diavolo, but keep that fork at the ready. Wrap your noodle around this: the pasta is delish! Don't know Caroline or Michael? Who cares. The pasta dishes named for them are so good you'll be blowing *baci*. Got room? Tuck into the grilled veal chop before retiring near the fireplace.

NYY Steak

Steakhouse ✗✗✗

1 E. 161st St. (In Yankee Stadium)

Subway: 161 St - Yankee Stadium
Phone: 646-977-8325
Web: www.nyysteak.com
Prices: $$$$

Lunch Mon – Fri
Dinner nightly

Yes, it's tucked inside Yankee Stadium, but you won't find any ballpark franks here. Instead, this steakhouse hits it out of the park with its traditional décor mixed with serious Yankee pride (the autographed walls are Kodak worthy).

You don't need to don a pinstriped suit but definitely skip the Sox, since this place is Yankee heaven. Even the steaks are branded with the interlocking NY. There's certainly plenty of room—these tender, dry-aged, and perfectly seared steaks are monsters but oh-so-good. Sides like lobster mac and cheese and onion rings are home runs and the A+ wine list will have you yelling "beer not here!" A natural during games (when tickets are necessary), NYY Steak keeps the party going even when the boys of summer aren't home.

Pine Bar & Grill

Italian ✗✗

1634 Eastchester Rd. (at Blondell Ave.)

Subway: Westchester Sq - Tremont Av
Phone: 718-319-0900
Web: www.pinebargrill.com
Prices: $$

Lunch & dinner daily

This hot younger sister to the always-bustling F & J Pine Restaurant used to be called Pine Tavern #2, but is now a destination in its own right. This bar and grill is not a typical Italian-American red sauce joint, but a decidedly spiffier spot with dark wood, coffered ceilings, and slick black-and-white photographs.

Since the Bastones do Italian so well, indulge in their perfect *pizzette* decked with milky-white fresh mozzarella and hearty *lasagne* that layer rich ground meat ragù with sweet ricotta and freshly made sheets of egg pasta. No need to meander off point with Latin notes like empanadas or coconut shrimp. If Frankie's in the back, he'll whip up practically anything you want. You want the spaghetti pomodoro? You get the spaghetti pomodoro!

Roberto's

C1

Italian ✗✗

603 Crescent Ave. (at Hughes Ave.)

Subway: Fordham Rd (Grand Concourse)
Phone: 718-733 9503
Web: www.roberto089.com
Prices: $$

Lunch Mon – Fri
Dinner Mon – Sat

Widely recognized as one of the best in the Bronx, this Southern Italian institution still rules its roost over what may be the county's most Italian food-focused neighborhood. Outside, the gruff cityscape is anything but contrived or fussy; while inside, owner Robert Paciullo's keen attention to detail, focused staff, and that sigh-inducing fare set upon rustic farmhouse tables have people swearing that this is the best food in the borough.

Favorites may include fresh pastas that manage to be both elegant and tasty, as in the soft, plump pillows of *agnolotti*, or a traditional Neapolitan *pastiera*, topped with a perfect little lattice. The daily specials are highlights, but remember to ask about prices, which can climb steeply when no one is looking.

Santa Clarita

A3

Mexican ✗

237 Willis Ave. (bet. 138th & 139th Sts.)

Subway: 3 Av - 138 St
Phone: 718-792-9399
Web: N/A
Prices: ⊖⊖

Lunch & dinner daily

Make your way past the Honduran and Puerto Rican restaurants that flank Willis Avenue in the Bronx's Mott Haven section to find this little taste of Mexico. Its rather theatrical façade (replete with a rosary-draped statue of the restaurant's namesake) belies a charming, tidy interior with small wooden tables, visible kitchen, and jukebox with vibrant music stocked by Chef/owner Conrado Ramos (affectionately known as El Chile).

The menu features abundant, if not downright humongous, courses; each dish vies to outdo the last with tender meats and a range of flavors from delicate to fiery hot. Try starting with *huraches* filled with spicy, tender pork before indulging in the fragrant, rich chicken mole, redolent of cinnamon, clove, and almonds.

Taqueria Tlaxcalli

Mexican ✗

B2

2103 Starling Ave. (bet. Odell St. & Olmstead Ave.)

Subway: Castle Hill Av   Lunch & dinner daily
Phone: 347-851-3085
Web: N/A
Prices:

It's the little touches at Taqueria Tlaxcalli (the fuchsia ribbon tied around the cutlery, the tortilla basket topped with a colorful painted lid, the myriad sauces served for each and every taco ordered) that make a visit up to this new Parkchester taqueria worth the hike. That the food is complex, authentic, and lip-smacking good is just the icing on the cake.

Locals and day-trippers pour into the tiny, crayola-bright space to pop open a beer to the strum of contemporary Mexican music, and tuck into *sopas del dia* blooming with smoky chipotle and bobbing with plump *camarones*, tender yucca, and bright carrots; tender tacos stuffed with chewy tripe; or a *molcajete* filled with fragrant beef, sautéed onions, Mexican sausage, and grilled cactus.

Tra Di Noi

Italian ✗

C1

622 E. 187th St. (bet. Belmont & Hughes Aves.)

Subway: Fordham Rd (Grand Concourse)   Lunch & dinner Tue – Sun
Phone: 718-295-1784
Web: N/A
Prices: $$

Standing proudly amid time-honored Italian markets and delis, Tra Di Noi radiates the kind of nostalgic warmth found only in the most authentic places and is really *the* place to escape the crowds on Arthur Ave. Loyal locals flock here for Chef Marco Coletta's (he was also Sophia Loren's personal chef for a brief time) deliciously satisfying Italian-American dishes, while his wife showers all with big doses of Abbruzzi-style hospitality.

The lasagna and *pizzaiola* alone are reason enough to dine here, but food lovers far and wide return for mouthwatering pasta *carbonara*, pounded veal chop, or fresh swordfish Siciliana. The jovial atmosphere hums with bits of bilingual banter rising from the tables—further evidence of a true Italian-American experience.

zero otto nove 😊

Italian ✗✗

C1

2357 Arthur Ave. (at 186th St.)

Subway: Fordham Rd (Grand Concourse)   Lunch & dinner Tue – Sun
Phone: 718-220-1027
Web: www.roberto089.com
Prices: $$

Named for the area code back in Chef/owner Roberto Paciullo's Italian hometown of Salerno, zero otto nove feels like the real deal—with the affable Paciullo (who also runs the popular Roberto's around the corner) hustling around the rustic, brick-lined interior from table to oven and back again, shaking hands with customers and overseeing his kitchen with an eagle's eye.

The Salerno-style dishes, served homestyle big with an excellent wine list for matching, include mouthwatering pizzas (sporting unique toppings like fresh butternut squash, pancetta, and smoked mozzarella); delicious baked pastas; and oven-baked meats and fish. Don't miss the *mafalde con ceci*, perfectly cooked wide ribbons of pasta with chickpeas, tomato, and crispy pork belly.

Feast for under $25 at all restaurants with 🍝.

Peter L. Wrenn/MICHELIN

Brooklyn

Brooklyn

Forage Brooklyn's trellis of neighborhoods and discover an exciting dining destination characterized by mom and pop stores, ethnic eateries, and trendy hot spots. Credit the influx of enterprising young chefs–many trained at Manhattan's top restaurants–for ushering in a new level of dining; while sedate establishments maintain the borough's rugged authenticity.

The sustainable food movement has taken root as eco-conscious communities expand, and local artisans gain popularity for their high quality, handcrafted goods. Locavores, want to support your neighbor's garden? Check out the handy website (www. eatwellguide.org) which offers a citywide directory of "green" gastronomy—family farms, farmers' markets, et al.

WILLIAMSBURG

Williamsburg, traditionally an Italian, Hispanic, and Hasidic neighborhood, is now home to hipsters and artists. Here in "Billyburg," artistic food endeavors abound: Find upscale eateries in former factories; an artisan chocolate line handcrafted from bean to bar (**Mast Brothers Chocolate**); and an online cooking show dedicated to making meals and mates (*Feed Me: The Brooklyn Cooking Dating Show*). If interested in learning how to pickle, bake a great pie, or ferment kombucha, sign up for a cooking class at the **Brooklyn Kitchen**.

Over on Metropolitan Avenue, cute takeout shop **Saltie** offers a short yet delish list of tempting sandwiches and sweets, to be (perfectly) chased down by a cuppa' at **Blue Bottle Coffee Co.** on Berry Street. Famous **Fette Sau** (also settled in boho-chic Billyburg) stokes legions of fans with its dry-rubbed smoked meats and sides; while **Pie 'n' Thighs** has returned to comfort with heaps of down-home goodness. Inspired by the art of butchery, **Marlow & Daughters**, boasts locally-sourced meats, house-made sausages, and a delightful spectrum of artisanal dry goods.

If meat and cheese are your daily staples, a visit to the boutique pizzeria **Best Pizza** is a must. In keeping with the mien of the neighborhood, their space may appear a bit dishevelled (slate-topped tables are scatterd throughout the small room), yet diners come in droves for their two varieties—a sliced cheese pizza embellished with pickled vegetables, and a sliced white pizza with dabs of creamy mozzarella and rich ricotta.

DUMBO

Besides DUMBO's breathtaking views, stroll down cobblestoned Water Street and into **Jacques Torres** for a taste of chocolate heaven. Bordering Prospect Park, verdant Park Slope boasts blocks of tony trattorias and cafés, catering to an army of stroller-rolling parents, including **Four & Twenty Blackbirds**—a charming bakeshop churning out a deluge of incredible pies. The **Park Slope Food Coop** is a member operated and owned cooperative selling locally-farmed produce, fair trade products, grass-fed meat, free-range poultry, and more. It is the largest of its kind in the country, and membership is offered to anyone willing to pay a small fee and work a shift of less than three hours each month. Carroll Gardens, a historically Italian neighborhood, offers shoppers a bevy of family-owned butchers and bakeries along Court Street. **Da'Mico** is coffee-lovers' nirvana, while **Caputo's** has sandwiches worth the wait... and...don't forget to grab a ball of their amazing mozzarella. As Court Street blends into family-friendly Cobble Hill, find **Staubitz Market**, the friendliest butcher around. Continue the stroll to Atlantic Avenue with its Middle Eastern goodies at **Sahadi's** and **Damascus Bakery**.

RED HOOK

On Brooklyn's waterfront rests Red Hook, attracting action with its large spaces and low rents. Industrious residents are transforming the neighborhood's aged piers and warehouses into cool breweries, bakeries, and bistros. Royalty reigns with the Queen Mary 2 docked here. In the mood for a sweet treat? Head to **Baked**; or follow the signs to **Steve's Authentic Key Lime Pie**. The **Red Hook Farmer's Market** features produce grown on Red Hook Community Farm. Both ventures are operated by Added Value, a mentoring organization that teaches urban youth how to till, sow, and harvest. On weekends from May through October, the ever-popular trucks and tents that line the Red Hook Ball Fields cater to hordes of New Yorkers in the know with their selection of homemade Latin American and Caribbean street foods.

The Global Highway

Saunter to Fort Greene for a taste of African delicacies: Ethiopian at **Bati's** and South African at **Madiba**, where the sidewalk offers some great alfresco dining. Land at Sunset Park, and be tantalized by the vibrant Mexican food and flavors as you bite into a *pambazo* from **Tacos Xochimilco**. Rows of grocery stores carry authentic ingredients; butcher shops offer unique meats; while bakeries carry sweets 'n treats.

Slightly south, Mexico meets China, and this fusion is best expressed in rare culinary offerings. Sidewalks teem with vendors steaming fresh tofu and fishmongers selling offbeat eats —bullfrog anyone? Chinatown encroaches into Bay Ridge where the dim sum is delicious and Asian markets aplenty. In a flock of Kosher restaurants, **Di Fara** is an unorthodox pizzeria and has called Midwood home for decades.

And at the end of Brooklyn, Brighton Beach is best known for its borscht and blintzes. **Café Glechik** is an Ukranian *bijou* replete with faithful fare— beef tongue chased by *syrniki*? And there is no confusing the Chesapeake with Sheepshead Bay, but **Clemente's Maryland Crab House** will provide you with a similar seafood experience.

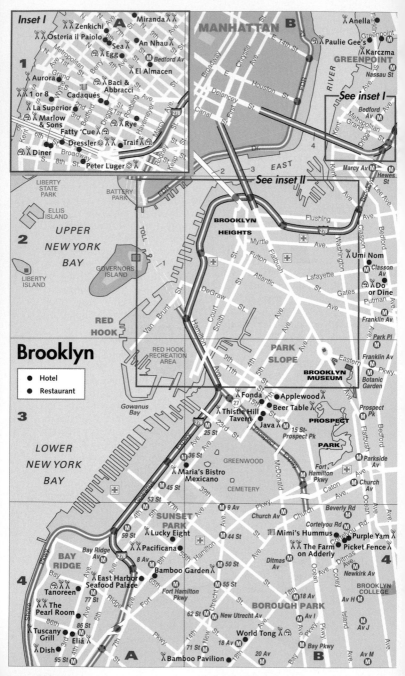

Inset I

Miranda

Zenkichi

Osteria il Paiolo

An Nhau

Sea

Egg

Bedford Av.

El Almacen

Aurora

Baci & Abbracci

1 or 8

Cadaqués

La Superior

Marlow & Sons

Rye

Fatty 'Cue

Dressler

Traif

Diner

Peter Luger

MANHATTAN

B

Anella

Paulie Gee's

Karczma

GREENPOINT

Nassau St.

RIVER

See inset I

Bedford Av.

Metropolitan

Grand

EAST

Marcy Av.

Hewes St.

Lee Av.

See inset II

Flushing Ave.

BROOKLYN HEIGHTS

Myrtle Ave.

Fulton St.

Atlantic Ave.

Lafayette Ave.

Gates Ave.

Washington

Umi Nom

Classon Av.

Do or Dine

Putman Ave.

Franklin Av.

Park Pl.

Franklin Av.

Eastern

BROOKLYN MUSEUM

Botanic Garden

Prospect Pk.

PARK SLOPE

Fonda

Applewood

Beer Table

Thistle Hill Tavern

Java

15 St-Prospect Pk

PROSPECT PARK

Parkside Av.

Church Av.

RED HOOK

RED HOOK RECREATION AREA

Brooklyn

● Hotel
● Restaurant

Gowanus Bay

2

LIBERTY STATE PARK

ELLIS ISLAND

UPPER NEW YORK BAY

LIBERTY ISLAND

GOVERNORS ISLAND

BATTERY PARK

TOLL

3

LOWER NEW YORK BAY

25 St

36 St

Maria's Bistro Mexicano

45 St

GREENWOOD CEMETERY

39th

9 Av

Church Av.

Beverly Rd

Cortelyou Rd

Mimi's Hummus

Purple Yam

The Farm on Adderly

Picket Fence

Ditmas Av

Newkirk Av

BROOKLYN COLLEGE

4

53 St

SUNSET PARK

59 St

Lucky Eight

44 St

Pacificana

8 Av

50 St

Bamboo Garden

55 St

Fort Hamilton Pkwy

BAY RIDGE

Bay Ridge Av.

East Harbor Seafood Palace

Tanoreen

77 St

The Pearl Room

86 St

Tuscany Grill

Elia

Dish

95 St

A

62 St

New Utrecht Av

BOROUGH PARK

World Tong

18 Av

71 St

Bamboo Pavilion

Av H

Av I

Av J

Bay Pkwy

20 Av

Av M

B

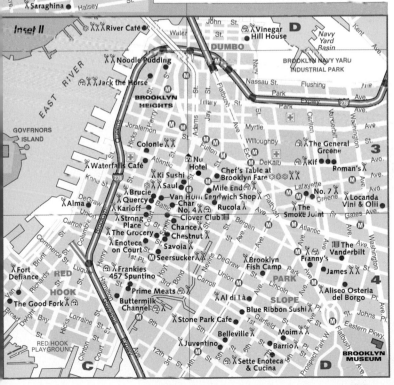

Al di Là

D4

248 Fifth Ave. (at Carroll St.)

Subway: Union St
Phone: 718-783-4565
Web: www.aldilatrattoria.com
Prices: $$

Lunch Wed – Mon
Dinner nightly

With its mouthwatering Northern Italian cuisine and a charming atmosphere, this neighborhood fixture, run by husband-and-wife team Emiliano Coppa and Anna Klinger, continues to be the first choice dining option for both nearby residents and foodies from afar. The high-ceilinged room boasts a faded chic, with church-pew seats and eccentric touches, such as coffee pots hanging from the wall and a blown glass chandelier.

Menu offerings may include perfectly seasonal salads, homemade ravioli filled with red beets and ricotta, or braised rabbit with black olives and polenta. Meals are not only delicious, but priced at what can clearly be considered a great deal. Al di Là also serves a lunch menu, which is pared down from the evening selections.

Aliseo Osteria del Borgo

D4

665 Vanderbilt Ave. (bet. Park & Prospect Pls.)

Subway: 7 Av (Flatbush Ave.)
Phone: 718-783-3400
Web: N/A
Prices: $$

Dinner Tue – Sun

Just a few blocks north of Prospect Park, this tiny sliver of a restaurant pokes a delightful hole in the fabric of low-end joints that line the neighborhood. The quaint interior of Aliseo Osteria del Borgo is decidedly romantic, from the rustic tables to the porcelain lights to the cute garden out back. Those who sidle up to the counter with a minute to spare can be charmed by the owner and stories about his labor of love. Mercifully, the food is just as lovely, with a scrumptious lineup of Italian specialties that might include the savory red beet flan, *sformatino*, with a salty-sweet Parmigiano sauce; or *agnello in brodo*—lamb that is so tender it verges on creamy, in a savory broth with winter root vegetables alongside thick, chewy pasta.

Alma

Mexican ✗

C3

187 Columbia St. (at Degraw St.)

Subway: Carroll St
Phone: 718-643-5400
Web: www.almarestaurant.com
Prices: $$

Lunch Sat – Sun
Dinner nightly

It might be a hassle to get to Alma via public transportation, but this contemporary Mexican charmer is well worth the hike to the water side of Brooklyn, where it sits overlooking the ship yards, right around the point where the neighborhoods of Carroll Gardens and Red Hook connect.

Duck into the Degraw St. entrance (the Columbia St. entrance takes you through the rollicking bar), and head up the stairs. There, you can choose from a whimsically-appointed dining room or an enormous rooftop dining area (that gets covered in winter) offering up gorgeous spreads of lower Manhattan. Don't miss the guacamole, chockablock with fresh avocado; or the fragrantly spiced Anaheim rellenos, stuffed with cheese, butternut squash, and cactus paddles.

Anella

Contemporary ✗

B1

222 Franklin St. (bet. Green & Huron Sts.)

Subway: Greenpoint Av
Phone: 718-389-8100
Web: www.anellabrooklyn.com
Prices: $$

Lunch Sat – Sun
Dinner Tue – Sun

Tucked away in Greenpoint, just a few blocks from the East River, Anella hosts diners in a slender, rough and tumble space that is wood-clad and enclosed by battered walls bearing nicks and scrapes. The back patio is pleasant and the welcoming bar, constructed out of a reclaimed work bench from the Steinway & Sons piano factory, is forever humming. While the kitchen has seen some transition since this establishment's opening in 2009, the recent team has sent out ambitious creations like an appetizer special of "panzanella" with *chicharrón* brilliantly substituting for bread, tossed with smoked cherry tomatoes and decadent romesco; and a bronzed boneless pork chop paired with barley pilaf, baby turnips, candied hazelnuts, and salted caramel sauce.

An Nhau

A1

172 Bedford Ave. (bet. N. 7th & N. 8th Sts.)

Subway: Bedford Av
Phone: 718-384-0001
Web: N/A
Prices: 🍴🍴

Lunch & dinner daily

Set along busy Bedford Avenue, this everyday Vietnamese restaurant is located alongside sister spot Banh Mi, a takeout shop specializing in the famed namesake sandwich. An Nhau offers table service in a room outfitted by wooden shutters, mirrors, and a wall decked with a big, delightful mural of a Vietnamese street scene.

Begin the affair with rolls and salads and make your way through the menu's home-style cooking featuring enjoyably aromatic preparations as well as myriad variations of the classic *pho*. Other delectable entrées include *bun*—lemongrass, garlic, and mint scented meats served over cool rice vermicelli; and pork belly braised in a sweet and savory coconut water-based broth, served with a hard boiled egg and pickled mustard greens.

Applewood

B3

501 11th St. (bet. Seventh & Eighth Aves.)

Subway: 7 Av (9th St.)
Phone: 718-788-1810
Web: www.applewoodny.com
Prices: $$

Lunch Sat – Sun
Dinner Tue – Sat

Skillfully prepared cuisine and a dainty setting reflect the seriousness of Applewood's owners David and Laura Shea. The pair is committed to promoting the work of organic and local farmers in a changing menu of small plates and entrées dedicated to reflecting the seasons.

The spare yet comfortable dining room, set in a century-old townhouse on a tree-lined street, is furnished with honey-toned wood tables and spindle-back chairs. When in use, a working fireplace warms the light-colored room, accented by the work of local artists.

Thick slices of fresh bread set the tone for an enjoyable meal of wild fish and hormone-free meats in delectable offerings such as lobster risotto with mascarpone and chili oil, or pan-seared bass with tomatillo jam.

Aurora

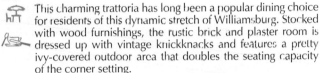

Italian ✗

A1

70 Grand St. (at Wythe Ave.)

Subway: Bedford Av
Phone: 718-388-5100
Web: www.auroraristorante.com
Prices: 💰💰

Lunch & dinner daily

This charming trattoria has long been a popular dining choice for residents of this dynamic stretch of Williamsburg. Stocked with wood furnishings, the rustic brick and plaster room is dressed up with vintage knickknacks and features a pretty ivy-covered outdoor area that doubles the seating capacity of the corner setting.

Aurora's enjoyable Italian cuisine speaks to the power of simplicity with minimally dressed market greens, expertly prepared pastas, and roasted meats. One can't go wrong with a meal of plump house-made sausage with lightly sautéed broccoli rabe and pickled Calabrian pepper; silky agnolotti stuffed with ricotta, spring peas, and fresh mint; or *affogato* with chocolate-crumb-coated vanilla gelato, all offered at impressive value.

Baci & Abbracci 😊

Italian ✗

A1

204 Grand St. (bet. Bedford & Driggs Sts.)

Subway: Bedford Av
Phone: 718-599-6599
Web: www.baciny.com
Prices: $$

Lunch Sat – Sun
Dinner nightly

This upbeat Williamsburg eatery features Italian cuisine with a wholehearted emphasis on pizza. With more than twenty permutations of pies baked in their wood-burning oven from Naples, these smoky-chewy crusts may be the foundation for sauce and freshly made mozzarella, or even *focaccia tartufata*—two thin layers filled with robiola cheese and topped with truffle oil. Beyond this, the adept kitchen also boasts homemade bread, enjoyable pastas, and an impressive short-list of *secondi* like juicy lamb chops with a crisp potato-rosemary crust.

The intimate space sports a contemporary design framed by a concrete floor, sleek furnishings, and glazed-tile accents. A charming little patch of backyard makes an especially popular setting for weekend brunch.

Brooklyn

415

Bamboo Garden

Chinese ✗

6409 Eighth Ave. (at 64th St.)

Subway: 8 Av
Phone: 718-238-1122
Web: N/A
Prices: 🌑🌑

Lunch & dinner daily

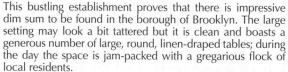

This bustling establishment proves that there is impressive dim sum to be found in the borough of Brooklyn. The large setting may look a bit tattered but it is clean and boasts a generous number of large, round, linen-draped tables; during the day the space is jam-packed with a gregarious flock of local residents.

The tables are attended to by Cantonese-speaking ladies, cheerfully dressed in fuchsia blouses and red vests, pushing cart after cart of steaming treats through the hungry hordes. Resist the urge to stock your table all at once; survey the delicacies and pace yourself for a spectrum of fresh, delish dumplings, buns, and pastries. The feast also includes some refreshingly unique preparations that steer away from the standard dim sum lineup.

Bamboo Pavilion

Chinese ✗

6920 Eighteenth Ave. (bet. Bay Ridge Ave. & 70th St.)

Subway: 18 Av
Phone: 718-236-8088
Web: N/A
Prices: $$

Lunch & dinner Mon – Sat

We may never know how this hot pot joint found its way onto Bensonhurst's predominantly Sicilian 18th Avenue (think *Saturday Night Fever*), alongside enough authentic Sichuan spots to have critics calling it the city's newest Chinatown. Here Bamboo Pavilion stands tall and unafraid to deliver you to that fiery, volcanic-like Sichuan dimension that actually makes you wish for more.

The space itself is rather nondescript, with bamboo-etched wallpaper, bright lights, big tables, and few of the comforts that promote lingering. Meals here are about those fragrant pots of bubbling broth and trays of soft noodles, succulent meats, leafy vegetables, and sauces–like the brew of chili oil, Sichuan peppers, and pink peppercorns–that bring new levels to each bite.

Barrio

D4

Mexican ✗

210 Seventh Ave. (at 3rd St.)

Subway: 7 Av (9th St.)
Phone: 718-965-4000
Web: www.barriofoods.com
Prices: $$

Lunch Thu – Sun
Dinner nightly

This cozy, fun neighborhood Mexican spot doubles its capacity in warmer weather with a cheery, covered outdoor dining space decorated with strings of colored lights overhead—a touch that makes it all the more a family favorite. The beautiful interior displays a glazed ceramic tile floor with pink and orange embellishments.

Even beyond this setting is the impressive cooking that pleases taste buds both young and old. The excellent tortilla chips accompanied by red or green salsa are a worthy introduction to an enjoyable meal here. Start with a melting crock of *queso fundido* or try the *platos del dia* which change with every passing day—think Taco Madness Monday, Kids Eat Free Tuesday, Crazy Quesadilla Wednesday; or Casa de Enchilada Thursday.

Beer Table

B3

Gastropub ✗

427 B Seventh Ave. (bet. 14th & 15th Sts.)

Subway: 7 Av (9th St.)
Phone: 718-965-1196
Web: www.beertable.com
Prices: ⊜⊜

Lunch Sun
Dinner nightly

This cozy neighborhood gastropub offers a simple yet creative menu of snacks and mains while remaining true to its name and focus with a rotating selection of draft beers. The attentive staff is at the ready with sage advice about the extensive and wisely organized beer list (lighter at the top, darker towards the bottom). The charming space is dominated by three communal tables and shelves of house-made pickles.

The menu is heavy on beer-friendly nibbles designed to pair nicely with rare brews from a spicy Belgian Christmas ale to the hoppy pale ales. The daily prix-fixe is simple but tasty with dishes like white bean purée laced with chili oil; a warmly spiced duck and beef meatloaf; or a creamy pudding full of toasty butterscotch flavors.

Belleville

D4

330 5th St. (at Fifth Ave.)

Subway: 4 Av - 9 St
Phone: 718-832-9777
Web: www.bellevillebistro.com
Prices: 💷

Lunch Sat – Sun
Dinner nightly

With windows that fly open to sidewalk seating along Brooklyn's bustling Fifth Avenue; a gaggle of closely nuzzled tables with mismatched wooden chairs; and vintage mirrored walls, Belleville could easily be plucked straight off the streets of the Parisian neighborhood it's named after. Luckily for us, it's right here in Park Slope—serving up delicious bistro staples like duck confit and steak frites to neighborhood families.

Kick things off with a fresh beet salad, drizzled with tart vinaigrette and topped with crumbles of soft, creamy goat cheese; and then move on to a spot-on coq au vin with plump lardons and tender sautéed mushrooms, then plated with a fluffy pile of mashed potatoes; or creamy lemon custard served in a dainty espresso cup.

Blue Ribbon Sushi

D4

278 Fifth Ave. (bet. 1st St. & Garfield Pl.)

Subway: Union St
Phone: 718-840-0408
Web: www.blueribbonrestaurants.com
Prices: $$

Dinner nightly

Consistent excellence in food and service has made this Brooklyn location of the Bromberg brother's notable restaurant lineup worthy of bearing the Blue Ribbon name. Slats of warmly polished wood and a cool grey palette lend a chic finish to this popular spot—filled with Park Slope parents towing along the next generation of sushi connoisseurs.

Classified according to ocean of origin (Atlantic or Pacific), the sushi here is delightful and is shored up by a creative menu of maki, such as the Blue Ribbon roll which lavishly combines lobster, caviar, and shiso. The lengthy list of appetizers may include king crab *sunomono* or *san diakon* (three radish salad).

Complement meals with a selection from the well-chosen sake list or a Japanese boutique beer.

Brooklyn Fish Camp

Seafood ✗

D4

162 Fifth Ave. (bet. De Graw & Douglass Sts.)

Subway: Union St
Phone: 718-783-3264
Web: www.brooklynfishcamp.com
Prices: $$

Lunch & dinner Mon – Sat

Inspired by the simplicity of rural Southern fish shacks, the menu at this Brooklyn offshoot of Mary's Fish Camp displays a reverence for seriously prepared seafood.

The welcoming bar upfront leads to a simple dining room furnished with warm-hued wood tables, topped with brown paper mats and bags of oyster crackers. Out back, picnic tables and folding chairs make a fine setting for a summertime meal, accompanied by movies shown on a whitewashed wall.

The excellent lobster roll, oyster Po' boy, and shrimp tacos are all fun favorites; but do not overlook more inspired entrées like whole fish served grilled or fried. Home-style desserts, like sundaes topped in house-made fudge, are fantastic, so be sure to check the wall-mounted blackboard.

Brooklyn Star

American ✗✗

C1

593 Lorimer St. (at Conselyea St.)

Subway: Lorimer St - Metropolitan Av
Phone: 718-599-9899
Web: www.thebrooklynstar.com
Prices: $$

Lunch Sat – Sun
Dinner nightly

Hooray for Brooklyn Star 2.0. The demise of the original was gut-wrenching—this hand-built restaurant was razed by a fire in 2010. But, perhaps a blessing in disguise? Because a just as alluring incarnation has sprouted nearby. The fresh setting heralds diners with a bar and dining room enlivened with a brick red terrazzo floor, eggshell walls, and chunky blonde wood tables topped with hot sauce, pepper vinegar, and wild flowers.

Chef Joaquin Baca's love letter to old-fashioned, down home specialties may reveal a green bean casserole coalesced by mushroom béchamel and showered with buttery crumbs and fried shallots; a hunk of a sandwich—warm bacon-wrapped meatloaf stuffed between thick slices of Pullman bread; and excellent buttermilk biscuits.

Brucie

C3

234 Court St. (bet. Baltic & Kane Sts.)

Subway: Bergen St (Smith St.)   Lunch & dinner Tue – Sat
Phone: 347-987-4961
Web: www.brucienyc.com
Prices: $$

With its nostalgia-hued vibe, Brucie is a welcome addition to the neighborhood. Housed in a former sushi den, the space now sports a considerably rustic scene devised by communal seating, a copper dining counter, and a corner designated for pasta prep.

The menu's old-world inspiration bears a new-world sensibility in its range of Italian specialties that reflect a product-driven commitment. "Smalls" feature olive oil-packed tuna crostini fashioned from slices of Caputo bakery bread, aïoli, and orange *fritti*. "Biggies" include a hearty hunk of lasagna—like a seasonal layering of ground lamb, butternut squash, and Parmesan-seasoned béchamel.

The Cobble Hill spot also functions as a market, proffering an assortment of goodies to take home.

Buttermilk Channel ☺

C4

524 Court St. (at Huntington St.)

Subway: Smith - 9 Sts.   Lunch Sat – Sun
Phone: 718-852-8490   Dinner nightly
Web: www.buttermilkchannelnyc.com
Prices: $$

Glossy, dark paint and large windows emanating a warm glow give this establishment an inviting, turn-of-the-century maritime feel. This befits its name, which references the (once crossable) strait separating Brooklyn from Governor's Island. The butter-yellow dining room attracts a lively and diverse crowd; regardless of one's tastes, the menu is bound to please, thanks to this very serious team of experienced professionals.

The menu begins with snacks like handmade mozzarella with basil and warm anchovy sauce, house-made charcuterie, and farmstead cheeses—perfect accompaniments to a local brew. The full offering of seasonal comfort food complements a separate (equally impressive) menu devoted to vegetarians. Mondays offer three courses for $25.

Cadaqués

Spanish

A1

188 Grand St. (bet. Bedford & Driggs Aves.)

Subway: Bedford Av
Phone: 718-218-7776
Web: www.cadaquesny.com
Prices: $$

Dinner nightly

Named for the Costa Brava town where legendary Spanish artists, including Dalí, Picasso, and Miró sojourned, this Williamsburg newcomer exhibits talent and creativity in its array of tapas that are alluded to as modern Catalan. The copious selection snares hungry eyes and pleases sharp palates with a tasty show of skill: plancha griddled *pan con tomate* rubbed with garlic and topped with freshly grated tomato; decadently thick, ivory white *sopa de almendras* drizzled with olive oil and balsamic vinegar; fried artichokes capped by fennel pollen aïoli; and delightfully tender octopus dressed with a pool of ink and crunchy, cool avocado fritters. The slender room is chic; done up with a galvanized metal ceiling (hung with linen pendants) and reclaimed wood.

Chance

Asian

C4

223 Smith St. (bet. Baltic & Butler Sts.)

Subway: Bergen St (Smith St.)
Phone: 718-242-1515
Web: www.chanceculsine.com
Prices:

Lunch & dinner daily

Chance continues to beautifully present its luscious, unique selection of Pan-Asian delights. The menu celebrates its varied influences in dishes ranging from spicy tuna rolls to pad Thai, and even includes an occasional nod to France, as evidenced in the foie gras appetizer or frozen crème brûlée for dessert. Inside, ivory leather seating and dark glossy tables give the space a modern look, and attractive red lanterns suspended over the bar allude to the Asian theme.

The dim sum assortment makes a fine starting point, followed by tasty pan-Asian specialties like orange crispy beef and spicy miso salmon. Other very good options include a short list of noodle and rice dishes. While the daily menus are reasonably priced, quality is not sacrificed.

Char No. 4

Gastropub ✗

196 Smith St. (bet. Baltic & Warren Sts.)

Subway: Bergen St (Smith St.)
Phone: 718-643-2106
Web: www.charno4.com
Prices: $$

Lunch Fri – Sun
Dinner nightly

More shrine than pub, this Smith Street watering hole offers a massive listing of whiskey, half of which are devoted to bourbon—a must for all "brown" fans. All are available in one or two ounce pours, allowing a civilized examination of the elixir's varied styles. The comfy bar radiates warmth with its wall of amber-filled bottles; and the slender dining room in the back, also dressed in brown, fits the mien.

The Southern-flecked menu unveils such decadent delights as a house-smoked brisket sandwich matched with *borracho* beans, or shrimp and grits redolent of sweet, spicy, and charred flavors. These pair stunningly with the stack of smoky bourbons. Close with a lick of house-made butter pecan ice cream, drizzled with a shot of bourbon, of course.

Chestnut

Contemporary ✗

271 Smith St. (bet. De Graw & Sackett Sts.)

Subway: Carroll St
Phone: 718-243-0049
Web: www.chestnutonsmith.com
Prices: $$

Lunch Sun
Dinner Tue – Sun

This Carroll Gardens eatery is the kind of place every neighborhood should have. Like its moniker, the philosophy here is comforting and seasonal. Chestnut's farm-reared chef spends time sourcing the best ingredients and then lets them shine in a menu reminding diners that the best supermarket is nature itself. The simple décor has just the right amount of personality, and the laid-back staff delivers genuinely warm service, starting your meal with fresh-baked bread and homemade pickles.

Come on Tuesday or Wednesday nights to take advantage of the three-course, prix-fixe value menus. Or, order à la carte any night to dine on skillfully-prepared items that may include salt cod *brandade*, roasted chicken breast with sausage filling, or chocolate *budino*.

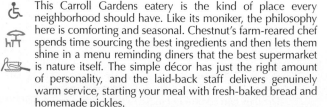

Chef's Table at Brooklyn Fare ✿✿✿

D3

200 Schermerhorn St. (bet. Bond & Hoyt Sts.)

Subway: Hoyt-Schermerhorn   Dinner Tue – Sat
Phone: 718-243-0050
Web: www.brooklynfare.com
Prices: $$$$

Douglas Kim

At this ambitious Chef's Table, copper pots shine more brightly, spotlights hit each plate at just the right angle, and devout foodies are quieting their delirium of joy at having scored a reservation—everyone and everything here is living up to the honor of adorning this extraordinary restaurant.

Despite its fame and amazing urban elegance, the understated entrance to this temple is found halfway down the block from the attached gourmet shop. It may be great theater and a most gorgeous incarnation, but dining here means sitting within a working, breathing kitchen. Of course, the brilliant and bespectacled Chef Cesar Ramirez steals this show that verges on religion. Your faith in Him is essential.

A brief printed overview is offered, but the intricacies of each dish (and there will be many) are yours to unveil as you are guided by the chef. A delicate *raviolo* is a play between earthy mushrooms and sweet ricotta. Buttery fluke is perfectly cut and served with pickled onion, daikon, lemon vinaigrette, and warm olive oil. Uni with truffle-oil gelée and brioche expresses the regret that we have but three stars to give. Though the chef is hopeful for a swift change, this table is BYO.

Clover Club

American

C4

210 Smith St. (bet. Baltic & Butler Sts.)

Subway: Bergen St (Smith St.)
Phone: 718-855-7939
Web: www.cloverclubny.com
Prices: $$

Lunch Tue – Sun
Dinner nightly

A former shoe store is now an atmospheric Smith Street rest stop that fashions a spot-on vintage vibe with mosaic tiled floors, glove-soft leather banquettes, and pressed-tin ceilings dangling etched-glass pendants that glow as warmly as single malt. The glossy mahogany bar (furnished with leather-upholstered bar stools) is overseen by a natty bartender artfully shaking and pouring a stellar selection of libations like the namesake Clover Club—a mixture of gin, dry vermouth, lemon, and raspberry syrup.

An excellent menu of savory bites is a perfect counterpoint to such liquid indulgences, with herb-marinated hanger steak over toasted baguette with horseradish cream, duck fat-fried potato crisps, oysters on the half-shell, or an American caviar service.

Colonie

Contemporary

C3

127 Atlantic Ave. (bet. Clinton & Henry Sts.)

Subway: Borough Hall
Phone: 718-855-7500
Web: www.colonienyc.com
Prices: $$$

Lunch Sat – Sun
Dinner nightly

Something special is happening on Atlantic Ave.—just west of Smith Street to be specific. Among the flurry of Middle Eastern fare, tavern grub, and faux Mexican is this shining jewel of a spot, serving up mouthwatering goodies to the fine folks of Brooklyn Heights. Inside, flickering candles, exposed brick, distressed wooded ceilings, and a verdant wall of greenery give the space a romantic feel; while the outstanding service team keeps the motor running.

Get to it with a delightful octopus salad of fennel, mizuna, apple, and pickled onions; seared artichokes served over blood orange hollandaise; and an earthy rabbit lasagna deliciously baked and sharply sprinkled with Parmesan. For a luxurious treat, try the fresh doughnuts with salty caramel custard.

Diner 😃

A1

American 🍴

85 Broadway (at Berry St.)

Subway: Marcy Av   Lunch & dinner daily
Phone: 718-486-3077
Web: www.dinernyc.com
Prices: **$$**

Do not let Diner's impossibly hip crowd and rather ramshackle setting deter you. Beneath all that plaid are ordinary folk who appreciate the renovated 1920s Kulman Diner setting and an impressively unfussy kitchen that knows how to make a perfect block of head cheese. Pioneering restaurateurs and publishers of *Diner Journal*, Mark Firth and Andrew Tarlow have run this establishment with heart and personality since 1998.

The kitchen uses spot-on technique in preparing specials that highlight seasonality, such as a Portuguese-inspired seafood stew. This neat pile of plump, tender mussels, sweet clams, cubes of firm fish, and thin slices of linguiça is served atop an olive oil-brushed crouton so a drop of brilliant sauce won't go to waste.

Dish

A4

Japanese 🍴

9208 3rd Ave. (bet. 92nd & 93rd Sts.)

Subway: Bay Ridge - 95 St   Dinner Tue – Sun
Phone: 718-238-7323
Web: www.dishbayridge.com
Prices: **$$**

Here in Bay Ridge, people just like this place. Attractive, with a classically minimalist Japanese design, Dish is easy to love. It turns out that bamboo grows in Brooklyn; stalks decorate one side of the dining room.

At first glance, the menu looks standard Japanese, with starters like negimaki and yakitori, but there are a few departures, such as barbecue scallop skewers with bacon. Starters like hot and spicy seafood soup showcase their very fine tuna, jumbo shrimp, and mackerel in a clear, piquant broth. Sushi features the usual suspects and rolls are creative, if at times slightly too much so. They also fire up the stove to prepare the likes of lobster teriyaki, Chilean sea bass with miso sauce, and filet mignon with red wine sauce.

Do or Dine 🐶

B2

Contemporary ✗

1108 Bedford Ave. (bet. Lexington Ave. & Quincy St.)

Subway: Bedford - Nostrand Avs   Dinner nightly
Phone: 718-684-2290
Web: N/A
Prices: $$

It's like a mafia of Michelin-starred runaways at Do or Dine, where honchos from The Modern and Daniel have decamped and are slumming it, Bed-Stuy style. Finding this place will try the patience of a saint, but whoa Nelly, channel your best Mother Teresa because it's definitely do or die.

Bring your bevs, but that's it, because this tiny kitchen cranks out mind-blowing food. The heart attack, a deep-fried jalapeño popper stuffed with salmon and chevre is a culinary coronary. You'll never dunk again after the foie gras doughnut and the artichoke escabeche is so good you'll be licking your lips; but really, just ask for some extra bread. Sake-steamed mussels, roasted lamb basted with cumin-lime dressing—it's another instance of Brooklyn at its best.

DuMont

C1

American ✗

432 Union Ave. (bet. Devoe St. & Metropolitan Ave.)

Subway: Lorimer St - Metropolitan Av   Lunch & dinner daily
Phone: 718-486-7717
Web: www.dumontrestaurant.com
Prices: $$

DuMont epitomizes its neighborhood's relaxed, edgy, and creative vibe. The multi-room space is warm and comfortably worn, furnished with dark wood tables topped with brown paper, vintage tile floor, and cool leather seating handmade by the owner. There is also a lovely backyard with elevated seating called "the treehouse."

Executive Chef Polo Dobkin fuels local crowds of Billyburg hipsters who clamor for his near-addictive comfort food menu. Favorites may include crispy artichokes with creamy garlic dressing; N.Y. strip steak with Bordelaise sauce; and of course, the DuMac and cheese (with *radiatore* pasta, richly coated in béchamel, under a molten blend of cheeses). Brunch keeps weekends groovy.

For a quick burger and a beer, try nearby DuMont Burger.

Dressler ✿

A1

American 🍴

149 Broadway (bet. Bedford & Driggs Aves.)

Subway: Marcy Av
Phone: 718-384-6343
Web: www.dresslernyc.com
Prices: $$

Lunch Sun
Dinner nightly

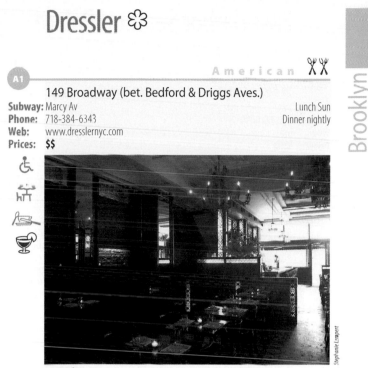

Stephanie Limpert

Dressler is a study in contrasts, yet remains a lovely experience from start to finish. The décor at this haute Williamsburg restaurant is at once masculine and simple with dark wood furnishings, brick walls, and low lights; yet feminine and ornate, amid elaborate chandeliers, floral etchings, and mosaic tiled floors.

Dishes may sound rustic and homey, yet they are prepared with the skill and superb ingredients of an exceptional kitchen. Inspired appetizers include the likes of *raviolini* made with velvety kabocha squash purée and ricotta cheese filling tender sheets of pasta, presented in a creamy, rich broth with Parmesan shavings, fried sage leaves, and butter-sautéed black trumpet mushrooms. The Hudson Valley chicken is beautifully roasted, moist and juicy with a crispy, golden-brown skin, over a mélange of roasted hen of the woods mushrooms, caramelized bacon lardons, pearl onions, and homemade dumplings.

Tantalizing desserts will surely leave you wanting more. Try the maple panna cotta, creamy and light with the woodsy flavor of maple and floral infusion of vanilla bean, sprinkled with candied pecans and coconut cream.

The wine and cocktail lists are focused and interesting.

427

East Harbor Seafood Palace

A4

Chinese ✗

714-726 65th St. (bet. Seventh & Eighth Aves.)

Subway: 8 Av

Lunch & dinner daily

Phone: 718-765-0098

Web: N/A

Prices: 🍴

East Harbor Seafood Palace is a haven for authentic dim sum devotees. Favored by Chinese locals, this behemoth presides over a commercial area that chronically rumbles with forklifts and foot-traffic—though closer scrutiny reveals tidy row houses and supermarkets. These residents are among the first to know that Brooklyn's N and D lines are coming to rival the foodie thrills found along the 7 through Queens.

Inside the lofty room flanked by fish tanks, the kindly staff circulates with steaming carts offering the likes of *cha siu bao* (barbecue pork buns); *cha siu soh* (barbecue pork puff pastry); and *zha liang* (fried cruller wrapped with *cheung fun* skin). Chef's specials like pan-fried *mei fun* with frogs legs and celery will leave you smitten.

Egg

A1

American ✗

135 N. 5th St. (bet. Bedford Ave. & Berry St.)

Subway: Bedford Av

Lunch daily

Phone: 718-302-5151

Dinner Thu – Sun

Web: www.pigandegg.com

Prices: 🍴

Boasting that famously laid-back Brooklyn personality, old-fashioned Southern soul, and a daily breakfast that lasts until 6:00 P.M., Egg's slender dining room seems to serve as a remote office for Williamsburg's work-from-home set. We may never know how many bestsellers were conceived here, while downing cups of sustainably-grown coffee or doodling with crayons provided on the paper-topped tables. On weekends, the wait for a table can be lengthy—jot your name on the flipchart stationed outside and be patient.

Southern-accented preparations begin with fresh-baked buttermilk biscuits (perhaps the city's best), homemade granola served with local yogurt, and griddle fare. Lunch and dinner hour bring the sinful plates of fried chicken and pulled pork.

El Almacen

Argentinian 🍴

557 Driggs Ave. (bet. N. 6th & N. 7th Sts.)

Subway: Bedford Av
Phone: /18-218-7284
Web: www.elalmacennyc.com
Prices: $$

Lunch Sat – Sun
Dinner nightly

This Argentinian grill is a carnivore's delight with its menu of meats prepared *de la parilla*: grass-fed cuts of beef, corn-fed pork, homemade chorizo, and *morcilla* (blood sausage). Tender empanadas, vibrant ceviches, and entrées like *Milanesa de pollo* or pappardelle with coffee-braised oxtail ragù are among the hearty offerings best followed by *dulce de leche* in one of its several guises.

El Almacen, which means general store in Spanish, boasts a dark and rustic interior and atmospheric setting replete with creaking wood furnishings, shelves filled with bric-a-brac, and cast iron skillets mounted on a brick wall. The inviting bar is amply stocked with bottles of wine and set against a backdrop of creamy white tile warmed by the candlelit room.

Eliá

Greek 🍴

8611 Third Ave. (bet. 86th & 87th Sts.)

Subway: 86 St
Phone: 718-748-9891
Web: www.eliarestaurant.com
Prices: $$

Dinner Tue – Sun

Oh my, Mykonos? Nope, it's Bay Ridge, but Eliá's weathered plank floors and whitewashed walls decorated with wooden shutters will have you convinced otherwise. And that's before you have even seen the charming backyard patio.

This sure isn't a weak Greek with plenty of top-of-mind classics (grilled shrimp, octopus) and a few newbies (lobster dumplings with white chocolate brown butter sauce) thrown in for good measure. Appetizers, like the tender pork ribs marinated in ouzo and roasted with Greek spices, are large enough to count as entrées, but with so many tempting choices, don't stop there. Definitely go for the pan-seared sheep's cheese *saganaki*, doused with a shot of ouzo for (ta-da!) flaming fun. Who doesn't love dinner and a show?

El Mio Cid

C2

Spanish 🍴

50 Starr St. (at Wilson Ave.)

Subway: Jefferson St
Phone: 718-628-8300
Web: www.elmiocidrestaurant.com
Prices: $$

Lunch & dinner daily

Right on a lovely corner in the middle of Bushwick, El Mio Cid is a pleasant surprise. This Spanish charmer dresses up the block with its polished presence—exposed brick walls covered with artist-painted murals of Spanish landscapes. The bar's wraparound seating is definitely a come-and-see-me magnet. Yes, those glass containers filled with addictive sangria blends are definitely calling your name.

Cold and hot tapas run the gamut from tender artichoke hearts and crispy sweetbreads, while stuffed chicken with spinach and cheese is delicious. *Paella Valenciana* is brimming with seafood like mussels, squid, clams, and monkfish as well as a few unusual suspects like lobster and shelled peas thrown in for good measure. Is this Bushwick or Barcelona?

Enoteca on Court

C4

Italian 🍴

347 Court St. (bet. President & Union Sts.)

Subway: Carroll St
Phone: 718-243-1000
Web: www.enotecaoncourt.com
Prices: 🐌🐌

Lunch & dinner daily

From the folks who run the old-school Marco Polo Ristorante, located just next door, comes this fresh-hearted take on *la cucina Italiana*. The wine bar-inspired room dishes out wood and brick details and serves as a cozy spot in which to enjoy a long line of snacks that include Italian cheeses, panini, and *marinati* (olives, roasted peppers, or eggplant).

The wood-burning oven is used to prepare the majority of offerings that include baked pastas; *carciofo ripieno* (stuffed artichokes); and an array of pizzas topped with a regionally influenced composition of ingredients. The *spiedini* are worthy of consideration—meaty skewers filled with the likes of house-made sausage, onions, and peppers, finished with red wine reduction and roasted new potatoes.

Fanny

Mediterranean 🍴

C1

425 Graham Ave. (bet. Frost & Withers Sts.)

Subway: Graham Av	Lunch & dinner daily
Phone: 718-389-2060	
Web: www.fannyfood.com	
Prices: $$	

Building the perfect neighborhood bistro is a delicate thing. It should be intimate and cozy, but lively when the mood fits; it should traffic in the kind of delicious, straightforward fare regulars won't tire of easily; and the owners ought to be folks you'd want to share a drink with.

Fanny, a romantic, low-lit charmer tucked into East Williamsburg's Graham Avenue, masters this formula with country house good looks, two French ex-pat owners, Julie Eck and Stephane Alix (who know all their regulars' names), and a tasty Southern French menu. Dishes may include baked eggs over ratatouille at brunch, salade Niçoise, sides of fried artichokes, and that final test of any bistro worth its salt—a perfect stack of crunchy frites with garlicky aïoli.

The Farm on Adderley

American 🍴🍴

B4

1108 Cortelyou Rd. (bet. 12th St. & Stratford Rd.)

Subway: Cortelyou Rd	Lunch & dinner daily
Phone: 718-287-3101	
Web: www.thefarmonadderley.com	
Prices: $$	

Tom Kearney, who earned his culinary stripes at Blue Hill and Jean Georges before crossing the river, doesn't need to bend over backward to expand his fan base—he has a plenty captive audience in the incoming mix of young families and professionals gentrifying Ditmas Park, a quickly-evolving neighborhood south of Prospect Park.

And yet he delivers sweet perfection with each dish, plying newcomers who make their way into his softly lit dining room with simple, seasonal fare like kale soup, bobbing with a poached egg and brown lentils; arctic char, grilled with roasted beets and green lentils; or a tender buttermilk tart, paired with irresistible blueberry compote. Morning birds will love the Fisherman's Eggs—poached eggs over smoked trout and hollandaise

Fatty 'Cue 😋

Asian ✗

91 S. 6th St. (bet. Bedford Ave. & Berry St.)

Subway: Marcy Av   Lunch & dinner daily
Phone: 718-599-3090
Web: www.fattycue.com
Prices: $$

Chef Zakary Pelaccio, of Fatty Crab fame, stoked the flames of his restless, creative energy to conjure up a lip-smacking mash-up of Southeast Asian influenced barbecue. Perched virtually underneath the Williamsburg Bridge, the roadhouse-looking space features a bar-dominated dining room supplemented by an alleyway used for outdoor seating.

Exotic and creative, Fatty 'Cue's menu boasts preparations like *ikan baker*, a smoky, banana leaf-seared mackerel seasoned with tumeric salt. Beef brisket brings deliciously hands-on eating—thin slices of lean meat and pieces of glazed fat arrive with chili jam, aïoli, and steamed buns for filling.

The cocktail list and unique drink specials perfectly complement this spirited, Brooklyn-soigné setting.

Fonda

Mexican ✗

434 Seventh Ave. (bet. 14th & 15th Sts.)

Subway: 7 Av (9th St.)   Lunch & dinner Tue – Sun
Phone: 718-369-3144
Web: www.fondarestaurant.com
Prices: $$

Chef Roberto Santibañez, a Le Cordon Bleu graduate and former culinary director of Rosa Mexicano, offers an updated take on Mexican cuisine at this cheerful Park Slope newcomer. Bright colors and bold artwork decorate the petite dining room, which is supplemented by warm-weather seating on the back patio.

Fonda's menu is endowed with a creative spin, evident in preparations such as fish *salpicon*—finely chopped with plenty of white onion, cilantro, and green chiles, then brightened with fresh lime juice and accompanied by warm hand-pressed tortillas. The banana leaf-wrapped *marco pollo* comes dressed with a crimson-hued sauce of achiote and roasted tomato, while desserts offer a home-style touch as in the softly set, citrus-scented *natillas*.

Fort Defiance

C4

American ✗

365 Van Brunt St. (at Dikeman St.)

Subway: Smith - 9 Sts (& bus B77)　　　　　Lunch daily
Phone: 347-453-6672　　　　　　　　　　Dinner Wed — Mon
Web: www.fortdefiancebrooklyn.com
Prices: $$

If you build it, they will come. Maybe that's what the owners were thinking, since this spot way out in Red Hook isn't exactly a hop, skip, and a jump away. But once you're tucked inside, expect to jump for joy over the very tasty and gussied up Southern-inspired food on the concise menu—think pimento cheese and Ritz crackers; deviled eggs; and shrimp and grits.

Plan on coming for more than just the food, since the drinks are out-of-this-world. From nods to old-world Waldorf–Astoria cocktails to new creations with literary namesakes (like Correspondence) and an ever-changing beer menu, there's something to quench the thirst of those true-blue artists, counter-culture denizens, and yes, even a few wealthy Wall Streeters, who populate Red Hook.

Frankies 457 Spuntino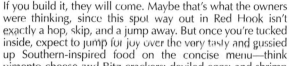

C4

Italian ✗

457 Court St. (bet. 4th Pl. & Luquer St.)

Subway: Smith - 9 Sts　　　　　　　　Lunch & dinner daily
Phone: 718-403-0033
Web: www.frankiesspuntino.com
Prices:

Courtesy of the Franks (Castronovo and Falcinelli) is this tremendously popular, homestyle Italian with a light, seasonal, and local touch. Although *spuntino* loosely translates as "snack," this menu satisfies both old-school Brooklynites and serious foodies—many of whom pick up a copy of the owners' cookbook.

While preparation is initially done in the basement kitchen, dishes are assembled in the casual dining room, behind stacks of charcuterie and crusty breads. This practice entices guests with mouthwatering aromas of meatballs with pine nuts and raisins, or sweet potato and sage ravioli in Parmesan broth.

Weather permitting, dine in the lovely back garden. Don't forget to try the Lower East Side or new Greenwich Village locations.

Franny's ☺

Italian ✗

D4

295 Flatbush Ave. (bet. Prospect Pl. & St. Marks Ave.)

Subway: Bergen St (Flatbush Ave.)   Lunch Sat – Sun
Phone: 718-230-0221   Dinner nightly
Web: www.frannysbrooklyn.com
Prices: $$

Run by husband-wife team Franny Stephens and Andrew Feinberg, and their contagious passion for sustainable agriculture, Franny's is an inviting spot. An affable staff, comfortable front bar, and stack of highchairs demonstrate that all are welcome.

The open kitchen's centerpiece is a wood-burning brick oven churning out a tandem of puffed and crispy pizzas; their clam pie with chilies and parsley is the stuff of local legends. While specials are tempting, open with a few snacks, like the wood-roasted olives, that really make this place unique.

Decorated with greenery, strings of white lights, and neat piles of firewood, the back patio is perfect for warm evenings. Be sure to visit nearby Bklyn Larder, proffering their gourmet provisions.

The General Greene ☺

American ✗

D3

229 DeKalb Ave. (at Clermont Ave.)

Subway: Lafayette Av   Lunch & dinner daily
Phone: 718-222-1510
Web: www.thegeneralgreene.com
Prices: $$

The rustic American revolution marches on with The General Greene, a solidly ensconced Fort Greene restaurant that taps the talents of an acclaimed kitchen which cooks up a creative, Southern-inflected menu guaranteed to steal the hearts of the upscale bohemian crowd that floods this neighborhood—its unkempt good looks and hip waitstaff only seal the deal.

The seasonal menu may include a silky chicken liver pâté dusted with sea salt; and their signature fried chicken accompanied by sweet potato and andouille hash, as well as braised collard greens. Or go for comfort with the 3 cheese mac n' cheese followed by homemade ice cream.

Also visit their attached country store for old-school goodies that range from house-rendered lard to candies.

The Good Fork 😊

Contemporary 🍴

C4

391 Van Brunt St. (bet. Coffey & Van Dyke Sts.)

Subway: Smith - 9 Sts (& bus B77)
Phone: 718-643-6636
Web: www.goodfork.com
Prices: $$

Dinner Tue – Sun

This is one restaurant that is truly worth the trip. In fact, it celebrates its environs with a range of local offerings, from AV Farms' produce in Red Hook to serving Steve's Key Lime pie.

It's a bit of a trek to get here, but once inside, guests settle into the quaint dining room (reminiscent of a train car from a bygone era) or head back to a patio with its iron gazebo and trees wrapped in twinkling lights. The setting is storybook, but Ben Schneider and his classically-trained Korean-American wife, Sohui Kim's lovingly prepared menu is earning everyone's devotion, gleefully trotting the globe and showcasing diverse sensibilities. Try the apple-braised wild boar shank with smoked bacon, creamy grits, mustard greens, and finished with pickled apple.

The Grocery

Contemporary 🍴

C4

288 Smith St. (bet. Sackett & Union Sts.)

Subway: Carroll St
Phone: 718-596-3335
Web: www.thegroceryrestaurant.com
Prices: $$

Lunch Thu – Sat
Dinner Tue – Sat

The longevity of this pioneering Smith Street restaurant is commendable. Open for more than a decade, The Grocery still has its fans. The quaint space (with its sage green walls and white trim) feels insouciant, especially when multi-tasking Chef Charles Kiely approaches your table to recite the specials he's crafted from the day's greenmarket offerings, or even just to chat.

The greenery-enhanced backyard is an idyllic landing place for a warm evening, but take note—seating here is first-come-first-serve. Sit back and relish the facile cooking that renders divine creations like boned, rolled, and roasted guinea hen with liver-cornbread stuffing and sage pan sauce; or East Coast halibut coated with lentils, scallions, and a carrot-Meyer lemon sauce.

435

Jack the Horse 😊

C3

American ✗✗

66 Hicks St. (at Cranberrry St.)

Subway: High St
Phone: 718-852-5084
Web: www.jackthehorse.com
Prices: $$

Lunch Sun
Dinner nightly

For all its upscale bohemian charm and perfect little brownstones, the picture-book neighborhood of Brooklyn Heights could use a few more restaurants like Jack the Horse—a homey, exposed brick tavern that's been kept under wraps by the locals who frequent it.

Who would want to share this gem? With its bright, window-lined walls and impossibly delicious cocktail list, this place would be a destination spot even without Tim Oltmans' gorgeous American fare like a savory artichoke, pancetta "cheesecake" starter topped with tomato-caper relish and crispy greens; creamy pan-seared hake with sweet red peppers, zucchini, chorizo, and plantains, dancing in a tomato cilantro-lime broth; or silky coconut panna cotta studded with crunchy sesame seeds.

James

D4

Contemporary ✗✗

605 Carlton Ave. (at St. Marks Ave.)

Subway: 7 Av (Flatbush Ave.)
Phone: 718-942-4255
Web: www.jamesrestaurantny.com
Prices: $$

Lunch Sat – Sun
Dinner nightly

The concise menu at Chef/owner Bryan Calvert's restaurant, James, first may appear simple and straightforward, like its name. However, roasted dorade with fennel, roasted pears, and anchovy vinaigrette; grilled lemon pound cake accompanied by blood orange compote; and the deceptively sophisticated "Burger Nights" and "Sunday Suppers" are all proof of the high level of talent and skill at work in the kitchen.

Likewise, the dining room housed on a tree-lined corner of Prospect Heights displays signs of refinement with a space accented in whitewashed brick walls and espresso-hued leather and wood furnishings. Warm lighting adds a gorgeous glow throughout, and the inviting bar further seduces with vintage mirrors and floral arrangements.

Java

B3

Indonesian ✗

455 7th Ave. (at 16th St.)

Subway: / Av (9th St.) Dinner nightly
Phone: 718-832-4583
Web: N/A
Prices: ⊕⊕

Meet Rofia, the delightful owner and chef here at Java, whose loving hospitality infuses this adorable spot with huge doses of charm. Get all cozy in the tiny dining room and prepare to get your Indonesian nosh on. Bamboo skewers of charbroiled lamb served with *kepac manis* are a delectable start; followed by velvety *semur*—thin slices of beef simmered in a rich garlicky sauce. The terrific *cumi baker* (baked tender squid topped with an aromatic ginger sauce) is a must try; but don't try to get the delicious details, as our tight-lipped chef won't divulge her secrets.

Bring a buddy and partake in the famous *Rijsttafel*, a feast of fifteen dishes plus dessert for under forty bucks. Note to the booze crowd: no alcohol is served.

Juventino

D4

American ✗

370 Fifth Ave. (bet. 5th & 6th Sts.)

Subway: 4 Av - 9 St Lunch daily
Phone: 718-360-8469 Dinner Mon – Sat
Web: www.juventinonyc.com
Prices: $$

The former Get Fresh Table and Market has been redone to do away with the market and focus on the table. The setting is inviting, and Park Slopers should feel fortunate to have such a sweet spot in the neighborhood. Those tables are lacquered with pages from old cookbooks, and the space is stocked with book-filled shelves and a generally countrified look.

Chef Juventino Avila offers brunch daily; eye-openers include homemade granola and cage-free truffled eggs. Heartier preparations embrace seasonality and product and share a south-of-the -order accent in items like a block of pan-seared cod cresting a flavorful mound of Mexican-style rice; and an offering of *tacos de mama*—over-stuffed handmade tortillas accompanied by a trio of salsas.

Karczma

Polish ✗

136 Greenpoint Ave. (bet. Franklin St. & Manhattan Ave.)

Subway: Greenpoint Av
Phone: 718-349-1744
Web: www.karczmabrooklyn.com
Prices: 🍪

Lunch & dinner daily

Located in a slice of Greenpoint that still boasts a sizeable Polish population, Karczma offers a lovely old-world ambience that may belie its age (opened in 2007) but perfectly matches its very traditional, budget-friendly menu. Hearty offerings may include peasant-style lard mixed with bacon and spices, or the plate of Polish specialties that heaps on pierogies (three varieties, steamed or fried, topped with sliced onions and butter), kielbasa, potato pancakes, hunter's stew, and stuffed cabbage. Grilled plates can be prepared for two or three, while others, like the roasted hocks in beer, could easily feed as many.

The charming, farmhouse-inspired interior is efficiently staffed by smiling servers in floral skirts and embroidered vests.

Karloff

Eastern European ✗

254 Court St. (bet. Butler & Kane Sts.)

Subway: Bergen St (Smith St.)
Phone: 347-689-4279
Web: www.karloffbrooklyn.com
Prices: 🍪

Lunch & dinner daily

Passersby may assume this Court St. eatery is a simple coffee shop, but in truth there's actually a lot more to offer than single-origin coffees and chai lattes. Open all day, Karloff is an enjoyable café serving up a variety of morning fare that includes organic kefir smoothies, eggs, and blintzes. Come evening, the mood is more substantial with a comprehensive range of Eastern European specialties: borscht; crisped latkes with apple sauce and sour cream; *vareniki*; and creamy beef stroganoff ladled over kasha pilaf. And there's ice cream, hand-churned in the Hudson Valley and offered in flavors like salted pretzel. A free scoop is given to children on their birthday.

Laid-back service and simple furnishings forge an easygoing ambience.

Kif 😊

Moroccan ✗

D3

219 DeKalb Ave. (bet. Adelphi St. & Clermont Ave.)

Subway: Lafayette Av   Lunch & dinner daily
Phone: 718-852-7273
Web: N/A
Prices: $$

After a brief shuttering in early 2010, Djamal Zoughbi's sweet little Moroccan darling is back in action —and not a moment too soon. Blessed with an open kitchen where diners can watch the chefs work their imported spices and oils into lip-smacking good small plates, Kif is perfectly outfitted for its upscale bohemian Fort Greene audience: a leafy outdoor garden opens up when the weather's nice, and snug velvet banquettes beckon come winter.

Classic staples like hummus and falafel are a solid notch above the competition, but don't miss the excellent grilled merguez, served over thick, smoky harissa; or the succulent chicken tagine, fragrant with preserved lemon, a heady blend of spices, and tender root vegetables.

Ki Sushi

Japanese ✗

C3

122 Smith St. (bet. Dean & Pacific Sts.)

Subway: Bergen St (Smith St.)   Lunch Mon – Sat
Phone: 718-935-0575   Dinner nightly
Web: www.ki-sushi.com
Prices: $$

Count sushi among Smith Street's wealth of dining options. At KI, the quality of fish and talented kitchen offer plenty to please its devoted clientele relishing the raw and the cooked in a Zen-chic space complete with a gently flowing wall of water and potted flowers.

The cheerful sushi team works from a long counter stocked with a tempting array of pristine fish. The sushi and sashimi are excellent, as is the whimsical and visually appealing maki, like the Fashion Roll of chopped tuna, jalapeño, and yuzu *tobiko* wrapped in slices of raw scallop. Dishes such as rock shrimp tempura drizzled with a creamy spiced mayonnaise emerge from the small kitchen located in back.

The friendly and attentive service adds to the charm of this Cobble Hill favorite.

La Superior

A1

295 Berry St. (bet. S. 2nd & S. 3rd Sts.)

Subway: Bedford Av   Lunch & dinner daily
Phone: 718-388-5988
Web: www.lasuperiornyc.com
Prices: 🍝

La Superior offers a fun and authentically delicious south-of-the-border dining experience that even the city's West Coast transplants should find impressive. The restaurant's name is scrawled tattoo-like across the front of its painted brick façade, alluding to the simplistic décor: chile-red walls, vintage Mexican movie posters, and food served on colorful plastic plates.

A "superior" Mexican bar stocked with tequila, rum, and cervezas are offered to wash down the inexpensive fare that may include crispy flautas dressed with excellent salsa verde; *panuchos de cochinita* (slow cooked pork and mashed black beans atop a thick tortilla); and tacos like the surprisingly decadent *rajas*, filled with strips of roasted poblanos and tangy *crema*.

Locanda Vini & Olii

D3

129 Gates Ave. (at Cambridge Pl.)

Subway: Clinton - Washington Avs   Dinner Tue – Sun
Phone: 718-622-9202
Web: www.locandany.com
Prices: $$

Ensconced in a restored century-old pharmacy, Locanda Vini & Olii is trimmed with a weathered white tiled floor and rustic furnishings. Glass cabinets stocked with colorful glass and curios flank the room and the kitchen is fronted by the original pick-up window. This lovely Italianate spot recently celebrated its tenth anniversary and experienced a change in ownership resulting from founding owners Francois and Catherine Louy handing over their pride and joy to the charge of Chef Michele Baldacci, Sommelier Rocco Spagnardi, and GM Michael Schall.

The cooking stays the course and continues to delight with the likes of *pappa al pomodoro*—slick, almost fluffy bread and tomato soup; or silky, parsley-flecked *fazzolettini* with shrimp and fish ragù.

Lucky Eight

Chinese 🍴

A4

5204 Eighth Ave. (bet. 52nd & 53rd Sts.)

Subway: 8 Av   Lunch & dinner daily
Phone: 718-851-8862
Web: N/A
Prices: ⊜⊜

With its plethora of dim sum spots, Chinese bakeries, and markets hawking everything from live bull frogs to fresh silky tofu, the south of Sunset Park area continues to grow as the borough's most prominent Chinatown. From this, Lucky Eight's excellent food, good service, and pristine setting is an authentic and rewarding find.

Until late afternoon, pick from a list of some 40 items priced at 80 cents each. The laminated dinner menu is crammed with pages illustrating unique, regional Chinese fare. The aptly named signature dish, Pride of Lucky Eight, offers a sumptuous stir fry of chives, celery, shiitake, and meaty abalone.

The highlight of the no-frills décor is the red-lacquer case at the back of the room, displaying interesting artifacts.

Maria's Bistro Mexicano

Mexican 🍴

B3

886 Fifth Ave. (bet. 37th & 38th Sts.)

Subway: 36 St   Lunch & dinner daily
Phone: 718-438-1608
Web: www.mariasbistromexicano.com
Prices: $$

A sunny streak of yellow signage sweeps along the storefront, name emblazoned across it, cheerfully beckoning diners into the lovely quarters. Inside, the narrow dining space is flanked by exposed brick on one side, and brightly painted walls on the other, and trimmed with foliage and colorful knickknacks. Here at Maria's Bistro, food is as fresh and tasty as the staff is warm and helpful.

Get things going with guac—perfectly made to order and served up in a lava rock mortar with homemade tortilla chips. Dive into the *barbacoa de Borrego*: lip smacking lamb, swathed in banana and avocado leaves, stewed in its own flavorful juices to tender perfection. Short on cash? Check out the website for specials like Unemployed Mondays and Ceviche Thursdays.

Marlow & Sons 😋

A1

81 Broadway (bet. Berry St. & Wythe Ave.)

Subway: Marcy Av   Lunch & dinner daily
Phone: 718-384-1441
Web: www.marlowandsons.com
Prices: $$

Lined with shelves of tastily selected groceries (think olive oil, heirloom beans, and vibrant preserves), Marlow & Sons is foodie heaven. Grab a pastry and coffee to go if you're in a hurry or take a seat in back and take the time to savor this special spot.

Morning sustenance is offered by way of scones with Devonshire cream and frittata sandwiches. While dinner unveils an animated scene stationed in a dusky den supping on a concise menu bolstered by an oft-changing list of specials: spaghetti tossed with mustard greens, toasted walnuts, white beans, and a luscious Parmesan-enriched pan sauce; bronze-skinned brick chicken—a menu mainstay; and simple but certainly impressive desserts like maple custard paired with crumbly as sand shortbread.

Mesa Coyoacán 😋

C1

372 Graham Ave. (bet. Conselyea St. & Skillman Ave.)

Subway: Graham Av   Lunch Thu – Sun
Phone: 718-782-8171   Dinner nightly
Web: www.mesacoyoacan.com
Prices: $$

Not that Brooklyn is wanting for exciting dining options, quite the opposite exactly, but the arrival of Chef Ivan Garcia's tempting spot has been greeted with open arms, and mouths. The Mexico City native ruled the roost previously at Barrio Chino and Mercadito, and now takes up residence in a glass fronted slab where wolfish appetites are sated.

It's not just the swank interior, fitted out with richly-patterned wallpaper, snug banquettes, and communal tables, but the mouthwatering Mexican food that makes this place such a jewel. Partake in tacos, perhaps the *carnitas*—braised Berkshire pork D.F.-style stuffed into handmade tortillas; or a choice from the *platos fuertes* that include *enchiladas de mole*, made from the chef's secret family recipe.

Mile End 😊

D3

97A Hoyt St. (bet. Atlantic Ave. & Pacific St.)

Subway: Hoyt-Schermerhorn   Lunch & dinner daily
Phone: 718-852-7510
Web: www.mileendbrooklyn.com
Prices: 💰💰

The star of the show at this gem of a spot is Montreal-style smoked meat: pasture-raised brisket that is spice-rubbed, then cured, oak-smoked, steamed, and finally hand cut onto slices of mustard-slathered rye. It's a revelatory sandwich, exactingly prepared, and has few peers in the city. Dinner brings further competition for your appetite with the likes of *poulet Juif*, a tantalizingly smoky, bronze-skinned chicken with wilted escarole and warm schmaltz-enriched vinaigrette. The petite room is rarely quiet. Beyond the handful of tables, there is a dining counter facing the white-tiled kitchen, accented with a blackboard of specials and treats such as Hungarian shortbread. To enjoy the goodness at home, walk up to the sidewalk window for takeout.

Mimi's Hummus

B4

1209 Cortelyou Rd. (bet. Argyle & Westminster Rds.)

Subway: Cortelyou Rd   Lunch & dinner daily
Phone: 718-284-4444
Web: www.mimishummus.com
Prices: 💰💰

Think snack taverna and you have the right idea about this adorable, warm spot in Brooklyn's ever-changing Ditmas Park. Though the space is teeny-tiny, excellent design and wise use of space give Mimi's a modern holistic feel—with large windows ferrying swaths of natural light into the dining room by day, and an open kitchen adding cheerful ambience come nightfall.

The menu is simple but scrumptious, with super-fresh ingredients and spot-on spices doing the work in dishes like silky fava bean hummus, served with fresh pita; chunky tomato stew paired with a plump poached egg and Israeli salad; or irresistibly thick and creamy *labne*, laced with fragrant herbs. At dinner, the menu opens up to include several entrées and takeout is available.

Miranda

A1

80 Berry St. (at N. 9th St.)

Subway: Bedford Av

Phone: 718-387-0711

Web: www.mirandarestaurant.com

Prices: $$

Lunch Sat – Sun
Dinner Wed – Mon

Run by husband-and-wife team, Sasha and Mauricio Miranda, this welcoming establishment located in Williamsburg has a lovely rustic charm accentuated by straw seat chairs, vintage crockery, and exposed brick walls. The duo has an impressive resume between them that includes work as such esteemed establishments as Spigolo and Alto.

The cuisine here weds the sunny flavors of Italy and Latin America for a menu of creative and vibrant treats. Small plate starters include *arancini* and empanadas; the pastas are made in house as in the perfectly delicious *garganelli*—embellished with sweet peas, fresh mozzarella, and diced *longaniza* (a chewy and slightly spiced sausage); and entrées include roasted pork tenderloin with tomatillo-fresh *mole verde*.

Moim

D4

206 Garfield Pl. (at Seventh Ave.)

Subway: 7 Av (Flatbush Ave.)

Phone: 718-499-8092

Web: www.moimrestaurant.com

Prices: $$

Dinner Tue – Sun

Set among an assemblage of bucolic brownstones, Moim serves a fresh take on Korean cuisine. Like its menu, the setting bears a contemporary vibe in a room of concrete grey and dark wood details. Moim translates as "gathering" and encourages sharing with oversized tables to be topped with any number of plates, small or large.

The kitchen rises above the pack with an array of items that begin with tapas such as stir-fried eggplant, and organic soft tofu in seasoned soy sauce. Small plates are also featured and include puffy steamed buns filled with a mixture of chopped pork and kimchi. Heartier plates and bowls offer the likes of *dak bok-kum*, a Korean-style *pot-au-feu* of rice wine-braised chicken, spicy chili soy, and Korean potato gnocchi.

Momo Sushi Shack

Fusion ✗

C1

43 Bogart St. (bet. Grattan & Thames Sts.)

Subway: Morgan Av
Phone: 718-418-6666
Web: www.momosushishack.com
Prices: $$

Lunch & dinner Tue – Sun

Feeling nostalgic for the days of Manhattan before its Disneyfication? Look no further than this Brooklyn 'hood, where tattooed bike-toting artists rule the roost and graffiti isn't a nuisance, it's an art form. Momo Sushi Shack is packed with hipsters all dancing to a different beat. There's nothing ersatz about its loading dock look, since it's not made to look warehousy—it is! Inside is true-blue industrial with cement floors and corrugated steel.

Wagyu beef "sushi" topped with crispy garlic and seaweed and a trio of flavored soy sauces made in-house is scary good. From the minced fresh scallops and the pressed tofu with basil-infused soy sauce, to the cold udon noodles swimming in shiso vinaigrette, it's a total tongue-teasing flavor bonanza.

Do not confuse ✗ with ✿! ✗ defines comfort, while ✿ are awarded for the best cuisine. Stars are awarded across all categories of comfort.

Noodle Pudding

Italian 🍴

C3

38 Henry St. (bet. Cranberry & Middagh Sts.)

Subway: High St   Dinner Tue – Sun
Phone: 718-625-3737
Web: N/A
Prices: $$

The mood is perfectly relaxed at this Brooklyn Heights restaurant, where old jazz tunes ooze from the speakers and the friendly waitstaff doles out killer Italian fare (pay attention to those daily specials). In warm weather, the windows fly open and the space has an indoor garden vibe, but you'll want to beat the crowds by arriving early: this neighborhood favorite doesn't take reservations.

Named for a savory pudding baked with noodles and traditionally served on the Sabbath, Noodle Pudding hits its wheelhouse with savory dishes. Dip into a soft bowl of rigatoni *arrabbiata* studded with sweet onions and pecorino; or succulent rabbit, braised in red wine with tomatoes, garlic, and fresh herbs, then paired with a fluffy side of polenta.

Northeast Kingdom

American 🍴

C2

18 Wyckoff Ave. (at Troutman St.)

Subway: Jefferson St   Lunch Sat – Sun
Phone: 718-386-3864   Dinner nightly
Web: www.north-eastkingdom.com
Prices: $$

You don't have to say goodbye to American pie at Northeast Kingdom, since this place is revered for its heavenly pot pies. It's a little taste of Americana-style food in the heart of warehouse-heavy and mega organic supermarket-enhanced Bushwick. Sure, it's a bitty gritty, but it has a burgeoning culinary scene, and Northeast Kingdom is running with the big dogs.

From fried green tomatoes and Vermont cheddar-stuffed pierogi to fricassee of wild mushrooms made silky with cream and sitting atop favas, carrot purée, and new potates, Northeast Kingdom's chef, Kevin Adely takes the best of the farmstand and brings it to life. Dishes like ginger-mint dressed pan-roasted duck are proof that it isn't your average country cookin', so leave Billy Bob behind.

No. 7

D3

American ✗

7 Greene Ave. (bet. Cumberland & Fulton Sts.)

Subway: Lafayette Av   Lunch Sat – Sun
Phone: 718-522-6370   Dinner Tue – Sun
Web: www.no7restaurant.com
Prices: $$

Emerging as a force in Brooklyn's anti-establishment foodie revolution, this Fort Greene hot spot is showing New York City what's what. Running the show is a young, fiercely talented team with the chops to deliver cuisine that's as inventive as it is mouthwatering.

Dive into the delicate, sashimi-grade raw mackerel, served with crunchy spaghetti squash and toasted pumpkin seeds. The duck and pork shoulder also deserves attention: tender, shredded meats in a savory broth, topped with battered, fried green beans, candied kumquats, and crème fraîche, with a side of the tastiest jasmine rice around. The apple tart with creamy dollops of cheddar, bacon, and whiskey exceeds expectation. The rustic, stylish space is packed with locals in the know.

1 or 8

A1

Japanese ✗✗

66 S. 2nd St. (at Wythe Ave.)

Subway: Bedford Av   Dinner Tue – Sun
Phone: 718-384-2152
Web: www.oneoreightbk.com
Prices: $$

Taking its moniker from a Japanese gambling expression that means all or nothing, this atelier of food is a sure thing for a truly creative meal. The lofty space boldly features a blank-canvas décor of monochromatic white, accentuated by an open kitchen.

A comfortable sushi counter indicates the kitchen's serious sushi offerings, while a menu of cooked preparations offers a unique take on Japanese cuisine. Dishes may include octopus ceviche, tender and refreshing, studded with green grapes and a gelée of bonito-infused vinegar; a terrine of beef sukiyaki stacking flavorful rib eye with carrots and shiitakes, with a soft-cooked egg; or a delicate fillet of tilefish grilled in phyllo, dressed with dashi-poached vegetables and classic sauce Américaine.

Osteria il Paiolo

Italian ✗✗

106 N. 6th St. (bet. Berry & Wythe Sts.)

Subway: Bedford Av
Phone: 718-218-7080
Web: www.ilpaiolonyc.com
Prices: $$

Lunch & dinner daily

Housed in a raw space of brick and concrete that is prettied by linen-draped, flower-topped tables and serviced by a team of natty veterans, Williamsburg's Osteria il Paiolo rocks a slick vibe that is decidedly urbane for this hipster enclave.

The impressive Northern Italian cuisine features an ingredient-driven menu incorporating several daily specials, such as shaved fennel salad studded with bits of oxtail and brightly dressed with fresh herbs. Also on offer is a listing of heirloom polenta and house-made pastas—the *maccheroncini alla crudaiola* combines rigatoni with blistered cherry tomatoes, a slab of cool imported *burrata*, and fresh basil that pools into a creamy pink sauce. Desserts include a rich vanilla bean-flecked panna cotta.

Pacificana

Chinese ✗✗

813 55th St. (at Eighth Ave.)

Subway: 8 Av
Phone: 718-871-2880
Web: N/A
Prices: $$

Lunch & dinner daily

You can thank Sunset Park's growing Asian population for the influx of excellent Chinese restaurants into this far-flung pocket of Brooklyn. Among the best of the lot is Pacificana, a bright, airy restaurant–think vaulted ceilings, jumbo windows, and an open kitchen sporting floor-to-ceiling fish tanks–tucked into a second floor space off bustling Eighth Avenue.

Dim sum carts packed to the gills with dishes like crispy pork over jelly fish, and tender shrimp dumplings, roll by like temptations-on-wheels, as dinner guests tuck into traditional fare like the rich, fragrant South China duck casserole; or chicken with crunchy, pale green preserved mustard greens, paired with preserved black beans and a steaming bowl of fluffy white rice.

Paulie Gee's 😈

B1

60 Greenpoint Ave. (bet. Franklin & West Sts.)

Subway: Greenpoint Av

Phone: 347-987-3747

Web: www.pauliegee.com

Prices: 💰💰

Lunch Sun

Dinner Tue – Sun

Owner Paul Gianonne, aka Paulie Gee, channeled a lifelong love of pizza into this charmingly delicious newcomer that feels as if it has been around forever. Rustic in appearance, the room's cool concrete and brick elements are warmed by the glow of the wood-burning pizza oven imported from Naples. It's from here that Gianonne and son work their magic.

The addictive crust is beguilingly moist and chewy, perfumed with smoke, and adroitly salted. Pizza dominates the menu with tempting combinations, excellent ingredients, and whimsical titles. Offerings may include the Arugula Shmoogala topped with baby arugula and Parmigiano Reggiano; and the Baconmarmalade Picante slathered with *fior di latte*, dollops of spiced bacon marmalade, and red onion.

The Pearl Room

A4

8201 Third Ave. (at 82nd St.)

Subway: 86 St

Phone: 718-833-6666

Web: www.thepearlroom.com

Prices: 💰💰

Lunch & dinner daily

With its jumbo garden and bright, sun-streaked dining room, this Brooklyn steady is a solid choice year-round. Most days, you'll catch a glimpse of the charming Chef/owner Anthony Rinaldi floating around, working his magic back in the kitchen and out in the dining room.

The Pearl Room is known for its vast seafood spread, and Rinaldi's wheelhouse is intricately designed fish plates like a lemon sole, coated in golden breading and pine nuts, and then tossed in a perfectly balanced lemongrass-kiwi sauce. But don't discount his other offerings—the menu boasts a wealth of vegetarian and meat dishes, many of them ample enough to split, as well as a few tongue-wagging desserts like a trio of luscious chocolate truffles rolled in bright green pistachios.

Peter Luger ✿

A1

178 Broadway (at Driggs Ave.)

Subway: Marcy Av
Phone: 718-387-7400
Web: www.peterluger.com
Prices: $$$

Lunch & dinner daily

Peter Luger

Peter Luger is not old, it's historic. The waiters are not gruff, they are focused. Dining here is not a meal; it is a right of passage. And these steaks are not just good—they are probably going to be the best you've ever had. This is the reason why Peter Luger has been receiving paramount praise since first opening to a very different Brooklyn in 1887.

In a room that harkens back to old New York and early German ale-houses, an unabashedly male crowd of tourists and businessmen sit elbow-to-elbow at bare tables, not worrying themselves with looking through a menu. When that steak for two (or three or four) arrives, slow yourself and take a long, hot look to appreciate its every perfection. The marbling is a thing of beauty, and becomes all the more appetizing as it is presented sliced and sizzling with drippings. Take a few mouthfuls before even considering trying the house sauce. It may be tasty, but c'mon. This steak is already nirvana in its nakedness.

Do allow your eyes to stray from the prize long enough to dig into their emerald-green and savory creamed spinach or thick, hand-cut fries. For dessert, the sinfully smooth cheesecake is simply delicious, *mit schlaag*, of course.

Picket Fence

B4   American ✘

1310 Cortelyou Rd. (at Argyle Rd.)

Subway: Cortelyou Rd   Lunch & dinner daily
Phone: 718-282-6661
Web: www.picketfencebrooklyn.com
Prices: $$

Nestled into Ditmas Park, a slowly gentrifying Brooklyn neighborhood lined with Victorian homes, Picket Fence is a sweet little gem. In spring, the doors swing open to the sidewalk, flooding light into the warm, sunny dining room, furnished with rattan chairs and cozy banquettes. Out back, a cheerful little garden is perfect for families to linger about and enjoy.

The food is free of fuss and full of comfort, so much so that it can feel like something of a throwback; yet its broad American menu does everything simply and deliciously. The familiar offerings include the likes of chicken pot pie; turkey meatloaf; fish and chips; healthy salads; and a range of burgers and toppings. Desserts build on the established theme with puddings, crisps, and cupcakes.

Prime Meats

C4   Eastern European ✘

465 Court St. (at Luquer St.)

Subway: Smith - 9 Sts.   Lunch & dinner daily
Phone: 718-254-0327
Web: www.frankspm.com
Prices: $$

Spreken ze...yummy? Don't worry about brushing up on your German to visit Prime Meats. Niceties aside, your mouth will be otherwise occupied.

It all starts with house-pickled vegetables and soft pretzels served with spicy hot mustard and continues with a cavalcade of carnivorous delights. Roasted bone marrow with gremolata, pickle-brined Amish chicken, and oh yes, sausages. *Sürkrüt garnie* is a threesome of meats with pork belly, calf tongue, and bratwurst for a very harmonious affair. Finish it with a piece of sea salt dark chocolate—so wunderbar.

Prime Meats doesn't just know how to suck out all the marrow of life, it looks good too. With dark woods, tall wooden booths, and wood framed glass windows, it nails that classic brasserie look.

Purple Yam

B4

1314 Cortelyou Rd. (at Rugby Rd.)

Subway: Cortelyou Rd
Phone: 718-940-8188
Web: www.purpleyamnyc.com
Prices: $$

Lunch Mon – Fri
Dinner nightly

What could be just another hip neighborhood restaurant gets elevated to destination restaurant heights in the hands of talented chef, Romy Dorotan, and his wife, Amy Besa. After losing their lease at Cendrillon, the Filipino restaurant they ran in SoHo, the pair relocated to Ditmas Park's Cortelyou Road, a Victorian-strewn street that's become a sort of restaurant row for the ever-gentrifying neighborhood.

With the new menu, Dorotan ventures into even more parts of Asia, most notably toward Korea, then ties the dishes together with a European sensibility. Don't miss the outstanding duck leg *betutu* with taro leaves, slow-cooked in Balinese spices and coconut milk to such silky perfection, that they should bottle the sauce and sell it.

Quercy

C3

242 Court St. (bet. Baltic & Kane Sts.)

Subway: Bergen St (Smith St.)
Phone: 718-243-2151
Web: N/A
Prices: $$

Lunch Sat – Sun
Dinner nightly

Named for the chef's hometown in Southern France, Quercy is a truly satisfying and authentic bistro that thankfully prefers tradition over change. With its cobalt blue façade, checkerboard-tile floor, and a chalkboard scrawled carte of daily specials like house-cured gravlax, this Cobble Hill charmer emanates a wonderfully familiar aura. The small art deco bar is a cozy spot to sip an aperitif, prior to a finely crafted meal at one of the paper-topped tables, tended by a cordial staff.

As one would hope and expect, the menu serves up heartwarming classics like *escargot au Cognac*; fork-tender bœuf Bourguignon; and tarte Tatin with a dense dollop of crème fraîche, along with a wine list that highlights the varietals of Southwestern France.

River Café ✿

Contemporary 🍴🍴🍴

C2

1 Water St. (bet. Furman & Old Fulton Sts.)

Subway: High St
Phone: 718-522-5200
Web: www.rivercafe.com
Prices: $$$$

Lunch & dinner daily

Noah Kalina/The River Café

Walking the plank is always enjoyable if it is bursting with flowers and leads into the River Café, the venerable New York institution situated on a decidedly upscale barge beneath the Brooklyn Bridge. A stroll across that bridge to the restaurant (where the dining room's legendary view of the Manhattan skyline is a breathtaking accompaniment to the seafood-stacked menu) is a seminal Big Apple experience for tourists and locals alike.

The extensive menu befits a restaurant that has been floating along a riverbank for over 25 years. Elegant and perfectly cooked starters may include the rainbow trout, first brined and smoked, dusted with flour, then lightly sautéed. The equally pleasing smoked salmon is silky, rich, and complemented by *raita* and *pappadams*.

Gladly, landlubbers need not despair. The Amish chicken, rolled in pancetta, arrives bronzed and juicy alongside a moist and herb-flecked cornbread stuffing atop bright, creamy sweet pea purée. Completely decadent treats include the chocolate sticky toffee cake covered in toffee sauce and paired with a pistachio ice cream sandwich; while seasonality is highlighted in a pumpkin pie matched with a scoop of maple frozen yogurt.

453

Roberta's 😊

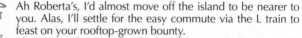

American ✗

261 Moore St. (bet. Bogart & White Sts.)

Subway: Morgan Av
Phone: 718-417-1118
Web: www.robertaspizza.com
Prices: $$

Lunch & dinner daily

Ah Roberta's, I'd almost move off the island to be nearer to you. Alas, I'll settle for the easy commute via the L train to feast on your rooftop-grown bounty.

The pizza here gets all the hype, and for sure it's amazing. Sample whichever one features as much of the urban garden as possible, or crucify your cholesterol with the Cheesus Christ. Then hone in on the seasonally-driven dishes from the kitchen which are the underdog. From Fairy Tale eggplant with mascarpone and wood sorrel to agnolotti with black truffle, Taleggio, and nasturtium, everything is delicious, product-driven, and creative in a whimsical way that works wonders. The best approach: get a few friends and sample one of everything, plus their dynamite cocktails swimming in Mason jars

Roman's

Italian ✗

243 DeKalb Ave. (bet. Clermont & Vanderbilt Aves.)

Subway: Lafayette Av
Phone: 718-622-5300
Web: www.romansnyc.com
Prices: $$

Dinner Tue – Sun

Your *mamma* didn't give you much of a choice for dinner, and neither will Andrew Tarlow and Mark Firth—at least not on the menu at their newest restaurant. But have faith, young Brooklyn—for this is the brilliant duo behind Diner and Marlow & Sons, two wildly successful Williamsburg restaurants that helped put a distinct Brooklyn cuisine on the map.

Housed in the duo's old Bonita space, Roman's is small and warm, with candlelight bouncing off white tiled walls, and blazing color mosaic tiles dotting the room. The menu offers a handful of simple, but delicious dishes that might include sweet, crisp carrot ribbons tossed with raisins, nuts, and parsley; tender pasta rings stuffed with fresh ricotta over chunky tomato sauce; or creamy chocolate gelato.

Rucola

190 Dean St. (at Bond St.)

Subway: Bergen St (Smith St.) Lunch & dinner Tue – Sun
Phone: 718-576-3209
Web: www.rucolabrooklyn.com
Prices: $$

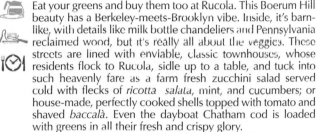

Eat your greens and buy them too at Rucola. This Boerum Hill beauty has a Berkeley-meets-Brooklyn vibe. Inside, it's barn-like, with details like milk bottle chandeliers and Pennsylvania reclaimed wood, but it's really all about the veggies. These streets are lined with enviable, classic townhouses, whose residents flock to Rucola, sidle up to a table, and tuck into such heavenly fare as a farm fresh zucchini salad served cold with flecks of *ricotta salata*, mint, and cucumbers; or house-made, perfectly cooked shells topped with tomato and shaved *baccalà*. Even the dayboat Chatham cod is loaded with greens in all their fresh and crispy glory.

You've been so good and ate all your vegetables, so reward yourself with a slice of that excellent chocolate torte.

Rye 😊

247 S. 1st St. (bet. Havemeyer and Roebling Sts.)

Subway: Marcy Av Lunch Sun
Phone: 718-218-8047 Dinner nightly
Web: www.ryerestaurant.com
Prices: $$

Chef/owner Cal Elliott's solo venture is housed in a nondescript section of south Williamsburg that coolly lacks any signage to promote its existence. The former bodega is outfitted with rough hewn wood flooring, zinc-topped tables, and exposed filament bulbs. The hefty bar, restored by the chef, dominates the intimate room; and arched, mirror-backed shelving is stocked with a collection of brown liquors. The succinct menu of snacks and grilled items boasts classic touches that reflect the kitchen's talents and skill. Offerings may include house-made gnocchi, topped with shreds of meltingly tender duck confit; golden and crisp, pan-roasted halibut drizzled with herb-flecked beurre blanc; or warm and fudgy chocolate cake with vanilla ice cream.

Saraghina

C2

435 Halsey St. (at Lewis Ave.)

Subway: Utica Av
Phone: 718-574-0010
Web: www.saraghinabrooklyn.com
Prices: $$

Lunch & dinner daily

Saraghina, named for a character in a Fellini film, may have lost its original owners but it hasn't lost any of its appeal. Bicycles are a plenty outside this building on a charming Bed-Stuy street lined with brownstones and Victorians. It's kitschy cute...old butcher signs, chairs hanging from the ceiling, and marmalade jars define the look, and there's even a leafy garden in the back for nice summer days.

This all-day spot is known for the pizza, which like the *capocollo* (topped with thick and searingly spicy *coppa* and buttery mozzarella) is definitely a don't-miss, but wait, there's more. Creamy risotto studded with sweet sausage; striped bass perfectly seasoned and simply cooked; even a grilled apple salad with tart goat cheese...it's all so *buono*!

Savoia

C4

277 Smith St. (bet. De Graw & Sackett Sts.)

Subway: Carroll St
Phone: 718-797-2727
Web: N/A
Prices: $$

Lunch & dinner daily

With its young at-home moms, lunching construction crews, and savvy foreign visitors, all walks of life are drawn to this Smith Street charmer, pastorally furnished with wooden tables and straw-seat chairs. Exposed brick and colorful tiles complement the two-room setting, equipped with a wood-burning pizza oven. Fittingly, Savoia devotes a large portion of its menu to manifold pizza offerings made in the Neopolitan tradition. Still, there is also an ample selection of gratifying homemade pastas, like the organic buckwheat *maltagliati* with porcini mushrooms, *bresaola*, and truffle oil; as well as heartier items like the roasted pork chop with eggplant caponata and grilled *orata* with sun dried tomatoes. Affable service adds to Savoia's casual vibe.

Saul ✿

Contemporary 🍴🍴

C3

140 Smith St. (bet. Bergen & Dean Sts.)

Subway: Bergen St (Smith St.)
Phone: 718-935-9844
Web: www.saulrestaurant.com
Prices: $$$

Dinner nightly

Daniel Krieger

Perhaps there is no grand entryway and no glittering glass artwork, but it is this modest mien that makes Saul a knock-out destination for true-blue NYers. The interior is a welcoming mix of hardwood floors, brick walls, and pressed-tin ceilings that keeps everyone relaxed but humming with anticipation. Maybe it's the tree-lined setting amidst charming stores and cheery playgrounds. Or, maybe it's the agreeable staff who makes everyone feel like regulars (and most are). Whatever it is, Saul is that iconic neighborhood restaurant that seems to have entered the realm of excellence.

For over a decade, Chef Saul Bolton has been earning his stripes and stars with his inspired American cooking that is both delicate and elegant. Curried lentil soup is silky and rich; handmade butternut squash gnocchi is melt-in-your-mouth tender; and roasted line-caught Chatham cod is caramelized perfection. Desserts are never an afterthought here: the goat cheesecake paired with a fan of poached pears and candied walnuts is a work of art.

Of course, you could go rogue and order the tasting menu, complete with six dishes and a choice of dessert nicely chased down by a supplemental cheese course.

Sea

A1

Thai ✗

114 N. 6th St. (bet. Berry St. & Wythe Ave.)

Subway: Bedford Av
Phone: 718-384-8850
Web: www.seathainyc.com
Prices: 🍜

Lunch & dinner daily

Resembling a trendy Manhattan lounge yet serving fresh, well-made Asian cuisine, Sea is an exotic bird among the small hipster bars of Williamsburg. The cavernous space pulsates with energy, and its popularity is enjoyed by a diverse clientele, from young families to large after-work groups. The dining room, flanked by two bars, has an industrial-chic vibe with its concrete floor and cement walls complemented by a section of seating around a reflecting pool crowned by a life-size Buddha.

Considering the festive environs, the staff is impressively gracious and attentive.

The Thai-focused menu may lack authenticity but is reasonably priced and extensive in its offerings of dumplings, spring rolls, and salads, along with curries and sautéed dishes.

Seersucker

C4

American ✗✗

329 Smith St. (bet. Carroll & President Sts.)

Subway: Carroll St
Phone: 718-422-0444
Web: www.seersuckerbrooklyn.com
Prices: $$

Lunch Sat – Sun
Dinner Mon – Sat

Folks have little difficulty guessing this concept, but here are a few clues: shaved country ham on a warm buttermilk biscuit; pan-fried sweetbreads with red eye gravy and spring peas; and crisp-skinned trout with risotto-style Carolina rice, favas, and mint. This is proudly Southern cooking with a sophisticated flair. For groups, the snack tray is loaded up with deviled eggs, pimento cheese, and homemade chips.

The graciously attended to setting is neat and tidy, done in a cool palette of pale gray, and the kitchen of Arkansas-born Chef /owner Robert Newton showcases a colorful and enticing display of pickled produce. Dapper yet comfortable, this 30-seat Smith Street spot is everything that one would hope to get from a place named Seersucker.

Sette Enoteca & Cucina 😊

Italian 🍴

D4

207 Seventh Ave. (at 3rd St.)

Subway: / Av (9th St.) Lunch & dinner daily
Phone: 718-499 7767
Web: www.setteparkslope.com
Prices: $$

This consistently excellent Park Slope Italian gem is popular with most everyone—from cool couples lingering over shared plates of light, crispy *fritto misto*, to hip moms twirling pappardelle with braised lamb, alongside their offspring sharing pizzas. Rustic entrées offer the likes of grilled salmon with arugula and fresh orange salad; these preparations can be observed from the open kitchen. Lunches here are a great value.

Complement meals with selections from the inexpensive Italian wine list, offering a range of bottles under $24, and many available by the glass or *quartino*.

This bustling corner location features covered outdoor dining, a bar, and a contemporary dining room with chunky, blonde wooden tables, and fabric-covered banquettes.

The Smoke Joint

Barbecue 🍴

D3

87 S. Elliot Pl. (bet. Fulton St & Lafayette Ave.)

Subway: Lafayette Av Lunch & dinner daily
Phone: 718-797-1011
Web: www.thesmokejoint.com
Prices: 🍴🍴

Just steps away from the Brooklyn Academy of Music (BAM), harmonic barbecue bliss awaits courtesy of pedigreed restaurateurs, Craig Samuel (of City Hall) and Ben Grossman (of Picholine and La Grenouille).

Unlike some of its too-cool-for-school Brooklyn cousins, Fort Greene is hip but playfully unpretentious—and those tired of the servers who skulk around Williamsburg will eat up the waitstaff's terrific energy. An irresistible combination when paired with lip-smacking fare like the tender, house-smoked chicken; meltingly good pulled pork; meaty, dry-rubbed ribs; or creamy macaroni and cheese, arguably some of the best in the city. Bourbon freaks should make their way to the adjoined Pig Bar, where brown liquor gets top shelf treatment.

Stone Park Cafe

Brooklyn

D4

Contemporary ✗

324 Fifth Ave. (at 3rd St.)

Subway: Union St
Phone: 718-369-0082
Web: www.stoneparkcafe.com
Prices: $$

Lunch Tue – Sun
Dinner nightly

At this corner location, large windows peer onto Park Slope's vibrant Fifth Avenue thoroughfare and small namesake park. Stone Park Café has remained popular with neighborhood couples and families seeking seasonally inspired, creative fare. Their $32 prix-fixe Daily Market menu offers the likes of house-made tagliatelle with andouille sausage, rock shrimp tempura, and lobster beurre blanc; Scottish salmon with horseradish spaetzle; and panna cotta with citrus compote—a very good value for such quality.

The light, airy interior has exposed brick, pale sage walls, a long bar near the entrance for pre-dinner cocktails, and a candlelit, sunken dining room with linen-topped tables. Weather permitting, alfresco sidewalk seating is available.

Strong Place

C4

Gastropub ✗

270 Court St. (bet. Butler & Douglass Sts.)

Subway: Bergen St (Smith St.)
Phone: 718-855-2105
Web: N/A
Prices: $$

Lunch & dinner daily

Fronted by a welcoming bar area that is unapologetically devoted to beer (more than 20 labels are served on tap bolstered by an additional selection of fifteen bottles), Strong Place invites everyone to kick back and unwind. The vibe is chill, as chunky wood tables and metal seating render a vaguely industrial look. An open kitchen and raw bar station embellish the amiable atmosphere.

Snacks such as deviled eggs, boiled peanuts, and waffle fries with onion dip serve as perfect partners for a frosty brew; while entrées offer market-focused pub-grub with a French accent. Dishes include fluke carpaccio with shaved fennel and pomegranate seeds, crispy duck leg confit, and a luscious spice-rubbed nugget of pork with black eye peas and baby bok choy.

Tanoreen 🐕

Middle Eastern 🍴🍴

A4

7523 Third Ave. (at 76th St.)

Subway: 77 St
Phone: 718-748-5600
Web: www.tanoreen.com
Prices: 💲💲

Lunch & dinner Tue – Sun

In a roomy new setting with glassed-in sidewalk dining and jewel-toned sconces, Tanoreen continues to impress with its extensive menu of Middle Eastern home-style specialties. Chef/owner Rawia Bishara may have started her career by feeding friends and families at countless dinner parties, but today she runs this popular operation with her daughter for the city's eager destination-driven foodies.

Meals graciously commence with house-pickled vegetables and warm breads, prepping the way for an array of exotic delights such as: *makdous*—pickled baby eggplant stuffed with walnuts; *sujok*—thin slices of Armenian dried beef in a crimson sauce of red pepper, garlic, and olive oil; and *musakhan*—grilled flatbread topped with sumac-seasoned chicken.

Thistle Hill Tavern

Contemporary 🍴

B3

441 Seventh Ave. (at 15th St.)

Subway: 15 St - Prospect Park
Phone: 347-599-1262
Web: www.thistlehillbrooklyn.com
Prices: 💲💲

Lunch & dinner daily

This South Slope newbie conjures a classic tavern ambience usually found in a longtime neighborhood favorite. The corner location is flanked by sidewalk seating for a leisurely al fresco lunch; inside, exposed brick and chocolate brown wainscoting paint a warm and inviting scene.

Light fare is on order for lunch, as in the market-fresh chopped salad of heirloom tomatoes, corn sliced off the cob, bacon, and ricotta *salata*; sandwiches may include a grilled mushroom *panino* stuffed with goat cheese and basil alongside fries paired with homemade ketchup. Dinner offerings are a hearty expansion of the seasonal, locally sourced dishes, while desserts feature the likes of an espresso semifreddo showered with dark cherries, Marcona almonds, and chocolate.

Traif 😋

Contemporary ✗

229 South 4th St. (bet. Havemeyer & Roebling Sts.)

Subway: Marcy Av
Phone: 347-844-9578
Web: www.traifny.com
Prices: $$

Lunch Sat – Sun
Dinner Tue – Sun

Rocking an affinity for pork and shellfish, this rollicking Williamsburg eatery serves up a vibrant array of flavor-packed small plates. The restaurant's moniker translates to "forbidden" in Yiddish, and the extensive menu offers more than 20 eclectic, global creations prepared by Chef/owner Jason Marcus and his team from a sliver of open kitchen that is brightly tiled and equipped with a single Vulcan range.

The team rises to the challenge, sending forth the likes of crispy salt and pepper shrimp with a *siracha*-spiced salad of pineapple, cucumber, watermelon and Thai basil; Catalonian black *fideos* with nuggets of octopus, escargot, and drizzles of creamy green garlic sauce; and warm bacon doughnuts with *dulche de leche* and coffee ice cream.

Tuscany Grill

Italian ✗

8620 Third Ave. (bet. 86th & 87th Sts.)

Subway: 86 St
Phone: 718-921-5633
Web: N/A
Prices: $$

Dinner nightly

Bay Ridge's ever-changing demographic does not deter this charismatic, quintessential neighborhood restaurant from serving Italian-American favorites to a loyal cadre of locals who come for dishes that burst with flavor as well as to share their latest adventures with the waitstaff.

The menu offers hefty portions of honest, good food, such as homey Hunter-style *farfalle* pasta baked in tomatoes, mushrooms, and cheese, with sweet and hot sausage. Crostini of fresh, milky ricotta, roasted red bell pepper, and basil leaf over toast brushed with quality olive oil makes a wonderful prelude to any meal. Save room for decadent house-made desserts such as the pignoli tart–lemony and piney–served in a crust that is truly worth every buttery calorie.

Umi Nom

Asian ✗

B2

433 DeKalb Ave. (bet. Classon Ave. & Taaffe Pl.)

Subway: Classon Av
Phone: 718-789-8806
Web: www.uminom.com
Prices: $$

Lunch & dinner Mon – Sat

You'll have to travel deep into Pratt's somewhat dodgy backyard for this one, but this popular Southeast Asian charmer is well worth the adventure to Bed-Stuy. The restaurant arrives courtesy of King Phojanakong, the man behind the Lower East Side's Kuma Inn, and owns a pretty, minimalist design fitted out with wooden pews, sultry lighting slung from brick walls, and a half-open kitchen emitting heavenly drafts from the wok.

Small plates abound on the menu, which might offer tender, market-fresh baby bok choy simmered with garlic and creamy butter, a plate of gorgeous prawns, served head-on in a devilishly spicy, lip-smacking chili sauce; or mackerel, grilled to a lovely char and paired with bright strips of pickled carrots and cool cucumber.

The Vanderbilt

Contemporary 〽

D4

570 Vanderbilt Ave. (at Bergen St.)

Subway: Bergen St (Flatbush Ave.)
Phone: 718 623-0570
Web: www.thevanderbiltnyc.com
Prices: $$

Lunch Sat – Sun
Dinner nightly

Chef Saul Bolton's yummy venture, opened in partnership with Ben Daitz, is the perfect contrast to his beloved namesake dining room on Smith Street. This lively, loud, and packed Prospect Heights spot, clad in reclaimed wood and marble-topped communal tables, is great for boisterous groups or a quick solo bite at the bar offering a worldly assemblage of mouthwatering small plates.

The fuss-free and fun fare may include the likes of caramelized Brussels sprouts tossed with lime, honey, and *sriracha*; a rich, luscious block of crispy pig's feet draped with tart and creamy sauce *gribiche*; or delicately fried spiced-apple turnover for dessert. A blackboard list of thirst-quenching spirits adds to the Vanderbilt's casually sophisticated appeal.

Van Horn Sandwich Shop

C3

231 Court St. (bet. Baltic & Warren Sts.)

Subway: Bergen St (Smith St.)
Phone: 718-596-9707
Web: www.vanhornbrooklyn.com
Prices: 🍷

Lunch & dinner Tue – Sun

Emanating a charmingly old-timey appearance and dishing up Southern-inspired fare, this Cobble Hill spot deliciously typifies au courant Brooklyn dining. The menu of hot and hearty sandwiches is fashioned from local ingredients in combinations that feature freshly prepared buttermilk-fried chicken on a sesame-seed bun and North Carolina-style pulled pork. The BLP slathers toasted sourdough slices with pimento cheese, makes a decidedly high-brow substitution of garlic aïoli for plain mayonnaise, then tops it off with crisp bacon and tender butter lettuce.

Side dishes like baked mac and cheese, jalapeño hushpuppies, craft beers, and cocktails round out a down-home menu that tastes even better when enjoyed seated outside in the backyard.

Vinegar Hill House 🎭

D2

72 Hudson Ave. (near Water St.)

Subway: York St
Phone: 718-522-1018
Web: www.vinegarhillhouse.com
Prices: $$

Dinner nightly

When Chef Brian Leth was brought on board Vinegar Hill House, the countrified child of husband-and-wife team Jean Adamson and Sam Buffa, a throng of hipster locals came knocking. The owners who live above, have showered this bucolic Brooklyn den with *mucho* charm in the form of well-worn wooden planks, pale grey walls, and tables armed with bent cane seating.

Peek in a petite open kitchen with a wood-burning oven churning out perfectly charred sourdough. Vintage crockery delivers a Mediterranean-flecked menu with dishes like oven roasted octopus moistened with lemon slices, green olives, and yogurt; *mezze maniche* slicked with spicy lamb ragù and frilled with picholine olives and ricotta; and Guiness cake polished with pretty cream cheese frosting.

Waterfalls Café

C3

Middle Eastern 🍴

144 Atlantic Ave. (bet. Clinton & Henry Sts.)

Subway: Borough Hall   Lunch & dinner daily
Phone: 718-488-8886
Web: N/A
Prices: 🥢

Deliciously uncompromised, made-to-order Middle Eastern food: what's not to love at the Waterfalls Café, a little café that rises above the rush of Arabic diners that cluster along this stretch of Atlantic Avenue? Perhaps the service, which can be a bit stilted and off-the-mark from time to time—that said, you'll soon realize that patience is a mighty big virtue here.

The reward is in the spectacularly creamy hummus; light-as-air falafel, fresh and crackling from the fryer; moist stuffed grape leaves; perfectly-spiced *moujadarra*, spiked with tender caramelized onions; and supremely tender chunks of lamb *shawarma*, served with fresh pita. No alcohol is served, but fragrant teas and Arabic coffee finish the meal; and takeout is available.

World Tong 😊

B4

Chinese 🍴

6202 Eighteenth Ave. (at 62nd St.)

Subway: 18 Av   Lunch & dinner daily
Phone: 718-236-8118
Web: N/A
Prices: 🥢

With its bland dining room and unadorned interior, this monochromatic Bensonhurst gem gets right down to business by putting its money where its customer's mouths would like to be—wrapped around some killer dim sum. And judging from the flood of locals who patron the joint, this no-nonsense approach appears to be right on cue.

Dreamy carts wheeling past showcase an endless array of tiny delights, like sticky-rice dumplings wrapped in lotus leaves; golden shrimp balls; or spare ribs with black bean sauce and taro. Don't miss the phenomenal parade of tender soup dumplings, a variety of soft pouches bursting with spice-infused broths, including star anise, clove, and ginger; or the strange-smelling, but oddly addictive, durian pastries.

Zenkichi

A1

77 N. 6th St. (at Wythe Ave.)

Subway: Bedford Av
Phone: 718-388-8985
Web: www.zenkichi.com
Prices: $$

Dinner Tue – Sun

Beyond a rather daunting wood-armored exterior, Zenkichi's small entryway is practically camouflaged. Once inside however, warm greetings ensue as groups small and large are escorted through the dim, three-level *izakaya* to private booths. Service is serious here; when ready to order, summon the staff with the tabletop button.

The menu features an assortment of Tokyo-style small plates designed to be enjoyed with alcohol, and lots of it. Set your own course or choose the well-priced omakase: an eight-course seasonal feast that may start with a chilled plate of pristine fish and then close with roasted honey-soy duck. Start off with some sake and oysters at adjacent Bar Akariba.

Return visits are inevitable—just remember to reserve.

Bib Gourmand 🐷
indicates our inspectors'
favorites for good value.

Queens

Queens

Nearly as large as Manhattan, the Bronx, and Staten Island combined, the borough of Queens covers 120 square miles on the western end of Long Island. Thousands of immigrants arriving here each year make Queens the most culturally diverse county in the country. They are all drawn to the relatively affordable housing, a familial quality of life, and the tight-knit cultural communities formed by extended immigrant families. Such a unique convergence results in the borough's international flavor, drawing throngs of New Yorkers eager to dine on affordable, ethnic eats.

ASTORIA'S GLOBAL BUFFET

Stroll through Astoria, a charming quarter of brick row houses and Mediterranean groceries. Discover grilled octopus and baklava at one of the many terrific Greek restaurants; then make your way to Little Egypt on Steinway Street for a juicy kebab; or chow on Czech kielbasas at the local *biergarten*. Along global lines, the **Hot Bread Kitchen** project is introducing NYers to a selection of traditional breads from around the world. The iconic *pasticceria*, **La Guli**, has been open since 1937 and dishes out a tandem of cakes, pastries (delicious pignoli tarts perhaps?), cookies, biscuits,

and seasonal specialties to everyone's heart's content.

Beer-lovers, on any lazy day, should frequent Astoria's newest beer havens. For an intimate setting with a serious selection head to **Sweet Afton**; and for the ultimate alfresco experience, **Studio Square** is *the* place! Order a dish from their Garden Grill menu (maybe jalapeño-spiced "Angry" chicken wings with a lick of blue cheese) and you will be floating for the rest of the night. Speaking of which, entertain crowds with a night of karaoke and peruse the unique beer offerings at **Mingle Beer House**.

FIERY FLUSHING

Flushing still reigns as Queens' most vibrant Asian neighborhood. Drop in for dim sum or slurp an avocado shake and a savory bowl of hot *pho* like you'd find street side in Saigon. Food vendors at Flushing's mini-malls offer a feast for the ravenous that's light on pockets with delights from every corner of China. You'll find anything at these stalls including hand-pulled noodles, fiery Sichuan chili-oil dishes, Peking duck pancakes, *bings*, and buns in a bustling setting that's right out of a Hong Kong alley. And the Chinese offerings don't stop here. If in the mood for vegetarian kosher Chinese delights, forge ahead on Main Street to **Buddha Bodai**. En-route to JFK, stop by **Warung**

Kario on Liberty Avenue for unique Indonesian-Surinamese cuisine. Traveling east is the **Queens County Farm Museum**. Considered one of the largest working farms in the city, it supports sustainable farming, offers farm-to-table meals, and is replete with livestock, a greenhouse complex, and educational programs.

EATING IN ELMHURST

Vivacity and diversity personify Elmhurst, the thriving hearth to immigrants primarily from China, Southeast Asia, and Latin America. The Royal Kathin, a celebration that occurs at the end of Thailand's rainy season, pays homage to the spirit of the monks. The Elmhurst adaptation may lack the floods, but offers a bounty of faithful Thai delicacies. Whitney Avenue houses a restaurant row with a range of tiny Southeast Asian storefronts. Indulge your *gado gado* craving at **Minangasli** or **Upi Jaya** and get your *laksa* on at **Taste Good**. Elmhurst spans the globe so if the powerful and pungent flavors of Southeast Asia aren't your thing, dive into an Argentinean *parilla* for a shift from Asia to the Americas.

A Marriage of Cultures

Jackson Heights is home to a distinct South Asian community. Take in the *bhangra* beats blaring from cars rolling along 74th Street—a dynamic commercial stretch of Indian markets, Bengali sweet shops, and Himalayan-style eateries. Some favorites include Indian tandoor specialties and Tibetan *momos* (beef dumplings). Latin Americans from Colombia, Ecuador, Argentina, Uruguay, Peru, and Mexico also make up a large part of the demographic here. Catering to their tastes, Roosevelt Avenue sizzles with a sampling of taquerias, Colombian coffee shops, and Argentinean bakeries. The commercial thoroughfare connects several neighborhoods, shape shifting from country to country.

WANDERING THROUGH WOODSIDE

Follow the Avenue west to Woodside, where Irish bars commingle with spicy Thai spots. Once home to a large Irish population, Woodside now shares its blocks with a small Thai and Filipino population. The kelly green awnings of decade-old pubs dot the streets and clover-covered doors advertise in Gaelic. Here **Donovan's** has one of the best (and juiciest) burgers in all the five boroughs. Alongside is Little Manila, an eight-block stretch of Roosevelt Avenue, where you can find Filipino groceries and restaurants galore. The recent opening of **Jollibee**, the ultra-popular fast-food chain, has folks lined up for a taste of home. On Queens Boulevard in Sunnyside (one of the most divergent 'hoods), eat your way through Korea, Columbia, Mexico, Romania, China, and Turkey. Of course, not in one day! In late June, check out The New York City Food Film Festival where food and film lovers gather to view screenings of food films while noshing on a variety of lip-smacking nibbles.

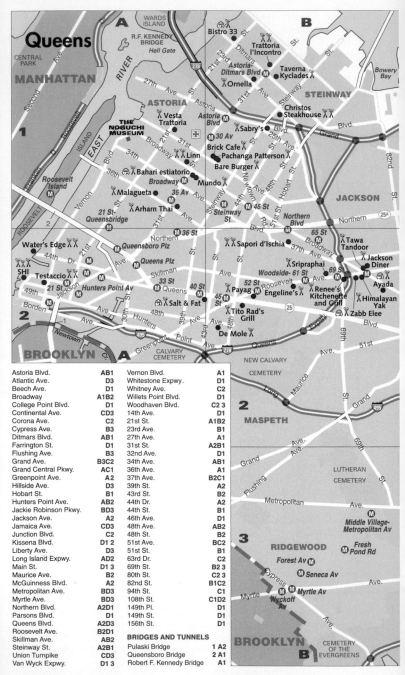

Queens

MANHATTAN

CENTRAL PARK

WARDS ISLAND

R.F. KENNEDY BRIDGE
Hell Gate

Bistro 33

Trattoria l'Incontro

Astoria-Ditmars Blvd

Taverna Kyclades

Ornella

STEINWAY

Bowery Bay

ASTORIA

THE NOGUCHI MUSEUM

Vesta Trattoria

Astoria Blvd

Christos Steakhouse

Sabry's

30 Av

Brick Cafe

Pachanga Patterson

Bare Burger

JACKSON

EAST

Roosevelt Island

ROOSEVELT I.

Bahari estiatorio

Broadway

Mundo

Malagueta

36 Av

Arharn Thai

21 St-Queensbridge

Steinway St

44th

46 St

Northern Blvd

Water's Edge

36 St

Queensboro Plz

Sapori d'Ischia

65 St

Tawa Tandoor

SHI

Testaccio

Queens Plz

Sripraphai

Jackson Diner

Hunters Point Av

33 St

40 St

Queens

Woodside- 61 St

52 St

69 St

Ayada

Payag

Engeline's

Renee's Kitchenette and Grill

Himalayan Yak

Salt & Fat

Tito Rad's Grill

Zabb Elee

De Mole

CALVARY CEMETERY

BROOKLYN

Newtown

Hunters Point

Greenpoint Ave.

NEW CALVARY CEMETERY

MASPETH

LUTHERAN CEMETERY

RIDGEWOOD

Middle Village-Metropolitan Av

Fresh Pond Rd

Forest Av

Seneca Av

Myrtle Av

Wyckoff Av

BROOKLYN

CEMETERY OF THE EVERGREENS

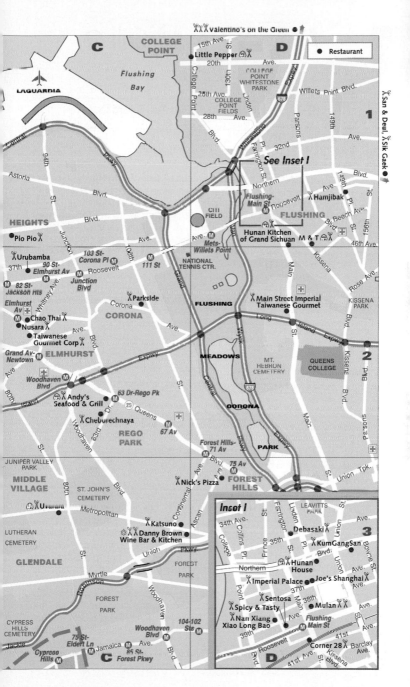

X X X Valentino's on the Green ●

● Restaurant

C COLLEGE POINT D

15th St.
Little Pepper ● 20th Ave.
LAGUARDIA
Flushing Bay
COLLEGE POINT WHITESTONE PARK
25th Ave. COLLEGE POINT FIELDS
28th Ave.
Willets Point Blvd.
149th
1
Central Pkwy.
94th St.
Astoria Blvd.
Blvd.
Blvd.
32nd Ave.
See Inset I
Northern Blvd.
149th Pl.
156th St.
46th Ave.
Linden
Parsons
Whitestone
Farrington St.
Flushing-Main St.
Roosevelt
Hamjibak X
FLUSHING
HEIGHTS Blvd.
Pio Pio ● X
CITI FIELD
Ave.
Mets-Willets Point
Hunan Kitchen of Grand Sichuan
M & T X
X Urubamba
103 St-Corona Pl.
Roosevelt
111 St
NATIONAL TENNIS CTR.
Beach Ave.
Kissena
37th
90 St-Elmhurst Av
M
Junction Blvd
M
Junction Ave.
Whitney Ave.
Corona
FLUSHING
Rose Ave.
KISSENA PARK
82 St-Jackson Hts
Elmhurst Av X
Chao Thai X
Nusara X
Taiwanese Gourmet Corp X
CORONA
X Parkside
Grand
Ave.
X Main Street Imperial Taiwanese Gourmet
Long
Island
Expwy.
Kissena Blvd.
Grand Av-Newtown
ELMHURST
Woodhaven Blvd
M
FLUSHING
MEADOWS
MT. HEBRON CEMETERY
QUEENS COLLEGE
2
80th St.
Island
Expwy.
Grand
Ave.
Queens
Blvd.
25
Andy's Seafood & Grill ● X
X Cheburechnaya
63 Dr-Rego Pk
67 Av
M
CORONA
PARK
Main St.
Parsons
REGO PARK
JUNIPER VALLEY PARK
Woodhaven
Forest Hills-71 Av
M
75 Av
M
FOREST HILLS
Union Tpk.
MIDDLE VILLAGE
80th St.
ST. JOHN'S CEMETERY
Metropolitan
X Nick's Pizza
Continental Ave.
Ascan
Blvd.
LEAVITTS PARK
Inset I
34th Ave.
Debasaki X
3
LUTHERAN CEMETERY
GLENDALE
X Katsuno
Danny Brown Wine Bar & Kitchen X X
Union
Pkwy.
FOREST PARK
X Usuarda
Myrtle
Robinson
FOREST PARK
Woodhaven Blvd
104-102 Sts
M
Collins Pl.
Prince St.
35th Ave.
Northern
Hunan House X
X KumGangSan
Bowne St.
Union St.
Imperial Palace X
Joe's Shanghai X
37th Ave.
X Sentosa
X Spicy & Tasty
Nan Xiang Xiao Long Bao X
X Mulan X
Flushing-Main St
38th Ave.
CYPRESS HILLS CEMETERY
75 St-Eldert Ln
M
Woodhaven Blvd
85 St-Forest Pkwy
M
Jamaica
Jackie Robinson Pkwy
Cypress Hills
M
C
Roosevelt
39th Ave.
41st St.
Corner 28 X
Barclay Ave.
41st Ave.
Kissena Blvd.
D

X San & Deul, X Sik Gaek ●

Andy's Seafood & Grill ☺

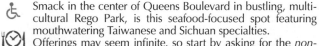

C2

95-26 Queens Blvd. (bet. 63rd Ave. & 63rd Dr.)

Subway: 63 Dr – Rego Park   Lunch & dinner daily
Phone: 718-275-2388
Web: N/A
Prices: ⊛⊛

Smack in the center of Queens Boulevard in bustling, multi-cultural Rego Park, is this seafood-focused spot featuring mouthwatering Taiwanese and Sichuan specialties.

Offerings may seem infinite, so start by asking for the *non-American* menu—yes, there are two—to focus your selections and heighten authenticity. Dishes may range from the fantastic "smelly tofu," aged and deep-fried, served with crunchy-sweet daikon and chili paste, to the restorative *hakku*-style soup, with chewy rice balls bobbing in a beautifully clarified, flavorful pork broth. Highlights include the über-fresh, steamed whole sea bass topped with ginger, scallions, and cilantro, bathed in a delicate broth, finished with fermented beans for a quintessential taste of umami.

Arharn Thai

A1

32-05 36th Ave. (bet. 32nd & 33rd Sts.)

Subway: 36 Av   Lunch & dinner daily
Phone: 718-728-5563
Web: www.thaiastoria.com
Prices: ⊛⊛

Just a block off the N train along this busy stretch of Astoria, Arharn Thai appears to be a fairly non-descript operation: clean, relatively unadorned, with Thai-inspired artifacts dotting the walls. However, the vibrant Thai specialties that swiftly land upon the minimally-dressed tables immediately break up the blandness of the room.

Each dish deftly balances the sweet, salty, spicy, bitter and sour elements that define the country's cuisine. While the heat is given the usual Western taming, there is still a great deal left to satisfy in plates like *mook ka prow*, sautéed pork with basil leaves and chili; crisp roasted duck with red curry; or *buad shee*, a dessert of banana steamed in coconut milk served with a warm coconut-banana soup.

Ayada 😊

B2

77-08 Woodside Ave. (bet. 77th & 78th Sts.)

Subway: Woodside 61 St   Lunch & dinner daily
Phone: 718-424-0844
Web: N/A
Prices: $$

Could Ayada, a seductive new restaurant on the Woodside Thai circuit, soon topple the area's reigning Thai sweetheart, Sripraphai? If rave reviews and smitten regulars have anything to say about it, the answer is most decidedly yes.

Owner Duangjai Thammasat hails from Pichit, an area of Central Thailand dominated by complex curries, coconut milk, and wok-fried noodles; and the chef shows a deft hand balancing sweet and sour flavors with salt and spice. Kick things off with a fiery raw shrimp salad marinated in lime, chili, and coriander; and then feast on plump steamed mussels dancing in coconut broth with lemongrass and basil; succulent crispy pork paired with tart Chinese broccoli; and tender frog legs bathed in a sharp basil sauce.

Bahari estiatorio 😊

A1

31-14 Broadway (bet. 31st & 32nd Sts.)

Subway: Broadway   Lunch & dinner daily
Phone: 718-204-8968
Web: www.bahariestiatorio.com
Prices: $$

Old, beloved Stamatis on Broadway got itself a hip make-over. Gone are the kitschy seafaring murals, usurped by the likes of exposed brick walls, an artsy display of window shutters, and wooden beams planking the ceiling. But don't fret, Astorians, though the name's different, this spruced-up replacement still has the same owners, same scrumptious menu, and same loving family feel.

So get in here, find your old favorite table, and get eating. *Kriya pikilia* is a fine way to start: a tasty assortment of traditional Greek spreads, from *skordalia* to *tzatziki*, with warm pita for dipping. Next, sink your chops into the succulent *hirines brizoles*—lightly seasoned, tender pork chops with rice and fresh veggies. Or stick to a classic—melt-in-your mouth *mousaka*.

Bare Burger

B1

33-21 31st Ave. (at 34th St.)

Subway: 30 Av   Lunch & dinner daily
Phone: 718-777-7011
Web: www.bareburger.com
Prices: $$

  ♿ 🍴

Funky chandeliers made out of spoons; spare, clean tables; and a whole lot of bustle welcome you to Bare Burger, a new organic burger joint set among Astoria's thriving neighborhood food scene. But burgers you can feel good about? Now that's a tasty idea.

The sustainable-minded restaurant occupies a well-exposed corner near the elevated train station. Once inside, customers have their choice of filling (everything from straight-up beef to elk, bison, and grilled pineapple); and the fun is just getting started. With salads and organic milkshakes in flavors like pistachio and raspberry rounding out the menu, you'd be hard-pressed to find a more appealing place for the young foodies moving into the hood. Don't miss the addictive dipping sauces.

Bistro 33 😊

B1

19-33 Ditmars Blvd. (at 21st St.)

Subway: Astoria - Ditmars Blvd   Lunch Sat – Sun
Phone: 718-721-1933   Dinner nightly
Web: www.lilbistro33.com
Prices: $$

  🍴

Located a few blocks from scenic Shore Blvd., Bistro 33 is home to Chef Gary Anza. This perfect little neighborhood spot serves a fusion cuisine that marries the chef's classic training with his experience in the art of sushi–he is a graduate of the French Culinary Institute and an alum of Bond Street– for a unique dining experience that does this borough proud. The resulting menu is well-prepared, neatly presented, and delights the palate with an array of sushi fare like freshly rolled maki topped with creamy, chopped lobster; as well as contemporary offerings that have included excellent pan-seared scallops sauced with warm, smoky-bacon dressing; and slow-cooked pork belly sweetened with an intriguing reduction of black cherry soda and palm sugar.

Brick Cafe

Mediterranean ✕

B1

30-95 33rd St. (at 31st Ave.)

Subway: Broadway
Phone: /18-267-2735
Web: www.brickcafe.com
Prices: $$

Lunch Sat – Sun
Dinner nightly

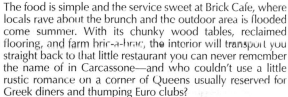

The food is simple and the service sweet at Brick Cafe, where locals rave about the brunch and the outdoor area is flooded come summer. With its chunky wood tables, reclaimed flooring, and farm bric-a-brac, the interior will transport you straight back to that little restaurant you can never remember the name of in Carcassone—and who couldn't use a little rustic romance on a corner of Queens usually reserved for Greek diners and thumping Euro clubs?

Best not to fight this kind of momentum and join the crowds digging into Southern French-and-Italian style dishes like grilled Maya shrimp, zucchini, and portobello mushroom caps tossed in a cilantro-garlic olive oil. The brunch menu carries the usual omelets and French toast, but also octopus carpaccio.

Chao Thai

Thai ✕

C2

85-03 Whitney Ave. (at Broadway)

Subway: Flmhurst Av
Phone: 718-424-4999
Web: www.demolenyc.com
Prices: 🍷🍷

Lunch & dinner daily

Tiny Chao Thai is not only a friendly escape from the cacophony of the LIRR, but a lovely culinary gem. Teeming with Asian diners, Chao Thai rises above its competition with earnest authenticity. The menu is manifold with classics, but most dishes hail from the North like *moo pad phrik ging*, juicy pork and crisp string beans stir-fried in a fragrant curry paste. It would be remiss to skip the daily specials (in Thai), so ask a waiter to explain.

All tables are dotted with complex, richly scented sauces that blend sublimely with classics like *massaman* curry (chicken and potatoes in a pungent coconut gravy); and grilled eggplant salad with ground pork and shrimp. The "potato chip bags" with deep-fried salted fish are a thrilling countertop takeaway.

Cheburechnaya

C2

92-09 63rd Dr. (at Austin St.)

Subway: 63 Dr - Rego Park   Lunch Sun – Fri
Phone: 718-897-9080   Dinner Sat – Thu
Web: www.cheburechnaya.com
Prices:

Make no mistake: the service can be halting, the halogen lighting is brutal, and the blaring Russian music videos don't exactly scream date night. But this boisterous Rego Park restaurant's inconveniences fade when the dining room's open grill lights up–crackling and sizzling with succulent kebabs–and gorgeous plates of food start flying out of the kitchen (sometimes all at once).

It's hard to miss with Cheburechnaya's gorgeous kosher food, which caters to the neighborhood's Bukharan Jewish population, but keep an eye peeled for the carrot salad, cut into noodle-thin strips and humming with chili, paprika, and cilantro; and the *noni toki* bread, a charred beauty that reads something like a cross between cumin seed-studded flat bread and matzo.

Christos Steakhouse

B1

41-08 23rd Ave. (at 41st St.)

Subway: Ditmars Blvd   Dinner nightly
Phone: 718-777-8400
Web: www.christossteakhouse.com
Prices: $$$

A dark red awning dips down over windows promising hearty portions of dry-aged beef while neat hedges line the entrance to this beloved Astoria institution. Inside, a front area serves as both bar and butcher shop, beautifully displaying their range of house-aged chops. Hardwood floors, warm tones, and mahogany tables draped in white linens complete the traditional setting.

But what sets Christos apart from its chophouse brethren is the uniquely Greek influence of the food: *taramosalata* and salads of Greek sausage over *gigante* beans share the menu with standards like roast chicken, lobster, and ribeye. Expertly prepared sides like tart and tender dandelion greens (*horta*) tossed in lemon juice and olive oil bring fresh flavors to steakhouse dining.

Corner 28

D3

Chinese 🍴

40-28 Main St. (at 40th Rd.)

Subway: Flushing - Main St   Lunch & dinner daily
Phone: 718-886-6628
Web: N/A
Prices: $$

Straddling a busy corner of Flushing is the bright, double-decker goliath, Corner 28. Choose from two entrances for different–albeit tasty–experiences. The left door leads to a chaotic take-out joint, where you can score a 75¢ Peking duck from early morning until 2:00 A.M. The right door leads guests up to the second floor, where a sunlight-flooded room finds diners flipping through glossy menus while friendly servers hustle to and fro with heaping plates of fragrant food. The space can get crowded quickly and the Chinese music can jangle the nerves, but oh-how-soothing it is to finally tuck your chopsticks into a heat-packing dish of soft, shredded pork, bathed in ruby-colored garlic sauce; or meltingly tender lamb chops, massaged with herbs and spices.

De Mole

Mexican 🍴

B2

45-02 48th Ave. (at 45th St.)

Subway: 46 St   Lunch & dinner daily
Phone: 718-392-2161
Web: www.demolenyc.com
Prices: 🍴🍴

Straddling a corner of Sunnyside dominated by Columbian bakeries, taco joints, and residential buildings, tiny, immaculate De Mole takes its namesake dish (and a wealth of other Mexican standbys) to new heights.

The flavors start rolling out at breakfast, which offers heavy hitters like *huevos rancheros* and De Mole buffalo burger. The pace marches on to a lunch and dinner menu that might include tender *chuleta*, a grilled pork chop smothered in caramelized onions and served with red rice, beans, and a fluffy stack of steaming corn tortillas; a spot-on torta boasting juicy strips of tender carne asada; or melt-in-your mouth coconut flan. Less adventurous eaters will find solace in Tex Mex standbys like fajitas, nachos, and taco salads.

Danny Brown Wine Bar & Kitchen ❀

Mediterranean ✗✗

C3

104-02 Metropolitan Ave. (at 71st Dr.)

Subway: Forest Hills - 71 Av   Dinner Tue – Sun
Phone: 718-261-2144
Web: www.dannybrownwinekitchen.com
Prices: $$

Gaetano Salvadore

Poised in the middle of stately Queens, this now "famous" kitchen and wine bar has brought along with it a host of newcomers to the Forest Hills nabe. Beset by a pretty pet shop, antique dealers, and a movie theater, Danny Brown further exalts the residential vibe with its large, enveloping windows and posse of devoted staff who are all warmth and candor.

You will feel like family upon entering this beaming space whose walls, floors, and windows are struck with neutral palettes. But amidst such sweet subtlety, lives some very striking and gracefully-lit artwork that *will* take your breath away. Coloring the very picture of an upscale bistro are wooden chairs with silken seating, high ceilings flecked with fans, well-spaced tables alluding to privacy, and that noble bar preening bottles, beers, and spirits.

As if to further romance you, sultry tunes hum as well-versed servers emerge from an open kitchen carrying such celebrated creations as warm Serrano ham croquettes sitting on a wave of saffron aïoli; *garganelli carbonara* richly tossed with truffles and cheese; a sweetly shined grilled Hampshire pork chop; and a little bit boozy yet incredibly light rum raisin cake to *finis*.

Debasaki

Japanese

33-67 Farrington St. (bet. 33rd & 35th Aves.)

Subway: Flushing - Main St   Dinner nightly
Phone: 718 886-6878
Web: N/A
Prices: $$

Surrounded by chop-shops and industrial outlets, this sexy Korean/Japanese chicken joint in Flushing gets a bit isolated after 8:00 P.M., though those who know where they're headed are in for a treat. Inside, you'll find a slick, stylish interior fitted out with cushy, high-backed striped booths, thumping Korean pop beats, and an intimate back bar that manages to be even darker than the restaurant.

The soups are notable at Debasaki, but it's the chicken that keeps this restaurant packed all hours of the night (the place stays open until 2:00 A.M.). Don't miss the *gyoza* of fried chicken wings stuffed with shrimp, corn, cheese, hot peppers, and corn kimchi; boneless barbecue chicken topped with crunchy fish eggs; or the tart kimchi fried rice with cheese.

Engeline's

B2

Filipino

58-28 Roosevelt Ave. (bet. 58th & 59th Sts.)

Subway: Woodside - 61 St   Lunch & dinner daily
Phone: 718-898-7878
Web: N/A
Prices: ⊜⊜

Sometimes you wake up and think—man, I would love some deep fried pork knuckles for breakfast. The good people at Engeline's won't judge you. In fact, this sweet little bakery-cum-restaurant, which doubles as a local hangout for the neighborhood's Filipino ex-pat scene, will serve it to you with a smile.

The bakery makes a mean pastry any way you slice it, but it's worth grabbing a seat at one of the simple wooden tables and plunking down some change for a full meal, for this kind of authentic Filipino comfort food doesn't come easy—try the *kare-kare*, a sweet, peanut butter-based stew of oxtail and tender honeycomb tripe, kicked up with a pungent, salty fish sauce; or *menudo*, a traditional peasant stew with addictive little cubes of spicy, perfumed pork.

Hamjibak

Queens

D1

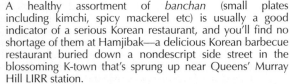

Korean ✗

41-08 149th Pl. (bet. Barclay & 41st Aves.)

Subway: Flushing - Main St Lunch & dinner daily
Phone: 718-460-9289
Web: www.hahmjibach.com
Prices: $$

A healthy assortment of *banchan* (small plates including kimchi, spicy mackerel etc) is usually a good indicator of a serious Korean restaurant, and you'll find no shortage of them at Hamjibak—a delicious Korean barbecue restaurant buried down a nondescript side street in the blossoming K-town that's sprung up near Queens' Murray Hill LIRR station.

The unassuming Hamjibak won't woo you with it's plain-Jane décor, but scores major points for the patient, oh-so-knowledgable waitstaff service, and masterful Korean specialties like *daeji bulgogi*, a plate of marinated pork ribs in chili-garlic sauce sprinkled with bright green scallions; or *boyang jeongol*, a traditional hot pot of lamb, dumplings, and vegetables swimming in a rich, spicy beef broth.

Himalayan Yak

B2

Tibetan ✗

72-20 Roosevelt Ave. (bet. 72nd & 73rd Sts.)

Subway: 74 St - Broadway Lunch & dinner daily
Phone: 718-779-1119
Web: www.himalayanyakrestaurant.com
Prices:

From the intricately carved doors and furnishings to the exposed brick and sultry sienna walls lined with masks and miniature yaks, the broadly appealing and exceptionally friendly Himalayan Yak is a place of care, restraint, and dining adventure

The menu may be best described as Indian-light, a hybrid that draws specialties from several cuisines including Nepali, Indian, Bhutanese, and most heavily Tibetan. Begin a culinary tour with *tsam thuk*, a thick, porridge-like soup served at room temperature, and bobbing with soft cubes of yak cheese; large beef dumplings in a rich, hot, and savory soup of tender greens and diced carrots; or a vegetarian tray which includes pickled mango strips, chutneys, greens, jasmine rice, and Indian pepper paper bread.

Hunan House

Chinese ✗

D3

137-40 Northern Blvd. (bet. Main & Union Sts.)

Subway: Flushing - Main St   Lunch & dinner daily
Phone: 718-353-1808
Web: N/A
Prices: 🍜

Sweet Flushing! Does New York's rising (and slowly reigning) Chinatown ever cease to delight those willing to trek out to its far-flung environs? Not if Hunan House has anything to say about it a plain, but tidy, little joint pushing out authentic, hard-to-find Hunanese fare.

The province's name means "south of the lake," and Hunan kitchens typically use more seafood than those of neighboring Sichuan—though they certainly share their neighbor's affinity for chili peppers. Witness a braised fish head in a spicy broth, topped with pickled chilies and cool cilantro; a fragrant, delicately preserved beef with pickled peppers and "white chili" (which turns out to be fried bean curd skin); or Hunan style spare ribs laced with red chili sauce.

Hunan Kitchen of Grand Sichuan 🍜

Chinese ✗

D1

42-47 Main Street (bet. Blossom & Franklin Aves.)

Subway: Flushing - Main St   Lunch & dinner daily
Phone: 718-888-0553
Web: www.thegrandsichuan.com
Prices: 🍜

As New York's Sichuan renaissance continues apace, this pleasant and unpretentious Hunanese spot has popped up on Flushing's Main Street. The look here is tasteful and uncomplicated; the cooking is fiery and excellent.

The extensive menu of Hunan specialties includes the likes of the classic regional dish, braised pork "Mao's Style" simmered in soy sauce, wine, oil, and stock, then braised to tender perfection. Boasting heat and meat in equal amounts, the spicy-sour string bean with pork expertly combines rich and savory aromatics, vinegary beans, and fragrant pork with tongue-numbing peppercorns. The barbecue fish Hunan-style is a brilliant menu standout.

Smaller dishes, like winter melon with seafood soup, round out an expertly prepared meal.

Imperial Palace

D3

136-13 37th Ave. (bet. Main & Union Sts.)

Subway: Flushing - Main St   Lunch & dinner daily
Phone: 718-939-3501
Web: N/A
Prices: $$

Grab a group of your fellow chowhounds and hop the 7 train to Flushing for plates of scrumptious classic Chinese cuisine. You'll be needing your nosh buddies to help you tackle the ample menu, which is jam-packed with delectable offerings like crunchy snow pea shoots with garlic; flavorful squid with chives; and fragrant preserved meat (sausage) with tart mounds of spinach. But the claim to fame at this frequented spot is the sticky rice and crab…did we say Dungeness? Oh, yes. Juicy, plump, sweet crabmeat served in a leaf-lined steamer with sublime bits of crisp, golden rice, along with black mushrooms, ginger, scallions, and dried shrimp.

Large, banquet style tables dot the dining space where the lively atmosphere brims with a prominently Asian crowd.

Jackson Diner

B2

37-47 74th St. (bet. Roosevelt & 37th Aves.)

Subway: Jackson Hts - Roosevelt Av   Lunch & dinner daily
Phone: 718-672-1232
Web: www.jacksondiner.com
Prices:

Jackson Diner is quite a trendsetter. When it trashed the tacky lights, requisite chandelier, and flat screen, the venerable Indian institution transformed itself into a sleek and mod eatery—and the neighborhood followed suit. While the inside has changed, the food is still the same: unapologetically simple and consistently solid.

Queens is dotted with the most marvelous, colorful fare, but Jackson Diner remains the favored spot for honest, authentic, and moderately priced *desi* food. Fans flock here for their tried-and-true preparations including garlicky *achari* mushrooms infused with ginger and turmeric; *sarson ka saag*, mustard greens tempered with mustard seeds; and the classic *dal makhani* spiced with coriander.

Joe's Shanghai

D3

Chinese 🍴

136-21 37th Ave. (bet. Main & Union Sts.)

Subway: Flushing - Main St   Lunch & dinner daily
Phone: 718-539-3838
Web: www.joeshanghairestaurants.com
Prices: $$

City kids that have given up on the banal kitchen at the Pell Street outpost of this popular soup dumpling house ought to take a little jaunt out to the original in Flushing, Queens. Because the doughy little pouches sure earn their pleated stripes at this location, thank you very much.

Kick things off with an order of the pork and crab soup dumplings—for the uninitiated, these are thin, soft purses of dough filled with a rich, lip-smacking-good hot broth. If you don't end up ordering back-to-back rounds of these heavenly dumplings, you might try any number of dishes like a trio of sweet and salty wine chicken, jellyfish strips, and duck's web feet; or tender sautéed pork, diced with minced jalapeño, diced squid, and dried tofu.

Katsuno

C3

Japanese 🍴

103-01 Metropolitan Ave. (at 71st Rd.)

Subway: Forest Hills - 71 Av   Dinner Tue - Sun
Phone: 718-575-4033
Web: www.katsunorestaurant.com
Prices: $$

Introduce a buddy from Manhattan to this outer borough Japanese gem and you'll forever be regarded as in the know. There is no sign to mark the entrance—only a tiny white lantern and pretty Noren curtains to usher you into the lovely little space—but make no mistake: this is authentic Japanese fare done right.

Chef Katsuyuki Seo crafts each and every plate with meticulous technique, employing seasonal fish flown in daily from Japan. Meanwhile, his wife hosts the crowd, who settles in for a parade of pristine dishes like shimmering fluke topped with ponzu sauce, tender seaweed, crunchy sea beans and a chiffonade of ginger and scallions; or a soft tangle of soba in fragrant duck broth, bobbing with *magret* duck and crunchy grilled scallion.

485

KumGangSan

Queens

D3

Korean ✗

138-28 Northern Blvd. (bet. Bowne & Union Sts.)

Subway: Flushing - Main St	Lunch & dinner daily
Phone: 718-461-0909	
Web: www.kumgangsan.net	
Prices: $$	

Lip-smacking Korean fare flows 24-7 from the kitchen of KumGangSan—a bright, busy restaurant tucked into Queens' bustling Northern Blvd. By day, customers pile into the dark wood tables or angle for a seat at the sushi bar, where big, windowed walls offer streams of sunlight and a nice view of the garden.

An excellent assortment of *banchan*, including grilled needlefish, kicks off a meal that might include seafood *pa jun*, a wonderfully crispy rice flour pancake filled with tender seafood, vegetables, and scallions, and served with sesame seed-studded soy sauce; or sweet and tender eel, carefully broiled and fanned out over a rich and earthy house sauce redolent of the sea.

Later, stock up on hard-to-find staples at the Korean grocery store next door.

Linn

A1

Japanese ✗✗

29-13 Broadway (bet. 29th & 30th Sts.)

Subway: Broadway	Dinner nightly
Phone: 718-204-0060	
Web: www.linnrestaurant.com	
Prices: $$	

It's not all kabobs and feta here in Astoria. Authentic Japanese cooking has made a heck of a mark. Enter Linn, a serious sushi spot helmed by Chef Tanaka Shigenori, formerly of Masa. Super sleek like an art-gallery, the minimal space is styled in sultry hues, tract lighting, and ever-changing oil-paintings, with an L-shaped sushi counter and two rows of simple, bare tables.

The outstanding omakase is to die for, and could include such delights as luscious and silky pork belly simmered in soy, ginger, and sake broth; grilled shiitake mushrooms; and an array of exceptionally fresh fish: Pacific scallops, Alaskan king salmon, Japanese snapper, striped bass, and toro, served with freshly grated wasabi, pickled ginger, and house-made soy.

Little Pepper 🏮

D1

Chinese 🍴

18-24 College Point Blvd. (bet. 18th & 20th Aves.)

Subway: Flushing - Main St (& bus Q20A)   Lunch & dinner Fri – Wed
Phone: 718-939-7788
Web: N/A
Prices: 💰💰

For those suffering the pain and heartbreak over the abrupt shut down of Little Pepper in Flushing last year, weep no more. The exquisite Little Pepper has re-emerged, this time in College Point and donning an entirely new look, replete with marble tiled floors, fresh white walls adorned with lovely "frescoes" (created by the owner's son), and a small service bar.

But the focus here is surely the sublime, delicate cuisine, which thankfully has not changed. Some irresistible selections: Fresh cucumber with mashed garlic sauce; thinly sliced, blanched ox organs tossed in chili oil; glass noodles in a heavenly pool of stir fried pork, scallions, and Sichuan peppercorns; and whole Chinese fish, deep-fried, and topped with a pickled cabbage sauce.

Main Street Imperial Taiwanese Gourmet

D1

Chinese 🍴

59-14A Main St. (bet. 59th & 60th Aves.)

Subway: Flushing - Main St   Lunch & dinner daily
Phone: 718-886-8788
Web: N/A
Prices: 💰💰

With its impossibly long name and simple, Zen-like interior, Main Street Imperial Taiwanese Gourmet isn't trying to woo anyone to Flushing for ambience. You can find that anywhere, after all. It's all about the food at this compact gem—and you'll have to take a subway ride and a bus to get there.

Rest assured it's worth it for the stinky tofu alone. The staff speaks little English, but with a dash of ingenuity you'll soon be on your way to exquisite delights like bamboo pork, served together in a hot cast iron vessel with scallions and a mouthwatering sauce; wildly fresh oyster pancakes sporting caramelized edges and a tantalizingly sweet sauce; and tender cuttlefish tossed with minced pork, crunchy Chinese celery, and seared green peppers.

Malagueta

A1

✗

25-35 36th Ave. (at 28th St.)

Subway: 36 Av   Lunch & dinner Tue – Sun
Phone: 718-937-4821
Web: www.malaguetany.com
Prices: $$

Just when it seemed like all of Brazil was on the Atkins diet, along comes this sweet little number where dinner is not dominated by stupefying amounts of meat. Not that there's anything wrong with getting your beef on—it's just that Herbet Gomes, Malagueta's Chef/owner, and his wife, Alda, prefer to run their place with an eye towards Brazil's diverse culinary offerings.

Set along a fairly residential street, Malagueta's parcel of tables fills up fast with neighborhood regulars and city slickers willing to hop the short train ride out to Long Island City.

Try the tender black-eyed pea fritters laced with *vatapá*, a creamy shrimp and coconut milk sauce; or the pork tenderloin, marinated and cooked to fork-tender perfection, then laced in dill sauce.

M & T

D1

✗

44-09 Kissena Blvd. (bet. Cherry St. & 45th Ave.)

Subway: Flushing - Main St   Lunch & dinner daily
Phone: 718-539-4100
Web: N/A
Prices: ☙☙

The décor—Spartan. The menu—vast and confusing. The cuisine...oh the cuisine...outstanding. Rejoice, residents of Flushing! The good folks at M & T Restaurant have brought you the cuisine of Qingdao, a seaside city in China's northeastern Shandong province, known for the popular beer Tsingtao.

Offerings are wonderfully exciting which may leave you a bit overwhelmed. Our advice? Skip straight to the terrific specials like succulent, sautéed kidney with veggies and crunchy slices of red jelly fish. Or the mouthwatering marriage of fragrant beef tendons with juicy shrimp. Though the sweet staff speaks little English, they're eager to help navigate the menu. If all else fails, point to a delicious looking dish on a neighboring table, and order that.

Mulan

Asian 🍴🍴

D3

136-17 39th Ave. (at Main St.)

Subway: Flushing - Main St
Phone: 718-886-8526
Web: www.mulan-restaurant.com
Prices: $$$

Lunch & dinner daily

Just a short walk from Flushing's bustling main drag, sits the Queens Crossing mall—a sort of Time Warner Center for the borough's Chinatown. And like its Manhattan counterpart, it prides itself on its delicious restaurants, notably Mulan.

This very modern Asian spot is gorgeous and unexpectedly chic filled with cherry blossom silk panels and creamy leather chairs, and has made a name for itself with polished service and a respectable wine list. The continental Cantonese fare includes delicately flavored and tender char-grilled salmon, varnished with a honey-tinged miso sauce and topped with sweet mango; or bone-in chicken, served in a pool of intensely dark, aromatic sauce swirling with mushrooms and creamy whole chestnuts.

Mundo

International 🍴

A1

31-18 Broadway (at 32nd St.)

Subway: Broadway
Phone: 718-777-2829
Web: www.mundoastoria.com
Prices: $$

Dinner Thu – Tue

Like the eclectic neighborhood it resides in, this Astoria charmer traffics in a unique mix of global fare. The locals respond with unflagging loyalty, and anyone who is lucky enough to accidentally wander in will find a bustling dining room filled with regulars lapping up the gracious hospitality and humor of Mundo's spirited host, Willy.

Kick things off with a Red Sonja, a cold starter of hand-formed red lentil and chickpea patties that allegedly count Donatella Versace as a fan; and then move on to plates like the creamy artichokes filled with diced carrots and peas, paired with braised fresh fava beans; moist, feather-light Turkish meatballs; or warm semolina cake soaked in a luscious syrup and stuffed with a cool lobe of vanilla ice cream.

Nan Xiang Xiao Long Bao

D3

38-12 Prince St. (bet. 38th & 39th Aves.)

Subway: Flushing - Main St
Phone: 718-321-3838
Web: N/A
Prices: 💰💰

Lunch & dinner daily

Also known as Nan Shian Dumpling House, it is easily found among a strip of restaurants reflecting the diversity of Flushing's dominant Asian population. Simply decorated, the comfortable dining room features rows of closely set tables and a mirrored wall that successfully gives the illusion of space.

This enjoyable and interesting menu focuses on noodle-filled soups, toothsome stir-fried rice cakes, and the house specialty, juicy pork buns. These are made in-house and have a delicate, silky wrapper encasing a flavorful meatball of ground pork or crab and rich tasting broth. Eating these may take some practice, but take your cue from the slurping crowd: puncture the casing on your spoon to cool the dumplings and avoid scalding your mouth.

Nick's Pizza

D3

108-26 Ascan Ave. (off Austin St.)

Subway: 75 Av
Phone: 718-263-1126
Web: N/A
Prices: 💰💰

Lunch & dinner daily

Pizza couldn't be hotter in New York right now, but this quiet little Forest Hills pie joint was kicking it long before the recent influx of newcomers. Located a stone's throw from the legendary Forest Hills Gardens, a lovely neighborhood featuring stunning Tudor homes, the pizzeria boasts a Norman Rockwell charm, with big glossy windows, a marble pizza counter, and cushy soda shop booths made for dinner with the family.

The menu is straightforward, with pizza, calzones, and a near-perfect cannoli, but don't be fooled by the simplicity—this is some of the city's finest pizza, its perfectly pliant crust lightly charred and laced with a lick-your-fingers red sauce, then loaded with toppings like crumbly sausage, fresh prosciutto, or tart anchovies.

Nusara

Thai ✗

C2

02 00 Broadway (at Whitney Ave.)

Subway: Elmhurst Av

Phone: 718-898-7996

Web: www.nusarathaikitchen.com

Prices: $$

Lunch & dinner daily

Tucked into an Elmhurst strip mall teeming with enough Asian food to send Asiaphiles into a coma, Nusara is indisputably the belle of the ball. Its edge? Ace Thai food, a pretty, softly lit dining room, and a staff willing to bend over backwards for their customers.

Newbies to authentic Thai will rejoice in Nusara's snappy, well-organized menu with its detailed explanations, but the spice-shy should proceed slowly. For all the sweetness of the staff, Nusara isn't afraid to bring the heat in dishes like whole red snapper, tossed in garlic and pepper; or sumptuous, seasonal Chinese watercress sautéed with ginger, red chili, and garlic. Cool your heels with a roasted duck salad, loaded with pineapple and cashews in a chili and lime vinaigrette.

Ornella

Italian ✗

B1

29-17 23rd Ave. (bet. 29th & 31st Sts.)

Subway: Ditmars Blvd

Phone: 718-777-9477

Web: www.ornellatrattoria.com

Prices: $$

Lunch & dinner daily

All hands are on deck at Ornella and Giuseppe Viterale's fantastic trattoria, where the husband-and-wife proprietors are always on hand to ensure smooth sailing. A cheery striped awning welcomes you into an intimate, narrow room fitted out with sunset-colored walls, but the real draw at this Astoria restaurant is the food—where a passion for homegrown veggies, fresh ingredients, and inspired sauces elevate otherwise rote Italian-American dishes to hubba-hubba homemade fare.

Dinner may begin with fluffy potato-and-ricotta gnocchi tossed with sweet gorgonzola cheese and cream, then baked into heaven on earth; and then move on to *pollo al Scarpariello*, an otherwise pedestrian chicken dish that graduates to excellence with a gorgeous reduction sauce.

Pachanga Patterson

B1

33-17 31st Ave. (at 34th St.)

Subway: 30 Av
Phone: 718-554-0525
Web: www.pachangapatterson.com
Prices: $$

Lunch & dinner daily

You don't need a lot of change in your purse to enjoy a good meal at Pachanga Patterson. Astoria's 31st Street, once known as Patterson Avenue, is quickly becoming a go-to spot for great food at even better prices, and Pachanga is one of its stand-outs.

Tacos stuffed with *moo shu* duck or Vietnamese pork shoulder offer something to tip your sombrero at. Pachanga is no typical Mexican restaurant, though the tortillas from Tortilleria Nixtamal are serious, the salsas are pretty darn good, and there's nary a burrito in sight. Unconventional dishes can be a bit wonky (think pork belly enchiladas with chocolate-laced fig sauce) but are tasty nonetheless. The food is matched only by the incredibly warm service. Small plates, small prices, and big smiles.

Parkside

C2

107-01 Corona Ave. (bet. 108th St. & 51st Ave.)

Subway: 103 St - Corona Plaza
Phone: 718-271-9871
Web: N/A
Prices: $$$

Lunch & dinner daily

Enter this warm, convivial Corona landmark and immediately feel welcomed by all—from hostess and bartender, to server and chef. A contagious, celebratory spirit fills the enthusiastic diners enjoying old-fashioned Italian-American dishes in a perennially packed, multi-room space. Its brick arches, twinkling white lights, wicker chairs, and hanging foliage conjure an upscale greenhouse, staffed by tuxedo-clad waiters.

Take a seat among the family-friendly patrons and order a plate of perfectly prepared *rigatoni all'Amatriciana*, served in a fresh tomato sauce with pancetta and basil; or thin cutlets of *veal piccata*, glazed in a luscious lemon-caper sauce. When the dessert tray rolls by, make sure you've saved room for biscotti or the beloved cannoli.

Payag

Filipino ✗

51-34 Roosevelt Ave. (at 52nd St.)

Subway: 52 St
Phone: 347-935-3192
Web: www.payagrestaurant.com
Prices: $$

Lunch & dinner Wed – Mon

The dearth of soulful, authentic Filipino food in the boroughs has been remedied to the tune of one restaurant, Payag. Here, owner Rena Avendula succeeds not just in satisfying hunger, but spirit as well. A *payag* is a simple Filipino hut, and the design of the dining room–airy and bright–is meant to evoke home. Calming touches of sea shells, bamboo, and rattan abound.

The food, which blends Spanish, Chinese, and Malay influences, is equally homey and hearty; portions are gargantuan and carefully presented. The classic Filipino stew, *kare-kare*, is full of tender, succulent oxtail and tripe in a peanut based sauce. The crispy *pata*, a deep-fried pig's knuckle, is almost overwhelmingly rich; juicy, crackling skin gives way to the fork-tender pork underneath.

Pio Pio

Peruvian ✗

84-02 Northern Blvd. (at 84th St.)

Subway: 82 St - Jackson Hts
Phone: 718-426-4900
Web: www.piopionyc.com
Prices: ⊖⊖

Lunch & dinner daily

The Peruvian rotisserie chicken joint that spawned a mini-empire (there are more than 8 locations now) moved from its colorful, exposed brick digs in Queens, but they didn't go far. Located just across the street from the old spot, the new Pio Pio is a sprawling, street level operation featuring a pleasant little garden and jumbo photos of the mother land.

The menu remains blissfully similar, with Peruvian goodies like crispy empanadas stuffed with sweet, fragrant chicken and a wicked salsa *criolla* (a house specialty that, when it appears on the menu accompanying any dish, should scream "order me"); or the *arroz con mariscos*, a Peruvian paella chockablock with fresh scallops, octopus, mussels, shrimp, and squid in a terrific red sauce.

Renee's Kitchenette and Grill

B2

69-14 Roosevelt Ave. (bet. 69th & 70th Sts.)

Subway: 69 St
Phone: 718-476-9002
Web: N/A
Prices: ⊝⊜

Lunch & dinner daily

Don't come for the setting–a rather utilitarian room located on a stretch of Roosevelt by the Grand Central Parkway overpass–but if you're looking for bang for the buck, you've found it. Renee's is a favorite among Filipinos who come for a taste of their homeland. The fact that you might be the only gringo here is just one more sign that this is the real deal.

Follow the next table's lead and start by slurping one of Renee's signature smoothies. You can't go wrong with classic Filipino staples like chicken *adobo* (in vinegar and soy sauce) and *tinolang manok* (a tart chicken soup with spinach); while items like *paksiw na lechon* (pork in liver sauce) are better suited for the adventurous palate. When you leave, your stomach will be as full as your wallet.

Sabry's

B1

24-25 Steinway St. (bet. Astoria Blvd. & 25th Ave.)

Subway: Astoria Blvd
Phone: 718-721-9010
Web: N/A
Prices: $$

Lunch & dinner daily

Located in an area of Astoria now known as Little Egypt, Sabry's uses Egyptian accents in preparing an array of well-priced, pristine seafood—a large ice-filled case displays the day's fresh catch at the entrance. In the style of many Mediterranean eateries, fish from this case are grilled or baked whole, permeated with Middle Eastern flavorings like garlic, cumin, cardamom, and red pepper. Aromatic *taogines*, including a shellfish version in rich and heady tomato sauce, are equally delicious. Smoky baba ghanoush is packed with flavor, especially when accompanied by fantastic pita bread, made fresh to order.

Be aware that the restaurant does not serve alcohol, nor is BYO permitted. However, your palate will be perfectly quenched by a tasty mint tea.

Salt & Fat 🐶

Contemporary ✗

A2

41-16 Queens Blvd. (bet. 41st & 42nd Sts.)

Subway: 40 St   Dinner Tue – Sun
Phone: 718-433-3702
Web: www.saltandfatny.com
Prices: $$

Oh, Sunnyside. Are you the next big foodie destination? Chef Daniel Yi seems to think so, springing open this brilliant and unique yet unpretentious little spot right in the heart of Queens Boulevard. Inside, dark wooden tables line exposed stone walls, and framed black-and-white photos perch on cream-colored wooden panes.

Here at Salt & Fat, beloved American classics are whipped up with global flare. Behold the braised short rib buns slathered in apricot mustard; outstanding oxtail terrine served with hon shimeji mushrooms; "crack" and cheese, topped with béchamel, and fatty, smoky bacon; Hampshire pulled pork sliders in sriracha barbecue sauce; and tender hanger steak served over *kobacha* purée. What are you waiting for? Hop on the 7 train stat.

San & Deul

Korean ✗

D1

251-05 Northern Blvd. (bet. 251st St & Browvale Ln.)

Subway: Flushing - Main St (& bus Q12)   Lunch & dinner daily
Phone: 718-281-0218
Web: N/A
Prices: $$

At the edge of the Queens' border, where the borough starts to meet Long Island, along a wide boulevard known as 25A, sits San & Deul—a Korean restaurant where the cooking is done table-top with real wood, the *panchan* is delightful, and the service is lovely.

If the décor (a clean, bright room with large windows overlooking the street) is a little on the functional end, you can probably look the other way. Food like this is ambience enough: A mashed soybean casserole is dotted with veggies and fresh clams; deep-fried dumplings are stuffed with pork, shiitake mushrooms, fish sauce, and tofu; and tender prime beef short ribs are cooked over a wood burning grill, then served with red rice, kimchi, and red-leaf lettuce for wrapping.

Sapori d'Ischia

Italian ✗✗

B2

55-15 37th Ave. (at 56th St.)

Subway: Northern Blvd   Lunch & dinner Tue – Sun
Phone: 718-446-1500
Web: N/A
Prices: **$$**

Part grocery store, part enoteca, all neighborhood gem, this Woodside spot brightens an otherwise desolate strip of warehouses and car repair shops. Step inside, past an unassuming façade and be transported: the rustic dining room is crowded with linen-covered tables from which emanate the quiet oohs and ahs of satisfied and delighted eaters.

The owners are very serious about their food. Cheeses and charcuterie, much of which is available to take home, are well-chosen and the dishes are uniformly scrumptious. For starters, ravioli filled with creamy butternut squash and dressed with brown butter and sage is generous and flavorful; while the osso buco is tender and tasty, especially when paired with a glass from their fine selection of wines.

Sentosa

Malaysian ✗

D3

39-07 Prince St. (at 39th Ave.)

Subway: Flushing - Main St   Lunch & dinner daily
Phone: 718-886-6331
Web: www.sentosausa.com
Prices:

Sentosa, the Malay word for tranquility, celebrates an agreeable intermingling of the mainly Chinese and Indian influences of Malaysia's multi-ethnic descendants. This very enjoyable restaurant features a contemporary setting with warm lighting, polished teak, and stone tiles.

Meals here include *mee siam* noodles, stir-fried with a sweet chili sauce, fried tofu, bean sprouts, and fresh shrimp. Other flavorful offerings include *rendang*, a rich stew of tender beef simmered in coconut milk, perfectly heated with chili paste; alongside a large selection of stir-frys and curries. Remember to save room for your vegetables here, which may highlight the alluring flavors of *belacan* (a funky ground, fermented shrimp paste) sautéed with halved okra.

Queens

SHI

Asian XXX

A2

17-20 Center Blvd. (bet. 47th & 48th Aves.)

Subway: Vernon Blvd - Jackson Av   Dinner nightly
Phone: 347-242-2450
Web: www.shilic.com
Prices: $$

Tucked into the base of a gorgeous high-rise building along the East River, SHI is the stamp Long Island City's been waiting for: consider this upscale hipster hub signed, sealed, and delivered.

Developers have poured millions into the new buildings that dot this area of the waterfront, and SHI is appropriately stunning— with floor-to-ceiling windows offering breathtaking views of the Manhattan skyline; sexy, plush white leather chairs flanking the beautiful bar area; and a dining room dripping in crystal chandeliers.

So how does the food fit into all this? Solidly, with simple, well-crafted Chinese-American and Japanese specialties like tender shrimp wrapped in smoky bacon; and crispy popcorn beef topped with chilies and bright cilantro.

Sik Gaek

Korean X

D1

161-29 Crocheron Ave. (bet. 161st & 162nd Sts.)

Subway: Flushing - Main St (& bus Q12)   Lunch & dinner daily
Phone: 718-321-7770
Web: N/A
Prices: $$

When David Chang and Anthony Bourdain have sunk their pincers into some far-flung outer borough joint, you know you're in for a treat. Sik Gaek, a Korean restaurant in Auburndale, is a riot of a place: think corrugated metal roofs, blaring rock music, neon aquariums, and flashing traffic lights, and you only start to get a picture.

But the fun atmosphere is only the beginning. Kick things off with a piping hot bowl of fish broth bobbing with thin noodles, fish cake, vegetables, boiled egg, and scallions; and then move on to the money shot: an enormous paella-style pan heaped with fresh vegetables, loads of shellfish, and a live—yes, live—octopus, which will probably try to make a run for it. Thankfully, there's not a yellow cab in sight.

Spicy & Tasty

D3

39-07 Prince St. (at 39th Ave.)

Subway: Flushing - Main St   Lunch & dinner daily
Phone: 718-359-1601
Web: N/A
Prices: 🍜

Spicy & Tasty has found its home in this bustling pocket of Queens, where a dizzying array of restaurants, bakeries, and stores jockey to win the favor of Flushing's booming Asian population. Its local love is clear in the diverse ethnicities scattered across the clean, contemporary, and spacious dining room, as well as in the cuisine—though it does seem to restrain its punchy Sichuan heat for fear of scaring the newbies.

Nonethess, this food is thoroughly enjoyable. It is likewise fun to watch the warm, knowledgeable staff walk first-timers through steaming plates of dumplings, plump with a spicy red chili sauce and minced meat; broad noodles in a powerful, rich, meaty sauce dancing with scallions and peppers; or tender and fiery cold tripe salad.

Sripraphai

B2

64-13 39th Ave. (bet. 64th & 65th Sts.)

Subway: Woodside - 61 St   Lunch & dinner Thu – Tue
Phone: 718-899-9599
Web: www.sripraphairestaurant.com
Prices: 🍜

A few years ago, this local favorite set off a critical firestorm for delivering killer, authentic-as-it-gets Thai food, then smartly expanded into roomier digs. In the current space, you'll find a large, elegant dining room with an enormous backyard garden, replete with gurgling fountain.

But with the flood of Westerners hovering like wolves outside the front door, has this beloved Woodside restaurant tamed her fiery ways? She has, but the bland food still remains quite popular regardless of diminished quality. The menu may feature bright green papaya salads; tender roasted duck over a bed of greens; fluffy Thai-style frittatas studded with ground pork; or fresh soft shell crab, lightly fried and pooled in delicious coconut-laced green curry.

Taiwanese Gourmet Corp

Chinese ✗

C2

84-02 Broadway (at St. James Ave.)

Subway: Elmhurst Av
Phone: 718-429-4818
Web: N/A
Prices: 💰💰

Lunch & dinner daily

A spotless semi-open kitchen is one of the first signs that this Taiwanese restaurant is just a little bit different than the other kids. Straddling a corner of Elmhurst, Taiwanese Gourmet is a bright spot on Queens' Chinatown circuit, with jumbo windows flooding the dining room with daylight and beautifully framed ancient warrior gear flanking the walls.

The menu reads minimalist, but the staff can be quite helpful if you approach them with questions. Skip the unimpressive oyster pancakes, and dive into dishes like shredded beef and dried tofu, stir-fried in a complex, dark sauce; a delicate, beer-infused duck hot pot teeming with juju beans and Chinese herbs; or a scrumptious clam and chicken hotpot bursting with flavor from smoky bonito flakes.

Taverna Kyclades

Greek ✗

B1

33 07 Ditmars Blvd. (bet. 33rd & 35th Sts.)

Subway: Astoria - Ditmars Blvd
Phone: 718-545-8666
Web: www.tavernakyclades.com
Prices: 💰💰

Lunch & dinner daily

This traditional and beloved Greek taverna, headed by a dedicated chef/owner and staff, continues to serve fresh fish daily, grilled or fried (note the showcase refrigerator in the semi-open kitchen), along with perfect portions tzatziki or *taramosalata*.

Years of non-stop service to a loyal and diverse clientele has not diminished the classic patina of the small, but warm and boisterous dining room. The setting here is no frills; this is a perfect spot to dine family style, elbow-to-elbow at simple wood chairs, on solid food with ambience to match. Meals can also be enjoyed year-round in the enclosed garden area. The surrounding space is crowded with back-to-back stores and restaurants. Service here is cool, helpful, and without attitude. *Opa*!

Tawa Tandoor

Indian ✗

B2

37-56 74th St. (bet. Roosevelt & 37th Aves.)

Subway: Jackson Hts - Roosevelt Av   Lunch & dinner daily
Phone: 718-478-2730
Web: www.tawatandoor74.com
Prices: $$

Tawa (Hindi for metal grill) Tandoor is long, dark, and handsome with wood floors, sumptuous leather chairs, and banquettes. Burrowed inside a recessed ceiling are modern light fixtures that shine upon a stunning fish tank and small service bar that keeps the crowd happy. Many of them are here for the hugely favored Indo-Chinese delicacies like *hakka* chicken and chicken *Manchurian*.

Beyond the specialties, let the ace staff keep you happy with expected classics such as vegetable *jalfrezi* dotted with black pepper; *kaleji masala* (mutton livers sautéed with onions, ginger, chillies, and cilantro); and *tawa*-grilled garlic naan that deliciously soaks up *navaratan* korma—vegetables married with fragrant spices in a silky almond sauce.

Testaccio

Italian ✗✗

A2

47-30 Vernon Blvd. (at 47th Rd.)

Subway: Vernon Blvd - Jackson Av   Lunch & dinner daily
Phone: 718-937-2900
Web: www.testacciony.com
Prices: $$

This new Italian gem arrives courtesy of one of the early owners behind TriBeCa's Pepolino, and those making their way to Long Island City's Vernon Blvd. will find a sexy, contemporary dining room fitted out in leather banquettes, votive candles, and white-washed exposed brick walls.

Excellent pizza and homemade pastas round out the dinner menu, and the latter should not be missed—the more traditional (think *bucatini all'Amatriciana*, *fettuccine alla ciociara*, and *spaghetti alla carbonara*), the better. Dinner might kick off with delicately fried baby risotto balls or a fresh tangle of tagliolini with pecorino romano, black truffle, and cracked pepper; before moving onto velvety oxtail braised in red wine with roasted vegetables and caramelized onions.

Tito Rad's Grill

B2

Filipino 🍴

49 12 Queens Blvd. (bet. 49th & 50th Sts.)

Subway: 46 St - Bliss St
Phone: 718-205-7299
Web: www.titorads.com
Prices: 💰💰

Lunch & dinner daily

When your breakfast coffee arrives with sardines and garlic fried rice, you'll know you're not really in Queens anymore. The welcome may be frosty and the Filipino-only crowd may wonder if you know what you're in for, but settle into one of the tightly packed tables and be rewarded.

First and foremost, Tito Rad's barbecue specialties are not to be missed. From tuna jaw to supremely tender pork, the barbecue presents the perfect yin and yang flavor combo of salty and sour. Be sure to sample some *menudo*, a pork-based stew, and the spicy tuna belly cooked in coconut milk, served soupy with bits of bitter melon and explosive heat. Tito's delight is the perfect finish with a trio of rich *leche* flan, cassava cake, and *ube*, a dense cake made from purple yam.

Trattoria l'Incontro

B1

Italian 🍴🍴

21-76 31st St. (at Ditmars Blvd.)

Subway: Astoria - Ditmars Blvd
Phone: 718-721-3532
Web: www.trattorialincontro.com
Prices: $$

Lunch & dinner Tue – Sun

Take the N train to the last stop to track down this feel-good Italian mainstay. Throngs of serious foodies flood this local favorite nightly; yet no matter how busy they get, Abruzzi native Tina Sacramone and her son, Rocco, always find time to pour on the hospitality.

In the back, a brick oven churns out a host of savory pies (as well as a chocolate-stuffed one for dessert), as endearing (if gushy) servers circulate the tranquil, well-appointed dining room, reciting a dizzying array of daily specials—there may be a half-dozen salads alone, not including those made with seafood. Outrageously generous pasta dishes highlight Italian-American sensibilities, with hearty amounts of everything from black linguini with seafood to gnocchi with rabbit ragù.

Urubamba

C2

86-20 37th Ave. (at 86th St.)

Subway: 82 St - Jackson Hts   Lunch & dinner daily
Phone: 718-672-2224
Web: N/A
Prices: **$$**

Handsome little Urubamba boasts a long, narrow space lined with Peruvian artifacts, indigenous paintings, brick walls, and an owner who has been serving Peruvian food to Queens since 1976.

At breakfast (served only on weekends), glimpse a crowd of devotees feast on *chanfainita*, a deliciously traditional beef stew; or *sopa de gallina*, a fragrant chicken noodle soup. At night, diners tuck into a variety of traditional Peruvian fare as well as popular Latin dishes. The menu may include moist, golden *tamal Peruano* filled with chicken, hard boiled eggs, and black olives; warm bowls of milky chowder brimming with shrimp, topped with bright green cilantro; and towering platters of fresh lime-marinated squid, shrimp, octopus, and fish ceviche.

Uvarara

C3

79-28 Metropolitan Ave. (at 80th St.)

Subway: Middle Village - Metropolitan Av (& bus Q54)   Dinner Tue – Sun
Phone: 718-894-0052
Web: www.uvararany.com
Prices: **$$**

The "location is everything" rule exempts the convivial Italian wine bar Uvarara, plunked between two cemeteries on a verdant stretch of Metropolitan Avenue. Housed in a former showroom for headstones, the interior is sultry and sexy now, with low, flickering candles, mismatched chairs, and curtains beaded with wine corks. Somehow the locale is perfect, because this kind of cozy bohemian charmer–with a wine list that gets more focused each year and *Mamma* Rosa's deliciously honest cooking–wouldn't be nearly as unexpected and cool anywhere else.

The menu shifts with the seasons, but *mamma* is sure to prepare *gnocchi alla Romana* as well as Neapolitan *pizzette*, with a decidedly Roman edge. Pay attention to the server's list of irresistible daily specials.

Valentino's on the Green

D1   Italian ✗✗✗

201-10 Cross Island Pkwy. (bet. 201st St. & Clearview Pk.)

Subway: N/A   Lunch Tue – Fri & Sun
Phone: 718-352-2300   Dinner Tue – Sun
Web: www.valentinosonthegreen.com
Prices: $$$

After a year-long closure, a lovingly restored Queens mansion overlooking Little Neck Bay is back in business and from a culinary standpoint, this particular go-around with the estate (which once belonged to Latin lover, Rudolph Valentino) looks very promising. Valentino's on the Green is divided into three separate dining experience areas, all of them elegant and romantic enough to beckon well-heeled residents from nearby Westchester and Long Island—an attentive service staff and a crackerjack kitchen ensures they'll be back.

Kick things off with a tangle of delicately fried calamari; then move on to silky homemade pastas, like one layered with mortadella, *scamorza*, and sausage; or tender herb-crusted rack of lamb cooked to juicy perfection.

Vesta Trattoria

A1   Italian ✗

21-02 30th Ave. (at 21st St.)

Subway: 30 Av   Lunch & dinner daily
Phone: 718-545-5550
Web: www.vestavino.com
Prices: $$

Named for the virgin god of the hearth in Roman mythology, the adorable Vesta continues to be popular with the local Astoria set. You can blame the low-lit, brick-lined interior, which offers the kind of easygoing weeknight meal the neighborhood was begging for, but our money's on the greenmarket-inspired Italian menu—where it's as easy to indulge in celebrated old-world steadies as it is to head into more intricate culinary territory. Add to that a slew of vegetarian options, and a small, but clever, wine list—and you've got a sleeper.

Don't miss the delicious *minestra*, thick with greens, cannellini beans, and a poached egg; the fresh, hand-rolled pastas; or the Baby Jesus cake, a fluffy spice cake with a toffee-like crust covered in caramel sauce.

Water's Edge

A2

4-01 44th Dr. (at the East River)

Subway: 23 St - Ely Av	Lunch Mon – Sat
Phone: 718-482-0033	Dinner nightly
Web: www.watersedgenyc.com	
Prices: $$$	

If New York is famous for blowing its use of waterfront land, Water's Edge didn't get the memo. A complimentary water ferry shuttles guests with reservations from Manhattan's 35th Street pier to this time-honored Queens fine dining institution, where a wall of windows offers breathtaking views of the East River and Manhattan skyline.

A recent face-lift has served the restaurant well, and the new interior is contemporary and stylish, fitted out in steely greys and ebony-rimmed chairs. Guests relax to live piano music and dip their forks into classic upscale fare like a plate of grilled lobster with roasted tomato hollandaise, leek fondue, and soft pillows of tarragon gnocchi; or cheesecake mousse paired with almond crumble and blueberry compote.

Zabb Elee

B2

71-28 Roosevelt Ave. (bet. 70th & 72nd Sts.)

Subway: 74 St - Broadway	Lunch & dinner daily
Phone: 718-426-7992	
Web: N/A	
Prices: 💰💰	

You don't come for the décor, you come for the food: Northeastern Thai cooking that is not afraid to bring the heat. Not to say the dining room at Zabb Elee is unpleasant—just a bit boring with its clean metal tables, cream colored walls, and flat screen televisions. Of course, maybe that's what makes the delightful service and authentic fare stand out even more.

Thailand's Isaan region is the culinary focus here, and dinner might include a fragrant pork spare rib soup bobbing with dried Chinese wood mushrooms, tomatoes, and basil in a spicy lemongrass broth; a delicious sour sausage salad, chockablock with vegetables, herbs, and tamarind sauce; or small plates of spice-laden meats like barbecue pork neck, chicken gizzards, and Thai meatballs.

Staten Island

Staten Island

Unless you live there, chances are that Staten Island is different from the perception. Think of ports, shores, and waterfronts perched at the gateway to New York Harbor. Then, consider that, in some ways, much of what enters the city has first passed through this most secluded borough.

It is only fitting that the bridge which opened it up and may have ended its previously bucolic existence be named for Giovanni da Verrazano, the Italian explorer who first arrived here in 1524. This is particularly apt, because one of the strongest and most accurate generalizations of Staten Island is that it is home to a large Italian-American population. No self-respecting foodie would consider a visit here without picking up a scungilli pizza from **Joe and Pat's**, or at least a slice from **Nunzio**...and maybe **Denino's**, too!

Display of Deliciousness

Beyond this, Staten Island continues to surprise with its ethnically diverse neighborhoods. Take a virtual tour of the eastern Mediterranean at **Dinora** or **Nova's** food market for imported olives, cheeses, and freshly butchered meat. Or, visit the old-world Polish delis, many of which seem to comfortably survive based on their large takeout business, and those mouthwatering homemade jams. Sri Lankan devotees can rejoice in the area

surrounding Victory Boulevard for its storefront diners and restaurants serving a range of this spicy, flavorsome, and fragrant cuisine, with perhaps a stop at the well-tread **Lakshmi's**. Close by these newcomers are a few authentic taquerias as well as the **St. George Greenmarket**, where one can find produce grown locally on Staten Island's own Decker Farm. Historic Richmond Town also organizes the family-focused festival *Uncorked!*, featuring the best in professional and homemade wine and food, offering recipes of traditional favorites. For rare and mature wines, visit **Mission Fine Wines**.

Food, Fun, and Frolic

With all this in mind, it should be no surprise to learn that the Staten Island of the future includes plans for a floating farmer's market, aquarium, and revamped waterfronts. So sit back and have a drink at one of the vibrant bars along Bay Street, and lament the world's myopic view of this much maligned borough.

Drive through some of the city's wealthiest zip codes, boasting splendid views of Manhattan and beyond. Whether here for those delicious Sri Lankan fish buns from **New Asha**; to glimpse the world's only complete collection of rattlesnakes at the S.I. Zoo; or to seek out the birthplaces of stars such as Christina Aguilera and Joan Baez, a visit to Staten Island is sure to surprise.

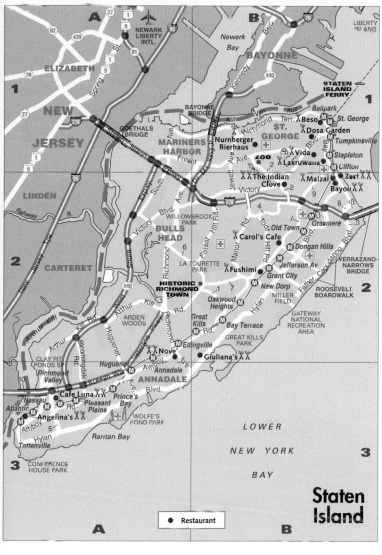

Angelina's

A3

Italian   ✗✗

399 Ellis St.

Bus: N/A   Lunch & dinner Tue – Sun
Phone: 718-227-2900
Web: www.angelinasristorante.com
Prices: $$$

Getting here requires perseverance and an excellent sense of direction: expect lefts, rights, and u-turns alongside smoke-stacks and tug boats before Angelina's emerges like a mirage before glistening water and a heart-stopping sunset at the tip of Staten Island. Your arrival, completed by uniformed valets, is transporting in itself.

Now occupying a gorgeous multi-level Victorian home, the beloved restaurant stuns with original woodwork, wide windows, and scene-stealing views. Loyal locals arrive in droves to savor the vast Italian offerings such as *linguini alle vongole* served al dente in garlic, parsley, and wine sauce with tender clams, topped with red pepper flakes; or a fontina-stuffed veal chop with mushroom-Marsala sauce. A trek, but worth it.

Bayou

B2

Cajun   ✗✗

1072 Bay St. (bet. Chestnut & St. Marys Aves.)

Bus: 51, 81   Lunch Mon – Sat
Phone: 718-273-4383   Dinner nightly
Web: www.bayounyc.com
Prices: $$

N'awlins via Staten Island? You heard right—and this longtime borough favorite just treated itself to a major face-lift. Bayou reopened in February of 2010 after extensive renovations, and the new digs feature a marble-lined bar area, linen-covered tables, and sumptuous chandeliers. Add live music during the week, and you've got one heck of a reason to stay on the island after dark.

Bayou's menu rounds the usual Creole-Cajun bases, but does so with panache: Cajun-seasoned alligator bites arrive grilled and served over chewy ciabatta bread, with Stella bleu cheese and tomato salad; while Steak Louie–a New York strip steak seasoned with Cajun spices–is served with a crunchy stack of onion rings and a side of chunky blue cheese and tomato.

Beso

B1

11 Schuyler St. (bet. Richmond Terrace & Stuyvesant Pl.)

Bus: N/A   Lunch & dinner daily
Phone: 718-816 8162
Web: www.besonyc.com
Prices: $$

With its pan-Castillian décor (a Spanish shawl for curtains, adobe walls, portraits of Flamenco dancing beauties), and sweet, helpful staff, this wildly popular spot–a stone's throw from the Staten Island ferry– is an excellent choice for big, lively groups or adventurous Manhattanites up for visiting their neighbor to the south.

Settle into one of the intricately carved, massive tables, order a glass of sangria, and let the grazing begin. Start with *relleno de gambas,* plantain stuffed with tangy shrimp, red peppers, onions, and garlic, with a sweet, tart sauce; and then move to *pollo Espanola*—sautéed chicken breast in mushroom sauce, served with yellow rice and pigeon peas. The house-made flan, served room temperature, is a lovely finale.

Cafe Luna

A3

31 Page Ave. (bet. Boscombe Ave. & Richmond Valley Rd.)

Bus: 74   Lunch Mon – Fri
Phone: 718-227-8582   Dinner nightly
Web: www.cafelunanyc.com
Prices: $$

When the moon hits your eye, it's amore at Cafe Luna. Staten Islanders have been fans of the Hyland Blvd original for years, but this new sister restaurant takes the cake for its more upscale, fresh, and contemporary setting. There's even ample parking—something of a rarity in this neck of the woods. Bright yellow and blue walls studded with sparkling star light fixtures lift your spirits, while a warm staff makes you feel like part of the *famiglia.*

From lasagna to linguini, the food is Italian-American to its core. Sicilian in spirit, the kitchen doles out the standards with favorites like chicken Parmigiana and veal Marsala. Homemade pastas, crispy pizzas, creamy cheesecake—it's all enough to make "The Chairman" proud.

Carol's Cafe

B2

American ✗

1571 Richmond Rd. (at Four Corners Rd. & Seaview Ave.)

Bus: 74, 76, 84, 86
Phone: 718-979-5600
Web: www.carolscafe.com
Prices: $$$

Dinner Wed – Sat

Chef/owner Carol Frazzetta knows her way around a kitchen. In fact, she even teaches these talents at the cooking school located through the rear of the main dining room, with classes like "My Sicilian Family Recipes."

Those seeking a less hands-on experience choose to relax in the wonderfully homey dining space and tear into the piping-hot basket of fresh breads. However, save room for the deep fried pizza—a crispy wedge of dough topped with fresh tomato, mozzarella, and basil. Other dishes offer refined sensibilities such as the sautéed salmon nestled against divine cinnamon-glazed carrots. End with a fantastic apple-cranberry-pecan crisp.

Pacing is challenged with courses arriving all at once, though you can request to have dishes staggered.

Dosa Garden

B1

Indian ✗

323 Victory Blvd. (bet. Cebra Ave. & Jersey St.)

Bus: 46, 48, 61, 66
Phone: 718-420-0919
Web: www.dosagardenny.com
Prices: $$

Lunch & dinner daily

Tucked into a Staten Island neighborhood slowly filling with Sri Lankan, Indian, and other South Asian restaurants, Dosa Garden cuts a warm but minimalist figure, with a few colorful wall murals, East Asian décor, and soft ethnic music playing in the background.

But with a kitchen manned by Tamil chefs from the Chettinad region of India (close to Sri Lanka), Dosa Garden's fare is a cut above the competition. The main draw is the irresistible *dosas* and *uthappams* made to order. The rest of the lengthy menu might unveil crispy lentil doughnuts soaked in a mild spiced yogurt and topped with fried green chillies, mustard seeds, and curry leaves; or *chettinadu curry*, silky lumps of fresh fish in an amazingly fragrant dark curry studded with mustard seeds.

Fushimi

B2

Fusion ✗

2110 Richmond Rd. (bet. Colfax & Lincoln Aves.)

Bus: 51, 81
Phone: 718-980-5300
Web: www.fushimi-us.com
Prices: $$$

Lunch & dinner daily

This local favorite remains in a league of its own as one of the better Japanese-leaning restaurants on Staten Island, serving an imaginative fare inclined towards fusion. While the ingredients may not be blue-ribbon, the presentation is nonetheless alluring, with large white platters elaborately decorated with fronds and bamboo tepees.

Despite its strip-mall location, the expansive outdoor seating and festive bar fashion a convivial mood, and is an ideal setting for the local crowd. Inside the more subdued yet busy dining room—accented with red lacquer, river stones, and autumnal branches—diners gather at brown banquettes and dark-wood tables to enjoy innovative maki, sushi, and entrées that boast surprising elements and perfectly balanced sauces.

Giuliana's

B2

Italian ✗✗

4105 Hylan Blvd. (at Osborn Ave.)

Bus: 54, 78, 79
Phone: 718-317-8507
Web: www.giulianasrestaurant.com
Prices: $$

Lunch & dinner Tue – Sun

Hylan Boulevard's bakeries, cafés, grocers, and bridal shops paint the perfect picture of Italian American culture, Staten Island's largest demographic. On this corner, framed in twinkling lights, is a lovely spot known for fresh-made mozzarella and toothsome Italian specialties.

Inside, framed photos of local diners, sports legends, and pop culture icons line the walls, setting an "everybody knows your name" kind of vibe. White linens drape wooden tables and walls are painted in warm golden hues. For a taste of a tried-and-true Sicilian dish, dig into the exquisite and authentically made *perciatelle con sarde*—piping hot pasta topped with flaky sardines, tender fennel, golden raisins, a touch of saffron, and crispy toasted breadcrumbs.

The Indian Clove

B2

1180 Victory Blvd. (at Clove Rd.)

Bus:	61, 62, 66	Lunch & dinner daily
Phone:	718-442-5100	
Web:	www.indianclove.com	
Prices:	**$$**	

♿

Poor Staten Island. With its spaghetti-and-meatballs reputation, New York City's oft-ignored borough has always been treated like a bit of a culinary stepchild. But change is in the air with The Indian Clove, a clever Indian restaurant with a fresh, modern interior soaked in beautiful, natural light, and a serious talent for Indian fare.

Try the orange and fig salad, a gorgeous minimalist number with skinless orange segments and crispy greens; or the *tandoori jhinga*, a perfectly-cooked plate of plump, tender shrimp in fragrant spices; or a silky, bone-in lamb chop curry, spiked with chili and garlic, then carpeted in fresh coriander. Non-meat eaters should head next door to Victory Bhavan—a vegetarian, kosher restaurant by the same owners.

Lakruwana

B1

668 Bay St. (at Broad St.)

Bus:	51, 76	Lunch & dinner daily
Phone:	347-857-6619	
Web:	www.lakruwana.com	
Prices:	💱	

S

It might be New York's most Italian-American borough, but Staten Island is home to a zillion Sri Lankan joints. Up until recently though, enjoying this country's food meant hunkering down in eateries that looked more like bodegas. No more: with the recent relocation of Lakruwana, the Sri Lankan food scene has officially arrived.

The over-the-top space is filled with wood masks, clay pots, and gold plaques, but the meticulously prepared food brings you home. Don't miss fish *lamprais*—banana leaf pouches of aromatic and nutty yellow rice laced with silky fish, cashews, and hard boiled egg; a moist fish croquette blending potato, onion, and mint served with a pepper sauce; or string hoppers, frilly pancakes of rice flour and coconut milk paired with curry.

Maizal

B2

Mexican ✗

990 Bay St. (bet. Lynhurst & Willow Sts.)

Bus: 51, 81
Phone: 347-825-3776
Web: www.maizalrestaurant.com
Prices: $$

Lunch Mon – Fri
Dinner Tue – Sun

If you've graduated beyond the thinking that Mexican food is just about burritos and nachos, then you're ready for Maizal. This lovely Staten Island restaurant is proof positive that you don't need to drink out of a sombrero shaped cup to enjoy the flavors of our south-of-the-border ally.

Sure, there are some traditional items on the menu, and you definitely can't go wrong with classics like chicken enchiladas with ancho chile sauce, and *enchilada de mole poblano*; but opt for one of the specials and you'll be in for a treat. From silky beef tongue with green tomatillo sauce to *pollo Patron*, chicken smothered in tequila and topped with *guajillo* chile sauce, mushrooms, and cream, the kitchen highlights the many, delicious dimensions of Mexican cooking.

Nove'

A2

Italian ✗✗

3900 Richmond Ave. (bet. Amboy Rd. & Oakdale St.)

Bus: 59, 79
Phone: 718-227-3286
Web: www.noveitalianbistro.com
Prices: $$$

Lunch & dinner Tue – Sun

Nove is Staten Island to a tee. Take a look around the room and see couples wearing sunglasses (even at night), dressed-to-the-nines. They are moneyed, mostly Italian-American, and all seem to know each other. Despite the elegant setting, the uninitiated may feel a bit like they're dining at the wrong cafeteria table. Then again, from coffered ceilings to carved wood moldings to a custom-made wine cabinet, no expense was spared in this opulent dining room, and that's exactly how this crowd wants it.

The menu varies from simple, unadorned pastas, like rigatoni with prosciutto and mozzarella cubes, to carefully constructed veal scaloppini with prosecco sauce. The offerings may sometimes seem bizarre, but it is just what the diva ordered.

Nurnberger Bierhaus

B1

817 Castleton Ave. (at Regan Ave.)

Bus: 46, 96

Phone: 718-816-7461

Web: www.nurnbergerbierhaus.com

Prices: $$

Lunch & dinner daily

This paen to the German art of stuffing yourself and throwing back beers is proof that despite its Italian connections, Staten Island proudly flies the flag of other culinary cultures.

There's no glitz with this schnitz. The feel is timeless, waitresses sport dirndls, and there's a requisite collection of beer steins. The crowd is boisterous, due in large to the ever-flowing beer, and covers everyone from little ones to old men packed around platters of meat. Their warm soft pretzels will forever ruin a hankering for the street cart variety. After tucking into *jagerschnitzel*, hearty goulash, and the menu's crowing jewel, *wusterller mit allem drum* and *dram* (with its four types of sausage piled high with sauerkraut), you'll be rolling out of here.

Vida 😊

B1

381 Van Duzer St. (bet. Beach & Wright Sts.)

Bus: 78

Phone: 718-720-1501

Web: www.vidany.com

Prices: $$

Lunch Fri – Sat

Dinner Tue – Sat

If you have a hankering for fresh food in a bright little interior, you're going to flip for Silva Popaz's charming Vida. An entryway filled with dried poblano braids leads to a sunny yellow room dotted with orange stools and wrought-iron café chairs, often filled with devoted locals and day-trippers in the know.

Popaz's extensive travels inform the menu, which dances across so many regions it's hard to define. Let a gorgeous bowl of vegan lentil soup, served with toasted country bread, do the talking; then move onto tender pulled pork and chicken, wrapped in a pair of fresh corn tortillas and topped with fresh cheese, tangy green onion, and a lick of salsa; or wildly fresh mussels and linguini dancing with Korean chili paste and shallots.

Zest

B2

977 Bay St. (bet. Lynhurst & Willow Sts.)

Bus: 51, 81
Phone: 718-390-8477
Web: www.zestsiny.com
Prices: $$

Dinner Tue – Sun

Staten Island dwellers need not hop the ferry for a nice evening out. Instead, just pick up the phone and make a reservation at Zest. Dark wood paneling, jazzy portraits, and crisp white linens lend a supper club feel to the charming ambience of this pleasing spot.

From foie gras to rack of lamb, expect French classics all the way—do not be tempted to veer from the wonderfully traditional dishes by their less successful, more complicated selections. Desserts like crêpes Suzette, with silky apricots poached in fresh orange and Grand Marnier, folded into thin, warm crêpes with a quenelle of vanilla ice cream, is pure pleasure.

The staff isn't speedy, but like the above-mentioned crêpe, you'll be enveloped in a warm and comfortable feeling.

Couverts (✗ ... ✗✗✗✗✗) indicate the level of comfort found at a restaurant. The more ✗'s, the more upscale a restaurant will be.

Staten Island

517

Where to Stay

Eventi

851 Sixth Ave. (bet. 29th & 30th Sts.)

Subway: 28 St (Broadway)
Phone: 212-564-4567 or 866-996-8396
Web: www.eventihotel.com
Prices: $$$

237
Rooms

55
Suites

Chris Sanders

Eventi is the latest addition to the Kimpton Hotels family, and like its siblings scattered across the country, this baby sister is fashion-forward and guest–and pet–friendly. Encompassing an entire block of Sixth Avenue in the thick of the hustle and bustle, Eventi is a chic 54-story tower of glass and steel. Inside, the lobby is a mix of hip library and sexy boudoir with shiny red marble, walnut paneling, and thick red velvet drapes. Guestrooms buck the city's trend toward tiny and instead offer spacious accommodations fitted with striking contemporary style and cushy comforts (think Frette linens and Etro toiletries). Take a gander at the spectacular views.

Head to the lobby for the evening wine happy hour (a Kimpton signature) or catch a flick on the 20-foot widescreen in the outdoor plaza. Need a nosh? Cozy up to one of the monitors at the Food Parc, and order from a handful of food court-style stalls (burger stand, dim sum, flatbread sandwiches, among others).

And then there's Bar Basque, with its impressive pedigree. Jeffery Chodorow is behind the authentic Basque menu, while set designer Syd Mead, of *Star Trek* and *Blade Runner* fame, has fashioned a futuristic look.

Manhattan ▶ Chelsea

The Maritime

B3

363 W. 16th St. (at Ninth Ave.)

Subway: 14 St - 8 Av
Phone: 212-242-4300 or 800-466-9092
Web: www.themaritimehotel.com
Prices: $$$

123
Rooms

3
Suites

The Maritime Hotel

Polka-dotted with porthole windows, The Maritime Hotel is a 2003 reincarnation of the truly unique, 12-story white-tile edifice designed by Albert C. Ledner in 1966 to house the National Maritime Union. The location, amid Chelsea's art galleries and the Meatpacking District's hip nightlife, assures the property a clientele encompassing artists and fashionistas as well as business travelers.

A complimentary bottle of wine and a personalized note welcome guests to the cabin-like rooms, each echoing the nautical feel with its five-foot porthole window and palette of sea blues and greens. All include a CD player and a flat-screen LCD TV. Marble baths and 500-thread-count bed linens add the luxury of an ocean-liner state room. A warning to guests seeking peace and quiet: request a room on a higher floor rather than try and engineer the noise-reducing "window plugs" in the middle of the night.

Dining options include La Bottega, an Italian trattoria with a large outdoor terrace; and chic Matsuri for Japanese cuisine. Between Cabanas rooftop bar and Hiro Ballroom, opportunities abound to drink in the Chelsea scene.

Manhattan ▶ Chelsea

The Bowery Hotel

335 Bowery (at 3rd St.)

Subway: Astor Pl
Phone: 212-505-9100 or 866-726-9379
Web: www.theboweryhotel.com
Prices: $$$$

128 Rooms

7 Suites

Gregory Goode

This nondescript block of what was once known as Skid Row might seem an unlikely location for a trendy boutique hotel, but Eric Goode and Sean MacPherson (who brought you the Maritime in Chelsea) are betting that their East Village property will draw hordes of hipsters and Europeans. Though the block can be dodgy late at night, it's within easy walking distance of New York's coolest 'hoods (East Village, SoHo, Nolita, Greenwich Village, Lower East Side).

From the outside, the hotel's new redbrick façade towers castle-like above neighboring structures. Giant black-paned windows give the building a pre-war charm. Step inside and you'll be engulfed in the dim, sultry lobby, where dark woods, fireplaces, velvet couches and mosaic mirrors create a distinctly old-world air.

Those huge, sound-proofed windows afford great city views, and paired with whitewashed brick walls, make the rooms seem larger. A mix of period and contemporary pieces add to the art deco-meets-21st century design, while 500-thread-count bed linens, HD TV, and rainfall showerheads add luxury.

The outdoor courtyard bar and restaurant Gemma are popular with the cool crowd.

Manhattan ▶ East Village

522

Cooper Square Hotel

25 Cooper Square (bet. 4th & 5th Sts.)

Subway: Astor Pl
Phone: 212-475-5700 or 888-251-7979
Web: www.thecoopersquarehotel.com
Prices: $$$$

139 Rooms

6 Suites

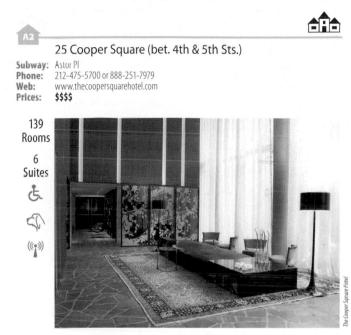

The Cooper Square Hotel

What's different about the Bowery these days? Well, besides the appearance of chic boutiques and restaurants, the curving 21-story glass and aluminum tower that rises above Cooper Square. Designed by Carlos Zapata Studio and opened in fall 2008, this hotel adds a sleek note to a once-gritty East Village neighborhood.

Unlike its façade, the lodging's intimate interior spaces take their cues from the 19th century tenement building around which the hotel is built. Check-in is not your standard experience. When guests walk through the huge wooden doors, they are escorted not to the front desk (there isn't one), but to the Library, a book-lined lounge area set up with an honor bar and warmed by a fireplace in winter. Here room keys are issued and a more personalized version of the check-in process is accomplished.

Guests are escorted to rooms that command striking views of the city and feature a warm minimalist décor courtesy of furnishings by B & B Italia. An eclectic collection of books is on hand in each room.

Downstairs, the repurposed dining room is now The Trilby restaurant offering European-inspired comfort food to the East Village.

Manhattan ▶ East Village

Andaz Wall Street

75 Wall St. (at Water St.)

Subway: Wall St (William St)
Phone: 212-590-1234 or 877-875-5036
Web: www.andaz.com
Prices: $$$

249
Rooms

4
Suites

Andaz Wall Street

Take what you know about Hyatt Hotels and toss it out the window before entering Andaz. This designer hotel, steps away from the Stock Exchange, is part of Hyatt's international empire, but it rips the rug out from the traditional hotel experience right from the beginning. Instead of a reception desk, arriving guests relax with drink in hand while hosts provide check-in services via handheld tablets (or skip it altogether– they'll check you in while you ride the elevator).

Andaz is Urdu for "however you want to express yourself," but this hotel knows exactly who it is with its chic, modern sensibility. Clean, uncluttered lines, exquisite fabrics, and distinct architectural touches define the public and private spaces. The rooms are exceedingly spacious and capped off with 11-foot ceilings. Gadget geeks drool over the technological touches, such as the bedside lighting controls and tastefully disguised data ports. Fear the fridge? Not here, where mini bars are stocked with complimentary snacks and beverages.

There is 24-hour room service for the time-starved, while others can kick back at Bar Seven Five or dine at the elegant Wall & Water restaurant.

Best Western Seaport Inn

33 Peck Slip (at Front St.)

Subway: Fulton St
Phone: 212-766-6600 or 800-937-8376
Web: www.seaportinn.com
Prices: $$

72
Rooms

Best Western Seaport Inn

This pleasant and welcoming Best Western hotel in Manhattan's Financial District is the perfect perch for history buffs seeking old New York with modern amenities to make any guest feel at home while traveling. Cobblestoned streets and Federal-style structures on the surrounding blocks transport visitors back in time to the 17th century, when the settlement known as Nieuw Amsterdam was taking shape. This hotel is steps from the historic ships docked at South Street Seaport.

Tidy, well-kept rooms have recently been refreshed; all come equipped with comforts including a safe for all your prized possessions. Rooms on the 6th and 7th floors offer private balconies overlooking the Brooklyn Bridge—a glittering sight after dark. The upgraded chambers also offer flat-screen TVs and whirlpool soaking tubs. Other perks include a complimentary continental breakfast each morning and fresh-baked cookies in the afternoon.

For shoppers, the mall at Pier 17 is a short walk away (where one can also catch a water taxi to Brooklyn). Also nearby are the skyscrapers of Wall Street and the greensward of Battery Park, which borders New York Harbor.

Manhattan ▶ **Financial District**

Gild Hall

15 Gold St. (enter on Platt St.)

Subway: Fulton St
Phone: 212-232-7700 or 800-268-0700
Web: www.thompsonhotels.com
Prices: $$$

116
Rooms

10
Suites

Thompson Hotels

A magnet for a young, hip, moneyed crowd, Gild Hall is an important member and integral part of the Thompson Hotel group. Located just steps from Wall Street, South Street Seaport, and some of downtown's best bars, this fashionable roost was conceived by interior-design guru Jim Walrod. The boutique property's style brings to mind a European gentlemen's club in the wood paneling, leather furniture, antler-shaped chandeliers, and shelves of fine literature. Yet there's nothing stodgy here; the leather furnishings sport sleek modern lines, and the chandeliers are crafted of chrome.

This clubby feel continues down the cranberry-colored hallways to the tranquil masculine-style guestrooms, where oversize leather-covered headboards, custom designed wood furnishings, and plaid throw blankets team with contemporary touches such as Sferra linens, mini-bar selections courtesy of Dean & DeLuca, and tinted glass tiles in the baths.

On the ground floor, Libertine does an ultra-modern take on an English tavern, spotlighting pub fare. Visit the Library Bar upstairs (2nd floor) if you're looking to sip on drinks and pump up the party vibe.

Manhattan ▶ Financial District

The Ritz-Carlton, Battery Park

2 West St. (at Battery Pl.)

Subway: Bowling Green
Phone: 212-344-0800 or 800-241-3333
Web: www.ritzcarlton.com
Prices: $$$$

259
Rooms

39
Suites

The Ritz-Carlton New York, Battery Park

If unique art deco furnishings, top-notch service, and stunning views of New York Harbor, the Statue of Liberty, and Ellis Island sound like your idea of a hotel, put on this Ritz. Occupying floors 3 to 14 of a 39-story glass and brick tower, the Ritz-Carlton, Battery Park lords it over a neighborhood that includes several museums as well as the greensward that defines the southwestern tip of Manhattan.

Guests nest here in spacious rooms and suites outfitted with Frette linens, featherbeds, and down duvets and pillows. Accommodations with harbor views have telescopes for checking out the dramatic waterscapes. All rooms provide classic Ritz luxury enhanced by plush robes, Bulgari bath amenities, and deep soaking tubs.

Of course, the hotel offers 24-hour room service, but you can dine on prime Angus beef on-site at 2 West; or lull over some classic cocktails in the lounge before retiring to your glorious room. Before you turn in, hand over your city-worn shoes for a complimentary overnight shine.

After a day of high-end shopping and sightseeing, return for a solid workout at the fitenss center, followed by luxurious pampering at their top-of-the-line spa.

Manhattan ▶ Financial District

Wall Street Inn

9 S. William St. (bet. Beaver & Broad Sts.)

Subway: Wall St (William St.)
Phone: 212-747-1500 or 877-747-1500
Web: www.thewallstreetinn.com
Prices: $$

46
Rooms

The Wall Street Inn

Although it's not actually on the street that traces the wood-plank wall erected by Dutch colonists in 1653, this charming inn is nonetheless a good option for travelers with business on Wall Street. Tucked away off William Street, the Wall Street Inn fills two landmark buildings that date back to 1895 and 1920.

Early American period reproductions, floral prints, and marble baths decorate the two classes (superior and deluxe) of tasteful rooms; and with such delightful amenities as an in-room refrigerators, a small basement exercise room, and complimentary continental breakfast, this low-key hotel offers good value for money. A small business center offers a full range of services. The back of the inn overlooks cobbled Stone Street, one of the narrow 17th century byways, which boasts some of the city's more renowned watering holes, namely Ulysses and Brouwers.

While party-loving guests appreciate the ability to stumble back to the hotel, there is a downside. Despite the soundproofed windows, lower rooms on this side of the property are privy to the noise made by other revelers on a nightly basis.

Ace Hotel New York

20 W. 29th St. (at Broadway)

Subway: 28 St (Broadway)
Phone: 212-679-2222
Web: www.acehotel.com/newyork
Prices: $$$

262
Rooms

3
Suites

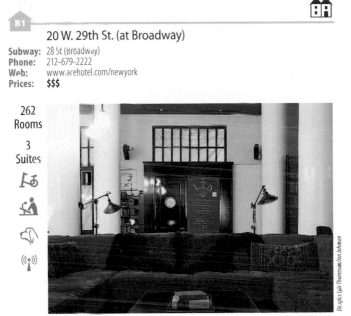

Douglas Lyle Thompson/Jon Johnson

You don't need to be an artist to stay at the Ace Hotel, but you'll certainly feel like one. Formerly known as the historic Breslin Hotel, which was once home to artists and personalities like "Diamond Jim" Brady, the design firm of Roman and Williams has completely redone the space, injecting it with an upscale bohemian flavor.

The rooms have an undeniably hip dorm room feel. The furnishings include vintage steamer trunks and other reclaimed items that give the rooms a certain thrift shop chic, while industrial furnishings (bent plumbing pipe clothes racks), plant the rooms firmly in the 21st century. Even the amenities play off the funky feel—instant ramen noodle soup sits next to the fridge, blank music sheets fill the bedside table, and the specially commissioned "bathrobes" are really more like hooded gray sweatshirts.

Forever ban the phrase "starving artist" from this hotel. Portland's famed Stumptown Coffee Shop set up its first East Coast spot here, while Fort Greene's hip No. 7 opened No. 7 Sub. The Breslin Bar and Dining Room and The John Dory Oyster Bar, both headed by April Bloomfield and Ken Friedman of Spotted Pig fame, crown the food and beverage offerings here.

Manhattan ▶ Gramercy, Flatiron & Union Square

The Carlton

88 Madison Ave. (at 29th St.)

Subway: 28 St (Park Ave. South)
Phone: 212-532-4100 or 800-601-8500
Web: www.carltonhotelny.com
Prices: $$$

294
Rooms

23
Suites

The Carlton Hotel

New and old dovetail seamlessly in this Beaux-Arts property, which premiered in 1904 as the Hotel Seville. The attractive property (complete with a showstopping and grand three-story lobby) screams luxury in the heart of harried (and commercial) midtown Manhattan. With its new entrance on Madison Avenue, this space synthesizes early-20th century style with sleek seating and crystal chandeliers shrouded in cylindrical metal-mesh covers—a Rockwell signature. A sepia-toned portrait of the Hotel Seville, the lobby's focal point, glitters like a rainy scene through the three-story waterfall that envelops it.

All 317 rooms have a modern aspect and include geometric-print fabrics, 42-inch flat-screen TVs, large work desks, and laptop-sized safes. Streamlined furnishings now complement such amenities as Frette linens, in-room wireless Internet access, plush robes, and Apple iHome sound systems. Molten Brown bath amenities will certainly help you unwind after a night on the town.

Off the lobby, the elegant Millesime dining room and bar feeds the hotel's spectrum of affluent guests in the balconied mezzanine.

Gramercy Park Hotel

2 Lexington Ave. (at 21st St.)

Subway: 23 St (Park Ave. South)
Phone: 212-920-3300 or 866-784-1300
Web: www.gramercyparkhotel.com
Prices: $$$$

140
Rooms

45
Suites

Gramercy Park Hotel

Reinvented by hip hotelier Ian Schrager and artist Julian Schnabel, the lobby of this 1925 Renaissance revival-style edifice could be an artist's home with its juxtaposition of true antiques and contemporary pieces. A custom-made Venetian glass chandelier hangs from the coffered ceiling, illuminating periodically changing works by modern masters such as Andy Warhol, Keith Haring, and Schnabel himself.

Velvet draperies in deep-rose hues with royal blue accents, tapestry-print fabrics, and louvered wood blinds lend a masculine feel to the rooms. Original photography and paintings adorn the walls. In keeping with its history of hosting artists, actors, and other glitterati, the hotel still pampers its guests. A landscaped private rooftop garden for dining (accessible only via a special key); a key to adjacent Gramercy Park—impossible to access unless you live on the square overlooking the gated greensward; personal trainers at the on-site Aerospace gym; and a "best of" collection of bathroom amenities carefully selected by Allure Magazine will give you the idea. Meanwhile, the celebutante scene at the Rose and Jade bars begs you to don your best Manolos.

Manhattan ▶ Gramercy, Flatiron & Union Square

Inn at Irving Place

B3

56 Irving Pl. (bet 17th & 18th Sts.)

Subway: 14 St - Union Sq
Phone: 212-533-4600 or 800-685-1447
Web: www.innatirving.com
Prices: $$$$

12 Rooms

Roy Wright/The Inn at Irving Place

Infused with a 19th century charm not often found in Manhattan hotels, this inn takes up two single-family brownstones built in 1834. To find it, look for the street number; the inn is unmarked. Walk inside and you'll be enveloped in a cozy parlor furnished with antique settees and armchairs covered in floral-patterned silk. If it's cold out, chances are the fireplace will be roaring.

A glass of Champagne and a plate of cookies welcome you to your room. Decked out with hardwood floors and period furniture, each of the 12 guestrooms offers a work desk, a well-stocked minibar and a Sony CD/radio. Pedestal sinks, antique mirrors, and black-and-white tile decorate the large bathrooms.

In the morning, a continental breakfast including fresh-baked croissants and sliced fruit is served in the parlor or delivered to your room—whichever you prefer. For a civilized afternoon break, make reservations for the five-course high tea at Lady Mendl's tea salon. Cibar Lounge, also on-site, is a clubby place for a martini and light fare.

One caveat: if you're traveling with heavy luggage in tow, note that there's a steep flight of stairs at the inn's entrance.

Manhattan ▶ Gramercy, Flatiron & Union Square

W Union Square

201 Park Ave. South (at 17th St.)

Subway: 14 St - Union Sq
Phone: 212-253-9119 or 877-782-0027
Web: www.whotels.com
Prices: $$$$

270
Rooms

18
Suites

W Hotels

Since its launch in New York City in 1998, the W brand has come to signify sophistication in its minimalist contemporary design and stylish comfort. This member of the Starwood group is no exception. Designed by David Rockwell, it recalls the grand gathering places of the early 20th century inside the landmark 1911 granite and limestone Guardian Life Building, but with a modern twist. In the two-story lobby, the Living Room provides a chic place to meet and greet under tall arched windows, while up the striking staircase, the Beaux-Arts-style Great Room preserves the past. Now used for conferences, this grand chamber is framed by splendid marble columns and original plasterwork on the coffered ceiling.

Rooms and suites each come in three sizes and even the least-expensive rooms are large by New York City standards. All see to your comfort with luxurious velvet armchairs, massive work desks, goose-down duvets and pillows, and beaming windows with an incredible view of Union Square.

The neighborhood's hip frequent the swank basement club, Underbar; while Olives caters to gourmands with a Mediterranean menu designed by Chef Todd English.

Manhattan ▶ **Gramercy, Flatiron & Union Square**

Gansevoort

18 Ninth Ave. (at 13th St.)

Subway: 14 St - 8 Av
Phone: 212-206-6700 or 877-462-7386
Web: www.hotelgansevoort.com
Prices: $$$$

166 Rooms

21 Suites

Hotel Gansevoort

In the Dutch language, the name "Gansevoort" refers to the goose (*gans*) at the head (*voort*) of a flock of geese, and indeed, this swanky hotel rises above; its 14 stories tower over the effervescent hip-dom of the Meatpacking District.

As you step into the ultra-chic lobby, you'll be launched into the 21st century through a 14-foot-high revolving door. Inside, the building seems to be supported by light, thanks to internally illuminated glass columns. Lofty rooms with 9-foot ceilings dress in dusky hues with splashes of blackberry; beds wear 400-thread-count Egyptian cotton sheets, and large lavish bathrooms are equipped with sleek steel sinks. On the high floors, huge windows command fabulous views of the Hudson River and surrounding city. Speaking of views, don't forget to check out the hotel's gorgeous rooftop. The neighborhood hot spot and the Gansevoort's signature, the rooftop holds the hip Plunge Bar and a heated swimming pool that pipes in underwater music. Special events are made even more so in the rooftop loft, where a landscaped garden can't quite compete with the 360-degree cityscape.

A newly opened sister property brings rooftop pool-cool to Park Avenue South.

The Standard

848 Washington St. (at 13th St.)

Subway: 14 St - 8 Av
Phone: 212-645-4646
Web: www.standardhotels.com
Prices: $$$

337
Rooms

Nikolas Koenig/The Standard, New York

Setting the standard for accommodations in the Meatpacking District, this modern slab of concrete and glass stands on concrete stilts above an area filled with low rise warehouses. The structure's lofty position insures that the hotel lords it over the neighborhood, drinking in every inch of this spectacular city. As if that weren't enough, the building is literally suspended above the High Line, the city's exciting and beloved greensward that has revamped an abandoned freight railway into a public park.

The lobby sets the sexy tone with its mirrored ceiling, sleek furnishings, and light-diffusing walls. Rooms are small, the décor funky and retro. Baths are open to the rest of the space, so privacy is in short supply. Hands-down, the floor-to-ceiling windows win the prize for their breathtaking panoramas of the Hudson River and the Manhattan skyline. Ask for a corner room to optimize your view.

Off the lobby, the Living Room cocktail lounge overlooks the grand plaza and spins tunes by live DJs on Friday and Saturday nights. But the fun doesn't stop there. The Standard is also outfitted with the outdoor Biergarten as well as Le Bain, a rooftop lounge.

Aloft Harlem

2296 Frederick Douglass Blvd. (bet. 123rd & 124th Sts.)

Subway: 125 St (Frederick Douglass Blvd.)
Phone: 212-749-4000 or 877-462-5398
Web: www.starwoodhotels.com/alofthotels
Prices: $$

124
Rooms

Frank Oudeman

For decades, Harlem was one neighborhood that most people avoided. Once a place buzzing with talent in its supper clubs, smoky jazz clubs, and famed Apollo Theater, Harlem fell into decline. My, how things change. It is now one of the city's most talked about and historic nabes (think Sugar Hill in Hamilton Heights)—even Bill Clinton had his offices here after leaving the White House. It was just a matter of time before it got a proper hotel and with the arrival of Aloft in late 2010, there is a now a spot for hipsters to hang their hat in Harlem.

You definitely won't walk by this hotel—its contemporary, gleaming façade screams cool. Inside, bright, stylish furnishings set a sleek tone. The rooms are spacious and packed with goodies like comfortable king-sized beds with neat, crisp linens. Oversized windows flood the rooms with plenty of sunlight, though the city views aren't anything to write home about.

The look and feel is boutique, but the Aloft collection of hotels is conceived by powerhouse Starwood Hotels. The W xyz bar is *the* in spot, often transforming into a stage showcasing serious talent. It's like your own version of American Idol—only way more trendy and hip.

The Hotel on Rivington

107 Rivington St. (bet. Essex & Ludlow Sts.)

Subway: Delancey St
Phone: 212-475-2600 or 800-915-1537
Web: www.hotelonrivington.com
Prices: $$$

89
Rooms

21
Suites

Hotel on Rivington

Grit and glamour collide on the Lower East Side, a neighborhood that has come into its own while retaining its diversity and refreshing lack of attitude. A great example of the area's newfound glamour, The Hotel on Rivington towers 21 stories above low-rise brick buildings. Floor-to-ceiling glass walls offer magnificent unobstructed views of Manhattan.

The remarkable result of a collaboration of cutting-edge architects, designers, decorators, and artists from around the world, this hotel combines sleek minimalist décor with ultramodern amenities, and, yes, comfort. If you notice anything else besides the view, you'll appreciate the Swedish sleep system that conforms to your every curve by sensing your body temperature and weight, as well as the Italian mosaic bathrooms decked out with heated floors, steam showers, and two-person Japanese-style soaking tubs. An on-site fitness facility, a DVD library of rare films, and the Co-Op Food & Drink restaurant serving global fare round out the amenities.

Largely populated by guests who work in the fashion, music, and media industries, The Rivington appeals to an artsy clientele who prefer not to stay in mainstream midtown.

Manhattan ▶ Lower East Side

The Benjamin

125 E. 50th St. (bet. Lexington & Third Aves.)

Subway: 51 St
Phone: 212-715-2500 or 866-222-2365
Web: www.thebenjamin.com
Prices: $$$$

112 Rooms

97 Suites

The Benjamin

From its ECOTEL certification to the cheerful and efficient staff who greet guests by name and care for them, The Benjamin ensures the comfort of its visitors. Before you arrive, just call the Sleep Concierge, who will help outfit your room with your preferred pillow (from a menu of 12 different types), aromatherapy fragrance, and relaxing lullaby. Then settle into the custom-designed mattress, wrap yourself in the fluffy duvet, and drift off to sleep. Argon-gas-filled windows should filter out any unwanted sounds. Canine guests can expect equally sweet dreams thanks to customized pet beds, puppy bathrobes, and gourmet food.

Rooms are designed as executive suites, encompassing all the technological amenities to facilitate working on-site. Many of the accommodations also have galley kitchens with state-of-the-art appliances. Given advance notice, the hotel will even stock your fridge with your favorite foods and beverages. Don't care to cook? The National Bar & Dining Room is located right downstairs.

In the public spaces, marble floors, upholstered walls, and Venetian mirrors reflect the spirit of this 1927 structure, which owes its elegant style to architect Emery Roth.

Elysée

60 E. 54th St. (bet. Madison & Park Aves.)

Subway: 5 Av - 53 St
Phone: 212-753-1066 or 800-535-9733
Web: www.elyseehotel.com
Prices: $$$

90
Rooms

13
Suites

&

((•))

Hotel Elysée

Low-key, intimate, and discreet, the Elysée has weathered the decades with grace since its opening in 1926. A timeless quality pervades the black-and-white marble flooring and gold-fabric-covered walls of the lobby, as well as the French-influenced old-world style in the guestrooms where cut-glass and polished brass sconces cast a warm glow. In its early days, this hotel was a haven for writers, actors, and musicians. Vladimir Horowitz once lived in the suite where his piano still stands; Tennessee Williams lived and died here (in the Sunset Suite); and Ava Gardner once made this her New York home.

The property's soft residential ambience appeals to a range of patrons. Moneyed or not, they appreciate the complimentary breakfast and evening wine and hors d'oeuvres, served in the second-floor Club Room; as well as the computer located there for guest use. Guests may also request a complimentary pass for nearby NY Sports Club including their daily fitness classes.

The Elysée is known and loved for its premier location, just steps away from 5th Avenue with its shopping galore, MoMA, St. Patrick's, Rockefeller Center, and many other midtown gems.

Manhattan ▶ Midtown East & Murray Hill

Four Seasons New York

57 E. 57th St. (bet. Madison & Park Aves.)

Subway: 59 St
Phone: 212-758-5700 or 800-487-3769
Web: www.fourseasons.com
Prices: $$$$

305 Rooms

63 Suites

Durston Saylor

In the heart of it all, New York's Four Seasons Hotel continues to have its finger on the pulse of this energetic city. Designed by renowned architect I.M. Pei, the Four Seasons chooses not to wow from the outside (it looks like any other nondescript midtown building), but step inside and you'll feel that you've been transported to an oasis of peace. There is an instant hush as you glide past the doors into this temple of luxury where French limestone columns, low lighting, and gleaming floors create a sophisticated, yet soothing, atmosphere.

The guest rooms and suites manage to feel luxurious while remaining exceedingly comfortable. Deep-soaking bathtubs that fill in just 60 seconds? Check. And jaw-dropping views? Check. Four Seasons' legendary white-glove service is just another part of the "standard" offerings at this posh hotel.

It doesn't stop there. Fine dining? It's here. From caviar (Calvisius Caviar Lounge) to Chablis (The Garden), the hotel offers a variety of settings for wining and dining. Serious foodies save their appetite for dinner at the stellar, show-stopper L'Atelier de Joël Robuchon, where French and Asian cuisines collide for spectacular results.

Hotel 57

130 E. 57th St. (at Lexington Ave.)

Subway: 59 St
Phone: 212-753-8841
Web: www.marriott.com
Prices: $$

169 Rooms

31 Suites

Cris Molina

It may be owned by mega-chain Marriott, but there's nothing typical about Hotel 57. This boutique-style hotel definitely has a personality of its own. Situated on 57th Street, this hotel has a prime location, but that's not the only reason it is packed with savvy sophisticates. Stylish surroundings, a perennially packed restaurant and bar, and a palatable price point that proves being hip doesn't have to hurt are among the top reasons.

From the intimate lobby dressed in funky furnishings and unique artwork to the chic yet comfortable accommodations, this hotel sports a modern metropolitan flair. The rooms and suites are well designed (spacious, marble bathrooms, ample closet space, convenient built-ins) and complete the urban, contemporary look with neutral colors, birch wood paneling, and sleek furnishings. Exposed brick and features like back-lit headboards lend a unique flavor to the accommodations.

Step outside onto buzzing 57th Street and a world of dining, shopping, and sightseeing awaits, but you don't need to go far to find a festive spirit. Opia Restaurant and Lounge is always hopping with a chic crowd of hotel guests and New Yorkers who come for the food and fun.

Manhattan ► **Midtown East & Murray Hill**

541

Library

299 Madison Ave. (enter on 41st St.)

Subway: Grand Central - 42 St
Phone: 212-983-4500 or 877-793-7323
Web: www.libraryhotel.com
Prices: $$$

60
Rooms

The Library Hotel

A welcoming inn well-located in midtown, The Library keeps to a literary theme with its collection of 6,000 volumes (if that's not enough books for you, the New York Public and the Pierpont Morgan libraries are just minutes away). Each floor is numbered after a category in the Dewey Decimal System, and rooms contain books on a particular subject. Math maven? Request a room on the fifth floor. Literature your thing? Head to the eighth floor.

Rooms, though small, are comfortable, and manage to squeeze a basic desk, an all-inclusive entertainment center (containing bookshelves, drawers, a small closet, a mini bar, and a flat-screen TV) into the cramped quarters. Modern bathrooms come equipped with a hairdryer, magnifying mirror, and scale.

On the second floor, the Reading Room is where you'll find the complimentary continental breakfast laid out in the morning, snacks throughout the day, and the wine and cheese reception each evening. The comfy Writer's Den and the terrace Poetry Garden are perfect for...what else?... reading.

When it's warm outside, head up to the rooftop bar (Bookmarks) for a cocktail and snack.

New York Palace

455 Madison Ave. (enter on 50th St.)

Subway: 51 St
Phone: 212-888-7000 or 800-697-2522
Web: www.newyorkpalace.com
Prices: $$$$

808
Rooms

86
Suites

The New York Palace

Best recognized by its lovely gated courtyard—formerly a carriage entrance—on Madison Avenue at 50th Street, The Palace serves up New York City on a silver platter. Enter through these gates and you'll be immersed in the old-world opulence that fills the 1882 Villard Houses, a U-shaped group of brownstones designed in the Italian Renaissance style by the firm of McKim, Mead and White.

Today the property blends the town houses with a 55-story tower added in 1980. Here, you'll find 808 guest rooms, 86 suites, a vast spa and fitness center, and 22,000 square feet of conference facilities. Guests in the modern tower rooms have access to a private lounge and concierge, as well as personal butler services. More modest deluxe rooms feature no less comfort, however, with their warm tones, new bedding, and oversize marble baths.

If you can tear yourself away from this palace be sure to check out the neighboring sights and sounds. Come back for afternoon tea in the lobby, or to experience cutting-edge cuisine in Gilt's sexy walnut-paneled space. Sophisticated cocktails abound in the contemporary Gilt Bar; and during warmer months, the opulent courtyard is home to the Palace Gate lounge.

Manhattan ▶ **Midtown East & Murray Hill**

Roger Williams

A6

131 Madison Ave. (at 31st St.)

Subway: 33 St
Phone: 212-448-7000 or 888-448-7788
Web: www.hotelrogerwilliams.com
Prices: $$$

191 Rooms

2 Suites

Roger Williams

Just blocks from the Empire State Building, this stylish boutique hotel makes a bright impression with its clean lines and pure colors. The "living room," as the lobby is called, is adorned with light wood paneling, soaring ceilings, and 20-foot-high windows creating an airy, cosmopolitan feel. Comfy contemporary furniture scattered throughout the lobby provides contemporary spaces to meet and greet.

Though on the small side, rooms at "the Roger" all feature flat-screen plasma TVs, mini bars, Aveda bath products, and wireless high-speed Internet access. Splashes of tangerine, lime green, cobalt blue, and red illuminate each room. The peppy colors aren't noisy and neither are the accommodations, thanks to well-insulated windows that help dampen the hustle and bustle of midtown. Japanese-inspired double rooms add shoji screens and sliding-glass bathroom doors, while 15 garden terrace rooms enjoy private patios and stirring cityscapes.

A help-yourself European style breakfast—ranging from fresh croissants, to smoked salmon and prosciutto—is available in the mezzanine lounge each morning, and it's a sunny spot for an afternoon espresso as well.

70 Park Avenue

A5

70 Park Ave. (at 38th St.)

Subway: Grand Central - 42 St
Phone: 212 973 2400 or 877 707-2752
Web: www.70parkave.com
Prices: $$$

201
Rooms

4
Suites

David Phelps

For sophisticated midtown digs located mere minutes away by foot from Grand Central Terminal, 70 Park can't be beat. This Murray Hill property embodies the Kimpton Group's signature elements: care, comfort, style, flavor, and fun.

Care highlights thoughtful amenities such as the pet-friendly policy, and a dedicated yoga channel on your flat-screen TV. In-room comfort surrounds you in the down comforters and pillows, terrycloth robes, and luxury bath products. Designed by Jeffrey Bilhuber in neutral hues of limestone gray, shimmering bronze, and light cocoa brown, the hotel's contemporary style speaks for itself. The complimentary wine reception held around the limestone fireplace on weeknights affords guests an opportunity for fun, as does the lively bar scene at the Silverleaf Tavern. You'll taste the 70 Park flavor in the tavern's limited menu of pub fare.

Other reasons to stay here? An easy walk to midtown offices and shopping, 24-hour room service, in-room spa services, and guest privileges at the NY Sports Club—a couple of blocks away. Strollers, cribs, and connecting rooms accommodate families.

Manhattan ▶ Midtown East & Murray Hill

The St. Regis

2 E. 55th St. (at Fifth Ave.)

Subway: 5 Av – 53 St
Phone: 212-753-4500 or 800-759-7550
Web: www.stregis.com/newyork
Prices: $$$$

164 Rooms

65 Suites

The St. Regis New York

Stylish and elegant, and with service close to perfection, the St. Regis reigns among the city's finest hotels. Commissioned by John Jacob Astor in 1904, this Beaux-Arts confection at the corner of Fifth Avenue is located just blocks from Central Park, MoMA, and other midtown attractions. Its public spaces and lobby, from the painted ceilings to the marble staircase, are steeped in Gilded Age opulence.

Floors fitted with elegant guestrooms are lined with silk wall coverings and custom-made furniture. Guests in the spacious suites (the smallest is 600 square feet and range up to 3,400 square feet) are cosseted with extra luxuries, such as a bouquet of fresh roses delivered daily. Unparalleled service includes a butler you can call on 24 hours a day, an on-site florist, complimentary garment pressing when you arrive, and the exclusive Remède Spa. Their signature massage calms jangled nerves with a mix of Shiatsu, Swedish, deep-tissue, and reflexology.

Be sure to stop in the King Cole Bar to peek at Maxfield Parrish's famous mural, and to sip a Bloody Mary, which was introduced here in the 1920s.

The Vincci Avalon

16 E. 32nd St. (bet. Fifth & Madison Aves.)

Subway: 33 St
Phone: 212-299-7000 or 888-447-8256
Web: www.theavalonny.com
Prices: $$

80 Rooms

20 Suites

Vincci Avalon

Right around the corner from the Empire State Building, this boutique property indulges business travelers with six meeting rooms and complimentary high-speed Internet access in each guestroom. Leisure travelers and theater lovers profit from The Avalon's setting, a short walk from Times Square and the bright lights of Broadway.

All appreciate large "Superior" rooms, each of which flaunt 27-inch flat-screen TVs, ample closet space, velour robes, and Irish cotton linens. Dark hardwood floors, earth tones (soft green, brown, and rust), and Italian marble baths accentuate the décor. At the top tier of room types, the 20 executive suites average 450 square feet and come with Jacuzzi tubs, fax machines, sofa beds, and Bose Wave radios.

Just off the elegant lobby, which is set about with pillars and paneling, the Library/Club room is a den-like area outfitted with a personal computer. Guests here will enjoy thoughtful and warm service from the affable staff, as well as passes to the nearby Equinox gym and fitness center. The SerRa Mediterranean Bistro serves a scrumptious spread for breakfast every morning and American fare for lunch and dinner.

Manhattan ▶ Midtown East & Murray Hill

The Waldorf=Astoria

301 Park Ave. (bet. 49th & 50th Sts.)

Subway: 51 St
Phone: 212-355-3000 or 800-925-3673
Web: www.waldorfastoria.com
Prices: $$$$

1085
Rooms

331
Suites

Waldorf=Astoria

Nothing says New York high society like The Waldorf=Astoria. Built in 1931, the hotel blends exquisite art deco ornamentation and lavish Second Empire furnishings. The original Waldorf, built in 1893, was demolished along with its companion, the Astoria, to make room for the Empire State Building. The huge "new" hotel (including its boutique counterpart with a private entrance, the Waldorf Towers) occupies the entire block between Park and Lexington avenues. Its lobby features a striking inlaid-tile mosaic and art deco chandelier, and emanates a generally palatial feel.

This grand dame pampers her affluent (and devoted) guests with richly appointed, beautifully maintained rooms and suites all dressed with antiques, deluxe fabrics, and sumptuous marble bathrooms. Original art deco effects lend to the accommodations a delightful residential ambience.

Long a midtown power scene, the mahogany-paneled Bull and Bear teems with brokers and finance types who come for the signature martinis, the dry-aged prime Angus beef, and the men's-club ambience. Also among the property's three restaurants, Peacock Alley (in the center of the main lobby) is worth seeking out for its elegant cuisine.

Manhattan ▶ Midtown East & Murray Hill

Algonquin

59 W. 44th St. (bet. Fifth & Sixth Aves.)

Subway: 42 St - Bryant Pk
Phone: 212-840-6800
Web: www.algonquinhotel.com
Prices: $$$

150
Rooms

24
Suites

The Algonquin Hotel

New York's oldest operating hotel remains true to its classically elegant roots and timeless aura. Best known for the the circle of literati, including Dorothy Parker and Robert Benchley, who lunched in the Round Table Room in the years after World War I, the Algonquin preserves the feel and look of a fine Edwardian club.

Rooms have been smartly upgraded to include all modern amenities (tastefully hidden); top-quality fabrics and fittings lend rich jewel tones to the accommodations. You may not want to rise from your pillow-top mattress, 350-thread-count linen sheets, down pillows, and the famous "Algonquin Bed." (Order one for home, if you like.) Each of the suites adds a fully stocked refrigerator.

For a taste of 1930s café society, step into the Oak Room, the legendary cabaret where famous audiences and performers (crooners Harry Connick Jr. and Diana Krall got their starts here) made merry. The mood lingers, and the shows still go on, with such talent as Andrea Marcovicci and Jack Jones. In the intimate Blue Bar, you'll find artwork by the late Al Hirschfeld, who was a regular.

Manhattan ▶ Midtown West

The Blakely

136 W. 55th St. (bet. Sixth & Seventh Aves.)

Subway: 57 St
Phone: 212-245-1800 or 800-735-0710
Web: www.blakelynewyork.com
Prices: $$

63 Rooms

55 Suites

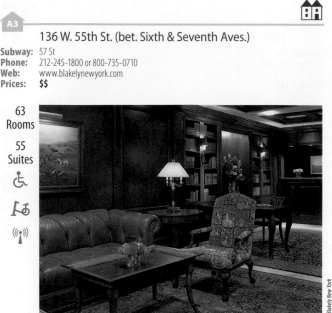

Blakely New York

Don't expect hipsters lounging in the lobby or rooms designed by the latest "it" decorator at The Blakely. Instead, this comfortable hotel is a perfect home-away-from-home for those looking for a terrific bang for the buck. Its enviable location puts this hotel smack dab in the heart of midtown's action. Business travelers flock here for access to area offices, but it's also a great choice for vacationers who want to traipse over to Central Park or hit up the shops on Fifth Avenue.

Everything about The Blakely feels like a classic New York residence. At first glance, the brick façade and blue awning could easily be mistaken for a private building, but it's the inside where guests feel immediately at home. The hotel shows off its old bones with terrific wood floors and large wood-framed windows.

The intimate English-style lobby is inviting, and the rooms and suites are well-designed to maximize comfort and function. Suites, equipped with kitchenettes and fully stocked pantries, are exceptionally large and are worth the extra bucks. If making your own coffee and snacks just isn't on your agenda, room service is available through the hotel's restaurant, Abboccato.

Manhattan ▶ Midtown West

Casablanca

147 W. 43rd St. (bet. Broadway & Sixth Ave.)

Subway: 42 St - Bryant Pk
Phone: 212-869-1212 or 888-922-7225
Web: www.casablancahotel.com
Prices: $$

43
Rooms

5
Suites

Christopher Ortnanik/IHK Fotos

Exotic tilework, warm wood paneling, and wrought-iron details greet guests at this European-style hotel. Convenient to Times Square and its many attractions, the Casablanca takes on the theme of the 1942 film starring Humphrey Bogart and Ingrid Bergman—without being kitschy. All the elements are here, from the pastel mural of the city of Casablanca that decorates the lobby stairway to the second-floor café called–you guessed it–Rick's.

With its tiled fireplace and bentwood chairs, Rick's Café is where you can wake up to a complimentary continental breakfast. In the afternoon, a selection of tea, coffee drinks, and cookies will tide you over until the wine-and-cheese reception at 5:00 P.M. Room service is provided by Tony's di Napoli restaurant, next door to the hotel.

The Moroccan ambience extends to the rooms, furnished with wooden headboards, damask linens, ceiling fans, and bathrobes. Guests enjoy free passes to the New York Sports Club, and a DVD library of films starring New York City.

No matter where you go when you leave this oasis, one thing's for sure: you'll always have Casablanca.

Manhattan ▶ Midtown West

Chambers

15 W. 56th St. (bet. Fifth & Sixth Aves.)

Subway: 57 St
Phone: 212-974-5656 or 866-204-5656
Web: www.chambershotel.com
Prices: $$$$

72
Rooms

5
Suites

Scott G. Morris/SGM Photography

Ideal for doing serious business or serious shopping (Bendel's is around the corner; Norma Kamali is next door; Bergdorf's is one block up), Chambers exudes a downtown feel despite its midtown location. It all begins with the two-story lobby where plenty of open space and a flickering fireplace provide a welcome cozy space. Sequestered seating on the mezzanine level above is the place to sneak away to with your laptop or a glass of wine—perhaps both.

The hotel's commitment to contemporary artists shows beautifully in the well-curated collection of more than 500 original pieces of art that is displayed throughout the public spaces, with different installations on each floor. Rooms continue the modern mood in SoHo-like appointments such as a plate-glass desktop balanced on a sawhorse-style base, and a poured concrete floor in the bathroom. Despite the cool aspect of the front-desk staff, service is very warm and accommodating.

Whether you're visiting for business or pleasure, one thing is for sure, the hotel will envelop you with their creativity and luxury.

Manhattan ▶ Midtown West

552

The Chatwal

130 W. 44th St. (bet. Sixth & Seventh Aves.)

Subway: Times Sq - 42 St
Phone: 212-764-5900 or 888-524-2892
Web: www.thechatwalny.com
Prices: $$$$

50
Rooms

26
Suites

The Chatwal/Phillip Ennis Photography

Everything old is white hot again at The Chatwal. From its landmark Stanford White-designed building to its striking art deco design to its scintillating history as the famous Lambs Club, The Chatwal revives the glamour of a bygone era. It is 1930s New York in all its glory from head-to-toe.

Guestrooms are a true work of art with details like suede-covered walls and leather-wrapped double closets. The Chatwal has truly thought of everything (envision radiant heated outdoor terraces, custom-designed Shifman mattresses, Frette linens, and Fili D'Oro towels). Gleaming woods, shining chrome, rich mocha and tobacco hues—the décor is as handsome as a dapper Don. Speaking of, there were plenty of those who frequented this haven in its previous incarnation as the Lambs Club, the first professional theater club. Everyone from Charlie Chaplin and Fred Astaire to Spencer Tracy and John Barrymore (for whom the 4,500 square-foot penthouse floor is named) communed here and their convivial spirit remains alive, especially at the Geoffrey Zakarian-run Lambs Club restaurant.

Nab a seat at the bar and drink in all of the action. Too many Manhattans or martinis? Detox at the luxe Kashwere Spa.

Manhattan ▶ Midtown West

City Club

55 W. 44th St. (bet. Fifth & Sixth Aves.)

Subway: 42 St - Bryant Pk
Phone: 212-921-5500
Web: www.cityclubhotel.com
Prices: $$$

62
Rooms

3
Suites

Matthew Hraneck

Originally conceived as an elite social club opened in 1904, the City Club now opens its doors to all. Located on 44th Street, the intimately scaled hotel is situated among a number of still active private clubs and has a sophisticated and exclusive ambience with a petite lobby that feels more like the entryway of a private residence than a hotel. The rooms are attractively designed to maximize square footage with a handsome beige and brown color scheme dominating. Marble bathrooms are outfitted with bidets and Waterworks showers.

All guests enjoy a plethora of modern day comforts including in-room DVD players, and electronic safe-deposit boxes. In the evening, turndown service includes a plate of freshly baked cookies. Truly spectacular are the hotel's three duplex suites, decked out with private terraces and circular stairways that lead up to the sleeping room from a well-appointed sitting room below. Room service is provided by Daniel Boulud's db Bistro Moderne which connects to the lobby via a paneled wine bar.

InterContinental Times Square

C2

300 W. 44th St. (at Eighth Ave.)

Subway: 42 St - Port Authority Bus Terminal
Phone: 212-803-4500 or 877-331-5888
Web: www.interconny.com
Prices: $$$

603
Rooms

4
Suites

Michael Kleinberg/InterContinental

Stylish digs and a great location with a price tag that doesn't have the accounting department keeling over is a business traveler's dream, but wake up, because you're not dreaming anymore. InterContinental Times Square has arrived. Opened in July 2010, this spanking new hotel has all of the bells and whistles and is even LEED certified (don't worry, since being green doesn't mean you're missing out on anything. Take those amazing rainfall showerheads, for one).

The rooms are tastefully appointed with a soothing neutral palette, but the bathrooms are really where InterContinental spoils its guests. Huge walk-in showers, gorgeous blue glass mosaic tiles, plentiful towels, it's all designed with comfort in mind. If honking taxis and New York City noises aren't your idea of an ambient soundtrack (this is Times Square, after all), opt for a higher floor.

There are ten meeting rooms, as well as 24-hour business and fitness centers. Their in-the-know concierge desk is invaluable, but the *pièce de résistance* is the signature restaurant, Ça Va, helmed by lauded Chef Todd English. There is all-day dining, as well as pre-theater (think of the neighborhood) in this sexy reinvented brasserie.

Manhattan ▶ **Midtown West**

Jumeirah Essex House

160 Central Park South (bet. Sixth & Seventh Aves.)

Subway: 57 St - 7 Av
Phone: 212-247-0300 or 888-645-5697
Web: www.jumeirahessexhouse.com
Prices: $$$$

428 Rooms

81 Suites

Jumeirah Essex House

Operated by the Dubai-based Jumeirah hospitality group, the venerable Essex House flaunts its enviable location at the foot of Central Park, with the shops and restaurants of 5th Avenue and the Time Warner Center right outside its door. This art deco gem, which opened its doors the same year as the Empire State Building (1931), underwent a $90-million face-lift after its new owners took over. Public spaces, outfitted with the likes of Macassar ebony chairs, and red wool carpets hand-knotted in Nepal, now pay homage to the hotel's vintage.

Why wouldn't you feel coddled in a room fitted with custom-designed furnishings, a glass-vessel sink, a touch-screen control pad, and lights underneath the nightstands to prevent stumbling in the dark? Access to the in-house spa and 24-hour health club are added perks.

The tower is crowned by the palatial 2,500-square-foot two-bedroom Presidential Suite, indeed fit for royalty with magnificent park views, original artwork, sumptuous fabrics, and bathrooms lined in marble and rosewood.

Tony Chi designed the dining room at South Gate, where contemporary cuisine takes on an urbane twist.

Manhattan ▶ **Midtown West**

Le Parker Meridien

118 W. 57th St. (bet. Sixth & Seventh Aves.)

Subway: 57 St
Phone: 212-245-5000 or 800-543-4300
Web: www.parkermeridien.com
Prices: $$$$

510
Rooms
221
Suites

Le Parker Meridien

To reach the lobby here, guests must pass through a columned, two-story lounge lined with marble, which sets the tone for Le Parker Meridien experience. The hotel, just steps away from Carnegie Hall, Central Park, and Fifth Avenue shops, divides its accommodations between the upper and lower tower—each has their own elevator bank.

Expect ergonomically designed rooms and suites to tout contemporary chic with platform beds, warm woods, 32-inch TVs, and CD/DVD players. There's a business center on-site, but if you wish to work in your room, a large, comfortable desk, and a halogen reading lamp provide all the necessities.

In the morning, fuel up on tasty breakfast dishes at Norma's. Then get in a workout at Gravity (the 15,000-square-foot fitness facility) or take a dip in the enclosed and heated rooftop pool that overlooks Central Park. For cocktails or an espresso choose Knave Cafe & Bar; or go for the simple burger at the rough-and-ready burger joint, arguably the best in the city.

Whimsical touches, like a "do not disturb" sign that reads "fuhgetaboudit," and vintage cartoons broadcast in the guest elevators, set this place apart from your standard midtown business hotel.

Manhattan ▶ Midtown West

557

The London NYC

A3

151 W. 54th St. (bet. Sixth & Seventh Aves.)

Subway: 7 Av
Phone: 212-307-5000 or 866-690-2029
Web: www.thelondonnyc.com
Prices: $$$$

552
Rooms
10
Suites

Tom Shelby/The London NYC

The London NYC is like a hop across the pond without the guilt of that pesky carbon footprint. Formerly the Righa Royal Hotel, The London with its ivy-covered façade rises a glorious 54 stories above Manhattan's midtown.

Guest suites epitomize modern sophistication with Italian linens, limed oak flooring, sectional sofas, and embossed-leather desks. Tones of soft gray, plum, sky-blue, and crisp white dominate. Styled by Waterworks, bathrooms have the last word in luxury, with white marble mosaic-tile floors, double rain showerheads, and sumptuous towels and bathrobes.

Since service is a hallmark of The London, the expert concierge services of Quintessentially are on hand to assist you with any business or personal requests. Novel extras include complimentary cleaning of your workout wear, and an iPod docking station in each room.

The hotel's elegant dining room, Gordon Ramsay at The London, is no longer home to the cantankerous chef, but continues to impresses with its polished service and contemporary cuisine. For a casual alternative, try boisterous Maze for its worldly menu of small plates served in a sleek brasserie setting.

Metro

45 W. 35th St. (bet. Fifth & Sixth Aves.)

Subway: 34 St - Herald Sq
Phone: 212 947-2500 or 800-356-3870
Web: www.hotelmetronyc.com
Prices: $$

161
Rooms
18
Suites

Hotel Metro

Though not hip or stylish, the Hotel Metro is nonetheless a good stay for the money. Located in the heart of the Garment District, near Penn Station (light sleepers take note that the hotel's location is not a quiet one), the building was constructed in 1901. An art deco-inspired lobby leads into a spacious breakfast room/lounge where tea and coffee are available throughout the day.

Guest rooms have been recently refurbished and are equipped with minibars, and upgraded "plush-top" mattresses. Many of the marble bathrooms benefit from natural light, and the overall standard of housekeeping is good. The hotel offers high-speed wireless Internet access, as well as a small business center. Room rates include a complimentary continental breakfast served in the lounge area.

From the large rooftop bar which has become quite popular, you can enjoy stunning views of the Empire State Building and the surrounding neighborhood, which includes Macy's, for all you hard-core shoppers.

Manhattan ▶ Midtown West

559

The Michelangelo

152 W. 51st St. (at Seventh Ave.)

Subway: 50 St (Broadway)
Phone: 212-765-1900 or 800-237-0990
Web: www.michelangelohotel.com
Prices: $$$

123
Rooms
55
Suites

James Starkman/Starquest Media LLC

Steps from Times Square, the Theater District, Rockefeller Center, and midtown offices, The Michelangelo caters to both leisure and business travelers. A recent renovation has polished the two-story lobby, regal in its liberal use of marble, rich fabric panels, and crystal chandeliers.

Winding hallways have been freshened with new paint and carpeting; shelves of books add a homey touch. Attractively appointed with marble foyers, small sitting areas, down pillows, and Bose radio/CD players, guest rooms are generous for Manhattan, with a standard king measuring about 325 square feet (upgrades get bigger from there). Marble bathrooms come equipped with hair dryers, make-up mirrors, deep soaking tubs, terrycloth robes, and even a small TV. Part of the Starhotels group, The Michelangelo interprets hospitality with *gusto di vivere italiano*. Turndown service, a complimentary continental breakfast, a small fitness center, and limo service to Wall Street on weekday mornings number among the amenities.

The Insieme lounge now quenches thirsts in a vividly-appointed, jewel box-inspired bar and salon featuring a spectrum of wines and cocktails.

The Peninsula New York

700 Fifth Ave. (at 55th St.)

Subway: 5 Av   53 St
Phone: 212-956-2888 or 800-262-9467
Web: www.peninsula.com
Prices: $$$$

185
Rooms
54
Suites

The Peninsula New York

When this magnificent 1905 hotel was built as The Gotham, it was the city's tallest skyscraper, towering 23 stories. Today the property still sparkles as the Peninsula group's U.S. flagship.

Plush rooms exude a timeless elegance, and art nouveau accents complement their rich colors and appointments. Ample in size and well-conceived for business travelers, each guest room provides a silent fax machine, and a bottled-water bar (with a choice of still or sparkling water). Service is a strong suit at The Peninsula, and the smartly liveried staff effortlessly executes your every request.

You could spend hours on the rooftop, site of the new ESPA, the state-of-the-art fitness center, and the glass-enclosed pool. Asian, European, and Ayurvedic philosophies inspire the spa treatments; check in early and relax in the Asian tea lounge, then loosen up those muscles in the steam room or sauna before your massage. Sharing this lofty perch, the stunning rooftop bar, Salon de Ning, wows patrons with its Fifth Avenue views and vivid Shanghai style. In addition to the interior bar, there are two large outdoor terraces furnished with Chinese-style day beds—perfect for a romantic liaison.

Manhattan ▶ **Midtown West**

The Plaza

B3

768 Fifth Ave. (at Central Park South)

Subway: 5 Av – 59 St
Phone: 212-759-3000
Web: www.theplaza.com
Prices: $$$$

180
Rooms

102
Suites

The Plaza Hotel

This storied Beaux-Arts masterpiece once again ushers the well-heeled and well-traveled through its gilded doors. Opened in 1907 and now managed by Fairmont Hotels & Resorts, this historic landmark has been lavishly renovated to restore the past and embrace the future. The hotel's Fifth Avenue lobby has an ethereal feel with gleaming marble flooring, Baccarat chandeliers, and picture windows framing the Pulitzer fountain in Grand Army Plaza.

Generously sized accommodations mix elegant appointments with a touch-screen monitor that dims the lighting, adjusts the temperature, and contacts guest services. You won't want to leave the mosaic stone-tiled bathroom complete with 24-karat-gold fixtures. And with each guest floor staffed by a team of affable butlers, the service is as impressive as the surroundings.

Purveyors of all things luxurious await the Shops at The Plaza and The Plaza Food Hall—a specialty arena steered by Chef Todd English, showcasing a range of fine, fresh, and gourmet food (and flower) options for guests, shoppers, and residents alike. For prime pampering, treatments at Caudalíe Vinothérapie Spa use beneficial polyphenols extracted from grapes.

The Ritz-Carlton, Central Park

50 Central Park South (at Sixth Ave.)

Subway: 5 Av – 59 St
Phone: 212-308-9100 or 800-876-8129
Web: www.ritzcarlton.com
Prices: $$$$

212
Rooms

47
Suites

The Ritz-Carlton New York, Central Park

Built in 1929 as the St. Moritz, the Ritz holds its place at the vanguard of luxury and graceful service among Manhattan's hotels. While the marble-floored reception lobby remains intimate, it opens into a grand two-story gathering space.

Sumptuous guestrooms are generously sized, beginning at 425 square feet and topping out at 1,900 for the Central Park Suite. Steeped in old-world elegance, rooms dress up in rich fabrics, crisp, white 400-thread-count linens, and a plethora of fluffy pillows. Gleaming, luxurious, and oversized marble baths are stocked with spacious vanities, hairdryers, and Frédéric Fekkai products.

If stress has sapped your energy, a visit to the on-site La Prairie Spa is in order. The massage menu tailors treatments to most every ailment of upscale urban life, including jet lag, shopping fatigue, and executive stress.

The presence of BLT Market brings a frequently changing menu of market-fresh breakfast and dinner fare designed by Chef Laurent Tourondel. For afternoon tea or a well-shaken martini, stop by the clubby Star Lounge, or relax in the lobby over an expertly-prepared and served refreshment.

Manhattan ▶ Midtown West

The Setai

400 Fifth Ave. (at 36th St.)

Subway:	34 St - Herald Sq
Phone:	212-695-4005 or 877-247-6688
Web:	www.setaififthavenue.com
Prices:	$$$$

157 Rooms

57 Suites

The Setai Fifth Avenue

It turns out that you can have your cake and eat it too. Always wanted the cache of Fifth Avenue but prefer the über-cool vibe of downtown? Meet halfway and check in to The Setai. Not far from the buzz of Herald Square, this super-sleek skyscraper has upped the ante for luxury lodgings. It is flat-out sweep-you-off-your feet stunning with its bird's eye view of Manhattan (with postcard-perfect vistas of the Empire State Building sound) and its chic interiors. It's a breeze to get anywhere from here...if you can tear yourself away.

From the Duxiana beds swathed in Pratesi linens to the Italian-crafted rosewood and walnut furnishings to the marble bathrooms, it is a world of luxury from head to toe. It may be in the heart of lower midtown, but the only noise heard here is the whisper of luxury. Spacious rooms, a first-rate spa, Julien Frel Salon...these are just some of the perks of being a guest here. One of the best perks? Proximity to the Ai Fiori Restaurant, where you don't just show up, you *arrive*.

Take the sweeping grand staircase straight out of Hollywood up to this sparkling spot by Chef Michael White and prepare to be dazzled by the setting and the delicious Italian food.

6 Columbus

D1

6 Columbus Circle (at 58th St.)

Subway: 59 St - Columbus Circle
Phone: 212-204-3000
Web: www.sixcolumbus.com
Prices: $$

72
Rooms
16
Suites
((•))

Thompson Hotels

This lovely addition to the Thompson Hotels collection (which includes 60 Thompson in SoHo) sparkles with a hip vibe. You can't beat the location, across the street from the Time Warner Center and Central Park. Despite its ritzy setting, the urban retreat is casual in style and surprisingly reasonable in price.

Sixties-mod describes the décor, which dresses the public spaces with teak paneling, molded chairs, and leather sofas in a palette of earthy tones. The same spirit (and teak paneling) infuses the sleek rooms, where custom-made furniture and chrome accents abound. Walls are decorated with artwork by fashion photographer Guy Bourdin. Frette linens, soft lighting, iPod docking stations, and complimentary WiFi Internet access round out the amenities. Bath products are by Fresh.

Adjacent to the lobby, Blue Ribbon Sushi Bar and Grill adds a beloved concept by the well-known Blue Ribbon restaurants group. Japanese fare here runs the gamut from hamachi to hanger steak. As for the young staff, they're friendly and helpful, catering to a clientele largely made up of savvy urban professionals and international visitors.

Manhattan ▶ Midtown West

Sofitel

45 W. 44th St. (bet. Fifth & Sixth Aves.)

Subway: 47-50 Sts - Rockefeller Ctr
Phone: 212-354-8844 or 877-565-9240
Web: www.sofitel-newyork.com
Prices: $$$$

346
Rooms

52
Suites

Sofitel

Located mid-block on 44th Street, this 30-story glass and limestone tower couldn't be more convenient to Fifth Avenue shopping, Times Square, and the Theater District. It's an easy walk from here to Grand Central Station too. Owned by the French hotel group–Accor–the Sofitel New York maintains a European feel throughout.

The art deco-style lobby is as welcoming as it is elegant, set about with blonde wood paneling, green marble, and groups of sleek leather club chairs arranged on a colorful floral-patterned carpet. Off the lobby, Gaby Bar offers a stylish lounge in which to sip a cocktail, while its sister restaurant (also called Gaby) features flavorful French classics along with more contemporary fare for lunch and dinner.

Honey-colored velvet drapes, red chenille armchairs, sumptuous damask linens, and marble baths outfit the attractive and well-maintained guest rooms. The glass-topped blonde wood desk paired with a cushioned leather chair caters to business travelers; WiFi Internet access is available for a fee. A thoughtful touch for European guests, a voltage adaptor is included in each room.

Manhattan ▶ Midtown West

Washington Jefferson Hotel

C2

318 W. 51st St. (bet. Eighth & Ninth Aves.)

Subway: 50 St (Eighth Ave.)
Phone: 212-246-7550 or 888-567-7550
Web: www.wjhotel.com
Prices: $

135
Rooms

Washington Jefferson Hotel

Fresh, contemporary design at a decent price in Manhattan was once a pipe dream, but the Washington Jefferson Hotel delivers style without a high price tag. Located in the ever-expanding neighborhood of Hell's Kitchen, the hotel is close to the bright lights of the Theater District.

The lobby is warm and welcoming, and the staff ensures that all guests feel at home from the moment they step inside the doors. Rooms are somewhat spartan, with platform beds dressed in crisp white linens, yet provide all the necessary amenities (TV with premium channels, radio/CD player). Clean lines extend to the bathrooms, outfitted with slate flooring and slate-tiled tubs. While standard rooms are on the small side, comfort is never sacrificed. Guests have 24-hour access to a small exercise room on-site, while serious athletes may have to resort to the running path along the Hudson River.

Although there is no room service, you can enjoy lunch and dinner at the hotel's restaurant, Shimizu. Sushi is a popular component here, but for those who prefer their fish cooked, the restaurant offers a delightful array of traditional Japanese dishes.

Manhattan ▶ Midtown West

Crosby Street Hotel

79 Crosby St. (bet. Prince & Spring Sts.)

Subway: Prince St
Phone: 212-226-6400
Web: www.crosbystreethotel.com
Prices: $$$$

75
Rooms
11
Suites

Firmdale Hotels

Tim and Kit Kemp, the very successful husband-and-wife team behind some of London's hottest properties, have hopped across the Pond for their American debut, and it looks like they've done it again. They picked the right spot —in the heart of SoHo on a charming cobblestoned street— but this hotel's attributes go far beyond location alone.

Kit Kemp has won awards for her inimitable design sense which is equal parts quirky and delightful. Distinctive artwork and objects are littered throughout the public and private spaces and are surefire conversation starters. The guest-only drawing room (perfect for afternoon tea) and its adjacent private garden provide an oasis in the Big City. Amenities include a well-equipped gym, private screening room, and The Crosby Bar & Restaurant.

Interesting patterns and pops of color define the guestrooms, which look and feel like an artist's pied-à-terre. Fabric-covered headboards, silk embroidered pillows, and eclectic decorative items prove that details are big here. Guests may linger at writing desks (turn-down service brings sharpened pencils), or enjoy the unobstructed views and fresh air (on the higher floors) from the lovely window seats.

The James

B2

27 Grand St. (at Sixth Ave.)

Subway: Canal St (Sixth Ave.)
Phone: 212-465-2000 or 888-526-3778
Web: www.jameshotels.com
Prices: $$$$

109
Rooms
5
Suites

The James New York

Just when you thought SoHo couldn't get any more chic, along comes The James. This hotel stands out from the pack with its curvy, current architecture, funky outdoor garden, and sky lobby. This is the *new* SoHo—glossy and sophisticated with nary an exposed pipe or brick wall in sight. The James is all about grown up hip with its blend of soothing palettes and serious amenities (think handmade pillows, iPads packed with local information, and yes, a solid commitment to green practices).

The rooms, complete with towering windows, look and feel more like aeries than hotel rooms. Note to toiletry fiends—there is still a barrage of those little plastic and "oh-so-pocketable" bottles available on request. Design-centric and artsy, The James is a showpiece of modern art. From a wall tiled in computer keys to cool canvases, light fixtures, and textiles, this hotel also echoes SoHo's dedication to the Arts evidenced in an impressive collection of up-and-comers and established artists.

The second-floor multi-tiered Urban Garden and rooftop pool are big highlights in the summer. While the appropriately favored Jimmy Bar, and famed celebrity chef David Burke's Kitchen draws an urbane crowd.

Manhattan ▶ SoHo & Nolita

The Mercer

147 Mercer St. (at Prince St.)

Subway: Prince St
Phone: 212-966-6060
Web: www.mercerhotel.com
Prices: $$$$

67 Rooms

8 Suites

Thomas Loof

Even if your name isn't Leonardo DiCaprio, Cher, or Calvin Klein, you'll be equally welcome at The Mercer. Housed in a striking Romanesque Revival-style building erected in 1890, the hotel caters to the glitterati with discreet, personalized service, and intimate elegance. The modern lobby feels like your stylish friend's living room, complete with comfy seating, appealing coffee-table books, and an Apple for guests' use.

A Zen vibe pervades the guestrooms, fashioned by Parisian interior designer Christian Liaigre with high, loft-like ceilings, large European-style windows, soothing neutral palettes, and Asian decorative touches. Don't fret if you get a room facing the street; soundproofing filters out the noise. You'll find everything you need for business or leisure travel in your room, right down to scented candles and oversize FACE Stockholm bath products. Forgot something? The hotel's warm and helpful staff will gladly accommodate you with a personal laptop.

Sure, the hotel offers 24-hour room service, but in this case the food comes from downstairs, Chef Jean-Georges Vongerichten's ever-alluring Mercer Kitchen.

Mondrian SoHo

9 Crosby St. (bet. Grand & Howard Sts.)

Subway: Canal St (Broadway)
Phone: 212-554-6120 or 800-697-1791
Web: www.mondriansoho.com
Prices: $$$$

264
Rooms
6
Suites

Morgans Hotel Group

Don't come with any lofty ambitions, since this is so *not* your typical SoHo hotel. In fact, there isn't an exposed pipe in sight, but you'll certainly get a dose of glamour at this smashing spot. Mondrian Soho quite literally stands out from the crowd. Set amidst the cobblestoned streets and low-lying buildings of Crosby Street, Mondrian catches you by surprise with its sleek glass tower exterior, but oh wow, come inside and you'll be even more surprised. Life certainly imitates art at this hotel, which was inspired by the 1946 Jean Cocteau classic film *"Le Belle et la Bête."*

Benjamin Noriega-Ortiz's design is surely eclectic but the dominant blue-and-white theme is simply dazzling. Rooms seem like jewel boxes tucked along corridors lined with plush blue carpets and oversized antique mirrors. Step inside these boudoirs and *voila—tres chic!* From the blue ceiling to the chrome desk to the patent leather furnishings, it's all very stylish in a mid-century mod kind of way, but floor-to-ceiling windows with drop-dead views remind you that you're in New York baby, not Paris.

The cocktail driven bar draws droves on the late night, while the white-hot Mister H is the latest it spot.

Manhattan ▶ **SoHo & Nolita**

571

60 Thompson

60 Thompson St. (bet. Broome & Spring Sts.)

Subway: Spring St (Sixth Ave.)
Phone: 212-431-0400 or 877-431-0400
Web: www.60thompson.com
Prices: $$$$

87 Rooms
10 Suites

Thompson Hotels

With its spare 1940s look inspired by French designer Jean-Michel Frank, 60 Thompson absolutely oozes SoHo style. The lobby, decorated in gray, brown, and moss-green tones, is accented by bouquets of fresh flowers, and natural light floods in from floor-to-ceiling windows.

Room sizes vary, but all sport a minimalist look, with crisp, white Frette linens standing out against a wall of dark, paneled leather. Business travelers take note that 60 Thompson has replaced the requisite in-room desk with a sitting area in its standard rooms. Bathrooms are tiled with chocolate-colored marble and stocked with spa products by Fresh. For those who don't appreciate the smell of cigarette smoke in their room, the hotel devotes the eighth floor to non-smoking chambers.

Check out the rooftop bar on the 12th floor, where you can sip a cocktail and drink in the great city views. In good weather, the rooftop scene is a hot one, whereas the lobby bar bustles year-round with a cool crowd. Downstairs, Kittichai puts out modern Thai cuisine in an Asian-chic setting. The small bar here mixes fantastic and creative cocktails.

Soho Grand

B2

310 West Broadway (bet. Canal & Grand Sts.)

Subway: Canal St (Sixth Ave.)
Phone: 212-965-3000 or 800-965-3000
Web: www.sohogrand.com
Prices: $$$$

361
Rooms
2
Suites

GrandLife Hotels

Cutting-edge fashion, fine art, and delicious dining beckon in the blocks right outside this hip hotel (whose equally chic sister, the Tribeca Grand, lies a short walk to the south). Inside, designer William Sofield calls to mind the neighborhood's industrial roots in the lobby's clean lines, concrete pillars, and cast-iron details.

Rooms are swathed in neutral tones, with leather headboards, Egyptian cotton sheets, and a host of modern amenities. Bose Wave CD/radios, DVD players, and in-room CD selections come in every room; iPods (for the suites) and docking stations are also available on request. For true grandeur, reserve one of the penthouse lofts. In these spacious custom designed suites, you will have the luxury of two bedrooms, as well as a 1,200-square-foot wraparound furnished terrace on which to entertain or simply to take in the killer view of the Manhattan skyline.

Bicycles are on hand for complimentary guest use when the weather permits; and the hotel's "grandlife" website provides a wealth of information about goings-on in the city. Families are welcomed with signature programs for babies and children, not to mention the hotel's pet-friendly policy. Ain't life grand?

Manhattan ▶ SoHo & Nolita

573

Trump SoHo

A1

246 Spring St. (at Varick St.)

Subway: Spring St (Sixth Ave.)
Phone: 212-842-5500 or 877-828-7080
Web: www.trumpsohohotel.com
Prices: $$$$

245
Rooms

146
Suites

Trump SoHo New York

You definitely won't need directions to find this hotel—just look up. Trump SoHo's lanky silver-glass skyscraper dominates the SoHo skyline.

This stylish hotel caters to well-heeled business and leisure travelers who appreciate the convenience of downtown but crave the creature comforts of a serious hotel. Whether it's the personal shopping and other individualized services of the Trump Attache or the 11,000 square-foot spa (the largest in the city!), the amenities are top-notch.

Milan meets Manhattan in the guestrooms and suites. Outfitted in sleek furnishings by Casa Fendi, they are the last word in modern elegance. Chocolate brown tufted leather headboards, curvy benches, chrome fixtures—it's all very glam in a masculine way. Whether it's the tech gadgets or the fluffy bedside rugs, the rooms have it all.

The public spaces are not to be outdone by the fabulous guestrooms, though. Whether you seek quiet reflection and a cappuccino at The Library, dig in to upscale Italian at Quattro Gastronomia, or hit up late-night hot spot Kastel, Trump SoHo has you covered. Feeling competitive? Take the elevator up to Bar d'Eau, the indoor/outdoor pool deck complete with a bocce court.

Cosmopolitan

95 West Broadway (at Chambers St.)

Subway: Chambers St (West Broadway)
Phone: 212-566-1900 or 888-895-9400
Web: www.cosmohotel.com
Prices: $

125
Rooms
((˙ȶ˙))

Cosmopolitan Hotel

This privately owned seven-story hotel enjoys a valuable location in the heart of TriBeCa, while catering to more budget-conscious visitors to the city. Just a few steps away from Wall Street, SoHo, and Chinatown, the Cosmopolitan pulls in a steady clientele of business travelers and European tourists, who may appreciate the hotel's low prices, convenient setting, and cigarette-friendly policy.

The Cosmopolitan may lack the frills of some grander city hostelries, but guests can use the money saved on a room here to splurge on a show or dinner in a fine restaurant. Basic rooms are well-maintained, fairly spacious, and they all have private baths. Scant in-room amenities include a hair dryer, cable TV, a ceiling fan, and free wireless Internet access. Ask for a room on the back side of the hotel if worried about the street noise. Despite the fact that the entire hotel is smoking-friendly, the halls and the rooms seems absent of cigarettes traces.

The hotel does not offer room service, but the Cosmopolitan Café is right next door. This tiny eatery, with its rustic country style, makes a good spot for a light breakfast or to catch a quick sandwich at midday.

Manhattan ▶ TriBeCa

575

Greenwich Hotel

377 Greenwich St. (at N. Moore St.)

Subway: Franklin St
Phone: 212-941-8900
Web: www.thegreenwichhotel.com
Prices: $$$$

75 Rooms

13 Suites

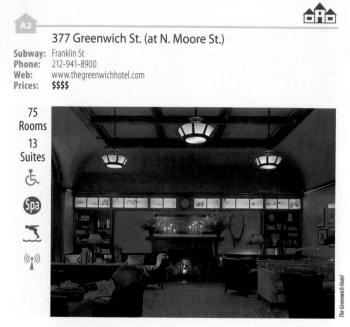

The Greenwich Hotel

Spanning the worlds of classic elegance and city chic, this TriBeCa stunner was unceremoniously unveiled in spring 2008. Though the hoopla was kept to a minimum–despite the fact that Robert DeNiro and his son are partners–the Greenwich is a hotel to crow about. Attention to detail is evident here from the construction materials to the organic bath amenities, all reflecting au courant Italian sensibilities.

Among the 88 rooms, no two are alike. Carved pine doors open into refined chambers boasting Duxiana beds, custom-designed settees, and hardwood floors. Ten foot-high ceilings create an airy feel. The same care is taken in the design of the bathrooms, with their brass hardware, Frette towels, and mosaic tiled showers. All the modern electronic amenities apply as well.

An on-site fitness center and a lantern-lit indoor swimming pool will take care of your exercise needs, while the Japanese-inspired Shibui Spa spotlights relaxation with a shiatsu room and a room for traditional bathing rituals. Italian fare takes top billing at Locanda Verde by Chef Andrew Carmellini.

Manhattan ▶ TriBeCa

Smyth

85 West Broadway (at Chambers St.)

Subway: Chambers St (West Broadway)
Phone: 212-587-7000 or 888-587-6984
Web: www.thompsonhotels.com
Prices: $$$

96
Rooms

4
Suites

Thompson Hotels

The latest in the Thompson Hotel Group's string of boutique properties around Manhattan, the Smyth is a 13-story condominium/hotel hybrid; the top four floors are dedicated to Smyth Upstairs, consisting of 15 luxurious apartments. Designer Yabu Pushelberg decked out the stunning public spaces in a modern mélange of marble, onyx, leather, and textured wall coverings. It all combines to create a playful sense and a sexy vibe—with attitude to spare.

Room décor reflects a mid-20th century sensibility, illustrated by clean lines, white walls, velvet fabrics, Sferra linens, and lots of wood. Despite the hotel's location right off busy Chambers Street, the windows do a surprisingly good job of blocking out noise from the street below. Suite upgrades add the likes of a wet bar, two full bathrooms, and perhaps a terrace with seating for six. In the bathrooms, gray-and-white marble subway tiles create a sparkling facing on the walls.

The Plein Sud restaurant provides room service; amenities such as in-room massage, valet parking, and a personal shopper are de rigueur. The jury is still out, but the Smyth may be destined as the TriBeCa hot spot for the hip traveling set.

Manhattan ▶ TriBeCa

Tribeca Grand

2 Sixth Ave. (at Church St.)

Subway: Canal St (Sixth Ave.)
Phone: 212-519-6600 or 877-519-6600
Web: www.tribecagrand.com
Prices: $$$

186 Rooms

15 Suites

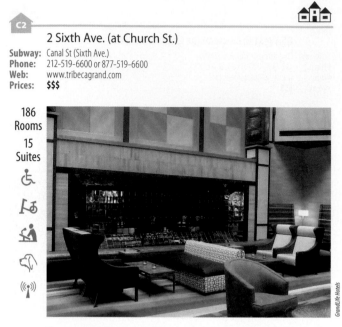

GrandLife Hotels

Frequented by celebrities and the oh-so-hip Euro-set, the Tribeca Grand gives every guest the star treatment. Sister to the Soho Grand, this hotel greets guests in its airy, vaulted atrium lobby (often used as a movie backdrop) whose clean lines evoke the Prairie style of architect Frank Lloyd Wright. In the evening, the lobby's swanky Church Lounge becomes a destination in itself, as it fills with the hot and hip music- and film-industry set. In summer, the party spills out to sidewalk seating along Sixth Avenue.

Deep earth tones, with bright sparks of orange and yellow, color the comfortable guest rooms, which are equally well-equipped for business and leisure travelers. Movie mavens may want to reserve an iStudio room, furnished with a video camera and a computer loaded with every program an amateur film buff could want.

Paris Hilton may feel perfectly at home here, but so would her pup. Owned by Leonard and Emanuel Stern, members of the family that founded Hartz Mountain Industries, the Tribeca Grand accommodates pets in equally high style. Had to leave your four-footed friend at home? Request a goldfish to keep you company in your room.

Manhattan ▶ TriBeCa

578

Bentley

500 E. 62nd St. (at York Ave.)

Subway: Lexington Av - 59 St
Phone: 212-644-6000 or 888-664-6835
Web: www.nychotels.com
Prices: $$

161
Rooms
36
Suites

((·))

The Bentley

It may be a little bit of a walk to the subway, Central Park, and the shops, but sitting on the East River, with easy access to-and-from the airports, it's worth the extra blocks for the value and accessibility. The Bentley may not be new or trendy, but it makes a fashionable first impression. Floor-to-ceiling windows, geometric-patterned carpets, marble flooring, and contemporary furnishings fill the art deco lobby of this 21-story glass-and-steel office building, which was converted into a hotel in 1998.

By New York City standard, rooms are surprisingly spacious. A bit the worse for wear, furnishings and carpeting adhere to a neutral color scheme. Seating nooks by the windows take in views of the East River and Queensboro Bridge. Families favor the extra space offered in the 36 suites, complete with pull-out sofas or futons. Given the location and moderate prices, this hotel is a good find.

The Bentley doesn't serve breakfast, but offers complimentary coffee during the day. If you don't feel up to dining out, the rooftop restaurant boasts panoramic city views with its limited menu. Valet parking, free daily newspapers, and concierge service count among other amenities provided.

The Carlyle

35 E. 76th St. (at Madison Ave.)

Subway: 77 St
Phone: 212-744-1600 or 800-227-5737
Web: www.thecarlyle.com
Prices: $$$$

124 Rooms

64 Suites

The Carlyle

Named for British historian Thomas Carlyle, this hotel epitomizes opulence with its fine artwork, Baccarat crystal light fixtures, and marble baths. Individually decorated Classic aka "standard" rooms are dressed in Louis XVI-style with original Audubon prints, 440-thread-count Italian linens, and elegant area rugs over wood floors. A select few of the Carlyle's roomy suites feature a baby-grand piano for the musically inclined.

Since it opened across from Central Park in 1930, The Carlyle has hosted every American president since Truman, along with a roster of foreign dignitaries from Prime Minister Nehru to Princess Diana—how's that for an A-list?

For entertainment, there's Café Carlyle, where Woody Allen regularly jams with the Eddie Davis New Orleans jazz band. Legendary Bemelmans Bar, renowned for its whimsical mural of characters from artist Ludwig Bemelmans' famous Madeline series of children's books, is a popular place for a cocktail.

With a contemporary menu almost as classy as the crowd it draws, the handsome Carlyle Restaurant proves a perfect complement to the hotel's sophistication. The hotel's new Sense Spa offers weary guests 4,000 square feet of soothing indulgence.

The Lowell

28 E. 63rd St. (bet. Madison & Park Aves.)

Subway: Lexington Av - 63 St
Phone: 212-838-1400 or 800-221-4444
Web: www.lowellhotel.com
Prices: $$$$

25
Rooms

47
Suites

The Lowell

From the moment you step inside the silk-paneled lobby, you'll sense the European elegance that defines The Lowell. Intimate and sumptuous, this place appeals to those who value discretion, in both the size of the property and the attitude of the staff.

With suites outnumbering rooms 47 to 25, the emphasis here is on residential luxury. Indeed, this art deco brick and glazed terra-cotta structure was completed in 1926 as an apartment hotel. While lavish suites boast wood-burning fireplaces, private terraces, kitchens, and more, all rooms are individually decorated with marble baths and original art and antiques.

The Lowell unveiled new healthful-living options in response to requests from its sophisticated travelers. Guests don't need to forsake their daily exercise routine since the hotel's fully equipped fitness center offers personal trainers and Pilates instructors, in addition to Cybex equipment and free weights. Maps of nearby Central Park are available for those who prefer to exercise outdoors. Come mealtime, menus for the Pembroke Room and in-room dining are now stocked with nutritious, low-calorie, and low-carb choices—so there's no excuse for cheating on your diet.

Manhattan ▶ Upper East Side

The Mark

25 E. 77th St. (at Madison Ave.)

Subway: 77 St
Phone: 212-744-4200
Web: www.themarkhotel.com
Prices: $$$$

100
Rooms
50
Suites

Todd Eberle/The Mark Hotel

This landmark hotel, originally opened in 1927, hits all of the right marks. Closed for three years for a top-to-bottom renovation by famed French designer Jacques Grange, The Mark has reopened with a bang. Grange's updates–like the dramatic black-and-white flooring–have given the hotel an incredibly fresh new look.

Set just off Madison Avenue, The Mark has a prime location. Close to it all, yet located on a side street, this hotel feels more like an exclusive private residence than an internationally known hotel. Even the white-glove amenities—Frédéric Fekkai salon, Jean-Georges Vongerichten restaurant, and John Sitaras 24-hour fitness center attest to the residential atmosphere.

Comfortably sized, the rooms and suites deliver top notch accommodations. Creamy coffered ceilings show off a classic style, while polished metal light fixtures, contemporary art, and sleek upholstered furnishings punch up the modern quotient. Creature comforts, including ample closet space that would make any New Yorker green with envy, are abundant. Even the mini bar goes above and beyond with three pullout, refrigerated drawers. Butler services ensure that guests never endure PC-related frustration.

Manhattan ▶ Upper East Side

The Regency

540 Park Ave. (at 61st St.)

Subway: Lexington Av - 59 St
Phone: 212-759-4100 or 800-233-2356
Web: www.loewshotels.com
Prices: $$$$

267
Rooms
86
Suites

ThiPaub Jeanson

Public spaces ooze personality at the Loews flagship, sitting right on Park Avenue. Accommodations are bland in comparison, but large by New York standards, with abundant closet space and enough room to stay comfortably for several days (as long as you don't mind that the mattresses and bathrooms could use upgrading). The pleasant team offers a high level of service, and if your pup is traveling with you, the hotel offers dog-walking services as well as a separate room-service menu for pets.

For good dining and entertainment options, you don't have to leave the hotel. The upscale restaurant, 540 Park, is always packed in the evening, attracting as much of a local following as it does hotel guests. At breakfast, this place shakes with major players brokering deals over bacon and eggs. The Library lounge is a cozy (and popular) spot for a cocktail any night of the week. Its menu runs to comfort food such as chicken pot pie and braised lamb shank.

Last but not least, there's Feinsteins at the Regency, named for its owner—pop vocalist and songwriter Michael Feinstein. This blast from the past still packs 'em in for cabaret headliners six nights a week.

Manhattan ▶ Upper East Side

The Surrey

20 E. 76th St. (at Madison Ave.)

Subway: 77 St
Phone: 212-288-3700 or 800-978-7739
Web: www.thesurrey.com
Prices: $$$$

158 Rooms

32 Suites

The Surrey Hotel

There is just something debonair about The Surrey. Maybe it's because this former private residence once housed the likes of Claudette Colbert, Bette Davis, and John F. Kennedy. After a $60 million renovation, it looks and feels swanky, suave, and sophisticated. It is the kind of place where the cast of *Mad Men* could easily take up residence.

In keeping with the building's history, the rooms and suites feel wonderfully private. The guestrooms are handsomely decorated in shades of gray and cream with polished wood furnishings. The in-room dining (or drinking) menu would make Don Draper seriously drool—a mixologist is sent up to your room to prepare cocktails with enough for 4-5 drinks.

First-rate amenities, such as the elegant spa and well-appointed 24-hour fitness room, are the calling card of The Surrey. The rooftop terrace is an exceptional private space reserved exclusively for hotel guests. Bar Pleiades, part art deco, part homage to Coco Chanel, personifies the luxury and class of the Upper East Side. Of course, Café Boulud's winning cuisine and elegant atmosphere make it the jewel in the Surrey's crown.

Mandarin Oriental

ﬁﬁﬁ

80 Columbus Circle (at 60th St.)

Subway: 59 St - Columbus Circle
Phone: 212-805-8800 or 866-801-8880
Web: www.mandarinoriental.com
Prices: $$$$

202
Rooms
46
Suites

Mandarin Oriental

Everything you could desire in New York City lies literally at the doorstep of the Mandarin Oriental. Occupying floors 35 to 54 in the north tower of the Time Warner Center, this hotel flaunts its enviable location overlooking Central Park. Also the site of such stellar restaurants as Per Se and Masa, hotel guests have direct access to the shops located inside the Time Warner Center at Columbus Circle. And don't pass up the contemporary fusion cuisine on-site at Asiate.

From the moment you enter to the moment you leave, the hotel's top-drawer service will make you feel like a VIP. Masculine yet delicate, modern yet timeless, guestrooms incorporate soigné touches such as cherry woods, silvery silks, and Fili D'oro linens. The view's the thing here; and the scenery is played up to full advantage with a wall of floor-to-ceiling windows in each room.

No visit to this unforgettable place is complete without a trip to the 36th-floor spa, which offers a customized "journey for the senses," booked in blocks of time rather than by treatment. The lobby lounge is an elegant spot to sip on a modern cocktail while taking in the panoramic view.

Manhattan ▶ Upper West Side

On the Ave

2178 Broadway (at 77th St.)

Subway: 79 St
Phone: 212-362-1100 or 800-497-6028
Web: www.ontheave.com
Prices: $$

274
Rooms
8
Suites

On the Ave

Broadway without the buzz is what awaits you On the Ave. Guests here get a respite from the bustle of midtown in this quiet Upper West Side neighborhood, where many of the city's natural and man-made treasures can be found. Fancy a walk in Central Park or a visit to the Museum of Natural History? Both are less than three blocks away. If you wish to explore farther afield, the subway station is just a two-block walk.

Shades of gray, ecru, and pewter color the restrained contemporary room décor, while baths sport brushed stainless-steel sinks and marble tiles. If you're not afraid of heights, rooms on the top three floors boast balconies with panoramas of the Hudson River and Central Park. Don't have a view? Take the elevator to the 16th floor, where you can relax and look out over uptown from the furnished and landscaped balcony. Backlit black-and-white photographs of Gotham City adorn the lobby and hallways of this hotel.

Exhilarated and ravenous after a day flooded with shopping and sightseeing? Step out of your room for a slew of comforting and contemporary dining delights from delicious (and well-tread) Fatty Crab.

Trump International Hotel & Tower

1 Central Park West (at Columbus Circle)

Subway: 59 St - Columbus Circle
Phone: 212-299-1000 or 888-448-7867
Web: www.trumpintl.com
Prices: $$$$

38 Rooms
129 Suites

Trump Hotel Collection

An icon for its association with its flamboyant owner, this 52-story tower does Donald Trump proud. The location is ideal, with upscale shopping at the Time Warner Center and the attractions of Central Park right outside the door.

More than two-thirds of the accommodations—located on the 3rd through 17th floors—are spacious one- or two-bedroom suites boasting custom-designed furniture and great city and park views. A blissful night's sleep awaits in lodgings that range from 460 square feet for a junior suite to 1,350 square feet for a two-bedroom unit. All have kitchens stocked with china and crystal; if you don't feel like cooking, you can arrange for a member of the staff from the stellar chef–Jean Georges' restaurant–to prepare a gourmet meal in your room.

The 55-foot-long indoor pool is perfect for swimming laps, and the Techno-Gym equipment at the fitness center supplies a challenging workout (personal training and one-on-one yoga sessions are available).

Offering everything from complimentary business cards to free local phone calls, Trump's signature Attaché service caters to The Donald in everyone.

Manhattan ▶ Upper West Side

Nu Hotel

85 Smith St. (bet. Atlantic Ave. & State St.)

Subway: Hoyt - Schermerhorn
Phone: 718-852-8585
Web: www.nuhotelbrooklyn.com
Prices: $

90
Rooms

3
Suites

Gridley & Graves Photography

Housed in a condominium tower near the quaint residential neighborhood of Cobble Hill, Nu Hotel opened in July 2008 and caters to the budget-conscious with contemporary style for reasonable rates. Located steps away from the government offices of downtown Brooklyn, the hotel is as ideally situated for those with business in the area as it is for guests visiting nearby family and friends.

Wide hallways lead to eco-friendly rooms dressed in organic white linens and modern light wood furnishings against a cool palette swathed in lead-free paint. White-tiled bathrooms incorporate a whimsical touch: a chalkboard wall for doodling or leaving messages for housekeeping. Inspired by urban lofts, suites may add a hammock or bunk beds as inventive sleeping spaces for extra guests.

The hotel has no restaurant, but does offer a complimentary daily buffet continental breakfast downstairs at Nu Bar.

And, sure, you can take the subway into Manhattan—there are a multitude of lines nearby—for shopping and dining, but why bother when the chic boutiques and culinary enticements of Smith Street are such an easy walk away?

Brooklyn

Indexes ▶ Alphabetical List of Restaurants

601

Restaurants by Cuisine

American

Argentinian

Asian

Chance	✗	421
China Grill	✗✗	259
Ember Room	✗✗	264
Fatty 'Cue	☺ ✗	432
Garden Court Café	☺ ✗	351
Hawkers	✗	104
Hung Ry	☺ ✗✗	148
Hurricane Club (The)	✗✗	105
Kuma Inn	🍴	194
Laut	❀ ✗	109
Momofuku Noodle Bar	☺ ✗	66
Mulan	✗✗	489
OBAO	☺ ✗✗	230
Purple Yam	✗	452
Radiance Tea House	✗	290
SHI	✗✗✗	497
Spice Market	✗✗	168
Tao	✗✗	240
Umi Nom	✗	463

Austrian

Blaue Gans	✗	324
Cafe Katja	✗	190
Café Sabarsky	✗	345
Edi & The Wolf	✗	53
Seäsonal	❀ ✗✗	294
Wallsé	❀ ✗✗	173

Barbecue

Daisy May's BBQ	✗	261
Dinosaur Bar-B-Que	✗	180
Hill Country	✗	104
Smoke Joint (The)	✗	459

Basque

Euzkadi	✗	53

Belgian

B. Café West	✗	376

Brazilian

Malagueta	✗	488

Cajun

Bayou	✗✗	510

Chinese

Andy's Seafood & Grill	☺ ✗	4/4
Bamboo Garden	✗	416
Bamboo Pavilion	✗	416
Chatham Square	✗	32
Chinatown Brasserie	✗✗	138
Congee Village	☺ ✗	192
Corner 28	✗	479
Dim Sum Go Go	☺ ✗	33
East Harbor Seafood Palace	✗	428
Fuleen Seafood	✗	34
Golden Unicorn	☺ ✗	34
Grand Harmony	✗	35
Grand Sichuan	✗	146
Great N.Y. Noodletown	✗	35
Great Sichuan	☺ ✗✗	103
Hunan House	☺ ✗	483
Hunan Kitchen of Grand Sichuan	☺ ✗	483
Imperial Palace	✗	484
Joe's Shanghai	✗	485
Legend Bar & Restaurant	✗	21
Liberty View	✗	80
Little Pepper	☺ ✗	487
Lucky Eight	✗	441
Main Street Imperial Taiwanese Gourmet	✗	487
Mapo Tofu	☺ ✗	227
Mr Chow	✗✗	229
M & T	☺ ✗	488
Nan Xiang Xiao Long Bao	✗	490
Nom Wah Tea Parlor	✗	38
Oriental Garden	☺ ✗	39
Pacificana	✗✗	448
Peking Duck House	✗	40
Philippe	✗✗	362
Phoenix Garden	☺ ✗	232
Shanghai Café	✗	41
Shanghai Pavilion	✗✗	364
South China Garden	☺ ✗	42
Spicy & Tasty	✗	498
Szechuan Chalet	✗✗	367
Szechuan Gourmet	☺ ✗	297
Taiwanese Gourmet Corp	✗	499

Brinkley's	✗	32
Char No. 4	☺ ✗	422
Clerkenwell (The)	✗	190
Jones Wood Foundry	✗	353
Marlow & Sons	☺ ✗	442
Minetta Tavern	✿ ✗	157
Molly's Pub & Shebeen	✗	112
P.J. Clarke's	✗	233
Redhead (The)	✗	71
Spitzer's Corner	✗	198
Spotted Pig	✿ ✗	170
Strong Place	✗	460

German

Heartbreak	✿ ✗✗	56
Nurnberger Bierhaus	✗	516

Greek

Ammos Estiatorio	✗✗	207
Avra Estiatorio	✗✗✗	209
Bahari estiatorio	☺ ✗	475
Eliá	✗	429
Estiatorio Milos	✗✗✗	265
Ethos	✗✗	217
Molyvos	✗✗	281
Periyali	✗✗	115
Pylos	✗✗	70
Snack	☺ ✗	320
Taverna Kyclades	✗	499

Indian

Amma	✗✗	207
Bombay Talkie	✗	16
Brick Lane Curry House	✗	48
Bukhara Grill	✗✗	213
Copper Chimney	✗✗	98
Dévi	✗✗	100
Dosa Garden	✗	512
Indian Clove (The)	✗✗	514
Jackson Diner	✗	484
Junoon	✿ ✗✗✗	108
Saravanaas	☺ ✗	118
Surya	☺ ✗	169
Taj Tribeca	✗	83
Tamarind	✗✗✗	119
Tamarind Tribeca	✿ ✗✗✗	338
Tamba	✗	120
Tawa Tandoor	✗	500
Tulsi	✿ ✗✗	242
Utsav	✗✗	299

Indonesian

Java	✗	437

International

Mundo	✗	489

Italian

Abboccato	✗✗	248
Ai Fiori	✿ ✗✗✗	249
Al di Là	✗	412
Alfredo's	✗✗✗	248
Aliseo Osteria del Borgo	✗	412
Angelina's	✗✗	510
Ápizz	☺ ✗✗	188
Armani Ristorante	✗✗	208
Aroma Kitchen & Wine Bar	☺ ✗	129
Asellina	✗✗	88
Aurora	✗	415
A Voce Columbus	✿ ✗✗✗	252
A Voce Madison	✿ ✗✗	90
Babbo	✗✗	131
Bacaro	✗	189
Baci & Abbracci	☺ ✗	415
Barbetta	✗✗✗	250
Barbuto	✗✗	132
Bar Luna	✗✗	375
Becco	✗✗	253
Beccofino	✗	398
Bianca	☺ ✗	132
Bice	✗✗	210
Bin 71	🍴	376
Bocca di Bacco	✗✗	256
Bottega del Vino	✗✗	212
Bread & Tulips	☺ ✗✗	95
Bread Tribeca	✗	324
Bricco	✗✗	258
Brucie	✗	420
Cacio e Pepe	✗	49
Cafe Luna	✗✗	511
Caffe Falai	✗	308
Caravaggio	✗✗✗	345
Casa Lever	✗✗✗	214
Cellini	✗✗	214
Centolire	✗✗	346
'Cesca	✗✗	378
Ciano	✗✗	98
Crispo	☺ ✗✗	139
Da Nico	✗	33

Indexes ▶ Restaurants by Cuisine

Sik Gaek	✗	497

Latin American

A Casa Fox	✗	188
Coppelia	⊛ ✗	18
Macondo	🍴	195
Nuela	✗✗✗	114
Rayuela	✗✗	196
Yerba Buena Perry	✗✗	174

Lebanese

al Bustan	⊛ ✗✗	204
Balade	✗✗	47
Naya	✗✗	230

Malaysian

Fatty Crab	⊛ ✗✗	142
New Malaysia	✗	37
Nyonya	⊛ ✗	38
Sentosa	✗	496

Mediterranean

Aldea	✿ ✗✗	89
Apiary	✗✗	46
Barbès	✗✗	210
Barbounia	✗✗	91
Belcourt	✗	48
Bistro de la Gare	✗	133
Bistro Lamazou	✗✗	92
Boulud Sud	✗✗✗	377
Brick Cafe	✗	477
Danny Brown Wine Bar & Kitchen	✿ ✗✗	480
Extra Virgin	✗	141
Fanny	✗	431
Fig & Olive	✗✗	349
Hearth	✗✗	57
Isabella's	✗✗	382
Kashkaval	✗	269
Mimi's Hummus	🍴	443
Nice Matin	✗	385
Vareli	✗✗	185
Villa Pacri	✗✗✗	172

Mexican

Alma	✗	413
Barrio	✗	417
Café el Portal	✗	307
Café Frida	✗	378
Cascabel Taqueria	✗	346

Crema	✗✗	19
De Mole	✗	479
El Parador	⊛ ✗✗	216
El Paso Taqueria	⊛ ✗	180
Empellón	✗✗	140
Estrellita Poblana III	✗	399
Fonda	✗	432
Hecho en Dumbo	⊛ ✗	147
Hell's Kitchen	✗	269
Itzocan Cafe	✗	58
La Esquina	✗	37
La Superior	✗	440
Maizal	✗	515
Maria's Bistro Mexicano	✗	441
Maya	✗✗	357
Maz Mezcal	✗	358
Mercadito Grove	✗	155
Mesa Coyoacán	⊛ ✗	442
Mexicana Mama	✗	156
MXco Cantina	✗	359
Noche Mexicana II	✗	386
Pachanga Patterson	✗	492
Pampano	✗✗	231
Papatzul	✗	315
Rocking Horse Cafe	✗	25
Rosa Mexicano	✗✗	234
Santa Clarita	✗	403
Sueños	✗	26
Taco Taco	⊛ ✗	368
Taqueria Tlaxcalli	✗	404
Toloache	✗✗	298

Middle Eastern

Balaboosta	✗	305
Taboon	✗✗	297
Tanoreen	⊛ ✗✗	461
Waterfalls Café	✗	465

Moroccan

Café Mogador	✗	49
Kif	⊛ ✗	439

New Zealand

Nelson Blue	✗	81

Persian

Persepolis	✗✗	362
Shalezeh	⊛ ✗✗	364

| Sigiri | ✗ | 72 |

Steakhouse

Ben Benson's	✗✗	254
BLT Prime	✗✗	93
BLT Steak	✗✗✗	211
Bobby Van's	✗✗	212
Christos Steakhouse	✗✗	478
Del Frisco's	✗✗✗	263
Frankie & Johnnie's	✗✗	266
Gallagher's	✗✗	267
Jake's Steakhouse	✗✗	400
Keens	✗✗	270
Le Relais de Venise	✗✗	226
MarkJoseph	✗✗	80
Michael Jordan's	✗✗	228
Morton's	✗✗✗	229
Nebraska Beef	✗✗	81
Nick & Stef's	✗✗	282
NYY Steak	✗✗✗	402
Parlor Steakhouse	✗✗	361
Peter Luger	☺ ✗	450
Porter House	✗✗✗	289
Primehouse New York	✗✗	116
Ricardo Steakhouse	✗✗	184
Smith & Wollensky	✗✗	237
Sparks	✗✗	238
Staghorn	✗✗	295
Wolfgang's (Midtown East)	✗✗	243
Wolfgang's (TriBeCa)	✗✗	339

Thai

Arharn Thai	✗	474
Ayada	☺ ✗	475
Chao Thai	✗	477
Jaiya	☺ ✗	107
Kin Shop	✗✗	151
Kittichai	✗✗	311

Nusara	✗	491
Qi Bangkok Eatery	✗✗	290
Sea	✗	458
Sookk	✗	389
Sripraphai	✗	498
Zabb Elee (East Village)	☺ ✗	75
Zabb Elee (Queens)	☺ ✗	504

Tibetan

| Himalayan Yak | ✗ | 482 |

Turkish

Antique Garage	✗	304
Beyoglu	☺ ✗	343
Bodrum	✗✗	377
Dardanel	✗✗	215
Pera	✗✗	232
Sip Sak	☺ ✗✗	237
Turkish Kitchen	☺ ✗✗	121

Uzbek

| Cheburechnaya | ✗ | 478 |

Vegan

| Blossom | ✗✗ | 16 |
| Pure Food and Wine | ✗✗ | 116 |

Vegetarian

| Dirt Candy | ☺ ✗ | 52 |
| Gobo | ✗✗ | 143 |

Vietnamese

An Nhau	✗	414
Cô Ba	☺ ✗	17
Pho Băng	✗	41
Thai So'n	✗	42
Xe Lua	✗	43

Indexes ▶ Restaurants by Cuisine

Cuisines by Neighborhood

Indexes ▶ Cuisines by Neighborhood

617

Indexes ▶ Cuisines by Neighborhood

618

Indexes ▶ Cuisines by Neighborhood

Starred Restaurants

*W*ithin the selection we offer you, some restaurants deserve to be highlighted for their particularly good cuisine. When giving one, two, or three Michelin stars, there are a number of elements that we consider including the quality of the ingredients, the technical skill and flair that goes into their preparation, the blend and clarity of flavours, and the balance of the menu. Just as important is the ability to produce excellent cooking time and again. We make as many visits as we need, so that our readers may be assured of quality and consistency.

A two or three-star restaurant has to offer something very special in its cuisine; a real element of creativity, originality, or "personality" that sets it apart from the rest. Three stars – our highest award – are given to the choicest restaurants, where the whole dining experience is superb.

Cuisine in any style, modern or traditional, may be eligible for a star. Due to the fact we apply the same independent standards everywhere, the awards have become benchmarks of reliability and excellence in over 20 countries in Europe and Asia, particularly in France, where we have awarded stars for 100 years, and where the phrase "Now that's real three-star quality!" has entered into the language.

The awarding of a star is based solely on the quality of the cuisine.

⌘⌘⌘

Exceptional cuisine, worth a special journey

One always eats here extremely well, sometimes superbly. Distinctive dishes are precisely executed, using superlative ingredients.

Chef's Table at Brooklyn Fare	✗✗	423
Daniel	✗✗✗✗	347
Eleven Madison Park	✗✗✗	101
Jean Georges	✗✗✗	383
Le Bernardin	✗✗✗	274
Masa	✗✗	279
Per Se	✗✗✗✗	287

⌘⌘

Excellent cuisine, worth a detour

Skillfully and carefully crafted dishes of outstanding quality.

Corton	✗✗✗	328	Marea	✗✗✗	277
Gilt	✗✗✗	220	Momofuku Ko	✗	67
Gordon Ramsay			SHO Shaun Hergatt	✗✗✗	82
at The London	✗✗✗✗	268	Soto	✗✗	167
Kajitsu	✗✗	61			
L'Atelier de					
Joël Robuchon	✗✗	224			

⌘

A very good restaurant in its category

A place offering cuisine prepared to a consistently high standard.

Adour	✗✗✗	205	Café Boulud	✗✗✗	344
Aldea	✗✗	249	Casa Mono	✗	97
Aldea	✗✗	89	Danji	✗	262
annisa	✗✗	130	Danny Brown Wine Bar		
Aureole	✗✗✗	251	& Kitchen	✗✗	480
A Voce Columbus	✗✗✗	252	Del Posto	✗✗✗✗	20
A Voce Madison	✗✗	90	Dovetail	✗✗	379
Blue Hill	✗✗	134	Dressler	✗✗	427
Bouley	✗✗✗✗	325	Gotham Bar		
Breslin (The)	✗	96	and Grill	✗✗✗	145
Brushstroke	✗✗✗	326	Gramercy Tavern	✗✗✗	102

Bib Gourmand

This symbol indicates our inspector's favorites for good value. For $40 or less, you can enjoy two courses and a glass of wine or a dessert (not including tax or gratuity).

631

Brunch

Late Dining

Alphabetical List of Hotels

The Michelin Adventure

It all started with rubber balls! This was the product made by a small company based in Clermont-Ferrand that André and Edouard Michelin inherited, back in 1880. The brothers quickly saw the potential for a new means of transport and their first success was the invention of detachable pneumatic tires for bicycles. However, the automobile was to provide the greatest scope for their creative talents. Throughout the 20th century, Michelin never ceased developing and creating ever more reliable and high-performance tires, not only for vehicles ranging from trucks to F1 but also for underground transit systems and airplanes.

From early on, Michelin provided its customers with tools and services to facilitate mobility and make travelling a more pleasurable and more frequent experience. As early as 1900, the Michelin Guide supplied motorists with a host of useful information related to vehicle maintenance, accommodation and restaurants, and was to become a benchmark for good food. At the same time, the Travel Information Bureau offered travellers personalised tips and itineraries.

The publication of the first collection of roadmaps, in 1910, was an instant hit! In 1926, the first regional guide to France was published, devoted to the principal sites of Brittany, and before long each region of France had its own Green Guide. The collection was later extended to more far-flung destinations, including New York in 1968 and Taiwan in 2011.

In the 21st century, with the growth of digital technology, the challenge for Michelin maps and guides is to continue to develop alongside the company's tire activities. Now, as before, Michelin is committed to improving the mobility of travellers.

MICHELIN TODAY

WORLD NUMBER ONE TIRE MANUFACTURER

- 70 production sites in 18 countries
- 111,000 employees from all cultures and on every continent
- 6,000 people employed in research and development

Moving
for a world

Moving forward means developing tires with better road grip and shorter braking distances, whatever the state of the road.

CORRECT TIRE PRESSURE

RIGHT PRESSURE

- Safety
- Longevity
- Optimum fuel consumption

-0,5 bar

- Durability reduced by 20% (- 8,000 km)

-1 bar

- Risk of blowouts
- Increased fuel consumption
- Longer braking distances on wet surfaces

forward together
where mobility is safer

It also involves helping motorists take care of their safety and their tires. To do so, Michelin organises "Fill Up With Air" campaigns all over the world to remind us that correct tire pressure is vital.

WEAR

DETECTING TIRE WEAR

The legal minimum depth of tire tread is 1.6mm.

Tire manufacturers equip their tire with tread wear indicators, which are small blocks of rubber moulded into the base of the main grooves at a depth of 1.6mm.

Tires are the only point of contact between vehicle and road.

The photo below shows the actual contact zone.

If the tread depth is less than 1.6mm, tires are considered to be worn and dangerous on wet surfaces.

NEW TIRE

WORN TIRE
(1,6 mm tread)

Moving forward
means sustainable mobility

By 2050, Michelin aims to cut the quantity of raw materials used in its tire manufacturing process by half and to have developed renewable energy in its facilities. The design of MICHELIN tires has already saved billions of liters of fuel and, by extension, billions of tons of CO_2.

Similarly, Michelin prints its maps and guides on paper produced from sustainably managed forests and is diversifying its publishing media by offering digital solutions to make travelling easier, more fuel efficient and more enjoyable!

The group's whole-hearted commitment to eco-design on a daily basis is demonstrated by ISO 14001 certification.

Like you, Michelin is committed to preserving our planet.